African American Films Through 1959

African American Films Through 1959

A Comprehensive, Illustrated Filmography

by LARRY RICHARDS

McFarland & Company, Inc., Publishers
Jefferson, North Carolina, and London

Front cover (from top): *The Bull-Dogger* (1923), *The Flaming Crisis* (1924), *The Crimson Skull* (1921)

British Library Cataloguing-in-Publication data are available

Library of Congress Cataloguing-in-Publication Data

Richards, Larry, 1950–
     African American films through 1959 : a comprehensive, illustrated
filmography / by Larry Richards.
          p.   cm.
     Includes index.
     ISBN 0-7864-0307-1 (case binding : 50# alkaline paper) ∞
     1. Afro-Americans in motion pictures.   2. Afro-Americans in the
motion picture industry.   3. Motion pictures — United States —
Catalogs. I. Title.
PN1995.9.N4R54   1998
791.43'6520396073 — dc21   97-23730
                                                                                      CIP

Manufactured in the United States of America

McFarland & Company, Inc., Publishers
   Box 611, Jefferson, North Carolina 28640

Dedicated to the memory of my father,
Earl A. Richards, Jr.,
who taught me to be kind and passionate,
and to be the best that I can be

CONTENTS

ACKNOWLEDGMENTS

There are a few organizations and people that I would like to thank for their assistance in helping me complete this book. First of all, I would like to thank the Free Library of Philadelphia and its resources, with a special thanks to Elaine Ebo of the Theater Collection, Maggie Hassett of the Database Center, and the Interlibrary Loan Department. I would also like to thank John Cunningham and Helen Miller for allowing me to run and grow unimpeded with the African American Film Festival for a decade and a half at the West Philadelphia Regional Library.

There are quite a few scholars and collectors who have over the years either assisted me in gathering information for this book or inspired me to publish it. Thanks to John Kisch, Bill McCrae, Pearl Bowser, Pam Thomas, Donald Bogle, Louise Spence, S. Torriano Berry, Pat Loughney, Gloria J. Gibson Hudson, Beth Deare, and Matthew Durington. A special thanks to the late Toni Cade Bambara who inspired me and made me realize this book was good and needed.

I would like to thank all of the universities, libraries and African American newspapers around the country that provided me with needed materials, with a special thank you to the University of Florida for lending me the George Johnson Collection on microfilm.

The biggest thank-you goes to my wife, Beverly Richards, for inspiring me, as well as putting up with nine years of me working constantly at the computer and not complaining, but rather, encouraging.

PREFACE

Derive pleasure from the art,
enlightenment from the history
and pride from the accomplishments
—Dr. Beverly Richards

The sentiments quoted above best explain my reasons for collecting early African American film memorabilia and for putting this book together. My passion for this subject and the reason for this book is to take what scholars have discovered and disseminate it to the public in a visually appealing, easy to read, and understandable form. The objective of this book is to present a complete list of African American films for the years 1895 through 1959. This filmography started out to be only of "race films" (films created especially for African American audiences with African American casts). But, over the last nine years it has grown to include predominantly African American cast films that try to represent the African American race (e.g., *Pinky*) and films that have an African American as its top star.

In 1982, I was asked to run a film festival during Black History Month at the Library. I decided to show race films since most people had no idea they existed. About four years into the now annual festival, a friend asked me if I wanted a race film poster (*The Bull-Dogger*) to exhibit. One look at that poster and I was hooked. I had never seen race film art, and from that point on became obsessed with learning and spreading the word about early African American film history. This book came about when opportunities to purchase posters and the lack of information available on the titles became evident.

In compiling and organizing the material contained in this book, I first relied on the material published by the two scholars Henry T. Sampson and Thomas Cripps. As I progressed, I realized that I was still missing material. As my collection grew, the films and memorabilia themselves became a great information source, as did the collections of others (e.g., the George Johnson Collection). My biggest source of information came from the written history of black Americans in the early African American newspapers. I studied thousands of newspapers and found a tremendous amount of information, and included many of the newspaper names and dates of previews and reviews in this book. I have tried to include every type of film possible. There are over 1300 titles: feature films, Soundies (the short music video of the forties), trailers, shorts, and documentaries, films produced by independents, the U.S. government, Hollywood and other major studios. I have also included, when available, the Library of Congress catalog number (e.g., FLA 4357). About one fifth of these films are available in video for home viewing.

The appendices at the end are unique. There is no other source presently available that can provide this type of information. There are over 1800 African American actors listed with their film credits in Appendix A. Appendix B lists the films by company, when available. Appendices C and D list the directors and producers, respectively, and their films. Appendix E lists the films in chronological order. Both new films and information about them are constantly being discovered by scholars. I hope this book contributes to the opening up of a new world of discovery and interest in African American film history and collecting.

A Note about Names, Titles and Other Data

Early African American films were generally very low budget and often were sold and redistributed shortly after their original release. The new owners sometimes changed titles or respelled or repunctuated them and changed production information; the addition of a musical scene, for instance, was not uncommon. Both the original producers and any new distributors created advertising materials that contained mispellings of actors' names and sometimes incorrect production information. The use of nicknames was inconsistent and arbitrary. So for instance the posters illustrated in this book sometimes bear information not in accord with the data given in the entry. I have tried to research and adjudicate the discrepancies to the best of my ability.

Larry Richards
Philadelphia
December 1997

HISTORICAL OVERVIEW

African American images and personalities in the movies are nothing new. They have been a part of American cinema from its beginnings. During the late nineteenth century, Thomas Edison, and his African American lab assistant, William Dixon, created the kinescope (1888), the first moving picture projector. Almost immediately blacks were on film, viewed as exotic, newsworthy and just different. Edison shot film called "Actualities"—unedited film footage, such as the 9th & 10th Colored Calvary during the Spanish-American War, black women bathing their children, African Americans eating watermelons during a contest, and many others.

At the beginning of the twentieth century, filmmakers learned the art of editing. Now the image projected on film could be manipulated. African American were now doomed to stereotypical images. One ray of light appeared in 1910, when William Foster started making all–African American cast shorts (e.g., *Pullman Porter*) for African American audiences in Chicago. But, it was D.W. Griffith's now legendary and controversial masterpiece *The Birth of a Nation* (1915) that almost single-handedly shocked an independent African American film industry into being.

Griffith's film, a commercial and critical hit because of its groundbreaking technical achievements, was also rife with virulent racist images: crazed ex-slaves running wild, raping and killing innocent whites. In response to *The Birth of a Nation*, efforts began in the African-American community to show a more honest depiction of black people by producing the first "all-colored cast" feature movies, or "race films."

In 1916, the Lincoln Motion Picture company released a positive counterpoint to Griffith in *The Realization of a Negro's Ambition* and went on to accidentally inspire the man who would become one of black America's most prolific artists, Oscar Micheaux.

The Lincoln Motion picture company was interested in adapting Micheaux's self-published novel *The Homesteader* for the screen. But when they refused Micheaux's request to direct the film, the novelist and salesman decided to make the movie himself. Fueled by his remarkable drive and knack for promotion, Micheaux—working in Chicago and New York—went on to write, direct and produce more than 40 films between 1918 and 1948, including Paul Robeson's screen debut, *Body and Soul* (1924).

The 1920s were boom years for black independent film making. Scrambling to embrace a powerful new medium, would-be *auteurs* used money raised from the black bourgeoisie and from white backers to open dozens of small studios in Philadelphia, Chicago, Kansas City, St. Louis, Los Angeles, New York and other large urban centers across the nation. Producing screen versions of African-American novels, uplifting melodramas and tragedies

5

about the consequences of trying to "pass" as white, these filmmakers spoke directly to black audiences about issues that concerned them. In the North, these "race films" were shown in ghetto movie houses, while down South, screenings were held in black school houses, churches, and special black-only shows at segregated theaters.

The boom years were short-lived. With the coming of the Great Depression and the advent of expensive-to-produce sound film technology, many of the black independents closed shop or went bankrupt. Hollywood, however, had become keenly aware of the profitability of African American films, and in 1929 produced their first of several all-colored-cast films, *The Hearts of Dixie*. By the mid–1930s, white owned companies producing all-colored-cast movies became the norm. Rather than the black-produced message movies, the new race films were low budget, African American–cast knockoffs of white commercial fare. There were African American cowboys in all-black westerns, African American gangsters in all-black mob films, and African American monsters in all-black science fiction. In 1943, Hollywood produced two memorable all–African American musicals, *Cabin in the Sky* and *Stormy Weather*.

Despite the generic formats, many African American stars emerged during this period. Spencer Williams, now best-known to millions as Andy from the 1950s television series *Amos 'n' Andy*, wrote, directed and starred in films, including the first all–African American horror picture, *Son of Ingagi* (1940). Mantan Moreland, famous for his later role as Charlie Chan's on-screen sidekick Birmingham, starred in over 20 "race films," including the original African American cast western *Harlem on the Prairie* (1938). Lena Horne's feature movie debut was in *The Duke Is Tops* (1938) — later re-released as *The Bronze Venus* (1943) — and Dorothy Dandridge debuted in the crime story, *Four Shall Die* (1940).

World War II put an interesting spin on race movies, with the U.S. government producing all–African American propaganda and service recruitment films. Films such as *Wings for This Man*, narrated by Ronald Reagan, and *The Negro Soldier* neglected to show the segregation and racial problems faced by the soldier, but instead showed an army warm and welcoming to African American G.I.s.

After the war, the focus of race films shifted again, with inexpensively produced "musicals" simply offering filmed versions of night club acts by recording stars such as Cab Calloway and Louis Jordan. Also, with attitudes having begun to change during the war, Hollywood started producing mixed-cast films, with blacks playing not merely servants or slaves, but sympathetic protagonists; *Pinky* and *Home of the Brave* were early examples of the genre. And, in the 1950s, all-black-cast movies, from *Carmen Jones* to *Porgy and Bess* to *Rock 'n' Roll Revue* from the Apollo Theater, reached wider audiences as whites began to recognize and appreciate some of the African American talent they had previously neglected on racial grounds.

Long overlooked and underpraised, the all-black-cast films of the teens through the fifties are the bedrock on which today's African American film art is built. Their existence is a tribute to the ingenuity, perseverance and fortitude of people who recognized the power of a medium they were locked out of and then successfully harnessed some of that power for themselves.

The preceding has been a very short historical overview and if one is interested in learning more about early African American film history in detail, I highly recommend the following books: *Blacks in Black and White*, 2nd ed., by Henry T. Sampson, and *Slow Fade to Black*, by Thomas Cripps.

THE FILMS

1   Absent 1928

Dir: Gant, Harry. *Prod:* Gant, Harry. *Co:* Rosebud Film Corporation. *Dist:* Ira McGowan & D.I.Thomas. *Cast:* Clarence Brooks, George Reed, Virgel Owens, Rosa Lee Lincoln, Floyd Shackeford. (B&W / Feature / Silent.)

The story of a shell-shocked veteran, memory gone, adrift on the mercy of civilization. It begins as he drifts, in search of health, wealth and happiness, into a mining camp. While there, he is given sustenance by an old miner and his daughter. He regains his memory fighting at the camp to save the life and property of his benefactors and gains a new start in life, with the help of the American Legion.

2   Abyssinia 1931

Co: Warner Bros. *Cast:* Eighteen Native Abyssinians, Hechla Tamanya, a dozen drummers and singers. (Documentary / Newsreel / B&W / Short / Sound.)

"This film short shows the natives crowding the Abyssinian capital, in a gala celebration to the King, Haile Selassie. Miss Tamanya's voice rings out in native Arabic and Hamharic"—*Philadelphia Tribune*, 6/21/31.

3   Adventure 1946

Dir: Anderson, Leonard. *Prod:* Alexander, William D. *Co:* Alexander Production. *Dist:* Soundies Distributing Corporation. *Cast:* Henry Woode and His Orchestra. (Soundies / Short / B&W / 12/30/46.)

4   Adventure in Boogie Woogie 1946

Dir: Crouch, William Forest. *Prod:* Crouch, William Forest. *Co:* Filmcraft Production. *Dist:* Soundies Distributing Corporation. *Cast:* Robert Crum. (Soundies 23505 / B&W / Short / Sound / Musical / 4/15/46.)

5   Africa Speaks! 1930

Co: Mascot Pictures Co. Photographed by Paul L. Hoefler. *Cast:* Paul Robeson. (B&W / Sound / Documentary / 40 min. / FEA 4763–4768.)

Documentary narrated by Paul Robeson.

6   Africa's Future 1959

Co: WCBS–TV & NET. (Ethiopia / Ghana / South Africa / Documentary / 16 mm / B&W / Sound / 29 min. / Short.)

Views of African teenagers on African independence.

7   Afrique sur Seine 1955

Dir: Vieyra, Paulin Souman & Mamamou Sarr. *Prod:* Groupe Africain. *Co:* Ethnographic Film Committee of the Museum. *Cast:* Paulin Soumanou Vieyra, Mamamou Sarr. (French / Commentary / Short / B&W / 22 min. / Sound.)

This film deals with the alienation and bitterness of emigration by a young African.

8   L'Afrique Vous Paris 1931

Co: French Film Company. (French / Feature / Documentary / B&W / Sound.)

"…This picture simply lifts one out of one's seat with its wild and primitive vigor, and fills one with admiration for the human beings who have been able to survive in this environment for thousands of years, for Africa is simply shot through with danger. And here we are speaking only of the natural perils, not of others such as slave raiders. Great herds of elephants; bands of highly-irritable rhinoceri which charge down at the slightest noise; troops of lions, bringing down and rendering their prey; leopards that creep on one unawares; flies, whose bite sends one into sleep from which one never awakes… Controversial scene of native being eaten by lion…"—excerpted from review in the *Philadelphia Tribune*, 4/30/31 & 5/7/31.

9   Ah, Yes, There's Good Blues Tonight 1946

Dir: Gould, Dave. *Prod:* Hersh, Ben. *Co:* RCM Production. *Dist:* Soundies Distributing Corporation. *Cast:* Liz Tilton, Matty Malneck and His Orchestra. (Soundies 25805 / B&W / Short / Sound / Musical / 9/30/46.)

10   Ain't Misbehavin' 1945

Co: RCM Production. *Dist:* Soundies Distributing Corporation. *Cast:* Fats Waller, Myra Johnson. (Soundies 4607 / B&W / Short / Sound / Musical / 12/15/45.)

11   Ain't My Sugar Sweet 1943

Co: RCM Production. *Dist:* Soundies Distributing Corporation. *Cast:* The Chanticleers. (Soundies 14408 / B&W / Short / Sound / Musical / 12/6/43.)

12   Ain't She Pretty   1944
Co: RCM Production. *Dist:* Soundies Distributing Corporation. *Cast:* The Three Peppers. (Soundies 18908 / B&W / Short / Sound / Musical / 11/20/44.)

13   Air Mail Special   1941
Co: RCM Production. *Dist:* Soundies Distributing Corporation. *Cast:* Count Basie and His Band. (Soundies 4501 / B&W / Short / Sound / Musical /12/8/41.)

14   Alabamy Bound   1941
Co: RCM Production. *Dist:* Soundies Distributing Corporation. *Cast:* Jackie Greene. (Soundies / B&W / Short / Sound / Musical / 12/22/41.)

15   Aladdin Jones   1915
Co: Historical Feature Films. *Cast:* Frank Montgomery, Florence McClain, Jimmy Marshall, Bert Murphy. (Silent / BW / Short / later released by Ebony Film Company.)

"Jonesy, dusky and shiftless, finds it much more pleasant to listen to the story of Aladdin as read by Buddy, his son, than to help Mandy with her arduous tasks. 'Tis washday, and after reluctantly grinding the wringer for his tyrannical wife, he decides that no washday can possibly be complete without a 'bucket of suds.' No sooner thought than done. The suds produce a peculiar effect and Jonesy drops off into a slumber with the story of Aladdin dominant in his dream mind. As he wanders alone he meets a patriarch dressed in flowing Oriental robes, who accosts him. 'Come with me and I will make you rich,' says the white-bearded man from the East, at the same moment 'with simple turn of the wrist' changing Jonesy's apparel from a weather-beaten shirt and patched trousers to the gaudy pantaloons and turban of the Arab. Jonesy follows the old man through the mazes of marvelous vegetation and experiences numerous surprises. At last he secures possession of the wonderful lamp and its supernatural powers and, escaping from the patriarch, brings life to the Genie, slave of the lamp. Now truly he has become Aladdin Jones, for he possesses the art by which his least desire may be satisfied. He asks for Budweiser, it flows freely. He asks for money, it descends from the skies. He asks 'fo' a shack to sleep in' and is confronted by an Oriental palace of wonderful size and magnificence. He lies on a divan and is entertained by a charming dancer. But in all his glory the fearful image of his wife rises before him. He runs for dear life, followed by his infuriated spouse. At last, with a cliff before him and his wife behind him, he chooses the lesser evil and plunges into the washtub! All Oriental splendor vanishes. He is plain Jonesy once more"— from *Blacks in Black and White*, 2nd ed., by Henry Sampson.

16   All American News Reel   1945
Co: All American News. *Cast:* "Sugar Chile" Robinson and many other Negro performers are featured. (Musical / 8 min. / Short / B&W.)

Seven-year-old "Sugar Chile" Robinson performs at the piano.

17   All American News Reel No. 4   1945
Co: All American News. (Newsreel / B&W / Short.)

"…The bulk of the events disclosed on the screen take place in New York and Chicago. Usually the events are a parade, a sports game, a cornerstone laying, a housing project, child's welfare center, a fashion revue, death of a celebrity, servicemen singing spirituals, a Negro receiving an appointment, the first of his race to be so honored, etc…"— excerpt of review from the *New York Amsterdam News*, 12/16/45.

18   All-Colored Vaudeville Show   1935
Dir: Mack, Roy. *Co:* Warner Bros. / Vitaphone. *Cast:* Adelaide Hall, The Nicholas Brothers, The Five Racketeers, Eunice Wilson, Cab Calloway. (35 mm / Sound / B&W/ 1 reel / 9 min./ Musical / Short / FEA 4770.)

This musical short features Adelaide Hall and the Nicholas Brothers. Music includes "Minnie the Moocher," "Sweet Sue," and "Stars and Stripes."

19   All Ruzzitt Buzzitt   1945
Co: RCM Production. *Dist:* Soundies Distributing Corporation. *Cast:* Dallas Bartley and His Orchestra, Female silhouetted dancers.

(Soundies 88908 / B&W / Short / Sound / Musical / 7/16/45.)

20   All's Fair   1938

Dir: Hall, Robert. *Prod:* Christie, Al. *Co:* Educational Film Corporation. *Cast:* The Cabin Kids (five colored harmonizers: Ruth Hall, Helen Hall, James "Darling" Hall, Winifred "Sugar" Hall, and little Frederick Hall), Tom Emerson's Mountaineers (white). Story by Arthur Jarrett & Marcy Klauber. (Sound / B&W / 1 reel.)

"Cute little pickaninny skit, with the Cabin Kids going to town and helping Mammy win the prize at the county fair for her pancakes. The youngsters do their numbers with their usual sprightliness, and in between have a lot of fun putting Mammy's rivals out of the running for the best cookery prize. They gum up the biscuit dough of one, and the sauce of another, and Mammy romps home an easy winner"—review from *Film Daily*, 3/16/38.

21   Along the Navajo Trail   1945

Co: RCM Production. *Dist:* Soundies Distributing Corporation. *Cast:* John Shadrack Horance, Johnnie Moore's 3 Blazers. (Soundies 21708 / B&W / Short / Sound / Musical / 10/15/45.)

22   Am I Guilty?   1940

Dir: Newfeld, Sam. *Prod:* Hackel, A.W. *Co:* Supreme Pictures Corporation. *Dist:* Hackel, A.W. *Cast:* Ralph Cooper, Sybil Lewis, Sam McDaniels, Lawrence Criner, Marcella Moreland (daughter of Mantan), Arthur T. Ray, Reginald Fenderson, Monte Hawley, Matthew Jones, Dewey "Pigmeat" Markham, Jesse Brooks, Napoleon Simpson, Clarence Brooks, Cleo Desmond, Ida Coffin, Lillian Randolph, Vernon McCalla, Eddie Thompson, Mae Turner, Alfred Grant, Guernsey Morrow. (6/21/40 / B&W / Sound / Feature.)

Am I Guilty?, 1940, was re-released in 1945 under the title *Racket Doctor*. Preview in *The Philadelphia Afro-American*, 5/11/40. Reviews

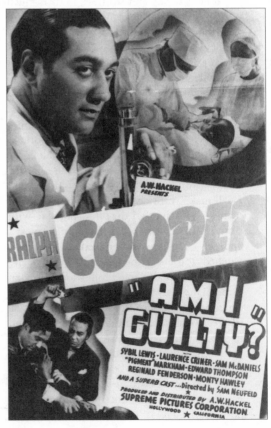

in the *Philadelphia Tribune*, 12/20/41, the *Philadelphia Afro-American*, 12/20/41, *New York Amsterdam News*, 10/5/40 & *Kansas City Call*.

The story tells of a courageous young Negro doctor whose high ideals lead him to attempt the establishment of a clinic in the slum district in which he was born. Dr. Dunbar falls into the hands of the Bennett gang, which is badly in need of a "mob doctor" to "fix up" wounded members. Bennett, through his lawyer, donates $8,000 to Dunbar to establish his clinic. Dunbar is eventually forced to accompany the gang on a series of breathtaking escapades, which finally end in the death of Bennett and the capture of the gang.

23   Am I Lucky? 1946

Dir: Gould, Dave. *Prod:* Hersh, Ben. *Co:* RCM Production. *Dist:* Soundies Distributing Corporation. *Cast:* Dusty Brooks. (Soundies 24M5 / B&W / Short / Sound / Musical / 10/28/46.)

24   American Soldier in Love & War, No. 3 pre–1910

(B&W / Silent / Short / FLA 3445.)

25   Anna Lucasta 1958

Dir: Laven, Arnold. *Prod:* Harmon, Sidney. *Co:* Longridge Enterprise, Inc. *Dist:* Longridge Enterprise, Inc. *Cast:* Eartha Kitt, Sammy Davis, Jr., Frederic O'Neal, Henry Scott, Rex Ingram, James Edwards, Georgia Burke, Isabelle Cooley, Rosetta Le Noire, Alvin Childress, Claire Leyea, John Proctor, Charles Swain, Isaac Jones, Eileen Harley.

Rare Hollywood all Black cast drama. Based on the play by Philip Yordan. Screenplay: Philip Yordan. Music: Elmer Bernstein. Title song: "That's Anna." Lyrics by Sammy Cahn. Director of photography: Lucien Ballard. Associate director: Irving Lerner. Graphic art: Charles White. Production supervisor: Leon Chooluck. Art director: John Poplan. Assistant director: Eugene Anderson, Jr. Set: Lyle Reifsbider. Property manager: Richard Rubin. Make-up: Ted Coodley. Hair: Helene Parrish. (Sound / Color / 97 min. / Feature.)

Melodrama about promiscuous Kitt who's forever at odds with her family and herself.

Anna's (Kitt) father wants to marry her off to a well-to-do young man. But Anna's taken up with a raunchy sailor (Davis) and there is constant bickering, quarrelling, carousing and carryings-on.

26   Are Working Girls Safe? 1918

Co: Ebony Film Company. *Dist:* General Film Company. *Cast:* Ebony Players (Sam Robinson, Samuel "Sambo" Jacks, Will Starks, Julia Mason, Bert Murphy, Evon Skekeeter, Mildred Price, Walter Brogsdale, Robert Duree, Frank Pollard, George Lewis Stock Company). (Silent / Short / B&W / 2 reels.)

27   Art in Negro Schools 1946

Co: Harmon Foundation Educational Films (Documentary / Short / B&W / Silent / 2 reels.)

The development and training in art expression through dramatics, music, dancing, and fine arts in several leading Negro colleges.

28   As Our Boyhood Is 1947

Co: American Film Center. (Documentary / B&W / Short / Sound.)

The best and worst of the education of Negro youth in the South.

29   As the World Rolls On 1921

Co: Andlauer Production Company. *Cast:* Jack Johnson, Blanche Thompson, Reed Thomas, Walter Simpson, Versia Rice, Capt. Sam Crawford of the K.C. Monarchs, Capt. Bruce Fetway of the Detroit Stars, Rube Foster & Chicago American Giants. (35 mm / Silent / B&W / Sport / 7 reels / 5,600 ft. / Feature.)

Jack Johnson plays himself in this film about Joe Walker, a physically weak young man who learns physical fitness and the art of self-defense from the great ex-heavyweight champion. Molly, Joe's girl, is framed and charged with conspiracy to defraud a doctor. The real crook is pointed out in court and tries to escape. Joe subdues him, frees Molly, and marries her. As newlyweds they visit Jack Johnson's home and are presented with a wedding gift of $1000.

30   Ask the OPA 1945

Prod: All American News. *Co:* All American News. *Dist:* All American News Reel. *Cast:* Canada Lee.

Sponsored by the Office of Price Administration. Announcement in the *Philadelphia Tribune*, 12/29/45. (16mm / B&W / Short / Documentary / Newsreel / Sound.)

This film is a short on rent control. It details the steps tenants may take to get relief from exorbitant rents in areas under the agency's control.

31   Babbling Bess   1943

Co: RCM Production. *Dist:* Soundies Distributing Corporation. (Soundies 13108 / B&W / Short / Musical / 8/30/43.)

32   Baby, Are You Kiddin?   1946

Dir: Dave Gould. *Prod:* Ben Hersh. *Co:* RCM Production. *Dist:* Soundies Distributing Corporation. *Cast:* Dusty Brooks and His Four Tones, Mildred Boyd. (Soundies 22M2 / B&W / Short / Sound / Musical / 8/12/46.)

33   Baby Don't Go Away from Me
1943

Dir: Crouch, William Forest. *Prod:* Crouch, William Forest. *Co:* Filmcraft Production. *Dist:* Soundies Distributing Corporation. *Cast:* Mabel Lee, Stepin Fetchit. (Soundies 16M1 / B&W / Short / Sound / Musical / 2/4/46.)

34   Baby Don't You Cry   1943

Co: RCM Production. *Dist:* Soundies Distributing Corporation. *Cast:* Warren Evans. (Soundies 14508 / B&W / Short / Sound / Musical / 12/13/43.)

35   Baby Don't You Love Me Anymore   1945

Co: RCM Production. *Dist:* Soundies Distributing Corporation. *Cast:* June Richmond. (Soundies 13M2 / B&W / Short / Sound / Musical / 11/26/45.)

36   Baby Jewels   1937

Dir: Wright, William Lord, Supervisor. *Co:* Universal Studios. (Sound / Shorts / 2 reels each / B&W / Scripts written by William Lester. All colored film series announced by Carl Laemmle, president of the Universal Pictures Corporation.)

Possibly never released, *Baby Jewels* is a series name for ten of the best Octavus Roy Cohen's

Saturday Evening Post stories about the Negro in his native haunts of the South. This series brought to the screen such well-known fictional characters as Florian Slappey, Lawyer Evens Chew, J. Caesar Clump, Septic Sims and Joe Bugg.

37   Back Beat Boogie   1944

Co: RCM Production. *Dist:* Soundies Distributing Corporation. *Cast:* The Burch Mann Dancers. (Soundies 18506 / B&W / Short / Sound / Musical / 10/16/44.)

38   Back Door Man   1946

Dir: Crouch, William Forest. *Prod:* Crouch, William Forest. *Co:* Filmcraft Production. *Dist:* Soundies Distributing Corporation. *Cast:* Vanita Smythe. (Soundies 19M4 / B&W / Short / Sound / Musical / 6/3/46.)

39   Backstage Blues   1943

Co: RCM Production. *Dist:* Soundies Distributing Corporation. *Cast:* Lynn Albritton, Lou Ellen, The Harlem Cuties. (Soundies 11905 / B&W / Short / Sound / Musical / 6/1/54.)

40   Bad Boy   1939

Dir: Meyer, Herbert. *Co:* Gateway Productions. *Cast:* Johnny Downs, Rosaline Keith, Helen MacKellar, James Robbins, Holmes Herbert, Matt Moore, Bobby Clark, Jr., Clem Wilenehech, Spencer Williams, and Clarence Brooks.

Screenplay by Richard C. Kahn, Cameraman Jack Greenhalgh. (B&W / Sound / Feature.)

41   Bally-Hoo Cake Walk   1901

Co: American Mutoscope / Biograph. (Newsreel / Short / B&W / Silent.)

Black Cake Walk dancers at the Pan American Exposition in Buffalo, New York, on June 17, 1901.

42   Baltimore News Revue   1950

(Newsreel / B&W / Short / Sound.)

Features Mary Daughtry parachute jumping from an altitude of 5,000 feet and takeoff of pilot Charles James from Curtis Field.

43   Band Parade   1943

Dir: Berne, Josef. *Co:* Berne, Josef. *Cast:* Count Basie and His Band. (Short / 10 min. / B&W / Sound.)

A couple of numbers performed by Count Basie and his band, with solos.

44   The Bar Sinister   1917

Prod: Lewis, Edgar. *Co:* Frank Hall Production. (Short / Dramatic / B&W / Silent.)

A tragic mulatto melodrama.

45   The Barber   1916

Co: Foster Photoplay Company. *Dist:* Foster Photoplay Company. *Cast:* Anna Holt, Howard Kelly, Edgar Wilson. (Silent / B&W / Short.)

An ambitious barber overhears a customer say he's looking for a Spanish music teacher for his wife. The barber grabs his mandolin and rushes over to the customer's house to earn money as a Spanish music teacher. The wife believes him, but shortly thereafter the man arrives, recognizes the barber and throws him out. Confusion reigns, the barber punches one of his ridiculing friends, who then calls the police. In the meantime, the wife, not knowing why her husband threw the music teacher out, sends for him to come back. He returns to the house only to be confronted again by the returning husband. A fight breaks out. The wife, fearing her husband is being hurt by the barber, hits him over the head with a vase. The barber runs out of the door only to be chased by police who were responding to a friend's call. The barber jumps in a lake, turns an old lady's boat over and is held by the old lady until the police arrive.

46   Barber of Darktown   1915

Co: Keystone. (Comedy / Short / Silent / B&W.)

Whites in blackface play the barber and his girlfriend.

47   Barbershop Blues   1937

Dir: Henabery, Joseph. *Co:* Vitaphone. *Cast:* Nicholas Brothers, Claude Hopkins Band, Four Step Brothers, Orlando Robinson.

Screenplay by Joseph Henabery. Review in *Film Daily*, 9/9/37. (Short / Musical / B&W / Sound / 1 reel.)

Dancing bootblacks (the Nicholas Brothers) in a black barbershop setting. The plot revolves around the winning of a new barbershop on a bet while the band plays on.

48   Bargain with Bullets   1937

Dir: Fraser, Harry. *Prod:* Popkin, Harry M. *Co:* Million Dollar Productions. *Cast:* Ralph Cooper, Frances Turham, Theresa Harris, Edward Thompson, Lawrence Criner, Clarence Brooks, Sam McDaniel, John Lester Johnson, Reginald Fenderson, Billy McClain, Al Duvall, Milton Shockley, Art Murray, Ray Martin, Halley Harding, Eight Covan dancers, Les Hite and His Cotton Club Orchestra.

Original story and play by Ralph Cooper and Phil Dunham. Reviews in *The Philadelphia Tribune*, 9/30/37, 11/10/38, *The Philadelphia Independent*, 11/13/38, the *Kansas City Call*, 9/17/37 and the *New York Amsterdam News*, 10/23/37. (B&W / Feature / Sound.)

"Mugsy" is the leader of a band of fur thieves. He is in love with the beautiful Kay and determined to hold her affection by giving her lavish presents and luxury. The plot is complicated by Grace, Mugsy's schoolday sweetheart. She remembers him only as Eddie, the boy who loved to be near her before he drifted away into underworld company and

the wiles of a heartless schemer. Still loving him, she becomes a famous radio singer when by the tides of fate their paths cross again. Lieutenant Lester finally solves the robberies and murders and runs down Mugsy's gang of criminals.

49   Barnstormers   pre–1910
(B&W / Silent / Short / FLA 4695.)

50   A Barnyard Mix-Up   1915
Prod: Lubin, Sigmund. *Co:* Lubin Manufacturing Company.
Cartoon comedy drawn by Vincent Whitman. Released on 7/20/1915. (Animated / Short / Silent / B&W / 400 ft.)
The chicken thieving of Rastus is discovered by Farmer Corntossel who pursues the thief through the haystacks. They have several encounters, but Rastus has peculiarly elastic legs and a strangely bulletproof body. The farmer's shots roll off his back like marbles, but finally an axe lays Rastus low. He is buried in the garden but is resurrected in the strangest manner by an explosion of dynamite. The sudden appearance of a ferocious white goat causes the two to forget their enmity and unite against the animal.

51   Basie's Boogie   1945
Cast: Count Basie and His Orchestra. (Musical / Short / Sound.)

52   Basin Street Boogie   1942
Co: Minoco Production. *Dist:* Soundies Distributing Corporation. *Cast:* Will Bradley and His Six Texas Hot Dogs, Ray McKinley. (Soundies / B&W / Short / Sound / Musical / 4/20/42.)

53   Basin Street Revue   1955
Dir: Kohn, Joseph. *Co:* Studio Films, Inc. *Cast:* Lionel Hampton, Sarah Vaughan, Martha Davis, Mantan Moreland, Nipsy Russell, The Larks, Little Buck, Nat "King" Cole, Count Basie, Helen Humes, Amos Wilburn, The Three Businessmen of Rhythm, Dinah Washington, Freddy and Flo, The Clovers, Paul Williams, Jimmy Brown. (35mm / Sound / Tinted / 8 reels / 58 min. / Feature / FGC 7520–7523.)
Acts from the Harlem Variety Revue at the Apollo Theater.

54   Bathing Beauty Parade, Pacific Beach   1925
(Newsreel / B&W / Short / Silent.)
Film coverage of a black bathing beauty contest at Pacific Beach in California.

55   Battling Amateurs   1941
Prod: Lewis, Edward. *Co:* Lewis, Edward W. (Newsreel / B&W / Sound / Short.) Produced as part of the *Colored Champions of Sport* series.

56   Beale Street Mama   1946
Dir: Williams, Spencer. *Prod:* Goldberg, Bert. *Co:* Hollywood Pictures Corporation. *Dist:* Sack Amusement Enterprises. *Cast:* July Jones, Spencer Williams, Rosalie Larrimore, Allen & Allen, Joyce McElrath, Don Albert's Band. (B&W / Sound / Feature / 60 min. / FDA 3665.) Closed after 3 days, called an insult to Negro race.
A street cleaner (Jones) and Bad News Johnson (Williams) find some stolen money, which they use to try to establish themselves in the good life. They are found out and end up losing everything. Very stereotypical.

57   Beale Street Revue   1955
Dir: Kohn, Joseph. *Co:* Studio Films, Inc. *Cast:* Cab Calloway, Sarah Vaughn, Bill Bailey. (B&W / Sound / Music / Feature / FBB 9706.)
Typical variety show on stage format.

58   Beat Me Daddy   1943
Co: RCM Production. *Dist:* Soundies Distributing Corporation. *Cast:* Maurice Rocco. (Soundies 15008 / B&W / Short / Sound / Musical / 12/29/43.)

59   The Beauty Contest   1921
Prod: Pathé. *Co:* Harris Dickson Film Corporation. *Dist:* Pathé. (Silent / B&W / Short / 2 reels / Comedy / Old Reliable series.)

60   Because I Love You   1942
Co: RCM Production. *Dist:* Soundies Distributing Corporation. *Cast:* Mamie Smith, Lucky Millinder and His Orchestra. (Soundies 2M1 / B&W / Short / Sound / Musical / 12/30/42.)

61   Bessie Coleman   1922
Co: Pathé. (Newsreel / B&W / Short / Silent.)

Bessie Coleman, famous aviatrix, performing airplane stunts in Berlin, Germany, and at the Tri-State Fair in Memphis, Tennessee, on August 14, 1922.

62   Bessie Coleman   1923

Co: Pathé. (Newsreel / B&W / Short / Silent.)

Bessie Coleman, famous aviatrix, swimming at Santa Monica Beach in California, and her subsequent airplane crash at Santa Monica Field, in which she was injured but fully recovered.

63   The Betrayal   1948

Dir: Micheaux, Oscar. *Prod:* Micheaux, Oscar. *Co:* Astor Pictures Corporation. *Dist:* Oscar Micheaux Corporation. *Cast:* Lou Vernon, Leroy Collins, Edward Fraction, Jesse Johnson, William Byrd, Myra Stanton, Frances DeYoung, Arthur McCoo, Vernetties Moore, Barbara Lee, Verlie Cowan, Alice B. Russell, Gladys Williams, Richard Lawrence, Harris Gaines, David Jones, Vernon B. Duncan, Curley Ellison, Sue McBride, Yvonne Machen.

Screenplay by Oscar Micheaux, based on book *The Wind from Nowhere,* by Micheaux. Reviews in the *New York Amsterdam News,* 6/19/48; —*New York Times,* 1/21/48, and *Moving Picture,* 6/26/48. (180 min. / B&W / Feature / Sound.)

Martin Eden, a young black who builds an agricultural empire in South Dakota, falls in love with a white woman. At first he rejects her, feeling that intermarriage would be unwise. In spite of his feelings, he marries her. Years of marital misunderstanding follow, combined with poverty and hardship. Finally, it is learned that the white woman is actually part Negro after all, and the marriage takes a turn for the better. A theme which Micheaux lived and tried to relate on many occasions in his films and books.

64   Beware!   1946

Dir: Pollard, Bud. *Prod:* Pollard, Bud. *Co:* Astor Pictures Corporation. *Dist:* Astor Pictures, Inc. *Cast:* Louis Jordan and His Tympany Five (William Davis, Joshua W. Jackson, Aaron Izenhall, Carl Hogan, Jesse Simpkins,

Eddie Byrd), Frank Wilson, Emory Richardson, Valerie Black, Milton Woods, Joseph Hilliard, Tommy Hix, Charles J. Johnson, John Grant, Walter Earle, Ernest Calloway, Dimples Daniels, The "Aristo Genes" Girls Club.

Executive producers: Berle Adams & R.M. Savini. Original screen story by John Gordon. Original music arrangement by Louis Jordan. Photography: John Malkames. Settings: Frank Nemczy. Makeup: Fred Ryle. Costumes: Variety. Sound recording: Walter Hicks. Assistant director: Ed Kelly. Film editor: Bud Pollard. Montages: Fred Barber. Lighting: Arthur Burns. Production manager: John Doran. Review in the *Film Daily*, 9/26/46. (16mm / Sound / B&W / 54 min. / FEA 7578 -7583.)

A crisis comes to Ware College: The dean says the college is broke and must shut down. A look at the college's finances sends alumnus Jordan's eyebrows up. The college it seems has enough cash to keep ticking for another century. Jordan advises the gloomy faculty in the dean's office and reveals that he has a trick up his sleeve to keep the college from closing. He plans a big dance to raise funds for his alma mater. The students cheer wildly when the dean is forced by Jordan to announce his "mistake" and declare that the college will stay open. Jordan ends up saving the school and getting the girl.

65   Big Bill Blues   1956
Cast: Bill Broonzy. (Belgium / Short / Musical / Documentary / 18 min. / Sound.)

Film record of "Big" Bill Broonzy singing and playing in clubs.

66   Big Bill Broonzy   1955
Cast: "Big" Bill Broonzy. (Documentary / Musical / Short / 9 min.)

Bill Broonzy sitting on a front porch and playing "Twelve Bar blues."

67   Big Fat Butterfly   1944
Co: RCM Production. *Dist:* Soundies Distributing Corporation. *Cast:* Gene Rodgers, The V's. (Soundies 89908 / B&W / Short / Sound / Musical / 12/31/44.)

68   Big Fat Mammas   1946
Dir: Anderson, Leonard. *Prod:* Alexander, William D. *Co:* Alexander Production. *Dist:* Soundies Distributing Corporation. *Cast:* "Bull-Moose" Jackson, Lucky Millinder and His Orchestra. (Soundies 22M3 / Short / Sound / Musical / B&W / 8/19/46.)

69   Big Fella   1938
Dir: Wills, J. Elder. *Co:* British Lion-Hammer. *Cast:* Paul Robeson, Elisabeth Welch, Eslanda Robeson, also white stars.

Story by Claude McKay. Mixed cast. (B&W / Sound / Feature / British.)

Paul Robeson is featured in this film story of the Marseilles waterfront. Loosely based on McKay's *Banjo*.

70   Big Timers   1945
Dir: Pollard, Bud. *Prod:* Glucksman, E.M. *Co:* All American News. *Dist:* Astor Pictures. *Cast:* Moms Mabley, Stepin Fetchit, Francine Everett, Duke Williams, Lou Swarz, Milton Woods, Dots Johnson, Walter Earle, Lucky

THE SECRETS OF A CHAMBERMAID IN A SUGAR HILL HOT

Brown, Gertrude Saunders, Ed Hunter, Elveta Hunter, Rocky Brown, Skylight, Tarzana, The All-American Girl Band.

Photography: Lester Lang. Set: Fred Thumm. Sound recording: Ed Fenton. Makeup: Dr. Liszt. Film editor: Bud Pollard. Production supervisor: Charles Krane. Review in the *New York Amsterdam News*, 11/17/45. (35mm / B&W / Sound / 4 reels / Feature / FEA 3694–3697.)

"This is a story about the rich black folks who live in Sugar Hill and the poor people that work for them" (from the first screen of film). A maid's daughter who wants to impress her male friend has her mother pretend that one of the rich folk apartments (the tenants are away) is theirs. Comedy reigns, but all ends well.

71 Bipp Bang Boogie 1944
Dir: Elljat, Sam. *Prod:* Sack, Alfred. *Co:* Harlemwood Studios. *Cast:* Ebony Trio, Alex Brown.

Features three musical numbers. (Short / B&W / Sound / 8 min. / FEA 8525.)

72 Birth Mark 1911
Dir: Foster, William. *Prod:* Foster, William.

Co: Foster Photoplay Company. *Dist:* William Foster. (Short / Silent / B&W.)

"The folly of a youth comes home…. Comes home twenty years after one of his deadly sins"— advertisement.

73 Birth of a Race (Lincoln's Dream) 1918
Dir: Noble, John W. *Prod:* Scott, Emmett J. *Co:* Birth of a Race Film Company. (Feature / Silent / B&W / 12 reel / 3 hours / only have 59 min. / FDA 4741 or FED 3368–3373.)

The film intended to counteract the effects and respond to the racial allegations in *The Birth of a Nation*. Ended up as a kind of patchwork extravaganza beginning in the Garden of Eden. It took over two years to make at a cost of over $1 million. Ended up not even concerning blacks.

74 Birthright 1924
Dir: Micheaux, Oscar. *Prod:* Micheaux, Oscar. *Co:* Micheaux Film Corporation. *Dist:*

Micheaux Film Corporation. *Cast:* Salem Tutt Whitney, Homer J. Tutt, Evelyn Preer, Callie Mines, E.G. Tatum, Edward Elkas, Alma Sewall, Lawrence Chenault, T.C. Crowell.

Preview in *The Philadelphia Tribune*, 11/22/24 and review in *The Philadelphia Tribune*, 11/29/24. (B&W / Feature / Silent / 35mm / 10 reels / 9,500 ft.)

He was a graduate of Harvard and so far above her in all intellectual things until she decided that it was useless to try to come to him. She told him she was immoral, therefore unfit, so he went away from her. But she was ambitious, she wanted to be somebody, but the Negroes told her she wasn't nothin'—just a "yallah, stuck-up, fly-by-night hussy"—and accused her of all kinds of things. She struggled, but how could a poor colored girl be anything in the face of such circumstances? Fate seemed to be against her; the more she tried to struggle up, the further she was pushed back into the grime and squalor of Niggertown. Then she was arrested for grand larceny—but was she guilty? Or was it because she refused to deliver her virtue—her body—to the seducer?

75   Birthright 1939

Dir: Micheaux, Oscar. *Prod:* Russell, A. Burton. *Co:* Micheaux Pictures Corporation. *Dist:* Micheaux Film Corporation. *Cast:* Ethel Moses, Alec Lovejoy, Carmen Newsome, J.A. Jackson, Laura Bowman, George Vessey (white).

Remake of 1924 film by Micheaux. From the novel by T.S. Stribling. (B&W / Feature / Sound.)

"… tells the story of a White man who took an interest in a young colored youth, took him into his home and tried to give him every advantage that a white boy would have. As the story takes place in a small Southern town, quite a bit of talk was caused. Then the boy wanted to marry Ethel Moses, and the white man tried to stop it"— review in *The Philadelphia Afro-American*, 3/11/39.

76   Black and Tan 1929

Dir: Murphy, Dudley. *Prod:* Currier, Dick. *Co:* RCA Phonophone / RKO Radio Pictures / Sack Amusement Enterprises. *Cast:* Duke

Ellington and His Orchestra, Fredi Washington, Alec Lovejoy, Cotton Club Chorus, Five Blazers, Hall Johnson Choir.

Produced at RCA Phototone Studios in New York under the supervision of Dick Currier. Review in *Film Daily* 11/17/29. (Musical / Short / 16mm / B&W / Sound / 20 min.)

This picture was produced primarily to showcase Duke Ellington and His Orchestra. The story deals with a dancer and her man who plays the piano in the orchestra of the show in which she is featured. Terribly ill, the brave dancer dances to her death at the finish of the picture, to the music of the song her sweetheart has written for her.

77   Black and Tan Mix Up 1918

Co: Ebony Film Company. *Dist:* General Film Company. *Cast:* Ebony Players (Sam Robinson, Samuel "Sambo" Jacks, Will Starks, Julia Mason, Bert Murphy, Evon Skekeeter, Mildred Price, Walter Brogsdale, Robert Duree, Frank Pollard, George Lewis Stock Company.) (Silent / B&W / Short / 2 reels.)

78   Black and White   1914

Co: Historical Feature Films. *Cast:* Frank Montgomery, Florence McClain, Bert Murphy. (Short / B&W / Silent.)

79   The Black Boomerang   1925

Co: William H. Clifford Photoplay Company. (Silent / B&W / 35mm / Feature.)

80   Black Cat Tales   1933

Cast: Buck and Bubbles. (B&W / Sound / Short.)

81   Black Gold   1928

Prod: Norman Film Manufacturing Company. *Co:* Norman Film Manufacturing Company. *Dist:* Norman Studios. *Cast:* Lawrence Criner, Kathryn Boyd, (Original Lafayette Players), Steve Reynolds, "Peg" Marshall, Alfred Norcom, United States Marshal, L.B. Tatums and the entire city of Tatums, Oklahoma. (B&W / Feature / Silent.)

Mart Aston, owner of the Bar Circle Ranch, had sunk all of his cash and cattle to raise cash to sink the first oil well on his ranch. On the adjoining claim, the Ohio Company brings in a well and this forces Aston to drill an offset well within 30 days or lose the permit to drill on his own ranch. At this point, crooks take over and try to thwart his drilling. Through superhuman effort, and without sleep for 48 hours, he fights a band of crooks — only to discover it is a dry hole. Aston winds up in jail. All this makes for an absorbing story of action and thrills with a great surprise at the end when everything is cleared up.

82   The Black King   1932

Dir: Heywood, Donald. *Prod:* Southland Pictures. *Co:* Metropolitan Films. *Dist:* Metropolitan Studios. *Cast:* A.B. Comathiere, Lorenzo Tucker, Vivianne Raber, Knolly Mitchell, Dan Michaels, Mike Jackson, Mary Jane Watkins, Harry Gray, Freeman Fairley, Ismay Andrews, Trixie Smith, James Dunmire.

The Black King was re-released in 1936 as *Harlem Big Shot. The Black King* is typical of the racist films produced in the 1930s by independent white film companies. The story was billed as a satire on the life of Marcus Garvey.

"Originally entitled *Empire, Inc.*" Production supervisor: Charles ?. Cinematographer: Dale Lawson. Recording engineer: Gerre Barton & Armand Schettini. Assistant director: Jos A. Bannon. Technical director: Marc S. Asch. Art director: Anthony Continer. Dialogue: Donald Heyward. Costumes: Brooks. Adapted and edited by Morris M. Levinson. Recorded at Metropolitan Studios, Fort Lee, New Jersey. Reviews in *The Philadelphia Tribune*, 6/20/32, the *Baltimore Afro-American*, 7/30/32 & *Chicago Defender*, 7/23/32. (Feature / 72 min. / B&W / 16mm / 2 reels / Sound.)

The story is about "Charcoal" Johnson, a crooked minister who ousts a kindly old reverend from his Logan, Mississippi, church and takes it over. Johnson's plan is to get the church members to give him money for a "Back to Africa" movement and to proclaim himself King of the United States of Africa. Film makes fun of Marcus Garvey's "Back to Africa" movement. Very stereotypical and unflattering to Negroes.

83   Black Magic   1932

Dir: Micheaux, Oscar. *Prod:* Micheaux, Oscar. *Co:* Micheaux Film Corporation. (B&W / Sound.)

84   Black Narcissus   1929

Dir: Foster, William. *Prod:* Foster, William. *Co:* Pathé. *Dist:* Supreme Distributing. *Cast:* Buck and Bubbles (Ford Lee Washington & John Sublette). (Sound / B&W / Short / Comedy.)

85   Black Network (A Broadway Brevity, 1936)   1936

Dir: Mack, Roy. *Prod:* Vitaphone. *Co:* Vitaphone. *Cast:* Nina Mae McKinney, The Nicholas Brothers, Emmett "Babe" Wallace, Amanda Randolph, Eddie Green, Thomas Chappelle, Washboard Serenaders. (16mm / Sound / B&W / 2 reels / Feature / 65 min. / FAB 1795-1796.)

"The story of a colored radio sponsor with an ambitious wife who wants to be the whole show. Already familiar to picture audiences, the Nicholas Brothers once more put on a dance routine that always clicks and Nina Mae McKinney sings in the new fashion of 'swing.'

Although the supporting cast is of smaller reputation, each member is effective, particularly three boys who supply music with a washboard, manipulated with thimbles and an assortment of pots and pans"—excerpt of review from *Film Daily*, 4/1/36.

86   Black Orpheus   1959

Dir: Camus, Marcel. *Prod:* Gordine, Sacha. *Co:* Lopert Films. *Cast:* Brenoo Mello, Marpessa Dawn.

Grand Prix, 1959 Cannes Festival. Marpessa Dawn, an American dancer, plays Eurydice. Story: Vinicius de Moraes, Screenplay: Jacques Viot. (Made in Brazil / Portuguese with English subtitles / also a dubbed version.) (16mm / 35mm / Color / Sound / Feature / 103 min.)

This Camus film loosely parallels the classic legend of Orpheus and Eurydice. The tragic love story unravels against the background of a carnival in Rio de Janeiro's black ghetto. The film, boasting an all–Negro cast, is based on the most popular of the legends of Orpheus, the musician-poet who could cause even the sun to rise with his playing of the lute, and the great love of Orpheus for his wife Eurydice. When she trod on a serpent and died while fleeing from Aristaeas, Orpheus was inconsolable and descended to the underworld to search for her. Charmed by his music, the deities of Hades allowed him to lead her back to the world of the living—provided he did not look back. But he forgot. Vowing never to look at a woman again, Orpheus returns to earth, but when he refuses to make love to a group of Bacchantes, they tear him to pieces. The film version follows the pattern of the legend, but with all the color, movement and excitement of the world's most famous carnival. A young Brazilian girl, Eurydice, arrives in Rio de Janeiro from the country to visit her cousin during carnival time. She is fleeing from a man whom she fears wants to kill her and is befriended by a trolley car motorman, Orpheus. They fall in love, despite the fact that Orpheus is engaged to the fiery Mira.

87   Black Preview Trailers   1939

Co: Hollywood Pictures Corporation. *Dist:* Sack Amusement Enterprises. *Cast:* Various stars. (16mm / Sound / B&W / 1 reel / 20 min. / Short.)

Contains original theatrical "preview" trailers from the following all-black films: *Bronze Buckaroo, Dark Manhattan, Harlem Rides the Range, Birthright, God's Stepchildren, Juke Joint*, etc.

88   A Black Sherlock Holmes   1917

Dir: Phillips, R.G. *Co:* Ebony Film Company. *Dist:* General Film Company. *Cast:* Ebony Players (Sam Robinson, Samuel "Sambo" Jacks, Will Starks, Julia Mason, Bert Murphy, Evon Skekeeter, Mildred Price, Walter Brogsdale, Robert Duree, Frank Pollard, George Lewis Stock Company), Yvonne Junior.

Very stereotypical comedy. (Short / B&W / Silent / 12 min. / FEA 6622.)

A black comic rendition of Sir Arthur Conan Doyle's story is the first offering of the Ebony Company under its new arrangement, and is the story of a man who believes himself to be a great detective. His efforts to capture a villainous kidnapper led him into many unexpected adventures, but he eventually saves the girl so she might marry her lover.

89   Black Thunderbolt   1921

Co: Millman, A.A. *Dist:* Comet Film Company. *Cast:* Jack Johnson, Marie Banos, Ray Gaby, Francisco Agulio, Asensio Rodriquez.

Filmed in Spain, while Johnson was in exile and released in the U.S. by A.A. Millman. Part of the series; The Blacks. (35mm / Silent / B&W / 7 reels / Feature.)

In the city of Silistra a change of government has not been satisfactory to the people and the restoration of the former monarch is desired. A political conspiracy is inaugurated to restore Prince Frederick to the throne. Prince Frederick, presiding over one of the clandestine meetings, entrusts to Jack Johnson his entire fortune of gold, precious stones, and state papers, telling him to bury them in a certain spot which he specifies and to guard that spot until his little daughter, the princess, is restored to her rightful place as the regent of Silistra. The little princess is then taken to a convent and Johnson is given instructions to never leave her alone. Johnson promises to faithfully carry out the instructions, not out of obedience to his benefactor, but because of his great heart and his desire to help those who suffer unjustly. His path is beset by innumerable dangers but he overcomes them all. The aid of a band of gypsies is enlisted and the little princess is stolen from her house and taken far away with them. When Johnson finds that she has disappeared, his intuition guides him almost unerringly to the little princess. Then begins a series of thrilling and dramatic episodes which carry Johnson far across the country into jungles, until he finally finds the little princess, brings her back and restores her, in time, to the throne.

90   Blackbird Fantasy   1942

Co: RCM Production. *Dist:* Soundies Distributing Corporation. *Cast:* Dorothy Dandridge, Billy Mitchell. (Soundies 9M1 / B&W / Short / Sound / Musical / 12/31/44.)

91   Blitzkreig Bombardier   1944

Co: RCM Production. *Dist:* Soundies Distributing Corporation. *Cast:* Skeets Tolbert and His Orchestra. (Soundies 9M1 / B&W / Short / Sound / Musical / 12/31/44.)

92   Block Party Revels   1943

Dir: Crouch, William Forest. *Prod:* Crouch, William Forest. *Co:* RCM Production. *Dist:* Soundies Distributing Corporation. *Cast:* Lynn Albritton, Billy and Ann, The Six Knobs, The Harlem Cuties. (Soundies 11802 / B&W / Short / Sound / Musical / 5/17/43.)

93   The Blood of Jesus   1941

Dir: Williams, Spencer. *Prod:* Sack, Alfred. *Co:* Amegro Films. *Dist:* Sack Amusement Enterprises. *Cast:* Spencer Williams, Cathryn Caviness, Juanita Riley, Heather Hardeman, Rogenia Goldthwaite, James B. Jones, Frank H. McClennan, Eddie DeBuse, Alva Fuller, R.L. Robertson and The Heavenly Choir.

Cinematographer: Jack Whitman. Sound: R.E. Byers. Screenplay: Spencer Williams. Music: Rev. R.L. Robertson and The Heavenly Choir. (68 min. / 6,065 ft. / 16mm / B&W / Sound / 2 reels / Feature / FBB 388-3889.)

The story of this religious folk drama concerns the accidental shooting of Williams' wife, Martha, and the faith in Jesus that brings her back to life. There are ceremonies with

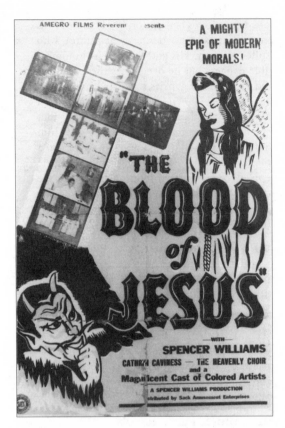

singing and angels. As she lies dying, her soul goes on a symbolic journey in which it rejects Hell for Zion, Satan for God, at the foot of the cross. When she awakens recovered, the choir of sisters and brothers from the church come to sing and celebrate the miracle with Martha and Frank.

94   Blowtop Blues   1945

Co: RCM Production. *Dist:* Soundies Distributing Corporation. *Cast:* Cab Calloway and His Orchestra. (Soundies 21808 / B&W / Short / Sound / Musical / 10/29/45.)

95   Blues in the Night   1942

Co: Minoco Production. *Dist:* Soundies Distributing Corporation. *Cast:* Cab Calloway and His Orchestra: Lamar Wright, Russell Smith, Shad Collins, Jonah Jones (trumpets); Key Johnson, Tyree Glenn, Quentin Jackson (trombones); Jerry Black, Hilton Jefferson, Andrew Brown, Teddy McRae, Walter Thomas, (reeds); Benny Payne (piano); Danny Barker (guitar); Milt Hilton (brass);

Cozy Cole (drums); The Cabaliers (the four Palmer Brothers) (vocal quartet). (Soundies 5201 / B&W / Short / Sound / Musical / 1/28/42.)

96   Boarding House Blues   1948

Dir: Binney, Josh. *Prod:* Glucksman, E.M. *Co:* All American News. *Cast:* Jackie "Moms" Mabley, John Mason & Company, Johnny Lee, Jr., Dusty Fletcher, Marcellus Wilson, Marie Cooke, Emery Richardson, James Cross & Harold Cromer (Stump & Stumpy), Sidney Easton, Freddie Robinson, J. Augustus Smith, Edgar Martin, John Piano, Lucky Millinder & His Band, Una Mae Carlisle, Bull Moose Jackson, Berry Brothers, Lewis & White, Anistine Allen, Paul Breckenridge, Lee Norman Trio & "Crip" Heard (one-armed and one-legged dancer).

Original story by Hal Seeger. Directory of photography: Sid Zucker. Cameramen: Frank Lafollette & George Stoetzel. Sound engineer: Harold Vivian. Art director: Sam Corso. Makeup: Doc Liszt. Assistant director:

Salvatore Scappa, Jr. Review in the *New York Age*, 9/14/48. (35mm / Sound / B&W / 90 min. / 1 reel / Feature / FEA 6071-6075, FEA 4685.)

The plot of the story is trivial and the film is primarily a showcase for the various entertainers appearing in the picture. Moms runs a boarding house of entertainers. When she can't make the rent she tells her boarders that if she can't pay then they'll all be out on the street. A plan is concocted: Moms plays a fortune teller and convinces a potential producer to do another show. He does, and hires mom's boarders to be in the show. Mom gets enough money to pay the landlord.

97   Bob Howard's House Party
1947

Co: Century Productions. *Cast:* Bob Howard, Noble Sissle and His Band. (10 min. / Musical / Short / B&W / Sound.)

98   Bobbling Over   1949
(B&W / Sound / Short.)

99   Body and Soul   1924

Dir: Micheaux, Oscar. *Prod:* Micheaux, Oscar. *Co:* Micheaux Film Corporation. *Dist:* Micheaux Film Corporation. *Cast:* Paul Robeson, Julia Theresa Russell, Mercedes Gilbert, E.G. Tatum, Percy Verwayen.

Paul Robeson's first film role. Preview in *New York Age*, 11/11/25. (16mm / B&W / Silent / Feature / 75 min.)

This is the story of a minister gone corrupt. He associates with the owner of a house of gambling, from whom he extorts money. He forces a girl of his church to steal her mother's savings and leave home. He later kills the girl's brother when he attempts to rescue the girl. But when it's all said and done it's only a dream.

In his first film, Robeson plays a dual role — a preacher who preys on the people of his congregation as well as the heroine, and he also plays his own brother, a good man. Required to give a balance to his theme by the New York Censors, Micheaux changed the preacher's role so that he is preacher, then detective, then finally an uplifting bourgeois future husband for the heroine.

100   Boogie Man   1943

Co: RCM Production. *Dist:* Soundies Distributing Corporation. *Cast:* Johnny Long and His Orchestra. (Soundies / B&W / Short / Sound / Musical / 10/18/43.)

101   Boogie Woogie   1944

Co: RCM Production. *Dist:* Soundies Distributing Corporation. *Cast:* Meade Lux Lewis, Dudley Dickerson, Joe Turner. (Soundies 16308 / B&W / Short / Sound / Musical / 4/24/44.)

102   Boogie Woogie Blues   1948

Co: All American News. *Cast:* Hadda Brooks. (16mm / Sound / B&W / 1 reel / 10 min. / 900 ft. / Musical / Short.)

Brooks, accompanying herself on the piano, sings several songs. Although the set is only one living room location, the cool beauty and low sultry voice of Brooks makes the film a delight. Of further interest is the manner in which the director obviously tries to "stretch" the three numbers into filling one "reel" of film. Several times he has her reprise a final chorus of a number that she obviously ended, even after we hear the director yelling "Cut!" off-screen.

103   Boogie Woogie Dream   1942

Dir: Burger, Hans. *Prod:* Goldberg, Jack & Dave. *Co:* Hollywood Pictures Corporation. *Cast:* Lena Horne, Albert Ammons, Pete Johnson, Teddy Wilson and His Orchestra.

Review in *Film Daily*, 7/6/44. (16mm / Sound / B&W / Musical / 13 min. / Short.)

Lena Horne, a dishwasher, sits with a painter and a piano player after the closing of a club, dreaming of jamming together. During the dream sequence they are performing as stars and are joined by Teddy Wilson and His Orchestra. When they awaken from their dream by the ringing phone they are surprised to find a white music producer and his wife (who had fallen asleep at their table) offering them an audition and contract.

104   Boogie Woogie Dream   1944

Dir: Burger, Hans. *Prod:* Goldberg, Jack & Dave. *Co:* Hollywood Pictures Corporation. *Dist:* Soundies Distributing Corporation. *Cast:* Lena Horne, Albert Ammons, Pete Johnson.

Excerpted from the Hollywood Production short "Boogie Woogie Dream" (1942). (Soundies / B&W / Short / Sound / Musical / 12/31/44.)

105   Boogie Woogie Piggy   1944
Co: RCM Production. *Dist:* Soundies Distributing Corporation.

106   Boogiemania   1946
Dir: Crouch, William Forest. *Prod:* Crouch, William Forest. *Co:* Filmcraft Production. *Dist:* Soundies Distributing Corporation. *Cast:* Nicky O'Daniel, The Sun Tan Four, Helen Bangs, Albert Reese Jones. (Soundies 18M6 / B&W / Short / Sound / Musical / 4/29/46.)

107   Booglie Wooglie Piggy   1941
Co: RCM Production. *Dist:* Soundies Distributing Corporation. *Cast:* The Deep River Boys. (Soundies 4102 / Short / Sound / Musical / B&W / 11/10/41.)

**108   Booker T. Washington's
            Industrial School**   1917
(Documentary / B&W / Short / Silent.)
Views showing the building, farms, and students working and learning trades at the Tuskegee Institute in Alabama; the cotton industry in the South; and the religious progress of the black churches of Boston.

109   Borderline   1929
Dir: Macpherson, Kenneth. *Co:* Pool Films. *Cast:* Paul Robeson, Eslanda Goode Robeson, Hilda Doolittle (white).
Robeson's first foreign film, shot in Switzerland. "A study in visual contrasts as well as a comment on racism." (B&W / Silent / Feature.)
Robeson plays Pete, a small town cafe worker whose wife Adah returns from an involvement with a white man. Thorne and his wife become estranged over the issue and the town blames Pete and Adah. Thorne's wife dies accidentally, thereby giving the town another excuse for making Pete the scapegoat for its hatred.

110   Bosko and the Pirate   1937
Co: Metro-Goldwyn-Mayer. *Cast:* Cab Calloway, Louis Armstrong, Mills Brothers. (8 min. / Animated / Short / B&W / Sound.)

In this animated short, a grog colony impersonates Cab Calloway, Louis Armstrong and the Mills Brothers.

111   Boy! What a Girl!   1946
Dir: Leonard, Arthur. *Prod:* Goldberg, Jack / Arthur Leonard. *Co:* Herald Pictures, Inc. *Cast:* Tim Moore, Elwood Smith, Duke Williams, Al Jackson, Warren Patterson (Patterson and Jackson), Sheila Guyse, Betti Mays, Sybil Lewis, Milton Wood, Slam Stewart Trio, Deek Watson and His Brown Dots, "Big" Sid Catlett and Band, Ann Cornell, The Harlemaniacs, Basil Spears, Ram Ramirez, and guest star Gene Krupa, Marva Louis.
Original screenplay: Vincent Valentini. Cinematographer: George Webber. Music supervision: John Gluskin. Art director: Sam Corso. Costumes: Ann Blazier. Makeup: Morgan Jones. Film editor: Jack Kemp. Sound: Mac Williams. Casting: Billy Shaw. Technical director: J.M. Lehrfeld. Announcement and preview in *The Philadelphia Tribune*,

8/27/46 and the *Philadelphia Independent*, 1/11/47. Reviews in the *Philadelphia Independent*, 2/1/47 and the *New York Amsterdam News*, 5/5/47. (16mm / Sound / B&W / 70 min. / Feature / 7 reels on 2.)

The story involves two would-be producers who get a promise from a Chicago financier to back half their show if they find another backer for the other half. When the other financier fails to show, they impersonate her to the other financier until she shows up, which creates a hilarious situation. Love wins out and the show goes on.

The Brand of Cain *see* **Murder in Harlem**

112   Breakfast in Rhythm   1943
Co: RCM Production. *Dist:* Soundies Distributing Corporation. *Cast:* The Three Chefs, Barry Paige's Orchestra.

Instrumental in background is "Be Careful." (Soundies 6M3 / B&W / Short / Sound / Musical / 10/29/43.)

113   Bright Road   1953
Dir: Mayer, Gerald. *Prod:* Fielding, Sol P. *Co:* Metro-Goldwyn-Mayer. *Cast:* Dorothy Dandridge, Harry Belafonte, Phillip Hepburn, Maidie Norman, Vivian Dandridge, Barbara Ann Sanders, Robert Horton (white), Renee Beard.

Screenplay: Emmett Lavery. Story based on "See How They Run," by Mary E. Vroman. (16mm / Sound / B&W / 2 reels / 69 min. / Feature.)

Dorothy Dandridge plays a young teacher trying to help a withdrawn, insecure student played by Philip Hepburn.

114   Broadway   1946
Dir: Anderson, Leonard. *Prod:* Alexander, William D. *Co:* Alexander Production. *Dist:* Soundies Distributing Corporation. *Cast:* Henry Woode and His Orchestra. (Soundies / B&W / Short / Sound / Musical / 12/30/46.)

115   Broadway and Main   1946
Dir: Crouch, William Forest. *Prod:* Crouch, William Forest. *Co:* Filmcraft Production. *Dist:* Soundies Distributing Corporation. *Cast:* Gloria Parker, Stepin Fetchit.

Sack Amusement Enterprises PRESENTS CLARENCE MUSE IN "THE BROKEN EARTH"

(Soundies / B&W / Short / Sound / Musical / 2/4/46.)

116   The Broken Earth   1939
Dir: Freulich, Roman. *Co:* Continental Pictures, Inc. *Dist:* Sack Amusement Enterprises. *Cast:* Clarence Muse, Freida Shaw Choir.

Screenwriter: Roman Freulich. Associate producer: Andrew V. White. Assistant director: Henry Spitz. Cinematographers: Jerome Ash, King Grey. Sound: Hans Wieren. Editor: George McGrath. Musical director: Freida Shaw. (Short / 11 min. / B&W / Sound.)

Joshua, a poor farmer with a dog and a son, works hard to care for his son. He visits his wife's grave and tells her that Little Joshua, their son, is going to get well. While out in the fields working, the dog comes to get him because his son has taken a turn for the worse. While praying for his son's life, a strong ray of sunlight breaks through the clouds over their cabin. Slowly, Little Joshua opens his eyes.

117   Broken Strings   1940
Dir: Ray, Bernard B. *Prod:* L.C. Borden

Productions. *Co:* International Road Shows. *Cast:* Clarence Must, Sybil Lewis, William Washington, Tommiwitta More, Stymie Beard, Pete Webster, Edward Thoompson, Buck Woods, Jesse Lee Brooks, Darry Jones, Earl J. Morris, Stevens Sisters, Elliot Carpenter, Curtis Mosby and His Orchestra.

Story & direction by Bernard B. Ray. Screenplay by Clarence Muse, Bernard Ray and David Arlen. Dialogue by Carl Krubada, Clarence Muse, David Arlen. Production manager: Bobby Ray. Photography: Max Stengle. Musical arrangements: Elliot Carpenter. Art director: Fred Preble. Film editor: Fredric Bain. Sound technician: Hans Weeren. Makeup: Harry Ross. Review in *Pittsburgh Courier,* 3/25/40. (16mm / B&W / Sound / 80 min. / Feature / 35mm / 6 reels FEA 8221-8226.)

A classical violinist (Clarence Muse) is in an accident and injures his fingers on his left hand, making it impossible for him to play. A devotee of the classics, he does not like swing

music. His son, played by William Washington, also plays the violin and although he is successful with the classics, his real love is swing. Needing money, the boy enters a contest where he is about to play a classical number. Unknown to him, his violin has been tampered with by another contestant and when two strings break, the boy is forced to play swing and is a handclapping success. The father unwittingly applauds his son and in doing so causes his injured fingers to move again, thereby regaining his playing ability. The son and father live happily ever after.

118   Broken Violin   1926

Dir: Micheaux, Oscar. *Prod:* Micheaux, Oscar. *Co:* Micheaux Film Corporation. *Dist:* Micheaux Film Corporation. *Cast:* Gertrude Snelson, J. Homer Tutt, Daisy Foster, "Boots" Horne, Ardella Dabney, W. Hill, Ethel Smith, Alice B. Russell.

Screenplay by Oscar Micheaux, based on his book, *House of Mystery.* Short preview in the *Philadelphia Tribune,* 5/29/29. (Feature / Silent / B&W.)

Lelia Cooper, a young washwoman with a proficiency for the violin, is unfortunately involved with an abusive father. In an argument with her mother, the father smashes Lelia's violin over her mom's head. Her younger brother tries to come to the mother's rescue, but one thing leads to another and the film culminates in a chase resulting in the father being hit by a truck — another daring approach by Micheaux.

119   The Bronze Buckaroo   1938

Dir: Kahn, Richard C. *Prod:* Buell, Jed. *Co:* Hollywood Pictures Corporation. *Dist:* Sack Amusement Enterprises. *Cast:* Herbert Jeffries, Flournoy E. Miller, Lucius Brooks, Clarence Brooks, Lee Calmes, Earl J. Morris (Drama editor for the *Pittsburgh Courier*), Artie Young, Rollie Hardin, W.C. Pumis, Spencer Williams, The Four Tones.

Picture was filmed at N.B. Murray's (black) dude ranch, then located near Victorville, California. Written by Richard C. Kahn. Photographed by Roland Price & Clark Ramsey. Production manager: Dick L'estrange. Art director: Vin Taylor. Sound engineer: Cliff

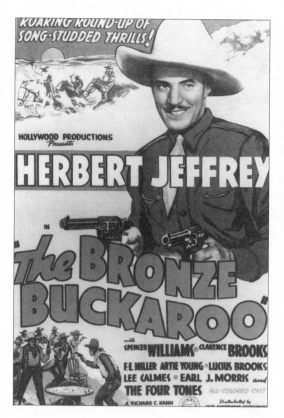

Ruberg. Music by Lew Porter. (Feature / Western / 57 min. / B&W / Sound / Video.)

Bob Blake and his sidekick, Dusty, go to the Jackson ranch to aid Betty Jackson, whose father has been shot in the back. Bob starts his search for the gang of outlaws who are responsible for the murder by questioning the ranchers in the area. In the end, Bob tracks down the villain, Buck Thorn, who is killed in a final shootout in the canyon.

120   The Bronze Venus (The Duke Is Tops)   1943

Dir: Popkin, Leo. *Prod:* Popkin, Harry M. *Co:* Toddy Pictures Company. *Dist:* Toddy Pictures Company. *Cast:* Ralph Cooper, Lena Horne, Lawrence Criner, Monte Hawley, Vernon McCalla, Edward Thompson, Neva Peoples, Charles Hawkins, Johnny Taylor, Everett Brown, Arthur Ray, Ray Martin, Guernsey Morrow, Basin Street Boys, The Cats and the Fiddle.

See *The Duke Is Tops. The Bronze Venus* is the re-released *The Duke Is Tops*, 1938. Originally made by Million Dollar Productions. (Sound / B&W / Feature.)

This is the story of a producer-performer team that has to break up when one, the lady, gets a better job in New York. The man's career fails; the lady is first a big hit, then also fails. They get together again for the finale, when combined efforts put them in the big time.

121   Brother   1918

Dir: Foster, William. *Prod:* Foster, William. *Co:* Foster Photoplay Company. *Dist:* Foster, William. (6 reels / Feature / Silent / B&W.)

A six-reel drama, starting back some 30 years. Showing four sides of life: the bad colored man, the bad white man, the good colored man, and the good white man. No race of men is better than its woman. Not every white man in the South is a race hater.

122   Brother Bill   1945

Co: RCM Production. *Dist:* Soundies Distributing Corporation. *Cast:* The Jubalaires.

(Soundies 20108 / B&W / Short / Sound / Musical 3/5/45.)

123   Brother Martin, Servant of Jesus   1942

Dir: Williams, Spencer. *Co:* Jenkins and Bourgeois. *Cast:* Spencer Williams.

Written by Spencer Williams. (B&W / Sound / Feature.)

124   Brown Bomber   1939

Dir: Lewis, Edward W. *Prod:* Lewis Edward W. *Co:* Million Dollar Productions. *Cast:* Joe Louis. (Documentary/ Newsreel / B&W / Short / Sound.)

Joe Louis, the world heavyweight boxing champion, reveals his training secrets.

125   Brown Gravy   1929

Prod: Christie, Al. *Co:* Paramount. *Cast:* Evelyn Preer, Spencer Williams, Edward Thompson.

Original story by Octavus Roy Cohen. Screenplay: Spencer Williams. (35mm / B&W / Sound / 2 reels / Comedy / Short.)

Dialect gags, black religious and fraternal life and black music abound in this Christie comedy, which also has a singing contest between black choruses in Memphis.

126   The Brute   1920

Dir: Micheaux, Oscar. *Prod:* Micheaux, Oscar. *Co:* Micheaux Film Corporation. *Dist:* Micheaux Film Corporation. *Cast:* Evelyn Preer, Sam Langford (prize fighter), Lawrence Criner, A.B. Comathiere, Susie Sutton.

George P. Johnson witnessed *The Brute* and said, "Plot good. Dramatic action good. Settings poor in all but one scene. Photography poor. Comedy very good. Sam Langford fight scene very good. Picture as a whole best he's produced" (Micheaux). (Feature / B&W / Silent.)

The story is of a beautiful and tender girl in the clutches of a shrewd gambler and boss of the underworld where the creed is "to make a woman love you, knock her down." Sam Langford, the boxer, battles against lynching in the South in this Micheaux melodrama which was shut down by Southern police. Evelyn Preer is the beautiful girl who falls into the clutches of the underworld brute.

127   Bubbling Over   1934

Dir: Jason, Leigh. *Co:* Van Beuren-Meyer, David / RKO Radio. *Cast:* Ethel Waters, Frank Wilson, Hamtree Harrington, Southernaires Quartet, William Edmondson.

Review in *Film Daily*, 1/9/34. (16mm / B&W / Sound / 2 reels / 20 min. / Comedy / Short / FBB 2379.)

The comings and goings in a Harlem tenement are featured in this musical comedy. Ethel Waters attempts to get rid of her lazy husband's out-of-work relatives. She sings "Darkies Never Dream." Frank Wilson plays the mind reader, Swami River.

128   Buck and Bubbles Laff Jamboree   1945

Co: Toddy Pictures Company. *Cast:* Buck and Bubbles. (B&W / Sound / Feature.)

129   A Bucket of Cream Ale   1904

Co: American Mutoscope / Biograph. (B&W / Short / Silent / FLA 4519.)

"A gruff Dutchman is seated in a sparsely

furnished room. A Negro servant woman enters, carrying a bucket of ale. She pours a glass for the man, and standing behind him, she takes a long swig on the bucket. He turns and angrily hurls his glass at her. In the blink of an eye, no pause to consider consequences, pure rage her only response, she dumps the bucket over the white man's head"—Thomas Cripps.

130   Bud Harris and Frank Radcliffe   1929

Co: Vitaphone. *Cast:* Bud Harris, Frank Radcliffe.

Songs: "St. Louis Blues," "She's Mine." (Comedy / Sound / B&W / Short.)

… a comedy skit called "At the Party."

131   The Bull-Dogger   1923

Prod: Norman Film Manufacturing Company. *Co:* Norman Film Manufacturing Company. *Dist:* Norman Film Company. *Cast:* Bill Pickett, Anita Bush, Steve Reynolds. (Feature / B&W / Silent.)

"A virile story of the golden west, featuring Bill Pickett, the Black hero of the Mexican bull ring, in death defying feats of courage and skill, such as wild horse racing, roping and tying wild steers. The picture also includes fancy and trick riding by Black cowboys and cowgirls and bull dogging and throwing with their teeth, the wildest wild steers on the Mexican border. This is the first feature picture of its kind, and proves conclusively that the Black cowboy is capable of doing anything the white cowboy does"— excerpt from *Exhibitor's Herald.*

132   The Bully   1918

Co: Ebony Film Company. *Dist:* General Film Company. *Cast:* Ebony Players (Sam Robinson, Samuel "Sambo" Jacks, Will Starks, Julia Mason, Bert Murphy, Evon Skekeeter, Mildred Price, Walter Brogsdale, Robert Duree, Frank Pollard, George Lewis Stock Company), Yvonne Junior, Rudolph Tatum. (Silent / B&W / Short.)

"This number, enacted by a cast composed

entirely of colored players, including Sam Robinson, Yvonne Junior and Rudolph Tatum, is exaggerated slapstick, the story dealing with a bully who works in a bakery and is finally overcome by a new cook who subdues him by means of a loaf of bread in which he has placed a horseshoe. It is about on the average with the previous issues of this brand and contains some laughs" — *The Moving Picture World*, 6/8/18.

133   A Bundle of Blues   1933

Co: Paramount. *Cast:* Duke Ellington and His Orchestra, Ivy Anderson. (16mm / B&W / Sound / 1 reel / 10 min. / Musical / Short.)

"Among other numbers, Ivy Anderson sings an elaborately staged version of 'Stormy Weather' in this musical short. The Duke plays an 'illustrated' conception of 'Stormy Weather' vocalized by a feminine sepia warbler (Ivie Anderson) with descriptive scenes showing rain in various places and from various angles. A nice bit of conception and quite artistically done. Some fast dancing by a couple of girls brings the short to a fast finish" — excerpt of review from *Film Daily*, 9/13/33.

134   The Burden of Race   1921

Co: Reol Productions. *Cast:* Edna Morton, Lawrence Chenault, Elizabeth Williams, Percy Verwayen, Mabel Young, Arthur Ray.

Review in *The Philadelphia Tribune*, 11/19/21. (Feature / B&W / Silent.)

At a great university he competed with the flower of young manhood and excelled both in academic achievement and in athletics. And then he met the girl — not of his own people — and for her he risked his life. In the greater university of life he grappled with the forces which made for success and or failure — and won. The girl, with no hope of that love's fruition, was his inspiration. He stood at the pinnacle of success fame. She loved him, but between them stretched a mighty chasm. Did a great love triumph? This is the story that grips the hearts of young and old and sends the blood coursing through the veins.

135   Burlesque in Harlem   1955

Dir: Alexander, William. *Prod:* Tuller, Joseph. *Co:* T.N.T. Pictures Corporation. *Cast:*

Dewey "Pigmeat" Markham, George Wiltshire, Vivian Harris, Dick Barrow, Jo Jo Adams, Mabel Hunter, Gertrude Baby Banks, Luella Owens, Princess Dorsey, Gloria Howard, Slip and Slide, Tarza Young, Betty Taylor Taylorettes, Olive Sayles, Maria Rout, Adella Gross, Ezella Lester, Marion L. Greene, Dorothy McCarty, Fannie Thornton, Griffen Trixie Terry, Rose Marie Foster, Gwendolyn Shaklett.

Costumes: Betty Taylor. Photography: G.G. Leontough & Vide Martino. Soundman: J. Suacure. Edited by Nathan of Braunstein & Sheldon Nemeyer. Technical advisor: Dewitt Jackson. (Feature / B&W / Sound / 60 min.)

Variety show type, with Markham, dancers, strippers, and musicians. Like *Rhythm and Blues Review*, typical for this period.

136   A Busted Romance   1917

Co: Ebony Film Company. *Dist:* General Film Company. *Cast:* Ebony Players (Sam Robinson, Samuel "Sambo" Jacks, Will Starks, Julia Mason, Bert Murphy, Evon Skekeeter, Mildred Price, Walter Brogsdale, Robert Duree, Frank Pollard, George Lewis Stock Company). (Short / Silent / B&W / 1 reel.)

"This one-reeler centers about a stray 'coon' living by his wits, a town gambler and a parson whose conscience can be made retroactive when money is shown. The transient wins the love of the gambler's sweetheart and is about to be married to her when his wife and four children appear on the scene" — *Exhibitor's Herald*, 2/22/17.

137   The Butler   1911

Dir: Foster, William. *Prod:* Foster, William. *Co:* Foster Photoplay Company. *Dist:* William Foster. (Short / Silent / B&W.)

A kidnap/detective melodrama.

138   Butt-ing In   1914

Dir: Lubin, Sigmund. *Prod:* Lubin, Sigmund. *Co:* Lubin Manufacturing Company. *Cast:* John Edwards, Clayborn Jones.

Written by Arthur D. Hotaling. Released on 11/10/14. (Silent / B&W / Short / 400 ft.)

"Brown does not like his cigar and having plenty of money, cast it away. Weary Nigger, who has no cigar and less money, seized the butt.

John Jinks, the cop, who is not allowed to spend any money buying cigars, sees a lost chance to secure the butt and gives Weary a lively chase. Weary is very unfortunate, for he encounters many obstacles to prevent his enjoying the butt, but not so with John, the cop, who captures Weary, secures the butt and smokes up to his heart's content"—*Herald Films.*

139 Buzz Me 1945

Dir: Crouch, William Forest. *Prod:* Adams, Berle. *Co:* Astor Pictures Corporation. *Dist:* Soundies Distributing Corporation. *Cast:* Louis Jordan and His Tympany Five.

Excerpted from the Astor two-reel short "Caldonia" (1945). (Soundies / 20308 / B&W / Short / Sound / Musical / 4/2/45.)

140 By an Old Southern River 1942

Co: RCM Production. *Dist:* Soundies Distributing Corporation. *Cast:* Bill Robinson. (Soundies 5907 / B&W / Short / Sound / Musical / 3/9/42.)

141 By Line Newsreel 1950

Dir: Alexander, William D. *Prod:* Alexander, William D. *Co:* Alexander Production. (4 newsreels / B&W / Sound / Short.)

Featuring footage of: Marian Anderson receiving an honorary Ph.D. from Morgan State University in Baltimore; a beauty contest; a Morgan State University vs. N.C. A. & T. University football game; a Pepsi-Cola commercial featuring an all-black cast.

142 By Request 1935

Dir: Mack, Roy. *Co:* Vitaphone. *Cast:* Claude Hopkins and His Orchestra, Tip, Tap and Toe.

Songs: "Sweet Horn," "To Call You My Own," "Every Day," and "Quarter to Nine." (B&W / Short / Sound.)

"A classy presentation of Claude Hopkins and His Orchestra .... The setting is a swanky night club ... with songs .... The work of the ivory-manipulator and the tapping of the three lads is something calling for cheers. Plenty of color in this black-and-white short — but it is all swell Harlem tints"— excerpt from review in the *Film Daily,* 10/18/35.

143 By Right of Birth 1921

Co: Lincoln Motion Picture Company. *Cast:* Clarence Brooks, Anita Thompson, Webb King, Lester Bates, Lew Meehan, Grace Ellenwood, Baby Ruth Kinbrough, Helen Childers, Beatrice George, Minnie Prevost (American Indian), Leo Bates, Dora Mitchell.

Review in *The Philadelphia Tribune,* 11/5/21. Screenplay: George P. Johnson. (16mm / B&W / Silent / 1 reel / Dramatic / Short / FAB 156.)

Juanita Cooper is the adopted daughter of Frank Cooper and Geraldine Cooper. Geraldine backs Manuel Romero, an unscrupulous Mexican-American stockbroker, on a trip to Oklahoma to secure oil leases from Freedmen allottees, who are ignorant of the real value of their holdings. Romero focuses on an allotment belonging to Helen, a missing allottee. He forges Helen's name to a lease, while searching for her. Geraldine discovers that Juanita is the missing Helen. After witnessing deceit and death, Juanita is reunited with her real mother and comes into the fortune and happiness which is hers.

144 Cab Calloway Medley 1945

Co: RCM Production. *Dist:* Soundies Distributing Corporation. *Cast:* Cab Calloway and Band. (Soundies 1M / B&W / Short / Sound / Musical.)

145 Cab Calloway's Hi-De-Ho 1934

Dir: Waller, Fred "Fats." *Prod:* Glucksman, E.M. *Co:* Paramount. *Cast:* Cab Calloway's Orchestra. (16mm / Sound / B&W / 1 reel / 10 min. / Musical / Short.)

Between swing numbers, Calloway finds time to flirt with the wife of a pullman porter, while her husband is away at work. Orchestra plays "Rail Rhythm" and "The Lady with the Fan."

146 Cab Calloway's Jitterbug Party 1935

Dir: Waller, Fred "Fats." *Co:* Paramount. *Cast:* Cab Calloway and His Band, Ethel Moses. (16mm / Sound / B&W / 1 reel / 10 min. / Musical / Short.)

"More of Cab's special brand of musical zaniness in a Harlem nightclub. A load of

Latouche. Music: Vernon Duke. Musical adaptation: Roger Edens. Musical direction: George Stoll. Orchestration: George Bassman. Choral arrangements: Hall Johnson. Director of photography: Sidney Wagner. Sound engineer: Douglas Sheaer. Art director: Cedric Gibbons, Associate: Leonid Vasian. Set: Edwin A. Willis. Costumes: Irene. Film editor: Harold Kress. Preview in *The Philadelphia Afro-American*, 9/12/42. Reviews in *The Philadelphia Tribune*, 4/3/43, *The Philadelphia Afro-American*, 4/3/43 and *Film Daily*, 2/15/43. (16mm / Sound / Sepia tones / B&W / 3 reels / 100 min. / Feature.)

A musical religious fantasy is the frame for the story of Little Joe and his wife Petunia. Little Joe is a "backslider"; a sweepstakes ticket and Georgia Brown put his soul in jeopardy. In heaven, a battle for it goes on between Lucifer, Jr., and a General of the Lord.

148   Cake Walk   pre–1910
(B&W / Silent / Short / FLA 3381.)

149   Caldonia   1945
Prod: Jordan, Louis. *Co:* Astor Pictures Corporation. *Cast:* Louis Jordan, Nicki O'Daniel,

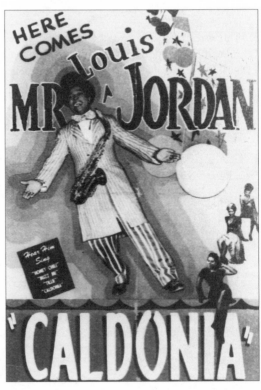

cotton club hotcha, mostly orchestra numbers and some hi-de-ho singing led by Cab Calloway, totaling up as fair entertainment. After a sequence in the night club, the party changes to street clothes and goes to a Harlem rendezous for what Calloway calls a jitterbug party, mostly shimmying and noisemaking" — review from *Film Daily*, 5/16/35.

147   Cabin in the Sky   1943
Dir: Minnelli, Vincente. *Prod:* Freed, Arthur. *Co:* Metro-Goldwyn-Mayer. *Cast:* Eddie Anderson, Lena Horne, Ethel Waters, Louis Armstrong, Rex Ingram, Duke Ellington and His Orchestra, The Hall Johnson Choir, Kenneth Spencer, Ernest Whitman, Mantan Moreland, Oscar Polk, Buck and Bubbles (Ford Lee Washington and John Sublett), Willie Best, Butterfly McQueen, Ruby Dandridge, "Moke" Fletcher Rivers, Bill Bailey, Nicodemus Stewart.

Minnelli's first feature. Screenplay: Joseph Schrank. Associate producer: Albert Lewis. Based on the book by Lynn Root. Lyrics: John

Roxie Joynes, Richard Huey, Sam Sporty-O-Dee, Taylor and Harris, George Wiltshire, Three Sun Tan Girls, Milton Woods.

Reviews in the *New York Age*, 8/5/45 and *Film Daily*, 10/4/45. (16mm / Sound / B&W / 18 min. / Musical / Short / Featurette.)

Typical Louis Jordan musical — thin plot but lots of music. Caldonia, Jordan's sweetheart, cannot bear to lose her sweetheart to a Hollywood contract. She cooks up a plot to trick Jordan into staying in New York. She convinces a friend to hire Jordan to make a movie in New York, only to be thwarted when creditors begin removing the set and equipment while filming. In typical Jordan fashion he sings "All This Trouble, and I Could Be in Hollywood," which ends the film.

150   Caldonia 1945

Dir: Crouch, William Forest. *Prod:* Adams, Berle. *Co:* Astor Pictures Corporation. *Dist:* Soundies Distributing Corporation. *Cast:* Louis Jordan and His Tympany Five, Roxie Joynes.

Excerpted from the Astor two-reel "Caldonia" (1945). (Soundies 20808 / B&W / Short / Sound / Musical / 6/11/45.)

151   Calhon — The Way to a Better Future 1945

Co: Harmon Foundation Educational Films. (Documentary / B&W / Short / Silent / 1 reel.)

The story of the work of the Calhon School serving the Negro people of Lowndes County, Alabama.

152   The Call of His People 1921

Co: Reol Productions. *Dist:* Cummings & Paul Distributing Co. *Cast:* George Brown, Edna Morton, Mae Kemp, James Stevens, Lawrence Chenault, Mercedes Gilbert, Percy Verwayen.

Based on the novel, *The Man Who Would Be White*, by Aubrey Bowser. Filmed at the Irvington-on-the-Hudson, NY, estate of Black millionairess, A. Lelia Walker, story by Aubrey Brower. Preview in *Billboard*, 7/16/21. (35mm / Silent / B&W / 6 reels / Feature.)

Nelson Holmes, a black man posing as a white man, had advanced from office boy to general manager. Nelson, hiding his true identity for obvious reasons, comes face to face with an old classmate during a job interview. Fearing that his friend will expose his true color, he hires him to be his personal secretary. When one of Nelson's competitors tries to steal important contracts, his secretary rescues the contracts. Nelson is deeply affected by his secretary's loyalty, and decides to confess his true color to his boss. His boss assures him that it is the man, not the color, that counts.

153   The Call to Duty 1946

Dir: Alexander, William D. *Prod:* Alexander, William D. *Co:* Alexander Production. *Cast:* Narrated by Walter Huston.

Review in the *Associated Negro Press* (NY), 1947. (Documentary / Sound / B&W / Short.)

A documentary film of Negro army exploits.

154   Callalco 1937

Dir: Nicholson, Irene & Brian Montagu. *Co:* British Film Company.

Songs by Edric Connor. (British / B&W / Sound / 16mm / Documentary / Short.)

"A documentary made for the Trinidad Guardian. Ursula Johnson, a worker in Port of Spain, is one of the Trinidadians in the film."

155   Camp Meeting 1936

Co: RKO Radio Pictures. *Cast:* Hall Johnson Choir, Clarence Muse. (B&W / Short / 2 reels / Sound / Musical.)

A musical rendition of an old-time camp meeting down in the South.

156   The Cannibal King 1915

Dir: Lubin, Sigmund. *Prod:* Lubin, Sigmund. *Co:* Lubin Manufacturing Company. *Cast:* Babe Hardy, Frances Ne Moyer, Harry Loraine, J. Frank Glendon, Frank C. Griffin.

Written by Edwin Ray Coffin. Released on 7/6/15. (Silent / B&W / Short / 500 ft.)

"Willie's desire to give his sweetheart a birthday present is responsible for his becoming a moving-picture actor. Unless he earns some money he cannot pay Grace the tribute she deserves. Willie's work consists in being made up for a cannibal and it is carried out to the smallest detail — so much that when Grace, accompanied by Willie's hated rival Fred, comes to the studio on a sightseeing visit, she does not recognize her Willie. But when Willie sees Fred making love to Grace he gives one whoop and flees. He is pursued by a howling mob and many policemen. He takes refuge in Grace's home and finds her badly upset over the studio happenings. When he throws himself before her to explain, Fred beats a hasty retreat and leaves Grace to her fate at the hands of the cannibal. This convinces Grace, once and for all, that Fred is unworthy and she gives her heart unreservedly to Willie. When Fred returns, shamefaced, Grace haughtily orders him from her and announces her immediate marriage to cannibal whose identity Fred never guesses"—*Lubin Bulletin.*

157   Can't See for Lookin' 1944
   Co: RCM Production. *Dist:* Soundies Distributing Corporation. *Cast:* Ida James. (Soundies 19608 / B&W / Short / Sound / Musical / 12/30/44.)

158   Caravan 1942
   Co: RCM Production. *Dist:* Soundies Distributing Corporation. *Cast:* The Mills Brothers. (Soundies 8907 / B&W / Short / Sound / Musical / 10/12/42.)

159   Carib Gold 1956
   Prod: Waters, Ethel. *Co:* Splendora Film Company. *Cast:* Ethel Waters, Cecily Tyson, Coley Wallace, Geoffrey Holder, Ruth Sawyer. (Sound / Feature / B&W.)
   This film tells the story of the search for sunken treasure off the Florida Keys.

160   Carmen Jones 1954
   Dir: Preminger, Otto. *Prod:* Preminger, Otto. *Co:* 20th Century–Fox Film Corporation. *Dist:* 20th Century–Fox. *Cast:* Harry Belafonte, Dorothy Dandridge, Pearl Bailey, Olga James, Joe Adams, Roy Glenn, Diahann Carroll, Brock Peters, Alvin Ailey, Nick Stewart.
   Book & lyrics by Oscar Hammerstein, 2nd. Music: Oscar Hammerstein. Screenplay: Harry Kleiner. Dandridge's singing is dubbed with Marilyn Horne's voice, Belafonte's with Le Vern Hucherson, and Joe Adam's by Marvin Hayes. Music: George Bizet. Screenplay: Harry Kleiner. Musical direction: Herschel Burke Gilbert. Cinematographer: Sam Leavitt.

Costumes: Mary Ann Nyberg. Art: Edward Ilou. Set: Claude Carpenter. Dandridge nominated for Best Actress, 1955 (a first for a black artist). (Cinemascope / Sound / Color / 3 reels / 107 min. / Feature.)
   Powerful melodrama adapted from Bizet's opera by Oscar Hammerstein, with exciting music and the equally exciting Dandridge as the ultimate femme fatale. A woman is caught between two men, one a pretty boy and the other a tough boxer. Carmen lures Joe (Belafonte) into deserting from the army and then leaves him for the boxer. Joe takes matters into his own hands and strangles Carmen.

161   Carnival of Rhythm 1944
   Co: Warner Bros. *Cast:* Katherine Dunham and her troupe, Archie Savage, Talley Beatty.
   Review in *Film Daily,* 7/18/41. (Short / B&W / Sound / 2 reels.)
   A short film devoted to Katherine Dunham and her ballet company; a mixture of classical and Afro-Cuban dance.

162   Case o' the Blues 1942
Co: RCM Production. *Dist:* Soundies Distributing Corporation. *Cast:* Maxine Sullivan, Benny Carter Orchestra. (Soundies 6501 / B&W / Short / Sound / Musical / 4/27/42.)

163   Cash Ain't Nothing but Trash 1945
Co: RCM Production. *Dist:* Soundies Distributing Corporation. *Cast:* Day, Dawn and Dusk. (Soundies / B&W / Short / Sound / Musical.)

164   Caterpillar Shuffle 1943
Co: RCM Production. *Dist:* Soundies Distributing Corporation. *Cast:* Johnny Long and His Orchestra. (Soundies / B&W / Short / Sound / Musical / 8/30/43.)

165   Cats Can't Dance 1945
Dir: Crouch, William Forest. *Prod:* Crouch, William Forest. *Co:* Filmcraft Production. *Dist:* Soundies Distributing Corporation. *Cast:* Mabel Lee. (Soundies 87608 / B&W / Short / Sound / Musical / 12/31/45.)

166   Cavalcade of Harlem 1937
Co: Harlem Productions. (B&W / Sound / Short.)

167   Cha-Chi-Man 1944
Co: RCM Production. *Dist:* Soundies Distributing Corporation. *Cast:* Little Four Quartet. (Soundies 18808 / B&W / Short / Sound / Musical.)

168   The Chair Song 1945
Dir: Crouch, William Forest. *Prod:* Crouch, William Forest. *Co:* Filmcraft Production. *Dist:* Soundies Distributing Corporation. *Cast:* Phil Moore. (Soundies 16M3 / B&W / Short / Sound / Musical.)

169   Chant of the Jungle 1943
Co: RCM Production. *Dist:* Soundies Distributing Corporation. *Cast:* Larry Clinton and His Orchestra. (Soundies / B&W / Short / Sound / Musical / 9/27/43.)

170   The Charge of the Black Brigade 1921
(Documentary / B&W / Silent / Feature / 4 reels.)

This film shows the activities of black soldiers in World War I, from the day they are drafted until the day they are mustered out after the armistice.

171   Charleston (Sur un Air de Charleston) 1927
Dir: Renoir, Jean. *Co:* Epinay Studios. *Cast:* Johnny Higgins, Catherine Hessling (white), Pierre Braunberger (white), Pierre Lestrinquez (white).
Screenplay by Pierre Lestrinquez. (France / Dramatic / Short / 35mm / Silent / B&W / 22 min.)
"Set in the year 2028, a Black explorer flies from Central Africa (the seat of civilization) to visit Europe which he thought was not inhabited. He discovers in Paris a primitive girl dancing the Charleston. Entranced, he gets into his space craft with her and goes back to Africa"—*Klotman.*

172   Chatter 1943
Co: RCM Production. *Dist:* Soundies Distributing Corporation. *Cast:* Charles Cook and Ernest Brown, The Sepia Steppers. (Soundies 14308 / B&W / Short / Sound / Musical / 11/29/43.) Music: "I Got Rhythm."

173   Check and Double Check 1930
Dir: Brown, Melville. *Prod:* LeBaron, William. *Co:* RKO Radio Pictures. *Dist:* RKO. *Cast:* Freeman Gosden (white), Charles Correll (white), Duke Ellington and His Cotton Club Orchestra, Sue Carol (white), Russell Powell [(white) Kingfish].
Screenplay: J. Walter Ruben. Story: Bert Kalmar & Harry Ruby. Cameraman: William Marshall. Recording engineer: George E. Ellis. (B&W / 16mm / Sound / 2 reels / 84 min. / Feature.)
"The only Amos and Andy film available stars the team of Gosden and Correll (white actors in burnt cork) in the roles they originated for radio. A haunted house, a wild taxi ride through the streets of New York, and a happy ending for two young lovers are ingredients for this black comedy set in Harlem and an upper class suburb"—*Klotman.*

174   Cherished Melodies   1950

Prod: Wilder, A.W. Lee. *Co:* United Artists. *Cast:* Jester Hairston and Choral Group.

Songs: "My Old Kentucky Home," "Oh Dem Golden Slippers." (Short / Musical / B&W / Sound.)

Songs of America series.

175   Chicago After Dark   1946

Dir: Binney, Josh. *Co:* All American News. *Cast:* Lollypop Jones, Allen McMillen, Edgar Lewis Morton, James Dunsmore, Artiebelle McGinty, Taps and Wilda. (35mm / B&W / Sound / 3 reels / Musical / Short / FEA 4864-4866.)

176   Chicken Shack Shuffle   1943

Co: RCM Production. *Dist:* Soundies Distributing Corporation. *Cast:* Mabel Lee. (Soundies 5M1 / B&W / Short / Sound / Musical / 9/21/43.)

177   A Child in Pawn   1921

Co: D.W.D. Film Corporation.

Made in Raleigh, North Carolina. (B&W / Silent / Feature / 5 reels.)

178   Children of Circumstance

1937

Prod: Sack, Alfred. *Co:* Gramercy Pictures. *Dist:* Alfred Sack. *Cast:* Catherine Alexander, Ollie E. Smith (drama instructor at Morgan College in Baltimore, MD), Tracey's "Kentuckians." (Sound / B&W / Feature.)

This story is about two children, a boy and a girl, whose mothers are killed in a car accident. The childhood sweethearts are placed in an orphanage; the boy is adopted and leaves the orphanage and years later becomes a lawyer. The girl, now a young lady, is in jail for murder, as a result of fending off a man trying to force himself on her. The young lawyer shows up and saves his childhood sweetheart in a courtroom drama. "You will cry at its tragedy, laugh at its comedy, thrill at its love and gleefully enjoy its music. Two hundred great colored stars"—*Philadelphia Tribune*, 8/15/37.

179   Children of Fate   1926

Prod: Starkman, David. *Co:* Colored Players Film Corporation of Philadelphia. *Cast:* Lawrence Chenault, Harry Henderson, Arline Mickey, Howard Agusta, Alonzo Jackson, Shingzie Howard, William A. Clayton, Jr. (B&W / Silent / Feature.)

The story is based on the theme "from out of the depths of evil there shall come good and from out of the pit of darkness shall come light." Ross Hampton, who made himself well-to-do by gambling, could not escape the grip of the white plague. In the days when he was lonesome and had to leave his friends in his search for health, the love of his childhood sweetheart, Virginia Lee, was the real power that brought him to health and happiness.

180   Chilly 'n' Cold   1945

Co: RCM Production. *Dist:* Soundies Distributing Corporation. *Cast:* The Little Four Quartet. (Soundies 10M / B&W / Short / Sound / Musical / 4/16/45.)

181   A Chocolate Cowboy   1925

Prod: Pizor, William M. *Co:* Cyclone Pictures. *Cast:* Fred Parker, Teddy Reavis. (B&W / Silent / Short.)

WILLIAM M. PIZOR
presents
FRED PARKER AND TEDDY REAVIS
....IN....
"A CHOCOLATE COWBOY"
A CYCLONE COMEDY

182   Chocolate Dandies 1924
Co: Pathé. *Cast:* Eubie Blake, Noble Sissle. (Newsreel / B&W / Silent / Short.)
Preview in *The Philadelphia Tribune*, 10/18/24.

183   Choo Choo Swing 1943
Co: Universal Studios. *Cast:* Count Basie and His Orchestra, Delta Rhythm Boys, Bobby Brooks.
Review in *Film Daily*, 11/12/43. (B&W / Musical / Short / 13 min. / Sound.)
Count Basie and His Orchestra title song and "Swingin' the Blues."

184   Chop Sticks 1943
Co: RCM Production. *Dist:* Soundies Distributing Corporation. *Cast:* Johnny Long and His Orchestra. (Soundies / B&W / Short / Sound / Musical / 11/8/43.)

185   Cielito Lindo 1944
Co: RCM Production. *Dist:* Soundies

Distributing Corporation. *Cast:* The Mills Brothers. (Soundies 19708 / B&W / Short / Sound / Musical / 12/31/44.)

186   Clarence Tisdale 1929
Co: Vitaphone. *Cast:* Clarence Tisdale. Songs: "The Sweetness of Song," "By and By," and "Oh, Didn't It Rain." (Musical / Short / B&W / Sound / Vitaphone #766.)
The great black tenor sings three songs.

187   Claude Hopkins and His Orchestra 1933
Co: Vitaphone. *Cast:* Claude Hopkins and His Orchestra, Orlando Robinson, Four Step Brothers. (Musical / Short / B&W / Sound / Vitaphone #8002.)

188   Claude Hopkins and His Orchestra 1935
Co: Vitaphone. *Cast:* Claude Hopkins and His Orchestra, Tip, Tap and Toe tap dancers. (Musical / B&W / Short / Sound / Vitaphone #1880.)

189   Clean Pastures 1937
Co: Warner Bros. *Dist:* United Artists. (Sound / 16mm / Animated / Short / B&W.)
An animated parody of "Green Pastures."

190   Clef Club Five Minutes for Train 1918
Co: Colored and Indian Film Company. *Cast:* James Reese Europe and His Clef Club Orchestra of New York City. (Short / Silent / B&W.)

191   A Close Call pre–1910
(B&W / Silent / Short / FLA 5301.)

192   Close Shave 1942
Co: RCM Production. *Dist:* Soundies Distributing Corporation. *Cast:* Aurora Greeley, LeRoy Broonfield, John Kirby. (Soundies 9608 / B&W / Short / Sound / Musical / 11/30/42.)

193   Coal Black and de Sebben Dwarfs 1942
Prod: Schlesinger, Leon. *Co:* Warner Bros. Screenplay: Warren Foster. Animation: Rod Scribner. (16mm / Sound / 1 reel / Animated / Short.)
A retelling of "Snow White and the Seven

Dwarfs," this wartime offering parodies Snow White by making her a "luscious chocolate cutie" threatened by the Queen (who appears to be "African"). The dwarfs (all enlisted men) protect her until the arrival of "Prince Chawmin."

194   Coffee Industry in Jamaica
1913

Dir: Lubin, Sigmund. *Prod:* Lubin, Sigmund. *Co:* Lubin Manufacturing Company.
Released on 7/24/13. (Silent / B&W / Short / 400 ft.)

"A very interesting educational picture, showing cultivating, gathering, drying, packing and shipping of the coffee berry. The work is all done by the natives, who seem to enjoy their job. They work very rapidly and wear little beyond the perpetual smile which is noticeable in the Negro race. Everything in life is a joke and so is coffee. The pictures were taken on one of the largest plantations in Jamaica and have faithfully photographed not only the industry, but the interesting atmosphere of the West Indies"—*Lubin Bulletin.*

195   Color of a Man   1946

Co: American Missionary Association. (Documentary / Short / B&W / Sound / Produced by the American Missionary Association of the Board of Home Missions of the Congregational Christian Churches.)

Living conditions of Negro families in the South.

196   Colored America on Parade
1940

Dir: Lewis, Edward W. *Prod:* Lewis, Edward W. *Co:* All American News. (16mm / B&W / Sound / 1 reel / 10 min. / Documentary / Short.)

"... a series of films on Colored people in America .... Washingtonians applauded the appearance on the score of such notables as Judge Myles Paige, James Watson, Toney, Jane Bolden, Colonel Davis of the 369th, shaking hands with Governor Lehman at the annual review of the 369th ... Elks parade ... Bill Robinson, J. Finley Wilson and his Cabinet"— excerpt from *The Philadelphia Afro-American,* 1/13/40.

197   Colored American Cavalcade
1939

Prod: Harding, Halley. *Co:* CAC News. *Cast:* Hattie McDaniel, Louise Beavers. (Cavalcade No. 6 / B&W / Sound / Short / FED 4817.)

The United Golfers Association (black) on its 14th annual outing in Los Angeles, California. Also shots of Hattie McDaniel and Louise Beavers, the big Hollywood stars.

198   The Colored American Winning His Suit   1916

Co: Frederick Douglas Film Company. *Dist:* Frederick Douglas Film Company. *Cast:* Thomas M. Mosley, Ida Askins, Florence Snead, Marshall Davis, F. King, Fred Leighton, Edgar Snead, Mrs. E. Snead, Thomas Wheeler, Minnie Smith, Fred Quinn and the local people from Jersey City and vicinity.

Screenplay by the Reverend W.S. Smith. Review in the *New York Age,* 7/20/16. (Short / B&W / Silent / 5 reels.)

Bob, whose father is the owner of an estate on which he once lived as a slave, returns home from college a lawyer. Bob falls in love with his sister's college roommate, but her mother wants her to marry the son of a wealthy farmer, Elton. Elton is framed and arrested for theft, and his accuser persuades other lawyers to keep their hands off the case. Finally, his sweetheart's mother relents and hires Bob to take Elton's case. Of course, Bob wins the case and marries his sweetheart.

199   Colored Americans   1918

Co: Mutual Film Corporation. (B&W / Silent / Documentary.)

Newsreel.

200   Colored Americans in the Nations Capitol   1946

Prod: Toddy, Ted. *Co:* Toddy Pictures Company. (Documentary / Sound / B&W / Short.)

Newsreel of coloreds in government.

201   Colored Champions of Sport
1940

Dir: Lewis, Edward W. *Prod:* Lewis, Edward W. *Co:* Lewis, Edward W.

Preview in *The Philadelphia Afro-American*, 6/8/40. (Newsreel / Documentary / Sound / B&W / Short.)

Newsreel subjects include John Borican and Gil Cruter, track and field stars. Track and field events featuring Eulace Peacock, hammer throw and javelin; Jimmy Herbert, John Woodruff, and Curtis Giddings, hurdles; Joe Louis, heavyweight boxing champion, in training at Pompton Lakes, New Jersey; the Harlem branch of the YMCA.

202   Colored Championship Baseball Game   1914

Dir: Foster, William. *Prod:* Foster, William. *Co:* Foster Photoplay Company. *Dist:* Foster Photoplay Company. *Cast:* Negro League Baseball Teams. (Newsreel / Documentary / B&W / Silent / Short.)

Actual footage of the Negro league championship game in Chicago, Illinois.

203   Colored Elks Parade   1916

Cast: Brotherhood of Elks. (Newsreel / B&W / Short / Silent.)

204   Colored Men in White   1943

Prod: Toddy, Ted. *Co:* Toddy Pictures Company. *Dist:* Toddy Pictures. (Documentary / Sound / B&W / Short.)

Activities of black doctors being trained for service in World War II.

205   Colored Soldiers Fighting in Mexico   1916

Dir: Jones, Peter P. *Prod:* Jones, Peter P. *Co:* Peter P. Jones Photoplay Company. (Newsreel / Short / B&W / Silent / 2 reels.)

Film covers the 8th Illinois crack black regiment under the command of Colonel Franklin (white).

206   Colored Troops at Chillicothe   1918

Co: Finely Film Company. *Cast:* U.S. Colored Troops. (Documentary / B&W / Silent / Short.)

207   Colored Troops Disembarking   1898

Co: Edison. (B&W / Short / Actuality / Documentary / Silent.)

Colored troops disembarking during the Spanish American War.

208   Come Back   1922

Prod: Whipper, Leigh. *Co:* Enterprise Film Company. *Cast:* Louise Fullen, K.D. Nolan, Ellen Ray, Ethel Watson, Victor Price. (B&W / Silent / Feature.)

209   Come Back, Africa   1959

Dir: Rogosin, Lionel. *Prod:* Rogosin, Lionel. *Co:* Lionel Rogosin Production. *Cast:* Lewis N'Kosi, Blake Modisane, Miriam Makeba.

Screenplay by Lionel Rogosin, Lewis N'Kosi, Blake Modisane. Won Italian Film Critics Award at the Venice Film Festival (1960). (South African / Dramatization / Documentary / 16mm / Sound / B&W / 3 reels / 90 min. / Feature.)

A semi-documentary about repressive life in apartheid South Africa. Miriam Makeba makes a brief appearance as singer in the slums of Sophiatown outside Johannesburg.

210   Come On, Cowboy!   1948

Co: Goldman Productions. *Dist:* Toddy Pictures Company. *Cast:* Mantan Moreland,

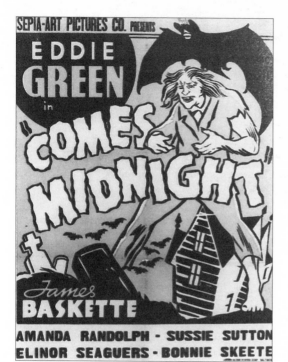

SEPIA-ART PICTURES CO. PRESENTS
EDDIE GREEN in "COMES MIDNIGHT"
James BASKETTE
AMANDA RANDOLPH · SUSSIE SUTTON
ELINOR SEAGUERS · BONNIE SKEETE

Mauryne Brent, Johnny Lee, Flournoy E. Miller. (B&W / Feature / Sound / Comedy.)

211   Come to Baby Do 1946
Dir: Crouch, William Forest. *Prod:* Crouch, William Forest. *Co:* Filmcraft Production. *Dist:* Soundies Distributing Corporation. *Cast:* The King Cole Trio (Nat "King" Cole, Oscar Moore, Johnny Miller). (Soundies 16M4 / B&W / Short / Sound / Musical / 2/25/46.)

212   The Comeback of Barnacle Bill 1918
Co: Ebony Film Company. *Dist:* General Film Company. *Cast:* Ebony Players (Sam Robinson, Samuel "Sambo" Jacks, Will Starks, Julia Mason, Bert Murphy, Evon Skekeeter, Mildred Price, Walter Brogsdale, Robert Duree, Frank Pollard, Yvonne Junior, George Lewis Stock Company). (B&W / Silent / Short / 11 min. / FEA 6570.)

Sam is in love with Skeeter, but when he learns that her former boyfriend is returning home, he becomes disconsolate and decides to commit suicide by shooting himself with a shotgun. He misses himself and accidently kills a thief hiding nearby. Sam, doubly surprised, finds that the thief was carrying a great deal of money, so he takes the money and pays off Skeeter's father's mortgage and wins her totally over.

213   Comedy Cake Walk pre–1910
(B&W / Silent / Short / FLA 3391.)

214   Comes Midnight 1940
Co: Sepia-Art Pictures Company. *Cast:* Eddie Green, Jimmy Baskette, Elinor Seaguers, Bonnie Skeete, Amanda Randolph, Sussie Sutton.
Preview in *The Philadelphia Afro-American*, 4/20/40. (Featurette / Short / B&W / Sound.)

Condemned Men *see* **Four Shall Die**

215   The Confederate Spy 1910
(B&W / Silent / Dramatic / Short.)
Uncle Daniel, a Negro spy for the Confederacy, dies in front of a Northern firing squad happy to have done it for his "massa's sake."

216   Congo Clambake 1942
Co: RCM Production. *Dist:* Soundies Distributing Corporation. *Cast:* Dorothy Dandridge. (Soundies 7906 / B&W / Short / Sound / Musical / 7/27/42.)

217   The Conjure Woman 1926
Dir: Micheaux, Oscar. *Prod:* Micheaux, Oscar. *Co:* Micheaux Film Corporation. *Dist:* Micheaux Film Corporation. *Cast:* Evelyn Preer, Percy Verwayen.
Screenplay adapted from Charles Chestnutt's novel by the same title. (35mm / Silent / B&W / Feature.)

218   Contrast in Rhythm 1945
Co: RCM Production. *Dist:* Soundies Distributing Corporation. *Cast:* Cecil Scott and His Orchestra, Robinson and Hill. (Soundies 11M1 / B&W / Short / Sound / Musical / 6/4/45.)

219   Coon Town Suffragettes 1914
Dir: Lubin, Sigmund. *Prod:* Lubin, Sigmund. *Co:* Lubin Manufacturing Company. *Cast:* John Edwards, Mattie Edwards.
Written by Arthur D. Hotaling. Review in the *Moving Picture World*, 2/21/14. Released on 2/28/14. (Silent / B&W / Short / 400 ft.)

Mandy Jackson, a colored wash lady, attends a white suffragette meeting and is inspired by their leader. She determines to start a suffragette party among her own people. The party is organized with Mandy as their leader, and they start out with a determination to raid the saloons. They proudly march into the gin mill and clear the place; each suffragette gets her husband and marches him out. The coon police are summoned but they are soon subdued. The husbands are then put to work and the militant colored suffragettes proudly claim their first victory.

220   Cootie Williams and His Orchestra 1944

Co: RCM Production. *Dist:* Soundies Distributing Corporation. *Cast:* Cootie Williams and His Orchestra, Sun Tan Four, Bud Powell. (Soundies / Musical / Short / B&W / Sound.)

221   Cora Green 1929

Co: Vitaphone. *Cast:* Cora Green.
Songs: "Brother-in Law Dan," "Travlin' All Along," and "I'll Tell the World." (Musical / B&W / Short / Sound.)
Cora sings three songs on this film.

222   Corn Pone 1945

Co: RCM Production. *Dist:* Soundies Distributing Corporation. *Cast:* Skeets Tolbert and His Orchestra, Lucy Carterio. (Soundies 9M2 / B&W / Short / Sound / Musical / 3/16/45.)

223   The Corpse Accuses 1946

Co: Toddy Pictures Company. (Feature / B&W / Sound.)
A mystery-comedy.

224   The Cotton Industry of the South 1908

Dir: Lubin, Sigmund. *Prod:* Lubin, Sigmund. *Co:* Lubin Manufacturing Company. (Documentary / Short / B&W / Silent.)
"The film depicts the development of cotton from the planting to the making of a sheet. The picture begins with the cotton planter's home. The cotton planter is riding to the cotton fields, where colored people are picking the cotton. After the baskets filled with cotton have been weighed, the cotton is loaded on wagons and brought to the mill. The cotton is then chopped, weeded, dried, pressed into bales, then weighed and brought to the ships or trains to be sent to the cotton mills. The picture continues showing the exterior of the cotton mill, a very large, well-lit and ventilated building. We next see the interior of the cotton mill showing the manufacturing of the finished product in all its details. We also see the making of spool cotton. We see the pictures of the original cotton gins and scenes as they are only found in the sunny South"— *Blacks in Black and White.*

225   Cotton-Pickin' Days 1934

Co: Tiffany Film Company. *Cast:* Forbes Randolph Kentucky Jubilee Singers. (1 reel / Musical / Short / B&W / Sound.)
The Forbes Randolph choir sings, among other things, "Camptown Races" and "Way Down Upon the Swanee River," among a background of Southern cabins and singing field hands.

226   Cotton Spinning on the Old Plantation 1904

Co: American Mutoscope / Biograph. (Documentary / Short / B&W / Silent.)
Blacks spinning cotton on a Southern plantation.

227   Count Me Out 1946

Dir: Crouch, William Forest. *Prod:* Crouch, William Forest. *Co:* Filmcraft Production. *Dist:* Soundies Distributing Corporation. *Cast:* Henry "Red" Allen, J.C. Higginbotham. (Soundies 20M3 / B&W / Short / Sound / Musical / 6/24/46.)

228   Cow-Cow Boogie 1942

Co: RCM Production. *Dist:* Soundies Distributing Corporation. *Cast:* Dorothy Dandridge, Dudley Dickerson. (Soundies 9104 / B&W / Short / Sound / Musical / 10/26/42.)

229   Crap Game 1930

Co: International Photoplay. *Cast:* Johnny Higgins, Eddie Green. (Short / B&W / Sound.)

230   Crawl Red Crawl 1946

Dir: Crouch, William Forest. *Prod:* Crouch,

THE NORMAN FILM MFG CO.
PRESENTS

THE CRIMSON SKULL

BAFFLING WESTERN MYSTERY PHOTOPLAY

CO-STARRING

ANITA BUSH   AND THE VERSATILE
LITTLE MOTHER of COLORED DRAMA   LAWRENCE CHENAULT

Supported by BILL PICKETT, World's Champion Wild West Performer
The One Legged Marvel, STEVE REYNOLDS and 30 Colored Cowboys

ALL COLORED CAST   PRODUCED BY
NORMAN FILM MFG CO.
JACKSONVILLE, FLA.   6 SMASHING REELS

William Forest. *Co:* Filmcraft Production.
Dist: Soundies Distributing Corporation. *Cast:*
Henry "Red" Allen, J.C. Higginbotham, Johni
Weaver. (Soundies 19M2 / B&W / Short /
Sound / Musical / 5/13/46.)

231   Crime Street   1946

Co: Toddy Pictures. (66 min. / Feature /
B&W / Sound.)

An action film about juvenile delinquency.

232   The Crimson Fog   1932

Prod: White, Charles Allman. *Co:* Paragon
Pictures. *Cast:* Thomas Moseley, Inez Clough,
Lawrence Chenault, Vera Temple, Billy
Andrews, Kitty Arblanche, Billy Sheppard,
Alvin Childress. (B&W / Feature.)

233   The Crimson Skull (aka The Scarlet Claw)   1921

Prod: Norman Film Manufacturing Company. *Co:* Norman Film Manufacturing Company. *Dist:* Norman Film Company. *Cast:*
Anita Bush, Lawrence Chenault, Bill Pickett,
Steve Reynolds, 30 Black cowboys.

Filmed on location in the then all–Black
town of Boley, Oklahoma. (30MM / Silent /
B&W / 6 reels / Feature.)

The peace-loving, all-black city of Boley,
Oklahoma, is invaded by "The Skull" and his
"Terrors." They have sown mortal fear into the
townsfolk and have the sheriff in their power.
"The Law and Order League" forces the sheriff's
resignation and offers $1,000 reward for the
capture of the gang. Lem Nelson is persuaded
to take the sheriff's job. Bob, Lem's ranch foreman, volunteers to join the gang with hopes of
capturing them. Bob aids some hostages of the
gang and is accused by the gang of being a trai-
tor. Uncertain of his guilt, he is tried by the test
of "The Crimson Skull." One drop of blood
decides his fate, if he shall live or die.

234   Croix du Sud   1932

Co: Pathé.

Shot in Africa and Joinville. (French /
B&W / Sound / Feature.)

"An African king spurns his white wife for
a black one"—*Klotman.*

Crooked Money *see* **While Thousands Cheer**

235   The Cry of Jazz   1958

Dir: Bland, Edward. *Prod:* Bland, Edward / Nelam Hill / M. Kennedy / E. Titus. *Co:* KHTB Productions. *Cast:* Sun Ra and His Orchestra, Dorothea Horton, George Waller, Linda Dillon, James Miller, Andrew Duncan.

Negro produced film with interracial cast. Music by Sun Ra and Paul Stevenson. (Color / Documentary / 33 min. / Short / Sound / 16mm.)

The film examines the meaning of jazz in the fabric of the experience of the American Negro. By highlighting the differences between experiences of the Negro and other Americans, it raises fundamental questions as to the worth and function of the Negro in America.

236   Cry, the Beloved Country   1952

Dir: Korda, Zoltan. *Prod:* Korda, Zoltan. *Co:* United Artists. *Cast:* Canada Lee, Sidney Poitier, Charles Carson, Michael Goodlife (white), Lionel Ngakane, Edric Connor, Albertina Temba.

Screenplay: Alan Paton. Story: Alan Paton. (16mm / Color / Sound / 3 reels / 105 min. / Feature.)

British, American, and South African filmmakers and actors collaborated in filming this drama in authentic locations. It focuses on Stephen Kumalo (Lee), an African minister who journeys to Johannesburg to find his wayward son. The tragedy of the South African experience unfolds during his search. Poitier is a young priest.

237   Cryin' and Singin' the Blues   1945

Co: RCM Productions. *Dist:* Soundies Distributing Corporation. *Cast:* Dallas Bartley and His Orchestra. (Soundies 88208 / B&W / Short / Sound / Musical / 10/8/45.)

238   Cuban Episode   1942

Co: RCM Production. *Dist:* Soundies Distributing Corporation. *Cast:* The Katherine Dunham Dancers. (Soundies 7703 / B&W / Short / Sound / Musical / 7/20/42.)

239   The Custard Nine   1921

Dir: Ginn, Haywood. *Prod:* Muse, Clarence. *Co:* Harris Dixon Film Company. *Dist:* Pathé. *Cast:* Virgil Custard, Baltimore Criddle, Clarence Muse, Wesley Jenkins, Tom Fletcher, Edward Tatum.

Based on Harris Dickson's "Colored stories" from the *Saturday Evening Post.* (Short / B&W / Silent / Comedy / 2 reels.) Filmed on location in Vicksburg, Mississippi.

A sketch of Virgil Custard leading Vicksburg's black baseball team through assorted farcical adventures.

240   Dance Your Old Age Away   1944

Co: RCM Production. *Dist:* Soundies Distributing Corporation. *Cast:* Tosh Hammed and Company. (Soundies / B&W / Short / Sound / Musical / 12/3/44.)

241   Dancemania   1943

Co: RCM Production. *Dist:* Soundies Distributing Corporation. *Cast:* Mabel Lee, Nicky O'Daniel, Slim Sham. (Soundies 4M4 / B&W / Short / Sound / Musical / 9/21/43.)

242   Dancers in the Dark   1932

Cast: Duke Ellington, Adelaide Hall.

Story: James A. Creelman (play). (76 min. / Feature / B&W / Sound.)

Film about the romance between a taxi driver and a jazz musician.

243   Dancing Darkey Boy   1896

Co: Thomas A. Edison, Inc. (Actualization / B&W / Silent / Short / FLA 3021.)

Actual footage of a young colored boy dancing on a box, surrounded by whites clapping their hands.

244   Dancing Darkies   1904

Co: American Mutoscope / Biograph. (Actuality / B&W / Short / Silent.)

Unrehearsed footage of a group of dancing blacks.

245   The Dancing Nig   1907

Co: Essanay. (Short / B&W / Silent.)

The company's film attests to the "well known fact" that a "darky" has trouble keeping his feet still when he hears the sound of

music. This film apparently means to demonstrate that "fact."

246   Dandy Jim's Dream   1914
Co: Afro-American Film Company. (Short / B&W / Silent.)

247   Dark and Cloudy   1919
Co: Gaiety Comedies. *Cast:* Lillian Byron, George Ovey. (35mm / Silent / B&W / 2 reels / Comedy / Short / FEA 3152.)

248   A Dark Lover's Play   1915
Dir: Sennett, Mack. *Co:* Keystone. (B&W / Silent / Comedy / Short.)

Sennett uses a pair of "coontown lovers" to elicit the humor in this comedy.

249   Dark Manhattan   1937
Dir: Fraser, Harry / Ralph Cooper / George Randol. *Prod:* Randol, George / Ben Renaldo. *Co:* Renaldo Films / Cooper-Randol. *Dist:* Sack Amusement Enterprises. *Cast:* Ralph Cooper, Cleo Herndon, Clarence Brooks, Sam McDaniels, Jess Lee Brooks, Corny Anderson,

Rubeline Glover, James Abamson, Nicodemus Stewart, Jack Liney, Roy Glenn, Sr., Clinton Rosemond.

Review in *The Philadelphia Tribune,* 2/25/37. Screenplay: Arthur Brooks. Story: George Randol. (16mm / B&W / Sound / 2 reels / 70 min. / Feature / FCA 6890-6891.)

The story is about a lad who rises to control of the policy racket in Harlem, meets a sweet and clean nightclub singer and falls in love with her. Before they can get married, a rival gang tries to muscle into the numbers racket and, at the end, the lad gets shotgunned and dies in the arms of his girl.

250   Dark Town Follies   1929
Dir: Foster, William. *Prod:* Pathé. *Dist:* Supreme Distributing Company. *Cast:* Buck and Bubbles.

Story from Hugh Wiley's *Saturday Evening Post* stories. Songs: "St. Louis Blues," "I'm Krazy for You," and "Some Rainy Day." (2 reeler / Short / Sound / Comedy.)

Broke and hungry, Wildcat, Buck, Denny

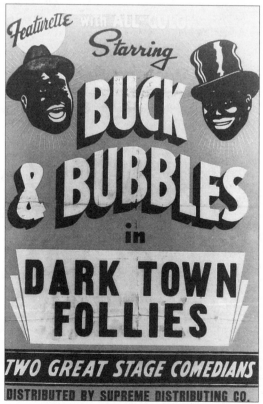

and Bubbles audition for the Darktown Follies doing songs, dance and jokes; they get hired.

251   Dark-Town Strutters' Ball
1941

Co: RCM Production. *Dist:* Soundies Distributing Corporation. *Cast:* The Charioteers. (Soundies 3603 / B&W / Short / Sound / Musical / 10/6/41.)

First music videos.

252   Darktown Affair   1921

Co: Mt. Olympus Distributing Co. *Dist:* Mt. Olympus Distributing Co. (Short / B&W / Silent.)

253   Darktown Blues   1929

Dir: Foster, William. *Prod:* Foster, William. *Cast:* Buck and Bubbles (Ford Lee Washington & John Sublette). (Sound / B&W / Short / Comedy.)

254   Darktown Jubilee   1914

Co: Biograph. *Cast:* Bert Williams. (16mm / Comedy / Short / Silent / B&W.)

Bert Williams, the famous comedian, actor, singer and mime, starred in this, his first film, which reportedly caused a race riot in Brooklyn.

255   The Darktown Revue   1931

Dir: Micheaux, Oscar. *Prod:* Russell, A. Burton. *Co:* Micheaux Film Corporation. *Dist:* Micheaux Film Corporation. *Cast:* Donald Heywood's choir, Tim Moore, Andrew Trible, Amon Davis.

Micheaux put this film together to take advantage of the new talk medium. (Short / B&W / Sound / 18 min. / FGE 2350.)

A short variety film with musical sequences and comedy.

256   Darktown Scandal's Revue
1930

Dir: Micheaux, Oscar. *Prod:* Russell, A. Burton. *Co:* Micheaux Film Corporation. *Cast:* Irvin Miller and His Brownskin Revue, Billy Fowler's Band, Sarah Martin, Maude Mills. (Sound / B&W / Feature.)

Harlem revue.

257   Darktown Strutters' Ball
1940

Dir: Randol, George. *Prod:* Randol, George /

Bert Goldberg. *Co:* George Randol Productions. *Dist:* International Road Shows.

Announcement in *New York Age*, 1/13/40. Screenplay by Shelton Brooks and F.E. Miller. (B&W / Sound / Feature / Musical.)

258   Darky Cake Walk   1904

Co: American Mutoscope / Biograph. (Newsreel / B&W / Short / Silent.)

Footage of black dancers doing the cake walk.

259   Dat Blackhand Waitah Man
1917

Co: Ebony Film Company. *Dist:* General Film Company. *Cast:* Ebony Players (Sam Robinson, Samuel "Sambo" Jacks, Will Starks, Julia Mason, Bert Murphy, Evon Skekeeter, Mildred Price, Walter Brogsdale, Robert Duree, Frank Pollard, George Lewis Stock Company). (Short / B&W / Silent / Comedy.)

260   A Date with Duke   1946

Prod: Pal, George. *Co:* Paramount. *Cast:* Duke Ellington and His Orchestra. (16mm / Color / Sound / 1 reel / 10 min. / Animated / Short.)

Duke Ellington plays his composition, "Perfume Suite," in this George Pal "puppetoon."

261   A Daughter of Pharaoh   1920

Co: Trinity Film Corporation. (B&W / Silent / Feature.)

262   A Daughter of the Congo
1930

Dir: Micheaux, Oscar. *Prod:* Russell, A. Burton. *Co:* Micheaux Film Corporation. *Dist:* Micheaux Film Corporation. *Cast:* Joe Byrd, Katherine Noisette, Wilhelmina Williams, Clarence Redd, Lorenzo Tucker, Roland Irving, Alice B. Russell, Charles Moore, Gertrude Snelson, Percy Verwayen, Madame Robinson, Salem Tutt Whitney, Willor Lee Guilford, "Speedy" Wilson, Daisy Harding, Rudolph Dawson.

With a few talking sequences and a music score. (35mm / B&W / Silent / Sound / 9 reels / Feature.)

"The central character is Lupelta, a beautiful mulatto girl who has been stolen as a baby and brought up among the savages of the jungle. The story opens with Lupelta on her way to the village to marry the tribal chief. She has paused to bathe in a brook when she is surrounded, captured and made a prisoner of slave hunters. In the meantime, Captain Paul Dale, colored U.S. Army, and his first lieutenant have been sent by their government to operate a constabulary, and are on a reconnaissance. They encounter the slave hunters and promptly take them prisoners and rescue Lupelta. She is taken to a mission school where she succumbs to learning and soon becomes a popular maid in spite of her frequent inclination to revert to the wild life of the jungle"— Henry Sampson.

263   Daughters of the Isle of Jamaica   1937

Co: Lenwall Productions. *Cast:* The people of Jamaica. (8½ min. / 739 ft. / Short / Sound / B&W / Documentary.)

The film opens in a Kingston night club, where the emcee introduces a very special tap dancer — it is a young Jamaican boy who tap dances barefooted by holding bottle caps between his toes! The film then goes outdoors for a trip through Kingston and the surrounding territory: We see black workers crushing rocks to make a new roadway, climbing coconut trees to bring down the fruit, cutting bananas and hauling them to the docks on their heads (where a supervisor with a machete hair-raisingly slashes at their loads, front and back, to remove excess stalk), riding burros to market, and finally, we see the famous waterfalls.

264   The Dawn of Truth   1916

Dir: Jones, Peter P. *Prod:* Jones, Peter P. *Co:* Peter P. Jones Photoplay Company. (Short / B&W / Silent.)

265   A Day at Tuskegee   1913

Co: Anderson-Watkins Film Company. (Newsreel / B&W / Short / Silent.)

This film shows 100 various scenes of industries and students at Tuskegee Institute.

266   A Day in an African Village   1929

Co: National Archives Gift Collection.

Part of Record Group 200 HF series, Harmon Foundation Collections. (16mm / Silent / (2) 1 reel units / B&W.)

"Tribal Customs, in Central Africa — hunting, food preparation, crafts, recreation"— Klotman.

267   A Day in the Magic City of Birmingham   1920

Co: Pyramid Picture Corporation. (Newsreel / Short / Silent / B&W.)

Scenes of the sites and sounds of Black Birmingham, Alabama.

268   A Day in the Nation's Capital   1918

Prod: Clifford, Lieut. J. Williams. *Co:* Monumental Pictures Corporation. *Dist:* Monumental Pictures Corporation. *Cast:* A.B. Truate, Tip Top. (Newsreel / Short / B&W / Silent / J. Williams Clifford, President.)

"Interesting and vivid the scenes flash by in a rapid succession from desperate military competition to clever tennis playing, to the jump of the horses at the gong in a Negro fire-fighting company, to splendid horsemanship in polo and racing, to water polo and high diving and finally a six foot hurdle by 'Tip Top' the winner of many blue ribbons"— advertisement.

269   A Day with the Tenth Cavalry at Fort Huachuca   1922

Co: Lincoln Motion Picture Company. (Newsreel / B&W / Short / Silent.)

This film covers the black cavalry in training at Fort Huachuca, Arizona.

270   The Dayton Guide   1924

(Newsreel / B&W / Short / Silent.)

The K of P Convention at Akron, Ohio; the K of P Band performing at Columbus, Ohio.

271   Dear Old Southland   1941

Co: RCM Production. *Dist:* Soundies Distributing Corporation. *Cast:* The Dixiairs.

Recorded by Ray Bloch and His Orchestra. (Soundies 4507 / B&W / Short / Sound / Musical / 12/8/41.)

272   The Debt   1912

(Dramatic / Short / 35mm / B&W / Silent / 2 reels.)

"Early example of the tragic Mulatto these in which the offspring of a white father/white mother and the same white father/Mulatto mistress meet and fall in love. As they are about to marry, they discover the awful interracial, almost incestuous truth"—Klotman.

273   A Debtor to the Law   1924

Prod: Norman Film Manufacturing Company. *Co:* Norman Film Manufacturing Company. *Dist:* Norman Films. (B&W / Silent / Feature / Short.)

274   Deceit   1921

Dir: Micheaux, Oscar. *Prod:* Micheaux, Oscar. *Co:* Micheaux Film Corporation. *Dist:* Micheaux Film Corporation. *Cast:* Ida Anderson, Evelyn Preer, Cleo Desmond, A.B. Comathiere, George Lucas, Norman Johnstone, Mabel Young, Mary Watkins, Louis De Bulger, Cornelious Watkins, Mrs. Irvin C. Miller, Ira O. McGowan, Lewis Schooler, Jerry Brown, James Carey, Viola Miles, N. Brown, J. Coldwell, F. Sandfier, Jesse R. Billings, Allen D. Dixon. White cast — Leonard Galezio, William Peterson, Sadie Carey, Milton Henry.

Review in *The Philadelphia Tribune*, 10/3/25. Based on "Behind the Hills" by Charles Chestnut. The plot of *Deceit*, closely parallels the events which occurred when Micheaux's picture *Within Our Gates*, was brought before the Chicago Board of Censors for approval. (Feature / B&W / Silent.)

Alfred Dubois organizes a film production corporation and produces its first picture, "The Hypocrite." On reaching the censor board for their approval, he finds his arch enemy, Rev. Bently, on the board. Rev. Bently succeeds in getting the film rejected. Alfred finally succeeds in having the case appealed and selecting an unbiased board to review the film — *Philadelphia Tribune*, 10/3/25.

275   Deed I Do   1944

Co: RCM Production. *Dist:* Soundies Distributing Corporation. *Cast:* Will Bradley and His Orchestra, Lloyd and Willis. (Soundies / B&W / Short / Sound / Musical / 8/7/44.)

276   Deep South   1937

Dir: Goodwins, Leslie. *Prod:* Gilroy, Bert.

Co: RKO Radio Pictures. *Cast:* Willie Best, Daisy Bufford, Clarence Muse, Hall Johnson Choir. (B&W / Short / Sound / 9 songs.)

"An atmospheric number of the South with the cotton fields as background. As the darkies work in the field, they are making ready to celebrate a wedding that evening of two of their number .... After the wedding in the evening they all troop to the new cabin to be inhabited by the happy couple, with a round of dancing, feasting and singing"— review from *Film Daily*, 1/9/37.

277   Democracy, or a Fight for Right   1919

Co: Democracy Photoplay Corporation. (Silent / Documentary / B&W / Short.)

A glorifying of Afro-American war heroes.

278   Devil for a Day   1917

Co: Ebony Film Company. *Dist:* General Film Company. *Cast:* Ebony Players (Sam Robinson, Samuel "Sambo" Jacks, Will Starks, Julia Mason, Bert Murphy, Evon Skekeeter,

Mildred Price, Walter Brogsdale, Robert Duree, Frank Pollard, George Lewis Stock Company). (Silent / B&W / Short / 2 reels.)

279   The Devil Sat Down and Cried   1942

Co: RCM Production. *Dist:* Soundies Distributing Corporation. *Cast:* Savannah Churchill, Les Hite and His Orchestra. (Soundies 6408 / B&W / Short / Sound / Musical / 4/20/42.)

280   Deviled Hams   1937

Dir: Schwarzwald, Milton. *Cast:* The Erskine Hawkins Orchestra, Wilbur Bascomb. (10 min. / Musical / Short / B&W / Sound.)

The Erskine Hawkins Orchestra displays its musical skill amid a satanic scene.

281   The Devils   1923

Co: E & H Distributing Company. *Dist:* E & H Distributing Company. (Short / B&W / Silent.)

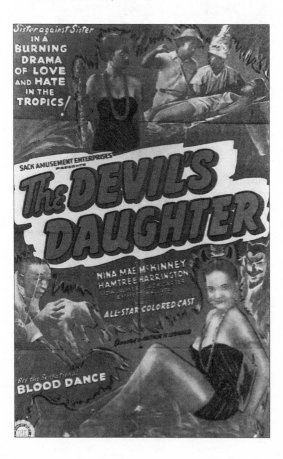

282   The Devil's Daughter   1939

Dir: Leonard, Arthur. *Prod:* Leonard, Arthur H. *Co:* Domino Film Corporation. *Dist:* Sack Amusement Enterprises. *Cast:* Nina Mae McKinney, Jack Carter, Ida James, Hamtree Harrington, Willa Mae Lane, Emmett "Baba" Wallace.

Filmed on location in Kingston, Jamaica. From the original story by George W. Terwilliger. Musical score: John Killam. Narrator: Leon Lee. Edited by Datlowe. Photography: Jay Rescher. Asst. cameraman: Tom Priestley. Sound: Dean Cole. Location manager: Syl Priestley. Makeup: Richard Willis. Wardrobe: Renee. A Variety Blue Seal Recording. (16mm / Sound / B&W / 2 reels / 70 min. / Feature.)

The plot of the story deals with two sisters whose father owns a West Indies rubber plantation. One of the sisters goes to New York City and later attains success, while the other remains at home. When the father dies, he leaves the plantation to the New York sister and she returns home to take over the plantation. The other sister, resentful, plans revenge through fake voodoo rites, hoping to frighten the favored one to return to New York. The plan fails, the sisters make up and agree to run the plantation together.

283   The Devil's Disciple   1926

Dir: Micheaux, Oscar. *Prod:* Micheaux, Oscar. *Co:* Micheaux Film Corporation. *Dist:* Micheaux Film Corporation. *Cast:* Evelyn Preer, Lawrence Chenault, Edward Thompson, Percy Verwayan.

Review in *The Philadelphia Tribune*, 2/9/28. (35mm / Silent / B&W / Feature.)

"The picture is really the first story of Negro night life in Harlem ever brought to the screen. Every scene is taken in the locality and every one will recognize the landmarks that are familiar to us. The story centers about a beautiful but vain girl who falls in love with a degenerate. She tries to reform him but fails miserably, and is in turn dragged down and down. Besides being intensely gripping and dramatic, the picture contains a good moral lesson for our stage struck sisters"— excerpt from review in the *New York Age*, 10/24/25.

284   The Devil's Match 1923

Co: North State Film Corporation. *Dist:* E & H Distributors. *Cast:* Walter Long, Bobby Smart. (Feature / B&W / Silent.)

"This is the story of a striving young minister, who is trying to build a church in a lawless section of the country run by a bully known as 'The Devil.' The minister's struggles and defeats are many and he finally agrees to right 'The Devil'; the loser is to leave town. What happens next is the climax of the film"—advertisement.

285   Dinah 1944

Dir: Crouch, William Forest. *Prod:* Crouch, William Forest. *Co:* RCM Production. *Dist:* Soundies Distributing Corporation. *Cast:* Bob Howard. (Soundies 17208 / B&W / Short / Sound / Musical / 7/3/44.)

First music videos.

286   Dinty McGinty 1946

Dir: Crouch, William Forest. *Prod:* Crouch, William Forest. *Co:* Filmcraft Production. *Dist:* Soundies Distributing Corporation. *Cast:* Johnny Woods, The Bailey Axton Trio. (Soundies / B&W / Short / Sound / Musical / 6/24/46.)

287   Dirty Gertie from Harlem, U.S.A. 1946

Dir: Williams, Spencer. *Prod:* Goldberg, Bert. *Co:* Sack Amusement Enterprises. *Dist:* Sack Amusement Enterprises. *Cast:* Francine Everett, Don Wilson, Katherine Moore, Alfred Hawkins, David Boykin, Lee Lewis, Inez Newell, Piano Frank, John King, Shelly Ross, Hugh Watson, Don Gilbert, Spencer Williams, July Jones, Howard Calloway.

Original story and screen adaptation by True T. Thompson. Assistant cameraman: Gordon Yoder. Sound engineer: Dick Byers. Properties: J.L. Bock. Art director: Ted Soloman. Makeup: Frillia. Director of photography: John Herrman. (60 min. / 5,378 ft. / 16mm / Sound / B&W / Feature / FEA 4952-4957.)

Gertie, having jilted her boyfriend in Harlem, runs off to the Paradise Hotel in Trinidad to perform along with her troupe. While she is being courted by the club's owner she is spotted by a friend of her jilted Harlem lover. When her Harlem boyfriend discovers where she is, he tracks her down and shoots her dead. Not a happy ending, but very little pity is felt for Gertie. Reminiscent of Dorothy Dandridge in *Carmen Jones* (1954).

288   The Disappearance of Mary Jane 1921

Co: Acme Film Distribution Corporation. *Dist:* Acme Film Distribution Corporation. *Cast:* Chicago Bathing Girls, Jimmie Cox (billed as the Black Charlie Chaplin), Shampo (trick mule). (Short / Comedy / Silent / B&W.)

289   Dispossessed Blues 1943

Co: RCM Production. *Dist:* Soundies Distributing Corporation. *Cast:* Lynn Albritton, The Four Knobs. (Soundies 12408 / B&W / Short / Sound / Musical 7/5/43.)

290   The Dixie Chase, 1931

(Documentary / Short / B&W / Sound.) Black men hunting possum.

291   Dixie Days 1928

Co: Vitaphone.

Review in the *Film Daily*, 9/2/28. Songs: "All Along the Mississippi," "All God's Chillun Got Shoes," "The Old Ark's A-Moving" and "Hallelujah to the Lamb." (B&W / Sound / Short / 6 min.)

These Negro spirituals have been built up by the group with some variations, and the voice recording is excellent. The backdrop used is cheap and flat, and fails to create the proper atmosphere for a high grade group of entertainers.

292   Dixie Love 1934

Dir: Hargrave, Myrtle. *Co:* Paragon Pictures. *Cast:* Lucille Pope, Richard Gregg, Alvin Childress.

Review in *New York Amsterdam News*, 10/6/34. (Silent / B&W / Feature.)

This story is about a sweet little Southern colored girl who heads north with her sweetheart. Once north her sweetheart becomes a monster and forces her to take to the streets. It does end happily, and the story is quite intriguing.

293 Dixie Rhythm 1945

Co: RCM Production. *Dist:* Soundies Distributing Corporation. *Cast:* Pat Flowers. (Soundies 89308 / B&W / Short / Sound / Musical / 4/23/45.)

294 Dixieland Jamboree 1935

Co: Warner Bros. / Vitaphone. *Cast:* Cab Calloway and His Band, Nicholas Brothers, Adelaide Hall, Eunice Wilson, The Tree Whippits, The Five Racketeers.

Songs: "I Don't Know Why I Feel This Way," "To Have You Hold Me and Love Me Again," and "Tiger Ray." (16mm / Sound / 1 reel / 9 min. / Musical / Short / B&W.)

Typical music revue.

295 Dixon-Chester Leon Contest pre–1910

(B&W / Silent / Short / FLA 5335.)

296 Do I Worry? 1941

Co: RCM Production. *Dist:* Soundies Distributing Corporation. *Cast:* Beverly Roberts.

Recorded by Ray Bloch and His Orchestra. (Soundies 13708 / Short / Musical / B&W / Sound / 6/30/41.)

297 Do I Worry? 1943

Co: RCM Production. *Dist:* Soundies Distributing Corporation. *Cast:* Patterson and Jackson. (Soundies 13708 / B&W / Short / Sound / Musical / 10/11/43.)

298 Do the Dead Talk? 1918

Dir: MacCullough, Jack. *Co:* Ebony Film Company. *Dist:* General Film Company. *Cast:* Ebony Players (Sam Robinson, Samuel "Sambo" Jacks, Will Starks, Julia Mason, Bert Murphy, Evon Skekeeter, Mildred Price, Walter Brogsdale, Robert Duree, Frank Pollard, George Lewis Stock Company), Hermina France, Willard Burt, Grant Forhman. (Silent / B&W / Short / 2 reels / written by Jack MacCullough.)

299 Does You Do, or Does You Don't 1946

Dir: Crouch, William Forest. *Prod:* Crouch, William Forest. *Co:* Filmcraft Production. *Dist:* Soundies Distributing Corporation. *Cast:* Vanita Smythe. (Soundies 22M1 / B&W / Short / Sound / Musical / 8/5/46.)

300 Doin' the Town 1935

Co: Mentone Production. *Dist:* Universal. *Cast:* The Five Rhythm Racketeers. (Musical / B&W / Short / Sound.)

Mixed variety show at the Club Alabam.

301 Doing Their Bit 1918

Co: Toussaint Motion Pictures Company. *Cast:* Documentary.

Review in *Philadelphia Tribune,* 4/13/18. (Silent / B&W / Documentary / Short / Newsreel.)

The famed 367th "Hell Fighters" Regiment marches up 5th Avenue in New York City and Harlem on March 23, 1918. Presentation of the stand of colors by Governor Whitman to the regiment in front of the Union League Club. The 367th Infantry parades down 5th Avenue in a snow storm. Acting Secretary of War dedicates the Buffalo Auditorium at Camp Upton. Colored troops drill at Camp Upton and Camp Dix. General Joffre reviews the black soldiers in the French Army. "Bob" Scanlon of the American Legion and a French soldier spar in a boxing match. Emmett J. Scott, the Special Assistant to the Secretary of War, leaves his office in Washington, D.C., at the end of the work day.

302 Don Redman and His Orchestra 1935

Co: Vitaphone. *Cast:* Don Redman and His Orchestra.

Songs: "Yeh Man," "Ill Wind," "Nagasaki," and "Why Should I Be Tall?" (Musical / B&W / Short / Sound.)

"With this aggregation of colored band artists, set up against a jazzy setting, Don Redman serves a nice little dish of novelty musical entertainment. It's mostly singing and instrumental stuff, with bits of romantic byplay flashed in, and also a little comedy supplied by a pair of singing comedians"— review from the *Film Daily,* 2/20/35.

303 Don't Be Late 1945

Co: RCM Production. *Dist:* Soundies Distributing Corporation. *Cast:* Cecil Scott and His Orchestra. (Soundies 89108 / B&W / Short / Sound / Musical / 4/23/45.)

304   Double Deal   1939

Dir: Dreifus, Arthur. *Prod:* Harwin, Dixon R. / Jack Goldberg. *Co:* Argus Pictures. *Dist:* Sack Amusement Enterprises. *Cast:* Monte Hawley, Jeni LeGon, Edward Thompson, Florence O'Brien, Freddie Jackson, Buck Woods, Maceo B. Sheffield, Charles Hawkins, Jack Clissby, Tommy Southern, Vernon McCalla, Charles Gordon, Arthur Ray, Flournoy E. Miller, Shelton Brooks.

Screenplay: Arthur Hoerl & Flournoy E. Miller. Additional dialogue: F.E. Miller. Musical direction: Ross DiMaggio. Photography: Mack Stengler. Assistant director: Ralph Slosser. Unit manager: William C. Kent. Furs: H.J. Stearns. Coiffures: Ruth, Gowns: J.J. Reed. Sound recording: Glen Glen. (Feature / 60 min. / B&W / Sound / FDA 2548.)

The typical two-guys-in-love-with-the-same-woman murder mystery. One is a thief who robs a jewelry store and gives the loot to his boss. In turn, it is stolen from his boss by the same thief, who then blames his rival for the theft. When the boss confronts his cohort with evidence of his crime, he murders his boss. In a daring escape attempt he is shot down by a policeman. Romance triumphs for the falsely accused rival.

305   Down, Down, Down   1942

Co: RCM Production. *Dist:* Soundies Distributing Corporation. *Cast:* Louis Jordan and His Tympany Five. (Soundies 1904 / B&W / Short / Sound / Musical / 12/31/42.)

306   Down on the Swanee River   1941

Co: RCM Production. *Dist:* Soundies Distributing Corporation. *Cast:* Forbes Randolph Choir. (Soundies / B&W / Short / Sound / Musical.)

307   Downbeat Revue   1955

Dir: Kohn, Joseph. *Co:* Studio Films, Inc. *Cast:* Count Basie, Nat "King" Cole, Dinah

Washington. (B&W / Sound / Feature / FBB 9706.)

Typical variety show on stage format.

308   The Dreamer   1948

Co: Astor Pictures Corporation. *Dist:* Astor Pictures. *Cast:* Mantan Moreland, June Richmond, Mabel Lee, Pat Rainey. (Sound / B&W / Feature.)

309   Dress Rehearsal   1939

Dir: Green, Eddie. *Prod:* Green, Eddie. *Co:* Sepia-Art Pictures Company. *Cast:* Eddie Green.

Eddie Green, President of Sepia Art Films. (Comedy / Short / B&W / Sound.)

Eddie Green is depicted as the star of a stage company that is waiting for him to show up at its dress rehearsal. The difficulties he encounters while en route and the embarrassment he suffers after he arrives furnish the comedy of the picture.

310   Drink Hearty   1946

Dir: Crouch, William Forest. *Prod:* Crouch, William Forest. *Co:* Filmcraft Production. *Dist:* Soundies Distributing Corporation. *Cast:* Henry "Red" Allen, J.C. Higginbotham.

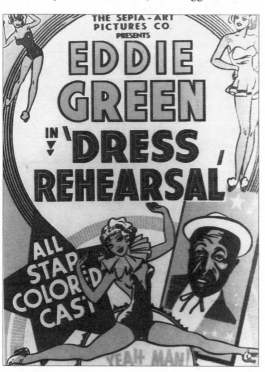

(Soundies 17M2 / B&M / Short / Sound / Musical / 3/11/46.

311   Drums o' Voodoo (aka Voodoo Drums)   1933

Dir: Hoerle, Arthur. *Prod:* Weiss, Louis / Robert Minz. *Co:* International Stage Play Pictures. *Dist:* Sack Amusement Enterprises. *Cast:* Laura Bowman, J. Augustus Smith, Chick McKinney, Lionel Monagas, Edna Barr, A.B. Comatheire, Fred Bonny, Alberta Perkins, Paul Johnson, Carrie Huff.

Drums o' Voodoo, 1933 was re-released in 1940 under the title *She Devil.* Screenplay based on stage play, "Louisiana," by J. Augustus Smith. Entire film cast is from stage play. Review in *The Philadelphia Tribune,* 8/17/33, 8/24/33. (Feature / B&W / Sound.)

"The conflict among a group of Louisiana Negroes between the Christian religion, voodooism and the entirely irreligious. The latter element is personified in Morris McKinney, owner of a jook, presumably a bawdy house, who is determined that he will have the niece of the local preacher, J. Augustus Smith, or expose the preacher's past. The grandson of the woman, who is high priestess of the voodoo worshippers, wants to marry the niece. Just as McKinney is disclosing to the preacher's congregation that Smith murdered a man, he is stricken blind. This is attributed to the voodoo woman's spell. Windup finds everybody happy and the forces of voodooism riding high"— review from *Film Daily,* 5/12/34.

312   Dry Bones   1945

Dir: Berne, Josef. *Co:* RCM Production. *Dist:* Soundies Distributing Corporation. *Cast:* The Delta Rhythm Boys. (Soundies 20508 / B&W / Short / Sound / Musical / 4/30/45.)

313   Duke Ellington and His Orchestra   1943

Dir: Bonafield, Jay. *Co:* Pathé / RKO Radio Pictures. *Cast:* Johnny Hodges, Betty Roche, Sandy Williams, Ben Webster, Ray Nance, Taft Jordan, Duke Ellington.

Songs: "Don't Get Around Much Any More," "Mood Indigo," "Go 'Way Blues," "It Don't Mean a Thing," and "Sophisticated Lady." Reviews in *The Philadelphia Tribune,*

7/10/43, *The Philadelphia Afro-American*, 7/3/43 and the *Film Daily*, 1/3/43. Filmed at the Movietone studios in Manhattan. (9 min. / Musical / Short / B&W / Sound.)

A musical Ellington short filmed against a background depicting the futuristic keyboard of a high piano.

314   The Duke Is Tops (The Bronze Venus)   1938

Dir: Nolte, William. *Prod:* Popkin, Harry M. *Co:* Million Dollar Productions. *Cast:* Ralph Cooper, Lena Horne, Lawrence Criner, Monte Hawley, Vernon McCallum, Edward Thompson, Neva Peoples, Charles Hawkins, Johnny Taylor, Everett Brown, Arthur Ray, Ray Martin, Guernsey Morrow, Willie Covan, Basin Street Boys, Rubber Neck Holmes, Cats and the Fiddle, Marie Bryant, Swing Band, Harlemania Orchestra.

The Bronze Venus, 1943 is the re-released *The Duke Is Tops*, 1938. Associate producer: Leo C. Popkin. Production manager: Walter Buck Jones. Supervising editor: Arthur A. Brooks. Screen adaptation: Phil Dunham. Supervisor: Halley Harding. Associate director: Herman Webber. Photography: Robert Cline, Henry Kruse. Recording engineer: Glen Glen. Set design: Vin Taylor. Musical director: Lou Frohman. Music arranger: Phil Moore. Film editor: Alice Greenwood. Ensemble numbers: Lew Crawford. Music: Ben Ellison & Harvey Brooks. Reviews in *The Philadelphia Tribune*, 8/4/38, the *Pittsburgh Courier*, 4/22/39, & 6/25/38 and the *Kansas City Call*, 6/24/38. (Feature / 80 min. / B&W / Sound.)

This is the story of a producer-performer team which has to break up when one, the lady, gets a better job in New York. The man's career fails, while the lady is at first a big hit; then she also fails. They both struggle to make ends meet — until they get together again for the finale, when combined efforts put them back in the big time.

315   The Dungeon   1922

Dir: Micheaux, Oscar. *Prod:* Micheaux, Oscar. *Co:* Micheaux Film Corporation. *Dist:* Micheaux Film Corporation. *Cast:* W.E. Fountaine, J.K. Goodman, Shingzie Howard, W.F. Crowell, Earl Brown Cooke, Blanch Thompson, Evelyn Preer.

Story by Oscar Micheaux. (B&W / Silent / Feature.)

Myrtle Downing, a beautiful young lady, is engaged to Stephen Cameron, a young lawyer. One morning she awakens to find out that she is married to "Gyp" Lassiter, a notorious crook and Cameron's worst enemy. She later discovers that "Gyp" is a bigamist, a man with many wives, all of whom he murdered when they tried to expose him. "Gyp," having political aspirations, plots to permit residential segregation in exchange for a Congressional seat. Myrtle overhears the plot and tries to escape and warn her people, but "Gyp" catches and locks her in a room. However, she escapes and exposes her husband. "Gyp," enraged at his wife's actions, sets out to murder her. He catches her and locks her in the dungeon. Cameron learns of her danger and proceeds to rescue her.

316   Dunkin' Bagels 1946

Co: RCM Production. *Dist:* Soundies Distributing Corporation. *Cast:* Slim Gaillard Trio. (Soundies / B&W / Short / Sound / Musical.)

317   Dusky Melodies 1930

Co: Ideal-Gainsborough. *Cast:* Lew Hardcastle Band, The Gainsborough Girls, Johnny Nit.

Made in London. (Musical / B&W / Short / Sound.)

Musical revue show.

318   The Dusky Virgin 1932

Prod: White, Charles Allman. *Co:* Paragon Pictures. *Cast:* Reginald Granger, Iris Daniels, Mildred Washington, Gertrude Fredericks, Walter Earl. (Sound / B&W / Feature.)

319   Easy Money 1921

Dir: Dudley, S.H. / Robert Levy. *Co:* Reol Productions. *Cast:* S.H. Dudley, H.L. Pryor, Inez Clough, Edna Morton, Alex K. Shannon, Percy Verwayen, Evelyn Ellis.

Dudley's first black-cast film. Original story by J. Rufus Brown. Reviews in *Billboard*, 4/15/22 & 5/11/22. (Silent / B&W / Feature.)

"He was poor. A rich man was courting his girl. He discovered the fake stock scheme of his rival. He exposed the plot and became the man of the hour. Then he turned the tables on the rich man and won back his sweetheart. See the exciting raid on the stock gambler's house. See the sensational leap from a tree to a speeding automobile. See the thrilling rescue of the banker's daughter from death. See the triumph of a small-town constable in the whirlwind climax of 'Easy Money'"—advertisement.

320   Easy Pickens 1937

Co: Educational Film Corporation. *Cast:* The Cabin Kids (five colored harmonizers, Ruth Hall, Helen Hall, James "Darling" Hall, Winifred "Sugar" Hall, and little Frederick Hall). (B&W / Short / Sound.)

"Employing but a slight plot, the entertaining Cabin Kids get a chance to offer more of their amusing singing. The setting is a ferry boat on which the colored youngsters are shining shoes. Becoming dissatisfied with business conditions they decide to try their luck as entertainers. They are so good, a troupe of professional musicians playing trade on the ferry becomes resentful and seeks to squelch them. But the kids get the crowd's applause and the captain's sympathy and the pros get the toe of the Captain's shoe"—review from the *Film Daily*, 5/7/36.

321   Easy Street 1930

Dir: Micheaux, Oscar. *Prod:* Russell, A. Burton. *Co:* Micheaux Film Corporation. *Dist:* Oscar Micheaux. *Cast:* Lorenzo Tucker, Willor Lee Guilford, Richard B. Harrison, William A. Clayton, Jr., Alice B. Russell. (Feature / B&W / Silent.)

"The plot deals around a sensational story of love, finance and gang life. It shows the 'inside actions' of city slickers in their attempt to swindle an old man of honestly earned money. Its plot is sensational with surprise, action, love, suspense, and intrigue"—excerpt from review in the *Pittsburgh Courier*, 8/6/30.

322   Easy Street 1941

Co: RCM Production. *Dist:* Soundies Distributing Corporation. *Cast:* Dorothy Dandridge. (Soundies 4805 / B&W / Short / Sound / Musical / 12/29/41.)

323   Easy to Get 1944

Co: U.S. Army. *Cast:* Paul Robeson, Joe Louis, Ralph Metcalfe. (Documentary / B&W / Sound / Short.)

Army training film (TF 8-1423), narrated by Paul Robeson, with direct appeals made by Sgt. Joe Louis and Lt. Ralph Metcalfe to the Negro soldier to avoid venereal disease either by abstinence or by the use of contraceptive devices. Dramatic incidents are used along with some animated segments. Emphasis is on the desirability of improving the health and mental status of the race.

324   Ebony Parade 1947

Co: Astor Pictures Corporation. *Dist:* Astor Pictures. *Cast:* Cab Calloway, Count Basie, Mantan Moreland, Mills Brothers, Ruby Hill, June Richmond, Dorothy Dandridge, Vanita Smythe, Mabel Lee, Francine Everett, Pat Flowers, Day, Dawn and Dusk, Jubilaires.

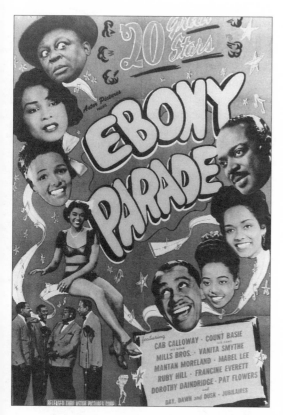

Company. *Cast:* Eddie Green, Ernestine Jones.

Is reissued combination of *Comes Midnight, What Goes Up* and *Dress Rehearsal.* (B&W / 50 min. / Feature / Sound.)

328   Ee Baba Leba   1947
Cast: Dizzy Gillespie, Helen Humes, Ralph Brown. (Sound / B&W / 10 min. / Musical / Short.)

Dizzy Gillespie and his Bebop Orchestra perform "Salt Peanuts" and "Ee Baba Leba" with Helen Humes doing the vocal on the latter. They also play the musical support for Ralph Brown's tap-dance number.

329   Eleven PM   1928
Dir: Maurice, Richard D. *Prod:* Maurice, Richard D. *Co:* Maurice Film Company. *Cast:* Richard Maurice, Leo Pope, Sammie Lane, H. Marion Williams.

Screenplay: Richard Maurice. (16mm / B&W / Silent / 6 reels / Feature / FDA 2151.)

A writer has several appointments set for eleven P.M. but falls asleep and dreams up the plot for a new drama which includes a strange element of reincarnation.

Songs: "Air Mail Special" and "The Skunk Song." (Sound / Musical / Feature / B&W.)

Musical variety type of the period.

325   Eddie Green and Company, Sending a Wire   1929
Co: Vitaphone. *Cast:* Eddie Green. (Comedy / B&W / Short / VBE 8158.)

Performing "Sending the Wire" skit from the Broadway show "Hot Chocolates."

326   Eddie Green's Rehearsal   1916
Dir: Green, Eddie. *Prod:* Green, Eddie. *Co:* Green, Eddie. *Dist:* Green, Eddie. *Cast:* Eddie Green.

Sound version released in 1939 by the title *Dress Rehearsal* by Sepia Arts. (Silent / Short / B&W.)

Eddie Green, desperate to get into show business, borrows a friend's clothes and car, and heads off to audition. He tells jokes, sings and generally performs to an encore.

327   Eddie's Laugh Jamboree   1944
Prod: Green, Eddie. *Co:* Toddy Pictures

330   Emily Brown 1943

Co: RCM Production. *Dist:* Soundies Distributing Corporation. *Cast:* Bob Parrish, Emily Brown, Chinky Grimes. (Soundies 12106 / B&W / Short / Sound / Musical / 6/14/43.)

331   Emperor Jones 1933

Dir: Murphy, Dudley. *Prod:* Krimsky, John & Gifford Cochran. *Co:* United Artists. *Cast:* Paul Robeson, Dudley Digges, Frank Wilson, Fredi Washington, Ruby Elzy, George Haymind Stampar, Jackie Mayble, Blueboy O'Connor, Rex Ingram, Gordon Taylor.

Adaptation of play by Eugene O'Neill, Screenplay: DuBose Heyward, Supervised by William C. de-Mille. Incidental music composed and directed by Frank Tours. Photography: Ernest Haller. Art director: Herman Rosse. Assistant director: Joseph H. Nadel. Sound: Joseph Kane. Production manager: Howard Shugrug. Film editor: Grant Whytock. Synchronization: Max Manne. Produced at Eastman Service Studios. Reviews in *The*

Philadelphia Tribune, 9/29/33, 10/26/33, 11/30/33 and the *Motion Picture Herald,* 9/23/33. (British made / 16mm / B&W / Sound / 2 reels / 73 min. / Feature / FCA 6017-6018.)

Robeson plays a Pullman porter who escapes from a chain gang and improbably becomes king (Brutus Jones) of a Caribbean island. His lust for power leads to disastrous consequences. Stereotypical, with some fancy camerawork at end. Robeson is excellent in his role as Brutus Jones.

332   Errand Boy for Rhythm 1946

Dir: Crouch, William Forest. *Prod:* Crouch, William Forest. *Co:* Filmcraft Production. *Dist:* Soundies Distributing Corporation. *Cast:* The King Cole Trio (Nat "King" Cole, Oscar Moore, Johnny Miller). (Soundies / B&W / Short / Sound / Musical / 5/27/46.)

333   Escapades of Estelle 1916

Dir: Palmer, Harry. *Co:* Mutual Film Corporation. (Animated / Silent / Short / 3 min. / 35mm / B&W / 1 reel / FEA 3306.)

Cartoon.

334   Eubie Blake Plays 1929

Co: Lee DeForrest Phonofilms. *Cast:* Eubie Blake. (35mm / Sound / B&W / 1 reel / Musical / Short / 6 min. / FEA 5456 or FAB 1823.)

Eubie Blake plays and sings "Way Down Upon the Swanee River."

335   Everybody Works But Father (Blackface) 1905

Co: Biograph. *Cast:* Lew Dockstader.

Black version most likely whites in blackface. (B&W / Silent / Short / FLA 5026.)

"A vehicle for a Lew Dockstader routine, featured two versions, one black, one white, of a family that rebels against its rocking-chair-bound father"— Thomas Cripps.

336   Everybody's Jumpin' Now 1946

Dir: Crouch, William Forest. *Prod:* Crouch, William Forest. *Co:* Filmcraft Production. *Dist:* Soundies Distributing Corporation. *Cast:* Noble Sissle and His Orchestra, Mabel Lee. (Soundies / Short / B&W / 12/30/46.)

Metropolitan Studios in New York. Preview in *The Philadelphia Tribune*, 2/19/31. (Feature / Sound / B&W / FBB 3489-3491.)

The central plot is concerned with a young black man whose fiancée comes into ownership of a mansion, located on South Parkway in Chicago, which serves as a combination cabaret and brothel. The young man, appalled, leaves the city for the plains of South Dakota. There he meets a pretty young girl whom he assumes to be white. He becomes her friend and protector but the race barrier stands between them until it is revealed that she is part Negro and all ends well.

339 Eyes of Youth 1920
Dir: Levy, Robert. *Co:* Quality Amusement Company. *Cast:* Abbie Mitchell, Lafayette Players Stock Company. (Silent / B&W / Short.)

The plot of the film concerns a woman who is trying to choose between several suitors. She consults a medium and deals with the future through the crystal ball concerning what would happen with each of her possible choices.

340 The Fall Guy 1913
Dir: Foster, William. *Prod:* Foster, William. *Co:* Foster Photoplay. *Dist:* William Foster. (Silent / B&W / Short / Comedy.)

341 The Fall of the Mighty 1913
Co: Al Bartlett Film Manufacturing Company. *Cast:* Billy Arnett, Clayburn Jones, I.D. Bradford, Grace Arnett, Ida Lochart, Jules McGarr, Ruby Taylor, George Fox. (Silent / B&W.)

342 Family of Ghana 1958
Prod: National Film Board of Canada. *Co:* National Film Board of Canada. (Documentary / 16mm / Sound / B&W / 1 reel / 30 min.)

"Experiences of a family in Ghana illustrate the culture of that country. Includes sequences of Accra and of native music and dancing"— Klotman.

343 Fan Tan Fanny 1945
Co: RCM Production. *Dist:* Soundies Distributing Corporation. *Cast:* Day, Dawn and Dusk. (Soundies 21008 / B&W / Short / Sound / Musical / 7/9/45.)

337 Everyday Is Saturday in Harlem 1944
Co: RCM Production. *Dist:* Soundies Distributing Corporation. *Cast:* Hilda Rogers. (Soundies 16608 / B&W / Short / Sound / Musical / 5/22/44.)

338 The Exile 1931
Dir: Micheaux, Oscar. *Prod:* Schiffman, Frank. *Co:* Micheaux Film Corporation. *Dist:* Micheaux Film Corporation. *Cast:* Eunice Brooks, Charles Moore, A.B. Comathiere, Carl Mahon, Lou Vernon, Katherine Noisette, Louise Cook, Roland Holder, George Randol, Donald Haywood's Band, Leonard Harper's Chorines, Stanley Morrell, Nora Newcome.

The first all Black cast independently produced talkie, written by Oscar Micheaux. Adapted from "The Conquest." Autobiographical, a story that he'll tell over and over. Photography: Lester Lang & Walter Strange. Score: Donald Heywood. Dance and ensemble: Leonard Harper. Produced at the

344   Fare Thee Well 1945

Co: RCM Production. *Dist:* Soundies Distributing Corporation. *Cast:* Day, Dawn and Dusk.

(Soundies 21008 / B&W / Short / Sound / Musical / 7/9/45.)

345   Father Said He'd Fix It 1915

Dir: Lubin, Sigmund. *Prod:* Lubin, Sigmund. *Co:* Lubin Manufacturing Company. *Cast:* Billy Higgins, Luke Scott, John Edwards, Mattie Edwards, Martha Brown.

Written by Will Louis. Released on 6/22/15. (Silent / Short / 500 ft.)

"The story has to do with Mrs. Mattie Wash who objects to the attentions paid by Deacon Dark's son Luke to Lynthia, her daughter. Luke returns home after his rebuff and tells his father that Mattie says he isn't 'good enough' for her girl. The Deacon's pride is given a shake-up by this news and, in a rage, he swears he will teach Mattie a thing or two about the distinguished ancestry of the Deacon's family. On arriving at Mattie's home he finds the widow in a flirta-

tious mood instead of the stubborn opposition he had hoped for. Instead of smoothing it for Luke he sets to work to win the widow. Luke and Lynthia, watching through the window, see Mattie nod her consent"—*Lubin Bulletin.*

346   Faust 1945

Co: RCM Production. *Dist:* Soundies Distributing Corporation. *Cast:* Day, Dawn and Dusk. (Soundies 20608 / B&W / Short / Sound / Musical / 5/14/45.)

347   Feeling Alright 1949

Co: Southern Educational Film Production Service. (Documentary / B&W / Sound / Short / Made in Mississippi.)

Non-professional blacks show a fictionalized version of what can happen if syphilis is not properly treated.

348   The Feud and the Turkey
pre–1910

(B&W / Silent / Short / FLA 5380.)

349   The Fight Never Ends 1947

Dir: Alexander, William D. *Prod:* Alexander, William D. *Dist:* Alexander Releasing Corporation. *Co:* Alexander Productions. *Cast:* Joe Louis, Ruby Dee, Harrel Tillman, Elwood Smith, Mills Brothers, William Greaves, Emmett "Babe" Wallace, Gwendolyn Tynes.

Reviews in the *New York Age,* 7/19/47 and 3/6/48. *New York Amsterdam News,* 2/28/48. (Feature / B&W / Sound.)

Joe Louis, portraying himself, is a good influence on a group of Harlem youths who are tempted to "go bad" by a gangster known as Caper, an older brother of one of the youths.

350   Fight That Ghost 1946

Dir: Newfield, Sam. *Prod:* Toddy, Ted. *Co:* Toddy Pictures Company. *Dist:* Toddy Pictures. *Cast:* Dewey "Pigmeat" Markham, John "Rastus" Murray, Sidney Easton, Percy Verwayen, David Beathea. (Sound / B&W / 62 min. / Feature.)

A comedy mystery feature replete with a ghost.

351   Fighting Americans 1943

Co: Toddy Pictures Company. *Cast:* Air Cadets at Tuskegee Army Air Field, Tuskegee,

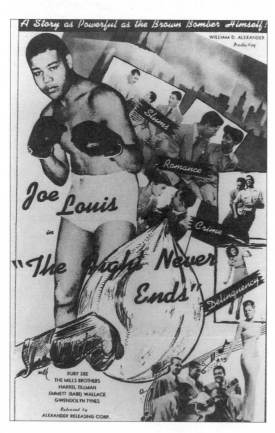

A Story as Powerful as the Brown Bomber Himself!

WILLIAM D. ALEXANDER Production

Joe Louis in "The Fight Never Ends"

Slums · Romance · Crime · Delinquency

RUBY DEE
THE MILLS BROTHERS
HARREL TILLMAN
EMMETT (BABE) WALLACE
GWENDOLYN TYNES

Released by
ALEXANDER RELEASING CORP.

Alabama, Wacs at Fort Devens, Massachusetts. (50 min. / Newsreel / Short / B&W / Sound.)

Shows black air cadets from Tuskegee Army Air Field, Alabama, and black Wacs from Fort Devens, Massachusetts.

352   The Fighting Deacon   1925

Prod: Flowers, Tiger & Walt Miller. *Co:* Flowers, Tiger & Walt Miller. *Dist:* Milton Star. *Cast:* Tiger Flowers, "Fighting Bob" Lawson.

Preview in the *New York Amsterdam News*, 4/8/25. (Dramatized / Documentary / Feature / Silent / B&W.)

The film tells the story of how Tiger Flowers, "The Fighting Deacon," rose from a delivery boy in a grocery store making $1.00 a week to become one of the highest paid prizefighters during the 1920s.

353   The Fighting Fifteenth Colored Regiment   1921

Co: Dunbar Film Corporation. (Silent / B&W / Newsreel / Short / Documentary.)

354   The Fighting Fool   1925

Prod: Norman Film Manufacturing Company. *Co:* Norman Film Manufacturing Company. *Dist:* Norman Films. (Silent / B&W / Feature.)

355   Fincho   1958

Dir: Zebba, Sam. *Prod:* Zebba, Sam. *Cast:* Patrick Akponu, Comfort Ajilo, Gordon Parryhobroyd, Harry Belafonte. (16mm / Color / Sound / 3 reels / 75 min. / Dramatized / Documentary.)

"Set in Nigeria, Fincho raises the problems of industrialization and modernization in emerging African nations. The cast is composed of non-professional Nigerian actors. Introduction by Harry Belafonte"—Klotman.

356   Fish   1916

Co: Biograph. *Dist:* General Films Company. *Cast:* Bert Williams. (Silent / B&W / Comedy / Short / 1 reel.)

"In this picture Bert goes fishing instead of chopping wood. He lands a ten pounder and despite his efforts to sell the fish, is unsuccessful. The reel closes with Bert being led back to the woodpile"—*The Moving Picture World*, 9/9/16.

357   Five Guys Named Moe   1942

Co: RCM Production. *Dist:* Soundies Distributing Corporation. *Cast:* Louis Jordan and His Tympany Five. (Soundies 11108 / B&W / Short / Sound / Musical / 12/31/42.)

358   Five Salted Peanuts   1945

Co: RCM Production. *Dist:* Soundies Distributing Corporation. *Cast:* The Counts and the Countess. (Soundies 88108 / B&W / Short / Sound / Musical / 10/22/45.)

359   Fixing the Faker   1918

Co: Ebony Film Company. *Dist:* General Films Company. *Cast:* Ebony Players (Sam Robinson, Samuel "Sambo" Jacks, Will Starks, Julia Mason, Bert Murphy, Evon Skekeeter, Mildred Price, Walter Brogsdale, Robert Duree, Frank Pollard, George Lewis Stock Company). (Comedy / Silent / B&W / Short.)

360   The Flames of Wrath   1923

Co: Western Film Production Company.

Cast: Roxie Mankins, John Burton, Charles Pearson, Anna Kelson, John Lester Johnson, Frank Colbert.

Made by the first Colored woman film producer, Mrs. Maris P. Williams. (35mm / B&W / Silent / 5 reels / Feature / Mystery.)

P.C. Gordon was killed and robbed of a valuable diamond, a birthday present from his wife. C. Dates, one of the robbers, was tried and prosecuted by a woman prosecuting attorney, Maria P. Williams, and sentenced to 10 years in the penitentiary, but later escapes and returns to the spot where he buried the ring. A boy, playing in a vacant lot, digs up the ring and gives it to his brother, Charles Pearson, who shows the ring to W.M. Jackson, who later causes the arrest of Charles Pearson. Pauline Keith, acting the part of a shrewd detective, succeeds in foiling the plot made between her employer, W.M. Jackson, the crooked lawyer, Frank Keither, her own father and Flora Fulton to rob Charles Pearson of the ring. A $2,000 reward is offered for the arrest of C. Dates, who surrenders and is pardoned.

361   The Flaming Crisis   1924

Prod: Goldman, Lawrence. *Co:* Monarch Productions / Mesco Productions. *Cast:* Dorothy Dunbar, Calvin Nicholson, Talford White, Henry Dixon, Kathryn Sherman, Marie Chester, Arthur Yeargan, William Butler.

Reviews in the *Kansas City Call* 5/30/24 and *Billboard* 1/29/24 & 5/24/24. (Feature / B&W / Silent.)

"Robert Mason, an aggressive newspaperman, exposes the methods of Mark Leithier, labor leader & political power. As a result, Mason's engagement to Vivian Leithier is broken. At the reception at the home of Dr. Walter McWalter, Leithier is murdered. Mason is accused and convicted. After several years in prison, he escapes and makes his way into the cattle lands of the southwest where he meets Tex Miller, a daughter of the prairie. He incurs the hatred of Buck Conley, who is also the mysterious 'Night Terror,' leader of an outlaw gang and Mason is soon involved in a series of thrilling adventures. After overcoming his enemies, he realized that he is an escaped convict. Then something big and entirely unexpected happens, which brings happiness to the lovers"— H. Sampson.

362   Flamingo   1942

Co: RCM Production. *Dist:* Soundies Distributing Corporation. *Cast:* Duke Ellington, The Katherine Dunham Dancers. (Soundies 4907 / B&W / Short / Sound / Musical / 1/5/42.)

363   Flamingo   1947

Prod: Pond, Stillman. *Co:* Stillman Pond Production. *Dist:* Stillman Pond Productions. *Cast:* Herbert Jeffries, Dorothy Dandridge. (B&W / Sound / Short?)

364   Flicker Up   1946

Dir: Alexander, William D. *Prod:* Alexander, William D. *Co:* Associated Producers of Negro Motion Pictures. *Cast:* Billy Eckstine, May Lou Harris. (Musical / B&W / Sound / Short.)

365   The Florian Slappey Series   1925

Prod: Cohen, Octavus. *Co:* Cohen, Octavus.

A series of all black comedies, 1925–1926. (Comedy / Shorts / B&W / Silent.)

366 Florida Crackers 1921

Dir: Foster, William. *Prod:* Foster, William. *Co:* Kalem Studio. (Short / Silent / B&W.)

A film which contained a graphic lynching scene and which was a source of real controversy. Made by pioneer black filmmaker Bill Foster.

367 The Flying Ace 1926

Prod: Norman Film Manufacturing Company. *Co:* Norman Film Manufacturing Company. *Dist:* Norman Studios. *Cast:* Kathryn Boyd, Lawrence Criner, Boise DeLegge, Harold Platts, Lions Daniels, Sam Jordan, George Colvin, Dr. R.L. Brown, Steve Reynolds. (B&W / Feature / Silent / FGE 4385-4387.)

A returning war hero, Captain Billy Stokes returns home to be given his old job back as chief security officer for the railroad company. The railroad has just been robbed of $25,000 and the case is handed over to Capt. Billy. After some great detective work, an airplane chase, and fist fights, he solves the mystery and gets the girl, Ruth Sawtelle, a female daredevil, in her most daring escapade. Ruth (Boyd) appears to climb a slender rope ladder suspended from a plane a mile up in order to escape from its burning fuselage. Lawrence Criner plays Captain Billy Stokes.

368 Folklore 1950

Prod: Wilder, A.W. Lee. *Co:* United Artists. (Musical / B&W / Short / Sound.) Songs: "Old Folks at Home," and "Swing Low, Sweet Chariot."

Negro choral group sings.

369 Foo, a Little Ballyhoo 1945

Co: RCM Production. *Dist:* Soundies Distributing Corporation. *Cast:* Cab Calloway and His Orchestra. (Soundies 21508 / B&W / Short / Sound / Musical / 9/17/45.)

370 Fool and Fire 1918

Dir: Foster, William. *Prod:* Foster, William. *Co:* Foster Photoplay Company. *Dist:* William Foster. (Silent / Short / B&W.)

A five-reel vampire drams. A story with a gasping situation that makes the world wonder can there be such a creature living. The climax will spellbound any audience.

371 Foolin' Around 1943

Co: RCM Production. *Dist:* Soundies Distributing Corporation. *Cast:* Harris and Hunt, Mabel Lee, The Harlem Honeys. (Soundies 14008 / B&W / Short / Sound / Musical / 11/1/43.)

372 Foolish Lives 1921

Co: Young Producers Filming Corporation. *Cast:* Frank Chatman, Henry Harris, Frank Carter, Jewel Cox, Marguerite Patterson, Jonella Patton. (35mm / Silent / B&W / Feature.)

A story of Negro life.

373 A Fool's Errand 1922

Dir: Micheaux, Oscar. *Prod:* Micheaux, Oscar. *Co:* Micheaux Film Corporation. *Dist:* Micheaux Film Corporation. *Cast:* William Fountaine, Shingzie Howard. (Feature / B&W / Silent.)

374 A Fool's Promise 1921

Co: White Film Corporation. (5 reels / Drama / Feature / B&W / Silent.)

375   For His Mother's Sake   1922

Co: Blackburn Velde Productions. *Cast:* Jack Johnson, Matty Wilkens, Adrian Joyce, Jack Hopkins, Jack Newton, Dick Lee, Hank West, Everett Godfrey, Edward McMowan, Ruth Walker.

Made at Cliffside Park, N.J. (5 reels / Feature / B&W / Silent.)

The story concerns a mother who has two sons, the youngest of whom is her idol and also the less industrious of the two. Both boys are employed by an express company, and when the younger brother steals a valuable parcel, the older brother, knowing what a blow the news of the younger brother's crime will be to his mother, takes the blame on himself and goes to Mexico, where he blossoms forth as a prizefighter. He wins several thousand dollars and returns home, pays for the theft and all ends happily.

376   For the Honor of the 8th Illinois Regiment   1914

Dir: Jones, Peter P. *Prod:* Jones, Peter P. *Co:* Peter P. Jones Photoplay Company. (Documentary / Newsreel / B&W / Silent / Short.)

This film shows the 8th Illinois in a dress parade; being reviewed by Governor Dunue of Illinois; marching in Cuba during the Spanish American War; being attacked and later repulsing the enemy on a bridge in Cuba with 1000 soldiers engaged in battle; taking a block house on San Juan Hill; firing cannons; and their victory celebration.

377   Forest People of Central Africa   1920

Prod: Dept. of Anthropology, Harvard University. *Co:* Dept. of Anthropology, Harvard University. (Documentary / 16mm / Silent / B&W / 1 reel / 20 min. / Short.)

"Shows the daily activities of Central African Pygmies; includes iron-making and dances"— Klotman.

378   Forty Seventh Street Jive   1944

Co: RCM Production. *Dist:* Soundies Distributing Corporation. *Cast:* June Richmond, Roy Milton and His Orchestra. (Soundies 17908 / B&W / Short / Sound / Musical / 8/28/44.)

379   Fought and Won   1921

Co: Gate City Feature Films. (Silent / B&W.)

380   Four Letters   1946

Dir: Crouch, William Forest. *Prod:* Crouch, William Forest. *Co:* Filmcraft Production. *Dist:* Soundies Distributing Corporation. *Cast:* Gloria Parker. (Soundies / B&W / Short / Sound / Musical / 3/4/46.)

381   Four or Five Times   1941

Co: RCM Production. *Dist:* Soundies Distributing Corporation. *Cast:* Sister Rosetta Tharpe, Lucky Millinder and His Orchestra. (Soundies 3608 / B&W / Short / Sound / Musical / 10/6/41.)

382   Four Shall Die   1940

Dir: Popkin, Leo C. *Prod:* Sanforth, Clifford. *Co:* Million Dollar Productions. *Dist:* Million Dollar Distributing Company. *Cast:* Dorothy Dandridge, Niel Webster, Jessie Lee Brooks, John Thomas, Mantan Moreland, Alfred Grant,

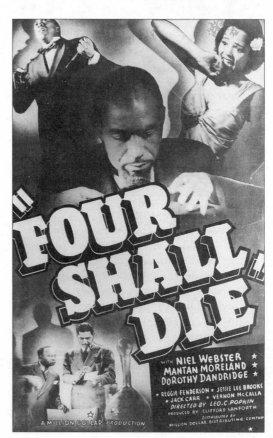

Edward Thompson, Reginald Fenderson, Jack Carr, Harry Levette, Vernon McCalla.

Condemned Men, 1948, is the re-released *Four Shall Die*, 1940. Dorothy Dandridge's first feature film. Cast announcement in *The Philadelphia Afro-American*, 8/31/40. Preview in the *Philadelphia Independent*, 9/22/40. (Feature / B&W / Sound.)

Dandridge plays a young heiress who is besieged by two young men, both of whom want to marry her. In addition to the love triangle and Haitian zombies, is the mystery of four deaths which Mantan Moreland, as the detective, tries to solve.

383   Fowl Play   1929

Dir: Foster, William. *Prod:* Foster, William. *Co:* Pathé. *Dist:* Supreme Distributing Company. *Cast:* Buck and Bubbles (Ford Lee Washington & John Sublette).

Songs: "Swanee River," "Oh, You Beautiful Doll," "When I Got You Alone Tonight," "Give Me a Little Kiss Will You, Huh," "Coal Black Mammy of Mine," "Chicken Reel." (Sound / B&W / Short / Comedy.)

Buck and Bubbles are hired to deliver an ostrich. This hilarious escapade gets complicated when they meet the "yaller-skinned" vamp.

384   The Framing of the Shrew   1929

Dir: Cohen, Octavus Roy. *Prod:* Christie, Al. *Co:* Christie Film Company. *Dist:* Paramount. *Cast:* Evelyn Preer, Spencer Williams, Roberta Hyson, Edward Thompson.

Screenplay: Octavus Roy Cohen & Spencer Williams. (Sound / B&W / 2 reels / Comedy / Short.)

An obstreperous wife (Preer) is tamed and trained by her smaller but wily husband.

385   France's Dusky Warriors   1918

Co: British & French Pictorial Film Service. *Dist:* Pathé. (Silent / Documentary / Newsreel / B&W / Short.)

This pictures the war work of Tunis, Algeria and Morocco. It is full of striking scenes from the native life of those countries, under the stirring influence of war preparations, equipping and mobilizing troops and sending them to the French front. The review of troops mounted on fine Arabian steeds is particularly colorful. There are also interesting views from the commercial life of Tunis, which is a great food center for the Allies.

386   Frederick Douglass's the House on Cedar Hill   1953

Dir: Moss, Carlton. *Prod:* Moss, Carlton. *Co:* Carlton Moss. *Cast:* Frederick Douglass. (16mm / B&W / Sound / 1 reel / 17 min. / Documentary / Short.)

A filmed biography of Frederick Douglass, eminent leader in the struggle against slavery. The narration is from Douglass' writings; the musical score is based on Afro-American folk songs.

387   Free and Equal   1925

Dir: Ince, Thomas. *Prod:* Ince, Thomas. *Co:* Thomas Ince. *Cast:* Jack Richardson. (Feature / B&W / Silent.)

This film was billed as an answer to *Birth of a Nation* when it opened at the Astor Theatre on Times Square, N.Y. It received negative reviews by the critics and was viewed by the mostly white audience with contempt. Premiered in New York in 1925. Intended to prove the Negro is naturally corrupt as well as inferior, the film is an exhortation against the "mixing of the races." Richardson (in blackface) plays Alexander Marshall, the Black character who after being taken into the home of a liberal Northern judge, pursues the judge's daughter, then rapes and strangles the maid" — Klotman.

Jack Richardson, who plays a Negro passing for white, is trying to exhort his fellows to make the most of their opportunities to assert themselves as the equals of the whites, socially and physically. At the close of the picture, he awakens from the dream which the picture is supposed to represent and says that Booker T. Washington is right — the Negro must stay in his place. The picture has as its central theme the question of the equality of the races. Judge Lowell believes that he can solve the question by taking a light skinned Negro into his home as his secretary and have him pose as white. In the end, the Negro commits a murder after having secretly married the daughter of his benefactor, the girl believing him to be white.

388   Freedom for Ghana 1957
Prod: Ghana Information Service. *Co:* Ghana Information Service. (Ghana / Documentary / 16mm / Sound / Color / 35 min. / Short.)

The anniversary celebration of Ghana's independence.

389   The French Way 1952
Dir: Debaroncelli, J. *Prod:* DeBaroncelli, J. / L. Barry Bernard. *Co:* Manor Films. *Dist:* Manor Films Release. *Cast:* Josephine Baker, Micheline Prelle, Georges Marchal, Aimos, Jean Tissier, Gabrielle Dorziat, Saturnin Fabre, Lucien Baroux, Marguerite Perry.

French with English subtitles. Music by WAL-BERG. English dialogue: Herman G. Weinberg. Editor: Reine Dorian. (B&W / Sound / Feature.)

Baker plays Madame Zazu, an entertainer during wartime France. She is loved by everyone, plays cupid, befriends hobos, and generally helps everyone. The basic plot involves the struggle of two young people in love, with feuding parents.

390   Frenzy 1946
Dir: Cornblum, Sherman. *Prod:* Cornblum, Sherman. *Co:* Cornblum, Sherman. *Cast:* Herb Jeffries, Dorothy Dandridge.

Songs: "Basin St. Blues," and "I Don't Want to Cry Anymore." (B&W / Sound / Short / Musical.)

Musical revue.

391   Frim Fram Sauce 1945
Dir: Crouch, William Forest. *Prod:* Crouch, William Forest. *Co:* Filmcraft Production. *Dist:* Soundies Distributing Corporation. *Cast:* The King Cole Trio (Nat "King" Cole, Oscar Moore, Johnny Miller). (Soundies 87408 / B&W / Short / Sound / Musical / 12/31/45.)

392   From Cotton Patch to Congress 1910
Co: M.W. Baccus Films Company. (B&W/ Silent / Biographical / Feature.)

The story of a colored man's rise to Congress.

393   From Harlem to the Rhine 1920
Co: U.S. War Department. *Cast:* Black Soldiers of World War I. (Newsreel / Documentary / Silent / B&W.)

"This documentary consists of five reels of pictures and over fifteen slides. The regiment is first shown in its infancy when Bert Williams was a member, later on the rifle range at Peekskill and subsequently in France and Germany. One of the scenes to occasion thunderous applause was that showing the regiment in action on the firing line. The triumphant march into Germany, 'Jim' Europe's band entertaining civilians of Teutonic extraction. The return of the 'Hell Fighters' to New York and the historic march up Fifth Avenue and through Harlem were the scenes which stirred the big audience"—excerpt from *New York Age*, 5/5/20.

394   The Funeral of Booker T. Washington 1916
Co: Pathé. (Newsreel No. 93 / B&W / Short / Documentary / Silent.)

Coverage of the funeral of Dr. Booker T. Washington at Tuskegee Institute, Tuskegee, Alabama, showing students carrying the body to its final resting place.

395   Fuzzy Wuzzy 1942
Co: RCM Production. *Dist:* Soundies Distributing Corporation. *Cast:* Louis Jordan and His Tympany Five, Ruby Richards. (Soundies 10305 / B&W / Short / Sound / Musical / 12/31/42.)

396   Fuzzy Wuzzy 1945
Prod: Sack, Alfred. *Co:* Sack Amusement Enterprises. *Dist:* Sack Amusement Enterprises. *Cast:* Louis Jordan and His Band, Una Mae Carlisle, Meade Lux Lews, Dudley Dickerson. (Musical / Short / B&W / Sound.)

Typical Jordanesque musical variety.

397   G.I. Jive 1944
Co: RCM Production. Dist: Soundies Distributing Corporation. Cast: Louis Jordan and His Tympany Five. (Soundies / B&W / Short/ Sound / Musical / 3/13/44.)

398   G.I. Jubilee, George Dewey Washington 1942
Cast: Ernest Whitman, Timmy Rogers, Lena Horne, Emett "Babe" Wallace. (Musical / B&W / Sound.)

Film climaxes in a car chase, crash, and capture. Nine Mae also gets the guy.

A filmed performance of this radio broadcast over America Free Radio stations during World War II.

399   Gang Smashers   1938

Dir: Popkin, Leo C. *Prod:* Popkin, Harry M. *Co:* Million Dollar Productions. *Cast:* Nina Mae McKinney, Lawrence Criner, Monte Hawley, Edward Thompson, Mantan Moreland, Vernon McCalla, Reginald Fenderson, Arthur Ray, John Criner, Charles Hawkins, Neva Peoples, Guernsey Morrow, Margaret Flemings, Bo Jenkins, Lester Wilkins, Everett Brown.

Screenplay by Ralph Cooper. Songs: "I Just Can't See It Your Way," "That's What You Get in Harlem." Preview in the *Philadelphia Afro-American*, 10/29/38, review in the *Los Angeles Sentinel*, 12/1/38. (Feature / B&W / Sound.)

Nina Mae McKinney, an undercover detective for the police, infiltrates the Dalton mob with the intentions of bringing them down.

400   Gang War   1939

Dir: Popkin, Leo C. *Prod:* Sanforth, Clifford. *Co:* Million Dollar Productions. *Dist:* Sack Amusement Enterprises. *Cast:* Ralph Cooper, Gladys Snyder, Reginald Fenderson, Lawrence Criner, Monte Hawley, Jesse Lee Brooks, Johnny Thomas, Maceo Sheffield, Charles Hawkins, Robert Johnson, Henry Roberts, Harold Garrison.

Original story by Walter Cooper. Screenplay: Lewis Sherman. Photography: Marcel A. Picard. Film editor: Michael Luciano. Sound: Earl Gille and Lambert Day. Art director: Paul Palmentola. Assistant director: Ben Chapman. Music and lyrics: Lou Porter & Johnny Lange. Music supervisor: Lou Porter. Executive producer: Harry M. Popkin. Associate producer: Sara Francis. Supervision of promotion: George D. Ringer. Production manager: Arthur C. Ringer. (Feature / B&W / Sound.)

"The story — Killer Meads rise from the streets of Harlem to the heights of gangdom

and his consequent fall from police bullets —
is familiar stuff from Hollywood ... But this
is the first time one has come out with Negroes
portraying a story of this caliber all the way
through. Minor annoyances are present in the
picture — especially in the last few scenes in
which Cooper is running across rooftops from
a squad of cops, one of whom fired his pistol
point blank at Ralph, a distance of only a few
feet separating him, and missed. Even the
audience became restive at the impossibility
of this sequence. But as a whole, we think
Cooper has finally made his best hoodlum picture"— review from the *New York Amsterdam
News*, 4/30/40.

**401   Gangsters on the Loose (Bar-
gain with Bullets)**   1944

Co: Million Dollar Productions. *Dist:* Toddy
Pictures Company. *Cast:* Ralph Cooper, Theresa
Harris, Lawrence Criner, Edward Thompson,
Clarence Brooks, Sam McDaniels, John Lester
Johnson, Billy McClain, Al Duvall, Milton

Shockley, Art Murray, Ray Martin, Halley
Harding, Frances Turham, Reginald Fenderson, Les Hite's Cotton Club Orchestra.

Gangsters on the Loose is the re-released *Bargain with Bullets*, 1937. (Feature / B&W /
Sound.)

"Mugsy" is the leader of a band of fur
thieves. He is in love with the beautiful Kay
and determined to hold her affection by giving her lavish presents. The plot is complicated by Grace, Mugsy's schoolday sweetheart.
She remembers him only as Eddie, the boy
who loved to be near her before he drifted
away into underworld company and the wiles
of a heartless schemer. Still loving him, she
has become a famous radio singer when, by
the tides of fate, their paths cross again. Lieutenant Lester finally solves the robberies and
murders and runs down the gang of criminals.

**402   The Gator and the
Pickaninny**   1903

Co: Edison. (Silent / B&W / Comedy /
Short / FLA 3647.)

"A Black man (blackface) chops open an
alligator and rescues a Black child who was
swallowed by the alligator"— Thomas Cripps.

403   Gayety   1929

Co: Vitaphone. *Cast:* Shelton Brooks,
Hamtree Harrington, Ida Anderson. (Short /
B&W / Sound.)

404   Gee   1944

Co: RCM Production. *Dist:* Soundies Dis-
tributing Corporation. *Cast:* Mabel Scott, The
Flennoy Trio. (Soundies 19305 / B&W / Short /
Sound / Musical / 12/18/44.)

**405   George Dewey Washington,
#1**   1928

Co: M-G-M Movietone. *Cast:* George
Dewey Washington. (Musical / Short /
Sound.)

Songs: "Chloe," and "Just Like a Melody
Out of the Sky."

**406   George Dewey Washington,
#2**   1929

Co: M-G-M Movietone. *Cast:* George Dewey
Washington. (Musical / B&W / Sound / Short.)

Songs: "There's a Rainbow 'Round My

Shoulder," "Pretty Little Bluebird," and "Sunny Boy."

407   George Dewey Washington, #3 1929

Co: M-G-M Movietone. *Cast:* George Dewey Washington. (Musical / B&W / Sound / Short.)

Songs: "Lonely Vagabond," and "The Sun Is at My Window."

408   George Dewey Washington, #4 1929

Co: M-G-M Movietone. *Cast:* George Dewey Washington. (Musical / B&W / Sound / Short.)

Songs: "Just Be a Builder of Dreams," and "Down Among the Sugar Cane."

409   George Dewey Washington, #5 1930

Co: M-G-M Movietone. *Cast:* George Dewey Washington. (Sound / B&W / Musical / Short / 7 min.)

Songs: "King for a Day," "Half Way to Heaven."

George Dewey Washington stands them up for three weeks in a row at the Paramount on Broadway. He's a colored Al Jolson and has that same knack of throwing himself completely into the mood of the song until it gets contagious.

410   George Washington Carver 1940

Dir: Parker, Ben. *Prod:* Green, Ira. *Co:* Bryant Productions. *Cast:* Dr. George Washington Carver, Booker T. Washington III, Ralph Edwards, Milton Sprague, Tim Campbell, Raye Gilbert.

Reviews in *The Philadelphia Afro-American*, 6/21/41, and the *New York Amsterdam News*, 4/14/40. Presented by Allen McDowell. Screenplay by Robert Starr. Narrated by John Martin. (Dramatized documentary / B&W / Sound / Feature.)

Dr. Carver tells the story of his life to a young boy who wonders what he will do when he graduates from college. He tells us about his life in flashbacks, as a slave child, the kidnapping of his mother, racial obstacles, and the studying of plants and animals as a young man.

411   Georgia Rose 1930

Dir: Gant, Harry. *Prod:* Rosebud Productions. *Co:* Aristo Films / Rosebud Productions. *Dist:* Rosebud Productions. *Cast:* Clarence Brooks, Evelyn Preer, Irene Wilson, Roberta Hyson, Allegretti Anderson, Edward Thompson, Webb King, Spencer Williams, Dora Dean Johnson, E.C. Dyer, Fred C. Washington and Orchestra.

The picture was filmed by Harry Gant, former cameraman with the Lincoln Motion Picture Company. Location scenes filmed at Dunbar Hotel, Jockey Club, and the Golden State Insurance Company building in Los Angeles. Filming was completed at the Disney Mickey Mouse Studios. Screenplay: Harry A. Gant. Music played and composed by Fred C. Washington & 111 piece orchestra. Preview in *The Philadelphia Tribune*, 5/1/30 & 9/28/30. Review in *The Philadelphia Tribune*, 10/2/30 & *The Pittsburgh Courier*, 4/18/30. (35mm / Sound / B&W / 7 reels / Feature.)

This story is about a minister's attempt to move his flock and daughter from Georgia to better farming land in the Midwest. While boarding up with a family, the minister's daughter is smitten by the love bug and led toward corruption by her new lover's brother. Of course, she is saved in the nick of time by her new lover and forgiven by her father.

412   Get It Off Your Mind   1946

Dir: Crouch, William Forest. *Prod:* Crouch, William Forest. *Co:* Filmcraft Production. *Dist:* Soundies Distributing Corporation. *Cast:* Vanita Smythe, Claude Demetrius. (Soundies 23M1 / B&W / Short / Sound / Musical / 9/2/46.)

413   Get with It   1943

Co: RCM Production. *Dist:* Soundies Distributing Corporation. *Cast:* The Bye Trio. (Soundies 6M5 / B&W / Short / Sound / Musical / 11/22/43.)

414   A Ghost Hunt   1921

Co: White Film Corporation. (B&W / Silent / Short / 2 reels / Comedy.)

415   Ghost of Tolston's Manor
1934

Dir: Micheaux, Oscar. *Prod:* Russell, A. Burton. *Co:* Micheaux Film Corporation. *Dist:* Micheaux Film Corporation. *Cast:* Andrew Bishop, Lawrence Chenault, Edna Morton, Monte Hawley, E.G. Tatum, Kink Stewart, W.B.F. Crowell, Shingzie Howard, Ida Anderson, Emmett Anthony, Mildred Smallwood, Blanche Thompson, Margaret Brown, Professor Hosay. (Feature / B&W / Sound / 8 reels / 35mm.)

Previews: *Billboard*, 4/7/23 & 5/5/23.

416   Ghosts   1917

Co: Ebony Film Company. *Dist:* General Film Company. *Cast:* Ebony Players (Sam Robinson, Samuel "Sambo" Jacks, Will Starks, Julia Mason, Bert Murphy, Evon Skekeeter, Mildred Price, Walter Brogsdale, Robert Duree, Frank Pollard, Yvonne Junior, George Lewis Stock Company). (Silent / Comedy / B&W / Short / 2 reels.)

"The good-natured darkey who plays the ghost in this picture is a very amusing ghost and, seeming to feel the dignity of his role, adds much to our enjoyment of the film. This is also a chase picture"—*Moving Picture World*, 12/8/17.

417   A Giant of His Race   1921

Prod: Strasser, Ben. *Co:* North State Film Corporation. *Cast:* Mabel Homes, Walter Holeby, Walter Long, Ruth Freeman.

Review in *Billboard*, 10/1/21 by Leigh Whipper. (Feature / B&W / Silent / 7 reels.)

The story tells of Munga who, although a slave in a new world, never renounces his faith and finally dies at a ripe old age, leaving behind the son who had been brought with him from Africa, now a young man. Under the name of Covington, he works his way through college, studies medicine, and after graduating, decides to devote his life to the uplifting of his people. The Yellow Plague breaks out and kills members of his race by the score. The doctor spends days searching for a cure, and finally fortune favors him. A young woman of his race is used in an experiment and is cured. Covington is awarded $100,000 for his discovery. The friendship of the doctor and the young woman has now ripened into love and they marry.

418   Gifts in Rhythm   1936

Co: Educational Film Corporation. *Cast:* Bob Howard, The Cabin Kids (five colored harmonizers, Ruth Hall, Helen Hall, James "Darling" Hall, Winifred "Sugar" Hall, and little Frederick Hall). (16mm / Sound / B&W / 1 reel / 10 min. / Musical / Short.)

The "Cabin Kids" along with Uncle Harry (Howard) put on a musical revue at the Fairmont Foundling Home.

419   Gig and Saddle   1933

Co: Goldberg Productions. *Cast:* Lucky Millinder, Putney Dandridge, George Williams, Gallie de Gaston, Billy Higgins, Joe Byrd, 12 Harlem Steppers, 3 Big Bands.

Original title: "Scandal." Announcement in the *Philadelphia Tribune*, 2/8/34. (Sound / B&W / Musical / Feature.)

OSCAR MICHEAUX'S
PRODUCTION

The
GIRL from CHICAGO

From the story
"JEFF BALLINGER'S WOMAN"
WITH

Grace **SMITH**   Carl **MAHON**

AND AN ALL STAR
COLORED CAST

A story of backstage life with an all-star colored cast.

420   The Girl from Chicago   1932

Dir: Micheaux, Oscar. *Prod:* Russell, A. Burton. *Co:* Micheaux Pictures Corporation. *Dist:* Micheaux Pictures Corporation. *Cast:* Grace Smith, Carl Mahon, Frank Wilson, Eunice Brooks, Minta Cato, Star Calloway, Juano Hernandez, Erwin, Gary, John Everett, Alice B. Russell, Cherokee Thornton, Chick Evans, Bud Harris, Rhythm Rascals Orchestra, Alfred "Slick" Chester.

Micheaux produced a slightly different version of this film in 1926 under the title, *The Spider's Web*. Story and adaptation by Oscar Micheaux, adapted from the story "Jeff Ballinger's Woman." Assistant director: Vere E. John. Photography: Sam Orleans. Recording engineer: Richard Halpenny. (16mm / B&W / Sound / 6 reels / 69 min. / Feature / FCA 7276-7277.)

Norma, a newly appointed school teacher, is boarding at the same house (Mary's) as Alonzo, a Secret Service agent staying over on a case. The two hit it off immediately, but little did Norma know that another tenant, Jeff, was eyeing her. Meanwhile, Jeff was being eyed by Alonzo, for he was the reason for his being there. Once Jeff was taken care of, Mary, Norma and Alonzo head off to Harlem. Mary gets involved with criminals and is eventually framed for murder. She is convicted and sentenced to die in the electric chair. Naturally, Alonzo solves the crime in the nick of time and then runs off to marry Norma.

421   The Girl from the Pepper Patch   1922

Co: Lone Star Motion Picture Company. (B&W / Silent.)

422   Girl in Room 20   1946

Dir: Williams, Spencer. *Prod:* Jenkins-Bourgeois. *Co:* United Films. *Dist:* United Films. *Cast:* July Jones, Geraldine Brock,

GERALDINE BROCK
AS THE

GIRL *in*
ROOM 20

Spencer **WILLIAMS** • *July* **JONES**

OUTSTANDING COLORED CAST SMASH HIT

Spencer Williams, John Hemmings, Myra Hemmings, Margery Moore, Mrs. F.D. Benson, R. Jore, Mamie Fisher, G.T. Sutton, James B. Edward, E. Celese Allen, Buzz Ayecock, Charles M. Reese, Katherine Moore, Frank Tanner, Howard Galloway, Montague McCord, Norma Johnson, Dorothy Scott.

Cinematographer: Frank Brodie & Jack Specht. Recording: Elmer Green. Editing: H.W. Kier. (Feature / B&W / Sound / FEA 6087, FEA 8415-8419.)

Small-town Texas girl leaves home, family and boyfriend to seek her dream of singing professionally in New York City. She's befriended by a cabby (Spencer Williams) who keeps an eye on her. She eventually, but innocently, gets wrapped up with a married man. His wife shows up and accidently shoots the young girl. The cabby calls her boyfriend in Texas to come to New York to assist her. She recovers, sings, and her boyfriend takes her and her good friends back to Texas.

423   Git It   1943

Co: RCM Production. *Dist:* Soundies Distributing Corporation. *Cast:* Patterson and Jackson. (Soundies 14808 / B&W / Short / Sound / Musical / 12/28/43.)

424   Give Me Some Skin   1941

Co: RCM Production. *Dist:* Soundies Distributing Corporation. *Cast:* The Delta Rhythm Boys. (Soundies 26M3 / B&W / Short / Sound / Musical / 12/30/46.)

425   Glory Filled Spirituals   1950

Prod: Wilder, A.W. Lee. *Co:* United Artists. (Musical / B&W / Sound.)

Songs: "All God's Chillun Got Wings," "Tramp, Tramp, Tramp," and "Dere's No Hiding Place Down Dere."

Negro choral group singing spirituals.

426   Glory Road   1945

Cast: Spencer Williams. (Sound / B&W.)

427   Gluttonous Negro   1905

Co: Pathé. (Newsreel / Short / B&W / Silent.)

Unreleased footage of obese black men.

428   Go Down, Death!   1944

Dir: Williams, Spencer. *Prod:* Sack,

Alfred N. / Spencer Williams. *Co:* Harlemwood Studios. *Dist:* Sack Amusement Enterprises. *Cast:* Spencer Williams, Myra Hemmings, Samuel H. Jones, the Heavenly Choir, Jimmie Green's Orchestra, Daniel Inma, Eddye L. Houston, Amos Droughan, Walter McMillion, Irene Campbell, Charles Washington, Helen Butler, Dolly Jones.

Inspired by James Weldon Johnson's poem, "Go Down Death." Screenplay: Sam Elljay. Dialogue director: Robert M. Moscow. Sound engineer: Bruce Jamieson. Photography: H.W. Kier. Editor: L.J. Powell. Story idea: Jean Roddy. (16mm / Sound / 2 reels / B&W / 54 min. / Feature / FBA 8623-8624.)

Folk-like drama, strong on religion. Minister tries to close down clubs on Sunday, but one club owner retaliates. He takes prearranged photos of the Minister in a compromising position, to blackmail him. One of the minister's church members knows what really happened and she also happened to be the woman who raised the corrupt club owner (Spencer Williams). When compromising photos are safely locked away by the club owner, his dead father's ghost leads the woman to the photos. While removing photos, she's discovered by Spencer Williams, a struggle ensues which results in her death. After attending the funeral, burial and church services, the club owner is haunted and taunted mentally by voices of guilt, until he goes crazy. Film ends with scenes of Hell as depicted from Dante's "Inferno," sucking in the corrupt club owner.

429   Go Man Go   1954

Dir: Howe, James Wong. *Prod:* Leader, Anton M. *Co:* United Artists. *Dist:* United Artists. *Cast:* Sidney Poitier, The Harlem Globetrotters, Slim Gaillard, Dane Clark (white), Patricia Breslin (white).

Screenplay: Arnold Becker. Song: "Go Man Go." (Feature / Color / Sound / Sports.)

The all-new, all-true, never-before-told story of the life and love of the man who brought Harlem Globetrotters fame and fortune. Obviously, this film is about the club's manager (played by Dane Clark).

430   God's Heaven   1943

Co: RCM Production. *Dist:* Soundies Distributing Corporation. *Cast:* George Washington Brown. (Soundies 12607 / B&W / Short / Sound / Musical / 7/19/43.)

431   God's Stepchildren   1938

Dir: Micheaux, Oscar. *Prod:* Micheaux, Oscar. *Co:* Micheaux Film Corporation. *Dist:* Sack Amusement Enterprises. *Cast:* Alice B. Russell, Trixie Smith, Jacqueline Lewis, Charles Thompson, Ethel Moses, Carmen Newsome, Gloria Press, Alec Lovejoy, Columbus Jackson, Laura Bowman, Sam Patterson, Charles Moore, Consuelo Harris, Tyler Twins, Sammy Gardiner, Leon Gross and His Orchestra.

Review in the *Kansas City Call*, 5/28/38. Film story adapted from *Naomi, Negress!* Screenplay: Oscar Micheaux. Film was withdrawn from showing at RKO's Regent Theater, May 1938, and not to be shown at any RKO Theaters. Picket lines in front of theater were formed by the Young Communist League. Claims film creates a false splitting of Negroes into light and dark groups. (16mm / B&W / Sound / 1 reel / 65 min. / Feature.)

Micheaux's attempt at showing the perils of "passing." Naomi, who does not want to be considered a Negro, is raised by her foster mother and forced to attend a Negro school. Naomi spreads a lie about her teacher and the principal, and a scandal develops. When her lie is discovered she is placed in a convent for 12 years. She eventually marries a dark-skinned Negro, and gives birth to a baby, which she promptly leaves with her foster mother. Wanting to be white, she goes over to the other side and marries a white man. When her true race is discovered she runs home disgraced. The film ends with her committing suicide by jumping off a bridge. A very serious message film by Micheaux.

432   Going to Glory, Come to Jesus   1946

Dir: Meyer, T. *Co:* Royal Gospel Productions. *Dist:* Toddy Pictures Co. Exchange. *Cast:* Irene Harper, Lloyd Howlett, Stella Van Derzee, Charles A. Freeman, John Watts, Marilyn Lawrence, Anne H. Francis, Thomas Quick, Josephine Gertrude, James Watts, Eddie L. Fluker, Wallace Harris, Thelma Lynch, Dorothy Thomas. (B&W / Sound / Religious / Feature.)

A young girl, an outcast and depressed because of her ugliness, falls to the temptations of the Devil. A prophet appears to save her and show her the way of the Lord.

433   Golden Pearls of Progress   1919

Co: Exquisite Productions. (Short / B&W / Silent.)

434   Goldilocks and the Jivin' Bears   1944

Dir: Freland, Fritz. *Co:* Warner Bros.

A Merrie Melody. (Animated / Short / 16mm / Technicolor / Sound / 1 reel / 10 min.)

A typical 1940s cartoon with blacks portrayed as boogie-woogie bears.

435   Gone Harlem   1939

Dir: Franklyn, Irwin R. & Hazele. *Co:* Creative Cinema Corporation. *Dist:* Sack Amusement Enterprises. *Cast:* Ethel Moses, Jimmy Baskette, Florence Hill, Chuck Thompson, Ovie Alston Orchestra, The Plantation Club Chorus. (Feature / B&W / Sound.)

"Passion, swing, rhythm, and crime behind locked doors of an artist studio" — from the film's poster.

436 Good Luck in Old Clothes
1918

Co: Ebony Film Company. *Dist:* General Films Company. *Cast:* Ebony Players (Sam Robinson, Samuel "Sambo" Jacks, Will Starks, Julia Mason, Bert Murphy, Evon Skekeeter, Mildred Price, Walter Brogsdale, Robert Duree, Frank Pollard, George Lewis Stock Company). (Comedy / B&W / Silent / Short.)

437 Good-Nite All 1943

Co: RCM Production. *Dist:* Soundies Distributing Corporation. *Cast:* Johnny Taylor. (Soundies 12508 / B&W / Short / Sound / Musical / 7/12/43.)

438 Got a Penny Benny 1946

Dir: Crouch, William Forest. *Prod:* Crouch, William Forest. *Co:* Filmcraft Production. *Dist:* Soundies Distributing Corporation. *Cast:* The King Cole Trio (Nat "King" Cole, Oscar Moore, Johnny Miller). (Soundies 18M5 / B&W / Short / Sound / Musical / 4/22/46.)

439 The Grafter and the Maid
1913

Dir: Foster, William. *Prod:* Foster, William. *Co:* Foster Photoplay Company. *Dist:* Soundies Distributing Corporation. *Cast:* Lottie Grady, Jerry Mills, Richard B. Harrison, Judy Moore, Marie Burton-Huyrain and her baby child, Kandy Kids, Burt and Grant, Kid Brown, Kinky Cooper.

Short melodrama. Also released under the title of *The Grafter and the Girl*. Written by Jerry Mills and Jesse Shipp. (Short / Silent / B&W.)

"The railroad scene, dancing in the hay, and the automobile ride were ample in variety. William Foster now has the best colored photoplays that the market can supply" — excerpt from the *Indianapolis Freeman*, 10/4/13.

440 The Greatest Sin 1922

Co: Trio Productions. *Cast:* Mae Evelyn Lewis, Victor Nix. (35mm / Silent / B&W / Feature / 3 reels.)

"A three-reel Colored drama produced in Dallas, Texas, received its premiere showing February 16, 17, and 18 at the Grand Central Theatre in Dallas. Messrs. John Ellis and Lewis, former insurance men of Dallas, are said to have invested about $8,000 in the venture" — review by J.A. Jackson from *Billboard*, 3/11/22.

441 The Green Eyed Monster
1921

Prod: Norman Film Manufacturing Company. *Co:* Norman Film Manufacturing Company. *Dist:* Norman Film Manufacturing Company. *Cast:* Jack Austin, Louise Dunbar.

Review by Leigh Whipper in *Billboard*, 10/1/21. (B&W / Silent / Feature / 8 reels / Drama.)

"The plot deals with the eternal triangle, two men in love with one girl, but the undercurrents bring in the interesting factor of two rival railroads and their fight for supremacy. Before the Government assumed chaperonage over the arteries of travel and transportation and when two roads ran on different routes to the same specific point, there was a rivalry between them as to which should carry the Government Fast Mail. In order to ascertain the fastest of these, a race is run — and it was by winning this race that the hero also won the hands of his sweetheart. $1,000,000 worth of railroad equipment was used and an $80,000 train wreck is part of the story" — Herald Films.

442   The Green Pastures   1936

Dir: Keighley, William / Marc Connelly. *Prod:* Keighley, William / Marc Connelly. *Co:* Warner Bros. *Dist:* Warner Bros. *Cast:* Rex Ingram, Oscar Polk, Eddie Anderson, Frank Wilson, George Reed. Abraham Gleaves, Myrtle Anderson, Ernest Whitman, William Cumby, Edna Mae Harris, Al Stokes, David Bethea, Clinton Rosemond, James Fuller, George Randol, Ray Martin, Charles Andrews, Dudley Dickerson, Jimmy Burress, Ivory Williams, Reginald Henderson, Slim Thompson, Hall Johnson Choir.

A fable by Marc Connelly, suggested by Roark Bradford's Southern Sketches "Ol' Man Adam and His Chillun," choral music arranged and conducted by Hall Johnson. Photography: Hal Mohr. Art direction: Allen Saalburg, Stanley Fleischer. Film editor: George Amy. Special effects: Fred Jackman. Reviews in Review in *The Philadelphia Tribune,* 7/30/36, and the *Film Daily,* 5/19/36. (16mm / B&W / Sound / 3 reels / 110 min. / Feature.)

A fable of life in heaven, and biblical stories which gives more meaning to Adam, Noah, and Moses than so-called biblical films. A hollywood attempt to depict black point of view. Heavenly choirs and fish-fries become metaphors for black culture.

443   The Green Pastures   1938

Co: Warner Bros. *Cast:* Cab Calloway, Fats Waller, and Louis Armstrong. (16mm / B&W / Sound / 7 min. / 1 reel / Animated / Short.)

Cartoon counterparts of Cab Calloway, Fats Waller, and Louis Armstrong perform.

Gridiron Graft *see* While Thousands Cheer

444   The Guerrilla   pre–1910

(B&W / Silent / Short / FLA 5422.)

445   Gun Moll (Gang Smashers)   1944

Dir: Popkin, Leo C. *Prod:* Popkin, Harry M. *Co:* Million Dollar Productions. *Dist:* Toddy Pictures Company. *Cast:* Nina Mae McKinney, Lawrence Criner, Monte Hawley, Edward Thompson, Mantan Moreland, Vernon McCalla, Reginald Fenderson, Arthur Ray, John Criner, Charles Hawkins, Neva Peoples, Guernsey Morrow, Margaret Flemings, Bo Jenkins, Lester Wilkins, Everett Brown.

Gun Moll is a re-release of the film *Gang Smashers* (1938).

446   The Gunsaulus Mystery   1921

Dir: Micheaux, Oscar. *Prod:* Micheaux, Oscar. *Co:* Micheaux Film Corporation. *Dist:* Micheaux Film Corporation. *Cast:* Lawrence Chenault, Evelyn Preer, Edward Abrams, Mabel Young, Eddie Brown, Hattie Christian, E.G. Tatum, Mattie Wilkes, Inez Clough, Bessie Beardon, Ethel Watts, Louis De Bulger, George Russell (white), W.D. Sindle (white), Alex Kroll (white).

Preview in the *New York Age,* 4/16/21, and review in the *Chicago Whip,* 5/7/21. Remake of *Within Our Gates.* Based on the Leo M. Frank's tale which took place in Georgia. The Leo Frank case concerned the murder of a factory girl whose body was found half-burned in the furnace, in the cellar of a factory. Frank was foreman of the factory and he was alone in the building when the girl called one afternoon to get her pay. It is alleged that he murdered her after having raped her, and with the assistance of the black janitor whom he threatened into aiding him, carried the body to the cellar and attempted to burn it. Frank tried to blame the whole crime on the janitor after his arrest but was finally convicted and executed. (Feature / 7 reels / B&W / Silent.)

Myrtle Gunsaulus, a young girl, is found mysteriously murdered in the basement of a factory by Arthur Gilpin, the black janitor, who is arrested and charged with the crime. The incidents surrounding the tragedy, the motive for the crime, and the strange manner in which the girl was killed make the case one of the most complicated the courts had ever been confronted with.

447   Hair Raid   1948

Dir: Alexander, William D. *Prod:* Alexander, William D. *Co:* Alexander Production. *Cast:* Patterson and Jackson, Lucky Millinder and His Band, Don Taylor, Clyde Jones, Emma Pope. (Musical / Comedy / B&W / Sound / Feature.)

448   Half Past Jump Time   1945

Dir: Crouch, William Forest. *Prod:* Crouch, William Forest. *Co:* Filmcraft Production. *Dist:* Soundies Distributing Corporation. *Cast:* Mabel Lee. (Soundies 22408 / B&W / Short / Sound / Musical / 12/30/45.)

449   Hall Johnson Choir in a Syncopated Sermon   1935

Co: Warner Bros. *Cast:* Hall Johnson Choir. (16mm / Sound / 1 reel / Musical / Short / B&W.)

Storyline surrounding such spirituals as "C Called Heaven," "Certainly Lord," and "Wade in the Water."

450   Hallelujah   1929

Dir: Vidor, King. *Prod:* Vidor, King. *Co:* Metro-Goldwyn-Mayer. *Dist:* Metro-Goldwyn-Mayer. *Cast:* Daniel L. Haynes, Nina Mae McKinney, William Fountaine, Everett McGarrity, Victoria Spivey, Harry Gray, Fanny Belle DeKnight, Milton Dickerson, Robert Couch, Walter Tait, Dixie Jubilee Singers.

Story: King Vidor. Scenario: Wanda Tuchock. Treatment: Richard Schayer. Dialogue: Ransom Rideout. Recording engineer: Douglas Shearer. Art director: Cedric Gibbons. Wardrobe: Henrietta Frazer. Photography: Gordon Avil. Film editor: Hugh Wynn. Western Electric Sound System. Preview in *The Philadelphia Tribune,* 12/27/28. Review in the *Philadelphia Tribune,* 8/2/29, and *Variety,* 8/28/29. (16mm / Sound / B&W / 107 min. / Feature.)

A stylized view of black life focusing on a Southern cottonpicker who becomes a preacher but retains all-to-human weaknesses. Beautifully filmed on location with some outstanding musical sequences. Hollywood's

second all-black cast film, Zeke (Haynes) becomes an evangelist after his brother is killed in a brawl, but he falls in with beautiful Chick (McKinney) and wanders from the path for a time. After such travail, including a stint on the chain gang, he returns to family and the "good" woman, Missy Rose (Spivey).

451   Ham and Eggs   1927

Dir: Ruth, Roy Del. *Co:* Warner Bros. *Dist:* Warner Bros. *Cast:* Tom Wilson, Heinie Conklin, Myrna Loy, William J. Irving, Noah Young, Cameo (dog). (White cast in blackface.)

Scenario: Robert Dillon, James A. Starr. Story: Darryl Francis Zanuck. Photography: Charles Clarke. Assistant director: Ross Lederman. (35mm / 6 reels / 5,613 ft. / B&W / Silent / Feature.)

A war picture with the actors playing in the dark. The entire cast is playing blackface. It deals with the Negro part of the war, fighting for Uncle Sam. Ham and Eggs, privates in an all–Negro regiment, become buddies while at training camp and are stationed together in a small French village. The innkeeper, Friml, an enemy spy, desirous of learning the number of soldiers in the Negro regiment, has Fifi, his Negro waitress, flirt with the soldiers so as to get this information. Ham and Eggs fall for her flirtation and go to her house that night, each trying to outstay the other. An officer commands the two to force her to disclose the location of Friml and to shoot her if she refuses to talk; she escapes them, but they uncover a coded enemy message. When the pair are sent to the front, Ham is wounded. They are accidentally cast adrift in a balloon, and in parachuting to safety, they "capture" Friml. They are later decorated for their bravery.

452   Hampton Institute Programs for Education   1946

Co: Harmon Foundation Educational Films. (Documentary / Newsreel / Short / Kodachrome / Silent / 3 Reels.)

The education programs at Hampton Institute, Hampton, Virginia.

453   Hanover Hangover   1946

Dir: Crouch, William Forest. *Prod:* Crouch, William Forest. *Co:* Filmcraft Production. *Dist:* Soundies Distributing Corporation. *Cast:* Johnny Long and His Orchestra, The Campus Cutups. (Soundies / B&W / Short / Sound / Musical / 4/29/46.)

454   A Hard Wash   pre–1910

(B&W / Short / Silent / FLA 3307.)

455   Hark! Hark! The Lark   1941

Co: RCM Production. *Dist:* Soundies Distributing Corporation. *Cast:* The Deep River Boys, Myra Johnson. (Soundies 4505 / B&W / Short / Sound / Musical / 12/8/41.)

456   Harlem After Midnight   1934

Dir: Micheaux, Oscar. *Prod:* Russell, A. Burton. *Co:* Micheaux Film Corporation. *Dist:* Micheaux Picture Company. *Cast:* Lorenzo Tucker, Dorothy Van Engle, Bee Freeman, Alfred "Slick" Chester, Rex Ingram, Lawrence Chenault, A.B. Comatheire, Count Le Shine. (Feature / B&W / Sound.)

"The story is built around Negro gangsters who kidnap a wealthy Jew and just about get away with it, until Micheaux, in the role of a clever sleuth, breaks up the racket"—excerpt from the *Atlanta Daily World*, 9/9/34.

457   Harlem After Midnight   1947

Cast: Billy Eckstine and his orchestra, Ann Baker, Nicky O'Daniel, Al Guster. (Musical / Short / B&W / Sound.)

Billy Eckstine and Ann Baker sing with his orchestra; O'Daniel and Guster dance.

458   Harlem Big Shot (The Black King)   1936

Dir: Pollard, Bud. *Prod:* Pollard, Bud. *Co:* Sack Amusement Enterprises. *Dist:* Sack Amusement Enterprises. *Cast:* A.B. Comathiere, Lorenzo Tucker, Vivianne Raber, Knolly Mitchell, Dan Michaels, Mike Jackson, Mary Jane Watkins, Harry Gray, Freeman Fairley, Ismay Andrews, Trixie Smith, James Dunmire.

Adapted from *The Black King*, 1932, by Donald Heywood. Cinematographer: Dal Lawson. Recording engineer: Gerre Barton & Armand Schettini. Assistant director: Jos A. Bannon. Technical director: Marc S. Asch. Art director: Anthony Continer. Dialogue: Donald Heyward. Costumer: Brooks. Adapted and edited by Morris M. Levinson. Recorded at Metropolitan Studios, N.J. (B&W / Feature / Sound / 70 min. / FCA 8235-8236.)

The story is about "Charcoal" Johnson, a crooked minister who ousts a kindly old reverend from his Logan, Mississippi, church and takes it over. Johnson's plan is to get the church members to give him money for a "Back to Africa" movement and to proclaim himself King of the United States of Africa. Film makes fun of Marcus Garvey's "Back to Africa" movement. Very stereotypical and unflattering to Negroes.

459   Harlem Bound   1935

Co: Universal Studios. *Cast:* Buck and Bubbles, Avis Andrews, Cook and Brown, "Pork Chops," Norman Ashwood. (B&W / Sound / Short / Musical.)

"The scene is a Harlem night club and such stellar Negro performers as Buck and Bubbles, Avis Andrews, swell songstress; Cook and Brown, hoofers; 'Pork Chops,' a comedy ace in a song and ukulele routine, and Norman Astwood in a blues number give the audience plenty of entertainment. Buck singing 'Trucking' is a vast delight. A line of girls is brought in for the final number"—review from *Film Daily*, 1/8/35.

460   Harlem Dynamite 1947
Cast: Dizzy Gillespie and His Orchestra. (Sound / B&W / Musical / Short.)
Three numbers are performed by Dizzy Gillespie and His Orchestra.

461   Harlem Follies 1950
Prod: Jarwood, Arthur. *Co:* Futurity Film Productions. *Cast:* "Chicago" Carl Davis, Princess R'Wanda, "Manhattan" Paul, Max Granville, Ruth Mason, "Fats" Noel, Clark Monroe, Audry Armstrong, "Chinky" Grimes, Lola Avasiago, "Shottsie" Keith, Monique, the "Hips Paraders," Savannah Club Chorus.
Filmed at the Savannah Club in Harlem, New York City. (Musical / Feature / B&W / Sound.)
Musical variety show.

462   Harlem Follies of 1949 1950
Prod: Goldberg, Jack. *Co:* Herald Pictures, Inc. *Cast:* Savannah Churchill, Sheila Guyse, John Kirby and His Band, Laveda Carter, Anna Cornall, Deek Watson and the Brown Dots, Sid Catlett's Band, Juanita Hall, Stepin Fetchit, Slam Stewart Trio, Paterson and Jackson, Rubel Blakey, Basil Spears, Leonardo and Zolo, Apus and Estellita, Al Young, Norma Shepard. (Variety / Musical / Feature / B&W / Sound.)
Variety musical and comedy show.

463   The Harlem Globetrotters 1951
Dir: Brown, Phil. *Prod:* Adler, Buddy. *Co:* Columbia Pictures. *Cast:* Thomas Gomez, Dorothy Dandridge, Bill Walker, The Harlem Globetrotters, Angela Clarke.
Written by Alfred Palca. (16mm / Sound / B&W / 2 reels / 80 min. / Feature.)
A film built around the famed basketball team, with a few romantic interludes.

464   Harlem Harmony 1935
Co: Educational Film Corporation. *Cast:* Ben Carter and His Pickaninny Choir. (B&W / Sound / Short / 1 reel.)
"Nicely produced and well-routined, this excellent novelty reel offers Ben Carter as a deacon conducting musical services with a choir of colored boys and girls about ten years old who sing and dance in very satisfactory fashion. Two of the girls are peppy song soloists and a male quartet slightly older than the others harmonize well. Carter conducts the entertaining services smartly and warbles agreeably himself"—review from *Film Daily*, 1/8/35.

465   Harlem Hot Shots 1945
Dir: Williams, Spencer. *Co:* Metropolitan Films. *Dist:* Sack Amusement Enterprises. *Cast:* Cora Harris, Leon Gross and His Orchestra, Stringbean Jackson, Lena Horne, The Red Lilly Chorus, Teddy Wilson. (16mm / Sound / B&W / 20 min. / Musical / Short / FEA 7332.)

466   Harlem Hotcha 1946
Dir: Crouch, William Forest. *Prod:* Crouch, William Forest. *Co:* Filmcraft Production. *Dist:* Soundies Distributing Corporation. *Cast:* Nicky O'Daniel, Harry Turner, The Sun Tan Four. (Soundies 20M1 / B&W / Short / Sound / Musical / 6/10/46.)

467   Harlem Is Heaven 1932
Dir: Franklin, Irwin R. *Prod:* Goldberg,

Bert. *Co:* Lincoln Productions. *Cast:* Bill Robinson, John Mason, Putney Dandridge, Jimmy Baskette, Anise Boyer, Henri Wressell, Alms Smith, Bob Sawyer, John Mason, Ferdie Lewis, Myra Johnson, Margaret Jenkins, Jeli Smith, Slick Chester, Thomas Mosley, George Nagel, Naomi Price, Jackie Young. Eubie Blake and His Orchestra.

Pre-release titles were *Take Your Time* (*The Philadelphia Tribune*, 1/14/32) and *Harlem Rhapsody* (*Baltimore Afro-American*, 3/2/32). Preview in *The Philadelphia Tribune*, 5/26/32. Jimmy Baskett played "Gabby" on Amos and Andy Radio Show. Bill Robinson's first film. (Feature / B&W / Sound / FEA 9804–9807.)

"The story is woven around the true life experiences of Robinson. It has to do with the adventures of a beautiful young actress just arrived from the South and the manner in which she is aided and befriended by Bill, star of a musical revue of a leading Harlem theatre. How the girl, Jean Stratton, played by Anise Boyer, falls in love with the juvenile of the show, Chummy Walker, is told with skill and the many complications and thrills that ensue are vividly portrayed"—excerpt of review from the *Atlanta Daily World*, 5/6/34.

468   Harlem Jazz Festival 1955
Dir: Kohn, Joseph. *Co:* Studio Films, Inc. *Cast:* Lionel Hampton and His Orchestra, Quincy Jones, Sarah Vaughn, Count Basie Septet, Dinah Washington, Nat "King" Cole. (51 min. / Musical / Feature / B&W / Sound.)
Musical revue.

469   Harlem Jubilee 1949
Cast: Billy Eckstine and Band, Dizzy Gillespie and Orchestra. (B&W / Sound / Musical / Variety Feature.)

470   Harlem Knights 1929
Co: Vitaphone. *Cast:* Flournoy E. Miller, Aubrey Lyles. (B&W / Sound / Short / 20 min. / VBE 8335.)

471   Harlem Mania 1929
Co: Vitaphone. *Cast:* Flournoy E. Miller, Aubrey Lyles, Norman Thomas Quintette. (B&W / Sound / Short / 10 min. / VBE 8161.)
"This aggregation of Colored boys play 'Sleep, Baby Sleep,' 'Listen to the Mocking Bird,' and 'Melody in F.' All of which means nothing by comparison with the antics of the crazy drummer who supplies the kick to this short subject. The Thomas bunch is well-known in vaudeville. Just as the drummer, by his wild and amusing antics, steals the show on the stage, so does it on the talking screen. He's guaranteed to dish out diversion to any and all bodies"—review from *Film Daily*, 8/18/29.

472   Harlem Mania 1938
Co: Creative Cinema Corporation. *Cast:* Ethel Moses, Jimmy Baskette, Count Basie and His Band. (B&W / Musical / Variety / Feature / Sound.)

473   Harlem Merry-Go-Round 1955
Dir: Kohn, Joseph. *Co:* Studio Films, Inc. (B&W / Feature / Sound / FBB 9813.)
Variety show type.

474   Harlem on Parade 1940
Prod: Goldberg, Jack & Dave. *Co:* Sack Amusement Enterprises. *Dist:* Sack Amusement Enterprises. *Cast:* Lena Horne, Lucky Millinder and His Band, Edna Mae Harris, Tim Williams, Teddy Wilson. (Musical / B&W / Sound / Variety / Feature.)

475   Harlem on the Prairie 1938
Dir: Newfield, Sam / Jed Buell. *Prod:* Buell, Jed. *Co:* Associated Features. *Dist:* Toddy Pictures Company. *Cast:* Herbert Jeffries, Mantan Moreland, Flournoy E. Miller, Connie Harris, Spencer Williams, Maceo B. Sheffield, Nathan Curry, The Four Tones (Lucius Brooks, Rudolph Hunter, Leon Buck, Ira Hardin), Edward Brandon, James Davis, The Four Blackbirds.

First all-colored cast Western made. This was filmed on location at N.B. Murray's Black dude ranch near Victorville, California. Additional dialogue by Flournoy E. Miller. Reviews in the *Philadelphia Afro-American*, 2/19/38, *New York Amsterdam News*, 5/5/38, *Film Daily*, 5/5/38, and the *Kansas City Call*, 7/1/38. (Feature / B&W / 54 min. / Sound.)

A former criminal returns home twenty years later to make things right by returning heisted gold left buried. En route, he is killed

by outlaws. Before he dies he entrusts a secret gold location map to his trusted companion. His companion encounters outlaws and comedians en route to restoring the gold to its rightful owners.

Harlem Rhapsody *see* Harlem Is Heaven

476   Harlem Rhumba   1942

Co: RCM Production. *Dist:* Soundies Distributing Corporation. *Cast:* The Chocolateers. (Soundies 9902 / B&W / Short / Sound / Musical / 12/21/42.)

477   Harlem Rhythm   1947

Cast: Dizzy Gillespie and His Orchestra. (Musical / short / B&W / Sound.)

The band is shown playing three numbers with dances created by Audrey Armstrong and Johnny and Henney.

478   Harlem Rides the Range 1939

Dir: Kahn, Richard C. *Prod:* Kahn, Richard

C. *Co:* Hollywood Pictures Corporation. *Dist:* Sack Amusement Enterprises. *Cast:* Herbert Jeffries, Lucius Brooks, Flournoy E. Miller, Artie Young, Spencer Williams, Clarence Brooks, Tom Southern, John Thomas, Wade Dumas, Leonard Christmas, The Four Tones.

Preview in the *New York Amsterdam News*, 2/5/38. Reviews in the *Film Daily*, 2/5/38, and the *Kansas City Call*, 7/1/38. Story written by Spencer Williams. Screenplay: Spencer Williams & Flournoy E. Miller. Photography: Roland Price & Clark Ramses. Production Manager: Dick L'estrange. Music: Lew Porter. Sound engineer: Cliff Ruberg. Art Director: Vin Taylor. (Feature / B&W / 58 min. / Sound / FCA 8104-8105.)

This is the classic "knight in shining armor" story. In an effort to steal an old man's radium mine, the villain tries to kidnap the old man's beautiful daughter. Herb Jeffries, wearing the white hat, arrives in the nick of time to save the young lady and her dad's mine.

479　Harlem Serenade 1942

Co: RCM Production. *Dist:* Soundies Distributing Corporation. *Cast:* Lucky Millinder and His Orchestra, Edna Mae Harris. (Soundies 11204 / B&W / Short / Sound / Musical / 12/31/42.)

480　Harlem Variety Revue 1955

Dir: Kohn, Joseph. *Co:* Studio Films, Inc. *Cast:* Lionel Hampton, Herb Jeffries, Faye Adams. (Short / Musical / B&W / Sound / FCA 9814.)

481　Harlem Wednesday 1959

Prod: Hubley, John. *Cast:* Benny Carter. (16mm / Sound / Color / Short.)

An ordinary day in Harlem depicted with jazz by Benny Carter.

482　A Harlemesque Revue 1943

Co: RCM Production. *Dist:* Soundies Distributing Corporation. *Cast:* Harry Roy and His Orchestra, Mabel Mercer. (Soundies 10806 / B&W / Short / Sound / Musical / 3/8/43.)

483　Harp Boogie 1946

Dir: Crouch, William Forest. *Prod:* Crouch, William Forest. *Co:* Filmcraft Production. *Dist:* Soundies Distributing Corporation. *Cast:* Adele Girard, Rusha Holden. (Soundies / B&W / Short / Sound / Musical / 8/12/46.)

484　Harriet 1945

Dir: Crouch, William Forest. *Prod:* Crouch, William Forest. *Co:* Filmcraft Production. *Dist:* Soundies Distributing Corporation. *Cast:* Chuck Foster and His Orchestra, Marilyn Paul. (Soundies / B&W / Short / Sound / Musical / 12/30/45.)

485　Harry the Hipster 1944

Dir: Blake, Ben K. *Prod:* Blake, Ben K. *Co:* RCM Production. *Dist:* Soundies Distributing Corporation. *Cast:* Harry "the Hipster" Gibson. (Soundies / B&W / Short / Sound / Musical / 9/18/44.)

486　Harry Wills in Training 1924

Co: Acme Film Distribution Corporation. *Dist:* Acme Film Distributors. *Cast:* Harry Wills (prize fighter) (Short / Silent / B&W.)

Shows Harry Wills the prize fighter in training.

487　The Haunted House 1915

Dir: Lubin, Sigmund. *Prod:* Lubin, Sigmund. *Co:* Lubin Manufacturing Company. *Cast:* John Edwards, Mattie Edwards, E. Roseburough.

Written by Will Louis. Released on 4/24/15. (Silent / 600 ft. / B&W / Short.)

"Owing to big doings in coon town the only hotel is over-crowded. John Edwards, traveling salesman, applies for a room, and is told there is nothing vacant, except a garret, that is haunted by a barber. John, not being afraid of spooks, takes the room. Blinks, the barber, next door, has a parrot, who delights in imitating his boss. At twelve o'clock at night he will yell 'Shave?' 'You're next.' The sound travels to the hotel through the two chimney holes in the wall, giving the impression that the garret is haunted. John has an exciting night, but discovers the ghost and all ends well"—*Lubin Bulletin.*

488　Haynes Newsreel No. 1 1914

Dir: Haynes, Hunter C. *Prod:* Haynes, Hunter C. *Co:* Haynes Photoplay Company. *Cast:* Sam Langford, Joe Walcott. (Newsreel / B&W / Silent / Short.)

Featured are: B.M.C. and Odd Fellows dress parade in Boston, Massachusetts; historical scenes in the city of Boston, Massachusetts; Field Day in New York City; notable Negro business enterprises in the Eastern U.S.; Joe Walcott, ex-welterweight boxing champion in training; Sam Langford, prizefighter, at his home in Boston, Massachusetts.

489　Haynes Newsreel No. 2 1916

Dir: Haynes, Hunter C. *Prod:* Haynes, Hunter C. *Co:* Haynes Photoplay Company. (Newsreel / Documentary / B&W / Short / Silent.)

Various scenes in the black community of Boston, Massachusetts; Field Day in New York City; notable Negro enterprises in the Eastern United States.

490　Haynes Newsreel No. 3 1917

Dir: Haynes, Hunter C. *Prod:* Haynes, Hunter C. *Co:* Haynes Photoplay Company. *Cast:* Sam Langford, Joe Walcott. (Newsreel / Documentary / B&W / Short / Silent.)

Joe Walcott and Sam Langford, famous prizefighters, in action.

491   Hazel Green and Company
1928

Dir: Foy, Bryan *Co:* Vitaphone. *Cast:* Hazel Green.

Complete title is *Hazel Green and Company, Foremost Female Director and Singer*, (Vitaphone, No. 2112). (B&W / Short / Sound / FEB 4764.)

492   He Was Bad   1914

Dir: Lubin, Sigmund. *Prod:* Lubin, Sigmund. *Co:* Lubin Manufacturing Company. *Cast:* John Edwards, Mattie Edwards, W. Higgins, H. Pennall, W. Carns.

Written by E.W. Sargent. Released on 7/14/14. (Silent / B&W / Short / 400 ft.)

"Sam Johnson was not regarded with great respect and usually got the worst of it. George Spratt cut him out with Mattie Washington. Henry Jefferson knocked him down when he demanded the return of a loan of four bits and a bunch of crapshooters cleaned him out. Then John Baxter gave him a job, sharpening razors. George was the first to see Sam laboring with a hone and enough razors to cut up the town. He spread the word that Sam had suddenly gone 'bad' and the excitement ran high. The crap players returned the money Sam had lost. Henry gave back the four bits and refused to take the change for a dollar and Mattie ran to the yard to ask him to take her to the ball. Then Baxter gave him a dollar and an old dress suit for the job and Sam, with his reputation for badness put it all over the others"—*Lubin Bulletin*.

493   Hearts in Bondage   1937
(Sound / B&W.)

494   Hearts of Dixie   1929

Dir: Sheehan, Winfield / Paul Sloan. *Prod:* Fox, William. *Co:* 20th Century–Fox Film. *Cast:* Clarence Muse, Stepin Fetchit, Mildred Washington, Eugene Jackson, Vivian Smith, A.C. Bilbrew Choir, Zack Williams, Bernice Pilot, Gertrude Howard, Clifford Ingram.

Hollywood's first all-black cast film. Clarence Muse aided in the direction. Preview and reviews in *The Philadelphia Tribune*, 3/7/29, *The Chicago Whip*, 5/18/29, and the *Los Angeles Evening Express*, 3/7/29. (35mm / B&W / Sound / 8 reels / 6,444 ft. / Feature.)

The tale of old Nappus, a black tenant who scratches a meager living from worn soil; his daughter Chloe (wife to shiftless Gummy) and their two children, Chiquapin and Trailia. The prologue focuses on the universal problem of making a living.

495   Hearts of the Woods   1921

Dir: Calnek, Roy E. *Co:* Superior Arts Motion Picture Company. *Cast:* Clifford Harris, Lawrence McGuire, Don Pierson, Anna Lou Allen, Mae Gibson. (Feature / B&W / Story.)

This is a story of a philandering married man who seeks to trick a young woman into a false marriage.

496   Hell Cats   1947

Co: Toddy Pictures Company. *Cast:* Dewey "Pigmeat" Markham. (B&W / Sound / Comedy / Short.)

497   Hello Bill   1927

Prod: I.B.P.O.E. *Co:* Famous Artists Company. *Cast:* Bill Robinson, Billy Higgins, Joe Byrd, Percy Verwayen, Floyd Hunter, Sarah Martin, Josephine Heathman, Marian Maris. (Silent / B&W / Feature / Newsreel.)

"Byrd and Higgins make the picture a laughing riot. These two prove that it does not take cork to make one funny, neither does it take illiterate speaking of lines. Their antics along the line of march doing the parade and at the big functions kept the fans in a continuous uproar. The picture stands as a tribute to the I.B.P.O.E. of the Elks and must be seen to be appreciated. It has a trend toward being a newsreel, but there are always Byrd and Higgins"—excerpt from review in the *Baltimore Afro-American*, 12/12/27.

498   Hello Bill   1946

Dir: Anderson, Leonard. *Prod:* Alexander, William D. *Co:* Alexander Production. *Dist:* Soundies Distributing Corporation. *Cast:* Lucky Millinder and His Orchestra. (Soundies 23M2 / B&W / Short / Sound / Musical / 9/9/46.)

499   Hell's Alley 1931

Co: Paragon Pictures. *Cast:* Thomas Moseley, Jean Webb, Alvin Childress, Fay Miller.

Screenplay: Hattie Watkins and Jean Webb. (Feature / B&W / Sound.)

500   Henry Brown, Farmer 1944

Dir: Barlow, Roger. *Co:* U.S. Department of Agriculture. *Dist:* USDA War Boards. *Cast:* Canada Lee (narrator). (Documentary / B&W / Sound / Short / 1 reel / 16mm.)

"In a tone that is sincere, reflecting wartime tension. Lee tells how the members of an average colored farm family are trying to do their part to help win the war. The film is climaxed at Tuskegee's air field where the Browns see their oldest son pilot his plane in a training flight along with two other cadets of the 99th Pursuit squadron"— review from *The Philadelphia Afro-American*, 10/24/42.

501   Hep Cat Serenade 1947

Dir: Crouch, William Forest. *Prod:* Sack, Alfred. *Co:* Sack Amusement Enterprises. *Dist:* Sack Amusement Enterprises. *Cast:* Louis Jordan and His Band, Una Mae Carlisle, The Chanticleers, Meade Lux Lewis, Dudley Dickason. (Musical / Short / B&W / Sound.)

502   Here Comes the Fattest Man in Town 1946

Dir: Crouch, William Forest. *Prod:* Crouch, William Forest. *Co:* Filmcraft Production. *Cast:* Gloria Parker. (Soundies / B&W / Short / Sound / Musical / 4/1/46.)

503   Here 'Tis Honey, Take It 1943

Co: RCM Production. *Dist:* Soundies Distributing Corporation. *Cast:* Myra Johnson, Dewey Brown. (Soundies 7M3 / B&W / Short / Sound / Musical / 12/21/43.)

504   Heroic Negro Soldiers 1919

Dir: Smith, Dr. William S. *Prod:* U.S. War Department. *Co:* Frederick Douglas Film Company. (Documentary / Newsreel / Short / B&W / Silent)

Film purchased from U.S. War Department.

Featured are activities of Negro soldiers during World War I showing civilians leaving home and joining the army, training of soldiers, going overseas, fighting in France, and the triumphant return to the United States.

505   Hey, Lawdy, Mama 1944

Co: RCM Production. *Dist:* Soundies Distributing Corporation. *Cast:* June Richmond, Roy Milton and His Orchestra. (Soundies 16808 / B&W / Short / Sound / Musical / 6/5/44.)

506   Hi-De-Ho 1934

Dir: Waller, Fred "Fats." *Prod:* Zukor, Adolph. *Co:* Paramount. *Dist:* U.M. & M. TV Corporation. *Cast:* Cab Calloway and His Orchestra.

Story by Milton Hooky & Fred Rath. Photography by William Steiner, Jr. Review in *Film Daily*, 8/16/34. (B&W / Sound / Short.)

This short starts out with Cab and his band rehearsing on the train. The porter is worried about his wife being home alone and asks Cab his advice. Cab suggest that he buy a radio to occupy his wife's time while he's away. He's very satisfied with the results, except he didn't realize that not only did the radio keep his wife occupied but so did Cab. All this is framed by Cab Calloway singing his hit song "Hi-De-Ho" and other specialty numbers by the dancers and other musical routines.

507   Hi-De-Ho 1937

Dir: Mack, Roy. *Co:* RKO Radio Pictures. *Cast:* Cab Calloway and His Orchestra. (B&W / Short / Sound.)

"A presentation of Cab Calloway and his colored band that dramatizes his life more or less. First he is seen as a poor colored boy with hopes of being a great band leader, as his mammy listens in awe to his ambitious plans. He goes to a fortune teller, and she forecasts the highlights of his career, they are re-enacted in the picture. Finishes with the big climax as he conducts his present-day band in the grand manner at a nite spot"— review from *Film Daily*, 2/20/37.

508   Hi-De-Ho 1947

Dir: Binney, Josh. *Prod:* Glucksman, E.M. *Co:* All-American News. *Cast:* Cab Calloway,

Jeni LeGon, Ida James, Peters Sisters, Miller Brothers and Lois, Dusty Fletcher, James Dunmore, George Wiltshire, Augustus Smith, Fredi Washington. (*Trailer* / 16mm / Sound / B&W / 2 reels / Musical / Short / 10 min. / FEA 8781.)

509 Hi-De-Ho 1947

Dir: Binney, Josh. *Prod:* Glucksman, E.M. *Co:* All-American News. *Cast:* Cab Calloway, Ida James, Jeni Le Gon, William Campbell, Virginia Green, George Wiltshire, James Dunmore, Augustus Smith, Edgar Martin, Leonard Rogers, David Belheu, Shepard Roberts, Frederick Johnson, Specialty acts by Dusty Fletcher, Peters Sisters, Miller Brothers and Lois.

Original story and screenplay: Hal Seegar. Director of photography: Don Malkames. Camera: Stoetzel, Zucker, & Lang. Art director: Frank Namczy. Musical arrangements: Buster Harding. Dance director: Addison Carey. Makeup: Rudolph G. Liszy. Film editor: Louis Hess. Sound: Nelson Minnerly. Costumes: Eaves Costume Co. Assistant director:

Thomas Darby. (B&W / Sound / Feature / 77 min. / FCA 5722-5723.)

Typical musical variety film of the period: heavy on acts, slim on plot. Cab and the boys are out of work; his manager finds him work in a small club; he becomes a hit. A rival club owner and hood try to knock him off. They accidently kill his conniving girlfriend, Minnie. Cab manages to kill his adversaries in a shootout and goes on to hitsville.

510 Hi-De-Ho Holiday 1944

Cast: Lena Horne. (B&W / Sound / Short.)

511 High Tones 1929

Dir: Foster, William. *Prod:* Foster, William. *Co:* Pathé. *Dist:* Supreme Distributing Company. *Cast:* Buck and Bubbles (Ford Lee Washington & John Sublette).

Songs: "My Old Kentucky Home," "Home Sweet Home," "13th Street Rag," "Clarinet Marmalade," "Lonely Me." (Sound / B&W / Short / Comedy.)

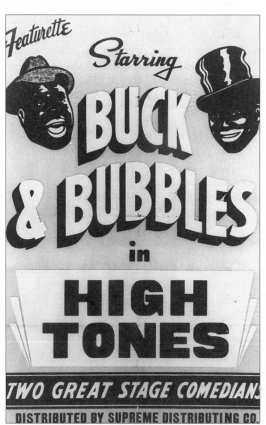

This Buck and Bubbles short shows how funny revenge can be. When Buck's job and woman is stolen from him by his arch enemy, he brings Bubbles and a goat to exact some revenge.

512 The Highest Tradition 1946

Dir: Alexander, William D. *Prod:* Alexander, William D. *Co:* Alexander Production. *Dist:* Astor Pictures. *Cast:* Fredric March (white) narrator. (Documentary / Newsreel / Short / B&W / Sound.)

Documentary depicting blacks in the United States Navy during World War II.

513 His Great Chance 1923

Prod: Strasser, Ben. *Co:* North State Film Corporation. *Cast:* Sandy Burns, Bobbie Smart, Tim Moore, Gertrude Moore, Walter Long, Fred Hart, Mark Slater, Fannetta Burns, Sam Russell.

Review by Leigh Whipper in *Billboard*, 5/19/22. (Feature / B&W / Silent.)

A heartwarming story about two young men who leave home for the bright lights of the entertainment business. Unfortunately, their success causes them to neglect their loving parents. While the parents mourn their boys' absence at holiday time, they are surprised when one shows up with a wife to help celebrate Christmas.

514 His Harlem Wife (Life Goes On) 1944

Dir: Nolte, William. *Co:* Million Dollar Productions. *Dist:* Toddy Pictures. *Cast:* Louise Beavers, Edward Thompson, Reginald Fenderson, Lawrence Criner, Monte Hawley, Hope Bennett, Jesse Brooks, May Turner, Artie Brandon, Edward Robertson, Oliver Farmer, Eloise Witherspoon, Lillian Randolph.

His Harlem Wife, 1944, is a reissue of *Life Goes On*, 1938. Louise Beavers first all-colored cast feature film. (Feature / B&W / Sound.)

Sally (Beavers) is a loving widowed mother who raises two sons, Bob and Henry. Bob grows up to become a lawyer while Henry grows up less successful and associates with the wrong crowd. Henry is wrongly accused of murder and his brother Bob is appointed his

lawyer. Bob is forced to fight against a powerful D.A. bent on sending his brother to the gallows.

515 His Last Chance 1923

Co: North State Film Corporation. (Silent / B&W / Feature.)

The story is about a country boy who gives show business a try.

516 His Rockin' Horse Ran Away 1944

Co: RCM Production. *Dist:* Soundies Distributing Corporation. *Cast:* Ida James. (Soundies / B&W / Short / Sound / Musical / 10/23/44.)

517 His Trust pre–1910

(B&W / Silent / Short / FLA 5445.)

518 His Trust Fulfilled pre–1910

(B&W / Silent / Short / FLA 5446.)

519 Hit That Jive Jack 1943

Co: RCM Production. *Dist:* Soundies

Distributing Corporation. *Cast:* The Musical Madcaps. (Soundies 12908 / B&W / Short / Sound / Musical / 8/9/43.)

520   Hollywood Boogie 1946
Dir: Gould, Dave. *Prod:* Hersh, Ben. *Co:* RCM Production. *Dist:* Soundies Distributing Corporation. *Cast:* Thelma White and Her All-Girl Orchestra. (Soundies / B&W / Short / Sound / Musical / 7/22/46.)

521   Home Brew 1920
Dir: Maurice, Richard D. *Prod:* Maurice, Richard D. *Co:* Quality Amusement Company. (Silent / B&W / Short.)

522   The Homesteader 1918
Dir: Micheaux, Oscar. *Prod:* Micheaux, Oscar. *Co:* Micheaux Book and Film Company. *Dist:* Micheaux Film Corporation. *Cast:* Charles Lucas, Evelyn Preer, Iris Hall, Charles S. Moore, Inez Smith, Vernon S. Duncan, Trevy Woods, William George.
Review in the *Chicago Defender*, 2/22/19. Based on the book *The Homesteader*, by Oscar Micheaux. (B&W / Silent / Feature.)
Jean Baptiste, a homesteader far off in the Dakotas is living where he is the only black. To this wilderness arrives Jack Stewart, a Scotsman, with his motherless daughter, Agnes. In Agnes, Baptiste meets the girl of his dreams. Knowing that a relationship with Agnes would not work, he goes back to his own people and marries the daughter of the preacher. The fact Baptiste does not get along with his father-in-law, eventually wears on the marriage. Baptiste heads back to the Dakotas where he finds the girl he first discovered. Later, he learns the truth about her race and the story has a beautiful ending. She has a little Negro blood racing through her veins.

523   Honest Crooks 1929
Dir: Foster, William. *Prod:* Foster, William. *Co:* Pathé. *Dist:* Supreme Distributing Company. *Cast:* Buck and Bubbles (Ford Lee Washington & John Sublette).
Songs: "Turkey in the Straw," "Old Black Joe." (Sound / B&W / Short / Comedy.)
A mysterious black bag, buried in a haystack by a couple of crooks, is found by Wildcat (Buck) and his pal Denny (Bubbles). It is full of money and when the boys try to return it, funny things happen.

524   Honey Chile 1945
Dir: Crouch, William Forest. *Prod:* Adams, Berle. *Co:* Astor Pictures Corporation. *Dist:* Soundies Distributing Corporation. *Cast:* Louis Jordan and His Tympany Five.
Excerpted from the Astor two-reel short, *Caldonia* (1945). (Soundies 19808 / B&W / Short / Sound / Musical / 1/29/45.)

525   Honeysuckle Rose 1941
Dir: Murray, Warren. *Prod:* Waller, Fred "Fats" *Co:* Minoco Production. *Dist:* Soundies Distributing Corporation. *Cast:* Fats Waller, Myra Johnson. (Soundies 4001 / B&W / Short / Sound / Musical / 11/2/41.)

526   Hot Biscuits 1929
Prod: Williams, Spencer. *Co:* Williams, Spencer.
Spencer Williams' first produced movie. (B&W / Short / Sound.)

527   Hot Chocklate (Cottontail) 1941
Dir: Berne, Josef. *Prod:* Coslow, Sam. *Co:* RCM Production. *Dist:* Soundies Distributing Corporation. *Cast:* Duke Ellington and His Orchestra, Whitey's (Arthur White's) Lindy Hoppers. (Soundies 5304 / B&W / Short / Sound / Musical / 12/31/41.)

528   Hot Dogs 1921
Co: White Film Corporation. (Silent / B&W.)

529   Hot Frogs 1942
Co: Harman-Ising. *Dist:* Soundies Distributing Corporation. *Cast:* Fats Waller, Bill Robinson, Ethel Waters, and the Mills Brothers (animation). (Soundies / B&W / Short / Sound / Animated / Musical / 3/2/42.)
An abbreviation of the 1937 Harman-Ising cartoon "Swing Wedding."

530   Hot in the Groove 1942
Co: RCM Production. *Dist:* Soundies Distributing Corporation. *Cast:* Erskine Hawkins and His Orchestra. (Soundies 9808 / B&W / Short / Sound / Musical / 12/14/42.)

531 The House Behind the Cedars 1924

Dir: Micheaux, Oscar. *Prod:* Micheaux, Oscar. *Co:* Micheaux Film Corporation. *Dist:* Micheaux Film Corporation. *Cast:* Shingzie Howard, Lawrence Chenault, Douglass Griffin, William Crowell "Big Bill."

Screenplay: Charles Chesnutt. Review in *The Philadelphia Tribune*, 12/13/24. (35mm / Silent / B&W / 9 reels / Feature.)

This "Pinky" style story deals with a beautiful "passing" mulatto who married a young white millionaire. The drama is presented to us through a court battle by the young man's parents trying to get the marriage annulled when they find out that his wife is colored. The young mulatto wins out in the end.

532 The House of Mystery 1923

Prod: Baker, Mary E. *Co:* Baker, Mary E.

Mary Baker of Philadelphia received a $10,000 check from a large film corporation, for producing this 5 reel drama. She also produced the 3 reel dramas, *The Lost Jewel*, *The Pink Slipper*, and *The Ruined Father*. Story on front page of the *Philadelphia Tribune*, 12/8/23. (Feature / B&W / Silent / 5 reels.)

533 House on 52nd Street 1944

Co: Henry "Red" Allen, J.C. Higginbotham. (Soundies 21M5 / B&W / Short / Sound / Musical / 7/24/44.)

534 House-Rent Party 1946

Dir: Newfield, Sam. *Prod:* Toddy, Ted. *Co:* Toddy Pictures Company. *Dist:* Toddy Pictures Company. *Cast:* Dewey "Pigmeat" Markham, John "Rastus" Murray, Lou Sealia Swarz, Claude Demetri, Rudolph Toombs, Macbeth's Calypso Band, "Lord Invader," Alberta Pryne, Ozzy Mallon's Jitterbugs.

Songs: "Yankee Dollar in Trinidad," "Rockaway," and "Mama's Got to Get That Rent." (Feature / B&W / Sound.)

"Pigmeat and Murray, who play the role of Shorty in *House Rent Party*, are barbers who work themselves into a lather when they hear that a reward is being offered for the capture of some rough customers bent on breaking up a house rent party. Pigmeat and Shorty get to the party just in time to see the gals and guys

go into a few hot songs and dances ... they start to go for the dames, but suddenly remember the money. Of course they catch the crooks ... but for a couple of barbers they certainly have some close shaves before the fast and furious fun is over"—excerpt from preview in the *New York Amsterdam News*, 6/22/46.

535 How Africa Lives 1929

Co: National Archives Gift Collection.

Part of Record Group 200 HF series, Harmon Foundation Collection. (35mm / Silent / B&W / 2 reels / Short.)

"Primitive life and how it is affected by the coming of the white man"—Klotman.

536 How an African Tribe Is Ruled Under Colonial Government 1929

Co: National Archives Gift Collection.

Part of Record Group 200 HF series, Harmon Foundation Collection. (16mm / 2 reels / Silent / Short / B&W.)

"Belgian Congo ruling as it employs tribal methods"— Klotman.

537 How Charlie Lost the Heiress pre–1910
(B&W / Silent / Short / FLA 3608.)

538 How High Is Up 1923
Dir: Grahm, Chatty. *Co:* Seminole Film Company. *Cast:* Moss & Fry, Corrine Smith, Richard B. Harrison.
    Made at the Lincoln Studios in New Jersey and finished in the Peter P. Jones laboratories at Ft. Lee. See review in *Billboard*, 9/29/23, by J.A. Jackson. (Silent / B&W / 2 reels / Comedy / Short.)
    Two-reel comedy concerned with Moss & Fry's effort to fly a plane.

539 How Rastus Got His Pork Chop 1908
Dir: Lubin, Fredric. *Prod:* Lubin, Fredric. *Co:* Lubin Manufacturing Company. (Short / B&W / Silent / Comedy.)

540 How Skinny Made Good 1915
Co: Afro-American Film Company.

541 How to Go to a French Restaurant 1941
Dir: Murray, Warren. *Prod:* Waller, Fred "Fats." *Co:* Minoco Production. *Dist:* Soundies Distributing Corporation. *Cast:* Willie Howard. (Soundies / B&W / Short / Sound / Musical / 12/31/41.)
    First music videos.

542 How to See a French Doctor 1941
Dir: Murray Warren. *Prod:* Waller, Fred "Fats." *Co:* Minoco Production. *Dist:* Soundies Distributing Corporation. *Cast:* Jean Porter.
    Recorded by Ray Noble and His Orchestra. (Soundies / B&W / Short / Sound / Musical / 12/31/41.)

543 Howard-Lincoln Football Game 1921
Prod: Smith, Dr. W. *Co:* Monumental Pictures Corporation. (Newsreel / Silent / Sport / B&W / Documentary / Short.)
    Film coverage of the football game between Howard University and Lincoln University

played on Thanksgiving Day in Philadelphia, Pennsylvania.

544 The Human Devil 1921
Co: Afro-American Exhibitors Company. (Silent / B&W.)

545 The Hunters 1958
Co: Harvard University Film Study Center. (Documentary / Sound / 16mm / Color / 2 reels / 76 min. / Feature.)
    "Depicts the life and culture of bushmen living in the Kalahari Desert of Africa. Illustrates the village life and the hunting practices of the bushman. Reveals the bare subsistence level of their lives"— Klotman.

546 The Hypocrite 1922
Dir: Micheaux, Oscar. *Prod:* Micheaux, Oscar. *Co:* Micheaux Film Corporation. *Dist:* Micheaux Film Corporation. (Feature / Silent / B&W.)

547 The Hypocrites 1917
Co: Ebony Film Company. *Dist:* General Film Company. *Cast:* Ebony Players (Sam Robinson, Samuel "Sambo" Jacks, Will Starks, Julia Mason, Bert Murphy, Evon Skekeeter, Mildred Price, Walter Brogsdale, Robert Duree, Frank Pollard, George Lewis Stock Company), Evelyn Preer, Cleo Desmond. (Silent / B&W / Short / 2 reels.)

548 I Ain't Gonna Open That Door 1949
Cast: Stepin Fetchit, Earl Bostic and His Orchestra. (Short / B&W / Sound / Comedy / Musical.)

549 I Ain't Got Nobody 1932
Co: Paramount. *Cast:* Mills Brothers.
    Songs: "Good-bye Blues," "Tiger Rag," & "I Ain't Got Nobody." (B&W / Sound / Short / 9 min.)
    "The fact remains that their [Mills Brothers] work in this short ought to prove plenty satisfying to most any audience. Then there is the usual singing to the accompaniment of the bouncing ball, and it's all good"— excerpt of review from *Film Daily*, 6/11/32.

550 I Can't Dance 1944
Co: RCM Production. *Dist:* Soundies

Distributing Corporation. *Cast:* Billy Haywood, Cliff Allen. (Soundies 17008 / B&W / Short / Sound / Musical / 6/19/44.)

551 I Can't Give You Anything But Love 1944

Co: RCM Production. *Dist:* Soundies Distributing Corporation. *Cast:* Hilda Rogers. (Soundies 17008 / B&W / Short / Sound / Musical / 6/19/44.)

552 I Cried for You 1946

Dir: Anderson, Leonard. *Prod:* Alexander, William D. *Co:* Alexander Production. *Dist:* Soundies Distributing Corporation. *Cast:* Billy Eckstine and His Orchestra, Ann Baker.

Excerpted from the featurette, *Rhythm in a Riff* (1946). (Soundies / B&W / Short / Sound / Musical / 12/30/46.)

553 I Dreamt I Dwelt in Harlem 1941

Dir: Snody, Robert R. *Co:* RCM Production. *Dist:* Soundies Distributing Corporation. *Cast:* The Delta Rhythm Boys.

Recorded by Steve Schultz. (Soundies 3506 / Short / B&W / Sound / Musical / 9/29/41.)

554 I Got It Bad, and That Ain't Good 1942

Co: RCM Production. *Dist:* Soundies Distributing Corporation. *Cast:* Ivie Anderson, Duke Ellington and His Orchestra. (Soundies 5105 / B&W / Short / Sound / Musical / 1/19/42.)

555 I Gotta Go to Camp and See My Man 1943

Co: RCM Production. *Dist:* Soundies Distributing Corporation. *Cast:* Edna Mae Harris (Soundies / B&W / Short / Sound / Musical / 7/26/43.)

556 I Had a Dream 1945

Co: RCM Production. *Dist:* Soundies Distributing Corporation. *Cast:* Johnny and George. (Soundies 88708 / B&W / Short / Sound / Musical / 7/16/45.)

557 I Heard 1932

Dir: Fleischer, Dave. *Prod:* Fleischer, Max. *Co:* Warner Bros. *Cast:* Betty Boop, Don Redman Orchestra. (Animated / Short / 16mm / B&W / 1 reel / 7 min. / Sound.)

Don Redman's Orchestra makes an appearance and furnishes the music with Betty Boop singing.

558 I Left My Heart in Texas 1945

Dir: Crouch, William Forest. *Prod:* Crouch, William Forest. *Co:* Filmcraft Production. *Dist:* Soundies Distributing Corporation. *Cast:* Chuck Foster and His Orchestra. (Soundies / B&W / Short / Sound / Musical / 12/30/45.)

559 I Like It Cause I Love It 1944

Co: RCM Production. *Dist:* Soundies Distributing Corporation. *Cast:* Una Mae Carlisle. (Soundies 18108 / B&W / Short / Sound / Musical / 9/18/44.)

560 I Miss You So 1943

Co: RCM Production. *Dist:* Soundies Distributing Corporation. *Cast:* Warren Evans. (Soundies 7M1 / B&W / Short / Sound / Musical / 12/21/43.)

561 I Need a Playmate 1946

Dir: Crouch, William Forest. *Prod:* Crouch, William Forest. *Co:* Filmcraft Production. *Dist:* Soundies Distributing Corporation. *Cast:* Vanita Smythe. (Soundies 24M3 / B&W / Short / Sound / Musical / 10/14/46.)

562 I Want a Big Fat Mama 1941

Co: RCM Production. *Dist:* Soundies Distributing Corporation. *Cast:* Lucky Millinder and His Orchestra. (Soundies 3807 / B&W / Short / Sound / Musical / 10/20/41.)

563 I Want a Little Doggie 1945

Co: RCM Production. *Dist:* Soundies Distributing Corporation. *Cast:* The Phil Moore Four. (Soundies 21908 / B&W / Short / Sound / Musical / 11/12/45.)

564 I Want a Man 1946

Dir: Anderson, Leonard. *Prod:* Alexander, William D. *Co:* Alexander Production. *Dist:* Soundies Distributing Corporation. *Cast:* Lucky Millinder and His Orchestra, Annisteen Allen. (Soundies 24M4 / B&W / Short / Sound / Musical / 10/21/46.)

565   I Want to Talk About You
1946
Dir: Anderson, Leonard. *Prod:* Alexander, William D. *Co:* Alexander Production. *Dist:* Soundies Distributing Corporation. *Cast:* Billy Eckstine and His Orchestra.

Excerpted from the featurette, *Rhythm in a Riff* (1946). (Soundies / B&W / Short / Sound / Musical / 12/30/46.)

566   I Was Here When You Left Me   1945
Co: RCM Production. *Dist:* Soundies Distributing Corporation. *Cast:* Cab Calloway and His Orchestra, Dotty Saulter. (Soundies 21608 / B&W / Short / Sound / Musical / 10/1/45.)

567   I Won't Miss You   1942
Co: RCM Production. *Dist:* Soundies Distributing Corporation. (Soundies 2M2 / B&W / Short / Sound / Musical / 12/30/42.)

568   I'd Love to Be a Cowboy
1944
Co: RCM Production. *Dist:* Soundies Distributing Corporation. *Cast:* Bob Howard. (Soundies / B&W / Short / Sound / Musical / 5/29/44.)

569   Idlewild   1927
Cast: Charles Chesnutt, and many other prominent Blacks. (B&W / Documentary / Short / 25 min. / Sound. FEB 4120-4122 or FBB 7022.)

A pictorial view of Idlewild, Michigan. This film was shot as an advertisement for the great Negro resort Idlewild. In one shot, Charles Chesnutt's face appears quickly on screen. Shot and narrated like an ad, long shots of homes, water, sporting events, people relaxing and playing, etc.

570   If a Boy Needs a Friend   1943
Co: Garrison Film Distribution Company. *Dist:* Garrison Film Distribution Company. (Documentary / Short / 1 reel / B&W / Sound.)

This is a film about race relations and friendship between several boys of different races.

571   If You Can't Smile and Say Yes   1944
Co: RCM Production. *Dist:* Soundies Distributing Corporation. *Cast:* Louis Jordan and His Tympany Five. (Soundies / B&W / Short / Sound / Musical / 5/8/44.)

572   If You Only Knew   1946
Dir: Gould, Dave. *Prod:* Hersh, Ben. *Co:* RCM Production. *Dist:* Soundies Distributing Corporation. *Cast:* Valaida Snow, The Ali Baba Trio. (Soundies 21M2 / B&W / Short / Sound / Musical / 7/8/46.)

573   If You Treat Me to a Hug
1943
Co: RCM Production. *Dist:* Soundies Distributing Corporation. *Cast:* The Chanticleers. (Soundies 14608 / B&W / Short / Sound / Musical / 12/20/43.)

574   I'll Be Glad When You're Dead, You Rascal You   1932
Dir: Fleischer, Dave. *Prod:* Fleischer, Max. *Co:* Warner Bros. *Cast:* Betty Boop, Louis Armstrong and His Orchestra. (Animated / Short / B&W / 16mm / Sound / 1 reel / 7 min.)

Betty Boop is on an island and captured by cannibals. She is helped by Bimbo and Koko. Louis Armstrong appears in the background (as Betty flees) singing the title song.

575   I'll Be Glad When You're Dead, You Rascal You   1942
Co: RCM Production. *Dist:* Soundies Distributing Corporation. *Cast:* Louis Armstrong and His Orchestra, Velma Middleton. (Soundies 7803 / B&W / Short / Sound / Musical / 7/27/42.)

576   Ill Wind   1946
Co: Toddy Pictures Company. (68 min. / Feature / B&W / Sound.)

577   Illinois National Half Century Exposition   1915
Dir: Jones, Peter P. *Prod:* Jones, Peter P. *Co:* Peter P. Jones Photoplay Company. (Newsreel / Documentary / Short / B&W / Silent.)

Film coverage of the Lincoln Jubilee held from August 21 to September 16 in Chicago, Illinois, showing progress of the Negro after 50 years of freedom from slavery. Also featured: Grand Elks Parade, Baptist Convention, Governor's Day Parade.

578   I'm a Good Good Woman
1944

Co: RCM Production. *Dist:* Soundies Distributing Corporation. *Cast:* Una Mae Carlisle. (Soundies 8M2 / B&W / Short / Sound / Musical / 8/28/44.)

579   I'm a Shy Guy   1946

Dir: Crouch, William Forest. *Prod:* Crouch, William Forest. *Co:* Filmcraft Production. *Dist:* Soundies Distributing Corporation. *Cast:* The King Cole Trio (Nat "King" Cole, Oscar Moore, Johnny Miller). (Soundies 16M2 / B&W / Short / Sound / Musical / 2/11/46.)

580   I'm Making Believe   1945

Co: RCM Production. *Dist:* Soundies Distributing Corporation. *Cast:* Cecil Scott and His Band, Warren Evans. (Soundies 20208 / B&W / Short / Sound / Musical / 3/19/45.)

581   I'm Tired   1944

Co: RCM Production. *Dist:* Soundies Distributing Corporation. *Cast:* Apus and Estrellita. (Soundies 17808 / B&W / Short / Sound / Musical / 8/21/44.)

582   Imitation of Life   1934

Dir: Stahl, John M. *Prod:* Laemmle, Carl Jr. *Co:* Universal Studies. *Cast:* Louise Beavers, Fredi Washington, Hazel Washington, Claudette Colbert (white), Warren William (white), Ned Sparks (white), Rochelle Hudson (white), Alan Hale (white).

Screenplay by William Hurlbut. Story by Fannie Hurst. Review in the *Philadelphia Afro-American*, 12/8/34 and *The Literary Digest*, 12/8/34. (16mm / Feature / Sound / B&W / 3 reels / 90 min.)

583   Imitation of Life   1959

Dir: Serk, Douglas. *Prod:* Hunter, Ross. *Co:* Universal Studios. *Cast:* Juanita Moore, Mahalia Jackson, John Gavin (white), Sandra Dee (white), Susan Kohner (white), Dan O'Herlihy (white), Ann Robeson (white),

Lana Turner (white), Robert Alda (white), Troy Donahue (white).

Review in the *New York Times*, 4/18/59, *New York Post*, 10/2/58, and *Commonweal*, 4/17/59. (Feature / Sound.)

A remake of the 1934 version features Susan Kohner (white) in the role of the tragic mulatto.

584   In and Out   1929

Dir: Foster, William. *Prod:* Foster, William. *Co:* Pathé. *Dist:* Supreme Distributing Company. *Cast:* Buck and Bubbles (Ford Lee Washington & John Sublette). (Sound / B&W / Short.)

585   In Honor of the 92nd Division   1917

Prod: Turpin, Charles H. *Co:* Turpin Film Company. (Newsreel / Documentary / Short / B&W / Silent.)

Film coverage of the celebration at St. Louis, Missouri, honoring the 92nd Division, held on April 14, 1917. Otis Duncan's speech is followed by a parade.

586   In the Depths of Our Hearts
1920

Co: Royal Garden Film Company. *Cast:* Herman DeLavalade, Augusta Williams, Irene Conn, Virgil Williams (president of the company), Charles Allen.

Virgil Williams (cast member) is also the president of the Royal Garden Film Company. (Silent / B&W / Feature / 7,000 ft.)

"The story is about a mother and her children who are of light complexion. She brings them up to believe that anyone of a darker hue is unfit as an associate. The son rebels, for his school sweetheart is not 'light,' and after an argument his mother sends him to his uncle's farm. After several years he returns to his former town and discovers his former sweetheart working as a waitress. They embrace and are caught by the proprietor, who discharges her. In the meantime, things have been going poorly for the mother and daughter. In the end the hero gets his girl's job back and convinces his family to change their hypocritical lifestyle"—excerpted from H. Sampson.

587   In the Shadows 1923
Co: Mesco Productions. (B&W / Silent.)

588   In Zululand 1915
Dir: Lubin, Sigmund. *Prod:* Lubin, Sigmund. *Co:* Lubin Manufacturing Company. *Cast:* Mattie Edwards, John Edwards.
(Released 9/28/15. Comedy / One Act / 1,000 ft. / B&W / Silent / Short.)
"In Zululand, lives Queen Cocoa, who loves Zebo, a good-for-nothing nigger. Zebo knows that if he can get the queen to marry him, a meal ticket and an easy life will be his. The Queen's two daughters are quietly displeased, so when the lovers become too engrossed in each other and the wedding is in sight, the daughters hit upon a scheme to spoil everything and thereby save their own meal ticket and the throne. One particular, moonlight night, when the Queen expects a visit from Zebo, the daughters disguise as ghosts, first one and then the other meets him on the way to visit the Queen. He becomes so frightened that he does not go near her and she becomes so alarmed that she goes to his hut to discover the reason. At the door of the hut she meets the two ghosts who warn her, as they did Zebo, that all attentions between them must cease or they will get her. The next day finds Zebo in the hands of the executioner, surrounded by the tribe, with the Queen on the throne ordering the execution"—*Lubin Bulletin.*

Injustice *see* **Loyal Hearts**

589   The Ink Spots 1955
Dir: Cowan, Will. *Co:* Universal-International. *Cast:* Georgie Auld and His Auld Stars are featured in a nightclub setting with numbers including "If I Didn't Care."

590   International Rhythms 1938
Co: RKO Radio Pictures. *Cast:* Ada Brown, Cecil Mack Choir, Princess Chiyo, Mara (white), Mogiloff's Balalika Orchestra. (Musical / B&W / Sound.)

591   Interrupted Crap Game
     1905
Co: Selig Company.
Whites in blackface. (Short / B&W / Silent.)

"Darkies" leave their crap game in order to chase a chicken.

592   Introducing East Africa 1950
Co: Editorial Film Productions. (British / Documentary / 35mm / B&W / 20 min. / 1758 ft. / Sound.)
Informational film on East Africa.

593   Is You or Is You Ain't My
     Baby 1944
Co: RCM Production. *Dist:* Soundies Distributing Corporation. *Cast:* The King Cole Trio (Nat "King" Cole, Oscar Moore, Johnny Miller, Ida James). (Soundies 15408 / B&W / Short / Sound / Musical / 2/21/44.)

594   It Happened in Harlem 1945
Dir: Pollard, Bud. *Co:* All-American News. *Cast:* Slick and Slack, Phil Gomez, Dotty Rhodes, Juanita Pitts, George Wiltshire,

Nicky O'Daniel, Milton Woods, Christopher Columbus and His Swing Crew, "Pitter-Patter" Pitts, The Paradise Chorus. (35mm / Sound / B&W / 3 reels / Featurette / Short / FEA 6003-6005.)

Ed Smalls is doing a tremendous business at Smalls Paradise Cafe in Harlem because Billy Bond is making a big hit with his singing. But when Smalls tells Bond that there will be a lot of celebrities in for the show, Bond shows his boss the paper — it's from Uncle Sam. Smalls is frantic, as he knows of no one who can replace Bond, so he starts accepting auditions to replace Bond. Frankie, a singer with a bobbysoxer crowd but little known, is turned away at the audition. Little Miss Brown, a Frankie fan, persuades Bond to listen to Frankie.

595   It Happened on Wash Day
1915

Dir: Lubin, Sigmund. *Prod:* Lubin, Sigmund. *Co:* Lubin Manufacturing Company. *Cast:* John Edwards, Mattie Edwards, David Roseborough.

Written by A.D. Hotaling. Released on 3/27/15. (Short / 400 ft. / Silent / B&W.)

"Speedy Smith spends his coin on a bottle of gin as a treat to Mattie with whom he is in love. But when John enters and presents a bouquet borrowed from a pot on a neighboring parch and his Beau Brummel self, Smith can't be seen. Smith indulges in a little brain work and makes of Mattie a target. Then he invites John to a little target practice. John shoots, Mattie falls, Smith tells Mattie that John did it, as he has the gun. Smith gets the gun and John hits on a scheme and accuses Smith of the shooting, but in the struggle that follows, Mattie is once more shot, and explains that John is trying to shoot her up. The officers chase John but Mattie being in a revengeful mood, gets a bomb and blows up the whole crowd"—*Lubin Bulletin.*

596   It Must Be Jelly (Cause Jam Don't Shake Like That)
1946

Dir: Crouch, William Forest. *Prod:* Crouch, William Forest. *Co:* Filmcraft Production. *Dist:* Soundies Distributing Corporation. *Cast:*

Johnny Long and His Orchestra, Doris York. (Soundies / B&W / Short / Sound / Musical / 3/18/46.)

597   It's a Sin to Tell a Lie   1946

Dir: Crouch, William Forest. *Prod:* Crouch, William Forest. *Co:* Filmcraft Production. *Cast:* Johnny Long and His Orchestra. (Soundies / B&W / Short / Sound / Musical / 6/3/46.)

598   It's Me, Oh Lord   1945

Co: RCM Production. *Dist:* Soundies Distributing Corporation. *Cast:* John Shadrack Horance, Johnnie Moore's 3 Blazers. (Soundies 87908 / B&W / Short / Sound / Musical / 11/20/45.)

599   I've Got to Be a Rug Cutter
1945

Co: RCM Production. *Dist:* Soundies Distributing Corporation. *Cast:* The Counts and the Countess. (Soundies 22008 / B&W / Short / Sound / Musical / 11/26/45.)

600   Jack Johnson vs. Jim Flynn
1912

(B&W / Silent / Short / FLA 5874.)
Jack Johnson fights Jim Flynn for the heavyweight boxing championship of the world in Las Vegas, New Mexico on July 4, 1912.

601   Jack, You're Playing the Game   1941

Co: RCM Production. *Dist:* Soundies Distributing Corporation. *Cast:* The Delta Rhythm Boys.

Recorded by Steve Schultz. (Soundies 4207 / B&W / Short / Sound / Musical / 11/17/41.)

602   The Jackie Robinson Story
1950

Dir: Green, Alfred E. *Prod:* Briskin, Mort. *Co:* Eagle Lion Films. *Cast:* Jackie Robinson, Minor Watson (white), Richard Lane, Louise Beavers, Ruby Dee, Joel Fluellen, Bernie Hamilton, Kenny Washington, Howard Louis McNeely, Billy Wayne.

Screenplay: Lawrence Taylor & Arthur Mann. (16mm / Sound / B&W / 76 min. / Feature.)

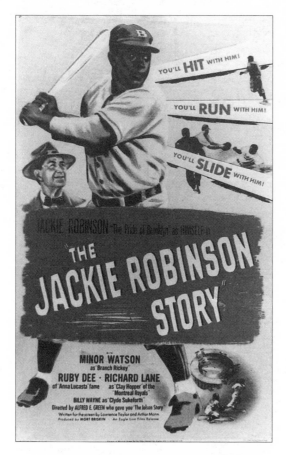

The story of Robinson's breakthrough to the major leagues and his early playing career. Louise Beavers plays Robinson's mother; Ruby Dee plays his sweetheart-then-wife Rae.

603   Jackpot   1943

Co: RCM Production. *Dist:* Soundies Distributing Corporation. *Cast:* Peggy Backus, The Harlem Honeys. (Soundies 7M6 / B&W / Short / Sound / Musical / 12/21/43.)

604   Jailhouse Blues   1934

Dir: Smith, Basil. *Co:* Columbia Pictures. *Cast:* Mamie Smith, Porter Grainger, Salem Tuft Whitney, Billy Mills. (Musical / Short / 9 min. / Sound / B&W.)

Mamie Smith is the featured artist.

605   Jam Session   1942

Dir: Berne, Josef. *Prod:* Coslow, Sam. *Co:* RCM Production. *Dist:* Soundies Distributing Corporation. *Cast:* Duke Ellington and His Orchestra: Ray Nance (fiddle), Rex

Stewart (trumpet), Ben Webster (saxophone), Joe Nanton (trombone), Barney Bigard (clarinet), Sonny Greer (drums). (Soundies 5503 / B&W / Short / Sound / Musical / 2/16/42.)

606   Jam Session   1944

Dir: Barton, Charles. *Co:* Columbia Pictures. *Cast:* Louis Armstrong and His Orchestra, Charlie Barnet (white) and His Orchestra, Clarence Muse. (16mm / B&W / Sound / 74 min. / Feature.)

Musical feature with a loosely sketched story line. Clarence Muse has a comic relief role.

607   Jamaica Negroes Doing a Two Step   1907

Co: Edison. (Newsreel / Actuality / B&W / Silent / Short.)

Unrehearsed footage of blacks doing a dance.

608   Jamboree (Disc Jockey Jamboree)   1957

Dir: Lockwood, Roy. *Cast:* Count Basie, Joe Williams, Fats Domino. (Sound / 86 min. / Feature / B&W.)

Popular entertainers are introduced through a sketchy story line and appearances are made by jazz artists. Numbers include "One O'Clock Jump" and "Wait and See."

609   Jammin' the Blues   1944

Dir: Mili, Gjon. *Prod:* Granz, Norman. *Co:* Gjon Mili Films / Warner Bros. *Cast:* Harry Edison, Lester Young, Illinois Jacquet, Marlowe Morris, John Simmons, Archie Savage, Joe Jones, Sid Catlett, Red Callender and His Orchestra, Marie Bryant, Barney Kessell (white).

Review in *Film Daily*, 4/2/44. Photographed by Gjon Mili. (16mm / B&W / Sound / 1 reel / 10 min. / Musical / Short.)

This is an excellent film of a "jam session" in a black nightclub. Great jitterbug dancing and special effects (multiple images).

610   The Janitor   1918

Co: Ebony Film Company. *Dist:* General Film Company. *Cast:* Ebony Players (Sam Robinson, cousin of Bill Robinson, Samuel Jacques, Yvonne Junior, Samuel "Sambo" Jacks, Will Starks, Julia Watson, Evon Skekeeter, Mildred Price, George Lewin, Bertie Moralis,

Elsie Whitely, Walter Brogsdale, Robert Dupree, Frank Pollard).

All members of the cast are members of the George M. Lewis Stock Company. (B&W / Silent / Short / 2 reels.)

Jasper Landry's Will *see* **Uncle Jaspers Will**

611   Jasper Series 1946
Dir: Pal, George. *Prod:* Pal, George. *Co:* Paramount.

Jasper in a Jam and *Jasper in a Haunted House* are two of the titles in series. (Animated/ Short / Color / Sound / 16mm / 10 min.)

"George Pal's series produced in the forties with Jasper as a Negro boy puppetoon — animated puppet, complete with bug eyes and a penchant for watermelon. He has a protective Mammy and together they have innumerable experiences, usually some confrontation with a black scarecrow hustler and his sidekick, a fast talking crow"—*Klotman.*

612   Jazz Festival 1955
Dir: Kohn, Joseph. *Prod:* Frye, Ben. *Co:* Studio Films, Inc. *Cast:* Mantan Moreland, Nipsey Russell, Lionel Hampton, Ruth Brown, Larry Darnell, Cab Calloway, The Clovers, Herb Jeffries, Bill Bailey, Dinah Washington, Duke Ellington, The Larks, Count Basie, and Sarah Vaughn.

Also released in a short version (tinted). (Musical / 35mm / B&W / Sound / 7 reels / Feature.) (FGC 7497-7498 short version.)

Musical variety type show of the period.

613   The Jazz Hounds 1922
Co: Reol Productions *Cast:* Edna Morton. (B&W / Silent / Short.)

614   Jeans Teacher and Her Work 1940
Co: Southern Education Foundation. (Documentary / B&W / Short / Sound / 1 Reel / 16mm.)

The activities of the Jeans teachers in all-black secondary schools in the South.

615   Jericho 1937
Dir: Freeland, Thornton. *Prod:* Futter, Walter. *Co:* Buckingham Films / Max Schach. *Cast:* Paul Robeson, Wallace Ford (white),

Henry Wilcoxon, Princess Kouka, John Laurie, James Darew, Laurence Brown, Rufus Fennell, Ike Hatch, Frank Cram, Frank Cochran, George Barraud, Frederick Cooper.

Original story: Walter Putter. Adaptation: Robert H. Lee & Peter Aurie. Scenario: George Barraud. Photography: John W. Boyle. Art director: Edward Darrick. Sound: A.S. Ross. Film editor: B.B. Jarvis. Assistant director: Donald Wilson. Original songs: Michael Carr & Jimmy Kennedy. Musical direction: Van Phillips. (British/ B&W / Feature / Sound / 75 min.)

Robeson flees from pre–World War II France after being wrongfully convicted of a crime. Arriving in North Africa, he becomes a desert sheik after rescuing a stranded caravan. He then becomes involved in a romance with a desert princess before his previous accuser arrives to return him to France.

616   Jim 1941
Co: RCM Production. *Dist:* Soundies Distributing Corporation. *Cast:* Judy Carroll. (Soundies 4308 / B&W / Short / Sound / Musical / 11/24/41.)

617   Jim Comes to Jo'Burg 1950
Dir: Swanson, Donald. *Prod:* Swanson, Donald. *Co:* Swanson, Donald. *Cast:* Daniel Adnewah, Dorothy Rathbe. (South African / Sound / B&W / Feature.)

"It tells the story of a youngster from the country who has spent his life in the pleasant pastoral surroundings of the Kraal. He minds the cattle and observes the ways and customs of country people. However, when adventure calls — he is lured to the big city and goes to Johannesburg. Big town sharpies and hoodlums waiting for easy pickings in the railroad terminal attacked and robbed him of his possessions. Befriended by a night watchman who finds him lying unconscious in a back alley after he had been attacked by the hoodlums, he takes residence at the samaritan's home and meets the latter's daughter who is featured as a night club entertainer"—excerpt of review from the *New York Amsterdam News*, 3/8/49.

618   Jim Town Cabaret 1929
Co: Vitaphone. *Cast:* Miller and Lyles. (Short / B&W / Sound / Comedy.)

619   Jimmie Lunceford and His Dance Orchestra   1936

Dir: Henabery, Joseph. *Co:* Vitaphone. *Cast:* Jimmie Lunceford and His Orchestra, Three Brown Jacks, Myra Johnson. (B&W / Sound / Short.)

"A typical sepia band, with a ritzy aggregation of hot-cha instrument men. The band does several numbers with different members doing their specialties with great gusto and zip. Also there are the Three Brown Jacks, lively steppers, and Myra Johnson doing a hit song number"— review from *Film Daily*, 1/7/37.

620   Jittering Jitterbugs   1943

Dir: Graham, Walter. *Co:* Sack Amusement Enterprises. *Dist:* Sack Amusement Enterprises. *Cast:* Hamtree Harrington, Lee Norman's Orchestra, Arthur White's Lindy Hoppers.

Review in *Film Daily*, 5/23/43. (16mm / B&W / Sound / 1 reel / 12 min. / Musical / Short.)

Harrington, et al., are the stars in this musical comedy which takes place in Harlem.

621   Jive Comes to the Jungle   1942

Co: RCM Production. *Dist:* Soundies Distributing Corporation. *Cast:* Edna Mae Harris, Slim Thomas, Ze Zullettes. (Soundies / Short / B&W / 11/16/42.)

622   Jivin' in Be-Bop   1946

Dir: Anderson, Leonard. *Prod:* Alexander, William D. *Co:* Alexander Production. *Dist:* Alexander Distributing Company. *Cast:* Dizzy Gillespie, Helen Humes, Ray Sneed, Freddie Carter, Ralph Brown, Dan Burley & Johnny Taylor, Phil & Audry, Jonny and Henny, Daisy Richardson, Pancho & Delores, Sahji, The Hubba Hubba Girls.

Photography: Don Malkames. Screenplay: Powell Lindsay. Film editor: Gladys Brothers. Sound: Nelson Minnerly. Makeup: Fred Ryle & Dave Gaston. (16mm / B&W / Sound / 2 reels / 60 min. / Feature / FGC 3203-3205 or FCA 7072-7073.)

Dizzy Gillespie heads this cast of entertainers; low on plot, but plenty of music, dancing, and comedy. Dizzy plays most of his bebop hits of the forties. Typical stage format of the period.

623   Jivin' the Blues   1946

Cast: Lena Horne, Sewanee Sweethearts. (Musical / Short / B&W / Sound.)

624   Joe, Joe   1946

Dir: Crouch, William Forest. *Prod:* Crouch, William Forest. *Co:* Filmcraft Production. *Dist:* Soundies Distributing Corporation. *Cast:* Noble Sissle. (Soundies / B&W / Short / Sound / Musical / 12/16/46.)

625   The Joe Louis Story   1953

Dir: Gordon, Robert. *Prod:* Silliphant, Stirling. *Co:* United Artists. *Dist:* United Artists. *Cast:* Coley Wallace, Paul Stewart (white), James Edwards, Hilda Simms, John Marley, Dotts Johnson, Primo Carnera (white), Max Baer (white), Max Schmeling (white), Jim Braddock (white), Rocky Marciano (white), Primo Canera (white).

Walter P. Chrysler, Jr. presentation. Original screenplay: Robert Sylvester. Music: George Bassman. Director of photography:

Joseph Brown. Film editor: David Kummins. Assistant director: Issac Jones & George Ackerson. Operative cameraman: Moe Harttzban. Sound engineer: James Shields. Continuity: Roberta Hode. Set design: Robert Gundlac. Makeup: Herman Buchman. Wardrobe: Florence Transfied. Hair: Helen Grizu. Technical advisor: Mannie Seamo. Production management & operation: Motion Picture Techniques, Inc. Associate producer: William F. Joyce. Unit manager: Thomas Whitesels. Assistant unit manager: Dorothy Bohes. Business manager: Philip Donoghue. (16mm / B&W / Sound / 3 reels / 87 min. / Feature.)

A fictional dramatization of Louis' career in the ring features actual sequences of his ring battles with Braddock, Baer, Carnera, and others.

626 Johnny Peddler 1941
Co: RCM Production. *Dist:* Soundies Distributing Corporation. *Cast:* Johnny Long and His Orchestra. (Soundies / B&W / Short / Sound / Musical / 3/2/41.)

627 The Joint Is Jumpin' 1941
Co: Minoco Production. *Dist:* Soundies Distributing Corporation. *Cast:* Fats Waller, Myra Johnson. (Soundies 4308 / B&W / Short / Sound Musical / 12/1/41.)

628 The Joint Is Jumping 1948
Dir: Binney, Josh. *Co:* All-American News. *Cast:* Rozelle Gale, Bob Howard, Una Mae Carlisle, Hadda Brooks, Slick & Slack, John Mason, Charles Ray (white), J. Patrick Patterson, Mattie Weave, Gertrude Saunders, John Oscar, Frog Edwards, Eddie South, Phil Moore Four.

Written by Hal Seeger. Preview in the *Chicago Defender*, 10/16/48. (35mm / B&W / Sound / 4 reels / Feature / FEA 7586–7589.)

629 Jonah and the Whale 1944
Co: RCM Production. *Dist:* Soundies Distributing Corporation. *Cast:* The Shadrach Boys. (Soundies 16108 / B&W / Short / Sound / Musical / 4/10/44.)

630 Jordan Jive 1944
Co: RCM Production. *Dist:* Soundies Dis-tributing Corporation. *Cast:* Louis Jordan and His Tympany Five. (Soundies / B&W / Short / Sound / Musical / 8/14/44.)

631 Jordan Melody #1 1946
Co: RCM Production. *Dist:* Soundies Distributing Corporation. *Cast:* Louis Jordan and His Band. (Soundies 3M / B&W / Short / Sound / Musical.)

632 Jordan Melody #2 1946
Co: RCM Production. *Dist:* Soundies Distributing Corporation. *Cast:* Louis Jordan and His Band. (Soundies 2M / B&W / Short / Sound / Musical.)

633 Joseph 'n' His Brudders 1945
Co: RCM Production. *Dist:* Soundies Distributing Corporation. *Cast:* June Richmond, Tiny Grimes and His Orchestra. (Soundies 88808 / B&W / Short / Sound / Musical / 7/16/45.)

634 The Judge's Story 1911
Co: Thanhauser. (B&W / Silent / Short.)
A young black worker is saved by a judge who in effect repays a debt of gratitude to the young man. The story is told in a flashback by a "Mammy" character.

635 Juke Box Boogie 1944
Co: RCM Production. *Dist:* Soundies Distributing Corporation. *Cast:* Gene Rodgers, the V's. (Soundies 19508 / B&W / Short / Sound / Musical / 12/30/44.)

636 Juke Joint 1947
Dir: Williams, Spencer, *Prod:* Goldberg, Bert. *Co:* Harlemwood Studies. *Dist:* Sack Amusement Enterprises. *Cast:* Spencer Williams, July Jones, Inez Newell, Leonard Duncan, Red Calhoun's Orchestra, Dauphine Moore, Melody Duncan, Katherine Moore, Tilford Patterson, Albert Smith, Howard Galloway, Frances McHugh, Clifford Beamon, Don Gilbert, Mac and Ace, Kit and Kat, The Jitterbug Johnnies, Duncan's Beauty Show Girls.

Original story by True T. Thompson. Cinematographer: George Sanderson. Screenwriter: Spencer Williams. Music: Red Calhoun and His Orchestra. Assistant cameraman: William Gulette. Sound engineer: Richard E. Byers.

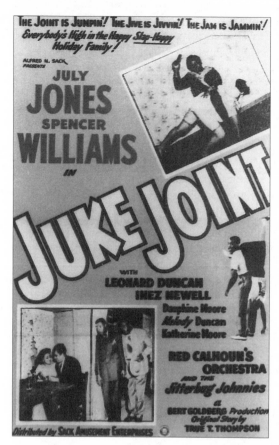

Makeup and hair: Farilla McGowan. Property master: Arthur Kendell. Musical director: George Randolf. Costumes: Julian Jullienne. Technical advisor: True T. Thompson. (60 min. / 5,378 ft. / 35 mm / B&W / Sound / 7 reels / Feature / FEA 418.)

Bad News Johnson and July Jones arrive in Hollywood with a quarter between them. Williams, Moreland and Jones star in a backstage plot set in Texas; includes a jitterbug contest, a staple of the forties.

637   Jules Bledsoe   1919

Co: Columbia Pictures. *Cast:* Jules Bledsoe (Musical / B&W / Short / Sound.)

Songs: "Old Man Trouble," and "Wadin' in the Water."

638   Jump Children   1946

Dir: Anderson, Leonard. *Prod:* Alexander, William D. *Co:* Alexander Production. *Dist:* Soundies Distributing Corporation. *Cast:* Anna Mae Winburn and the International Sweethearts of Rhythm. (Soundies / Short / B&W / 8/26/46.)

639   Jump In   1942

Co: RCM Production. *Dist:* Soundies Distributing Corporation. *Cast:* The Four Toppers, Cee Pee Johnson and His Orchestra. (Soundies 10605 / B&W / Short / Sound / Musical / 12/31/42.)

640   Jumpin' at the Jubilee   1944

Co: RCM Production. *Dist:* Soundies Distributing Corporation. *Cast:* Louis Jordan and His Tympany Five, The Swing Maniacs. (Soundies 16208 / B&W / Short / Sound / Musical / 4/17/44.)

641   Jumpin' Jack from Hackensack   1943

Co: RCM Production. *Dist:* Soundies Distributing Corporation. *Cast:* Tommy Thompson, The Chanticleers. (Soundies 13908 / B&W / Short / Sound / Musical / 10/25/43.)

642   Junction 88   1947

Dir: Quigley, George P. *Prod:* Sack, Alfred.

Co: Sack Amusement Enterprises. *Dist:* Sack Amusement Enterprises. *Cast:* Dewey "Pigmeat" Markham, Bob Howard, Wyatt Clark, Noble Sissle and His Orchestra, Marie Cooke, Abbey Mitchell, Artie Belle McGinty, George Wiltshire, Herbert Junior, Alonzo Bosan, Maude Simmons, Al Young, J. Augustus Smith, Choir (Eugene Thompson, Rumena Matson, Mable Berger, Dephine Roach, Henry Nelson). (35mm / Sound / B&W / 6 reels / 60 min. Feature / FEA 4202–4209.)

Typical musical variety film. A songwriter, writing under an alias, is finally discovered and rewarded with a lucrative contract and romance.

643   Jungle Drums   1929

Co: Tiffany Film Company (Documentary / Short / B&W / Sound.)

Documentary on African natives.

644   Jungle Jamboree   1943

Co: RCM Production. *Dist:* Soundies Distributing Corporation. *Cast:* Pauline Bryant, Cook and Brown, The Jungle Jivesters. (Soundies / 13608 / B&W / Short / Sound / Musical / 10/4/43.)

645   Jungle Jig   1941

Dir: RCM Production. *Dist:* Soundies Distributing Corporation. *Cast:* Dorothy Dandridge, Cee Pee Johnson. (Soundies 1802 / B&W / Short / Sound / Musical / 6/2/41.)

First musical videos.

646   A Jungle Jinx   1932

Co: Official Films. (Animated / B&W / Short / Music only.)

This cartoon takes place down in Dixie, replete with stereotypical images, watermelon eating, dancing, shuffling, cottonfield happiness, slaves, slave auction, master with ship, slow-minded and ball-and-chain action black images.

647   Jungle Jitters   1942

Prod: Schlesinger, Leon. *Co:* Warner Bros. / Vitaphone.

A Merrie Melodies. Supervisor: I. Freleng. Story: George Manuell. Animation: Phil Monroe. Musical direction: Carl W. Stalling. (Animation / Color / Sound / Short.)

This cartoon takes place in Africa, a tribe doing all of the stereotypical things meet a goofy white salesman. He ends up in a stew pot; queen falls in love with salesman; salesman sees ugly queen and decides to get back in the stew pot.

648   Junior   1946

Dir: Crouch, William Forest. *Prod:* Crouch, William Forest. *Co:* Filmcraft Production. *Dist:* Soundies Distributing Corporation. *Cast:* Johnny Long and His Orchestra, Francey Lane. (Soundies / B&W / Short / Sound / Musical / 4/1/46.)

649   Junior Jeeps   1947

Prod: Weiss, George. *Co:* Weiss, George. *Cast:* Uncredited.

Narrator: Edward Mason. Cinematographer: Hal Malvern. Continuity: Sam Elljay. Sound: Melvin D'Anton. (10 min. / 910 ft. / B&W / Sound / Short.)

A young man reads in a newspaper of an upcoming auto race at the local track — Bonelli Stadium. He shows the notice to a younger friend, and they begin to dream of being racedrivers themselves. Walking through the neighborhood, they spy an old race car at a garage. Through much eloquent arguing and bargaining, they manage to talk the owner out of the machine. He even helps them fix it up. They enter the race, with the younger boy driving, and their fantasy is fulfilled as he wins!

650   Just a Note   1914

Dir: Lubin, Sigmund. *Prod:* Lubin, Sigmund. *Co:* Lubin Manufacturing Company. *Cast:* John Edwards, Mattie Edwards, Charles Porter, Harold Hevener (white), Marguerite Ne Moyer (white), James Levering (white).

"Sam, a valet to Harry Reynolds, asks him to write a love letter to Roxy, who is maid to Lucy Clayton, Harry's sweetheart. Roxy leaves the letter in Lucy's room and she recognizes the handwriting and cannot understand why he would write to Roxy. When Harry calls at the house, old man Clayton chases him with a gun. Then Tough Jake, another of Roxy's admirers, also chases Sam with a gun. Nobody, however, is hurt until they all meet on the road and explanations follow. As Jake's gun is now empty, Sam draws his razor and had it not been for Roxy's interference bid fair to send another black angel aloft" — *Lubin Bulletin.*

Henry Jackson is the pride of his small town. He wins a Golden Gloves title and later goes to New York with his manager Ed Watson, despite opposition from his father and sweetheart, Fanny. He meets an old school chum, Frank, who turns out to be a cold-blooded gambler betting that Henry loses the fight. On the day of the fight, a plot to drug Henry's liquor just before he leaves to fight is thwarted. A companion sees the drug administered to Henry's drink and switches them when no one is looking. Henry wins the bout and events move pleasingly to the end, where Henry and Fanny are together again and Frank and his cohorts are confounded.

653   Keep Smiling 1943

Co: RCM Production. *Dist:* Soundies Distributing Corporation. *Cast:* The Four Ginger Snaps. (Soundies 13008 / B&W / Short / Sound / Musical / 8/23/43.)

654   Keep Waitin' 1943

Co: RCM Production. *Dist:* Soundies Distributing Corporation. *Cast:* George Washington Brown. (Soundies 12008 / B&W / Short / Sound / Musical / 6/7/43.)

655   Kentucky Jubilee Singers 1928

Co: Fox-Movietone. *Cast:* Kentucky Jubilee Singers.

Song: "Shout All Over Gods Heavens." (B&W / Sound / Short / Musical.)

"This well known aggregation does two numbers in a close harmony setting. It shows the outside of the old Southern cabin, with the darkies grouped lazily outside, or sitting on the fence. Their first number is 'Carry Me Back to Old Virginny' and their harmonizing comes through clear and melodious. They finish with a pep number, 'All God's Chillen Got Wings,' with one member carrying the song and the other members breaking in with typical vocalizing and harmony that gets over big"—review from *Film Daily*, 6/10/28.

656   Kentucky Jubilee Singers 1929

Co: Fox-Movietone. *Cast:* Kentucky Jubilee Singers.

Songs: "My Old Kentucky Home," and "Swing Low, Sweet Chariot." (Musical / Short / B&W / Sound.)

Written by E.W. Sargent. Released on 3/14/14. (Silent / B&W / Short / 400 ft.)

651   Just a-Sittin' and a Rockin' 1945

Co: RCM Production. *Dist:* Soundies Distributing Corporation. *Cast:* The Delta Rhythm Boys. (Soundies 21308 / B&W / Short / Sound / Musical / 8/20/45.)

652   Keep Punching 1939

Dir: Clein, John. *Prod:* Clein, John. *Co:* Film Art Studios, Inc. *Dist:* M.C. Pictures / Sack Amusement Enterprises. *Cast:* Henry Armstrong, Lionel Monagas, Francine Everett, Willie Bryant, Mae Johnson, Hamtree Harrington, Canada Lee, Arthur (Dooley) Wilson, Alvin Childress, Hilda Offey, J. Rosamond Johnson, George Wiltshire, Lee Norman's Orchestra, Arthur White's Lindy Hoppers.

Story: J. Rosamond Johnson. Screenplay: March Klauber. Photography: J. Burgi Contner & Jay Rescher. Film editor: Al Harburger. Sound engineer: N. Dean. Music score: Lee Norman Cole. (B&W / Sound / Feature / 80 min.)

657   Kid Chocolate and Jack Kid Berg 1930

(Newsreel / Short / B&W / Sound.)

Footage of a prizefight between Kid Chocolate and Jack Berg.

658   Killer Diller 1948

Dir: Binney, Josh. *Prod:* Glucksman, E.M. *Co:* All-American News. *Cast:* King Cole Trio, Dusty Fletcher, Andy Kirk and His Orchestra, Butterfly McQueen, Jackie "Moms" Mabley, Clark Brothers, George Wiltshire, Freddie Robinson, Nellie Hill, Beverly White, William Campbell, Edgar Martin, Sidney Easton, Augustus Smith, Ken Renard, Four Congaroos, Patterson & Jackson and the Varietiettes Dancing Girls.

Story and Screenplay: Hall Seegar. Musical arrangements: Rene J. Hall. Dance director: Charles Morrison. Assistant director: Walter Sheridan. Director of photography: Lester Lang. Film editor: L. Hesse. Costumes: Madames Bartha & Eaves Costume Co. Sound engineer: Harold Vivian. Draperies: Frank W. Stevens. Art director: Sam Corso. (16mm / B&W / Sound / 2 reels / 80 min. / Feature / FGC 2380-2383.)

Typical variety musical plot for this period. Slim on plot but packed full of entertainment. Dusty, while on stage, makes the manager's girl disappear in a magic cabinet. When he can't bring her back, the manager calls the police, and for the remainder of the picture Dusty is chased by the police in the theater, à la Keystone Kops. Comedic scenes with Kops entwined and with various musical performers.

659   Kilroy Lives Here 1940

Dir: Pollard, Bud. (Sound / B&W.)

660   King Cole and His Trio 1950

Dir: Cowan, Will. *Co:* Universal-International. *Cast:* Nat "King" Cole, Irving Ashby, Joe Comfort, Jack Costanzo, Benny Carter and His Orchestra, Delores Parker, "Scatman" Crothers. (Musical / Short / 15 min.)

661   King Cole Trio and Benny Carter 1950

Co: Universal Studios. *Cast:* Nat "King" Cole and His Trio, Benny Carter and His Orchestra, Bunny Briggs, "Scatman" Crothers, Delores Parker.

Review in *Film Daily*, 5/15/50 (B&W / Short / Sound.)

Enjoyable musical variety footage.

662   King for a Day 1934

Co: Vitaphone. *Cast:* Bill Robinson, Muriel Rahn, Hattie Noel, Dusty Fletcher, Babe Matthews, Ernest Whitman. (B&W / Sound / Musical / Short.)

"Bill, refused a job in a show that is rehearsing, shoots dice with the producer — using two bucks the latter gave him. After the production opens and is going great, the ex-owner comes around looking for a handout, and in turn he rolls them with Bill until he gets his show back. In between these incidents are some dancing and singing specialties in typical Negro vein" — review from *Film Daily*, 7/9/34.

663   Kinky 1923

Co: Educational Film Corporation. *Cast:* Black Boy. (Silent / Short / B&W.)

664   A Kiss in the Dark pre–1910

(B&W / Silent / Short / FLA 3663.)

665   Knock Me Out 1945

Co: RCM Production. *Dist:* Soundies Distributing Corporation. *Cast:* Apus and Estrellita, Dewey Brown. (Soundies 89508 / B&W / Short / Sound / Musical / 3/16/45.)

666   The Lady Fare 1929

Dir: Watson, William. *Prod:* Christie, Al. *Co:* Christie Film Company. *Dist:* Paramount. *Cast:* Spencer Williams, Evelyn Preer, Edward Thompson, Roberta Hyson, Leroy Broomfield, Lawrence Criner, Claude Collins, Gus Jones, Zack Williams, Herbert Skinner, Leon Hereford's Cotton Club Jazz Orchestra, the Cotton Club dancing chorus, Rutledge and Taylor.

Original story by Octavus Roy Cohen. Screenplay: Spencer Williams. (B&W / 2 reels / Sound / Comedy / Short.)

One of the Christie comedy series which like others, uses "Negro dialect." It has dusky singing and dancing teams featured in fast numbers and is a combination of a typical Octavus Roy Cohen story and revue entertainment of the kind for which the colored performers are especially noted.

Lady Luck *see* **Lucky Ghost**

667   Laughing Ben pre–1910
(B&W / Silent / Short / FLA 3194.)

668   The Law of Nature 1917
Co: Lincoln Motion Picture Company. *Cast:* Noble M. Johnson, Clarence Brooks, Albertine Pickens.

Review in the *Chicago Defender*, 7/17/17. (Silent / B&W / Feature.)

"A beautiful eastern society girl is the governess of the children of a wealthy cattleman whom she eventually marries. The lure of the bright lights, dances and cabarets prove irresistible for her, so she, with her husband and children, returns east. The humiliation she suffers because of the crudeness of her rancher husband in society and the persistent attentions of a former admirer lead to innumerable complications which result in her husband and children returning to the west. Cast aside, alone, deserted, homeless, ill, she finally realizes her folly and the inevitable consequences of the violation of 'Nature's Law'; she returns west to her husband and children. The regeneration complete, she succumbs to the will of God"— H. Sampson.

669   Lazy Lady 1945
Dir: Crouch, William Forest. *Prod:* Crouch, William Forest. *Co:* Filmcraft Production. *Dist:* Soundies Distributing Corporation. *Cast:* The Phil Moore Four. (Soundies 22208 / B&W / Short / Sound / Musical / 12/24/45.)

670   Lazy River 1944
Co: RCM Production. *Dist:* Soundies Distributing Corporation. *Cast:* The Shadrach Boys. (Soundies 15508 / B&W / Short / Sound / Musical / 2/28/44.)

671   Lazy River 1944
Co: RCM Production. *Dist:* Soundies Distributing Corporation. *Cast:* The Mills Brothers. (Soundies 19108 / B&W / Short / Sound / Musical / 12/4/44.)

672   The Leaders of His Race 1922
Co: Reol Productions. *Cast:* Booker T. Washington. (Documentary / Short / Newsreel / B&W / Silent.)

The life and achievements of Dr. Booker T. Washington, founder and president of Tuskegee Institute, Tuskegee, Alabama.

673   Legs Ain't No Good 1942
Co: Minoco Production. *Dist:* Soundies Distributing Corporation. *Cast:* Edna Mae Harris, Slim Thomas. (Soundies 10006 / B&W / Short / Sound / Musical / 12/28/42.)

Lem Hawkins' Confession *see* **Murder in Harlem**

674   Let My People Live 1938
Dir: Ulmer, Edgar G. *Prod:* National Tuberculosis Association. *Co:* Motion Picture Service Corporation. *Cast:* Rex Ingram, Erostine Coles, Peggy Howard, Wilbert Smith, Students from the Tuskegee Little Theatre (Robert Anderson, Jackson Burnside, Christine Johnson).

Film notes in the *Philadelphia Tribune*, 5/19/38. (16mm / Sound / B&W / 14 min. / Short / Dramatized / Documentary.)

This dramatization shows the dangers of neglecting tuberculosis. After several inspirational and informational scenes the homes and churches of common colored folk are visited. The message comes in loud and clear what could happen to anyone without treatment.

675   Let's Do the Black Bottom 1926
Co: Castle Films. (Documentary / Newsreel / B&W / Short / Silent.)

Development of the Black Bottom dance featuring blacks.

676   Let's Get Away from It All 1943
Co: RCM Production. *Dist:* Soundies Distributing Corporation. *Cast:* Johnny Long and His Orchestra. (Soundies / B&W / Short / Sound / Musical / 10/4/43.)

677   Let's Get Down to Business 1943
Co: RCM Production. *Dist:* Soundies Distributing Corporation. *Cast:* Myra Johnson,

Dewey Brown. (Soundies 5M2 / B&W / Short / Sound / Musical / 9/21/43.)

678   Let's Go 1942

Co: RCM Production. *Dist:* Soundies Distributing Corporation. *Cast:* The Four Toppers, Cee Pee Johnson and His Orchestra. (Soundies 11305 / B&W / Short / Sound / Musical / 12/31/42.)

679   Let's Shuffle 1942

Co: RCM Production. *Dist:* Soundies Distributing Corporation. *Cast:* Bill Robinson. (Soundies 5006 / B&W / Short / Sound / Musical / 1/12/42.)

680   Life Goes On (His Harlem Wife) 1938

Dir: Nolte, William. *Co:* Million Dollar Productions. *Dist:* Toddy Pictures. *Prod:* Popkin, Harry. *Cast:* Louise Beavers, Edward Thompson, Reginald Fenderson, Lawrence Criner, Monte Hawley, Hope Bennett, Jesse Brooks, May

Turner, Artie Brandon, Edward Robertson, Oliver Farmer, Eloise Witherspoon, Lillian Randolph.

His Harlem Wife, 1944, is a reissue of *Life Goes On*, 1938. Louise Beavers first all-colored cast feature film. Screenplay: Phil Dunham. Reviews in the *Philadelphia Tribune*, 3/24/38, and the *Kansas City Call*, 4/13/38. (Feature / B&W / Sound.)

Sally (Beavers) is a loving widowed mother who raises two sons, Bob and Henry. Bob grows up to become a lawyer and Henry grows up less successful and associates with the wrong crowd. Henry is wrongly accused of murder and his brother Bob is appointed his lawyer. Bob is forced to fight against a powerful D.A. bent on sending his brother to the gallows.

681   Life in Harlem 1940

Dir: Lewis, Edward W. *Prod:* Lewis, Edward W. *Co:* Sack Amusement Enterprises. *Dist:* Sack Amusement Enterprises. *Cast:* E.W. Lewis (narrator).

Life in Harlem is part of the documentary series, *Colored America on Parade,* produced for all-black theaters. Edward W. Lewis, producer of film was photographer on the staff of the *New York Daily News.* (Newsreel / 16mm / B&W / Sound / Short.)

This newsreel shows scenes of poverty and opulence taken at random on 125th Street on a busy day. Edgecombe Avenue, the Eighth Avenue pushcart markets, Harlem at dawn and Harlem after dark, with scenes at the Savoy Ballroom, Smalls' Paradise and other night spots.

682   Life Is Real 1935

Co: Lincoln Productions / Gaumont British Studios. *Cast:* Scott and Whaley, Nina Mae McKinney, Debroy Somers (white) and His Band. (British made / B&W / Sound / Feature.)

Referenced in the *Philadelphia Independent*, 7/31/38.

683   Life of Booker T. Washington 1940

Co: Duo Art Pictures, Inc. (Documentary / B&W / Sound / Biographical / Short.)

The story of Booker T. Washington.

684   Life of Florence Mills 1940

Dir: Brodie, Don. *Prod:* Blake, Sid. *Co:*

Duo Art Pictures, Inc. *Cast:* Bobbye Gwynn, Laura Newman, Leroy Antoine, Madam Sul-Te-Wan, The Four Toppers, The Hi-Hatters.

Music: Joe Greene. Assistant director: Howard Fawcett. Story is based on an original by Thaddeus Jones. Film announcement in the *Philadelphia Afro-American,* 9/20/40. (B&W / Sound / Feature.)

This film will touch the highlights of the little songbird's life.

685   Life of George Washington Carver 1940

Prod: Blake, Sid. *Co:* Duo Art Pictures, Inc. *Cast:* Clinton Rosamond. (B&W / Sound / Documentary / Short.)

The life of George Washington Carver.

686   The Life of the Party 1935

Dir: Watson, William. *Prod:* Christie, Al. *Co:* Educational Film Corporation. *Cast:* The Cabin Kids (five colored harmonizers, Ruth Hall, Helen Hall, James "Darling" Hall, Winifred "Sugar" Hall, and little Frederick Hall), Six Mountain Melodeers (white). (B&W / Sound / Short.)

"Lively and melodic number featuring those cute pickaninnies, the Cabin Kids. At a house party the hostess finds herself shy of the expected talent and discovers the five youngsters in the kitchen with their mammy. They are doing their stuff for their own amusement, so they are brought in to entertain the guests" — review from *Film Daily,* 5/9/35.

687   Life of Today 1937

(Documentary / B&W / Short / Sound.)

A film study of life among the black folks of Kansas City, Missouri.

688   Lifting as We Climb 1953

Co: Artisan Productions / National Association of Colored Women. (16mm / Sound / 1 reel / 15 min. / Documentary / B&W / Short.)

Discusses the activities and the program of the National Association of Colored Women. Traces the growth of the organization from 1896 to 1953. Points to the past achievements of the organization and outlines its program for the future.

689   Lincoln-Howard Football Game 1934

Co: Brown-America Studios. (Newsreel / Documentary / B&W / Short / Sound.)

Footage of the annual football classic between Howard University and Lincoln University.

690   Lincoln Pictorial 1918

Co: Lincoln Motion Picture Company. (Newsreel / Short / Documentary / B&W / Silent.)

Views of the black community of Los Angeles, California.

691   Linda Brown 1943

Co: RCM Production. *Dist:* Soundies Distributing Corporation. *Cast:* The Musical Madcaps. (Soundies 13208 / B&W / Short / Sound / Musical / 9/6/43.)

692   Lionel Hampton and Herb Jeffries 1955

Dir: Cowan, Will. *Co:* Universal-International. *Cast:* Lionel Hampton and His Band. Vicky Lee, Loray White and the Four Hamptons, Herb Jeffries. (Sound / 15 min. / Musical / Short.)

Focuses on the artists above performing, for example, "Baby, Don't Love Me" and "Black Coffee."

693   Lionel Hampton and His Orchestra 1949

Dir: Cowan, Will. *Co:* Universal-International. *Cast:* Lionel Hampton and His Orchestra, Kitty Murray, Sonny Parker, Lorene Carter, Lawrence and Lillian Williams, Curley Hamner, Joe Adams, Attorney Belford Lawson, Governor William Hastie, Dr. Mary McLeod Bethune.

Announcement in the *Philadelphia Tribune,* 3/12/49. Originally planned for a feature. Made for the *Negro Marches On* series. (Sound / 14 min. / Musical / Short / B&W.)

Lionel Hampton performing.

694   Listen to the Mocking Bird 1941

Dir: Primi, John. *Prod:* Waller, Fred "Fats." *Co:* Minoco Production. *Dist:* Soundies Distributing Corporation. *Cast:* The Korn Kobblers. (Soundies / B&W / Short / Sound / Musical / 10/20/41.)

695   Little Black Sambo 1933

Dir: Iwerks, Ub. *Prod:* Celebrity Pictures. *Co:* Celebrity Pictures Cartoon. (16mm / Color / Sound / 1 reel / 10 min. / Animated / Short.)

This film is an animated version of the old story with Sambo and a black child with a dog, and a mother who seems to be part of the American scene. This tiger doesn't turn to butter but is outwitted and physically beaten by Sambo and his dog.

696   Little Carol Jackson 1942

Cast: Carol Jackson. (Musical / Short / B&W / Sound.)

697   Little Daddy 1931

Prod: Roach, Hal. *Co:* Metro-Goldwyn-Mayer. (Documentary / B&W / Short / Sound.)

Two young Negro boys discuss Noah and other biblical stories.

698   A Little Jive Is Good for You 1941

Co: RCM Production. *Dist:* Soundies Distributing Corporation. *Cast:* Martha Tilton, The Three Slate Brothers.

Recorded by Ben Pollack Orchestra. (Soundies / B&W / Short / Sound / Musical / 8/25/41.)

699   Lobola 1954

Prod: Perold, Jan M. *Co:* Jan M. Perold. (South Africa / Documentary / Sound / 16mm / B&W / 26 min. 1 reel / Short.)

"Pictures some of the personal and social problems arising out of cultural differences between two tribes and also the movement of Blacks into the urban areas of the white man. Uses photography and a narration frequently interposed with native proverbs"—Klotman.

700   Lonesome Lover Blues 1946

Dir: Anderson, Leonard. *Prod:* Alexander, William D. *Co:* Alexander Production. *Dist:* Soundies Distributing Corporation. *Cast:* Billy Eckstine and His Orchestra.

Excerpted from the Featurette *Rhythm in a Riff* (1946). (Soundies / B&W / Short / Sound / Musical / 12/30/46.)

701   The Lonesome Road 1941

Co: RCM Production. *Dist:* Soundies Distributing Corporation. *Cast:* Sister Rosetta Tharpe, Lucky Millinder and His Orchestra. (Soundies 4106 / B&W / Short / Sound / Musical / 11/10/41.)

702   The Long and Short of It 1943

Co: RCM Production. *Dist:* Soundies Distributing Corporation. *Cast:* Johnny Long and His Orchestra. (Soundies / B&W / Short / Sound / Musical / 11/29/43.)

703   Long Remembered 1950

Prod: Lee, A.W. *Co:* United Artist. *Dist:* United Artists. (Musical / B&W / Short / Sound.)

Songs: "Carry Me Back to Old Virginny" and "Cert'n'y Lord."

Black choral group performs.

704   Look-Out Sister 1948

Dir: Pollard, Bud. *Prod:* Adams, Berle. *Co:* Astor Pictures Corporation. *Dist:* Astor Pictures. *Cast:* Louis Jordan and His Tympany Five (Aaron Izenhall, Paul Quinchette, William Doggett, William Hadnott, Chris Columbus and James Jackson), Louise Franklin, Louise Ritchie, Maceo B. Sheffield, Napoleon Whiting, Bobby Johnson, Peggy Thomas, Monte Hawley, Bob Scott, Jack Clisby, Tommy Southern, Suzette Harbin, Glenn Allen, Anice Clark, Dorothy Seamans, Glenn Leedy, Jack Williams, Curtis Hamilton, Eugene Jackson, Freddy Baker, James Davis (stunt man).

Review in the *Baltimore Afro-American*, by Harry Levette, 4/10/48. Executive producer: R.M. Savini. Screenplay: John Gordon. Additional dialogue: Will Morrissey. Photography: Carl Barger. Editor: Bud Pollard. Sound: Glen Glen & Harry Eckles. Assistant director: Willard Sheldon. Costumes: Western Costume Co. Montage and Special effects: Nat Sobel. Chief Grip: William Johnson. (16mm / B&W / Sound / 2 reels / 67 min. / Feature / FEA 4211–4217.)

Musical Western satire with a minor plot and a lot of music. The film, named after Jordan's original musical number with this title, has as most of its locale a modern dude ranch with a swimming pool and conveniences.

Louisiana *see* **Drums o' Voodoo**

705   Love and Undertakers 1918

Co: Colored and Indian Film Company. *Cast:* Daniel Michaels, Montgomery and his wife. (Short / B&W / Silent / 1 reel / 1,000 ft.) Released 1/1/18.

706   The Love Bug 1920

Prod: Norman Film Manufacturing Company. *Co:* Norman Film Manufacturing Company. *Dist:* Norman Studios. *Cast:* Billy Mills Stock Company (Billy Mills, Maud Frisbie, Robert Stewart, Maud Johnson), a 425-pound fat lady and a set of triplets. (Feature / B&W / Silent / 2 reels / Comedy.)

707   Love Grows on a White Oak Tree 1944

Co: RCM Production. *Dist:* Soundies Distributing Corporation. *Cast:* The Little Four Quartet. (Soundies 19408 / B&W / Short / Sound / Musical / 12/28/44.)

708   Love in Syncopation 1946

Dir: Alexander, William D. *Prod:* Alexander, William D. *Co:* Astor Pictures Corporation. *Dist:* Astor Pictures. *Cast:* Ruby Dee, Maxine Johnson, Harrel Tillman, Powell Lindsey, June Eckstine, Taps and Wilda, Ronnell and Edna, Henri Woode and His Band. (Feature / Sound / B&W.)

This typical forties musical is a showcase for the Henri Woode Band. It traces the band's rise in show business, starting with its origins in the Navy during World War II and their struggle to make it.

709   Love Me, Love My Dog 1914

Prod: Haynes, Hunter C. *Co:* Afro-American Film Company. (Short / B&W / Silent.)

710   Lovie Joe's Romance 1914

Co: Afro-American Film Company. *Cast:* Robert A. Kelly, Stella Wiley, Bruxton Carter, Anthony Byrd. (Silent / Short / B&W.)

"The [photo] play is disconnected all through. The scenery is bad ... is static, even in the announcements. The camera in most instances, was out of focus and the gun used was a toy weapon that would not shoot. 'Lovie Joe' is in evidence, but the 'Romance' was not discernible. The general action of the piece is absolutely absurd and is to be regretted ...."— excerpted from the *Indianapolis Freeman*, 3/28/14, review by Herbert T. Meadows.

711   Lovin' Up a Solid Breeze 1943

Co: RCM Production. *Dist:* Soundies Distributing Corporation. *Cast:* The Chanticleers. (Soundies 12808 / B&W / Short / Sound / Musical / 8/2/43.)

712   Low Down: A Bird's Eye View of Harlem 1929

Co: Vitaphone. *Cast:* Monette Moore, Gertie Chambers, Mary Burnes, Washboard Serenaders.

Songs: "Dynamite," "Weary River," "Georgia Is Always on My Mind," and "That Thing Called Love." (B&W / Sound / Short / 8 min. / FEB 4706.)

"We are treated to some musical antics that are not exactly invigorating, though, it must be admitted, there is some dancing of the hot variety and a passable amount of humor"— excerpt from review in *Film Daily*, 2/23/30.

713   Low Down Dog 1944
Co: RCM Production. *Dist:* Soundies Distributing Corporation. *Cast:* Meade Lux Lewis, Joe Turner. (Soundies 16508 / B&W / Short / Sound / Musical / 5/15/44.)

714   Low, Short and Squatty 1946
Dir: Crouch, William Forest. *Prod:* Crouch, William Forest. *Co:* Filmcraft Production. *Dist:* Soundies Distributing Corporation. *Cast:* Vanita Smythe. (Soundies 26M1 / B&W / Short / Sound / Musical / 12/2/46.)

715   Loyal Hearts 1919
Dir: Peacocke, Leslie / Sidney P. Dones. *Prod:* Peacocke, Leslie. *Co:* Democracy Photoplay Corporation. *Dist:* Bookertee Films Exchange. *Cast:* Sidney Preston Dones, Thais Nehli Kalana, Dorothy Yvonne Dumont, Maurice Stapler, Vera Lavassor, Mrs. Wilhelmina Owens, Mrs. Hamer Burrell, Mrs. Seith Webb, Margaret Grace-Boon, Mrs. W.W.E. Gladden, Gwendoline Gordon, Mary Strange, Veronica Smith, Jeanette Criner, Mrs. James Seager, Mrs. Crystal Reed. Cora Reed, Miss Dryfus, Mrs. Otis Banks, Chaplain W.W.E. Gladden, Robert Fortson, Lt. Journee White, Eldridge Lee, Otis Banks, Robert Owens, Mr. Christian, Dr. W.A. Tarleton, Lt. Matthews, Lt. Eugene Lucas, F.L. Banks, J.B. Banks, Harry Jones, Herbert Bost, J.W. Coleman, Julia Stuart, Lt. Hankin, Lt. Jackson.
Reviews in *The Leader*, 8/5/19, and the *Chicago Defender*, 5/5/20. (Silent / B&W / 7 reels / 35mm / Feature.)
Original Title *Injustice* never released.
The story is about a young society woman who is rumored to have Negro blood in her veins. The rumor is confirmed by her rival and, in order to avoid disgrace, she goes to France during World War I as a Red Cross nurse. While attending to the wounded, she is attacked by a band of Huns and the unspeakable outrage is about to be visited upon her when she is rescued by her former butler, who slaughters the Huns singlehandedly. He is seriously wounded, but is nursed back to life and the reward she pays him is far better than the decorations he receives for bravery.

716   The Loyalty of a Race 1918
Dir: Tyler, Ralph W. *Co:* National Colored Soldier's Comfort Committee. *Cast:* Vivian Thompson Taylor, Walter Scott Turner, Jr., Prof. J. Henry Lewis, Miss Estelle Collier, Isadore Kenney.
Scenario by Mark Edmund Jones. Preview in the *Philadelphia Tribune*, 4/20/18. (Documentary / B&W / Silent / Short.)
The study and contributions of the prominent Negroes of Washington, D.C.

717   Luck in Old Clothes 1918
Co: Ebony Film Company. *Dist:* General Film Company. *Cast:* Ebony Players (Sam Robinson, Samuel "Sambo" Jacks, Will Starks, Julia Mason, Bert Murphy, Evon Skekeeter, Mildred Price, Walter Brogsdale, Robert Duree, Frank Pollard, George Lewis Stock Company). (Short / Silent / B&W / 2 reels.)

718   Lucky Gamblers 1946

Dir: Binney, Josh. *Co:* All-American News. *Cast:* Lollypop Jones, Edith Graves, J. Augustus Smith, Frederick Johnson. (16mm / B&W / Sound / 1 reel / 20 min. / Comedy / Short.)

Lollypop Jones' character gets a job as a waiter at the 7-11 Club. Shortly after, he overhears a plot by ruthless gamblers to defraud the club owner of his ownership. Eventually, the gamblers using loaded dice, almost gain control of the club but Jones ends up saving the day.

719   Lucky Ghost (Lady Luck) 1941

Dir: Crowley, William Xavier. *Prod:* Buell, Jed. *Co:* Dixie National Pictures, Inc. *Dist:* Toddy Pictures. *Cast:* Mantan Moreland, Flournoy E. Miller, Eddie Anderson, Maceo B. Sheffield, Arthur Ray, Florence O'Brien. "Slickem" Harold Garrison, Jessie Cryer, Nappie Whiting, Jess Lee Brooks, Ida Coffin,

Nathan Curry, Millie Monroe, Louise Franklyn, Lucille Battles, Aranelle Harris, Monte Hawley, Vernon McCalla, Buck Woods, Henry Hastings, Florence Fields, John Lester Johnson, Edward Thompson, Leonard Christmas, Reginald Fenderson, Mildred Boyd, Conga Night Club Band of Los Angeles, California.

Original title was *Lady Luck* (1940, announced in the *Philadelphia Afro-American*, 8/27/40), but never released. Released a year later with the title *Lucky Ghost* (1941). Successor to *Mr. Washington Goes to Town*. Co-produced by Ted Toddy. Associated producer, Maceo B. Sheffield. Review in the *Philadelphia Tribune*, 5/30/42. (Sound / B&W / Feature.)

Mantan Moreland and Flournoy E. Miller do a bug-eyed bit in this fun-filled supernatural comedy filled with pratfalls and wacky situations. The two, having been sent to another state by a judge, have a supernatural run of luck. Mantan's luck at dice wins them clothes, a car, his life, a club and money.

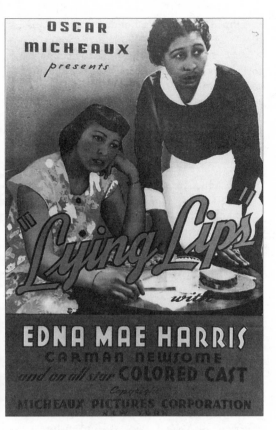

720 Lucky Millinder 1946

Dir: Alexander, William D. *Prod:* Alexander, William D. *Co:* Astor Pictures Corporation. *Dist:* Astor Pictures. *Cast:* Lucky Millinder and His Orchestra. (Musical / Short / B&W / Sound.)

Songs: "Hello Bill," "I Wan' a Man," and "Big Fat Mamma and Little Fat Mamma Are Back in Style."

A filmed musical presentation of Lucky Millinder and His Orchestra.

721 The Lure of a Woman 1921

Dir: Simms, John M. *Prod:* Progress Picture Producing Association. *Co:* Progress Picture Producing Association. *Dist:* Afro-American Exhibitors Co. *Cast:* Regina Cohee, Dr. A. Porter Davis, Charles K. Allen, Mrs. J.D. Brown, Roberto Taylor, Lenore Jones, John Cobb, Alonzo Dixon, Susie Dudley, Veronica Miller, Emily Gates, Alice Johnson.

The first Black film produced in Kansas City. Written by: John M. Simms. Photography: Howard Curtis. Assistant director: Mrs. Osborne. (35mm / Silent / B&W / Feature / 5 reels.)

722 Lure of the Woods 1922

(Silent / B&W.)

723 Lying Lips 1939

Dir: Micheaux, Oscar. *Prod:* Micheaux, Oscar. *Co:* Micheaux Pictures Corporation. *Dist:* Sack Amusement Enterprises. *Cast:* Edna Mae Harris, Carman Newsome, Amanda Randolph, Frances Williams, Frank Costell, J. Lewis Johnson, Teddy Hall, Slim Thompson, Juano Hernandez, Robert Earl Jones, Cherokee Thornton, Gladys Williams, Henry "Gong" Cines, Don D. Lee, Charles Latorre, Robert Paquin, George Reynolds.

Written by: Oscar Micheaux. Cinematography: Lester Lang. Recorded by: Nelson Minnerly. Editor: Leonard Weiss. Musical director: Jack Shilkret. Director of dialogue: John Kollin. (16mm / Sound / B&W / 60 min. / Feature / FCA 8237–8238.)

Elsie Ballwood, a young nightclub singer, is convicted and sent to prison for the murder of her aunt. Benjamin, who is in love with Elsie, and Detective Wanzer set out to prove her innocence. They do and Elsie and Benjamin are married after she is pardoned and released from prison.

724 MacNamara's Band 1941

Dir: Murray, Warren. *Prod:* Waller, Fred "Fats." *Co:* Minoco Production. *Dist:* Soundies Distributing Corporation. *Cast:* Gus Van.

Recorded by Ray Bloch and His Orchestra. (Soundies / B&W / Short / Sound / Musical / 11/3/41.)

725 The Magic Garden 1952

Dir: Swanson, Donald. *Prod:* Swanson, Donald. *Co:* Swan Films. *Cast:* Tommy Ramokgopa, Dolly Rathebe, Harriet Qubeka, David Mukwanazi.

Screenplay: Ferdinand Webb, Donald Swanson, C. Pennington Richards. (South Africa / Feature / Sound / B&W / 16mm / 63 min.)

"The misadventures of a thief who steals forty pounds from an old man who has just donated it to the church. How the money affects the various people who come in contact with it is the core of this light comedy"— Klotman.

726   Mama Had a Little Lamb
1944
Co: RCM Production. *Dist:* Soundies Distributing Corporation. *Cast:* The Three Peppers. (Soundies 18408 / B&W / Short / Sound / Musical.)

727   Mama, I Wanna Make Rhythm 1943
Co: RCM Production. *Dist:* Soundies Distributing Corporation. *Cast:* Patterson and Jackson. (Soundies 15108 / B&W / Short / Sound / Musical / 12/30/43.)

728   Mammy's Boy 1932
Prod: Binney, Josh. *Co:* Lichtman Theatre Enterprises. (Short / B&W / Sound.)
Never released.

729   Mamprusi Village 1944
Dir: Pal, John. *Co:* British Information Service. (British / Documentary / Sound / B&W / 1 reel / 16mm / 20 min. / Short.)
"Shows self-government of an African tribal society in the mid-1940s. Depicts village life in an agricultural community of the African Gold Coast where the governing body composed of native chiefs must handle such complex matters as flood control, taxes, education, police, and transportation — all carried out in spite of the fact that very few of the populace can read and write" — Klotman.

730   The Man from Texas 1921
Dir: Wilson, Ben D. *Prod:* Wilson, Ben D. *Co:* Ben Roy Productions. (Western / Silent / B&W / Feature / 5 reels.)

731   The Man in Ebony 1918
Co: T.H.B. Walker's Colored Pictures. *Cast:* Jack Johnson. (Silent / B&W / Short / 3 reels.)

732   Man of the Worlds (Kisenga, Man of Africa) 1946
Dir: Dickinson, Thorold. *Co:* Two Cities Film Company. *Cast:* Robert Adams, Eric Portman (white), Orlando Martins, Sam Blake, Napolean Florent, Viola Thompson, Eseza Makumbi, Tunji Williams, Phyllis Calvert (white), Rudolph Evans, Uriel Porter.

Filmed mainly in a London studio. This film was released in the United States as *Kisenga, Man of Africa* in 1952. Screenplay: Joyce Cary, Herbert Victor, Thjorold Dickinson. (British / Feature / B&W / Sound.)
"The film depicts the struggle against fear and superstition that an educated Black African faces upon his return to his country, Tanganyika. Robert Adams plays Kisenga, Orlando Martins, the witch doctor" — Klotman.

733   Mandy's Choice 1914
Prod: Haynes, Hunter C. *Co:* Afro-American Film Company. *Cast:* Charles Gilpin, Billy Harper, Sarah Green Byrd. (Silent / B&W / Short.)

734   A Man's Duty 1919
Prod: Johnson, George P. *Co:* Lincoln Motion Picture Company. *Dist:* George P. Johnson. *Cast:* Clarence Brooks, Webb King, Tasmania Darden, Ethel Gray, Eva Johnson, Anita Thompson. W.H. Saunders, Mrs. Conners, Frank White, Jeanette Criner. (Feature / B&W / Silent.)
"Wealthy man about town, Richard Beverly, and Hubert Gordon are rivals for the affections of Myra Lewis. A drunken binge, contrived by Hubert to embarrass Richard in public, winds up with Richard spending the night in a bordello with a girl named Helen. Learning of the trick the next day, Richard, seeking revenge, engages Hubert in a fight. Hubert hits his head on a rock when he falls down after being hit by Richard. Richard, thinking that he has killed Hubert, flees to a distant city where he spends his time drinking booze all day. It is there that Richard meets Merriam Givens …. Hoping to clear himself of his disgrace so that he can marry Merriam, he writes home and learns that, although Hubert survived the accident, the prostitute Helen is pregnant as a result of their night together in the bordello. Richard confides in Merriam who tells him that the child she has raised is not hers and that he should return home to marry Helen. Upon Richard's return, he learns that Hubert, who has married Myra, is really the father of Helen's unborn child. Richard summons Merriam to marry him" — Henry Sampson's *Blacks in Black and White*.

735 Mantan Messes Up 1946

Prod: Toddy, Ted. *Co:* Lucky Star Productions. *Dist:* Toddy Pictures. *Cast:* Mantan Moreland, Monte Hawley, Lena Horne, Eddie Green, Buck and Bubbles, Nina Mae McKinney, Red Caps, Neva Peoples, Bo Jinkins, Four Tones. (B&W / Short / Comedy / Sound.)

736 Mantan Runs for Mayor 1946

Prod: Toddy, Ted. *Co:* Lucky Star Productions. *Dist:* Toddy Pictures Company. *Cast:* Mantan Moreland, Flournoy E. Miller, Ruth Jones, John Dee, Jr., Fred D. Gordon, Johnny Lee, Terry Knight, McKinley Reeves. (B&W / Comedy / Feature / Sound.)

737 Marching On! 1943

Dir: Williams, Spencer. *Prod:* Sack, Alfred. *Co:* Astor Pictures Corporation. *Dist:* Astor Pictures Corporation. *Cast:* Lawrence "Pepper" Neely, Georgia Kelly, Hugo Martin, Emmett Jackson, Mickey McZekkashing, Clarissa Deary, Myra Hemmings, Wash & Wimpy, George T. Sutton, L.K. Smith.

Written by: Spencer Williams. Photography: Clark Ramsey. Recorded by: H.W. Kier, R.C.A. High Fidelity. This film was re-released in 1944, titled *Where's My Man To-Nite*, (music acts added). (Sound / B&W / 83 min. / 7,516 ft. / Semi-Documentary / Feature.)

Williams' film depicts black soldiers in a fictional story against the background of army life in the all-black 25th Infantry. A young man fighting with the emotional baggage of being in the service, black and afraid of war eventually deserts the army. While escaping on a freight train, he befriends a hobo. Both jump off the moving train to escape being detected; the hobo is hurt and dies. Before the hobo dies, it is revealed that the hobo was the soldier's dad, who had been reported killed in World War I. Instead he had been roaming around with amnesia all along. The young man passes out in the desert and unbelievably is found by his grandfather. He and his grandfather accidently discover a Japanese radio post in the mountains. Grandfather is killed during a struggle with the Japanese, as other U.S. soldiers arrive to save the day. The AWOL soldier is given a second chance as he has seen the err of his ways. This film stresses patriotism and the contribution of blacks to the war effort.

738   Marcus Garland 1928

Dir: Micheaux, Oscar. *Prod:* Micheaux, Oscar. *Co:* Micheaux Film Corporation. *Dist:* Micheaux Film Corporation. *Cast:* Salem Tutt Whitney, Amy Birdsong. (Feature / Silent / B&W.)

A film based on Marcus Garvey's life.

739   Maria Elena 1943

Co: RCM Production. *Dist:* Soundies Distributing Corporation. *Cast:* Johnny Long and His Orchestra. (Soundies / B&W / Short / Sound / Musical / 12/13/43.)

740   Marian Anderson 1953

Prod: World Artist, Inc. *Co:* World Artist, Inc. *Cast:* Marian Anderson. (16mm / Sound / B&W / 1 reel / 27 min. / Short / Documentary.)

Presents Marian Anderson as she sings a program of songs in rehearsal as well as on the concert stage. Provides details of her life, including her birthplace, friends that have helped her, her farm home in Connecticut, and the honors bestowed upon her.

741   The Matchless Key 1921

Co: White Film Corporation.

Film was supposed to be produced as a 15-part serial. First chapter shown in April 1921, at the Lincoln Theatre in Baltimore, Maryland. There is no record of production after the 7th episode. (B&W / Silent / Short / 7 episodes / Serial.)

742   Mayor of Jimtown 1929

Co: Metro-Goldwyn-Mayer. *Cast:* Aubrey Lyles, Flournoy E. Miller.

Screenplay: Aubrey Lyles and Flournoy E. Miller. (Silent / B&W.)

Miller and Lyles are the mayor and police chief, respectively, of Jimtown with dialect-dialogue in this MGM musical comedy.

743   Meet the Maestro 1938

Co: Paramount. *Cast:* Cab Calloway, Isham Jones and His Orchestra. (B&W / Sound / 9 min. / Musical / Short.)

This musical short features the above musicians as Cab Calloway plays "Zah-zuh-zag."

744   Meetin' Time 1943

Co: RCM Production. *Dist:* Soundies Distributing Corporation. *Cast:* The Radio Aces. (Soundies 11708 / B&W / Short / Sound / Musical / 5/10/43.)

745   Melancholy Dame 1929

Dir: Gillstrom, Arvis. *Prod:* Christie, Al. *Co:* Christie Film Company. *Dist:* Paramount. *Cast:* Evelyn Preer, Edward Thompson, Spencer Williams, Roberta Hyson, Charles Olden, John Williams.

First black short sound film. Screenplay: Octavus Roy Cohen. Claude Collins sang a specially written song by Sterling Sherwin "Melancholy Mama." Reviews: *The Motion Picture World,* 4/20/29, and *Film Daily,* 2/3/29. (35mm / B&W / Sound / 2 reels / Comedy / Short.)

The story relates the troubles of "Permanent Williams," darktown cabaret owner, who is forced to hire his divorced wife and her new husband as entertainers. His second wife doesn't relish the fact, so, in the words of Cohen, "troubles is somethin' Permanent ain't got nothing else exceptin'."

746   Melodic Spirituals 1950

Co: United Artists. *Dist:* United Artists. *Cast:* Jessie Hairston, Choral Group.

Songs of America series. Songs: "Roll Jordan, Roll" and "Walk Together Children." (Short / B&W / Musical / Sound.)

747   Melodies Reborn 1950

Co: United Artists. *Cast:* Jessie Hairston, Choral Group.

Songs of America series. Songs: "Steal Away to Jesus" and "In Dat Great Gittin' Up Mornin'." (Musical / B&W / Short / Sound.)

748   Melody Makers Series 1932

Co: Wardour Films. *Cast:* Frank Wilson. (B&W / Short / Sound.)

Stephen Foster's songs are background for familiar shots of blacks "in the quarter." Wilson is the only one of the black company to get a credit line.

749 Melody Takes a Holiday
1943

Co: RCM Production. *Dist:* Soundies Distributing Corporation. *Cast:* The Harlem Honeys, Dewey Brown. (Soundies 6M2 / B&W / Short / Sound / Musical / 10/29/43.)

750 Memorial Services at the Tomb of "Prince Hall" 1922

Co: Peacock Photoplay Company. (Newsreel / Short / B&W / Silent.)

751 Memories and Melodies 1935

Prod: Patric, Fitz. *Co:* Metro-Goldwyn-Mayer. (Short / B&W / Sound.)

752 Mercy, the Mummy Mumbled 1917

Dir: Phillips, R.G. *Co:* Ebony Film Company. *Cast:* Ebony Players (Sam Robinson, Samuel "Sambo" Jacks, Will Starks, Julia Mason, Bert Murphy, Evon Skekeeter, Mildred Price, Walter Brogsdale, Robert Duree, Frank Pollard, George Lewis Stock Company). (Short / B&W / Silent / 11 min. / FEA 6621.)

753 Merrie Howe Carfe 1939

Co: Argus Pictures. *Cast:* Freddie Jackson, Jeni LeGon, Monte Hawley. (B&W / Sound / Short.)

754 Message from Dorothy Maynor 1949

Prod: Yorke, Emmerson. *Co:* National Tuberculosis Association. *Cast:* Dorothy Maynor, Hall Johnson Choir.

Public Service Film. Songs: "Brahms Lullaby," "Nobody Knows the Trouble I've Seen," and "America the Beautiful." (Sound / Short / B&W / Musical / Newsreel.)

Dorothy Maynor issues a message on the cure and diagnosis of tuberculosis and the Hall Johnson Choir sings a few songs.

755 The Midnight Ace 1928

Dir: Wade, John H. *Prod:* Micheaux, Swan. *Co:* Dunbar Film Corporation. *Cast:* A.B. Comathiere, Mabel Kelly, Susie Sutton, William Edmondson, Walter Cormick, Oscar Roy Dugas, Roberta Brown, Bessie Givens, Anthony Gaytzera, Pete Smith, Clarence Penalver, War Day.

Of 15 in cast, 5 were white. Susie Sutton was Miss Lincoln of the Howard-Lincoln 1927 football classic. Film shot in Warner Bros. studio in Brooklyn, N.Y. Previews in the *Philadelphia Tribune*, 6/28/28, and the *Chicago Defender*, 3/31/28. (Silent / B&W / Feature / 7 reels.)

The ace of spades is the only clue in a series of masterful robberies. The police are baffled, but a young detective is given a clue by the crook's jealous wife. The criminal's wife has found a picture of her husband's girlfriend who just happens to be the detective's girlfriend also. The unexpected clue leads to the arrest and daring escape from court by the crook who lives long enough to drive off a cliff during his getaway. Of course, the detective gets the girl.

756 Midnight Lodger 1930

Co: Vitagraph. *Cast:* Aubrey Lyles, Flournoy E. Miller. (Sound / B&W / Short.)

This film is about the treasurer of a black lodge who is confronted by members about missing lodge funds, interspersed with songs by lodge members.

757   Midnight Menace 1946

Dir: Binney, Josh. *Co:* All-American News. *Cast:* Sybil Lewis, Lollypop Jones, George Wiltshire, James Dunsmore, Harold Coke, Leon Poke, Amos Austin, Alma Jones, Jimmy Walker, Black Diamond Dollies. (B&W / Feature / Sound.)

758   Midnight Shadow 1939

Dir: Randol, George. *Prod:* Randol, George. *Co:* George Randol Productions. *Dist:* Sack Amusements Enterprises. *Cast:* Frances Redd, Pete Webster, Clinton Rosemond, Jesse Lee Brooks, John Criner, Buck Woods, Richard Bates, Charles Hawkins, Ruby Dandridge, Napoleon Simpson, Edward Brandon, Ollie Ann Robinson.

Cinematographer: Arthur Reid. Sound: Carson Jowett. Editor: Robert Jahns. Production manager: Wilfred Black. Assistant director: Charles Hawkins. Music director: Johnny Lang, with Lou Porter. Film editor: Robert Jahn. (54 min. / 4,833 ft. / 35mm / B&W / Sound / 6 reels / Feature / FEA 4259–4264.)

A light murder mystery. A man is killed while sleeping by a midnight intruder. The murderer steals a deed to land and oil fields from the dead man. Amateur detectives bumble through the case and manage to capture the thief and murderer.

759   A Milk-Fed Hero 1918

Co: Ebony Film Company. *Dist:* General Film Company. *Cast:* Ebony Players (Sam Robinson, Samuel "Sambo" Jacks, Will Starks, Julia Mason, Bert Murphy, Evon Skekeeter, Mildred Price, Walter Brogsdale, Robert Duree, Frank Pollard, George Lewis Stock Company).

Possibly re-released in 1918 as the *Comeback of Barnacle Bill.* (Short / Silent / B&W / 2 reels.)

"This film is chock full of slap-stick. The scenes are laid out on a farm and concern the activities of a farmhand in love with the daughter of the farmer. A rebuff from the girl sets the suicide microbe working, but [he] cannot hit himself with a shotgun. The report, however, frightens two burglars in the act of dividing their spoils and the farmhand finds the loot and assumes ownership. He finally saves the farm by paying off the mortgage and is awarded the daughter and the farmer's gratitude"— Review from *Exhibitors Herald,* 2/22/17.

760   Miller and Lyles 1929

Co: Vitaphone. *Cast:* Flournoy E. Miller, Aubrey Lyles. (Comedy / Musical / B&W / Sound.)

Songs: "Shuffle Along," "Rang Tang," "The Great Temptations," and "Runnin' Wild."

A comedy skit called "They Know Their Groceries" is performed.

761   The Millionaire 1927

Dir: Micheaux, Oscar. *Prod:* Micheaux, Oscar. *Co:* Micheaux Film Corporation. *Dist:* Micheaux Pictures Corporation. *Cast:* Grace Smith, Lawrence Criner, Lionel Monagas, Cleo Desmond, William Edmondson, Vera Bracker, S.T. Jacks, E.G. Tatum, Robert S. Abbott.

Micheaux filmed a cabaret scene in this movie using the patrons of the Plantation Cafe in Chicago, Illinois. Review in the *Philadelphia Tribune,* 11/24/27. (Feature / B&W / Silent.)

This unusual story is about a Negro solider of fortune in South America. After years of working and accumulating his fortune he returns to America, where he meets a young lady. Unfortunately, the woman he likes is part of a crime family and she is used in a plot to steal his fortune.

762   Mills' Blue Rhythm Band 1933

Co: Vitaphone. *Cast:* Mills' Blue Rhythm Band, Fredi Washington, Hamtree Harrington. (B&W / Sound / Short / 10 min.)

"Lively music, hot singing and fast dancing make this a very entertaining subject of its kind. After a night club introduction, Hamtree Harrington takes the gang up to his Harlem penthouse apartment for a rent party, and several more numbers are put on there"— review from *Film Daily,* 11/13/33.

763   A Minister's Temptation 1919

Co: Democracy Photoplay Corporation. (Short / Silent / B&W.)

764   Minnie the Moocher 1932
Prod: Fleischer, Max. *Co:* Warner Bros.
Cast: Cab Calloway. (16mm / Sound / 1 reel /
B&W / 6–8 min. / Animated Short.)

Betty Boop cartoon series, with characters
swinging and singing using Cab's voice and
band.

765   Minnie the Moocher 1942
Co: Minoco Production. *Dist:* Soundies
Distributing Corporation. *Cast:* Cab Calloway
and His Orchestra: Lamar Wright, Russell
Smith, Shad Collins, Jonah Jones (trumpets);
Keg Johnson, Tyree Glenn, Quentin Jackson
(trombones); Jerry Blake, Hilton Jefferson,
Andrew Brown, Teddy McRae, Walter
Thomas (reeds); Benny Payne (piano); Danny
Barker (guitar); Milt Hilton (brass); Cozy Cole
(drums). (Soundies 5405 / B&W / Short /
Sound / Musical / 2/9/42.)

766   Minstrel Days 1929
Co: Vitaphone. *Cast:* Mosby's Blue Blow-
ers Band (whites in blackface). (Sound /
B&W / Short.)

767   Minstrel Days 1930
Prod: Laemmle, Carl, Jr. *Co:* Universal Stu-
dios. *Dist:* Comedy House. *Cast:* Nine Mae
McKinney, Scott and Whaley, 8 Black Streaks,
Debroy Somers and His Band (white), Harry
Pepper's "White Coons." (Variety / B&W /
Sound / Feature / Comedy.)

A typical musical variety minstrel show,
with whites and blacks in blackface. Vaudeville on film. The highlight is the young and
pretty Nina Mae McKinney singing.

768   Miracle in Harlem 1948
Dir: Kemp, Jack. *Prod:* Goldberg, Jack.
Co: Herald Pictures, Inc. *Dist:* Screen Guild
Productions. *Cast:* Juanita Hall and Her
Choir, Savannah Churchill, Sheila Guyse,
Sybil Lewis, Hilda Offley, William Greaves,
Stepin Fetchit, Lawrence Criner, Jack Carter,
Monte Hawley, Alfred "Slick" Chester, Ken-
neth Freeman, Creighton Thompson, Milton
Williams, Ruble Blakey, Laveda Carter,
Norma Sheperd, Lynn Proctor Trio.

Preview in the *New York Age,* 10/25/47.
Original story and Screenplay: Vincent Valentini. Editor: Don Drucker. Musical director:

Jack Shaindlin. Cinematographer: Don Malkames. Sound: Nelson Minnerly. Wardrobe:
Ann Blazier. Makeup: Dr. Rudolph G. Liszt.
Technical advisor: J.M. Lehrfeld. Musical
supervision: John Gluskin. Dialogue director:
James Light. (73 min. / 6,569 ft. / 16mm /
B&W / Sound / 3 reels [spliced from original
8] / Feature / FCA 3030–3032 or FEB 1274–
1282.)

Dear Sweet old Aunt Hattie and her niece
run a candy store that is in competition with a
major candy store chain. Disliking competition,
the candy store chain owner's son swindles
Aunt Hattie out of her candy store. Eventually, the chain-store owner is found murdered and his son is fingered as the culprit.
The scene that fingers the son has Aunt Hattie rising from a coffin and scaring out a confession.

769   The Mis-Directed Kiss pre-
     1910
(B&W / Silent / Short / FLA 4725.)

770   Miss Jewett and the Baker Family of Negroes 1905

Co: American Mutoscope / Biograph. (Newsreel / Documentary / B&W / Short / Silent.)

Footage of a well-dressed white woman visiting a poor black family at their cabin.

771   The Mississippi 1934

Dir: Mack, Roy. *Co:* Vitaphone. (B&W / Sound / Short.)

"This is classed as 'tone journey' with Ferde Grofe's tuneful composition 'Mississippi Suite' employed as the inspiration. It is one of the most delightful shorts produced in many months and despite its highly artistic treatment, it cannot fail to please all types of audiences. The mood of the Mississippi has been woven into the pictures which move with classic finese from Indians to Huckleberry Finn, from steamboat darkies to the plantation scenes. It is a restful yet entertaining, enjoyable and impressive"— review from *Film Daily*, 1/17/34.

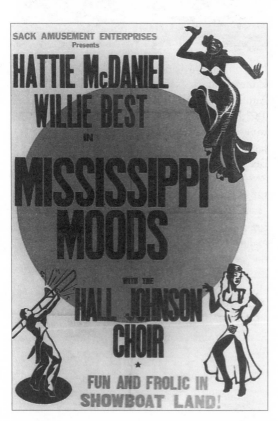

772   Mississippi Moods 1937

Dir: Goodwins, Leslie. *Prod:* Gilroy, Bert. *Co:* RKO Radio Pictures. *Cast:* Hall Johnson Choir, Hattie McDaniel, Willie Best.

Story: Gay Stevens, Jester Hairston. Film editor: John Lockert. Music: Hall Johnson. Photography: Harry Wild.

RKO Radio Pictures, Inc. (2 reels / Sound / B&W / Short / Musical.)

"Plenty of good Negro atmosphere, with the choral numbers all the way through and an appropriate and humorous story vein keeping a neat suspense sustained to the end"— excerpt of review from *Film Daily*, 7/23/37.

773   Mistaken Identity 1941

Dir: Quigley, George P. & Arthur Leonard. *Prod:* Quigley, George P. & Arthur Leonard. *Co:* Century Productions. *Cast:* Nelle Hill, George Oliver, Bill Dillard, Ruth Cobbs, Ken Renard, Andrew Maize, Bob Brown, Pinky Williams, Alston & Young, Skippy Williams and His Jazz Band.

Screenplay: Victor Vicas & Norman Borisoff. Photography: George Weber. Sound recording: Robert E. Rosmen. Based on story by George Freedland. Original music: Skippy Williams. (Feature / B&W / Sound / 60 min. / FDA 3303.)

A mystery musical, set against the background of a big city nightclub. It is about a murder that occurs in a nightclub and its possible connection to a singer's relationship with an escaped convict.

774   Mr. Atom's Bomb 1949

Dir: Green, Eddie. *Co:* Sepia-Art Pictures Company. *Dist:* Sepia Film Company. *Cast:* Eddie Green, Gene Ware. (35mm / Sound / B&W / Short / 20 min. / FEA 4378-4379.)

775   Mr. Black Magic 1956

Co: Universal-International. *Cast:* Billy Daniels, Eileen Barton, Benny Payne, Giselle Szony, The Cabots. (Sound / B&W.)

776   Mr. Creeps 1938

Co: Toddy Pictures Company. *Cast:* Mantan Moreland, Flournoy E. Miller. (B&W / Sound / Comedy.)

777   Mr. Jackson from Jacksonville 1945

Co: RCM Production. *Dist:* Soundies Distributing Corporation. *Co:* June Richmond. (Soundies 89108 / B&W / Short / Sound / Musical / 6/4/45.)

778   Mr. Miller's Economics 1916

Co: Triangle Film Company. (Silent / B&W / Short.)

A black washerwoman steals clothes from "the big house" for her husband's appearance at an "Afro-Aryon Ball."

779   Mr. Smith Goes Ghost 1940

Dir: Markham, Dewey and Heckle. *Prod:* Markham, Dewey and Heckle. *Co:* Markham and Heckle. *Dist:* Toddy Pictures Company. *Cast:* Johnny Taylor, Florence O'Brien, Lawrence Criner, Dewey "Pigmeat" Markham, Monte Hawley, Lilian Randolph, Vernon McCalla, Millie Monroe.

Screenplay by Dewey Markham. (B&W / Sound / Short.)

TODDY PICTURES CO. PRESENTS
'PIGMEAT' MARKHAM

You'll Quiver
You'll Chill
You'll Roar
With Him
—IN—

"MR. SMITH GOES GHOST"

A Featurette with
LAWRENCE CRINER
JOHNNY TAYLOR
FLORENCE O'BRIEN

HOT DIGGITY BELLY LAFFS GALORE!

© TODDY PICTURES COMPANY 723 Seventh Avenue New York

780   Mr. Washington Goes to Town 1940

Dir: Buell, Jed. *Prod:* Buell, Jed / James K. Friedrich. *Co:* Dixie National Pictures, Inc. *Dist:* Toddy Pictures Company. *Cast:* Flournoy E. Miller, Mantan Moreland, Maceo B. Sheffield, Arthur Ray, Margarette Whitten, Clarence Morehouse, Monte Hawley, Zoreta Steptoe, Florence O'Brien, John Lester Johnson, DeForrest Covan, Edward Boyd, Clarence Hargraves, Johnny Taylor, Walter Knox, Geraldine Whitfield, Cleo Desmond, Charles Hawkins, Harold Garrison.

Review in *New York Amsterdam News* by Lawrence F. LaMar, 4/20/40, the *Pittsburgh Courier* by Earl J. Morris, 3/20/40, and the *Philadelphia Tribune*, 7/27/40. (Sound / B&W / 62 min. / Feature.)

Prisoner Syracuse (Moreland) finds he inherited a hotel, falls asleep and dreams up some very weird, frightening hotel guests. He awakens to being kicked out of the jail and when his cell mate says "Let's go to your new hotel," he replies, "I just come from that hotel and I don't want nothing more to do with it."

781   Mr. X Blues 1945

Co: RCM Production. *Dist:* Soundies Distributing Corporation. *Cast:* Cecil Scott and His Orchestra. (Soundies 11M3 / B&W / Short / Sound / Musical / 6/4/45.)

782   Mistletoe 1946

Dir: Anderson, Leonard. *Prod:* Alexander, William D. *Co:* Alexander Production. *Dist:* Soundies Distributing Corporation. (Soundies / B&W / Short / Sound / Musical / 12/30/46.)

783   A Modern Cain 1921

Prod: Fife, J.W. *Co:* J.W. Fife Productions. *Dist:* Comet Film Exchange. *Cast:* Norman Ward, Vivian Carrols, Theodore Williams, Harriett Harris, Fred Williams, Z.V. Young, Youth Mason, Munzell Everett.

Released by Comet Film Exchange (1331 Vine St. Phila.) (Feature / B&W / Silent / 6 reels.)

John and Paul, twin brothers, are left orphans when very young by the death of their father, who appoints his brother guardian over the two boys. John is of a meek, humble nature, with a sterling character that believes in doing good to his fellow man. Paul, on the contrary, is avaricious and a genuine ne'er-do-well. The boys grow up and are co-partners in a business that their uncle has established with the money left them by their father. Incidentally, they are both in love with a girl who realizes the sterling worth of John and the mean character of Paul. Paul becomes enraged one day while they are out riding in an automobile and throws his brother over a cliff. He then comes back home and reports him missing. The family mourns John as dead, and Paul forces his attentions upon the girl almost to the point of marrying her. In the meantime John is rescued, but, due to the injury to his head, he forgets who he is and goes through life more or less half-witted, until one day a doctor happens to see him and performs a very delicate operation which cures John. John then sets out to search for his old friends, and returns to his family. Paul in the meantime, becomes a dope fiend. Torn by nightly dreams, when weird figures appear to him, he finally, one day, becomes so excited and nervous that his already weakened frame gives way, and he dies in a terrible delirium. Just about this time John has found his people again, and returns home to find his brother dead. He then marries his sweetheart, and all ends happily.

784   A Modern Dixie 1938

Co: Twentieth Century–Fox Film Corporation. (Documentary / Newsreel / B&W / Short / Sound.)

The modern lifestyle of the Southern black.

785   Money Talks in Darktown 1916

Co: Historical Feature Films. *Dist:* Ebony Film Company (later). *Cast:* Frank Montgomery, Florence McClain, Bert Murphy, Jimmy Marshall.

This film was later released by the Ebony Film Company (Short / Silent / B&W.)

The plot of this film revolves around Flossie, a charming lady who must decide between suitors. As her suitors spend money and jump through hoops to impress her, she finally lets money decide for her.

786   Monumental Monthly Negro Newsreel 1921

Prod: Monumental Pictures Corporation. *Co:* Monumental Pictures Corporation. *Dist:* True Films Company.

"*News Reel for Negro Movie Fans.* J. Williams Clifford, president of the Monumental Picture Corporation, who states, writing a Negro news weekly entitled the 'Monumental Monthly,' that this subject will be a complete chronicle of the events of concern and interest to the Negroes of the world"— article in *Motion Picture News,* 4/16/21.

787   Monumental News Reel No. 2 1921

Co: Monumental Pictures Corporation. *Dist:* True Films Company. (Newsreel / Documentary / B&W / Short / Silent.)

Negro political leaders are being received by President Harding at the White House in Washington, D.C.; Negro children participating in a May Day Festival in Baltimore,

Maryland; President Harding's black cook; New York Giants (white) baseball team play an exhibition game against a black professional team in Atlanta, Georgia.

788 Moo Cow Boogie 1943

Co: Sack Amusement Enterprises. *Dist:* Sack Amusement Enterprises. *Cast:* Dorothy Dandridge, Stepin Fetchit, Troy Brown, Eugene Jackson. (Musical / Short / B&W / Sound.)

789 Moon Over Harlem 1939

Dir: Ulmer, Edgar G. *Prod:* Ulmer, Edgar G. *Co:* Meteor Film Production Company. *Dist:* Meteor Studios. *Cast:* Cora Green, Bud Harris, Izinetta Wilcox, Earl Hough, Mercedes Gilbert, Walter Richardson, Alec Lovejoy, Rosetta Williams, Slim Thompson, Patrina Waples, Perita Moore, Mariluise Bechet, Freddie Robinson, Archie Cross, William Woodward, John Fortune, Audrey Telbird, Marie Young. John Bunn, Sidney Bechet and His Swing Band, a chorus of 20 girls, Christopher Columbus and His Swing Crew, a choir of 40 voices and a mixed symphony orchestra of 60 pieces.

Associate producer: Peter E. Kassler. Screenplay: Sherle Castle. Story: Frank Wilson. Original story and dialogue: Mathew Mathews. Photography: J. Burdi Conmer & Edward Hyland. Film editor: Jack Kemp. Sound: Edwin Schabbha & Edward Renton. Set: Eugene Woll. Assistant director: Fred Kabble & Gustave Heim. Musical score: Donald Heywood. Score arranged by Lorenzo Caldwel & Kenneth Macombe. Music conductor: Donald Heywood. Reviews in the *New York Amsterdam News*, 8/19/39, and 6/17/39. (16mm / B&W / Sound / 8 reels / 67 min. / Feature / FCA 6892–6893.)

"This film is centered around the pushcart racket in Harlem and the efforts of a young colored lawyer to break it up in opposition to the hoodlums controlled by the stepfather of his sweetheart. Incidental music and nightclub sequences were freely used and some brand new talent was flashed across the screen"— excerpt from the *New York Amsterdam News*, 8/19/39.

790 Mop 1946

Dir: Crouch, William Forest. *Prod:* Crouch, William Forest. *Co:* RCM Production. *Dist:*

Soundies Distributing Corporation. *Cast:* Henry "Red" Allen, J.C. Higginbotham. (Soundies 18M4 / B&W / Short / Sound / Musical / 4/15/46.)

791 Mother 1917

Dir: Foster, William. *Prod:* Foster, William. *Co:* Foster Photoplay Company. *Dist:* William Foster. (Feature / 6 reels / Silent / B&W.)

A six-reel war drama. Some fifty scenes, 4000 people. Presenting the race of this great World's War.

792 A Muffin Lesson 1905

Co: American Mutoscope / Biograph. (Newsreel / Documentary / B&W / Short / Silent.)

Footage showing a cooking class for black women, who are neatly dressed in white uniforms.

793 Murder in Harlem (aka Lem Hawkins' Confession, *The Brand of Cain*) 1935

Dir: Micheaux, Oscar. *Prod:* Micheaux,

Oscar. *Co:* Micheaux Film Corporation. *Dist:* Oscar Micheaux. *Cast:* Andrew Bishop, Dorothy Van Engle, Clarence Brooks, Laura Bowman, Lionel Monagas, Bee Freeman, Alec Lovejoy, Alice B. Russell, "Slick" Chester, Oscar Micheaux, Sandy Burns, Lea Morris, Joie Brown, Jr., Eunice Wilson, Henrietta Loveless, Lorenzo McClane, Helen Lawrence, David Hanna, Byron Shore.

Originally named *Lem Hawkins' Confession* (Alternate title — *The Brand of Cain*), released as *Murder in Harlem.* Micheaux makes appearance as detective. Songs by Eunice Wilson and Clarence Williams. Running time: 98 minutes (8,794 ft.) Using a different cast Micheaux produced a silent version of this picture entitled *The Gunsaulus Mystery.* Story based on the Stanfield murder case. Cinematographer: Charles Levin. Sound: Harry Belock and Armand Schettin. Screenwriter: Oscar Micheaux. Production manager: Charles P. Nason. Art director: Tony Continenta. (B&W / Feature / Sound.)

Myrtle Gunsaulus, a young girl, is found mysteriously murdered in the basement of a factory by Arthur Gilpin, the black janitor, who is arrested and charged with the crime. The incidents surrounding the tragedy, the motive, and the strange manner in which the girl was killed, make the case one of the most complicated the courts had ever confronted.

794   Murder in Swingtime 1937

Dir: Dreifuss, Arthur. *Co:* Movietone Studios / RKO Radio Pictures. *Dist:* Sack Amusement Enterprises. *Cast:* Les Hite and His Orchestra, June Richmond, Ben (Shadrack) Carter, Zack Williams, James Adamson, Joe Bailey, Jess Hurley, Charles Andrews, Rhythm Pals. Guests: Mesdames Hattie Bailey, Henry Prince, Marvin Johnson, Luther "Soldier Boy" Gafford, Louis Cole. Chorus: Lois Bright, Connie Harris, Rosalee Lincoln, Patsy Hunter, Mildred Boud, Louise Robinson, Ethel Boyde, Catherine Atkinson.

Reviews in *Philadelphia Tribune,* 5/20/37, the *California Eagle,* 5/13/37, and the *Film Daily,* 8/20/37. Made at the Conn Studios on Santa Monica Boulevard in Hollywood. (Short / 17 min. / Musical / B&W / 1 reel / 35mm.)

"The piece is as unique as its name, and instead of being a pot-pourri of tunes as an excuse for the band to play, it has a definite plot that moves right along on the waves of

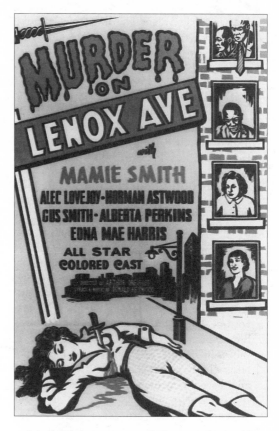

music until the unexpected climax. The lively sketch includes a crime, the arrest, trial by jury and the confession"—*Philadelphia Independent,* 5/23/37.

795   Murder on Lenox Ave. 1941

Dir: Dreifuss, Arthur. *Prod:* Dreifuss, Arthur / Jack Goldberg. *Co:* Colonade Pictures Corporation. *Cast:* Sidney Easton, Alberta Perkins, Alec Lovejoy, Dene Larry, J. Augustus Smith, Ernie Ransom, Earl Sydnor, Norman Astwood, Mamie Smith, George Williams, Herman Green, Edna Mae Harris, Cristola Williams, Emily Santos, Flo Lee, Wahneta San.

Original story: Frank Wilson. Screen adaptation: Vincent Valentini & Bryna Ivens. Music and Lyrics: Donald Heywood. Orchestral arrangements: Ken Macomber. Cinematographer: George Weber. Unit manager: Irving C. Miller. Costumes: Als Stevens. Art direction: William Salter. Sound: Ed Fenton. Assistant director: Charles Wasserman. Editor: Robert Crandall. (16mm / B&W / Sound / 2 reels / 65 min. / Feature/ FCA 8213–8214.)

A promoter in Harlem forms a Better Business League, but is kicked out after being accused of mismanagement. They replace him with Pa, a respected man in the community. Ola, Pa's daughter, is in love with a teacher, but Pa wants her to marry Jim (Ernie Ransom), who is loved by Mercedes. Ola marries the teacher and moves down South. Meanwhile, the former league president plots to get even with Pa. He gets Jim to plant a bomb in the hall where Pa will be speaking. The bomb is discovered and removed, but Ola reads of the threat and returns from the South. Ola arrives at the hall while her father is giving a speech denouncing the attempt on his life. As a last desperate attempt to regain power, one of the conspirators tries to shoot Pa, butco-conspirator Jim steps in the way of the bullet and is killed.

796   Murder Rap 1948

Prod: Million Dollar Productions. *Co:* Goldseal Productions. *Dist:* Consolidated National Film Exchange. *Cast:* Monte Hawley, Jeni LeGon, Jack Carter, Harlem Dead End Kids (Freddie Baker, Eugene Jackson, Paul White, Eddie Lynn, Deforrest Covan), Lovey Lane, Harry Levette, Robert Webb, Guernsey Morrow, Herbert Skinner, Arthur Ray.

Murder Rap, 1948, is the re-released *Take My Life*, 1941. (B&W / Feature / Sound.)

The Harlem Dead End Kids are brought to the brink of tragedy when one of their gang members is framed for murder. They see the error of their ways and join the United States Army and learn what it's like to be real men.

797   Murder with Music 1941

Dir: Quigley, George P. *Prod:* Quigley, George P. *Co:* Century Productions. *Dist:* Sack Amusement Enterprises. *Cast:* Bob Howard, Nellie Hill, Milton Williams, Ken Renard, George Oliver, Bill Dillard, Marjorie Oliver, Ruth Cobb, Andrew Maize, Noble Sissle and His Orchestra, Pinky Williams and the Skippy Williams Orchestra, Dance teams Alston and Young, Johnson and Johnson.

Based on a story by George Freedland. Pho-

tography: George Webber & John Visconti. Sound: Robert Rosien. Screenplay: Victor Vicas, Norman Borisoff, Gus Smith. Music: Sidney Easton, Gus Smith, Skippy Williams. (16mm / Sound / B&W / 2 reels / 59 min. / Feature / FEA 5461 / FEA 6060–6064.)

Typical musical film of the forties. The story is about a reporter's jealousy which leads to murder. The plot is thin and the picture is primarily concerned with musical and dance numbers by the performers.

798   Music Hath Harms 1929

Dir: Graham, Walter. *Prod:* Christie, Al. *Co:* Christie Film Company. *Dist:* Paramount. *Cast:* Evelyn Preer, Edward Thompson, Spencer Williams, Florian Slappey, Zenia Sprawl, Sam Ginn, Lawyer Cheev, Roscoe Griggers, Harry Porter, Leon Hereford, Nathan Curry, Roberta Hyson, Harry Tracy.

Original story by Octavus Roy Cohn. Screenplay and Assistant director: Spencer Williams. (Sound / B&W / 2 reels / Comedy / Short / 20 min.)

Stereotypical dialect. This film is about a scam where Spencer Williams, an orchestra leader, is offered $500 to play two clarinet solos. Not knowing how to play the clarinet he hires a musician to play under the stage while he lip-synchs the playing, except when he starts the musician plays a saxophone instead. In the end he gives his newly earned money to his new honey. They get married and she opens her new beauty shop.

799   My, Ain't That Somethin' 1944

Co: RCM Production. *Dist:* Soundies Distributing Corporation. *Cast:* Gene Rodgers. (Soundies 18708 / B&W / Short / Sound / Musical.)

800   My Bottle Is Dry 1946

Dir: Crouch, William Forest. *Prod:* Crouch, William Forest. *Co:* Filmcraft Production. *Dist:* Soundies Distributing Corporation. *Cast:* June Richmond. (Soundies 24M2 / B&W / Short / Sound / Musical / 10/7/46.)

801   My First Love 1921

Prod: Dones, Sidney P. *Co:* Bookertee Investment Company. *Cast:* Leon Hereford, Harry Porter, Evelyn Preer. (Silent / B&W / Feature.)

802   My Girl Loves a Sailor 1943

Co: RCM Production. *Dist:* Soundies Distributing Corporation. *Cast:* Johnny Long and His Orchestra. (Soundies / B&W / Short / Sound / Musical / 8/2/43.)

803   My New Gown 1944

Dir: Burger, Hans. *Prod:* Goldberg, Jack & Dave. *Co:* Hollywood Pictures Corporation. *Dist:* Soundies Distributing Corporation. *Cast:* Lena Horne, Albert Ammons, Teddy Wilson and His Orchestra (Emmett Berry, Jimmy Hamilton, Benny Morton, John Williams, J.C. Heard, Pete Johnson).

Excerpted from the Hollywood Productions short, *Boogie Woogie Dream* (1942). (Soundies / 21M1 / B&W / Short / Sound / Musical / 12/30/44.)

804   My Song Goes Forth 1947

Prod: Church, Gilbert. *Co:* Ambassador Films. *Cast:* Paul Robeson. (Documentary / Short / Sound / B&W.)

805   Mystery in Swing 1940

Dir: Dreifuss, Arthur. *Prod:* Dreifuss, Arthur / Jack Goldberg. *Co:* Aetna Films Corporation. *Dist:* International Roadshow. *Cast:* Monte Hawley, Margarette Whitten, Edward Thompson, Tommie Moore, Jesse Lee Brooks, Flournoy E. Miller, Josephine Edwards, Sybil Lewis, Robert Webb, Buck Woods, Thomas Southern, Alfred Grant, Halley Harding, Leonard Christmas, Charles Andrews, Earl Morris, John Lester Johnson, The Four Toppers, Ceepee Johnson and His Orchestra.

Screenplay: Arthur Hoerl. Additional dialogue: Flournoy E. Miller and William Werckenthien. Entire score played by Cee Pee Johnson and His Orchestra. Cinematographer: Mack Stengler. Technical direction: Ross Di Maggio. Coiffures: Ruth. Settings: Louis Diage. Editor: Robert Crandall. Special Effects: Ray Mercer. Sound: Glen Glenn. Associate producer: Rudolph Brent. Songs: "Jump, the Water's Fine," "Let's Go to a Party," "The Killer," "Can't Fool Yourself About Love," "I Want to Play Tom Toms," "Swing It Lightly." Reviews in the *Kansas City Call*, 5/3/40, and the *Chicago Defender*, 3/2/40. (16mm / Sound / B&W / 8 reels / Feature / FCA 5720–5721.)

The story is based on the murder of a "hot" trumpeter, through the placing of poison in the mouthpiece of an instrument. This, in turn, causes a second murder. Both crimes are solved in logical fashion and with a high quotient of accompanying comedy and music.

806   Nat "King" Cole and Joe Adams' Orchestra 1951

Co: Universal-International. *Cast:* Nat "King" Cole and his trio, Joe Adams' Orchestra, Mauri Lynn, Clarence Metcaff. (Sound / 15 min. / Musical / Short.)

Musical short of Joe Adams' Orchestra. Nat "King" Cole sings three numbers, including the popular "Too Young."

807   Nat "King" Cole and Russ Morgan's Orchestra 1953

Co: Universal Studios. *Cast:* Nat "King" Cole, (white — Russ Morgan's Orchestra, Gene Louis Dancers, Mar-Vels, John Elms). (Sound / 18 min. / Musical / Short.)

Nat "King" Cole plays and sings.

808   The Nat "King" Cole Musical Story 1955

Dir: Cowan, Will. *Prod:* Cowan, Will. *Co:* Universal-International. *Cast:* Nat "King" Cole. (Sound / TechniColor / 18 min. / Musical / Short / Featurette.)

Details Cole's discovery and rise to fame. Includes "Sweet Lorraine," "Route 66," and "Straighten Up and Fly Right." Commentary by Jeff Chandler (white).

809   National Negro Business League 1913

Co: Afro-American Film Company. (Newsreel / Documentary / B&W / Short / Silent.)

The National Negro Business League's meeting is held in Philadelphia, Pennsylvania; various black business enterprises in the "City of Brotherly Love."

810   National Negro Business League 1914

Co: Afro-American Film Company. (Newsreel / Documentary / B&W / Silent / Short.)

The National Negro Business League's meeting is held at Muskogee, Oklahoma; various business enterprises in the all-black town of Boley, Oklahoma.

811   Native Son 1951

Dir: Chenal, Pierre. *Prod:* Prades, James. *Co:* Argentina Sono / Classic Pictures / Walter Gould. *Dist:* Classic Pictures, Inc. *Cast:* Richard Wright, Jean Wallace (white), Gloria Madison, Nicholas Joy, Charles Cane, George Rigaud, George Greer, Willa Pearl Curtiss, Gene Michael, Don Dean, Ned Campbell, Ruth Roberts, George Nathanson, George Roos, Lewis MacKenzie, Cecile Lezard, Charles Simmonds, Leslie Straugh, Lidia Alves.

Adapted from the novel by Richard Wright. Screenplay: Pierre Chenal & Richard Wright. Dialogue: Richard Wright. Director of Photography: A.U. Merayo. Location sequences: R.A. Hollahan. Editor: George Garate. Sets: Gori Munoz. Sound recording: Mario Fezia & Charles Mari. Music: John Elhert. (35mm / B&W / Sound / 10 reels / 91 min. / Feature.)

Based on the classic novel by Richard Wright, the film concerns a young black man, Bigger Thomas, who is hardened by life in the slums of Chicago and whose efforts to free himself prove hopeless. Richard Wright plays the role of Bigger; Gloria Madison is Bessie Mears. Footage of Chicago's south side, locale of the novel, is intercut with scenes shot in Argentina.

812   Native Woman Coaling a Ship at St. Thomas, D.W.I. 1895

Co: Thomas A. Edison, Inc. (B&W / Silent / Actualities / Short / FLA 4742.)

813   Native Woman Washing a Negro Baby in Nassau, B.I. 1895

Co: Thomas A. Edison, Inc. (B&W / Silent / Actualities / Short / FLA 3635.)

814   Native Woman Washing Clothes at St. Vincent, D.W.I. 1895

Co: Thomas E. Edison, Inc. (B&W / Silent / Actualities / Short / FLA 3651.)

815   Native Women Coaling a Ship and Scrambling for Money 1895

Co: Thomas A. Edison, Inc. (B&W / Silent / Actualities / Short / FLA 4741.)

816   Natural Born Gambler 1916

Dir: Bitzer, G.W. *Co:* Biograph. *Dist:* General Films Company. *Cast:* Bert Williams.

One of the last films made by Biograph. In this film Williams appears in blackface makeup and black gloves, his usual custom when appearing in vaudeville or in minstrel shows. He was a solo performer in Ziegfeld Follies. (16mm / B&W / Sound added / Silent / 1 reel / 12 min. / Comedy / Short.)

The plot of this comedy is trivial, dealing with a poker game which is raided by the local police. The participants, all black, are hauled to court but all are released with the exception of Williams. While in jail he does his famous routine of playing poker with himself.

817   Natural Born Shooter 1913

Co: Historical Feature Films. *Dist:* Ebony Film Company. *Cast:* Bert Murphy, Frank Montgomery, Florence McClain. (Short / B&W / Silent.)

818   The Negro and Art 1931

Co: National Archives Gift Collection.

Record Group 200 HF series, Harmon Foundation Collection. (Short / B&W / Silent / 1 reel / 16mm.)

A 1931 exhibit of work of Negro artists featuring their work as well as the artists.

819   Negro Colleges in Wartime 1943

Prod: Office of War Information. *Co:* U.S. War Department. *Dist:* Republic Pictures. (Documentary / B&W / Short / Sound / 1 reel / Newsreel / 16mm / 8 min.)

Documents black participation in World War II. This film shows academic, sports, and war preparations at Howard University, Prairie View University and Hampton Institute.

820   Negro Education and Art in the United States 1931

Co: National Archives Gift Collection.

Several films are sublisted under this title.

Among those included are: "Art and Sculpture and Negro Notables." Part of Record Group 200 HF series, Harmon Foundation Collection.

821 The Negro Farmer 1938
Co: U.S. Department of Agriculture. (Documentary / Newsreel / B&W / Short / Sound / 16mm / 30 min.)

The training of Negro farmers at Tuskegee Institute, Tuskegee, Alabama.

822 The Negro in Art 1947
Co: Harmon Foundation Educational Films. (Documentary / B&W / Short / Sound.)

This film is a study on famous black artists.

823 The Negro in Entertainment 1950
Dir: Trent, William, Jr. *Prod:* Glucksman, E.M. *Co:* Chesterfield Company. *Cast:* W.C. Handy, Ethel Waters, Louis Armstrong, Bill Robinson, Duke Ellington, Fats Waller. (16mm / B&W / Sound / 1 reel / 10 min. / Musical / Short.)

A short featuring many black stars, hosted by Bill Lund and Etta Moten, smoking cigarettes. Presented by Chesterfield cigarettes.

824 The Negro in Industry 1952
(Newsreel / Documentary / Short / B&W / Sound.)

Featured are Claude A. Barnett of the Associated Negro Press; Willard Townsend, president of the International Transport Service Employees Union; Horace Sudduth, president of the National Negro Business League; Hon. William Dawson, congressman from Illinois.

825 The Negro in Sports 1950
Dir: Trent, William, Jr. *Prod:* Glucksman, E.M. *Co:* Chesterfield Company. *Cast:* Jesse Owens. (16mm / B&W / Sound / 1 reel / 10 min. / Short / Documentary.)

A Chesterfield cigarette–produced short featuring many black athletes of the period. Narrated by Jesse Owens; Bill Lund acts as host.

826 Negro Life 1929
Co: National Archives Gift Collection.

Part of Record Group 200 HF series, Harmon Foundation Collection.

Film of Negro life in the twenties.

827 The Negro Logging in Louisiana 1921
Co: Dunbar Film Corporation. (Documentary / B&W / Silent / Newsreel / Short.)

Negro loggers at work in Louisiana.

828 The Negro Marches On 1938
Co: Goldberg Productions. *Cast:* Elder Soloman Lightfoot Micheaux. (Newsreel / Documentary / B&W / Sound / Short.)

Evangelist Micheaux figures prominently in this documentary about the "progress" of the Negro.

829 Negro News Reel 1923
Prod: Herman, Will. *Co:* Will Herman. *Cast:* Baptist Convention / U.N.I.A. and Marcus Garvey, local scenes around Los Angeles. (Newsreel / Documentary / B&W / Short / Silent / Narrated.)

Contains segments of a Baptist convention, U.N.I.A. and Marcus Garvey.

830 The Negro Rich Farmer 1922
Co: Dunbar Film Corporation. (Documentary / B&W / Silent / Newsreel / Short.)

Negroes at work in the rice fields in Louisiana.

831 The Negro Sailor 1945
Dir: Lieven, Henry. *Prod:* All-American News. *Co:* U.S. Navy Department. *Cast:* Joel Fluellen, Leigh Whipper, Monica Carter, Joan Douglas, Mildred Boyd, Louise Franklin.

The Negro Sailor was a propaganda film, emphasizing the need for racial harmony for victory. The film was photographed by Navy camera crews and completed at Columbia Studios. Released February 1946. Preview in the *Philadelphia Independent*, 7/14/45. (16mm / B&W / 1 reel / Sound / 29 min. / Documentary.)

Another war propaganda film meant to inspire the colored "folk" to join the Navy. This story shows a young man being bombarded with inspirational speeches and lessons on Negro history as reasons to join the Navy. Scenes of him learning and working as a Navy man are faded in and out, but the biggest inspirational scene is when he sees a colored skipper commanding a Navy oiler.

832   The Negro Soldier 1944

Dir: Capra, Col. Frank / S. Heisler. *Prod:* U.S. War Department. *Co:* U.S. War Department. *Dist:* U.S. War Department. *Cast:* Bertha Wolford, Lt. Norman Ford, Carleton Moss, Clarence Brooks.

Preview in the *Philadelphia Tribune*, 4/1/44, reviews in the *Philadelphia Tribune*, 4/29/44, *Philadelphia Independent*, 4/2/44, 5/7/44, the *New York Age*, 4/20/44, and *Time* magazine, 3/27/44. Lawsuit by the Negro Marches on Company, the *Philadelphia Tribune*, 4/29/44. War Dept. rebuttal in the *Philadelphia Tribune*, 5/13/44. Filmed by the Special Coverage Section of the U.S. Army Signal Corps under the supervision of Col. Frank Capra. Carleton Moss wrote the script and served as technical advisor. Screenplay: Carleton Moss. (16mm / B&W / 4 reels / 45 min. / Dramatized Documentary / Sound.)

Sequences in the film trace the Negro soldier's participation in past wars including: Negro Minutemen; Peter Salem, Negro hero of Bunker Hill; Prince Whipple at Valley Forge with General George Washington; Negro sailors with Perry at Lake Erie; Negro troops with Andrew Jackson at New Orleans; the famous Massachusetts 54th Regiment of volunteers in the Civil War; the 9th and 10th Calvary and 34th Infantry at San Juan Hill; and Negro troops in World War I. In the last part of the film, dramatic continuity is conveyed through a Negro mother who at a church service reads a letter from her son detailing his routine from induction to his preparation for Officer's School.

833   Negro Soldiers Fighting for Uncle Sam 1916

Dir: Jones, Peter P. *Prod:* Jones, Peter P. *Co:* Peter P. Jones Photoplay Company. (Documentary / Newsreel / B&W / Short / Silent.)

The activities of Negro soldiers training for active duty during World War I.

834   The Negro Today 1921

Co: C.B. Campbell Studio. (Newsreel / B&W / Silent / Short.)

835   Nellie, Beautiful Housemaid pre–1910

(B&W / Silent / Short / FLA 4428.)

836   Never Too Old to Swing 1945

Co: RCM Production. *Dist:* Soundies Distributing Corporation. *Cast:* Tiny Grimes and His Orchestra. (Soundies 88008 / B&W / Short / Sound / Musical / 11/5/45.)

837   A New Way to Win 1915

Dir: Lubin, Sigmund. *Prod:* Lubin, Sigmund. *Co:* Lubin Manufacturing Company. *Cast:* Mattie Edwards, "Baby" Mack, John Edwards, D. Roseborough.

Written by E.W. Sargent. Released on 7/20/15. (Silent / B&W / Short / 600 ft.)

"The popular colored players are here exploited in a short farce which they play with their accustomed laughter producing results. Mattie Edwards has never had a better part than that of the mother-in-law who turns the tables on her daughter's husband. He ejects her from the house on account of the reasons which usually go with a mother-in-law. But her daughter gives her courage and promises a speedy reinstatement. Babe, the daughter, then refuses to do any of the work which her mother always did; consequently John, the husband, finds that he has cut off his nose to spite his face. Everything goes wrong. When John finally falls on his knees and begs his mother-in-law to return and again run things to suit herself, the triumphant woman asserts herself in a manner calculated to make the spectator rock with mirth"—*Lubin Bulletin*.

838   News Reel #1 1922

Co: Eagle Film Company. (Newsreel / B&W / Silent / Short.)

Contained many fraternal scenes.

839   News Reel #1 1930

Co: Bilmore Film Company. *Cast:* Chappie Gardner (narrator). (B&W / Short / Sound / Newsreel.)

Subjects include: parachute jump by Mary Doughtry, the only black parachute jumper of the American Aviation School; and Charles James' flight at Curtis Field.

840   News Reel #2 1922

Co: Eagle Film Company. (Newsreel / B&W / Silent / Short.)

Fraternal uniform ranks of two different orders and the first Negro Motion Picture Ball and Cabaret made in St. Louis.

841 The Nigger in the Woodpile
1904

Co: Biograph. (B&W / Silent / Short / FLA 5118.)

A white landowner discovers blacks (whites in blackface) stealing wood from his woodpile. To end this he sticks dynamite in the end of a log and waits for the blacks to steal wood. Eventually the blacks take the wood for their fire and when lit they're blown to bits. The owner is very satisfied with the results.

842 Night Club Girl (One Dark Night) 1944

Dir: Popkin, Leo C. *Co:* Million Dollar Productions. *Dist:* Toddy Pictures Company. *Cast:* Mantan Moreland (his first feature role), Bettie Treadville, Josephine Pearson, Bobby Simmon, Lawrence Criner, Arthur Ray, Monte Hawley, Ruby Logan, Alfred Grant, Herbert Skinner, the Four Tones, Jesse Grayson, John Thomas, Earl Hall, Guernsey Morrow, Vernon McCalla, Ray Martin, John Lester Johnson, Ruth Givins, A.K. Slim, Mae Turner, Effie Smith.

Night Club Girl, 1944, is the re-released *One Dark Night*, 1939. Story by Billy Meyers. (B&W / Sound / Feature.)

Mantan Moreland plays a lazy and shiftless father of two children who lets his wife support the family. He is continually insulted and annoyed by his in-laws who live with him, and finally he does a disappearing act. Meanwhile, life goes on as usual, with an old suitor trying to marry Moreland's wife when it is believed he is dead. However, Moreland discovers a radium mine in his wanderings on the desert. Later he returns home, scares off his rival, buys a local nightclub, dresses up his family and all is forgiven.

843 A Night in a Night Club
1937

Co: Universal Studios. *Cast:* Buck and Bubbles, Martha Raye (white). (Comedy / Short / B&W / Sound.)

844 A Night in Dixie 1926

Co: Deforest Phonofilm. *Cast:* Abbie Mitchell.

Songs: "Mighty Like a Rose," and "Old Kentucky Rose." (B&W / Short / Sound—FEA 4180 / Silent—FEA 4050.)

845 Night in Harlem 1947

Cast: Dizzy Gillespie and His Bebop Orchestra. (Sound / 10 min. / Musical / Short / B&W.)

Musical short featuring Dizzy Gillespie and His Bebop Orchestra.

846 A Night with the Devil 1946

Prod: Toddy, Ted. *Co:* Toddy Pictures Company.

No record of release. Story: Wilson and Grant. (Sound / B&W / 71 min. / Feature.)

847 Nine Lives 1926

Co: Colored Motion Picture Producers. *Cast:* Butterbeams and Susie (Joe and Susie Edwards). (Silent / B&W / Comedy / Short.)

848 Ninety-Second Division on Parade 1919

Prod: Turpin, Charles H. *Co:* Turpin Film Company. (Newsreel / B&W / Short / Silent / 900 ft.)

Film coverage of the 92 Division (black) on parade in St. Louis, Missouri, on March 14, 1919.

849   Ninth U.S. Cavalry Watering Horses 1898

Co: Thomas A. Edison, Inc.

Spanish-American War. (B&W / Silent / Short / Actualities / FLA 4756.)

850   No Mr. Ghost, Not Now 1947

Cast: Cecil Gant, Master of the Boogie. (Sound / B&W / Short.)

851   No, No, Baby 1945

Co: RCM Production. *Dist:* Soundies Distributing Corporation. *Cast:* Skeets Tolbert and His Orchestra. (Soundies 89608 / B&W / Short / Sound / Musical / 3/16/45.)

852   No Time for Romance 1948

Prod: Anderson, Byron O. *Co:* Norwanda Pictures. *Dist:* Embassy Pictures. *Cast:* Eunice Wilson, Austin McCoy, Joel Fluellen, Bill Walker, Shirley Haven, Ray Martin, Jay Brooks, Mildred Boyd, DeForrest Covan, Austin McCoy's Band, Louise Franklyn, Byron Ellis.

First all–Negro cast film shot in cinecolor. Original story: Vivian Cosby. Sound recording: Telefilm Corporation. Set designs: Hal Cramp. Dialogue: Bill Walker. Makeup: Harry Gillette. Costume design: Billie Chestwood. (Feature / B&W / Sound.)

"The story tells the struggle of a young musician, despite his superior talent, in the effort to reach the top. He does. Forty-six Negro actors and actresses comprise the case required to make the film"— excerpt of preview from the *New York Amsterdam News*, 8/21/48.

853   Noah 1946

Dir: Crouch, William Forest. *Prod:* Crouch, William Forest. *Co:* Filmcraft Production. *Dist:* Soundies Distributing Corporation. *Cast:* The Jubalairs. (Soundies 15M1 / B&W / Short / Sound / Musical / 1/28/46.)

854   Noble Sissle and Eubie Blake 1927

Co: Vitaphone. *Cast:* Noble Sissle, Eubie Blake. (9 min. / Musical / Short / B&W / Sound.)

Sissle and Blake perform numbers which include "I Wonder Where My Sweetie Can Be."

855   Nobody's Children 1920

Dir: Maurice, Richard D. *Prod:* Maurice, Richard D. *Co:* Maurice Film Company. *Dist:* Maurice Film Company. *Cast:* Richard Maurice, Jacque Farmer, Alex Griffin, Joe Green, Vivian Maurice, Howard Nelson, Max Johnson.

Alternate title *Our Christianity and Nobody's Children.* (B&W / Silent / Feature / Crime / 5,500 ft.)

"It tells of the death of the mother of two illegitimate children, a boy and a girl. A deathbed promise is made by the former that he will look after and protect his sister. The stepfather is a no-account type whose time is spent in the resorts of the underworld. It is during the search in a resort for him by the boy that a murder is committed and for which the lad is falsely accused, tried, convicted and sentenced to hang. The stepparent abducts the girl and takes her to one of the resorts where he is known. The actual slayer is a dope fiend. He discovers the girl's presence and decides to aid the brother to escape from jail so that he might rescue his sister. The consummation of this escape and the hand-to-hand fight which takes place in the room in which the stepfather had placed the girl, and in which the boy kills the unnatural parent, furnishes one of the most gripping climaxes ever seen on the screen"— excerpted from review in the *Norfolk Journal and Guide*, 2/19/21.

856   Norman Thomas Quintette, Harlem Mania 1929

Co: Vitaphone. *Cast:* Norman Thomas and His Quintette. (B&W / Short / Sound / 20 min. / Vitaphone #827 / VBE 8161.)

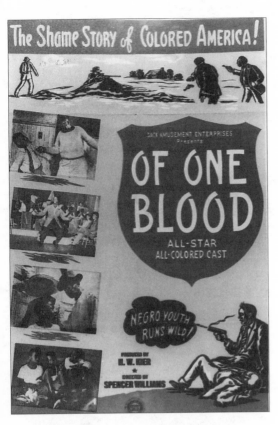

857   The Notorious Elinor Lee
1940

Dir: Micheaux, Oscar. *Prod:* Micheaux, Oscar, Hubert Julian. *Co:* Micheaux Film Corporation. *Dist:* Micheaux Pictures Corporation. *Cast:* Edna Mae Harris, Carmen Newsome, Gladys Williams, Robert Earl Jones, Ella Mae Waters, Sally Gooding, Vera Burelle. (Sound / B&W / Feature / 72 min. / FBB 3896–3899.)

The story concerns a great Negro boxing champion who is in the hands of crooks who want him to lose his most important fight so that they can settle some big bets. The champ is put in the toils of a clever woman who has been told to make him like her, to soften him up so that when the "time came" he could be "persuaded." What happens provides tense and thrilling screen entertainment.

858   Of One Blood 1944

Dir: Williams, Spencer. *Prod:* Kier, H.W. *Co:* Sack Amusement Enterprises. *Dist:* Sack Amusement Enterprises. *Cast:* Spencer Williams, Geraldine Maynard.

Written by Spencer Williams. (35mm / Sound/ B&W / 7 reels / 5,498 ft. / Feature / 61 min. / FEA 4671–4677.)

Spencer Williams plays a deaf mute who is actually an undercover FBI agent in this film which contains some of his religious/moral symbols.

859   Oft in the Silly Night 1929

Prod: Christie, Al. *Co:* Paramount. *Cast:* Spencer Williams, Evelyn Preer, Edward Thompson.

Screenplay: Octavus Roy Cohen and Spencer Williams. (Sound / B&W / 2 reels / Comedy / Short.)

Romance blossoms between a black chauffeur and the boss's daughter.

860   Oh, Susannah 1941

Co: Minoco Production. *Dist:* Soundies Distributing Corporation. *Cast:* The Charioteers.

Recorded by George Steiner Orchestra. (Soundies 3402 / B&W / Short / Sound / Musical / 9/22/41.)

861   Oh-H-E-E My, My 1945

Co: RCM Production. *Dist:* Soundies Distributing Corporation. *Cast:* The Counts and the Countess, The King Cole Trio (Nat "King" Cole, Oscar Moore, Johnny Miller). (Soundies 87808 / B&W / Short / Sound / Musical / 12/3/45.)

862   Ol' King Cotton 1931

Dir: Cogine, Ray. *Co:* Paramount. *Cast:* George Dewey Washington.

Story by Walton Butterfield. Review in *Film Daily*, 1/4/31, and 10/11/31. (B&W / Sound / Short / 9 min.)

"A river boat, workers on it and a girl who stows away just to be near her boyfriend, provide background here for several numbers, including solo and group. George Dewey Washington, moves around the boat from the deck to the pilot house with his singing. For an effective close, he and his stowaway girl, who's pardoned for coming on the boat by the white captain, do a double with the boat hands below dressing up"—review from the *Philadelphia Tribune*, 1/28/32.

863   Old Black Joe 1933

Co: Tiffany Film Company. *Cast:* Forbes

Randolph Kentucky Jubilee Singers. (Short / B&W / Sound / Musical.)

864   Old Dan Tucker 1946
Dir: Crouch, William Forest. *Prod:* Crouch, William Forest. *Co:* Filmcraft Production. *Dist:* Soundies Distributing Corporation. *Cast:* The Swing Stars, Joann Cavanaugh. (Soundies 17M1/ B&W / Short / Sound / Musical / 3/4/46.)

865   Old Man Mose 1942
Co: RCM Production. *Dist:* Soundies Distributing Corporation. *Cast:* Louis Jordan and His Tympany Five. (Soundies 10506 / B&W / Short / Sound / Musical / 12/31/42.)

866   Old Man Rhythm 1932
Co: Paramount. *Cast:* George Dewey Washington. (B&W / Sound / Short.)
"…. melodies in a setting representing the hold and deck of a river steamer. The rendition is in a measure effective, but the subject is rather too prolonged to be striking in any way"— excerpt of review from the *Motion Picture Herald*, 2/6/32.

867   Old Man Trouble 1929
Dir: Smith, Basil. *Co:* Columbia Victor Gems. *Cast:* Jules Bledsoe. (B&W / Sound / Short / 7 min.)
"The set shows a Southern plantation with the family of father, mother, and son grouped about the cabin door. Bledsoe, as the son, comes on and after talking with his mammy goes into song numbers. One of the best things in its class that has yet been presented in sound shorts. Bledsoe's voice registers beautifully and has an appealing quality that is bound to get over with any type of audience"— review from *Film Daily*, 6/9/29.

868   Old Time Songs 1928
Co: Vitaphone. *Cast:* Clarence Tisdale. (B&W / Short / Sound / 9 min.)
"Scene shows a cotton field with Tisdale, the Colored Tenor, outside the cabin singing. He leads off with 'The Sweetness of Your Song,' follows with 'By and By,' and finishes with 'Oh, Didn't It Rain.' None of the numbers clocked, in spite of his fine tenor voice and good recording. The material was at fault, for it lacked popular appeal"— review from *Film Daily*, 6/2/28.

869   On a Plantation 1930
Co: Tiffany Film Company. *Cast:* Forbes Randolph's Kentucky Jubilee Singers. (Musical / B&W / Short / Sound.) Songs: "Great Camp Meetin' in the Promised Land," "Shine On," and "Let My People Go."

870   On the Levee 1930
Co: Columbia Pictures. *Cast:* Jules Bledsoe. (Musical / B&W / Sound / Short.) Song: "Since I Went Away."

871   One Big Mistake 1940
Prod: Markham, Dewey and Heckle. *Co:* Markham and Heckle. *Dist:* Toddy Pictures Company. *Cast:* Dewey "Pigmeat" Markham, Lillian Randolph, Johnny Taylor, Monte Hawley, Millie Monroe. (Featurette written by Dewey "Pigmeat" Markham / B&W / Sound / Short.)

872   One Dark Night 1939
Dir: Popkin, Leo C. *Co:* Million Dollar Productions. *Dist:* Toddy Pictures Company.

Cast: Mantan Moreland (his first feature role), Bettie Treadville, Josephine Pearson, Bobby Simmon, Lawrence Criner, Arthur Ray, Monte Hawley, Ruby Logan, Alfred Grant, Herbert Skinner, The Four Tones, Jesse Grayson, John Thomas, Earl Hall, Guernsey Morrow, Vernon McCalla, Ray Martin, John Lester Johnson, Ruth Givins, A.K. Slim, Mae Turner, Effie Smith.

One Dark Night, 1939, was re-released in 1944 under the title *Nightclub Girl*. Story by Billy Meyers. Preview in the *Los Angeles Sentinel*, 8/3/39. (Feature / B&W / Sound.)

Mantan Moreland plays a lazy and shiftless father of two children who lets his wife support the family. He is continually insulted and annoyed by his in-laws who lives with him, and finally he does a disappearing act. Meanwhile, life goes on as usual, with an old suitor trying to marry Moreland's wife when it is believed he is dead. However, Moreland discovers a radium mine in his wanderings on the desert. Later he returns home, scares off his rival, buys a local nightclub, dresses up his family and all is forgiven.

873   One Large Evening 1914

Co: Afro-American Film Company. *Cast:* Charles Gilpin, Marie Young, Leon Williams, Sara Green Byrd, Anthony Byrd, Eva Johnson.

Very offensive to Blacks (stereotypical). Film was released in white theaters under the title *A Night in Coontown*. Black protest kept it out of black theaters. (Silent / B&W / Short.)

"There are many scenes of excruciatingly funny complications that reflect much credit on the author ... as the story develops, one scene leads to another in such rapid succession that one's interest is held with a break. The action is such as might and actually occur, at times in our every-day life.... The picture caused great laughter among the previewers, the actors seemed to catch the spirit of the situation and succeeded in bringing out all the laughable points artistically"—excerpted from review in the *New York Amsterdam News*, 4/10/14.

874   One Round Jones 1948

Dir: Green, Eddie. *Prod:* Green, Eddie. *Co:* Sepia-Art Pictures Company. *Dist:* Toddy Pictures Company. *Cast:* Eddie Green, Lorenzo Tucker. (Sound / B&W / Feature.) Comedy about a prizefighter, played by Eddie Green.

875   One Tenth of Our Nation 1940

Dir: Rodakiewicz, Henwar. *Co:* American Film Center. (Sound / B&W / Documentary / Short.)

Documentary for blacks showing inadequate conditions of education in the South.

876   Oop Boop Sh'Bam 1947

Cast: Dizzy Gillespie and His Bebop Orchestra, Taylor and Burley, The Hubba Hubba Girls, Ray Smith. (Sound / B&W / 10 min. / Short / Musical.)

Variety show type.

877   Open the Door, Richard! 1947

Co: All-American News. *Cast:* Dusty Fletcher. (Short / Sound / B&W.)

878   Opus 12 EEE 1944

Dir: Blake, Ben K. *Prod:* Blake, Ben K. *Co:* RCM Production. *Dist:* Soundies Distributing Corporation. *Cast:* Harry "The Hipster" Gibson. (Soundies / B&W / Short / Sound / Musical / 12/18/44.)

Othello in Harlem *see* Paradise in Harlem

879   Our Boys at Camp Upton 1918

(Newsreel / B&W / Short / Silent.)

The training of the 367th Infantry at Camp Upton, New York. The film was shown to raise funds for the benefit of the 367th under the auspices of the Upton Thrift Committee.

880   Our Colored Boys Over There 1921

Co: U.S. War Department. (Newsreel / B&W / Documentary / Short / Silent.)

Film coverage of black and white soldiers in action during World War I in Chateau Thierry and the Argonne Forest in France.

881   Our Colored Fighters 1918

Prod: Division of Films, U.S. War Department. *Co:* Downing Film Company. *Cast:* Activities of black soldiers in World War I.

The official United States War picture released by the Division of Films of the Committee on Public Information, and exhibited by the Downing Film Company. (Silent / B&W / Documentary / Short / 2 reels.)

"A picture illustrating the important place the American Negro fighters are taking in World War I. The film pictorializes the enlistment and training of the colored soldiers in the cantonments and also shows their work overseas"— excerpted from review in *New York Age*, 10/24/18.

882   Our Hell Fighters 1918

(Silent / B&W / Documentary / Short / 1 reel.)

This film is about the 369th all–Negro Regiment and its contribution to the World War I effort.

883   The Outskirts of Town 1942

Co: RCM Production. *Dist:* Soundies Distributing Corporation. *Cast:* Louis Jordan, Theresa Harris, Dudley Dickerson. (Soundies 9005 / Musical / Sound / Short / B&W / 10/19/42.)

884   O'Voutie O'Rooney 1947

Dir: Rieger, Jack. *Prod:* Rieger, Jack. *Co:* Astor Pictures Corporation. *Cast:* The Slim Gaillard Trio, Mabel Lee. (Sound / B&W / Feature.)

885   Painting in Oil 1946

Co: Harmon Foundation Educational Films. (Harmon Foundation Series / Short / Silent / Kodachrome / B&W / 1 reel / 16mm.)

A film study of Palmer Hayden, a famous artist.

886   Paper Doll 1942

Dir: Berne, Josef. *Prod:* Coslow, Sam. *Co:* RCM Production. *Dist:* Soundies Distributing Corporation. *Cast:* Erskine Hawkins and His Orchestra. (Soundies 9706 / B&W / Short / Sound / Musical / 12/7/42.)

887   Paradise in Harlem 1940

Dir: Seiden, Joseph. *Prod:* Goldberg, Jack & Dave. *Co:* Jubilee Pictures Corporation. *Dist:* International Road Show Release. *Cast:* Lucky Millinder and His Orchestra, Frank Wilson, Mamie Smith, Alec Lovejoy, Edna

Mae Harris, Juanita Hall Singers, Babe Mathews, Sidney Easton, Norman Astwood, Percy Verwayen, Madeline Belt, Herman Green, George Williams, Lionel Monagas, Francine Everett, Joe Joe Thomas, Perry Bradford, Alphabetical Four, Merritt Smith.

Original title was *Othello in Harlem*. Songs: "Harlem Serenade," "Why Have You Left Me Blue?" "Harlem Blues." Screenplay: Vincent Valentini. Story: Frank Wilson. Cinematography: Don Malkames & Charles Levine. Sound recording: Murray Dichter & Paul Jacobs. Unit manager: Irvin C. Miller. Production supervisor: Jack Goldberg. (16mm / B&W / Sound / 2 reels / 85 min. / Feature / FEA 4301–4306.)

Gangster plot set against a backdrop of late thirties jazz, with Lucky Millindar and His Orchestra. Typical musical: short on plot, heavy on musical variety.

888 Pardon Me, but You Look Like Margie 1943

Co: RCM Production. *Dist:* Soundies Distributing Corporation. *Cast:* The Three Chefs, Barry Paige's Orchestra. (Soundies 12308 / B&W / Short / Sound / Musical / 6/28/43.)

889 Patience and Fortitude 1946

Dir: Gould, Dave. *Prod:* Hersh, Ben. *Co:* RCM Production. *Dist:* Soundies Distributing Corporation. *Cast:* Valaida Snow, The Ali Baba Trio. (Soundies 18M3 / B&W / Short / Sound / Musical / 4/8/46.)

890 Paul J. Rainey's African Hunt pre–1910

(B&W / Silent / Short / FLA 5919–5921.)

891 Peacock News Reel #1 1921

Co: Peacock Photoplay Company. (Documentary / Short / B&W / Silent.)

Various colored news bits.

892 Peacock News Reel #2 1922

Co: Peacock Photoplay Company. (Newsreel / Documentary / B&W / Sound / Short.)

Subjects include: Ned Gourdin, Harvard athlete, winning the 100-yard dash over Abraham of England, and breaking the world's record in the running broad jump; Florence Parlam, the child actress; a review of Tuskegee Institute looking back at its first 10 years.

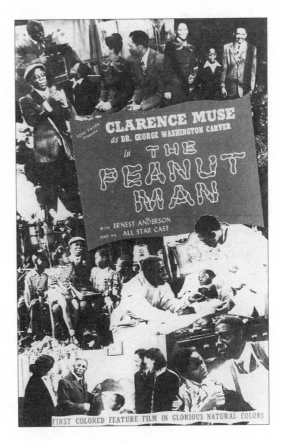

FIRST COLORED FEATURE FILM IN GLORIOUS NATURAL COLORS

893 The Peanut Man 1947

Prod: Paton, Tony. *Co:* Consolidated Pictures. *Cast:* Clarence Muse, Ernest Anderson, Maidie Norman. (Technicolor / Sound / Feature.)

A film depicting the life and achievements of Dr. George Washington Carver (Muse).

894 Peckin' 1942

Co: RCM Production. *Dist:* Soundies Distributing Corporation. *Cast:* The Chocolateers. (Soundies 9303 / B&W / Short / Sound / Musical / 11/2/42.)

First music videos.

895 The Perfect Dreamer 1922

Co: Young Producers Filming Corporation. (35mm / Silent / B&W / Feature.)

A story of "Negro" life.

896 Phantom of Kenwood 1933

Dir: Micheaux, Oscar. *Prod:* Russell, A. Burton. *Co:* Micheaux Film Corporation. *Dist:* Micheaux Film Corporation. *Cast:* Frank

Wilson, Babe Townsend, Bea Freeman, Pearl McCormack, Carlton Moss.

Bea Freeman, a Philadelphia girl. (Silent / B&W / Feature.)

"This feature deals with the theme of a perfect murder and in telling how it is solved holds intense and intriguing moments from start to finish"—*Philadelphia Tribune*, 5/4/33.

897   Pickaninnies and Watermelon 1912

Co: Imp. (Newsreel / Documentary / B&W / Short / Silent.)

Film footage of black kids eating watermelon.

898   The Pickaninny 1921

Co: Pathé. *Cast:* "Sunshine Sammy" Morrison. (Silent / B&W / Short.)

899   Pickaninny's Dance 1903

Co: American Mutoscope / Biograph. (Newsreel / Documentary / B&W / Short / Silent.)

Film footage of black teenagers doing the buck-and-wing and the cake-walk dances.

900   Pickin' Cotton 1930

Co: Tiffany Film Company. *Cast:* Forbes Randolph Kentuck Jubilee Singers. (B&W / Sound / Short / 1 reel / 8 min.)

"Darky melody interpretations. Nothing particularly new, with the usual old Southern cabin setting, and the Black boys harmonizing outside the door. The singing is up to the standard of the famous aggregation"—review excerpt from *Film Daily*, 12/7/30.

901   Pie Eating Contest 1903

Co: American Mutoscope / Biograph. (Newsreel / Documentary / B&W / Short / Silent / Actuality.)

Film footage of a group of black men eating pies.

902   Pie Pie Blackbirds 1932

Dir: Mack, Roy. *Prod:* Warner Bros. *Co:* Warner Bros. / Vitaphone. *Cast:* Nine Mae McKinney, Eubie Blake and His Band. Nicholas Brothers (Harold and Fayad).

Songs: "Blackbird Pie" and "You Rascal You." Reviews in the *Motion Picture Herald*, 6/25/32, and the *Film Daily*, 6/11/32. (Sound / B&W / 1 reel / 9 min. / Musical / Short.)

A Vitaphone short featuring instrumental, vocal and dance numbers, with a backdrop of a giant pie (Eubie and Band rise up from within), among them: "Blackbird Pie" and "You Rascal You."

903   Pigmeat Throws the Bull 1945

Dir: Crouch, William Forest. *Prod:* Crouch, William Forest. *Co:* Filmcraft Production. *Dist:* Soundies Distributing Corporation. *Cast:* Dewey "Pigmeat" Mark, Mabel Lee. (Soundies 14M1 / B&W / Short / Sound / Musical / 12/2/45.)

904   Pigmeat's Laugh Hepcats 1944

Co: Toddy Pictures Company. *Dist:* Toddy Pictures. *Cast:* Dewey "Pigmeat" Markham, Monte Hawley, Lillian Randolph, Vernon McCalla, Millie Monroe, Lawrence Criner, Johnny Taylor.

Pigmeat's Laugh Hepcats is a combination re-release of *One Big Mistake* and *Mr. Smith Goes Ghost*. (Sound / B&W / 36 min. / Feature.)

905   Pink Lemonade 1936

Dir: Hammons, E.W. *Prod:* Christie, Al. *Co:* Educational Film Corporation. *Cast:* The Cabin Kids (five colored harmonizers, Ruth Hall, Helen Hall, James "Darling" Hall, Winifred "Sugar" Hall, and little Frederick Hall).

Story by Art Jarrett. (Sound / B&W / 990 ft. / Short.)

"The popular pickaninnies, the Cabin Kids, appear in a circus skit where they crash the gate of the big top by crawling under the canvas. Caught by the cops, the clowns intercede for them, and Toto the Clown puts on a private act for them on condition that they reciprocate by singing one of their darky harmonies"— review from the *Film Daily*, 10/21/36.

906   Pinky 1949

Dir: Kazan, Elia. *Prod:* Zanuck, Darryl F. *Co:* Twentieth Century–Fox Film Corporation. *Cast:* Jeanne Crain, Ethel Barrymore, Ethel Waters, Evelyn Varden, Frederick O'Neal, Nina Mae McKinney.

Based on a novel by Cid Ricketts Sumner. Screenplay by Philip Dunne and Dudley Nichols. (Feature / Sound / B&W.)

907   Pitch a Boogie Woogie 1948

Dir: Lord, William. *Prod:* Warner, John. *Co:* Lord-Warner Pictures. *Cast:* Tom Foreman, Herman Forbes, Esther Mae Porteur, Joe Little, Beatrice Atkinson, Evelyn Whorton, Dorothy Lee, Cleophus Lyons, Rosa Burrell, Eleanor Hines, the "Count and Harriet," Irvin C. Miller and girls, Billy Cornell and Chorus.

Story by: John W. Warner and William Lord. Musical synchronization: Charles Woods. Songs: "Pitch a Boogie Woogie," "Te Quiero," "I Heard You Say," "Vini, Vidi, Vinci." Filmed in Greenville, South Carolina. (Musical / Sound / B&W / Short.)

908   Play It, Brother 1947

Cast: Billy Eckstine and His Band, Lucky Millinder and His Band. (Featurette / Sound / B&W.)

Musical short featuring the above artists.

909   Policy Man 1938

Prod: Franklyn, Irwin & Hazele. *Co:* Creative Cinema Corporation. *Dist:* Sack Amusement Enterprises. *Cast:* Ann Harleman, Henry Wessels, Jimmie Baskette, Ethel Moses, Count Basie and His Orchestra, the N.Y. Plantation Club Chorus, Al Taylor Orchestra, Savoy Lindy-Hoppers and Big Applers. (Sound / B&W / Feature.)

910   The Pollard Jump 1946

Dir: Crouch, William Forest. *Prod:* Crouch, William Forest. *Co:* Filmcraft Production. *Dist:* Soundies Distributing Corporation. *Cast:* Nicky O'Daniel, The Sun Tan Four. (Soundies 18M2 / B&W / Short / Sound Musical / 4/1/46.)

911   Pompey's Honey Girl
pre–1910
(B&W / Silent / Short / FLA 3820.)

912   Poppin' the Cork 1943

Co: RCM Production. *Dist:* Soundies Distributing Corporation. *Cast:* The Sepia

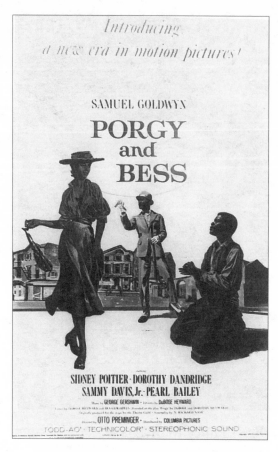

Steppers, Billy and Ann. (Soundies 12208 / B&W / Short / Sound / Musical / 6/21/43.)

913   Porgy and Bess 1959

Dir: Preminger, Otto. *Prod:* Goldwyn, Samuel. *Co:* Columbia Pictures. *Dist:* Columbia Pictures. *Cast:* Sidney Poitier, Dorothy Dandridge, Sammy Davis, Jr., Pearl Bailey, Brock Peters, Diahann Carroll, Ivan Dixon, Clarence Muse, Joel Fluellen.

Music: George Gershwin. Music arranged by: Andre Previn and Ken Darby (won Oscars). Final film of producer Samuel Goldwyn. Screenplay: N. Richard Nash. Libretto and lyrics: DuBose Heyward. Story: Dubose and Dorothy Heyward (Opera). (16mm / Color / Sound / 4 reels / 138 min. / Feature.)

A poignant love story set against the backdrop of Catfish Row in the post–Civil War South. The film showcases many black stars: Poitier plays Porgy, Dandridge is Bess, Peters is Crown, Davis is Sportin' Life. A very stereotypical film — most of the actors were upset at their roles and attempted a boycott.

914   The Porters 1903

Co: American Mutoscope / Biograph. (Newsreel / Documentary / B&W / Silent / Short / Actuality.)

Film footage of a group of Pullman Porters.

915   The Porters 1918

Co: Ebony Film Company. *Dist:* General Film Company. *Cast:* Ebony Players (Sam Robinson, Samuel "Sambo" Jacks, Will Starks, Julia Mason, Bert Murphy, Evon Skekeeter, Mildred Price, Walter Brogsdale, Robert Duree, Frank Pollard, George Lewis Stock Company). (B&W / Silent / Short / 2 reels.)

"Showing the trials of hotel boys whose hours are from six to six. It is full of lively business, has a few feet somewhat objectionable vulgarity, and has fairly amusing rough and tumble, knock-about business. It is a good film for the rougher audience" — review from the *Moving Picture World*, 12/8/17.

916   Porters' Parade 1903

Co: American Mutoscope / Biograph. (Newsreel / Documentary / B&W / Silent / Short.)

Rare film footage of Pullman Porters on parade.

917   The Possum Hunt 1910

Co: Edison. (Newsreel / Documentary / B&W / Short / Silent.)

Film footage of blacks on a possum hunt.

918   Prairie Comes to Harlem 1941

Prod: Toddy, Ted. *Co:* Toddy Pictures Company. *Dist:* Toddy Pictures Company.

A sequel to "Harlem on the Prairie." (Sound / B&W / 61 min. / Feature.)

919   Prancing in the Park 1943

Co: RCM Production. *Dist:* Soundies Distributing Corporation. (Soundies 7M2 / B&W / Short / Sound / Musical / 12/21/43.)

920   The Preacher and the Bear 1945

Co: RCM Production. *Dist:* Soundies

Distributing Corporation. *Cast:* The Jubalairs. (Soundies 20408 / B&W / Short / Sound / Musical / 4/16/45.)

921   A Prince of His Race
1926

Dir: Calnek, Roy / Bob Martin. *Prod:* Starkman, David / Louis Groner. *Co:* Colored Players Film Corporation of Philadelphia. *Cast:* Harry Henderson, Lawrence Chenault, Shingzie Howard, William Clayton, Ethel Smith, William Smith, Arline Mickey.

Review in the *Philadelphia Tribune,* 5/15/26. Reviews in the *Philadelphia Tribune,* 6/19/26, 7/17/26, and 7/15/26. Written by Roy Calnek. (Silent / B&W / Feature.)

The story deals with a young man who is sent to prison on the evidence of one whom he thought was his friend. The hero is ostracized by the townfolk after his release from prison. This forces him to leave town and incidentally leads him toward success. The friend whom he went to prison to save proves false and bribes the father of the hero's sweetheart to persuade her to marry him. Having successfully intercepted all of the letters of the missing lover, he feels all is going according to plan, and proceeds to plan the wedding. The bride is all ready, and the bridesmaids are in waiting, the preacher arrives — what happens next is the climax of the picture.

922   Prinsesse Tam-Tam 1935

Prod: Nissotti, Arys. *Co:* Pathé Nathan-Joinville. *Dist:* ARYS Productions. *Cast:* Josephine Baker, Albert Prejean, Robert Arnoux, Germaine Aussey, Georges Peclet, Viviane Romance, Jean Galland, Teddy Michaud, Henry Richard, Marion Malville, Paul Demange.

Realization: de Edmond T. Greville. Dialogue: Yves Mirande. Artistic direction: Pepito Abatino. Photo: G. Benoit. Montage: J. Feyte. Sound engineer: A. Archimbaud. Décor de la Fête: L. Meerson. Autres décors: De Gastyne. Music: Dallin, Grenet, Goehr, Al Romans. Lyrics: Badet. Musical director: Arthur Nissotti. Edited by: Choudens. Danses: Floyd Du Pont. Assistant: Robert Rips. Administrator: Joseph Macaluso. Régisseur: Jacques Pelosof. Robes: Philippe el Gaston. Costumes: Zanel.

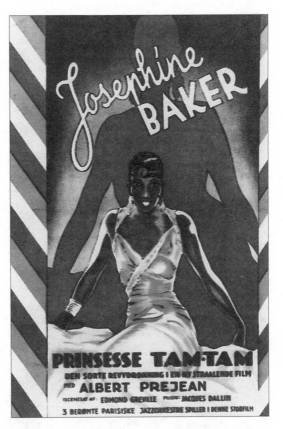

R.C.A. High Fidelity. Copie: Éclair-Tirage. (B&W / Sound / Feature.)

"This film is about a Parisian novel writer who in order to escape a marital quarrel decided to separate from his wife for a while. He goes to Tunis to gain his moral equilibrium abroad and inspiration at the same time and also in order to increase his wife's affection by his absence. In Africa he gets interested in a young beggar girl, Acuina (Baker), who symbolizes the carefree joy of the native who can live from little while fully enjoying the independence which her simplicity and love of nature gives her. The novelist studies the amusing reactions of Acuina in opposition to the Western world. He works out a book he is to write on the poetical dream of Acuina's inspiration. This dream is worked out. The little native girl goes to France with the novelist whom she loves. For a while she is happy but cannot get used to occidental life and its restrictions and she returns to her country" — review from the *New York Amsterdam News,* 5/21/38.

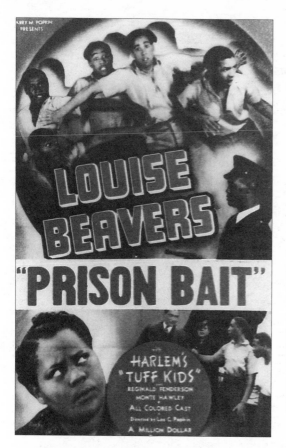

Prison Bait *see* **Reform School**

923   Prize Drill Team 1919

Co: Colored and Indian Film Company.
(Newsreel / Documentary / B&W / Silent / Short.)

924   Professor Creeps 1941

Prod: Buell, Jed. *Co:* Dixie National Pictures, Inc. *Dist:* Toddy Pictures Company.
Cast: Mantan Moreland, Flournoy E. Miller, Arthur Ray, Zack Williams, John Lester Johnson, Florence O'Brien, Margarette Whitten, Billy Mitchell, Maceo Sheffield, Shelton Brooks, John Criner, Clarence Hargrave, Nappie Whiting, Jesse Cryer.

Review in the *Pittsburgh Courier*, 3/7/42.
(Sound / B&W / 63 min. / Feature.)

Jefferson and Washington operate a failing detective agency. Washington dozes and dreams that they are hired by a wealthy heiress to rid her of her diabolical uncle, Professor Wackingham Creeps. The professor develops a chemical to turn men into animals and then the fun begins. Washington awakens to find out that it was only a dream.

925   Progress of the Negro 1916

Dir: Jones, Peter P. *Prod:* Jones, Peter P. *Co:* Peter P. Jones Photoplay Company. (Newsreel / Documentary/ B&W / Silent / Short.)

This film shows Booker T. Washington and Tuskegee Institute and a Negro city, Mound Bayou, Mississippi, built by ex-slaves.

926   Pudgy Boy 1942

Co: RCM Production. *Dist:* Soundies Distributing Corporation. *Cast:* Les Hite and His Orchestra. (Soundies 6707 / B&W / Short / Sound / Musical / 5/11/42.)

927   The Pullman Porter 1910

Dir: Foster, William. *Prod:* Foster, William. *Co:* Foster Photoplay Company. *Dist:* Foster Photoplay Company. *Cast:* Lottie Grady, Jerry Mills, Kid Brown, Bill Cole.

William Foster's death notice and Pullman Porter remarks in the *Philadelphia Tribune*, 4/18/40. (Silent / B&W / Comedy / Short.)

"The story deals with a young wife who, thinking her husband had gone out on 'his fun,' invited a fashionably dressed chap, who was a waiter at one of the colored cafes on State street, to dine. However, the husband did not go out and, upon returning home, found wifey sitting at the table serving the waiter all the delicacies of the season. Mr. Husband proceeds to get his revolver, which he uses very carelessly, running the unwelcome visitor to his home. Then the waiter gets his revolver and returns the compliment. However, nobody is hurt, despite all the shooting and all ends happily"— review excerpted from the *New York Age*, 9/25/13.

928 Put Your Arms Around Me, Honey 1943

Co: RCM Production. *Dist:* Soundies Distributing Corporation. *Cast:* Ruby Hill, Virgil Van Cleve. (Soundies 4M1 / B&W / Short / Sound / Musical / 9/21/43.)

929 Pygmies of Africa 1938

Prod: Haven, H.C. *Co:* Encyclopaedia Britannica Films. (Central Africa / Documentary / Sound / 16mm / B&W / 20 min. / 1 reel / Short.)

"This film shows the pygmies' unending search for food, stalking techniques used, various handicrafts and sacrificial ceremonies"— Klotman.

930 Pythian Conclave and League Parley 1930

Prod: Walker, C.J. *Co:* Madam C.J. Walker Manufacturing Company.

Review in the *Philadelphia Tribune*, 1/30/30. (Newsreel / Documentary / B&W / Short / Sound.)

Filmed in Indianapolis, Indiana.

Pythian Conclave and League Parley; K of P Supreme Lodge; National Negro Business League.

931 Pythian Parade and 19th Biannual Encampment 1920

Prod: Turpin, Charles H. *Co:* Turpin, Charles H. (Newsreel / Documentary / B&W / Silent / Short.)

Film coverage of the 19th Encampment of the Pythians at St. Louis, Mo.

932 Quarry Road 1943

Co: RCM Production. *Dist:* Soundies Distributing Corporation. *Cast:* Sam Manning, Belle Rosette. (Soundies 10802 / B&W / Short / Sound / Musical / 3/8/43.)

933 Queen of the Boogie 1947

Co: All American News. *Cast:* Hadda Brooks. (35mm / Sound / B&W / 1 reel / Short / 9 min. / FEA 8674.)

Hadda Brooks is at the piano in this musical short.

934 Quick Watson, The Question 1943

Co: RCM Production. *Dist:* Soundies Distributing Corporation. *Cast:* Myra Johnson, The Harlem Honeys. (Soundies 5M5 / B&W / Short / Sound / Musical / 10/29/43.)

935 The Quiet One 1958

Dir: Meyers, Sidney. *Prod:* Meyers, Sidney, Jane Loeb. *Co:* Independent. *Cast:* Estelle Evans, Sadie Stockton, Donald Thompson, Gary Merrill (white), Clarence Cooper (white), Paul Bawam (white), Staff of the Wiltwyck School.

Screenplay: James Agee, Helen Levitt, Sidney Meyers, Janet Loeb. (Feature / Drama / Documentary / 16mm / B&W / Sound / 67 min. / 2 reels.)

This film tells the story of a Harlem boy who grows up feeling withdrawn and rejected, eventually drifting into delinquency. While attending the Wiltwyck School for Boys, he becomes known as the "Quiet One." He builds up a wall of silence to hid his bitterness.

936 Racket Doctor (Am I Guilty?) 1945

Dir: Newfeld, Sam. *Prod:* Hackel, A.W. *Co:* Supreme Pictures Corporation. *Dist:* Toddy Pictures Company. *Cast:* Ralph Cooper, Sybil Lewis, Sam McDaniels, Lawrence Criner, Marcella Moreland (daughter of Mantan), Arthus Ray, Reginald Fenderson, Monte Hawley, Matthew Jones, Dewey "Pigmeat" Markham, Jesse Brooks, Napoleon Simpson, Clarence Brooks, Cleo Desmond, Ida Coffin, Lillian Randolph, Vernon McCalla, Eddie Thompson, Mae Turner, Alfred Grant, Guernsey Morrow.

Racket Doctor, 1945, was originally released as *Am I Guilty?*, 1940. See *Am I Guilty?* for Review dates. (Feature / B&W / Sound.)

The story tells of a courageous young Negro doctor whose high ideals lead him to attempt the establishment of a clinic in the slum district in which he was born. Dr. Dunbar falls into the hands of the Bennett gang, which is badly in need of a "mob doctor" to "fix up" wounded members. Bennett, through his lawyer, donates $8,000 to Dunbar to establish his clinic. Dunbar is eventually forced to accompany the gang on a series of breathtaking escapades, which finally end in the death of Bennett and the capture of the gang.

937   Radio Rascals   1935

Co: Educational Film Corporation. *Cast:* The Cabin Bids (five colored harmonizers, Ruth Hall, Helen Hall, James "Darling" Hall, Winifred "Sugar" Hall, and little Frederick Hall), Mountain Melodeers (white), Austin Fairman (white), Elmira Sessions (white), Ruth Denning (white). (B&W / Sound / Short / 9 min.)

"An amateur hour on the radio, featuring the five pickaninnies, the Cabin Kids. These clever youngsters do several song numbers with fine harmony effects. The comedy relief is secured through interspersing several so-called amateur acts built for the absurdities"—excerpt of review from the *Film Daily*, 8/1/35.

938   The Railroad Porter   1912

Dir: Foster, William. *Prod:* Foster, William. *Co:* Foster Photoplay Company. *Dist.* Foster Photoplay Company. *Cast:* Lottie Grady, Jerry Mills, Edgar Litterson. (Short / Silent / B&W.)

Was first race comedy made inaugurating the chase idea, later copied by Lubin, Keystone Cops, etc.

939   Rakoon Hose Company   1913

Dir: Lubin, Sigmund. *Prod:* Louis, Will. *Co:* Lubin Manufacturing Company. *Cast:* John Edwards, Luke Scott, Mattie Edwards, D. Roseborough.

Written by Will Louis. Released on 8/3/15. (Silent / B&W / Short / Comedy / 600 ft.)

"Mattie, the belle of Ethiopia, is much sought after, but she is loved by John, the fireman, and while John is an honest man and has a regular job, he hasn't the fine clothes and the smooth tongue that has Rastus, the town sport. But when Rastus attempts to steal her away from him, John gives chase and after locating them at the meeting house he gives Rastus the most exciting time of his life, finally chasing Rastus to an abandoned old hut and with the aid of a bomb sets the hut on fire. John's fire department answers the call of fire, but when John tells them the circumstances they walk away and let it burn. At this point Mattie comes to the rescue of the unfortunate Rastus and pleads with John to release him. John finally succumbs and demands of Mattie to take her choice. She of course chooses John, and Rastus is given one hour to leave town"—*Lubin Bulletin*.

940   Rastus Among the Zulus   1913
Dir: Lubin, Sigmund. *Prod:* Lubin, Sigmund. *Co:* Lubin Manufacturing Company.
Released on 7/28/13. (Silent / B&W / Short / 600 ft.)
"Rastus is taking a nap on the dock when three roughs shanghai him and put him onboard a vessel bound for Africa. The ship is wrecked and Rastus is the only soul saved. He is captured by Zulus and condemned to the cooking pot. The King's daughter pleads for his life that she may marry him, but Rastus decides to accept the cooking pot. He is then beaten so hard that he wakes up and finds a policeman clubbing his feet"—*Lubin Bulletin.*

941   Rastus Knew It Wasn't   1914
Dir: Lubin, Sigmund. *Prod:* Lubin, Sigmund. *Co:* Lubin Manufacturing Company. *Cast:* John Edwards, Royal Byron (white), Mabel Paige (white), Ed Lawrence (white).
Written by E.W. Sargent. Released on 9/15/14. (Silent / B&W / Short / 400 ft.)
"Rastus Remington, porter of the police station, leaves his scrubbing pail in the road of the Chief, who stumbles over it. For this Rastus thinks it wise to make a get-away. The Chief throws the pail after him and Rastus, dodging, it strikes Lugi Ferranti, who is out walking with his sweetheart. Lugi's hot sicilian blood boils and when he remonstrates the Chief beats him up. Rastus goes to see a picture show wherein a bomb discovered proves to be nothing but an alarm clock. He saunters to the station where he finds great agitation among the men who have found an alarm clock planted by Lugi. Rastus knows that it is harmless and proceeds to open it with an axe. He leaves the earth and goes up into space"—*Lubin Bulletin.*

942   Ration Blues   1944
Dir: Crouch, William Forest. *Prod:* Crouch, William Forest. *Co:* RCM Production. *Dist:* Soundies Distributing Corporation. *Cast:* Louis Jordan and His Tympany Five. (Soundies / B&W / Short / Sound / Musical / 3/27/44.)

943   Readin', Writin' and Rhythm   1939
Co: RKO Radio Pictures. *Cast:* Lucky Millinder and His Band, Don Bayas, Frankie Newton. (Musical / B&W / Sound / Short.)

944   The Real Joe Louis   1946
Cast: Joe Louis. (Sound / B&W / Short.)
The Brown Bomber's own story.

945   The Realization of a Negro's Ambition   1916
Co: Lincoln Motion Picture Company. *Dist:* Lincoln Motion Picture Company. *Cast:* Noble Johnson, Clarence Brooks, Webb King, G.H. Reed, A. Burns, A. Collins, Beulah Hall, Lottie Boles, Bessie Mathews, Bessie Baker, Gertrude Christmas. (Silent / B&W / 2 reels / Feature.)
James Burton, a young Negro graduate from Tuskegee, as a civil engineer finds no satisfaction working on his father's farm and heads west. Unable to find a job because of his color, he is despondent. He chances upon a runaway two-horse rig and risks his life to stop it. Unknowingly, he has saved the daughter of an oil company owner. Out of gratitude he's given a job as head of oil expeditions. He convinces the owner to let him drill on his father's farm and surrounding farms. After a round of trickery and romance he strikes oil and is soon wealthy. He buys a home and gets married. The last scene shows James in later years, with ambition realized: home and family, a nice country to live in and nice people to live by and enjoy it with him.

946   Re-Birth of a Nation   1916
Dir: Jones, Peter P. *Prod:* Jones, Peter P. *Co:* Peter P. Jones Photoplay Company. (Silent / B&W.)
Possible answer to *The Birth of a Nation.*

947   Reckless Money   1926
Dir: Dudley, Sherman H., Jr. *Prod:* Dudley, Sherman H., Jr. *Co:* Dudley Film Company. *Cast:* Sherman H. Dudley, Jr., John La Rue.
Choreographer: Mrs. Mary Dudley. Cameraman: Watkins of Durham. Film made in Durham, N.C. (Serial / Comedy / Silent / B&W / Feature.)
Comedy.

948   A Reckless Rover   1918
Dir: David, N.C. *Co:* Ebony Film Company. *Dist:* General Film Company. *Cast:* Ebony

Players (Sam Robinson, Samuel "Sambo" Jacks, Will Starks, Julia Mason, Bert Murphy, Evon Skekeeter, Mildred Price, Walter Brogsdale, Robert Duree, Frank Pollard, George Lewis Stock Company.) (B&W / Short / Silent / 10 min. / FEA 6620.)

949 Reet-Petite and Gone
1947

Dir: Crouch, William Forest. *Prod:* Crouch, William Forest, R.M. Savini, Berle Adams. *Co:* Astor Pictures Corporation. *Cast:* Louis Jordan and His Orchestra. Bea Griffith, June Richmond, Milton Woods, David Bethea, Lorenzo Tucker, Vanita Smythe, Mabel Lee, Dots Johnson, Pat Rainey, Rudy Toombs, J. Lewis Johnson, Joe Lillard.

Screenplay: Irwin Winehouse. Story: William Forrest. Photographer: Don Malkames. Film editor: Leonard Anderson. Recording engineer: Nelson Minnerly. Settings: Frank Namczy. Preview in the *Philadelphia Tribune,* 10/28/45.

(16mm / B&W / Sound / 2 reels / 65 min. / Feature / FEA 5450, 7348–7353.)

The search is on to find the girl whose measurements fit those prescribed in a will of the hero's uncle. Louis Jordan's orchestra and the musical talents of blacks are showcased to support the thin plot.

950 Reform School 1939

Dir: Popkin, Leo C. *Co:* Million Dollar Productions. *Cast:* Louise Beavers, Reginald Fenderson, Monte Hawley, Eugene Jackson, Freddie Jackson, Eddie Lynn, DeForest Covan, Bob Simmons, Maceo Sheffield, Edward Thompson, Vernon McCalla, Alfred Grant, Milton Hall, Clifford Holland, Edward Patrick, Charles Andrews, Harold Garrison, Edward Ony, "Harlem Tuff Kids" (Jackson, Covan, Lynn and Simmons).

Reform School, 1939, was re-released in 1944 under the title *Prison Bait.* Story: Joseph O'Donnell and Hazel Jamieson. Associate

producer: Harry M. Popkin. Supervisor: A.A. Brooks. Assistant director: V.O. Smith. Reviews in the *Philadelphia Afro-American*, 5/6/39, and the *New York Amsterdam News*, 6/17/39. (Feature / B&W / Sound.)

The picture deals with the brutal manner in which petty offenders are disciplined in reform school for juveniles, and with the campaign waged by a woman probation officer to substitute kindness and education. A parole violator is sentenced to reform school and while there becomes the victim of the superintendent and guard's cruelties. Later, his case is brought to the attention of the probation officer. Through her efforts the superintendent is removed and more humane and progressive discipline methods are implemented. Later, the guard steals and plants evidence to cast suspicion on the boy. The boy and his pals, however, take matters into their own hands. Breaking confinement, they round up the guard and force him to confess his guilt.

951   Reformation   1919

Dir: Peacocke, Captain Leslie T. *Prod:* Dones, Sidney P. *Co:* Democracy Photoplay Corporation. *Cast:* Sidney P. Dones, Geraldine Steele, Webb King, Vera Lavassor, Yvonne Dumont, Bert Haily, Fred Scott, Vernol Moore. (Silent / B&W / Feature / 5 reels.) Detective story written by Sidney P. Dones and adapted to screen by Captain Leslie T. Peacocke.

Carter Spencer lives alone with his mother, who is a devout church member. Carter is a fine young fellow, but wild and dissolute; he spends most of his time flirting, gambling and drinking. He is also a prominent member of one of the fashionable tennis clubs. He falls in love with Clarice Penlow, a sweet, pretty girl and devout church member who sings in the choir. She is in love with Carter but will not engage herself to him because of his wild ways. Finally, when national Prohibition goes into effect, she influences Spencer to apply for a position as a Secret Service agent to help enforce Prohibition. Against his will, yet because of his love for Clarice, Carter decides to become an official enemy of John Barleycorn.

952   Regard sur l'Afrique Noire
1947

Prod: Mahuzier, A. *Co:* Les Actualités Françaises. (Chad / Documentary / Sound / 16mm / 1 reel / B&W / 20 min. / Short.)

This film shows 20th century influences on French Equatorial African life.

953   Regeneration   1923

Prod: Norman Film Manufacturing Company. *Co:* Norman Film Manufacturing Company. *Dist:* Norman Films. *Cast:* Carey Brooks, Stella Mayo, M.C. Maxwell, Charles Gains, Alfred Norcom, Clarence Rucker, Dr. R.L. Brown, Steve Reynolds.

Review in *Billboard*, 11/17/23/ by J.A. Jackson. (Silent / B&W / Feature.)

"Violet Daniels, the only child of a widowed sea captain, is left an orphan by the death of her father. He leaves her a strange legacy in the form of a map showing the location of buried treasure on an island. She enlists the aid of her friend Jack in the search. 'Knife' Hurley, mate

of Jack's ship, is a villain who has managed to collect the scum of the waterfront for the crew with the intention of seizing the treasure chart. Aboard ship a fight ensues, a fire starts, 'Knife' grabs the map and escapes on the only lifeboat. Violet and Jack construct a raft and after enduring hardships from thirst and hunger they land on an uninhabited island which they call 'Regeneration.' It's treasure island; 'Knife' arrives and they defeat him"— review from the *Film Herald*.

954   A Regeneration of Souls   1921
Dir: Whipper, Leigh. *Prod:* Whipper, Leigh. *Co:* Whilco Film Corporation. *Cast:* Kid Noland (lightweight boxing champion), Lila Walker Jones.
Publicity in *Billboard*, 3/12/21. (Short / B&W / Silent.)

955   Renaissance Newsreel   1921
Dir: Whipper, Leigh. *Prod:* Whipper, Leigh. *Co:* Whipper, Leigh. (Newsreel / Documentary / B&W / Short / Silent.)
Film footage of a black YMCA, Booker T. Washington Sanitarium, the Imperial Elks Lodge, and 15th Regiment parade.

956   Return of Black Hawk   1921
Dir: Maurice, Richard D. *Prod:* Maurice, Richard D. *Co:* Maurice Film Company. (Silent / B&W.) No record of release.

957   Return of Mandy's Husband   1948
Co: Lucky Star Productions. *Dist:* Toddy Pictures Company. *Cast:* Mantan Moreland, Flournoy E. Miller, John D. Lee, E. Hensley, McKinley Reeves, Terry Knight. (Sound / B&W / Feature / Comedy.)

958   A Review of the B.M.C. and the Colored Business World   1914
Co: Hunter C. Haynes Photoplay Company. (Newsreel / Documentary / B&W / Silent / Short.)
Film footage of prominent black politicians and other subjects.

959   Revival Day   1929
Co: Vitaphone *Cast:* Slim Timblin. (Vita-

phone no. 3679 / B&W / Sound / Short / 10 min. / VBE 8336.)

960   The Revue des Revues   1927
Prod: Nalpas, Alex. *Co:* France. *Cast:* Josephine Baker, Gabrielle Dixon, Andre Luquet, Jeanne de Balzac, Erna Carise, The John Tiller Girls, The Eccentric Stanford, The Russian Trio Kamarowa, Henri Varna. (B&W / Short / Sound.)
Gabrielle, a minor helper at the famous couturier Paquin, becomes a music hall star thanks to the protection of the comedian Georges Barsac.

961   Revue in Rhythm   1955
Co: Studio Films, Inc. *Cast:* Duke Ellington, Dinah Washington, Nat "King" Cole. (Sound / B&W / Musical / Short.)

962   Rhapsody in Black   1934
Dir: McGuire, Neil. *Co:* Organologue. *Cast:* "Uncle" Billy McClain. (16 mm / Sound / B&W / 1 reel / 10 min. / Dramatic / Short.)
A sing-a-long with Negro spirituals. A

typical sequence shows a black man climbing a literal stairway to heaven with giant dice in the sky.

963   Rhapsody of Love   1944

Co: RCM Production. *Dist:* Soundies Distributing Corporation. *Cast:* Hilda Rogers. (Soundies 17408 / B&W / Short / Sound / Musical / 7/24/44.)

964   Rhapsody of Negro Life   1949

Dir: Williams, Spencer. *Prod:* Williams, Spencer. *Co:* Williams, Spencer. (Sound / B&W / Short.)

No record of release.

965   Rhumboogie   1943

Co: RCM Production. *Dist:* Soundies Distributing Corporation. *Cast:* Maurice Rocco. (Soundies 15308 / B&W / Short / Sound / Musical / 12/31/43.)

966   Rhythm and Blues Revue   1956

Dir: Kohn, Joseph. *Prod:* Frye, Ben. *Co:* Studio Films, Inc. *Cast:* Lionel Hampton, Count Basie, Cab Calloway, Nat "King" Cole, Joe Turner, Sarah Vaughan, Little Buck, Delta Rhythm Boys, The Larks, Herb Jeffries, Freddy and Flo Robinson, Martha Davis, Amos Milburn, Faye Adams, Bill Bailey, Mantan Moreland, Nipsey Russell, Ruth Brown, Paul "Hucklebuck" Williams and His Orchestra, M.C. Willie Bryant.

There were two versions made. (Long version / 10 reels / 35mm.) (Short version / 16 mm / B&W / Sound / 2 reels / 70 min. / Feature / FGC 7512–7515.)

Filmed on stage at Harlem theaters, this variety musical was produced for all-black audiences.

967   Rhythm in a Riff   1946

Dir: Birch, Maceo. *Prod:* Alexander, William D. *Co:* Associated Producers of Negro Motion Pictures. *Cast:* Billy Eckstine, Emmett "Babe" Wallace, Ray Moore, Sarah Harris, Ann Baker, Garfield Love, Hortense (The Body) Allen.

Songs: "I'm in the Mood for Love," "Prisoner of Love," "Rhythm in a Riff," "Lonesome

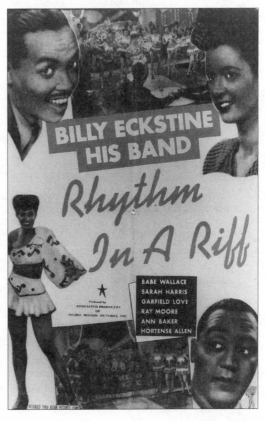

Lover," "You Call It Madness," "What Is This Thing Called Love," "Exactly Like You," and "Second Balcony Jump." Review in the *Houston Informer*, 11/23/46. (Sound / B&W / 45 min. / Feature.)

"Bill Eckstine, the bronze singing idol, makes his screen debut.... Unlike the majority of orchestra features, this film was made sans the usual corny dialogue and meaningless story, but instead highlighted the singing maestro and his crew in a topnotch presentation"—excerpt from *Houston Informer*, 11/23/46.

968   Rhythm in a Riff   1946

Dir: Birch, Maceo / Leonard Anderson. *Prod:* Alexander, William D. *Co:* Alexander Production. *Dist:* Soundies Distributing Corporation. *Cast:* Billy Eckstine and His Orchestra. Excerpted from the Featurette "Rhythm in a Riff" (1946). (Soundies / B&W / Short / Sound / Musical / 12/30/46.)

969   Rhythm in Harlem   1955

Dir: Kohn, Joseph. *Co:* Studio Films, Inc. (B&W / Sound / 31 min. / FCB 0231.)

Typical variety show format.

970   Rhythm Mad   1943

Co: RCM Production. *Dist:* Soundies Distributing Corporation. *Cast:* The Musical Madcaps. (Soundies 6M4 / B&W / Short / Sound / Musical / 10/29/43.)

971   Rhythm Mania   1943

Co: RCM Production. *Dist:* Soundies Distributing Corporation. *Cast:* Harris and Hunt, Mabel Lee, The Harlem Honeys. (Soundies / Short / B&W / 10/29/43.)

972   Rhythm of Africa   1947

Prod: Cocteau, Jean & Francois Villiers. *Co:* Cocteau, Jean & Francois Villiers. *Cast:* Kenneth Spencer.

Screenplay by Langston Hughes. (Documentary / Sound / 16mm / B&W / 1 reel / 17 min. / Short.)

Shows people of Chad working at various jobs and interactions at the marketplace. This film also shows daily village life and gives a special look at the ceremonial dance of atonement.

973   Rhythm of the Rhythm Band   1943

Co: RCM Production. *Dist:* Soundies Distributing Corporation. *Cast:* The Musical Madcaps, Nikki O'Daniels. (Soundies 13408 / B&W / Short / Sound / Musical / 9/20/43.)

974   Rhythm on the River   1932

Co: Paramount. *Cast:* George Dewey Washington. (B&W / Sound / Short.)

"Some fine vocal work by a group of Negro singers, headed by the popular George Dewey Washington, against a river boat setting. The numbers appear to have been specially written for his skit, and they are good. There is also a touch of love interest in George's sweetheart being found stowing away on the boat because she couldn't stay behind, and the girl then contributes her ringing voice to the proceedings"—review from the *Film Daily*, 1/31/32.

975   Rhythm on the Run   1942

Co: RCM Production. *Cast:* Lucky Millinder, Edna Mae Harris. (Sound / B&W / Short / Musical.)

976   Rhythm Rodeo   1938

Dir: Randol, George. *Prod:* Randol, George. *Co:* George Randol Productions. *Cast:* Jackson Brothers, Rosa Lee Lincoln, Jim Davis, Four Tones, Troy Brown.

A musical western, produced for all-black theaters, employs an all-black cast. Screenplay: George Randol. (16 mm / B&W / Sound / 1 reel / 20 min. / Musical / Short.)

977   Rhythm Sam   1946

Dir: Crouch, William Forest. *Prod:* Crouch, William Forest. *Co:* Filmcraft Production. *Dist:* Soundies Distributing Corporation. *Cast:* The Lennox Trio, The Three Peppers. (Soundies 20M2 / Short / B&W / 6/17/46.)

978   Rhythm Saves Day   1937

Dir: Kane, Raymond. *Prod:* Christie, Al. *Co:* Educational Film Corporation. *Cast:* The Cabin Kids (five colored harmonizers, Ruth Hall, Helen Hall, James "Darling" Hall, Winifred "Sugar" Hall, and little Frederick

Hall), Alice Dawn (white), Buddy Page and his band (white).

Story by: Marcy Klauber & Arthur Jarrett. Photographed by: George Weber. (Sound / B&W / 996 ft. / Short.)

"Buddy Page and his orchestra are laboring in uniforms under the guidance of an old-fashion band leader. Threatened with dying a slow death if they continue the dull program, and the maestro will not have his contract renewed unless they draw crowds, Page calls in the Cabin Kids and they lock the maestro up. They picket the town with signs advertising a free swing band. A crowd flocks to the park to hear them and the maestro gets his contract renewed" — review from the *Film Daily*, 11/22/37.

979   Ride On, Ride On   1944

Co: RCM Production. *Dist:* Soundies Distributing Corporation. *Cast:* June Richmond, Roy Milton and His Orchestra. (Soundies / B&W / Short / Sound / Musical / 6/26/44.)

980   Ride, Red, Ride   1941

Co: RCM Production. *Dist:* Soundies Distributing Corporation. *Cast:* The Charioteers. (Soundies 3202 / B&W / Short / Sound / Musical / 9/8/41.)

First music videos.

981   Riff   1943

Co: RCM Production. *Dist:* Soundies Distributing Corporation. *Cast:* The Winnie Hoveler Dancers. (Soundies / B&W / Short / Sound / Musical / 12/6/43.)

982   Rigoletto Blues   1941

Co: RCM Production. *Dist:* Soundies Distributing Corporation. *Cast:* The Delta Rhythm Boys. Recorded by Steve Schultz. (Soundies 4005 / B&W / Short / Sound / Musical / 11/3/41.)

983   Rinka Tinka Man   1944

Co: RCM Production. *Dist:* Soundies Distributing Corporation. *Cast:* Billie Haywood, Cliff Allen. (Soundies 16908 / B&W / Short / Sound / Musical / 6/12/44.)

984   Rise of a Race   1945

Co: Board of Missions of the Presbyterian Church. (Documentary / Newsreel / B&W / Sound / Short.)

Film footage of the wonderful work done by the Presbyterian Church among the blacks of the South.

985   The Road Home   1931

Co: Tiffany Film Company. *Cast:* Forbes Randolph Kentucky Jubilee Singers. (Musical / B&W / Short / Sound.)

Musical presentation.

986   The Roar of the Crowd   1938

Co: Monogram Pictures. *Cast:* Joe Louis, Max Baer, Primo Carnera, Levinsky, Schmeling, Sharkey, Ettore, Braddock. Biographical documentary, (Feature / B&W / Sound.)

Biographical documentary of Joe Louis: his rise, fall, and rise again to fame.

987   Rocco Blues   1943

Co: RCM Production. *Dist:* Soundies Distributing Corporation. *Cast:* Maurice Rocco. (Soundies 15608 / B&W / Short / Sound / Musical / 12/31/43.)

988   Rocco Blues 1947

Prod: Sack, Alfred. *Co:* Sack Amusement Enterprises. *Dist:* Sack Amusement Enterprises. *Cast:* Maurice Rocco, Louis Jordan and His Band, The Chanticleers, The Four Gingersnaps. (Sound / B&W / Featurette / Short.)

Musical short.

989   Rock It for Me 1943

Co: RCM Production. *Dist:* Soundies Distributing Corporation. *Cast:* Maurice Rocco. (Soundies 14708 / B&W / Short / Sound / Musical / 12/27/43.)

990   Rock 'n' Roll Revue 1955

Dir: Kohn, Joseph. *Prod:* Frye, Ben. *Co:* Studio Films, Inc. *Cast:* Nat "King" Cole, Lionel Hampton and His Orchestra, Dinah Washington, Joe Turner, Duke Ellington and His Band, Larry Darnell, The Clovers, Ruth Brown, Coles & Atkins, Martha Davis, Little Buck, Delta Rhythm Boys, Mantan Moreland,

Leonard Reed, Nipsey Russell, Willie Bryant. (16 mm / Tinted / Sound / 70 min. / Feature / FGC 7499–7502.)

Live concert at the Apollo Theater in Harlem, New York. Willie Bryant is the MC.

991   Rockin' Chair 1942

Co: RCM Production. *Dist:* Soundies Distributing Corporation. *Cast:* The Mills Brothers. (Soundies 9292 / B&W / Short / Sound / Musical / 11/2/42.)

992   Rockin' the Blues 1955

Prod: Pollard, Fritz. *Co:* Studio Films, Inc. *Cast:* Mantan Moreland, Flournoy E. Miller, Connie Carroll, Harpstones, Linda Hopkins, Wanderers, Pearl Woods, Hurricanes, Miller Sisters, Reese La Rue, Marilyn Bennett, Elyce Roberts, Lee Lynn, Cuban Dancers. (35 mm / 7 reels / Sound / B&W / Feature.)

Typical musical variety show.

993   Roll Along 1929

Prod: Christie, Al. *Co:* Christie Film Company. *Dist:* Paramount. (Short / B&W / Sound.)

"This film is a comedy in which all of the cast, made up of the well-known Christie players, appears in black face. Negro comedies have been attempted before, but with Negro actors. Christie's innovation lies in the idea that white players, under careful direction can bring out the comedy of the Negro with the skill of the trained White comedian"— newspaper article from the George Johnson Collection.

994   Roll 'Em 1944

Co: RCM Production. *Dist:* Soundies Distributing Corporation. *Cast:* Meade Lux Lewis, Dudley Dickerson, Joe Turner. (Soundies 16008 / B&W / Short / Sound / Musical / 4/3/44.)

995   Romance on the Beat 1945

Dir: Pollard, Bud. *Co:* All American News. *Cast:* Lloyd Randall, Lionel Monagas, Tiny Dickerson, Jimmy Fuller, Percy Verwayne, Hughie Walker, The Four Master Keys and Doc Rhythm, Ida James, Dotty Rhodes.

A Streamlined All American Feature. (16mm / B&W / Sound / 1 reel / 30 min. / Musical / Short / FEA 8317–8320.)

996   Romance Without Finance 1945

Dir: Crouch, William Forest. *Prod:* Crouch, William Forest. *Co:* Filmcraft Production. *Dist:* Soundies Distributing Corporation. *Cast:* Tiny Grimes and His Orchestra. (Soundies 87508 / B&W / Short / Sound / Musical / 12/31/45.)

997   Rufus Green in Harlem 1946

Prod: Toddy, Ted. *Co:* Toddy Pictures Company. *Dist:* Toddy Pictures Company. (Sound / B&W / Short.)

998   Rufus Jones for President 1933

Dir: Mack, Roy. *Co:* Vitaphone. *Cast:* Ethel Waters, Hamtree Harrington, Sammy Davis, Jr., Dusty Fletcher, Edgar Connor, The Will Vodery Girls, The Russell Wooding Jubilee Singers.

Story: Dorian Otvos and Cyrus Wood. Musical score: Cliff Hess. Announcement in *Philadelphia Tribune*, 12/21/33. Review in the *Motion Picture Herald,* 9/2/33. Songs: "Am I Blue," and "I'll Be Glad When You're Dead, You Rascal You." (16mm / Sound / B&W / 16 min. / Comedy / Short.)

A very stereotypical Hollywood musical. This film starts with a 7-year-old Sammy Davis in the arms of Ethel Waters, being told that he could be president one day. He falls asleep and dreams of being president. Plenty of singing and dancing with lots of stereotypical dialect and scenes like, "Vote for Rufus Jones for president and get two pork chops," or scenes of dice-playing in Congress or everyone walking around holding a pork chop.

999   Rug Cutters Holiday 1943

Co: LOL Production. *Dist:* Soundies Distributing Corporation. *Cast:* Freddie and Flo, Slap and Happy, Snap and Snappy. (Soundies 10704 / B&W / Short / Sound / Musical / 3/1/43.)

1000   S.S. Booker T. Washington 1942

Dir: Sherman, Vincent. *Co:* Warner Bros. Screenplay: Lillian Hellman. (Documentary / B&W / Sound / 2 reels / Short / Newsreel.)

"Story of the new cargo vessel, and the background which preceded its launching.... This is the first vessel ever built to honor a colored leader, and to be officered by colored ship's officers"—from the *Philadelphia Afro-American,* 10/24/42.

1001   Saddle Daze 1926

Cast: Wild West Rodeo. (B&W / Silent.)

1002   St. Louis Blues 1929

Dir: Murphy, Dudley. *Prod:* Sack, Alfred. *Co:* Blackhawk Films. *Dist:* Sack Amusement Enterprises. *Cast:* Bessie Smith, Jimmy Mordecai, Isabel Washington, Shingzie Howard, Johnny Lee, Hall Johnson Chorus.

This 17 min. short was Bessie Smith's only film appearance. Produced at Gramercy Studio

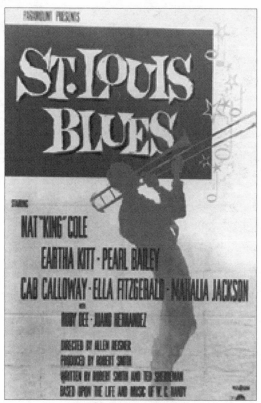

of RCA Photophone, Inc. under the supervision of Dick Currier. Choral arrangements: W.C. Handy and Rosamund Johnson. Cinematographer: Walter Strenge. Written by: Russell Shields. Recordist: George Oschmann. (16mm / B&W / Sound / 1 reel / 17 min. / Dramatic / Short.)

Bessie Smith falls in love with an unfaithful man, who constantly takes her money and throws her down and generally treats her like dirt, and then she sings "The St. Louis Blues."

1003   St. Louis Blues 1958

Dir: Reisner, Allen. *Prod:* Smith, Robert. *Co:* Paramount. *Dist:* Paramount. *Cast:* Nat "King" Cole, Eartha Kitt, Pearl Bailey, Cab Calloway, Ella Fitzgerald, Mahalia Jackson, Ruby Dee, Juano Hernandez, Billy Preston, Teddy Buckner, Barney Bigard, George "Red" Callender, Lee Young, George Washington.

Written by: Robert Smith and Ted Sherdeman. Director of photography: Kaskell Boggs. Art direction: Hal Pereira & Roland Anderson. Special effects: John P. Fulton. Set decoration: Sam Comer & Robert Benton. Assistant direc-

tor: Richard Caffey. Costume: Edith Head. Edited by: Eda Warren. Makeup: Wally Westmore. Hair: Nellie Manley. Sound recordings: Gene Merritt & Charles Grenzbach. Music arranged & conducted by: Nelson Riddle. (16mm / B&W / Sound / 3 reels / 93 min. / Feature.)

Based on the life and music of W.C. Handy (the "Father of the Blues"). The story tells of Handy's struggle to write and play music. His father, a minister, is against the "devil's" music, and, therefore, against his son. He becomes temporarily blind, and of course there's the standby problem, romance.

1004   St. Louis Gal 1938

Co: Creative Cinema Corporation. *Cast:* Nine Mae McKinney, Jack Carter. (Sound / B&W / Short.)

1005   Salute to Duke Ellington
1950

Dir: Cowan, Will. *Co:* Universal-International. *Cast:* Duke Ellington and His Orchestra, Kay Davis, Chubby Kemp, Ray Nance,

Johnny Hodges, Harry Carney, Tyree Glenn, Lawrence Brown.

Review in *Film Daily*, 9/25/50. Songs: "Things Ain't What They Used to Be," "Hello Little Boy," "History of Jazz," "She Wouldn't Be Moved," "Violet Blue," "Take the 'A' Train" (Musical / Short / B&W / 15 min. / Sound.)

Features performances by Duke Ellington and His Orchestra.

1006   Sam and the Bully   1914

Dir: Lubin, Sigmund. *Prod:* Lubin, Sigmund. *Co:* Lubin Manufacturing Company. *Cast:* John Edwards, Mattie Edwards, Speedy Smith.

Written by E.W. Sargent. Released on 12/12/14. (Silent / B&W / 400 ft. / Short.)

"Sam Johnson is not a coward, but he lacks confidence in himself and lets Bully Bill put it all over him. Sam and Bill both love Mattie, or perhaps Bill just butts in to be contrary. Sam sees an advertisement of the Courage Corporation which professes to teach bravery by mail. He puts up five dollars and sends a letter telling what the trouble is. All he gets is the assurance that he can kill Bill if he wants to. Sam thinks that is a great joke and he goes to tell Mattie. On the way he meets Bill and gets another mussing up. Bill enjoys it so much that he follows Sam down to Mattie's and orders him out of her yard. That gets Sam so sore that he commences to believe the letter. He sails in and before astonished Bill quite realizes the situation, he has been chased up a tree and had his pants pulled off. Sam lays the pants at Mattie's feet as a trophy of love and his cup of joy spills over at the sight of Bill being lead off to jail in a barrel. He decides he was not swindled after all. A nice hardworking laundress is worth five dollars any day"—*Lubin Bulletin.*

1007   Sam Langford–Jim Flynn Prize Fight   1910

Co: Western Film Production Company. (Newsreel / Documentary / B&W / Silent / Short.)

Film footage of the Sam Langford–Jim Flynn prize fight.

1008   Samba   1928

Dir: Bruckner, August. *Co:* Münchener Lichtspielkunst Emelka / Coloniale du Film. (Germany / Feature / B&W / Tint / 35mm / 1685 meters / Silent.)

"The first Negro film concieved and realized by French Blacks; it is a faithful rendering of the life of Samba and Fatou made with nonprofessional actors"— Klotman.

1009   Sambo and Jemima   1900

(B&W / Silent / Short / FLA 435.)

Two white comedians in blackface.

1010   Sambo Comedies   1919

Co: Baby Marie Productions. (B&W / Silent / Short.)

1011   Sanders of the River   1935

Dir: Korda, Zoltan. *Prod:* Korda, Alexander. *Co:* Alexander Korda London Films. *Dist:* Film Classic, Inc. *Cast:* Paul Robeson, Leslie Banks, Nina Mae McKinney, Robert Cochran

(white), Martin Walker (white), Toto Ware, Richard Gray, Tony Wane, Marquis de Portago, Eric Haturin, Allen Jeayes, Charles Carson, Chiefs of the Wagenia (Congo) Tribe, Chief of the Acholi Tribe, Members of the Acholi, Sesi, Tefik, Juruba, Mendi, & Kroo Tribes.

Screenplay: Edgar Wallace. Scenario continuity & dialogue: Jeffrey Dell, Lajos Biro. Lyrics: Arthur Wimperis. Musical composition: Michael Spolianski. Photography: George Perinal, Osmond Borrodaile, Louis Page. Recording director: A.W. Watkins. Camera: Bernard Brown. Production manager: E.T. Grossmith. Supervising editor: William Hornbeck. Technical advisors: Major C. Wallace, C.O. Lemon, Cecil Grosse. Film editor: Charles Crichton. Assistant director: Stanley Irving. Musical director: Muir Mathieson. Sound: L. Fisher, D. Field & J. Paddon. (British made / 16mm / B&W / Sound / 2 reels / 88 min. / Feature.)

Sanders was shot in Africa and England. Robeson in loincloth plays Bosambo, a self-appointed leader of the river people who respect "Sandi," the representative of the English crown in this part of West Africa. Complications arise when a bellicose tribal chief foments bloody rebellion by attacking Bosambo's beautiful wife. Sanders rescues Lilongo and re-establishes Bosambo as king.

1012   Sarah Vaughn and Herb Jeffries, Kid Ory, Etc.   1950

Dir: Cowan, Will. *Co:* Universal-International. *Cast:* Sarah Vaughn, Herb Jeffries, Kid Ory and His Creole Jazz Band, The Treniers.

Review in *Film Daily*, 9/25/50. Songs: "Tiajuana Teaparty," "Don't Blame Me," "Muskrat Ramble," "A Woman Is a Worrysome Thing," "You're a Sweetheart," and "I Cried for You." (Sound / B&W / 15 min./ Musical / Short.)

Musical variety short.

1013   Satchel Mouth Baby   1946

Dir: Gould, Dave. *Prod:* Hersh, Ben. *Co:* RCM Production. *Dist:* Soundies Distributing Corporation. *Cast:* Dusty Brooks and His Four Tones, Mildred Boyd. (Soundies 21M4 / B&W / Short / Sound / Musical / 7/22/46.)

1014   Satchmo the Great   1954

Prod: Murrow, Edward R./ Fred Friendly. *Co:* United Artists. *Dist:* United Artists. *Cast:* Louis Armstrong, Edward R. Murrow, Leonard Bernstein, W.C. Handy. (Sound / 64 min. / Feature.)

Louis Armstrong and His All Stars' tour of Africa and Europe is recorded on this footage originally shot for an Ed Murrow show.

1015   Scandal   1933

Co: Goldberg Productions. *Cast:* Lucky Millinder, Putney Dandridge, George Williams, Gallie de Gaston, Billy Higgins, Joe Byrd, 12 Harlem Steppers, 3 Big Bands.

Released under the title "Gig and Saddle." Has also been seen as "Scandals of 1933." Announcement in the *Philadelphia Tribune*, 2/8/34. (Sound / B&W / Musical / Feature.)

A story of backstage life with an all-star colored cast.

1016   The Scapegoat   1917

Dir: McGill, Lawrence B. *Co:* Frederick Douglas Film Company. *Cast:* Abbie Mitchell,

Walker Thompson, Maude Jones, Sidney Kirkpatrick, Leon Williams, Mabel Young, "Little Jeff," Jack Thornton, Lorrine Harris, Josephine Thornton. Original Story: Paul Lawrence Dunbar. (Silent / B&W / Feature.)

"This film is in three parts and lacks a certain cohesiveness of sequence … [characters] at times, are thrust into new environments and new conditions with startling abruptness. As a case in point, Asbury is seen as a single man and in the next scene shows him with his wife and child — quite a hurdling of periods.… — It was gratifying to note that when Asbury's child was sick a Colored doctor was summoned, even if few Colored lawyers were in evidence at his trial" — review excerpted from the *New York Age*, 5/17/17.

1017   The Scar of Shame   1927

Dir: Perugini, Frank. *Prod:* Dudley, Sherman H., Jr. *Co:* Colored Players Film Corporation of Phila. *Cast:* Harry Henderson, Lucia Moses, Ann Kennedy, Norman Johnstone, William E. Pettus, Pearl McCormick, Lawrence Chenault. (16mm / Silent / B&W / 3 reels / 90 min. / Feature / FEA 7342–7347.)

Made in Philadelphia, Pennsylvania. Story: David Starkman. Photographed by: Al Liguori. Preview in review in the *Philadelphia Tribune*, 4/11/29. Major story on *Scar of Shame* and Colored Players Film Corporation of Philadelphia in the *Philadelphia Bulletin* (magazine), 11/17/74.

This is the story of a marriage between Alvin, a black music student, and a poor lower-class black girl, Louise. Alvin is ashamed of his wife and keeps their marriage a secret from his class-conscious mother. However, Louise's drunken father plans to kidnap her so that she can sing at the nightclub of Spike, one of his gangster friends. During an argument between Louise and Spike, Alvin accidentally shoots and wounds Louise. Alvin is sent to prison but later escapes. He begins his life anew and falls in love with another woman, Alice. Eventually Louise sees Alvin again and begs him to leave Alice and return to her. Alvin refuses because he knows she can never be his equal. Rejected, Louise commits suicide. Later, Alvin marries Alice and starts a new life.

Scarlet Claw see The Crimson Skull

1018   The Schemers   1922

Dir: Reol Productions. *Cast:* Edna Morton, G. Edward Brown, Lawrence Chenault. (Silent / B&W / Feature.)

This is the story of a struggling young chemist who is employed by a drug firm and who has made several important discoveries, among which is a formula for making gasoline. This fact is discovered by a syndicate of international swindlers, who, after finding they could not bribe the young chemist to sell the formulas, attempt to steal them. However, they are thwarted in the attempt by the chemist's sweetheart, who overhears the plot.

1019   Scotch Boogie   1945

Co: RCM Production. *Dist:* Soundies Distributing Corporation. *Cast:* Pat Flowers. (Soundies 88508 / B&W / Short / Sound / Musical / 9/10/45.)

1020   A Scrap in Black and White   1903

Co: Thomas A. Edison, Inc. (B&W / Silent / Short / FLA 4865.)

"Two boys, one black, one white, pummel each other without a clear decision, although the climax is a knockdown by the black boy, who hovers menacingly over his white victim" — Thomas Cripps.

1021   Second News Reel   1942

Co: All-American News. (Sound / B&W / Newsreel / Documentary / Short.)

Subjects include: victory parade; football game between New York Bombers and Washington Lions; black calvary troops at Ft. Myers, Virginia; training of black doctors and nurses at Meharry Medical College, Nashville, Tennessee; Fisk University Choir.

1022   Secret Sorrow   1921

Prod: Levy, Robert. *Co:* Reol Productions. *Cast:* Edna Morton, G. Edward Brown, Percy Verwayen, Inez Clough, Ida Anderson, Lawrence Chenault, J.H. Woodson, Henry Pleasants.

Review in *Billboard*, 11/16/21, by J.A. Jackson. (Silent / B&W / Feature.)

This is the story of two brothers, one living with their mother, the other adopted by a doctor. The adopted one, Arthur, grew up to be an assistant district attorney and Joe, raised by his mother, grew up to be a notorious gangster. Joe works for Sam Dungan, a power in city politics and the owner of several notorious dives. Arthur is in love with Sam's daughter, Grace. Joe is falsely arrested for murder. Arthur, the prosecutor, calls Joe's mother to the stand (not knowing that she is also his mother) and tears at her to prove that Joe is a degenerate. Through clever work of Grace, the real murderer is apprehended and the mother and the two boys are again united, with Grace as an addition to the happy group.

1023   Seeing Kansas City in Action   1921

Co: St. Paul Presbyterian Church. (Newsreel / Documentary / B&W / Short / Silent.)

Black business and professional life in Kansas City, Missouri.

1024   The Seeress   pre–1910

(B&W / Silent / Short / FLA 4394.)

1025   Selected Negro Work Songs   1952

Provided by Center for Southern Folklore. (16mm / B&W / Sound / 9 min. / Documentary / Short.)

Two black laborers' songs, "Let the Church Roll On" and "Dis Old Hammer," sung by a mixed chorus.

1026   Sepia Cinderella   1947

Dir: Leonard, Arthur. *Prod:* Goldberg, Jack / Arthur Leonard. *Co:* Herald Pictures, Inc. *Cast:* Sheila Guyse, Billy Daniels, Tondelayobrillianis, Ruby Blake, Emery Richardson, Jack Carter, Ruby Verwayen, Dusty Freeman, George Williams, Fred Gordon, Al Young, Freddie Bartholomew, June Proctor, John Kirby and His Band, Walter Fuller Orchestra, Deek Watson and His Brown Dots, Apus and Estellita, Leonardo and Zolo, Lorenzo Tucker.

Film announcement in the *Philadelphia Independent,* 1/11/47. Previews in the *Philadelphia Tribune,* 1/10/48, and the *New York Age,*

7/26/47. Screenplay and story: Vincent Valentini. Director of Photography: George Webber. Film editor: Jack Kemp. Musical direction: John Gluskin. Art direction: Frank Namczy. Sound engineer: Nelson Minnerly. Costumes: Ann Blazier. Casting director: Billy Shaw. Makeup: Edward Scanlon. Technical advisor: Jacob M. Lehrfeld. (16mm / Sound / B&W / 67 min. / Feature / FEA 7342–7347.)

In a very loose plot: boy loses girl, boy finds girl. He is a songwriter and she is a singer, and they plan to get married. He gets a job in a nightclub and falls in love with the proprietress, to the consternation of her boyfriend. The boy is fired. His girl gets a job in a cafe, sings a song written by him, and they finally get back together.

1027   Sergeant Joe Louis on Tour   1943

Prod: Toddy, Ted. *Co:* Toddy Pictures Company. *Cast:* Joe Louis. (Sound / B&W / Documentary / Short.)

Follows the great boxer's tours for the Army during World War II.

1028   Set My People Free   1948

(B&W / Sound / Short.)

1029   Shadowed by the Devil   1916

Co: Unique Film Company. *Cast:* Orville Fletcher, Gertrude Mills.

The film is based on an original story by Mrs. M.M. Webb. (3 reels / Silent / B&W / Short.)

The theme of this story should be "The good, the bad, and the ugly." It is based on three different characters: a frivolous, spoiled girl (ugly), a Satan-guided businessman (bad), and a loving father and husband (good). How their lives develop is the plot of this story.

1030   Shadrach   1941

Co: RCM Production. *Dist:* Soundies Distributing Corporation. *Cast:* The Deep River Boys. (Soundies 3903 / B&W / Short / Sound / Musical / 10/27/41.)

1031   Shake It Up   1929

Co: Vitaphone. *Cast:* Eddie Moran, Beth Challis, Six Cheerful Steppers. (Vitaphone No.

854 / B&W / Sound / Short / 10 min. / VBE 8159.)

1032   Shango   1953

Dir: Henle, Fritz. *Cast:* Geoffrey Holder and his troupe. (Sound / Color / 10 min. / Short.)

Trinidad's musical heritage is illustrated through the authentic tribal dances performed by Geoffrey Holder and his troupe. One of the dances is a ritual dance in which a chicken is sacrificed.

She Devil   *see*   **Drums o' Voodoo**

1033   She's Crazy with Heat   1946

Dir: Anderson, Leonard. *Prod:* Alexander, William D. *Co:* Alexander Production. *Dist:* Soundies Distributing Corporation. *Cast:* Anna Mae Winburn and the International Sweethearts of Rhythm. (Soundies 25M1 / B&W / Short / Sound / Musical / 11/3/46.)

1034   She's Too Hot to Handle   1944

Co: RCM Production. *Dist:* Soundies Dis-

tributing Corporation. *Cast:* Bob Howard. (Soundies 18208 / B&W / Short / Sound / Musical / 9/25/44.)

1035   She's Too Mean for Me   1948

Prod: Toddy, Ted. *Co:* Goldman Productions. *Dist:* Toddy Pictures Company. *Cast:* Mantan Moreland, Johnny Lee, Flournoy E. Miller. (Sound / B&W / Feature.)

1036   Shine   1942

Dir: Berne, Josef. *Prod:* Coslow, Sam. *Co:* RCM Production. *Dist:* Soundies Distributing Corporation. *Cast:* Louis Armstrong and His Orchestra. (Soundies 18008 / B&W / Short / Sound / Musical / 6/29/42.)

1037   Shine   1944

Co: RCM Production. *Dist:* Soundies Distributing Corporation. *Cast:* Bob Howard. (Soundies 18008 / B&W / Short / Sound / Musical / 9/4/44.)

First musical videos.

1038   Shine Johnson and the Rabbit Foot   1917

Co: Ebony Film Company. *Dist:* General Films Company. *Cast:* Ebony Players (Sam Robinson, Samuel "Sambo" Jacks, Will Starks, Julia Mason, Bert Murphy, Evon Skekeeter, Mildred Price, Walter Brogsdale, Robert Duree, Frank Pollard, George Lewis Stock Company). (Comedy / B&W / Short / Silent.)

1039   Sho Had a Wonderful Time   1946

Dir: Crouch, William Forest. *Prod:* Crouch, William Forest. *Co:* Filmcraft Production. *Dist:* Soundies Distributing Corporation. *Cast:* Vanita Smythe, Claude DeMetrius. (Soundies 25M3 / B&W / Short / Sound / Musical / 11/18/46.)

1040   Shoe Shine Boy   1945

Co: Metro-Goldwyn-Mayer. *Cast:* Walter Catlett, Melvin Bryant. (B&W / Sound / Short.)

"This short tells how a Colored shoe shine boy realizes his ambition to own a trumpet. When the youth is offered an attractive contract after demonstrating his talent as a trumpeter, he turns the offer down with the explanation he wanted the trumpet just so he could practice to be a bugler in the Army"— excerpt of review from *Film Daily*, 2/12/45.

1041   Shoot 'Em Up, Sam   1922

Co: Black Western Film Company. *Cast:* Kid Nolan (Heavyweight boxing champion of New England). (Silent / B&W / Western / Feature.)

1042   Shoot the Rhythm to Me   1943

Co: RCM Production. *Dist:* Soundies Distributing Corporation. *Cast:* The Musical Madcaps. (Soundies 4M3 / B&W / Short / Sound / Musical / 9/21/43.)

1043   A Shot in the Night   1922

Prod: Strasser, Ben. *Co:* North State Film Corporation. *Cast:* Bobby Smart, Walter Hoelby, Walter Long, Ruth Freeman, Tom Amos, Tolliver Brothers.

Preview in *Billboard*, 3/4/22 by J.A. Jackson. (Silent / B&W / Feature / Mystery.)

The city is in the grip of the "Masked Terror," a criminal who has just stolen a half million dollars and killed a banker in the process. The story is stolen by an 8-year-old boy, who while playing detective discovers the "Midnight Terror's" hideout. Naturally, he is discovered and about to be disposed of when he is rescued by the district attorney. Not to be outdone the "Masked Terror" finds and kidnaps the dead banker's daughter. But, once again just as he is about to dispose of her, the district attorney rescues her and eventually catches the "Masked Terror."

1044   Shout, Brother, Shout   1946

Dir: Gould, Dave. *Prod:* Hersh, Ben. *Co:* RCM Production. *Dist:* Soundies Distributing Corporation. *Cast:* Dusty Brooks and His Four Tones. (Soundies 23M3 / B&W / Short / Sound / Musical / 9/16/46.)

1045   Shout! Sister, Shout!   1941

Co: RCM Production. *Dist:* Soundies Distributing Corporation. *Cast:* Sister Rosetta Tharpe, Lucky Millinder and His Orchestra. (Soundies 3701 / B&W / Short / Sound / Musical / 10/13/41.)

1046   Shuffling Jane   1921

Co: Tropical Photoplay Company. *Cast:* Elizabeth Boyer. (Silent / B&W / Short.)

1047   Shut My Big Mouth   1947

Prod: Toddy, Ted. *Co:* Toddy Pictures Company. *Cast:* Dewey "Pigmeat" Markham, John Murray (white). (Sound / B&W / 63 min. / Feature.)

1048   Simba   1955

Dir: Hurst, Brian D. *Prod:* Sarigny, Peter de. *Co:* Arthur Rank Productions. *Cast:* Earl Cameron, Orlando Martins, Ben Johnson, Joseph Tomelty, Dirk Bogarde (white), Virginia McKenna (white).

Screenplay: John Baines & Robin Estridge. (British / Feature / Sound / B&W.)

Story of terrorism and revenge, a semi-documentary of the Mau-Mau movement in Kenya. Earl Cameron is Karaja; Ben Johnson, Kimani; Orlando Martins, a Headman; and Joseph Tomelty, Dr. Hughes, the martyred physician.

1049   The Simp   1921

Co: Reol Productions. *Cast:* S.H. Dudley, Jr., Inez Clough, Edna Morton, Alex K. Shannon, Percy Verwayan. (35mm / Silent / B&W / Feature.)

1050   Sing and Swing   1943

Co: RCM Production. *Dist:* Soundies Distributing Corporation. *Cast:* The Fast Steppers, The Roberts Brothers. (Soundies / B&W / Short / Sound / Musical / 7/12/43.)

1051   Singin' the Blues   1948

(Sound / B&W / Feature.)
The life story of W.C. Handy, the father of the blues.

1052   A Sinner Kissed an Angel   1942

Co: RCM Production. *Dist:* Soundies Distributing Corporation. *Cast:* Johnny Johnston, Judith Gibson.
Recorded by Darrell Calker. (Soundies / Short / B&W / 1/19/42.)

1053   Siren of the Tropics   1927

Dir: Nalpas, Mario / Henri Etierant. *Co:* Centrals Cinematographique. *Dist:* Gold Talking Picture Company. *Cast:* Josephine Baker, Reginia Dalthy, Regina Thomas, Georges Melchior (white), Signor Albertini (white), Count Pepito DiAbatino (white), Pierre Batcheff (white), Adolphe Cande (white), Kiranine.
Produced in France (*La Sirens des Tropiques*) and later released in America. Screenplay: Maurice De Kobra. Review in *New York Amsterdam News*, 7/31/29 & 11/20/29. (Silent / B&W / Feature.)
Josephine Baker is Papitou, the beautiful West Indian mulatto daughter of a white man and a black woman, who falls in love with Berval, a visiting Frenchman. A number of complicated circumstances bring her to Paris where she performs in a music hall, shoots a villainous marquis (for the sake of her lover) and manages to survive a disappointing denouncement of her love affair.

1054   Sissle and Blake   1923

Dir: De Forrest, Lee. *Prod:* De Forrest, Lee. *Co:* Lee De Forrest Phonofilms. *Cast:* Noble Sissle, Eubie Blake.

This film short is one of the earliest experimental sound films made, and it is the first appearance of blacks on sound film. (35mm / Sound / B&W / 1 reel / Musical / Short / 3 min. / FEA 5455.)
The famous team performs "I'll Never Roam from My Swanee Home," "Affectionate Doll," and "All God's Children."

1055   Sissle and Blake   1930

Co: Vitaphone. *Cast:* Noble Sissle, Eubie Blake. (Sound / B&W / Short.)
Sissle and Blake perform "The Big Parade."

1056   Sizzle with Sissle   1946

Dir: Crouch, William Forest. *Prod:* Crouch, William Forest. *Co:* Filmcraft Productions. *Dist:* Soundies Distributing Corporation. *Cast:* Noble Sissle, Mabel Lee. (Soundies 26M2 / B&W / Short / Sound / Musical / 12/9/46.)

1057   The Skunk Song   1942

Co: Minoco Production. *Dist:* Soundies Distributing Corporation. *Cast:* Cab Calloway and His Orchestra: Lamar Wright, Russell Smith, Shad Collins, Jonah Jones (trumpets); Keg Johnson, Tyree Glenn, Quentin Jackson (trombones); Jerry Blake, Hilton Jefferson, Andrew Brown, Teddy McRae, Walter Thomas (reeds); Benny Payne (piano); Danny Barker (guitar); Milt Hilton (bass); Cozy Cole (drums); The Cabaliers (the Four Palmer Brothers, vocal quartet). (Soundies 6105 / B&W / Short / Sound / Musical / 3/30/42.)

1058   The Slacker   1917

Dir: Jones, Peter P. *Prod:* Jones, Peter P. *Co:* Peter P. Jones Photoplay Company. (Silent / B&W / Short.)
This inspirational World War I film uses ghost of wars past and a sweetheart to convince a young man to join in the war effort. Of course, he ends up a hero in France.

1059   Slave Days   1930

Dir: Randolph, Forbes. *Co:* Tiffany Film Company. *Cast:* Forbes Randolph Kentucky Jubilee Singers. (B&W / Sound / Short / 9 min.)
"A rendition of Civil War darky melodies by the Singers. They interpret some of the

old-time songs with some splendid work. For lovers of the real darky melodies, this should prove a treat. The set shows an old plantation, and the recording is excellent"— review from *Film Daily*, 12/7/30.

1060   The Slaver 1917

Dir: Jones, Peter P. *Prod:* Jones, Peter P. *Co:* Peter P. Jones Photoplay Company. (Silent / B&W / Feature.)

A tribal chieftain on the coast of Africa reverses the slavery pattern: He makes a deal with a white sea captain to buy a white girl. A black cabin boys saves her, sacrificing himself in the process.

1061   Slavery 1953

Co: NET. Series: History of the Negro People. (16mm / Sound / B&W / 1 reel / 30 min. / Documentary / Short.)

Based on actual testimony of former slaves, it tells of the tragic and sometimes humorous experience of life in the Old South. Tells of small incidents in the lives of many slaves and depicts the liberation of slaves by the Yankee troops. Uses Negro spirituals to help tell the story of slavery.

1062   Sleep Kentucky Babe
1945

Dir: Berne, Josef. *Prod:* Crouch, William Forest. *Co:* RCM Production. *Dist:* Soundies Distributing Corporation. *Cast:* Day, Dawn, and Dusk. (Soundies 21408 / B&W / Short / Sound / Musical / 9/3/45.)

1063   Sleepy Time Down South
1942

Co: RCM Production. *Dist:* Soundies Distributing Corporation. *Cast:* Louis Armstrong and His Orchestra. (Soundies 6906 / B&W / Short / Sound / Musical / 5/25/42.)

1064   Slim-the-Cow-Puncher
1914

Co: Al Bartlett Film Manufacturing Company. (Silent / Short / B&W.)

1065   Slow Poke 1932

Dir: Herzig, Sid. *Prod:* Hammons, E.W. *Co:* Educational Film Corporation. *Cast:*

Stepin Fetchit, Bunny and the Cotton Girls, Lethia Hill, Una Labek, Katherine Smith.

Screenplay: Sid Herzig. Supervised by: B.K. Blake. Musical supervision: Sunia S. Samuels. Edited by: Leonard Weiss. Photographed by: Frank Zucker. Series: Song Hit Stories. (16mm / B&W / Sound / 1 reel / 10 min. / Musical / Short.)

A typical stereotypical performance by Stepin Fetchit with music. His wife sings a song about the laziest man on earth while he complains and nods in his rocking chair surrounded by variety acts.

1066   Smash Your Baggage
1932

Dir: Mack, Roy & Joseph Henabery. *Co:* Vitaphone. *Cast:* Roy Eldridge, Dickie Wells, Small's Paradise Entertainers, Emett "Babe" Wallace, "Rubber Legs" Williams, Doris Rheubottom, Vic, Ace, and Danny, Dewey Brown. Review in *Film Daily*, 1/14/33. (16mm / Sound / 1 reel / Musical / Short.)

The plot revolves around the treasurers of the railroad brotherhood losing funds shooting craps. The locale is Grand Central Station where the redcaps work and the high point is a benefit revue with a half dozen musical/ dance numbers.

1067   Smiling Hate 1924

Prod: Calnek, Roy. *Co:* Superior Arts Motion Picture Company. *Cast:* Harry Henderson, Josephine Talley, Howard Agusta, William Milton, William Clayton, Ethel Smith, Will Lee.

Story: Ray Ujffy, adapted by Paul K. Alger, under the supervision of Albert A. Fish. Review in the *Philadelphia Tribune*, 7/8/25. (Silent / B&W / Feature / Western / 6 reels.)

Warren Headley, owner of the "Glory Hole" gold mine, seeks the source of high-grading at his mine. He sends Bane, his future son-in-law, to investigate with the assistance of his son, Bob. Bob falls in love with Ruth, the pretty canteen girl, and is assisted in his efforts to discover the thieves by a twisted deformed creature known as "Smiling Hate." Lusting after Ruth, Bane attacks her and leaves evidence. Bob starts a furious search for Bane and his search culminates in a titanic struggle. "Smiling Hate" reveals that his twisted, distorted shape has been assumed and that he is none other than James Randall, owner of a gold mine which previously had been ruined by high-graders. He is also an old buddy, who helped obtain proof that Bane is the leader of high-graders.

1068   Snappy Tunes 1923
Co: Lee De Forrest Phonofilms. *Cast:* Noble Sissle, Eubie Blake.

They perform three songs including "Affectionate Dan" and "All God's Children Got Shoes." (Silent / B&W / Musical / Short.)

1069   Snoqualomie Jo Jo 1945
Co: RCM Production. *Dist:* Soundies Distributing Corporation. *Cast:* The Delta Rhythm Boys. (Soundies 89008 / B&W / Short / Sound / Musical / 6/4/45.)

1070   The Snowman pre–1910
(B&W / Silent / Short / FLA 5706.)

1071   Solid Senders 1941
Cast: Edna Mae Harris, "Rubberneck" Holmes. (Sound / B&W / Short.)

1072   Some Baby 1917
Co: Ebony Film Company. *Dist:* General Film Company. *Cast:* Ebony Players (Sam Robinson, Samuel "Sambo" Jacks, Will Starks, Julia Mason, Bert Murphy, Evon Skekeeter, Mildred Price, Walter Brogsdale, Robert Duree, Frank Pollard, George Lewis Stock Company).

Review in the *Philadelphia Tribune*, 2/13/26. (Silent / B&W / Short / 2 reels.)

"A somewhat diverting chase picture by Negro players. It ought to go pretty well in many houses partly on account of the novelty of a dark-skinned cast and partly because it is light and inconsequential to fit the mood of some who do not want to think"—review from the *Moving Picture World*, 12/8/17.

1073   Some of These Days 1942
Co: RCM Production. *Dist:* Soundies Distributing Corporation. *Cast:* Maxine Sullivan. (Soundies 6205 / B&W / Short / Sound / Musical / 4/6/42.)

1074   Son of Ingagi 1940
Dir: Kahn, Richard C. *Prod:* Kahn, Richard C. *Co:* Hollywood Pictures Corporation. *Dist:* Sack Amusement Enterprises. *Cast:* Laura Bowman, Zack Williams, Spencer Williams, Daisy Bufford, Alfred Grant, Earl J. Morris, Arthur Ray, Jesse Graves, The Four Toppers.

The first black-cast horror film. Story: Spencer Williams, originally titled *House of Horror*. Screenplay, story and continuity: Spencer Williams. Supervisor of production: Dr. Herbert Meyer. Production manager: Dick L'estrange. Cinematography: Roland Price & Herman Schope. Sound engineer: Cliff Ruberg. Film editor: Dan Milner. Reviews in the *Pittsburgh Courier*, 12/28/39, and 1/27/40. (Sound / B&W / Feature / 70 min.)

A scientist who is wealthy and a recluse wills her fortune and a gloomy old house to a newlywed, the daughter of the man that she once loved but who did not return her love. The scientist has brought back from Africa an

blacks drinking, carousing and crap shooting. Preview in the *Philadelphia Tribune*, 2/13/26. Review in the *Chicago Defender*, 1/31/25. (Silent / B&W / Feature.)

The story revolves around the experiences of a man going to a haunted house and staying all night because of a bet.

1076   Song After Sorrow   1929

Co: National Archives Gift Collection.

Part of Record Group 200 HF series, Harmon Foundation Collection. (B&W / Silent / 16mm / 3 reels / Short.)

At the Bibanga Laper Camp patients learn to be self-supporting during treatment.

1077   A Song and Dance Man   1943

Co: RCM Production. *Dist:* Soundies Distributing Corporation. *Cast:* Taps Miller. (Soundies 14208 / B&W / Short / Sound / Musical / 11/22/43.)

1078   The Song of Freedom   1938

Dir: Wills, J. Elder. *Prod:* Wills, J. Elder. *Co:* British Lion–Hammer Production / Trio Exchange. *Cast:* Paul Robeson, Elizabeth Welch, George Mozart, Esme Percy, Arthur Williams, Robert Adams, Orlando Martins, James Solomon (white), Ecce Homo Toto, Ronald Simpson, Jenny Dean, John Fred Emney, Bernard Ansell, Johnnie Schofield, Ambrose Manning, Honorable Arthur Eliot, Miss C. Smith.

British-made film. Story: Claude Wallace & Dorothy Holloway. Screen adaptation & scenario: Ingram D'Abbes & Fenn Sherie. Music: Eric Ansell. Lyrics: Henrik Ege. Photography: Eric Cross, Harry Rose, Thomas Glover. Art: Norman Arnold. Assistant director: Arthur Allcott. Sound: Harold King. Edited by: Arthur Tavares. Production supervisor: H. Fraser Passmore. Review in the *Philadelphia Tribune*, 8/25/38. (16mm / Sound / B&W / 2 reels / 80 min. / Feature.)

Paul Robeson plays a London stevedore, a descendant of slaves, who longs to return to his homeland in Africa to help his oppressed people. To this end, he becomes an opera singer which gives him the opportunity to

ape man who drinks a potion she has concocted in the laboratory. The ape-man turns on her and kills her. Later, he murders an attorney who is searching for $20,000 in gold that the scientist has hidden in her home. Zeno, brother of the scientist and ex-convict, finds the money but is discovered by the ape-man. Zeno fires on the ape-man but the ape-man kills the brother before dying. A detective finally recovers the gold and presents it to the newlyweds.

1075   Son of Satan   1924.

Dir: Micheaux, Oscar. *Prod:* Micheaux, Oscar. *Co:* Micheaux Film Corporation. *Dist:* Micheaux Film Corporation. *Cast:* Andrew Bishop, Lawrence Chenault, Emmette Anthony, Edna Morton, Monte Hawley, Shingzie Howard, Ida Anderson, E.G. Tatum, Marie Dove, Margaret Brown, Walter Robinson, Mildred Smallwood, the chorus from "Runnin' Wild" show.

This is one of the few films that Micheaux produced which showed numerous scenes of

raise money and to sing for the film audience.

1079   Souls of Sin   1949

Dir: Lindsay, Powell. *Prod:* Alexander, William D. *Co:* Alexander Production. *Cast:* Savannah Churchill, William Greaves, Jimmy Wright, Billie Allen, Emory Richardson, Louise Jackson, Powell Lindsay, Charlie Mae Rae, Bill Chase, Jessie Walter, Harris and Scot Henry Glover.

Written by Powell Lindsay. Cinematographer: Louis Andres. Editor: Walter Kruder. Production supervisor: Harriette A. Miller. (Sound / B&W / 65½ min. / 5,878 ft. / Feature / FGC 2388–2390.)

In a wonderful slice of Harlem, this story takes place in a boardinghouse full of aspiring, but poor artists. The calm is disrupted when Dollar Bill, a cheap hoodlum, moves in. His aspirations to be a big time hood and his relationship with life and the boardinghouse tenants are, at the least, tumultuous. The ten-

ants try in vain to guide him to the straight and narrow, but eventually he dies in a mob shoot-out.

1080   The Sound of Jazz

1957

Dir: Smight, Jack. *Prod:* Hentoff, Nat / Whitney. *Co:* Studio Films, Inc. *Cast:* Henry "Red" Allen (white) and His All Stars, Billie Holiday, Mal Waldron All Stars (white), Count Basie's All Stars, Jimmy Rushing, Jimmy Giuffre Trio, Thelonius Monk. (Sound / 60 min. / Musical / Feature.)

Musical extravaganza including the above listed artists performing numbers such as "Wild Man Blues," "Fine and Mellow," and "I Left My Baby."

1081   Southern a Cappella

1950

Prod: Wilder, A.W. Lee. *Co:* United Artists. *Cast:* Jester Hairston, Male choral group.

Songs of America Series. Songs: "Dis Ol' Hammer" and "Git on Board Little Chillun." (Musical / Short / B&W / Sound.)

1082   The Southern Negro Baptism   1921

Co: Dunbar Film Corporation. (Documentary / Silent / Newsreel / Short / B&W.)

Film footage of Negro religious services.

1083   Southern Revellers   1928

Co: Vitaphone. Songs: "Goin' Fly All Over God's Heaven," "G'wine Home," and "Hallelujah." (Musical / B&W / Short / Sound.)

"They have good character vocal numbers built around them. The characters are seen around a cabin door taking the part of field hands on a plantation after a day of cotton picking ... a basso solo, later a comedy spiritual with many extra verses complete a repertoire that is sure to please any audience" — review from the *Philadelphia Tribune*, 9/6/28.

1084   The Spider's Web   1926

Dir: Micheaux, Oscar. *Prod:* Micheaux, Oscar. *Co:* Micheaux Film Corporation. *Dist:* Micheaux Film Corporation. *Cast:* Evelyn Preer, Billy Gulfport, Marshall Rogers,

Edward Thompson, Lorenzo McLane, Henrietta Loveless, Grace Smythe.

Using a different cast, Micheaux produced a sound version of this picture in 1932 under the title *The Girl from Chicago*. From the story "The Policy Player." (35mm / Silent / B&W / 7 reels / 6,913 ft. / Feature.)

Mary Austin, a widow dwelling in a small Southern delta town, is visited by her niece, Norma of New York. At the depot Norma meets and makes a date with Ballinger for later that night. Meanwhile, Elmer Harris, a detective with the U.S. Secret Service, has come from Chicago looking for a criminal. When Harris comes to Mary's house that night, he recognizes Ballinger as the man he's seeking. Ballinger's associates force Norma and Mary to return. Despondent, Mary takes up gambling; when she hits big and tries to collect her money she is framed for murder. Harris and Norma unravel the mystery and find the persons who committed the crime which leads to Mary's release from prison.

1085   Spirit of Boogie Woogie
1942
Co: RCM Production. *Dist:* Soundies Distributing Corporation. *Cast:* Meade Lux Lewis, The Katherine Dunham Dancers. (Soundies 8103 / B&W / Short / Sound / Musical / 8/17/42.)

1086   The Spirit of the
Hellfighters   1932
Co: Calverton Motion Picture Service. *Cast:* The 369th (Black) Regiment. (Documentary / Newsreel / B&W / Short / Sound.)

The story of the famed 369th Regiment in World War I.

1087   The Spirit of Youth   1937
Dir: Fraser, Harry. *Prod:* Golder, Lew. *Co:* Globe Pictures / Vintage Films. *Dist:* Thunderbird Films. *Cast:* Joe Louis, Anthony Scott, Jesse Lee Brooks, Clarence Muse, Edna Mae Harris, Janette O'Dell, Mae Turner, Mantan Moreland, Cleo Desmond, Tom Southern, Clarence Brooks, Jewel Smith, Margarette Whitten, The Plantation Boys Choir, The Creole Chorus, The Big Apple Dancers.

Released through Thunderbird Films. Screenplay: Arthur Hoerl. Associate producer: Edward Shanberg. With original score by Clarence Muse & Elliot Carpenter. Supervisor: Clarence Muse. Photography: Robert Cline. Art: F. Paul Sylos. Musical conductor: Lee Zahler. Technical advisors: Julian Black, John Roxborough. Production manager: Nack Griffith. Film editor: Carl Pierson. Recording engineer: Farrell Redd. Paper (posters, lobby cards, etc.) has Grand National listed as company. Review in the *Philadelphia Tribune*, 1/13/38. TV preview in the *New York Amsterdam News* by S.W. Garlington, 5/20/49. (16mm / B&W / Sound / 2 reels / 70 min. / Feature — FEA 6453–6459.)

A country boy (Joe Louis) leaves home in search of work, so that he might take care of his crippled father. Louis gets involved in a fight and is discovered to have a dynamite punch. Persuaded to get into boxing he goes on to win the Golden Gloves and gains tremendous success. Louis takes to a woman and the party life, neglecting his training. He proceeds to lose a fight and his woman. Louis finally is given a short at the world championship, but having lost his girl his heart is not in it. Luckily, while Louis is taking a beating he sees his girl in the audience and is inspired to go on and win the world championship.

1088   Spiritual Sing-a-Long 1-A
1948
Co: Sack Amusement Enterprises. *Dist:* Sack Amusement Enterprises. *Cast:* Heavenly Choir. (Musical / B&W / Short / Sound.)

Songs: "Great Day," "Steal Away," and "Couldn't Hear Nobody Pray."

1089   Spiritual Sing-a-Long 2-B
1948
Co: Sack Amusement Enterprises. *Dist:* Sack Amusement Enterprises. *Cast:* Heavenly Choir. (Musical / Sound / B&W / Short.)

Songs: "All God's Children," "Nobody Knows the Trouble I've Seen" and "Cross the River of Gold."

1090   Spiritual Sing-a-Long 3-C
1948
Co: Sack Amusement Enterprises. *Dist:* Sack Amusement Enterprises. *Cast:* Heav-

enly Choir. (Musical / B&W / Sound / Short.)

Songs: "Give Me That Old Time Religion" and "I Ain't Gonna Study War No More."

1091   Spiritual Sing-a-Long 4-D
1948

Co: Sack Amusement Enterprises. *Dist:* Sack Amusement Enterprises. *Cast:* Heavenly Choir. (Musical / B&W / Sound / Short.)

Songs: "Good News" and "Where Shall I Be When the First Trumpet Sounds."

1092   Spitfire 1922

Co: Reol Productions. *Cast:* G. Edward Brown, Edna Morton, Lawrence Chenault, Daisy Martin, Mabel Young, Sam Cook, Edward Williams.

Reviews in the *Philadelphia Tribune,* 2/23/24, 8/1/25, and *Billboard,* 8/26/22, by J.A. Jackson. (16mm / Sound / B&W / Feature.)

A young colored novelist has written a novel dealing with colored folks, but is told by his publisher that it lacks the aura of reality because he has not lived among the lowly folk about whom he attempts to write. In search of such experience, he goes to a little Maryland settlement and there meets the daughter of a farmer who, by reason of her quick temper, has been nicknamed "Spitfire." Her father is in the clutches of a gang of horse thieves headed by Bradley, and it is the rounding up of the gang and the love that springs up between the young novelist and the country lass that provide the theme.

1093   Spooks 1917

Co: Ebony Film Company. *Dist:* General Film Company. *Cast:* Ebony Players (Sam Robinson, Samuel "Sambo" Jacks, Will Starks, Julia Mason, Bert Murphy, Evon Skeeeter, Mildred Price, Walter Brogsdale, Robert Duree, Frank Pollard, George Lewis Stock Company). (Silent / B&W / Short /2 reels.)

1094   Spooks 1936

Dir: Watson, William. *Prod:* Christie, Al. *Co:* Educational Film Corporation. *Cast:* The Cabin Kids (five colored harmonizers, Ruth Hall, Helen Hall, James "Darling" Hall,

Winifred "Sugar" Hall, and little Frederick Hall) (B&W / Sound / Short.)

"The pickaninny outfit lands in a deserted cabin on a stormy night and do their numbers interspersed with a lot of excitement and scares as various spooky things occur to upset them. They get over the songs with their own original style and plenty of pep"—review in the *Film Daily,* 6/10/36.

1095   The Sport of the Gods
1921

Prod: Levy, Robert. *Co:* Reol Productions. *Dist:* Cummings & Paul Distributing Company. *Cast:* Elizabeth Boyer, Edward R. Abrams, G. Edward Brown, Leon Williams, Lucille Brown, Lindsay J. Hall, Stanley Walpole, Walter Thomas, Lawrence Chenault, Ruby Mason, Edna Morton, Jim Burris.

Story by Paul Lawrence Dunbar. Preview in the *Philadelphia Tribune,* 7/2/21, and review in *California Eagle,* 7/30/21. (Silent / B&W / Feature.)

The story deals with a man whose fidelity and loyalty are rewarded by his being thrown into prison for the crime of another. His wife, son and daughter, rather than suffer the humiliation and disgrace brought upon them by their friends in old Virginia, move to New York. The son associates with evil companions and the daughter's character is placed in jeopardy while she is working as a singer in an underworld cabaret. The mother, having been convinced that a prison sentence is the same as a divorce, is persuaded to marry a man who has schemed to get her money. The husband is finally released from jail after the real criminal has confessed and he goes to New York to join his family, only to find his wife married. After many complications, it all works out.

1096   Sports Cavalcade 1944

Co: All-American News. *Cast:* Fay Young (narrator). (35mm / B&W / Sound / 2 reels / Newsreel / Short / FEA 6069–6070.)

Newsreel with introductions by Young, "Dean of American Negro Sportswriters."

1097   Spying the Spy 1918

Co: Ebony Film Company. *Dist:* General Film Company. *Cast:* Ebony Players (Sam

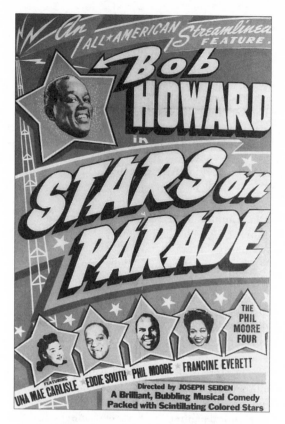

Robinson, Samuel "Sambo" Jacks, Will Starks, Julia Mason, Bert Murphy, Evon Skekeeter, Mildred Price, Walter Brogsdale, Robert Duree, Frank Pollard, George Lewis Stock Company), Yvonne Junior. (16mm / B&W / Silent / 1 reel / 10 min. / Dramatic / Short / FEA 6757.)

The central character of the film is Sambo Sam, who dreams of becoming a hero by catching German spies. Sambo Sam sets out from his office and immediately gets into trouble by capturing Herman Schwartz, who turns out to be a "respectable colored gentleman." Next, Sam runs afoul of some black lodge members who decide to teach him a lesson. They capture Sam and, while dressed in black-hooded robes, proceed to scare him by threatening to chop off his head. They finally free the terrified Sam and in the last scene of the film he is seen running down the railroad tracks out of town.

1098   Square Joe   1922
Dir: Edwards, J. Harrison. *Co:* E.S. & L. Colored Feature Photoplay Company. *Cast:* Joe

Jeanette, John Lester Johnson, Marian Moore, Bob Slater, Mrs. Fred Moore, Fred Miller, Bobby Fitzgerald, Mrs. Eugene L. Moore, Fredrica Washington, Minnie Summer.

Review in *New York Age*, 6/24/22. (35mm / Silent / B&W / Feature / Sport / Drama.)

The plot of the story deals with an innocent man who is charged and convicted of shooting a policeman in a raid on a neighborhood gambling house. How the real murderer is captured and finally punished makes a story which thrills and holds the interest of the spectators from beginning to end.

1099   Standin' Joe   1945
Co: RCM Production. *Dist:* Soundies Distributing Corporation. *Cast:* Dallas Bartley and His Band, Dancing Duo. (Soundies 12M2 / B&W / Short / Sound / Musical.)

1100   Stars on Parade   1946
Dir: Seiden, Joseph. *Co:* All-American News. *Cast:* Bob Howard, Una Mae Carlisle, Eddie South, Francine Everett, Phil Moore, The Phil Moore Four, King Cole Trio, Benny Carter Choir. (Sound / B&W / 50 min. / Feature.)

Musical film featuring the above in instrumental and vocal numbers.

1101   Stars Over Harlem   1956
Dir: Kohn, Joseph. *Co:* Studio Film, Inc. *Cast:* Count Basie, Nat "King" Cole, Delta Rhythm Boys, Joe Turner. (Sound / Musical / Short / B&W.)

Typical stage show type film of the period.

1102   Steak and Potatoes   1944
Co: RCM Production. *Dist:* Soundies Distributing Corporation. *Cast:* Mabel Scott, The Flennoy Trio. (Soundies 19008 / B&W / Short / Sound / Musical / 11/27/44.)

1103   Steamer Mascotte Arriving at Tampa   1898
(Newsreel / Actuality / Documentary / Silent / Short.)

Film footage of a battalion of the 24th Infantry arriving at Tampa, Florida, on the steamer *Mascotte*.

1104   Steppin' Along   1929
Co: Metro-Goldwyn-Mayer. *Cast:* Ernest

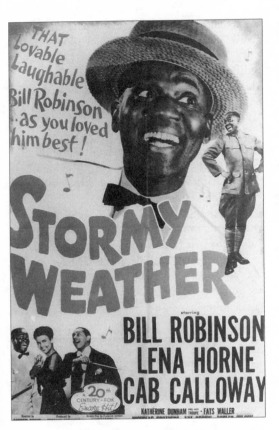

loway and His Band, Katherine Dunham and Her Troupe, Fats Waller, The Nicholas Brothers, Ada Brown, Ralph Cooper, Dooley Wilson, Babe Wallace, Ernest Whitman, Zuttie Singleton, Flournoy E. Miller, Nicodemus Stewart.

Review in *Film Daily*, 5/28/43. Fats Waller sings "Ain't Misbehavin'," Lena Horne sings title song, the Nicholas Brothers are on last because no one wanted to follow them. Screenplay: Frederick Jackson & Ted Koehler. Adaptation by H.S. Kraft. From the original story by Jerry Horwin & Seymour Robinson. Dance staged by: Clarence Robinson. Costumes: Helen Rose. Supervised by: Franchon. Assistant producer: Irving Wills. Cinematographer: Leon Shanroy. Art Direction: James Basevi & Joseph C. Wright. Set design: Thomas Little & Fred J. Rode. Film editor: James D. Clark. Makeup: Guy Pearce. Special effects: Fred Sersen. Sound: Alfred Bruzlin & Roger Herman. Musical direction: Emil Newman. A Western Electric recording. Review in the *Philadelphia Tribune*, 10/9/43. (16mm / B&W / Sound / 2 reels / 77 min. / Feature.)

A semi-biography of Bill Robinson, the film is the story of a black dancer who woos a beautiful woman, Selina, played by Horne, and wins her after the usual complications. Most of the time is spent with the musical-dance performances of the entire cast. Extraordinary talent.

"Sunshine Sammy" Morrison. (Musical / Sound / B&W / Short.)

Features the child star "Sunshine Sammy."

1105   Steppin' High   1924

Co: Superior Arts Motion Picture Company. *Cast:* William Lee. (Silent / B&W / Short.)

1106   Stepping Along   1943

Co: RCM Production. *Dist:* Soundies Distributing Corporation. *Cast:* Evelyn Keyes, The Sepia Steppers. (Soundies 14108 / B&W / Short / Sound / Musical / 11/8/43.)

1107   Sticks and Stones   1943

Co: RCM Production. *Dist:* Soundies Distributing Corporation. *Cast:* Rita Rio (Dona Drake). (Soundies / B&W / Short / Sound / Musical / 1/4/43.)

1108   Stormy Weather   1943

Dir: Stone, Andrew L. *Prod:* LeBaron, William. *Co:* Twentieth Century–Fox Film Corporation. *Dist:* Twentieth Century–Fox. *Cast:* Bill Robinson, Lena Horne, Cab Cal-

1109   Story of Dr. Carver   1939

Dir: Smith, Pete. *Prod:* Smith, Pete. *Co:* Metro-Goldwyn-Mayer. *Dist:* Metro-Goldwyn-Mayer. *Cast:* Clinton Rosemond, John Lester Johnson, Bernice Pillot.

Film note in the *Philadelphia Tribune*, 5/19/83 and the *Philadelphia Afro-American*, 1/30/43. (16mm / B&W / Sound / 1 reel / 10 min. / Dramatization / Documentary Short.)

A slave boy with a keen interest in studying is educated by his master, Carver. The young scientist, George Washington Carver, then devotes his life to the development of uses of the peanut and other agricultural products of the South. Shows some of his experimental work and his achievements at Tuskegee Institute.

1110 The Story of Dr. George Washington Carver 1935

Co: Teaching Film Custodians. *Cast:* Clinton Rosemond, Walter Stoderling, Frank McGlynn, Jr. (Documentary / B&W / Short / Sound / 10 min.)

Documentary based on the life and work of the great Negro scientist.

1111 Story of the American Negro Theatre 1944

(Documentary / Newsreel / B&W / Short / Sound.)

A short film showing members of the American Negro Theatre.

1112 Straight to Heaven 1939

Dir: Leonard, Arthur. *Prod:* Popkin, Harry M. *Co:* Million Dollar Productions / Lenwal Productions. *Dist:* Sack Amusement Enterprises. *Cast:* Lorenzo Tucker, Nina Mae McKinney, Jack Carter, Bernice Vincent, Thomas Mosley, Pearl Bains, George Williams, James Fuller, Jimmie Baskett, Emmory Evans, Teddy Hale, Jackie Ward, Lionel Monogas, Percy Verwayen. The Three Peppers, Millie and Bubbles, Sherman Dirkson, Jules Smith, Martin and Williams, Tuffy Hawkins, Mae Francis, Edna Slatten, Lenore White, Marion Galloway, Marcelle Wescott.

This film was later purchased and distributed by Million Dollar Productions. Review in the *New York Amsterdam News*, 11/18/39. (Sound / B&W / Feature / 52 min. / FBB 3884–3885.)

Lucky John is head of a syndicate which is distributing rotten canned food to unsuspecting Negroes in Harlem. Joe Williams is sent to jail for murder and placed on trial for his life. Williams' wife plays a big part in clearing her husband of murder charges engineered by Lucky John.

1113 The Stranger from Way Out Yonder 1922

Co: Lone Star Motion Picture Company.

Released under the title *You Can't Keep a Good Man Down*. (Silent / B&W / Short / Comedy.)

1114 Streamlined Swing 1938

Co: Metro-Goldwyn-Mayer. *Cast:* The Original Swing Band. (Musical / B&W / Short / Sound.)

The band members use their voices as instruments.

1115 A Study of Negro Artists 1945

Co: Harmon Foundation Educational Films.

Part of Record Group 200 HF series, Harmon Foundation Collection. (Documentary / B&W / Silent / 4 reels / 16mm.)

"Methods of work and productions of several artists. Indicates range of bread-winning activities which keep art work going"—Klotman.

1116 The Subpoena Server pre–1910

(B&W / Silent / Short / FLA 5725.)

1117 Sugar Chile Robinson 1947

Co: All-American News. *Cast:* Sugar Chile Robinson (7 yrs. old). (Musical / Sound / B&W / Short.)

Songs: "Sugar Chile Boogie," "Hen House Blues," "Tuxedo Junction," and "Robinson Boogie."

1118 Sugar Chile Robinson 1950

Dir: Cowan, Will. *Prod:* Cowan, Will. *Co:* Universal-International. *Cast:* Count Basie, Billie Holiday, Frankie "Sugar Chile" Robinson, Basie Sextet.

Complete title—*Frankie "Sugar Chile" Robinson, Billie Holiday, Count Basie and His Sextet.* (Musical / Sound / B&W / Short.)

Songs: "God Bless the Child That's Got His Own," "Now Baby, or Never," "Numbers Boogie," and "After School Boogie." (Musical / Sound / B&W / Short.)

The above listed artists perform such numbers as "God Bless the Child," "Now Baby, or Never," "After School Boogie," and "One o'Clock Jump."

1119 Sugar Hill Baby 1937

Co: Creative Cinema Corporation. *Cast:* Harlemania's Swing Band, Ken Renard. (Sound / B&W / Short.)

1120 Sugar Hill Masquerade 1942

Co: RCM Production. *Dist:* Soundies Distributing Corporation. *Cast:* Whitey's (Arthur White's) Lindy Hoppers. (Soundies 9505 / B&W / Short / Sound / Musical / 11/23/42.)

1121 Sun Tan Ranch 1948

Co: Norwanda Pictures. *Cast:* Byron and Bean, Eunice Wilson, Mildred Boyd, Joel Fluellen, Austin McCoy, Bill Walker. (Sound / B&W / Feature.)

1122 Sun Tan Strut 1946

Dir: Crouch, William Forest. *Prod:* Crouch, William Forest. *Co:* Filmcraft Production. *Dist:* Soundies Distributing Corporation. *Cast:* Jeni Freeland, Emile Petti and His Orchestra. (Soundies 24M1 / B&W / Short / Sound / Musical / 9/30/46.)

1123 Sunday Sinners 1941

Dir: Dreifuss, Arthur. *Prod:* Dreifuss, Arthur / Jack Goldberg. *Co:* Colonade Pictures

Corporation. *Cast:* Mamie Smith, Frankie Wilson, Edna Mae Harris, Alec Lovejoy, Norman Astwood, Sidney Easton, Earl Sydnor, Christola Williams, Gus Smith, Alberta Perkins, Dene Larry, Thelma Norton, Ernie Ransom, Percy Verwayen, Al Young, Herman Green, George Williams, The Sunkissed Brownskin Chorus.

Original story: Frank Wilson. Screen adaptations: Vincent Valentini. Music and lyrics: Donald Heywood. Orchestral arrangements: Ken Macomber. Cinematographer: George Webber. Unit manager: Irvin C. Miller. Costumes: Al Stevens. Art director: William Salter. Sound: Ed Fenton. Assistant director: Chuck Wasserman. Editor: Robert Crandall. (16mm / Sound / B&W / 2 reels / 65 min. / Feature.)

The story is of a courageous minister who battles the forces of the underworld. His son is accused (framed by racketeers) of robbery and murder. In the darkest hour of gloom, his followers enroll in the army of righteousness and drive out the racketeers.

1124   Sunshine Sammy   1929
Prod: Movietone. *Co:* Metro-Goldwyn-Mayer. *Cast:* Ernest "Sunshine Sammy," a mammy, and two black children. (Sound / B&W / Short.)

1125   Super Sleuths   1947
Prod: Toddy, Ted. *Co:* Toddy Pictures Company. *Cast:* F.E. Miller, Jones Boys, Mantan Moreland.

Released under the title *Professor Creeps.* (Sound / B&W / Feature.)

1126   Swami Sam   1914
Dir: Lubin, Sigmund. *Prod:* Lubin, Sigmund. *Co:* Lubin Manufacturing Company. *Cast:* John Edwards, Mattie Edwards, Harry Lorain, Ed Lawrence, Don Ferrando.

Written by E.W. Sargent. Released on 10/13/14. (Silent / B&W / Comedy / Short / 400 ft.)

"The Chief of Smithville telegraphs the Riverside police to arrest Sam Johnson, who is calling himself Swami Sam, on charges of forgery. This embarrasses the force, for they have to take up a collection to pay for the telegram. The chief details two men to arrest Sam, who is running a fortune-telling parlor. Sam hypnotizes the two men and persuades one that he is the other one's prisoner. The Chief is sore and the whole force starts out to arrest Sam. Percy, a perfect gentleman, wants to make the arrest single-handed, and the others are very willing to see him do so, but when Percy sees the two guns that Sam is fondling, he makes a round trip of it. Sam opens fire and the cops don't stop running until they get back to the station. The Chief sends this telegram to Smithville—'If you want Sam, come and get him. We can't.' Then Mattie, a colored laundress, walks in with Sam and prefers a charge of assault"—*Lubin Bulletin.*

1127   Swanee Showboat   1945
Co: Ajax Pictures. *Cast:* Nina Mae McKinney, Dewey "Pigmeat" Markham, Mabel Lee, Helen Barys, the Eight Black Streaks, the Lindy Hoppers, Scott and Whaley, Swanee Swingsters, The Sun Tan Four. (Sound / B&W / Feature.)

1128 Swanee Smiles 1943

Co: RCM Production. *Dist:* Soundies Distributing Corporation. *Cast:* The Cabin Kids (five colored harmonizers, Ruth Hall, Helen Hall, James "Darling" Hall, Winifred "Sugar" Hall, and little Frederick Hall). (Soundies 11704 / B&W / Short / Sound / Musical / 5/10/ 43.)

1129 Swanee Swing 1944

Co: RCM Production. *Dist:* Soundies Distributing Corporation. *Cast:* LaVilla Tullos. (Soundies 17308 / B&W / Short / Sound / Musical / 7/10/44.)

1130 Sweet Kisses 1943

Co: RCM Production. *Dist:* Soundies Distributing Corporation. *Cast:* The Mitchell Brothers, Evelyn Keyes, The Sepia Steppers. (Soundies 7M5 / B&W / Short / Sound / Musical / 12/21/43.)

1131 Sweet Shoe 1947

Cast: Rita Rio and Her All-Girl Band, Anita Colby, the Four Horsemen Male Quartet. (Sound / B&W / Short.)

1132 Sweethearts of Rhythm 1947

Dir: Alexander, William D. *Prod:* Alexander, William D. *Co:* Associated Producers of Negro Motion Pictures. *Cast:* Sweethearts of Rhythm (All Girl Band). (Musical / Sound / B&W / Short.)

All female orchestra from Piney Woods School, Piney Woods, Mississippi.

1133 Swing 1938

Dir: Micheaux, Oscar. *Prod:* Russell, A. Burton. *Co:* Micheaux Film Corporation. *Dist:* Micheaux Pictures Corporation. *Cast:* Cora Green, Hazel Diaz, Carman Newsome, Dorothy Van Engle, Alec Lovejoy, Mandy Randolph, Larry Seymour, Tyler Twins, Trixie Smith, Nat Reed, Sammy Gardiner, Doli Armena, Columbus Jackson, George R. Taylor, Leon Gross and His Orchestra.

Written by Oscar Micheaux. Photography by Lester Lang. Recording engineer: Ed Fenton & E.A. Schhabbehor. Edited by Patricia Rooney. A Blue Seal Noiseless Recording. Review in the *Baltimore Afro-American*,

10/1/38. Theatrical backer, George Taylor. (Sound / B&W / Feature / 80 min. / FCA 7712–7713.)

Mandy is a cook and, as the story opens, is living in Birmingham. She is in love with a "yaller" man whom her friends called "no good." His name is Cornell: occupation, "hustler." He takes Mandy's money and blows it on Eloise, a "high yaller." Eloise, gorgeous and striking, belongs to "Lem" Jackson, a fireman who vows to kill any man, dude loafers included, if he ever catches one hanging around her. Other cooks know Cornell is unfaithful and send one of their number to warn Mandy. But Cornell has taken the pains to set Mandy right, so she refuses to listen to them. But one night she is persuaded and goes to a roadhouse where one look at him, with Eloise in his arms and their faces together, convinces Mandy — and the fun begins! The scenes shift to New York where Mandy goes and meets little Lena, whom she had helped put through school, and through Lena, Ted Gregory, tall and handsome and Lena's sweetie who is rehearsing a show. They give Mandy a job. Meanwhile, Eloise and Lem Jackson have preceded Mandy to New York and changed their names to "Big" Jones and "Cora Smith." Cora has been cast as the female lead in the show but is overbearing, disagreeable, boastful and unruly—finally climaxing it all by getting drunk, falling down stairs and fracturing her leg. Panic-stricken, Lena recalls that Mandy had a wonderful voice and persuades her to assume Cora's role. All is going well when Mandy announces abruptly that she is quitting. All wonder why. She admits that it is Cornell, who has hoboed his way to New York. He is in truth a piano player, so is taken on to play for Mandy. The show has a grand opening, they let Mandy have her Cornell to spend her money as he wishes to, Ted and Lena get each other, the show goes over and all ends well.

1134   Swing Cats Ball   1943
Co: RCM Production. *Dist:* Soundies Distributing Corporation. *Cast:* Evelyn Purvis, Rusti Sanford. (Soundies 14908 / B&W / Short / Sound / Musical / 12/28/43.)

1135   Swing for Sale   1941
Co: RCM Production. *Dist:* Soundies Distributing Corporation. *Cast:* The Charioteers. (Soundies 2802 / B&W / Short / Sound / Musical / 8/11/41.)
First music videos.

1136   Swing for Your Supper
1941
Co: RCM Production. *Dist:* Soundies Distributing Corporation. *Cast:* Dorothy Dandridge, Cee Pee Johnson. (Soundies 1406 / B&W / Short / Sound / Musical / 5/5/41.)

1137   Swing It Harlem   1941
Cast: Ralph Brown, Ella Mae Walters. (Sound / B&W / Short.)

1138   Swingin' in the Grove
1945
Co: RCM Production. *Dist:* Soundies Distributing Corporation. *Cast:* Tiny Grimes and His Orchestra. (Soundies 13M1 / B&W / Short / Sound / Musical / 10/22/45.)

1139   Swingin' on Nothin'
1942
Co: RCM Production. *Dist:* Soundies Distributing Corporation. *Cast:* Louis Armstrong and His Orchestra, Velma Middleton, George Washington. (Soundies 8004 / B&W / Short / Sound / Musical / 8/10/42.)

1140   Swingtime Jamboree
1949
Co: Astor Pictures Corporation. *Cast:* Louis Jordan and His Tympany Five, Stepin Fetchit. (Sound / B&W / Musical / Short.)

1141   The Symbol of Sacrifice
1918
Co: African Films. *Cast:* Mabel May.
Made in Johannesburg, South Africa. (Drama / Feature / 8 reels.)
Zulu War drama.

1142   The Symbol of the Unconquered   1920.
Dir: Micheaux, Oscar. *Prod:* Micheaux, Oscar. *Co:* Micheaux Film Corporation. *Dist:* Micheaux Film Corporation. *Cast:* Lawrence Chenault, Iris Hall, Walker Thompson, E.G. Tatum, Leigh Whipper, Jim Burns, Mattie Wilkes.
Original title, *Wilderness Trail.* Screenplay: Oscar Micheaux. (Silent / B&W / Feature.)
"Eva Mason, beautiful quadroon, has inherited property from her father, and while looking it over becomes lost. She is found by Hugh von Allen who mistakes her for white. They later fall in love. Later, Drescola, villainous scoundrel, learns that Eva's property has valuable oil on it and, unable to buy the property from her, he uses his influence with a Negro-hating squaw man and a band of 'white riders' to run Eva off the property"—*Film Herald.*

1143   Symphonic Shades
1950
Co: United Artists. *Cast:* Jester Hairston, Negro choir.
Songs of America Series. (Musical / B&W / Sound / Shorts.)
Songs: "Rise Up Shepherd and Follow" and "Ring de Banjos."

1144   Symphony in Black: A Rhapsody of Negro Life
1935

Dir: Waller, Fred "Fats." *Prod:* Zukor, Adolph. *Co:* U.M. & M. TV Corporation. *Cast:* Duke Ellington and His Orchestra, Billie Holiday, Earl "Snake Hips" Tucker.

Composed by Duke Ellington. Photographed by William Steiner. Continuity by Milton Hocky & Fred Rath. (Short / B&W / Sound / 10 min. / 1 reel / 16mm.)

The Duke plays music in tune with scenes of Negro life, in four suites. A very young Billie Holiday croons the blues in one scene.

1145   Symphony in Swing   1949
Co: Universal-International. *Cast:* Duke Ellington and His Orchestra, Delta Rhythm Boys. (B&W / Sound / Short / 15 min. / Musical.)

A bandstand setting, with the typical musical variety theme of the period.

1146   Syncopated Sermon   1930
Dir: Mack, Roy. *Co:* Vitaphone. *Cast:* Hall Johnson Choir, Willard Robison.

Songs: "The Devil's Afraid of Music," "City Called Heaven," "Certainly Lord," "Stay Away to Jesus," "Wade in the Water," and "The Great Gettin' Up Mornin'." Preview in the *Philadelphia Tribune*, 7/31/30. (Musical / B&W / Short / Sound.)

"The group is introduced by Willard Robison, composer .... Robison, who is conductor of the Maxwell House radio hours, plays and sings in conjunction with the choir, all presented with the spirit and fervor of the camp meetings"—review in the *Philadelphia Tribune*, 4/23/31.

1147   T.G. Boogie Woogie   1945
Dir: Crouch, William Forest. *Prod:* Crouch, William Forest. *Co:* RCM Production. *Dist:* Soundies Distributing Corporation. *Cast:* Tiny Grimes and His Orchestra. (Soundies 87708 / B&W / Short / Sound / Musical / 12/17/45.)

1148   Taint Yours   1944
Co: RCM Production. *Dist:* Soundies

Distributing Corporation. *Cast:* Una Mae Carlisle. (Soundies 17608 / B&W / Short / Sound / Musical / 8/7/44.)

1149   Take Everything   1945
Co: RCM Production. *Dist:* Soundies Distributing Corporation. *Cast:* The Three Peppers. (Soundies 89408 / B&W / Short / Sound / Musical / 4/23/45.)

1150   Take Me Back, Baby   1941
Co: RCM Production. *Dist:* Soundies Distributing Corporation. *Cast:* Count Basie and His Band, Jimmy Rushing. (Soundies 4406 / B&W / Short / Sound / Musical / 12/1/41.)

1151   Take My Life   1941
Co: Million Dollar Productions / Goldseal Productions. *Dist:* Consolidated Film Exchange. *Cast:* Monte Hawley, Jeni LeGon, Jack Carter, Harlem Dead End Kids (Freddie Baker, Eugene Jackson, Paul White, Eddie Lynn, De Forrest Covan), Lovey Lane, Harry Levette, Robert Webb, Guernsey Morrow, Herbert Skinner, Arthur Ray.

Previews in the *Philadelphia Tribune*, 10/3/42, 10/10/42, and the *New York Amsterdam News*, 7/4/42. *Take My Life*, 1941, was re-released in 1948, under the title *Murder Rap*. (Sound / B&W / Feature.)

The Harlem Dead End Kids are brought to the brink of tragedy when one of their gang members is framed for murder. They suddenly see the error of their ways and join the United States Army and learn what it's like to be real men.

1152   Take the "A" Train   1941

Co: RCM Production. *Dist:* Soundies Distributing Corporation. *Cast:* The Delta Rhythm Boys.

Recorded by Steve Schultz. (Soundies 3803 / B&W / Short / Sound / Musical / 10/20/41.)

1153   The Tale of a Chicken   1914

Dir: Lubin, Sigmund. *Prod:* Lubin, Sigmund. *Co:* Lubin Manufacturing Company. *Cast:* John Edwards, Mattie Edwards, Maha Rajah, Luke Scott.

Written by Arthur D. Hotaling. Released on 4/28/14. (Silent / B&W / Short / Comedy / 1,000 ft.)

"Sam Johnson and Rastus Hudson are suitors for the hand of Mandy Jones, but Mandy's attentions are strong towards Sam. When Mandy gives Rastus the cold shoulder his Negro blood is aroused. Rastus loses no time in telling his troubles to his gang. They decide to cook up a scheme whereby they steal a chicken and hide it by Sam's house. They also put some feathers in Sam's pocket. Then they inform the owner of the chicken. He gets a policeman and has Sam arrested. The chicken is produced in the court-room and the feathers are found in Sam's pocket. Sam is thrown into jail, much to the delight of Rastus and his gang. But Mandy, knowing Sam's innocence, presses into service the great detective of international fame, Sherlock Jackson Holmes. Sherlock finds a trail of chicken feathers and in the course of a couple of hours he traps the gang in their den. He marches them to the court where they are thrown into a dungeon and Sam is then released. Sherlock receives for his reward, a smile from Mandy"—*Lubin Bulletin.*

1154   Tall, Tan and Terrific   1946

Dir: Pollard, Bud. *Prod:* Pollard, Bud. *Co:* Astor Pictures Corporation. *Dist:* Astor Film Exchange. *Cast:* Francine Everett, Monte Hawley, Milton Wood, Mantan Moreland, the Golden Slipper All Girl Band, Dots Johnson, Perry "Butterbeans" Bradford, Rudy Toombs, Lou Swartz, Johnny and George, Edna Mae Harris, Myra Johnson, Thelma Codero, The Two Fat Men, The Gorgeous Astor Debutants, All Girl Golden Slipper Band.

Executive producer: R.M. Savini. Screenplay: John S. Gordon. Photography: Jack Etra. Sound engineer: Nels Mindlin. Sets: Billy. Costumes: Variety. Assistant director: Ed Kelly. Edited by Bud Pollard & Shirley Stone. Original story: John E. Gordon. Original music score: Gene Rowland. Special musical arrangement: Emile Vlasc. Dance arranged by Art Selectman. Preview in the *Philadelphia Independent*, 1/25/47. (Sound / B&W / 60 min. / Feature / FCA 0706.)

Miss Tall, Tan and Terrific is the star of the Golden Slipper nightclub, which is in danger of being taken over by a couple of crooks. First they fail at their attempt to woo Miss Tall, Tan and Terrific away from the club so they frame the owner for murder. Mantan Moreland stumbles into some evidence to help save the club owner from the electric chair.

1155   The Tango Queen   1916

Dir: Haynes, Hunter C. *Prod:* Haynes, Hunter C. *Co:* Afro-American Film Company. (Short / B&W / Silent.)

1156   Tap Happy   1943

Co: RCM Production. *Dist:* Soundies Distributing Corporation. *Cast:* Slim and Sweets. (Soundies 15208 / B&W / Short / Sound / Musical / 12/31/43.)

1157   Teamwork   1946

Co: U.S. War Department. *Dist:* Mayer-Burstyn.

Documentary. Sequel to *The Negro Soldier*. Screenplay by Carlton Moss. (B&W / Short / 20 min. / Sound / Documentary / Newsreel.)

"The film 'Teamwork' depicts many highlights of the service of Negro soldiers in the Army's Ground, Air and Service Forces during the battle for Europe. It includes action shots taken on the beaches of Normandy and emphasizes the integral role played by these troops as part of the great Allied team that defeated the German armies"— excerpt of preview from the *New York Age*, 7/7/46.

1158   Temple Belles 1946
(B&W / 1 reel / 35mm / Short.)

1159   Temptation 1936
Dir: Micheaux, Oscar. *Prod:* Micheaux, Oscar. *Co:* Micheaux Film Corporation. *Dist:* Micheaux Pictures Corporation. *Cast:* Andrew Bishop, Bernice Gray, Ethel Moses, Ida Forest, Lorenzo Tucker, Hilda Rogers, Alfred "Slick" Chester, Larry Seymore, Pope Sisters, Lillian Fitzgerald, Dot and Dash, Bobby Hargreaces and His Kit Kat Club Orchestra.
Preview in the *Houston Informer*, 11/27/37. (Sound / B&W / Feature.)
"The story deals with a beautiful model who, through no fault of her own, innocently becomes involved with a mob of gangsters and smugglers and is eventually accused of murder which she did not commit. In the musical sequences which take place in the Mad Mullah, a notorious night club, will be seen some of your most famous musical comedy stars"—from the *Philadelphia Independent*, 4/24/38.

1160   Ten Minutes to Kill 1933
Dir: Micheaux, Oscar. *Prod:* Micheaux, Oscar. *Co:* Micheaux Film Corporation. *Dist:* Micheaux Film Corporation. (Sound / B&W / Feature.)

1161   Ten Minutes to Live 1932
Dir: Micheaux, Oscar. *Prod:* Russell, A. Burton. *Co:* Micheaux Film Corporation. *Dist:* Micheaux Picture Corporation. *Cast:* Lawrence Chenault, William Clayton, Jr., Alice B. Russell, Ethel Smith, A.B. Comathiere, Laura Bowman, Tressie Mitchell, Mabel Garrett, Carl Mahon, Lorenzo Tucker, Galle De Gaston, George Williams, Willor Lee Guilford, Donald Heywood's Chorus.
Adaptation, dialogue: Oscar Micheaux. Assistant director: A.B. Comathiere. Master of

ceremonies, musical arranger, floor show: Donald Heyward. Photography: Lester Lang. From a collection of short stories entitled, "Harlem After Midnight." Crudely cut and edited. Producers note: "This Photoplay is adapted from the following short stories of Negro night life in Harlem: Story No. 1, 'The Faker'; Story No. 2, 'The Killer.'"
Reviews in the *Philadelphia Tribune*, 8/25/32, and the *Kansas City Call*, 7/15/32. (16mm / Sound / B&W / 2 reels / 65 min. / Feature / FDA 2120.)
A mystery-musical built around a threatening note which gives the heroine only ten minutes to live. Much nightclub business (musical variety) as the mystery unravels with song and dance numbers and a stand-up comedy routine.

1162   Ten Nights in a Bar-Room
1926
Dir: Calnek, Roy E. *Prod:* Starkman, David/ Louis Groner. *Co:* Colored Players Film Corporation of Philadelphia. *Cast:* Charles Gilpin,

Lawrence Chenault, Myra Burwell, William Clayton, Jr., Harry Henderson, Ethel Smith, Arline Mickey, Edward Moore, William Johnson.

Preview in the *Philadelphia Tribune*, 8/15/25, and reviews in the *Philadelphia Tribune*, 11/20/26, and the *Chicago Defender*, 1/1/5/27. (35mm / Silent / B&W / 5 reels / 60 min. / Feature.)

Black version of William Pratt's temperance novel. The story shows, in brief, how Joe Morgan, part proprietor of the lumber mill, loses his interests in that property by his drinking habits and the accidental death of his daughter. Finally he reforms and there is promise of peace if not happiness between him and his wife. Gilpin plays the father who is overcome by the demon drink.

1163   The Ten Thousand Dollar Trail ($10,000 Trail)   1921

Prod: Dones, Sidney P. *Co:* Bookertee Investment Company. *Dist:* E.L. Cummings (white). *Cast:* Sidney P. Dones, Nina Rowland, Dorothy Dumont, Frances Henderson, Clinton Ross, "Kid" Herman, Joel Teal, Master Henry Feltenburg, E. Patrick, Henry Smith, J. Crockett, E.M. Dennis.

Screenplay and scenario by Dolores L. Mitchell. Review in *California Eagle*, 9/10/21. (Silent / B&W / Feature.)

The picture tells the story of a Western-born girl, Kate Allison, who returns from the East and scorns the crudities of "Smiling Bob," to whom she is engaged. Rosemary, along with her aunt and cousin Archie, is visiting Kate at

her ranch. El Modrego, an outlaw whose den is hidden in the mountains, plans to kidnap Archie. Bob is mistakenly kidnapped and carried to their stronghold. Rosemary receives the ransom note and chooses to handle it alone. El Modrego keeps Rosemary and frees Bob. However, while being led back by the outlaws, Bob destroys the bills ($10,000 he kept hidden from his captors) and strews the torn bits along the trail in order to find his way back with help. Upon returning, Bob's boys and El Modrego's minions battle until Bob wins.

1164   Ten Thousand Years Ago   1945

Co: RCM Production. *Dist:* Soundies Distributing Corporation. *Cast:* The Jubalairs. (Soundies 20708 / B&W / Short / Sound / Musical / 5/28/45.)

1165   Tenderfeet   1928

Dir: Williams, Spencer. *Prod:* Williams, Spencer. *Co:* Midnight Productions. *Cast:* Spencer Williams, Mildred Washington, Flora Washington, Spencer Bell, James Robinson. (35mm / Silent / B&W / Short.)

1166   That Man of Mine   1946

Dir: Anderson, Leonard. *Prod:* Alexander, William D. *Co:* Alexander Production. *Dist:* Soundies Distributing Corporation. *Cast:* Anna Mae Winburn and the International Sweethearts of Rhythm. (Soundies 23M4 / B&W / Short / Sound / Musical / 9/23/46.)

1167   That Man of Mine   1947

Dir: Alexander, William D. *Prod:* Alexander, William D. *Co:* Associated Producers of Negro Motion Pictures. *Dist:* Astor Pictures. *Cast:* Ruby Dee, Powell Lindsay, Harrel Tillman, Rhina Harris, Flo Hawkins, Betty Haynes, Tomi Moore, Henri Woode and His Six Hepcats, The International Sweethearts of Rhythm (all-female band).

Songs: "That Man of Mine," "Don't Get It Twisted," "The Thing," "Just Like That," "Woode Would," "Dear One," "Vi Viger," "How 'Bout That Jive," "Standing Room Only," and "Jam Session." (Sound / B&W / Feature / Musical / 7 reels on 3 / 16mm.)

Musical variety show, featuring exotic dancing.

1168   That Man Samson   1937

Co: RKO Radio Pictures. *Cast:* Lawrence Stewart, Edna Mae Harris, George Randol, Clinton Rosemond, Hall Johnson Choir. (B&W / Sound / Feature.)

A black version of the biblical story of Samson and Delilah presented in *Green Pastures-*style.

1169   That Ol' Ghost Train   1942

Co: RCM Production. *Dist:* Soundies Distributing Corporation. *Cast:* Les Hite and His Orchestra. (Soundies 7006 / B&W / Short / Sound / Musical / 6/1/42.)

1170   That's the Spirit   1932

Co: Vitaphone. *Cast:* Noble Sissle and His Band, Cora La Redd, The Washboard Serenaders, Flournoy E. Miller, Mantan Moreland.

Review in the *Film Daily*, 6/10/33. (16mm / Sound / 1 reel / 9 min. / Musical / Short.)

Moreland and Miller are nightwatchmen easily terrorized by "ghostly" happenings. La Redd and the Washboard Serenaders provide the song and dance numbers. Sissle and his band play "Tiger Rug" and "St. Louis Blues."

1171   There Are Eighty-Eight Reasons Why   1945

Co: RCM Production. *Dist:* Soundies Distributing Corporation. *Cast:* Johnny and George, Billy Daniels, Benny Payne. (Soundies 88408 / B&W / Short / Sound / Musical / 9/10/45.)

1172   They Know Their Groceries   1929

Co: Vitaphone. *Cast:* Miller and Lyles. (Comedy / B&W / Short / Sound.)

1173   They Raided the Joint   1946

Dir: Crouch, William Forest. *Prod:* Crouch, William Forest. *Co:* Filmcraft Production. *Dist:* Soundies Distributing Corporation. *Cast:* Vanita Smythe. (Soundies 21M3 / B&W / Short / Sound / Musical / 7/15/46.)

1174   They're Not Warm   1905

Co: American Mutoscope / Biograph. (Newsreel / Documentary / B&W / Short / Silent.)

Unrehearsed footage of female and male blacks dancing on a levee.

1175   The Thirteen Club   1905

Co: Biograph. (B&W / Silent / Short / FLA 5741.)

"A black waiter at the Thirteen Club is frightened into shakes and bugeyes as he suddenly sees a dead head centerpiece while setting the table" — Klotman.

1176   Thirty Years Later   1928

Dir: Micheaux, Oscar. *Prod:* Micheaux, Oscar. *Co:* Micheaux Film Corporation. *Dist:* Micheaux Film Corporation. *Cast:* A.B. Comatheire, Ardelle Dabney, Barrington Carter, Gertrude Snelson, Arthur Ray, Ruth Williams, Mabel Kelly, William Edmondson, Mme. Robinson.

Review in the *Philadelphia Tribune*, 2/2/28. Screenplay based on the stage play *The Tangle*. (Sound / B&W / Feature.)

A premise that Micheaux tells over and over. A Negro man, raised thinking he is white, falls in love with a young Negro girl. Natural complications arise keeping them apart. As in Micheaux's *Birthright* the hero discovers that he is not white but had a Negro mother. The way now is opened for him to marry the young girl.

1177   Those Pullman Porters   1930

Co: Vitaphone. *Cast:* Kings of Harmony Quartette. (Musical / B&W / Sound / Short / Vitaphone #2101.)

1178   Those Who Dance   1950

Co: Warner Bros. (Documentary / B&W / Short / Sound.)

This film traces dancing from African origins through the waltz, minuet, jitterbug, foxtrot, rumba, tango, and square dance.

1179   Three Songs by Leadbelly   1945

Prod: Folklore Research Films. *Co:* Folklore Research Films. *Cast:* Huddie Ledbetter. (16mm / 8 min. / Color / Sound / Documentary / Short.)

In his only film, Huddie "Leadbelly" Ledbetter is seen at his prime (in 1945) singing three well-known folk songs: "Pick a Bale of Cotton," "Grey Goose" and "Take This Hammer."

1180   Ties of Blood   1921

Co: Reol Productions. *Cast:* Inez Clough, Arthur Ray, Henry Pleasant. (35mm / Silent / B&W.)

1181   Till Then   1944

Co: RCM Production. *Dist:* Soundies Distributing Corporation. *Cast:* The Mills Brothers. (Soundies 18308 / B&W / Short / Sound / Musical / 10/2/44.)

1182   Tillie   1945

Dir: Crouch, William Forest. *Prod:* Adams, Berle. *Co:* Astor Pictures Corporation. *Dist:* Soundies Distributing Corporation. *Cast:* Louis Jordan and His Tympany Five.

Excerpted from the Astor two-reel short, "Caldonia" (1945). (Soundies 21108 / B&W / Short / Sound / Musical / 7/23/45.)

1183   Time Takes Care of Everything   1946

Dir: Crouch, William Forest. *Prod:* Crouch, William Forest. *Co:* Filmcraft Production. *Dist:* Soundies Distributing Corporation. *Cast:* June Richmond. (Soundies 25M2 / B&W / Short / Sound / Musical / 11/10/46.)

1184   'Tis You, Babe   1945

Co: RCM Production. *Dist:* Soundies Distributing Corporation. *Cast:* Skeets Tolbert and His Orchestra. (Soundies 12M1 / B&W / Short / Sound / Musical / 9/10/45.)

1185   To Live as Free Men   1943

Co: Penn School Trustees.

Adapted by Mr. C. Elliott Barb from the book entitled "School Acres" by Miss Rossa B. Cooley. Review in the *Philadelphia Tribune* 3/6/43. (Sound / Color / Documentary / Short.)

This picture, which tells the story of Penn School — the oldest Negro school in the South — founded in 1832, depicts the rise of the Negro from slave days to the present on the Sea Islands of the Deep South.

1186   Tony's Shirt   1923

Co: Dunbar Film Corporation. (Silent / B&W / Short.)

1187   Toot That Trumpet!   1941

Co: RCM Production. *Dist:* Soundies Distributing Corporation. *Cast:* Deep River Boys. (Soundies 4703 / B&W / Short / Sound / Musical / 12/22/41.)

1188   Toot That Trumpet   1943

Co: RCM Production. *Dist:* Soundies Distributing Corporation. *Cast:* Francine Everett, Cook and Brown, The Sepia Steppers. (Soundies 13808 / B&W / Short / Sound / Musical / 10/18/43.)

1189   Toot That Trumpet   1946

Co: All American News. *Dist:* Astor Pictures. *Cast:* Louis Jordan and His Band, Monte Hawley, Apus and Estrellita, Francine Everett. (Musical / Sound / B&W / Short.)

1190   Toppers Take a Bow   1941

Dir: Kahn, Richard C. *Co:* Hollywood Pictures Corporation. *Cast:* Four Toppers, Spencer Williams. (Sound / B&W / Musical / Short.)

The story is about a quartet that applies for work in a radio station which is operated by the announcer (Williams). As they try out for a sponsor, they go through their routine of four numbers with attendant changes of costume and camera effects.

1191   Toussaint L'Ouverture   1921

Dir: Muse, Clarence. *Prod:* Muse, Clarence. *Co:* Blue Ribbon Pictures. *Cast:* Clarence Muse. (Biography / B&W / Silent.) (May have never been released.)

The story of the great black Haitian general and liberator.

1192   The Tradition   1950

Prod: Wilder, A.W. Lee. *Co:* United Artists. *Cast:* Jester Hairston, Choral Group.

Songs of America Series. (Musical / B&W / Short / Sound.)

Songs: "Deep River" and "Little David Play on Your Harp."

1193   Trailer Paradise   1937

Co: Educational Film Corporation. *Cast:* The Cabin Kids (five colored harmonizers, Ruth Hall, Helen Hall, James "Darling" Hall, Winifred "Sugar" Hall, and little Frederick

Hall), Bob Howard. (Musical / Comedy / B&W / Short / Sound.)

1194 Trooper of Troop K (Trooper of Company K)
1916

Co: Lincoln Motion Picture Company. *Cast:* Noble Johnson, Beulah Hall, Jimmie Smith, Mexican Soldiers, former Ninth and Tenth U.S. Cavalrymen. (Silent / B&W / Feature.)

"Shiftless" Joe, unkempt and careless of dress, spends his last cent for flowers to give to Clara, a high school girl who has taken a sisterly and charitable interest in him. Jimmy, an ardent admirer and chum of Clara's, is not pleased with Clara's unselfish, broadminded interest in Joe. Joe bumbles job after job so Clara suggests that he join the army, much to Jimmy's pleasure. Several months later, Joe is seen doing duty with Company K in Mexico, while Jimmy at home is finding clear sailing with Clara. During a battle with Mexican troops at Carrizal, Joe distinguishes himself by heroic deeds during the fight. Clara reads in the papers of Joe's deeds and denounces Jimmy. Joe is decorated for bravery, arrives home and is welcomed by Clara with open arms.

1195 Troubles of Sambo and Dinah 1914

Dir: Jones, Peter P. *Prod:* Jones, Peter P. *Co:* Peter P. Jones Photoplay Company. *Cast:* Matt Marshall, Ethel Fletcher, Tom Lemonier, Ethel Ridley, Earl Watson. (Short / B&W / Silent.)

1196 Tunes That Live 1950

Prod: Wilder, A. W. Lee. *Co:* United Artists. *Cast:* Jester Hairston, Negro Choral Group.

Songs of America Series. (Musical / B&W / Short / Sound.)

Songs: "Old Black Joe" and "Religion Is a Fortune."

1197 Turpin's Real Reels 1916

Prod: Turpin, Charles H. *Co:* Charles H. Turpin. (Newsreel / Documentary / B&W / Short / Silent.)

Featured are: Black children and teachers during recess and at the end of the school day at the black church schools in St. Louis, Missouri; fraternal organizations on parade; the new Booker T. Washington Theatre, St. Louis, as a matinee performance is letting out; views of the Black Old Folks and Orphans Home; the colored business league in session; views of Charles H. Turpin, the first black man ever elected to the office of constable in the state of Missouri.

1198 Tuskegee Finds a Way Out
1923

Co: Crusader Film Company. *Cast:* Tuskegee Institute. (Silent / B&W / Documentary / Feature / 7 reels.)

"This film tells the story of Booker T. Washington's life work. It is the great educator's vision … there is a note of human interest that is sustained throughout. One is both entertained and educated by this latest screen novelty. The photography is worthy of praise"— excerpt of review from *New York World,* 6/9/23.

1199 A Tuskegee Pilgrimage 1922

Co: Reol Productions. (Documentary / Newsreel / B&W / Short / Silent.)

Film footage of the student and faculty at Tuskegee Institute, Alabama.

1200 Tuskegee Trains New Pilots
1931

Co: National Archives Gift Collection.

Part of Record Group 200 HF series, Harmon Foundation Collection. (2 reels / Short / 16mm / Silent / Partly edited.)

1201 Tuxedo Junction 1942

Co: RCM Production. *Dist:* Soundies Distributing Corporation. *Cast:* Edna Mae Harris, The Lindy Lenox Hoppers. (Soundies 10206 / B&W / Short / Sound / Musical / 12/31/42.)

1202 Tweed Me 1942

Co: RCM Production. *Dist:* Soundies Distributing Corporation. *Cast:* The Chocolateers, John Kirby. (Soundies 10107 / B&W / Short / Sound / Musical / 12/31/42.)

1203 Two Black Crows in Africa
1929

Co: Educational Film Corporation. *Cast:*

George Moran (white), Charles Mack (white)—(Moran & Mack). (Sound / B&W / 2 reels / Comedy / Short.)

One of a number of two-reel comedy shorts made by the blackface comedy team, "Two Black Crows."

1204   Two-Gun Man from Harlem 1938

Dir: Kahn, Richard C. *Prod:* Kahn, Richard C. *Co:* Hollywood Pictures Corporation. *Dist:* Merit Pictures / Sack. *Cast:* Herbert Jeffries, The Four Tones, Clarence Brooks, Margaret Whitten, Spencer Williams, Rose Lee Lincoln, Mantan Moreland, Stymie Beard, Tom Southern, Mae Turner, Jesse Lee Brooks, Paul Blackman, The Cats and the Fiddle.

Produced at International Studios, Hollywood. Written by Richard C. Kahn. Production manager: Al Lane. Film editor: W.M. Earis. Sound engineer: Cliff Ruberg. Art director: Vin Taylor. Music by Herbert Jeffrey & the Four Tones. (Sound / B&W / Feature / 60 min. / FBB 6105–6106.

Musical Western in which a phony deacon becomes a two-gun-totin' man. Faithful Mary, a former Father Divine "angel," appears.

1205   Two Knights of Vaudeville 1916

Co: Historical Feature Films. *Dist:* Ebony Films Company. *Cast:* Frank Montgomery, Florence McClain, Bert Murphy, Jimmy Marshall. (Short / B&W / Silent / FEB 6837.)

1206   Two of a Kind 1955

Dir: Alexander, William D. *Prod:* Alexander, William D. *Co:* Alexander Production. *Cast:* Scotty and Harris. (Sound / B&W / Feature.)

1207   Uncle Jasper's Will 1922

Dir: Micheaux, Oscar. *Prod:* Micheaux, Oscar. *Co:* Micheaux Film Corporation. *Dist:* Micheaux Film Company. *Cast:* William E. Fountaine, Shingzie Howard.

Original title, *Jasper Landry's Will.* (Silent / B&W / Feature.)

1208   Uncle Remus' First Visit to New York 1914

Dir: Haynes, Hunter C. *Prod:* Haynes,

Hunter C. *Co:* Hunter C. Haynes Photoplay Company. *Cast:* Wesley Jones, Maude Jones, Tom Brown, Leorine Harris, Abbie Mitchell, Allie Gilliam, Billy Harper, Leon Williams, Edna Morton, Mr. and Mrs. Charles H. Anderson. (Silent / B&W / Short / 2 reels / Comedy.)

"The story revolves around the visit of 'Uncle Remus,' an unsophisticated old farmer from Awfulville, Miss., to his fashionable nephew in New York City. The mishaps and mixups which befall the old man and his wife from the time they left their delta farm to the close of their sojourn in Gotham, together with the embarrassment of the high-toned city nephew and his wife and stylish friends, form a series of situations that make for laughter, mingled with a bit of pathos"— excerpt from review in the *Indianapolis Freeman*, 11/26/14.

1209   Uncle Tom's Cabana   1947

Prod: Quimby, Fred. *Co:* Metro-Goldwyn-Mayer. (Animation / Short / Sound / Color.)

An animated version of "Uncle Tom's Cabin."

1210   Uncle Tom's Cabin   1903

Prod: Porter, Edwin S. *Co:* Thomas A. Edison, Inc.

First ever film of "Uncle Tom's Cabin." Porter plays Uncle Tom in blackface. (Dramatic / B&W / Silent / Short / 15 min. / 1,000 ft. / 2 reels / FLA 5913.)

This film adaptation (watered-down version) of Harriet Beecher Stowe's novel showing the cruelties of slavery, courage, family devotion, and the possible freeing of the slaves. A string of animated tableaux with painted backdrops, cakewalk, and various theatrical illusions.

1211   Uncle Tom's Cabin   1909

Co: Thanhauser.

The first remake. (Short / B&W / Silent.)

1212   Uncle Tom's Cabin   1914

Dir: Daly, William R. *Prod:* Laemmle, Carl, Jr. *Co:* World Film Company. *Cast:* Sam Lucas, Irving Cummings (white), Marie Eline (white).

Sam Lucas may have been the first black man to have a leading role in films. Screenplay by Harriet Beecher Stowe. Story by Harriet Beecher Stowe (novel). (Feature / B&W / Silent / 75 min.)

This version stars Sam Lucas as Uncle Tom.

1213   Uncle Tom's Cabin   1918

Dir: Dawley, J. Searle *Co:* Paramount. *Cast:* Marguerite Clark (white). (Silent / B&W / Short.)

This version was shot in Mississippi. Marguerite Clark plays both Topsy (in blackface) and little Eva.

1214   Uncle Tom's Cabin   1927

Dir: Pollard, Harry. *Co:* Universal Studios. *Cast:* James Lowe, Margarita Fischer (white), George Seigmann (white), Arthur Edmund Carew (white), Madam Sul-te-Wan. (Feature / Silent / 16mm / B&W / 93 min.)

James Lowe plays Uncle Tom in this version.

1215   Under the Old Apple Tree
pre–1910

(B&W / Silent / Short / FLA 5780.)

1216   The Undertaker's Daughter
1915

Dir: Lubin, Sigmund. *Prod:* Lubin, Sigmund. *Co:* Lubin Manufacturing Company. *Cast:* John Edwards, Mattie Edwards, Mr. Kelly, Mr. Higgins, Luke Scott.

Written by Will Louis. Released on 5/1/15. (Short / 400 ft. / B&W / Silent.)

"Mattie Cook, the Undertaker's daughter, loves John Scott, who has no job, but father wants her to marry Sime Sloan, who has one and it takes all of Mattie's persuasive power to overcome Dad, but she is equal to the occasion. She gets rid of Sime and Bime by promising to marry them if they will prove their love for her. One must sleep in one of her father's coffins and the other sit by it all night. Unbeknown to one another they come to fulfill their promise and settle down to the task. It really looks as if she would have to marry both, when she hits on the thought that a little noise would help some and with the aid of John she manages to get rid of them. In their fright they run through the meeting house presided over by Dad, who gets a couple of spills. He finally decides that John is the most sensible and can help in the undertaking business"—*Lubin Bulletin*.

1217   Underworld   1937

Dir: Micheaux, Oscar. *Prod:* Micheaux, Oscar. *Co:* Micheaux Pictures Corporation. *Dist:* Micheaux Pictures Corporation. *Cast:* Oscar Polk, Sol Johnson, Ethel Moses, Bee Freeman, Larry Seymour, "Slick" Chester, Angel Gabriel, Lorenzo Tucker, Dottie Salter, The Pope Sisters, Bobby Hargreaves Orchestra.

Adapted from the story *Chicago After Midnight* by Edna Mae Baker. Photographed by Lester Lang. Edited by Nathan Cy Braunstein. Continuity by Jack Kemp. Reviews in the *Philadelphia Tribune*, 1/6/38, and the *Philadelphia Independent*, 1/16/38. (Sound / B&W / 60 min. / Feature / FCA 9584–9585.)

Story of a young man, a graduate of a Southern black college, who goes to Chicago, becomes romantically involved unknowingly with the "Big" man's deceitful girl. "Hell hath no fury like a woman scorned" is the rest of the plot. When the naive young man becomes aware of her status, he leaves her and dates another. The scorned lady frames him for the murder of her husband; he's convicted and sentenced to death. At the last minute, an eyewitness to the murder comes forth and saves the young man.

1218   Undisputed Evidence   1922

Co: Cotton Blossom Film Company. (Silent / B&W / 5 reels / Feature.)

1219   The Unknown Soldier Speaks   1934

Dir: Goldberg, Jack. *Prod:* Rossen, Robert & Jack. *Co:* Lincoln Productions. *Cast:* Documentary with narration by Alan Bunce (white).

Dialogue by Robert Rossen. Preview in the *Philadelphia Tribune*, 4/19/34. (Silent / B&W / Documentary / Short.)

"Documents the contributions of Black soldiers in American wars ... the film is pretty much a succession of soldiers on parade, firing of cannons, and the general spectacle of destruction on a wholesale scale"—excerpt of review from the *Film Daily*, 5/26/34.

1220   Unlucky Woman   1944

Dir: Burger, Hans. *Prod:* Goldberg, Jack & Dave. *Co:* Hollywood Pictures Corporation. *Dist:* Soundies Distributing Corporation. *Cast:* Lena Horne, Teddy Wilson and His Orchestra (Emmett Berry, Jimmy Hamilton, Benny Morton, John Williams, J.C. Heard, Pete Johnson).

Excerpted from the Hollywood Productions short "Boogie Woogie Dream" (1942). (Soundies 19208 / B&W / Short / Sound / Musical / 12/11/44.)

1221   Up Jumped the Devil   1941

Dir: Crowley, William Xavier. *Prod:* Buell, Jed. *Co:* Dixie National Pictures, Inc. *Dist:* Toddy Films. *Cast:* Mantan Moreland, Maceo Sheffield, Shelton Brooks, Clarence Brooks, Florence O'Brien, J. Lawrence Criner, Arthur Ray, Susette Johnson, Ariel Harris.

Review in the *Pittsburgh Courier*, 9/20/41. (Sound / B&W / 62 min. / Feature.)

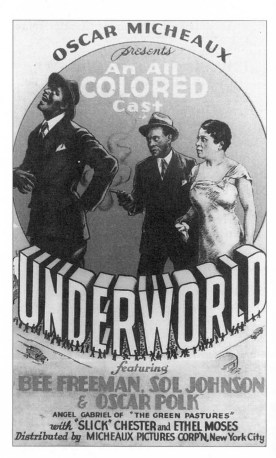

A very funny and silly movie with Mantan Moreland and Shelton Brooks. They play two parolees out looking for a job. They apply and get a job on a wealthy estate as a butler and a maid. Of course, Mantan plays a big chested maid and Shelton the butler. The plot basically involves a shady swamie trying to steal the lady of the estate's jewelry and succeeding. Enter Mantan and Shelton to trick the swamie into getting the jewelry back and having him arrested.

1222   Upbeat in Music   1943

Prod: March of Time. *Co:* March of Time. *Cast:* Duke Ellington, Marian Anderson, Art Tatum, George Gershwin (white).

Series: The March of Time. (16mm / Sound / Documentary / Short.)

1223   Upward Path   1919

Co: Democracy Photoplay Corporation. (Silent / B&W / Short.)

1224   Utica Jubilee Singers   1930

Co: Vitaphone. *Cast:* Utica Jubilee Singers. (Mississippi). (Musical / B&W / Sound / Short.)

1225   Vanities   1946

Dir: Alexander, William D. *Prod:* Alexander, William D. *Co:* Alexander Production. *Cast:* Charles Keith, Joesfred Portee, Audrey Armstrong. (Sound / B&W / Short.)

This is another nightclub performance film, with young Charles Keith as MC. Before he introduces the other acts, he confesses that he is an out-of-work actor whose idol is Bette Davis. He does a masterful impersonation of her role in *The Letter* in which he first sounds remarkably like the actress, then even begins to look like her. The next act is Joesfred Portee, who sings. Then, Keith introduces "Little Audrey" Armstrong, who demonstrates her remarkable muscle control and persistence in a gyrating dance. For a finale, Ms. Portee comes back and sings.

1226   Veiled Aristocrats   1932

Dir: Micheaux, Oscar. *Prod:* Micheaux, Oscar. *Co:* Micheaux Film Corporation. *Dist:* Micheaux Pictures Corporation. *Cast:* Lorenzo Tucker, Barrington Guy, Lawrence Chenault, Walter Fleming, Laura Bowman, Lucille Lewis, Carl Mahon. Willor Lee Guilford, Bernardine Mason, Aurora Edwards, Arnold Wiley, Mabel Garrett.

Written by Oscar Micheaux. Originally lost, film restored with segment missing. Possibly from the 1923 novel by Miss Gertrude Sanborn (white) of Chicago, Illinois, entitled *Veiled Aristocrats* published by Colored Publishers of Washington, D.C. Story in the *Philadelphia Tribune*, 12/29/23. (Sound / B&W / Feature / 48 min.)

The story of a lawyer who returns home to find that his light-skinned sister is about to marry a dark-skinned man. He and the mother agree that he should take her away to a better situation. The lawyer (Lorenzo Tucker) introduces her to a wealthy white man, who falls in love with her. She realizes that she's not white and is still in love with her dark-skinned man. She leaves her brother's house and returns to her real life.

1227   The Vicious Circle   1936

Prod: Morris Wax Management Company. *Co:* Cramerly Picture Corporation. *Cast:* Actors from the Philadelphia area.

Produced under the auspices of the Wax Theater Interest, the Royal Theater Management in Philadelphia. (Sound / B&W / Feature.)

"'The Circle' is an exposé of the vice rackets that rule so many of America's big cities. The story is laid in Philadelphia and most of the action centers around the efforts of a 'numbers' writer, protected by a shady political boss, to entangle innocent people in his net of iniquity. How he is hunted down in the story makes for a whirlwind climax to a bullet spattered melodrama of high tension"— *Philadelphia Tribune*, 11/12/36.

1228   The Virgin of the Seminole   1922

Dir: Micheaux, Oscar. *Prod:* Micheaux, Oscar. *Co:* Micheaux Film Corporation. *Dist:* Micheaux Film Corporation. *Cast:* Shingzie Howard, William Fountaine.

Preview in the *Philadelphia Tribune*, 5/8/26. (Silent / B&W / Feature.)

This story amplifies Micheaux's belief that the colored should own land. This story tells of a young colored man who becomes a member of the Canadian Mounted Police. His heroic deeds reward him enough to buy a ranch and retire. His adventures in romance and business

SHE WAS DOOMED TO DIE !

TODDY PICTURES CO. PRESENTS

VOODOO DEVIL DRUMS

SEE--
FOR THE FIRST TIME --
THE VIRGIN DANCE OF DEATH !
THE ALTAR OF SKULLS!
THE WALKING DEAD!

STRANGE SECRETS *never before* REVEALED!

lead the viewer through a good part of the picture.

1229   Virginia, Georgia and Caroline   1942

Co: Minoco Production. *Dist:* Soundies Distributing Corporation. *Cast:* Cab Calloway and His Orchestra: Lamar Wright, Russell Smith, Shad Collins, Jonah Jones (trumpets); Keg Johnson Tyree Glenn, Quentin Jackson (trombones); Jerry Blake, Hilton Jefferson, Andrew Brown, Teddy McRae, Walter Thomas (reeds); Benny Payne (piano); Danny Barker (guitar); Milt Hilton (bass); Cozy Cole (drums); The Cabaliers (the Four Palmer Brothers, vocal quartet). (Soundies 4606 / B&W / Short / Sound / Musical 2/23/42.)

1230   Voodoo Devil Drums   1946

Prod: Toddy, Ted. *Co:* Toddy Pictures Company. *Dist:* Toddy Pictures Company. (Sound / B&W / 44 min. / Feature / Semi-documentary.)

Voodoo rites, zombies, witchcraft, and magic are included in this film.

Voodoo Drums   *see*   Drums o' Voodoo

1231   Voodoo in Harlem   1938

Dir: Zamora, Rudy. *Prod:* Lantz, Walter. *Co:* Universal Studios.

Story by Victor McLeod & Win Smith. Musical Score: Frank Churchill, Animators: Frank Tipper & Merle Gilson. (B&W / Sound / Animation / Short.)

An animator leaves his work station at the end of the day, leaving his ink bottle open. Later that night a storm brews, the wind blows in the window and knocks over the ink bottle. Drops of ink drip off the edge of the table onto the paper on the floor. The black droplets begin to form into little black Africans in straw wraps, who then begin dancing around singing "Voodoo in Harlem."

1232   The Wages of Sin   1928

Dir: Micheaux, Oscar. *Prod:* Micheaux, Oscar. *Co:* Micheaux Film Corporations. *Dist:* Micheaux Film Corporations. *Cast:* Lorenzo Tucker, Sylvia Birdsong, William A. Clayton, Jr., Katherine Noisette, Alice B. Russell, William Baker, Bessie Gibbens, Gertrude Snelson, Ethel Smith.

Adaptation from the story "Alias Jefferson Lee." This story is remarkably close to Oscar Micheaux's Company and the hiring of his brother, Swan Micheaux. Review in the *Philadelphia Tribune*, 11/29/28. (Silent / B&W / Feature.)

This tragic story involves two brothers. Winston, the eldest, and J. Lee, the youngest. Sworn to take care of his younger brother at the request of his mother on her death bed. Winston soon regrets his promise. Winston hires his brother, who immediately begins to steal from the company. Winston eventually fires his brother, goes away, falls in love, returns home only to weaken and rehire his brother. J. Lee continues to ruin the company, but as usual everything ends well.

1233   Walker Newsreel No. 1   1921

Co: T.H.B. Walker's Colored Pictures. (Newsreel / B&W / Short / Silent / 3 reels.)

Featured are: views of seventeen black colleges; banks and factories owned by blacks; Jack Johnson, former world heavyweight boxing champion.

1234 Walking with My Honey
1945

Co: RCM Production. *Dist:* Soundies Distributing Corporation. *Cast:* Cab Calloway and His Orchestra, Dotty Saulter. (Soundies 21208 / B&W / Short / Sound / Musical / 8/6/45.)

1235 Waller Medley 1946

Co: RCM Production. *Dist:* Soundies Distributing Corporation. *Cast:* Fats Waller. (Soundies 4M / B&W / Short / Sound / Musical.)

1236 The Walls Keep Talking
1942

Co: RCM Production. *Dist:* Soundies Distributing Corporation. *Cast:* Paul White, Artie Brandon. (Soundies / B&W / Short / Sound / Musical / 4/13/42.)

1237 Watch Out! 1946

Dir: Crouch, William Forest. *Prod:* Crouch, William Forest. *Co:* Filmcraft Production. *Dist:* Soundies Distributing Corporation. *Cast:* Johnny Long and His Orchestra, Tommy Morton, Joan Mann, Bill Skipper. (Soundies / B&W / Short / Sound / Musical / 5/13/46.)

1238 The Water Boy
1929

Co: Pathé / RCA Phonophone. *Cast:* Kentucky Jubilee Singers. (Musical / Short / B&W / Sound.)

1239 A Watermelon Contest
1895

Co: Thomas A. Edison, Inc. (B&W / Silent / Short / Actualities / FLA 4940.)

Unedited footage of a group of black men eating watermelons in a contest.

1240 Watermelon Feast 1903

Co: American Mutoscope / Biograph. (Newsreel / B&W / Short / Silent.)

Film footage of black men once again eating watermelons.

1241 Way Down South 1903

Co: American Mutoscope / Biograph. (Newsreel / Documentary / B&W / Short / Silent.)

Film footage of various scenes of Southern blacks working on plantations.

1242 Way Down South 1939

Dir: Vorhaus, Bernard / Clarence Muse. *Prod:* Lessor, Sol. *Co:* Variety Film Company / RKO Radio Pictures. *Dist:* Variety Film Distributors. *Cast:* Bobby Breen (white), Clarence Muse, Allan Mowbray (white), Ralph Morgan (white), Steffi Duna, Sally Blane, Lillian Yarbo, Matthew Beard, Jack Carr, Marguerite Whitten, Hall Johnson Choir.

Screenplay: Clarence Muse & Langston Hughes. Story: Langston Hughes. Musical direction: Victor Young. Vocal arrangement: Hall Johnson. Photography: Charles Schoenbaum. Art director: Lewis L. Rachmil. Film editor: Arthur Hilton. Assistant director: John Sherwood. Wardrobe: Albert Deanno. Sound technician: Richard Van Hessen. (Sound / B&W / Feature / 62 min.)

When the master of the plantation is killed and before the heir becomes of age, a mean Simon LeGree–type administrator is appointed. How the heir and slaves join forces to oust the administrator is the movie plot.

1243 Way Down Yonder 1934

Dir: Watson, William. *Prod:* Christie, Al. *Co:* Educational Film Corporation. *Cast:* The Cabin Kids (five colored harmonizers, Ruth Hall, Helen Hall, James "Darling" Hall, Winifred "Sugar" Hall, and little Frederick Hall), Frank Wilson. (Sound / B&W / 1 reel / Short.)

1244 Way Out West 1935

Dir: Watson, William. *Prod:* Christie, Al. *Co:* Educational Films Corporation. *Cast:* The Cabin Kids (five colored harmonizers, Ruth Hall, Helen Hall, James "Darling" Hall, Winifred "Sugar" Hall, and little Frederick Hall), Range Ramblers (white), Eight Serenaders (white). (B&W / Silent / Short.)

"Those clever little pickaninnies are introduced to the wild west atmosphere in a comedy skit with near-thrills, and they succeed in making a big hit with the big rough men of the great outdoors"—excerpt of review from the *Film Daily*, 10/30/35.

1245   The Way to Happiness
1943
(Sound / B&W / Short.)

1246   We Pitched a Boogie Woogie 1946
Dir: Crouch, William Forest. *Prod:* Crouch, William Forest. *Co:* Filmcraft Production. *Dist:* Soundies Distributing Corporation. *Cast:* Johni Weaver, Lou Crawford, Dallas Bartley and His Orchestra. (Soundies 17M3 / B&W / Short / Sound / Musical / 3/18/46.)

1247   We the Cats Shall Hep Ya
1945
Co: RCM Production. *Dist:* Soundies Distributing Corporation. *Cast:* Cab Calloway and His Orchestra. (Soundies 22108 / B&W / Short / Sound / Musical / 12/10/45.)

1248   We Work Again 1936
Co: WPA Film. (Sound / B&W / Newsreel / Short.)

Newsreel showing scenes of blacks participating in various WPA work projects in the United States.

1249   Welcome Home 1931
Co: Tiffany Film Company. *Cast:* Forbes Randolph Kentucky Jubilee Singers. (Musical / B&W / Short / Sound.)

1250   The Well (Deep Is the Well) 1951
Dir: Rouse, Russell & Leo C. Popkin. *Prod:* Popkin, Leo C. & Clarence Green. *Co:* United Artists. *Cast:* Maidie Norman, Ernest Anderson, Bill Walker, Alfred Grant, Benjamin Hamilton, Gwendolyn Laster, George Hamilton (white), Christine Larsen (white).

Screenplay by Clarence Muse, Russell Rouse. (Feature / Sound / B&W / 16mm / 3 reels / 89 min.)

"Racial tensions mount when a missing Black girl is last seen talking to a white stranger. The town is on the verge of open riot, but when the girl is discovered down an abandoned well, all sides join in to save her"—Klotman.

1251   West Indian Boys Diving for Money 1897
Co: Thomas A. Edison, Inc. (B&W / Silent / Short / Actualities / FLA 4943.)

1252   West Indian Girls in Native Dance 1897
Co: Thomas A. Edison, Inc. (B&W / Silent / Short / Actualities / FLA 3379.)

1253   We've Come a Long, Long Way 1943
Dir: Goldberg, Jack. *Prod:* Goldberg, Jack / Elder Micheaux. *Co:* Negro Marches on Corporation. *Cast:* Dr. George Washington Carver, Joe Louis, Bill Robinson, Lena Horne, Paul Robeson.

Previews in the *Philadelphia Tribune*, 6/19/43, 1/20/45, the *Philadelphia Independent*, 1/26/45, and the *New York Amsterdam News* 6/24/44. NAACP protest against, *Philadelphia Independent*, 2/20/44. Coproduced and narrated by Elder Solomon Lightfoot Micheaux, then pastor of the Radio Church in Washington, D.C. Additional commentary by Dr. Mary McLeod Bethune and Major R. Wright, banker and former college president. (Sound / B&W / Newsreel / Short Documentary.)

The picture opens with a funeral eulogy of a young black officer killed in action which is used to depict pictorially the opportunities and achievements of the race in peace and war. The film also warns the black man of the dangers of Nazi or Japanese domination. Blacks are shown working on the farm and in Harlem, at work in schools, colleges, in laboratories, factories, in the armed services and in varied entertainment fields. Included are shots of Dr. George Washington Carver, Joe Louis, Paul Robeson, Lena Horne, and Bill Robinson.

1254   We've Got the Devil on the Run 1934
Prod: Micheaux, Elder Solomon Lightfoot. *Co:* Elder Solomon Lightfoot Micheaux. *Cast:* Elder Micheaux. (Documentary / Sound / B&W / Short.) The Reverend Lightfoot was the pastor of the Radio Church in Washington, D.C.

The religious services filmed at the Reverend Lightfoot's Church in Washington, D.C.

1255 Wham 1943

Co: RCM Production. *Dist:* Soundies Distributing Corporation. *Cast:* The Four Ginger Snaps. (Soundies 13308 / B&W / Short / Sound / Musical / 9/13/43.)

1256 Wharf Scenes and Natives Swimming at St. Thomas, D.W.I. 1897

Co: Thomas A. Edison, Inc. (B&W / Silent / Short / Actualities / FLA 3607.)

1257 What a Guy 1947

Prod: Toddy, Ted. *Co:* Lucky Star Productions. *Dist:* Toddy Pictures Company. *Cast:* Mantan Moreland, Ruby Dee, Monte Hawley, Lawrence Criner, John Bouie, Ken Freeman, Al Curtis, Anna Lucasta. (Sound / B&W / Feature.)

1258 What Goes Up 1939

Dir: Green, Eddie. *Prod:* Green, Eddie. *Co:* Sepia-Art Pictures Company. *Dist:* Toddy Pictures Company. *Cast:* Eddie Green, Dick Campbell, Honey Boy Johnson, Sidney Easton, Carol Purlow. (Comedy / Sound / B&W / Feature.)

1259 What Happened in the Tunnel pre–1910

(B&W / Silent / Short / FLA 3660.)

1260 What to Do 1942

Co: RCM Production. *Dist:* Soundies Distributing Corporation. *Cast:* Savannah Churchill, Les Hite and His Orchestra. (Soundies 6601 / B&W / Short / Sound / Musical / 5/4/42.)

1261 Whatcha Know, Joe? 1941

Co: RCM Production. *Dist:* Soundies Distributing Corporation. *Cast:* Johnny Long and His Orchestra, Swede Neilson. (Soundies / B&W / Short / Sound / Musical / 3/30/41.)

1262 What's the Use? 1918

Co: Trowship Film Company. (Silent/ B&W / Short.)

1263 When Cupid Went Wild 1917

Co: Ebony Film Company. *Dist:* General Film Company. *Cast:* Ebony Players (Sam Robinson, Samuel "Sambo" Jacks, Will Starks,

Julia Mason, Bert Murphy, Evon Skekeeter, Mildred Price, Walter Brogsdale, Robert Duree, Frank Pollard, George Lewis Stock Company). (Silent / B&W / Short / 2 reels.)

1264 When Giants Fought 1926

Co: England. *Dist:* England. *Cast:* Tom Molyneux. (Silent / Sport / Feature.)

The career of black boxer Tom Molyneux.

1265 When Good Luck Comes Our Way 1917

Prod: Deans, William. *Co:* William Deans. *Cast:* William Deans, Spurlock. (B&W / Silent / 35mm / Short.)

1266 When Men Betray 1929

Dir: Micheaux, Oscar. *Prod:* Micheaux, Oscar. *Co:* Micheaux Film Corporation. *Dist:* Micheaux Pictures Company. *Cast:* Bessie Gibbens, Gertrude Snelson, Lorenzo Tucker, Ethel Smith, Alice B. Russell, William Clayton, Jr. (Silent / B&W / Feature.)

"A soul stirring drama of a girl who did not know there is one vital question to be answered — see 'When Men Betray'" — *Film Herald*.

1267   When True Love Wins
1915

Co: Southern Motion Picture Company. Written by Mr. Isaac Fisher. (Silent / B&W / Feature.)

"Skillfully constructed story that only the highest human characteristics and impulses are portrayed. He has woven a plot around love affairs of Thelma Drayton. Possessing those maidenly charms which compel the admiration of the young people in her church, Thelma Drayton finds herself surrounded with many suitors, three of whom are very desirable young men. As the action of the play progresses, Thelma frequently finds herself unable to make a definite choice between these three young men, as each one in turn reveals some hidden strength which appeals to her. In the climax there is a strong scene in which the hero has to choose between the opportunity to win Thelma and to do his duty for his country. To the surprise of Thelma he states positively that to him love of country precedes love of sweetheart, and he prepares to take up arms to defend his country. The very thought of parting with him pains her very keenly, and she finally decides that after all she loves the hero. Of course, there is a happy ending and good moral" — excerpt from review in the *Atlanta Independent*, 12/3/15.

1268   When You and I Were Young, Maggie   1944

Co: RCM Production. *Dist:* Soundies Distributing Corporation. *Cast:* Will Bradley and His Orchestra, Billie Joyce. (Soundies / B&W / Short / Sound / Musical / 9/4/44.)

1269   When You Are Scared, Run
1918

Co: Ebony Film Company. *Dist:* General Film Company. *Cast:* Ebony Players (Sam Robinson, Samuel "Sambo" Jacks, Will Starks, Julia Mason, Bert Murphy, Evon Skekeeter, Mildred Price, Walter Brogsdale, Robert Duree, Frank Pollard, George Lewis Stock Company). (Comedy / B&W / Short / Silent.)

1270   When You Hit, Hit Hard
1918

Co: Ebony Film Company. *Dist:* General Film Company. *Cast:* Ebony Film Players (Sam Robinson, Samuel "Sambo" Jacks, Will Starks, Julia Mason, Bert Murphy, Evon Skekeeter, Mildred Price, Walter Brogsdale, Robert Duree, Frank Pollard, George Lewis Stock Company). (Silent / B&W / Short / 2 reels.)

1271   Where the Sweet Mammas Grow   1941

Co: RCM Production. *Dist:* Soundies Distributing Corporation. *Cast:* The Korn Kobblers. (Soundies / B&W / Short / Sound / Musical / 11/3/41.)

1272   Where's My Man To-Nite?
1944

Dir: Williams, Spencer. *Prod:* Sack, Alfred. *Co:* Bourgeois-Jenkins Pictures. *Dist:* Sack Amusement Enterprises. *Cast:* Irvin C. Miller's "Brownskin Models," Peachy Pinups, Emmet

Jackson, George T. Sutton, L.K. Smith, Myra J. Hemming, Hugh Martin, Georgia Kelly, Clarissa Deary, Lawrence "Pepper" Neely, Estrica McZekkashine.

Written by Spencer Williams, this film is the re-released. *Marching On*, 1943, with musical variety acts added in. Photographed by Clark Ramsey. Recorded by H.W. Kier, R.C.A. High Fidelity. (Feature / B&W / Sound.)

Williams' film depicts black soldiers in a fictional story against the background of army life in the all-black 25th Infantry. A young man, fighting with the emotional baggage of being in the service, black and afraid of war, eventually deserts the army. While escaping on a freight train, he befriends a hobo. Both jump off the moving train to escape being detected; the hobo is hurt and dies. Before the hobo dies, it is revealed that the hobo was the soldier's dad, who had been reported killed in World War I. Instead he had been roaming around with amnesia all along. The young man passes out in the desert and unbelievably is found by his grandfather. He and his grandfather accidently discover a Japanese radio post in the mountains. Grandfather is killed during a struggle with the Japanese, as other U.S. soldiers arrive to save the day. The AWOL soldier is given a second chance as he has seen the error of his ways. The film stresses patriotism and the contribution of blacks to the war effort.

1273   While Strolling in the Park
pre–1910
(B&W / Silent / Short / FLA 5252.)

1274   While Thousands Cheer
1940
Prod: Popkin, Harry M. *Co:* Million Dollar Productions. *Dist:* Popkin, Leo C. *Cast:* Kenny Washington, Gladys Snyder, Jeni LeGon, Florence O'Brien, Ida Belle Kauffin, Mantan Moreland, Reginald Fen-derson, Lawrence Criner, Monte Hawley, Edward Thompson, Lena Torrance, Joel Fluellen, Harry Lavette.

Kenny Washington, former all-American football player at UCLA. Original title was *Gridiron Graft*, but released with *While Thousands Cheer* title, then re-released in 1945 under the title *Crooked Money*. Preview in the

Philadelphia Independent, 9/22/40. Reviews in the *Philadelphia Tribune*, 11/14/40, and the *California Eagle*, by John Kinloch, 11/28/40. (Sound / B&W / Feature.)

This "Mickey Rooneyish" type story is about a young colored college football player. As the story goes, he is being pursued by fix-minded racketeers, but he and his college chums foil their plans with some quick thinking.

1275   Who Dunit to Who   1946
Dir: Crouch, William Forest. *Prod:* Crouch, William Forest. *Co:* Filmcraft Production. *Dist:* Soundies Distributing Corporation. *Cast:* June Richmond. (Soundies 25M4 / B&W / Short / Sound / Musical / 11/24/46.)

1276   Who Said Chicken?   pre–1910
(B&W / Silent / Short / FLA 3146.)

1277   Who Threw the Whiskey in the Well?   1945
Dir: Crouch, William Forest. *Prod:* Crouch, William Forest. *Co:* Filmcraft Production. *Dist:* Soundies Distributing Corporation. *Cast:* The Phil Moore Four. (Soundies 22308 / B&W / Short / Sound / Musical / 12/30/45.)

1278   Who's Been Eating My Porridge?   1944
Co: RCM Production. *Dist:* Soundies Distributing Corporation. *Cast:* The King Cole Trio (Nat "King" Cole, Oscar Moore, Johnny Miller), Ida James. (Soundies 15808 / B&W / Short / Sound / Musical / 3/27/44.)

1279   Who's Who   1914
Dir: Lubin, Sigmund. *Prod:* Lubin, Sigmund. *Co:* Lubin Manufacturing Company. *Cast:* John Edwards, Mattie Edwards, Bessie Brown.

Written by Will Louis. Released on 12/19/14. (Silent / B&W / Short / 400 ft.)

"Jim Luke stops to tell Dr. Black that his wife is a little off in the top piece. The doctor promises to do what he can for her. The daily paper gives an account of a negro with unbalanced mind roaming about. In making his visit, the doctor gets into the wrong house and the occupants, having read an account of the crazy negro, think the doctor is the crazy man. On entering the room Doc finds the woman as he thinks in a terrible frame of mind and tries to humor her. There are a number of shots fired. The noise brings the neighbors and police, and the doctor is told of his mistake"—*Lubin Bulletin*.

1280   Who's Who in Colored America   1945
Prod: Toddy, Ted. *Co:* Toddy Pictures Company. *Dist:* Toddy Pictures Company. (Sound / B&W / Documentary.)

1281   Why Worry?   1923
Co: Lone Star Motion Picture Company. *Cast:* Byron Smith, Mae Morris, Frank Brown. (Silent / B&W / Comedy / Short.)

A country bumpkin and his little sister finally make it to the big city only to find out that it is not as nice as they thought it would be. He falls in love and decides he needs money. He enters a boxing contest and wins $10,000.

1282   The Widow's Bite   1929
Prod: Christie, Al. *Co:* Paramount. *Cast:* Spencer Williams, Evelyn Preer, Edward Thompson. (Sound / 35mm / B&W / 2 reels / Comedy / Short.)

One of the Christie series done in "Negro dialect."

1283   The Wife Hunters   1922
Dir: White, Bob. *Co:* Lone Star Motion Picture Company. *Cast:* Bob White, Jessie Purty, Edward Townsend, V. Stevens, P. Massey, H.C. Grant, J.T. Walton. J.G. Selby, and other local citizens in San Antonio, Texas.

Filmed on location in San Antonio, Texas. Photography by B.L. Teycer. (35mm / Silent / B&W / Short / 2 reels / Comedy.)

1284   Willie and Eugene Howard in a Theater Manager's Office   1927
(B&W / Sound / Short / 20 min. / VBE 8160.)

1285   Willie and Eugene Howard, Music Makers   1928
(B&W / Sound / Short / 20 min. / VBE 8155.)

1286   Willie and Eugene Howard, My People   1929
(B&W / Sound / Short / VBE 8156–8157.)

1287   The Willie Mays Story   1955
Co: RKO Radio Pictures. *Cast:* Willie Mays. (Biography / B&W / Feature / Sound.)

The story of the great black baseball player, Willie Mays of the San Francisco Giants and New York Giants.

1288   Willie Willie   1943
Co: RCM Production. *Dist:* Soundies Distributing Corporation. *Cast:* Sam Manning, Belle Rosette. (Soundies / B&W / Short / Sound / Musical / 2/1/43.)

1289   Wings for This Man   1944
Co: U.S. Army, Air Force Production. *Cast:* U.S. Air Force (blacks). (Sound / B&W / Documentary.)

Filmed at Tuskegee Army Air Field, Alabama. Blacks in the Army Air Force.

1290   The Witching Eyes   1930
Cast: Salem Tut Whitney, Lorenzo Tucker, Sylvia Birdsong. (Silent / B&W / Feature.)

1291   With the Help of Uncle Eben   1915
Co: Afro-American Film Company. (Silent / B&W / Short.)

1292   Within Our Gates   1919
Dir: Micheaux, Oscar. *Prod:* Micheaux, Oscar. *Co:* Micheaux Book and Film Company. *Dist:* Micheaux Book and Film Co. *Cast:* Evelyn Preer, William Starks, Mattie Edwards, E.G. Tatum, Grant Edwards, Charles D. Lucas, Lawrence Chenault, Flo Clements, Ralph Johnson, Grant Gorman, James D. Ruffin, William Smith.

Produced at Capitol Film Studios. Copy of film found in Spain in 1991, dubbed in Spanish entitled "La Negra." Lost for 72 years and restored by the Smithsonian Institute. Review in the *Chicago Defender*, 2/7/20. (8,000 ft. / 35mm / 7 reels / 79 min. / Silent / B&W / Feature / Video.)

It is late September, the cotton has been picked, ginned, baled and delivered, and Jasper Landry, a cropper, has prospered, clearing $685. In the same community dwells "Eph," the "tattle-tale" whom the blacks call a "white folks nigger." He is a pest who makes no effort toward his own betterment, but makes it his business to "spread news." Jasper gets into a dispute with Girdlestone, a wealthy planter, aristocrat and owner of everything for miles around. Girdlestone is shot and Jasper is seen holding a smoking revolver. This picture contains a lynching and rape scene which caused controversy in cities where it was shown.

1293 Woman's a Fool 1947

Co: Astor Pictures Corporation. *Cast:* Jean LaRue, Alabama Blossom, Birdina Hackett, Billy Fuller, Hollywood Jitterbugs, Red Calhoun and His Royal Swing Band, Ida Cox. (Sound / B&W / Feature.)

Late forties style musical revue with very little plot.

1294 Woman's Error 1922

Prod: Saunders, Tressie. *Co:* Tressie Saunders. (Silent / B&W.)

1295 A Woman's Worst Enemy
1918

Dir: Foster, William. *Prod:* Foster, William. *Co:* Foster Photoplay Company. *Dist:* William Foster. (Silent / B&W / 5 reels / Feature.)

"A five-reel drama starting in Oklahoma oil fields, ending in Chicago, when a clever vampire starts the social and business world going wrong. There's no telling what the ending will be" — advertisement.

1296 The Wooing and Wedding of a Coon 1905

Co: Biograph. (Silent / B&W / Comedy / Short.)

Two actors in blackface in an early derisive depiction of a newlywed Negro couple.

1297 Write That Letter Tonight
1945

Co: RCM Production. *Dist:* Soundies Distributing Corporation. *Cast:* Johnny and George. (Soundies 11M2 / B&W / Short / Sound / Musical / 6/4/45.)

1298 Wrong All Around 1917

Co: Ebony Film Company. *Dist:* General Film Company. *Cast:* Ebony Players (Sam Robinson, Samuel "Sambo" Jacks, Will Starks, Julia Mason, Bert Murphy, Evon Skekeeter, Mildred Price, Walter Brogsdale, Robert Duree, Frank Pollard, George Lewis Stock Company).

Reviews in the *Moving Picture World*, 12/8/17, and the *Exhibitors Herald*, 12/22/17. (Silent / B&W / Short / 2 reels.)

"A farce played by Negroes and the trial of a young man who is in love with the village belle as its motive. She has also a rich suitor. Her poor lover has many jobs and is the victim of bad luck in many different ways. The lady is always turning up at the moment when he is in some not wholly dignified predicament" — review from the *Moving Picture World*, 12/15/17.

1299 Wrong All Around
1922

Co: Lone Star Motion Picture Company. (Silent / B&W.)

1300 The Wrong Mr. Johnson
1922

Co: Lone Star Motion Picture Company.

Produced out of San Antonio, Texas. (Serial / 16 episodes / Silent / B&W / Shorts / Comedy.)

1301 The Wrong Mr. Wright
1947

Prod: Toddy, Ted. *Co:* Toddy Pictures Company. *Cast:* Dewey "Pigmeat" Markham, John Murray (white). (Sound / B&W / Short.)

1302 Xavier University — Negro Catholic College 1946

Co: Harmon Foundation Educational Films. (Documentary / Newsreel / B&W / Silent / 1 reel / 16mm / Short.)

Film footage of Xavier University, New Orleans, Louisiana.

1303 Y.M.C.A., Harlem, N.Y.
1945

Co: Harmon Foundation Educational Films. (Documentary / B&W / Short / Silent / 1 reel / 16mm.)

The Harlem Branch of the Y.M.C.A. showing the recreational facilities.

1304   Ya Fine and Healthy Thing
1945

Co: RCM Production. *Dist:* Soundies Distributing Corporation. *Cast:* Dallas Bartley and His Orchestra. (Soundies 88608 / B&W / Short / Sound / Musical / 9/10/45.)

1305   Yamekraw   1930

Dir: Roth, Murray. *Co:* Vitaphone. *Cast:* Jimmy Mordecai, Margaret Simms, Marianni's Mediterraneans, Murray Roth, Louise Cook.

An entirely new type of one reeler, subtitled "A Negro Rhapsody," is modernistic to the extreme and displays a new camera and lighting technique. No camera shot lasts for more than 20 seconds. "Yamekraw" is named after a Negro settlement in Savannah, Georgia. Composition by James P. Johnson. Ed Dupar chief cameraman. Preview in the *Philadelphia Tribune*, 5/30/30. Review in the *Philadelphia Tribune*, 5/15/30. (B&W / Short / Sound / Musical / 1 reel / Vitaphone #1009 / FEB 6957.)

A picturization of a jazz symphony. This short is an impressionistic expression of the moods and emotions of the Negro. A vignette of black life — the dilemma surrounding the move from country to city, leaving the security of the known for the uncertain promise of opportunity ahead.

1306   Yankee Doodle Never Went to Town   1944

Co: RCM Production. *Dist:* Soundies Distributing Corporation. *Cast:* Mabel Scott, The Flennoy Trio. (Soundies 89808 / B&W / Short / Sound / Musical / 12/31/44.)

1307   Yes! Indeed   1941

Dir: Murphy, Dudley / Josef Berne. *Prod:* Coslow, Sam. *Co:* RCM Production. *Dist:* Soundies Distributing Corporation. *Cast:* The Spirits of Rhythm. (Soundies 4304 / B&W / Short / Sound / Musical / 11/24/41.)

1308   You Always Hurt the One You Love   1944

Co: RCM Production. *Dist:* Soundies Distributing Corporation. *Cast:* The Mills Brothers. (Soundies 18508 / B&W / Short / Sound / Musical / 10/16/44.)

1309   You Call It Madness   1946

Dir: Anderson, Leonard. *Prod:* Alexander, William D. *Co:* Alexander Production. *Dist:* Soundies Distributing Corporation. *Cast:* Billy Eckstine and His Orchestra.

Excerpted from the featurette "Rhythm in a Riff" (1946). (Soundies / B&W / Short / Sound / Musical / 12/30/46.)

1310   You Can't Fool About Love   1943

Co: RCM Production. *Dist:* Soundies Distributing Corporation. *Cast:* Josephine Edwards, The Four Toppers, Cee Pee Johnson and His Orchestra. (Soundies 4M2 / B&W / Short / Sound / Musical / 9/21/43.)

1311   You Can't Keep a Good Man Down   1922

Co: Lone Star Motion Picture Company. (Silent / B&W / Comedy / Short.)

1312   Young Pushkin   1935

Dir: Narodistky, Arady. *Co:* Len Films. *Cast:* V. Litovsky (white), L. Paramof (white), A. Aharazia White). (Feature / Sound / B&W.)

A Russian film on Alexander Pushkin's life covering the years 1811–1817.

1313   Your Feet's Too Big   1941

Co: Minoco Production. *Dist:* Soundies Distributing Corporation. *Cast:* Fats Waller. (Soundies 4203 / B&W / Short / Sound / Musical / 11/17/41.)

1314   Your Feet's Too Big   1946

Dir: Gould, Dave. *Prod:* Hersh, Ben. *Co:* RCM Production. *Dist:* Soundies Distributing Corporation. *Cast:* The Ali Baba Trio. (Soundies 19M1 / B&W / Short / Sound / Musical / 5/6/46.)

1315   Zeb, Zack and the Zulus   1913

Dir: Lubin, Sigmund. *Prod:* Lubin, Sigmund. *Co:* Lubin Manufacturing Company.

Released on 7/24/13. (Silent / B&W / 600 ft. / Short.)

"Zeb Jackson and Zack Johnson, two colored Missionaries, land in an African Village and are seized by Zulus. They are put in a cage to fatten up before being cooked. When the King and his counselors go to look at the prisoners, they find that Zeb and Zack have charmed the guards by singing 'Everybody's Doing It' and dancing the trot. The King and counselors become infected with the song and they dance through the village. During the riot, the Missionaries see a chance to bolt. They beat it to the shore and there find a boat, the sailors quickly take them on board, thus escaping a terrible fate"—*Lubin Bulletin*.

1316 Zircon 1923

Prod: Norman Film Manufacturing Company. *Co:* Norman Film Manufacturing Company. *Dist:* Norman Studios. *Cast:* Clarence Brooks, Anita Thompson.

Fifteen-chapter all-black serial which was never released. (Silent / B&W / Serial / Short / 2 reels each.)

*Chapter 1. *The Spider's Web*. John Manning, a young chemist and mining engineer in the employ of the Egyptian Potash Company, discovers a new wonder substance, naming it "Zircon." A rival interest, the Potash Corporation, hires a criminal known as "The Spider" to steal the formula and the manufacturing process. Manning and his sweetheart, Helen, are enmeshed in "The Spider's Web," with apparent death staring them in the face because of their refusal to give up the secret. *Chapter 2. *The Wheel of Death*. "The Spider," after securing by force a sample of Zircon, leaves Manning to die on the spinning hub of one of the monstrous wheels of the potash pump. *Chapter 3. *The Poison Cloud*. "The Fox," in the employ of the Potash Trust, while analyzing the sample of Zircon, is surprised by Manning. "The Fox" releases a poison cloud in his laboratory and leaves Manning to die. *Chapter 4. *The Desert Trap*. On a journey into the desert to rescue Helen, Manning is trapped by "The Spider's" gang and left to die in a raging sandstorm. *Chapter 5. *The Living Tomb*. Helen and Manning seek shelter in an ancient tomb of "Cliff Dwellers" and are trapped there and left to die of suffocation. *Chapter 6. *The Crocodile's Jaws*. Upon their rescue from the liv-

ing tomb, Manning and Helen are attacked by an army of crocodiles, with no apparent escape from death in sight. *Chapter 7. *The Sky Demon*. A colored aviator, who has been of assistance to Manning, rescues them from the crocodiles, but they are again captured by the Spider's gang. They are bound in the airplane. One of the Spider's gang takes them aloft in the airplane, then jumping with a parachute, leaves them to certain death in the pilotless plane. *Chapter 8. *The Ship Killer*. Falling into the ocean, the occupants of the plane are rescued by a ship, on which "The Spider" is fleeing to a foreign country with the formula of "Zircon" which he has arranged to sell to foreign interest and double-cross the Potash Company. Manning regains the formula and "The Spider" traps him and Helen in the hold of the ship, then scuttles the ship. The water slowly rises in the hold of the ship, swirling higher and higher around Manning and Helen. *Chapter 9. *Flames of Fear*. Failing in his purpose, "The Spider" escapes in a life boat after having set fire to the ship, leaving Manning and Helen helpless to roast alive. *Chapter 10. *Tigers of the Sea*. Drifting on a raft at sea, Manning is forced to fight for his life with a monstrous tiger shark. *Chapter 11. *Jungle Death*. Making land, "The Spider" is surprised to see that Manning and Helen have been cast upon the island. Manning and Helen are left bound to trees to be devoured by a monstrous snake. *Chapter 12. *Sands of Death*. Managing to escape, Manning discovers on the island the richest deposits of potash in the world. Potash is rich in mineral "Zircon." "The Spider," with the formula, leaves Manning at the mercy of the quicksand, taking Helen, with him. *Chapter 13. *Trail of the Spider*. Manning is rescued from the island and trails Helen, who is about to suffer dishonor at the hands of "The Spider." *Chapter 14. *The Vanishing Prisoner*. Manning rescues Helen from "The Spider's" clutches and captures him. But "The Spider" vanishes with the help of one of his confederates, who has a mysterious substance which makes him invisible. Manning is bound in a cabin by the invisible "Spider" and the cabin is blown up.* Chapter 15. *Millions*. Peg, a one-legged friend of Manning's secures some of the invisible powder, and making himself invisible, rescues Manning from the cabin just before it is blown up. "The Spider" is killed by a piece of rock debris from the explosion. "The Spider's" gang is rounded up and captured. Helen, who is the daughter of Manning's employer, is married to Manning and with the newly discovered rich deposits of potash and the secret formula of "Zircon," the Potash Trust is forced out of business and Manning becomes a millionaire.

1317   Zoot 1946

Dir: Gould, Dave. *Prod:* Hersh, Ben. *Co:* RCM Production. *Dist:* Soundies Distributing Corporation. *Cast:* Thelma White and Her All-Girl Orchestra, Ellen Connor. (Soundies / B&W / Short / Sound / Musical / 8/5/46.)

1318   A Zoot Suit (With a Reet Pleat) 1942

Co: RCM Production. *Dist:* Soundies Distributing Corporation. *Cast:* Dorothy Dandridge, Paul White. (Soundies 5801 / Short / B&W / Sound / Musical / 3/9/42.)

1319   Zouzou 1934

Dir: Nissotti, Arys. *Prod:* Allgret, Marc. *Co:* Pathé Nathan-Joinville / B. Goldberg. *Dist:* ARYS Production. *Cast:* Josephine Baker, Jean Gabin (white), Yvette Lebon, Illa Meery, Palau, Madeleine Guitty, Claire Gerard, Marcel Vallee, Pierre Larquey, Serge Grave, Andree Wendler, Adreinne Trenkel, Vivian Romance, Pierre Palau, Phillippe Richard, Geo Forster, Roger Blin, Lucin Walter.

French. Scenarios & Dialogues by: Carlo Rim. Story by: G. Abatino. Artistic direction by: G. Abatino. Chief operator: Kelber. Operators: Louiz Nee & Kaufman Mercanton. Ingénieur du Son: Archimbaud. Décors: L. Meerson et Trauner. Montage: D. Batcheff. Music by Van-Parys-Scotto et Al. Romans, Coupletz de R. Bernstein et Koger. Edited by Salabert. Music direction: Louis Wins. Dance: Floyd du Pont. Administrator: Macaluzo. Régisseur: Pelozoff. Costumes: Pascaud et Zanel. Studios et tirage: Pathé-Nathan, R.C.A. High Fidelity. (French / Sound / B&W / 90 min. / Feature.)

"Zouzou (Baker), a little mulatto girl, and Jean, both orphans, were raised by Father Mele. Jean falls in love with Claire, Zouzou's friend, even though Zouzou loves him passionately. But she draws back in order to devote her life to the stage on which, by chance, she has already achieved a resounding success"—from *Blacks in Black and White.*

1320   Zululand 1947

Co: Twentieth Century–Fox Film Corporation. *Cast:* Ed Thorgenson (white) narrator. (Documentary / B&W / Short / Sound.)

A narrator describes the customs and traditions of the Zulus of Africa.

1321   A Zulu's Devotion 1916

Co: African Films. *Cast:* Zulu tribesmen.

Made in South Africa. Part of the Zulutown series, based on Zulu life. (Comedy / B&W / Feature / Silent.)

1322   The Zulu's Heart 1910

Co: Biograph. (B&W / Silent / Short / FLA 5837.)

"In it the Zulus are deterred from attacking a Boer wagon when one of their number kills three of his fellows in defense of the whites. The fadeout is on the Zulu, who clasps to his breast a doll given by the grateful Afrikaners"—Thomas Cripps.

1323   Zulutown 1916

Co: African Films. *Cast:* Zulu native actors.

Made in South Africa. The first in a series of comedies adapted from well-known sketches of Zulu life. (Comedy / B&W / feature / Silent.)

"A Zulu native returns to his native village after working at a skating rink in a nearby town. He floats a company amongst his dusky compatriots to start a rink in their town and very amusing scenes are witnessed on the opening day"—*Bioscope*, 9/27/17.

1324   Zulutown Races 1916

Co: African Films. *Cast:* Zulu actors.

Made in South Africa. Second in the Zulutown series. (Comedy / B&W / Feature / Silent.)

"The folk of Zulutown, having heard of the great sport of horse racing among the whites in town, try their hand at the same thing with very successful results"—*Bioscope*, 9/27/17.

APPENDIX A:
ACTOR CREDITS

Abbott, Robert S.
Millionaire (1927)

Abrams, Edward
Gunsaulus Mystery (1921), Sport of the Gods (1921)

The Acholi Tribe Chief
Sanders of the River (1935)

Adams, Faye
Harlem Variety Revue (1955), Rhythm and Blues Revue (1956)

Adams, Jo Jo
Burlesque in Harlem (1955)

Adams, Joe
Lionel Hampton and Orchestra (1949), Nat "King" Cole and Joe Adams Orchestra (1951)

Adams, Robert
Man of the Worlds (1946), The Song of Freedom (1938)

Adamson, James
Dark Manhattan (1937), Murder in Swingtime (1937)

Adnewah, Daniel
Jim Comes to Jo'Burg (1950)

Aguilo, Francisco
Black Thunderbolt (1921)

Agusta, Howard
Children of Fate (1926)

Ailey, Alvin
Carmen Jones (1954)

Albert, Don
Beale Street Mama (1946)

Albritton, Lynn
Backstage Blues (1943), Block Party Revels (1943), Dispossessed Blues (1943)

Alexander, Catherine
Children of Circumstance (1937)

The Ali Baba Trio
If You Only Knew (1946), Patience and Fortitude (1946), Your Feet's Too Big (1946)

All American Girl Band
Big Timers (1945)

Allan, E. Celese
Girl in Room 20 (1946), Go Down, Death! (1944), Marching On! (1943), Where's My Man To-Nite? (1944)

Allen, Anistine
Boarding House Blues (1948)

Allen, Anna Lou
Hearts of the Woods (1921)

Allen, Annisteen
I Want a Man (1946)

Allen, Billie
Souls of Sin (1949)

Allen, Charles
In the Depths of Our Hearts (1920), Lure of a Woman (1921)

Allen, Cliff
I Can't Dance (1944), Rinka Tinka Man (1944)

Allen, Glenn
Look-Out Sister (1948)

Allen, Hortense (The Body)
Rhythm in a Riff (1946)

The Alphabetical Four
Paradise in Harlem (1940)

Alston, Olive (Orchestra)
Gone Harlem (1939)

Alston and Young
Mistaken Identity (1941), Murder with Music (1941)

Amena, Doli
Swing (1938)

Ammons, Albert
Boogie Woogie Dream (1942), Boogie Woogie Dream (1944), My New Gown (1944)

Amos, Tom
Shot in the Night (1922)

Anderson, Allegretti
Georgia Rose (1930)

Anderson, Charles H. (Mr & Mrs.)
Uncle Remus' First Visit to New York (1914)

Anderson, Corny
Dark Manhattan (1937)

Anderson, Eddie "Rochester"
Cabin in the Sky (1943), Green Pastures (1936), Lady Luck (1940), Lucky Ghost (1941)

Anderson, Ernest
The Peanut Man (1947), Well (1951)

Anderson, Ida
Deceit (1921), Gayety (1929), Ghost of Tolston's Manor (1934), Secret Sorrow (1921), Son of Satan (1924)

Anderson, Ivy
Bundle of Blues (1933), I Got It Bad, and That Ain't Good (1942)

Anderson, Marion
Marian Anderson (1953), Upbeat in Music (1943)

Anderson, Myrtle
Green Pastures (1936)

Andrews, Avis
Harlem Bound (1935)

Andrews, Billy
Crimson Fog (1932)

Andrews, Charles
Green Pastures (1936), Murder in Swing Time (1937), Mystery in Swing (1940), Prison Bait (1944), Reform School (1939)

Andrews, Ismay
The Black King (1932), Harlem Big Shot (1932)

Anthony, Emmett
Ghost of Tolston's Manor (1934)

Antoine, Leroy
Life of Florence Mills (1940)

Apus and Estellita
Harlem Follies of 1949 (1950), I'm Tired (1944), Knock Me Out (1945), Sepia Cinderella (1947), Toot That Trumpet (1946)

Arblanche, Kitty
Crimson Fog (1932)

Arista Genes Girls Club
Beware (1946)

Armstrong, Audrey
Harlem Follies (1950), Vanities (1946)

Armstrong, Henry
Keep Punching (1939)

Armstrong, Louis
Bosko and the Pirate (1937), Cabin in the Sky (1943), Green Pastures (1938), I'll Be Glad When You're Dead You Rascal You (1932), I'll Be Glad When You're Dead You Rascal You (1942), Jam Session (1944), Negro in Entertainment (1950), Rhapsody in Black and Blue (1932), Satchmo the Great (1954), Shine (1942), Sleepy Time Down South (1942), Swingin' on Nothin' (1942)

Arnett, Billy
Fall of the Mighty (1913)

Arnett, Grace
Fall of the Mighty (1913)

Ashby, Irving
King Cole and His Trio (1950)

Ashkins, Ida
Colored American Winning His Suit (1916)

Astwood, Norman
Harlem Bound (1935), Paradise in Harlem (1940), Sunday Sinners (1941)

Atkins, Charles
Rock 'n' Roll Revue (1955)

Atkinson, Beatrice
Pitch a Boogie Woogie (1948)

Atkinson, Catherine
Murder in Swingtime (1937)

Auld, George (Auld Stars)
Ink Spots (1955)

Austin, Amos
Midnight Menace (1946)

Austin, Jack
The Green Eyed Monster (1921)

Avasiago, Lola
Harlem Follies (1950)

Axton, Bailey (Trio)
Dinty McGinty (1946)

Ayecock, Buzz
Girl in Room 20 (1946)

Backus, Peggy
Jackpot (1943)

Bailey, Bill
Basin Street Revue (1955), Cabin in the Sky (1943), Jazz Festival (1955), Rhythm and Blues Revue (1955)

Bailey, Joe
Murder in Swingtime (1937)
Bailey, Mesdames Hattie
Murder in Swingtime (1937)
Bailey, Pearl
Carmen Jones (1954), Porgy and Bess (1959), St. Louis Blues (1958)
Bains, Pearl
Straight to Heaven (1939)
Baker, Ann
Harlem After Midnight (1947), I Cried for You (1946), Rhythm in a Riff (1946)
Baker, Bessie
Realization of a Negro's Ambition (1916)
Baker, Danny
Virginia, Georgia and Caroline (1942)
Baker, Freddy
Look Out Sister (1948)
Baker, Josephine
The French Way, (1952), Prinsesse Tam-Tam (1935), Revue des Revues (1927), Siren of the Tropics (1928), Zouzou (1934)
Baker, William
Wages of Sin (1928)
Bangs, Helen
Boogiemania (1946)
Banks, Gertrude "Baby"
Burlesque in Harlem (1955)
Banks, J.B.
Injustice (1919), Loyal Hearts (1919)
Banks, Lesley
Sanders of the River (1935)
Banks, Otis
Injustice (1919), Loyal Hearts (1919)
Banks, Mrs. Otis
Injustice (1919), Loyal Hearts (1919)
Banos, Marie
Black Thunderbolt (1921)
Barr, Edgar
Drums o' Voodoo (1933), She Devil (1940)
Barrow, Dick
Burlesque in Harlem (1955)
The Barry Sisters
Ink Spots (1955)
Bartholomew, Freddie
Sepia Cinderella (1947)
Bartley, Dallas (Orchestra)
All Ruzzitt Buzzitt (1945), Cryin' and Singin' the Blues (1945), Standin' Joe (1945), We Pitched a Boogie Woogie (1946), Ya Fine and Healthy Thing (1945)

Barton, Eileen
Mr. Black Magic (1956)
Barys, Helen
Swanee Showboat (1945)
Bascomb Wilbur
Deviled Hams (1937)
Basie, Count
Air Mail Special (1941), Band Parade (1943), Basie's Boogie (1945), Basin St. Revue (1955), Choo-Choo Swing (1943), Downbeat Revue (1955), Ebony Parade (1947), Harlem Jazz Festival (1955), Harlem Mania (1938), Jamboree (1957), Jazz Festival (1955), Policy Man (1938), Rhythm and Blues Revue (1956), Sound of Jazz (1957), Stars Over Harlem (1956), Sugar Chile Robinson (1950), Take Me Back, Baby (1941)
Basin Street Boys
The Bronze Venus (1943), Duke Is Tops (1938)
Baskette, James (Jimmy)
Comes Midnight (1940), Gone Harlem (1939), Harlem Is Heaven (1932), Harlem Mania (1938), Policy Man (1938), Straight to Heaven (1939)
Bates, Leo
By Right of Birth (1921)
Bates, Lester
By Right of Birth (1921)
Bates, Richard
Midnight Shadow (1939)
Battles, Lucille
Lady Luck (1940), Lucky Ghost (1941)
Bayas, Don
Readin', Writin' and Rhythm (1939)
Beamon, Clifford
Juke Joint (1947)
Beard, Matthew (Stymie)
Broken Strings (1940), Two Gun Man from Harlem (1939), Way Down South (1939)
Beardon, Bessie
Gunsaulus Mystery (1921)
Beathea, David
Fight That Ghost (1946)
Beatty, Talley
Carnival of Rhythm (1944)
Beavers, Louise
Colored American Calvacade (1939), His Harlem Wife (1944), Imitation of Life (1934), Jackie Robinson Story (1950), Life

Goes On (1938), Prison Bait (1944), Reform School (1939)

Bechet, Marilouise
Moon Over Harlem (1939)

Bechet, Sidney (Band)
Moon Over Harlem (1939)

Belafonte, Harry
Bright Road (1953), Carmen Jones (1954), Fincho (1958)

Belheu, David
Hi-De-Ho (1947)

Bell, Spencer
Tenderfeet (1928)

Belt, Madeline
Paradise in Harlem (1940)

Bennett, Hope
His Harlem Wife (1944), Life Goes On (1940)

Bennett, Marilyn
Rockin' the Blues (1955)

Benson, Mrs. F.D.
Girl in Room 20 (1946)

The Berry Brothers
Boarding House Blues (1948)

Best, Willie
Cabin in the Sky (1943), Deep South (1937), Mississippi Moods (1937)

Bethune, Mary McLeod
Lionel Hampton and Herb Jeffries (1955)

The Big Apple Dancers
Policy Man (1938), Spirit of Youth (1937)

Bigard, Barney
Jam Session (1942), St. Louis Blues (1958)

Bilbrew, A.C. (Choir)
Hearts of Dixie (1929)

Billings, Jesse R.
Deceit (1921)

Billy and Ann
Poppin' the Cork (1943)

Birdsong, Amy
Marcus Garland (1928)

Birdsong, Sylvia
Wages of Sing (1928), Witching Eyes (1930)

Bishop, Andrew
Ghost of Tolston's Manor (1934), Lem Hawkins' Confession (1935), Murder in Harlem (1935), Son of Satan (1924), Temptation (1936)

Black, Valerie
Beware (1946)

The Black Diamonds Dollies
Midnight Menace (1946)

Blackman, Paul
Two-Gun Man from Harlem (1938)

Blake, Eubie
Chocolate Dandies (1924), Eubie Blake Plays (1927), Harlem Is Heaven (1932), Noble Sissle and Eubie Blake (1927), Pie Pie Blackbird (1932), Sissle and Blake (1923), Sissle and Blake (1930), Snappy Tunes (1923)

Blake, Jerry
Blues in the Night (1942), Minnie the Moocher (1942), Skunk Song (1942), Virginia, Georgia and Caroline (1942)

Blake, Ruby
Sepia Cinderella (1947)

Blake, Sam
Man of the Worlds (1946)

Balkey, Rubel
Harlem Follies of 1949 (1950), Miracle in Harlem (1948)

Blane, Sally
Way Down South (1939)

Bledsoe, Jules
Jules Bledsoe (1929), Old Man Trouble (1929), On the Levee (1930)

Blossom, Alabama
Woman's a Fool (1947)

Boles, Lottie
Realization of a Negro's Ambition (1916)

Bonny, Fred
Drums o' Voodoo (1933), She Devil (1940)

Bosan, Alonzo
Junction 88 (1947)

Bost, Herbert
Injustice (1919), Loyal Hearts (1919)

Bostic, Earl (Orchestra)
I Ain't Gonna Open That Door (1949)

Boud, Mildred
Murder in Swingtime (1937)

Bouie, John
What a Guy (1947)

Bowman, Laura
Birthright (1939), Drums o' Voodoo (1933), God's Stepchildren (1938), Louisiana (1934), She Devil (1940), Son of Ingagi (1940), Ten Minutes to Live (1932), Veiled Aristocrats (1932), Murder in Harlem (1935).

Boyd, Edward
Mr. Washington Goes to Town (1940)

Boyd, Kathryn
Black Gold (1928), The Flying Ace (1926)

Boyd, Mildred
Baby, Are You Kiddin? (1946), Lucky Ghost (1941), Lady Luck (1940), No Time for Romance (1948), Satchel Mouth Baby (1946), Sun Tan Ranch (1948)

Boyde, Ethel
Murder in Swingtime (1937)

Boyer, Anise
Harlem Rhapsody (1932), Harlem Is Heaven (1932)

Boyer, Elizabeth
Shuffling Jane (1921), Sport of the Gods (1921)

Boykin, David
Dirty Gertie from Harlem, U.S.A. (1946)

Bracker, Vera
Millionaire (1927)

Bradford, I.D.
Fall of the Mighty (1913)

Bradford, Perry
Paradise in Harlem (1940)

Bradley, Will (Orchestra)
Basin Street Boogie (1942), Deed I Do (1944), When You and I Were Young, Maggie (1944)

Brandon, Artie
His Harlem Wife (1944), Life Goes On (1940), Walls Keep Talking (1942)

Brandon, Edward
Harlem on the Prairie (1938), Midnight Shadow (1939)

Breckenridge, Paul
Boarding House Blues (1948)

Brent, Mauyne
Come On, Cowboy (1948)

Briggs, Bunny
King Cole Trio and Benny Carter (1950)

Brock, Geraldine
Girl in Room 20 (1946)

Brogsdale, Walter
Are Working Girls Safe (1918), Black and Tax Mix Up (1918), Black Sherlock Holmes (1917), Bully (1918), Busted Romance (1917), Comeback of Barnacle Bill (1918), Dat Blackhand Waitah Man (1917), Devil for a Day (1917), Do the Dead Talk? (1918), Fixing the Faker (1918), Ghosts (1917), Good Luck in Old Clothes (1918), Hypocrites (1917), Janitor (1918), Luck in Old Clothes (1918), Mercy, the Mummy Mumbled (1917), Milk-Fed Hero (1918), Porters (1918), Reckless Rover (1918), Shine Johnson and the Rabbit Foot (1917), Some Baby (1918), Spooks (1917), Spying the Spy (1918), When Cupid Went Wild (1917), When You Are Scared, Run (1918), When You Hit, Hit Hard (1918), Wrong All Around (1917)

Brooks, Bobby
Choo Choo Swing, (1943)

Brooks, Carey
Regeneration (1923)

Brooks, Clarence
Absent (1928), Am I Guilty (1940), Bad Boy (1939), Bargain with Bullets (1937), The Bronze Buckaroo (1938), By Right of Birth (1921), Dark Manhattan (1937), Gangsters on the Loose (1944), Georgia Rose (1930), Harlem Rides the Range (1939), Law of Nature (1918), Lem Hawkins Confession (1935), A Man's Duty, (1919), Murder in Harlem (1935), The Negro Soldier (1943), Racket Doctor (1945), Realization of a Negro's Ambition (1916), Spirit of Youth (1938), Two-Gun Man from Harlem (1939), Up Jumped the Devil (1941), Zircon (1923)

Brooks, Dusty (Four Tones)
Baby, Are You Kiddin? (1946), The Bronze Buckaroo (1938), Harlem on the Prairie (1938), Harlem Rides the Range (1939), Mantan Messes Up (1946), Night Club Girl (1944), One Dark Night (1939), Rhythm Rodeo (1938), Satchel Mouth Baby (1946), Shout, Brother, Shout (1946), Two-Gun Man from Harlem (1938)

Brooks, Eunice
Exile (1931), Girl from Chicago (1932)

Brooks, Hadda
Boogie Woogie Blues (1948), The Joint Is Jumping (1948), Queen of the Boogie (1947)

Brooks, Jay
No Time for Romance (1948)

Brooks, Jess Lee
Am I Guilty? (1940), Broken Strings (1940), Condemned Men (1948), Dark Manhattan (1937), Four Shall Die (1940), Gang War (1939), His Harlem Wife (1944), Lady Luck (1940), Life Goes On (1938), Lucky Ghost (1941), Midnight Shadow (1939), Mystery in Swing (1940), Racket Doctor (1945), Spirit of Youth (1939), Two-Gun Man from Harlem (1939)

Brooks, Lucius
The Bronze Buckaroo (1938), Harlem on the Prairie (1938), Harlem Rides the Range (1939)

Brooks, Shelton
Double Deal (1939), Gayety (1929), Professor Creeps (1941), Up Jumped the Devil (1941)

Broomfield, Leroy
The Lady Fare (1929)

Broonfield, Larry
Close Shave (1942)

Broonzy, Bill
Big Bill Blues (1956), Big Bill Broonzy (1955)

Brown, Ada
International Rhythms (1938), Stormy Weather (1943)

Brown, Alex
Bipp Bang Boogie (1944)

Brown, Andrew
Blues in the Night (1942), Minnie the Moocher (1942), Skunk Song (1942), Virginia, Georgia and Caroline (1942)

Brown, Bessie
Who's Who (1914)

Brown, Bob
Mistaken Identity (1941)

Brown, Dewey
Here 'Tis Honey, Take It (1940), Knock Me Out (1945), Let's Get Down to Business (1943), Melody Takes a Holiday (1943), Smash Your Baggage (1932)

Brown, Eddie
Gunsaulus Mystery (1921)

Brown, Emily
Emily Brown (1943)

Brown, Ernest
Chatter (1943)

Brown, Everett
The Bronze Venus (1943), The Duke Is Tops (1943), Gang Smashers (1938), Gun Moll (1944)

Brown, Frank
Why Worry? (1923)

Brown, G. Edward
Schemers (1922), Secret Sorrow (1921), Spitfire (1922), Sport of the God's (1921)

Brown, George
Call of His People (1921)

Brown, George Washington
God's Heaven (1943), Keep Waitin' (1943)

Brown, J.D.
Lure of a Woman (1921)

Brown, Jerry
Deceit (1921)

Brown, Jimmy
Basin Street Revue (1955)

Brown, Joie
Lem Hawkins' Confession (1935), Murder in Harlem (1935)

Brown, Kid
Grafter and the Maid (1913), Pullman Porter (1910)

Brown, Lucille
Sport of the Gods (1921)

Brown, Lucky
Big Timers (1945)

Brown, Margaret
Ghost of Tolston's Manor (1934), Son of Satan (1924)

Brown, Martha
Father Said He'd Fix It (1915)

Brown, N.
Deceit (1921)

Brown, Dr. R.L.
Flying Ace (1926), Regeneration (1923)

Brown, Ralph
Ee Baba Leba (1947), Jivin' in Be-Bop (1946), Swing It Harlem (1941)

Brown, Roberta
Midnight Ace (1928)

Brown, Rocky
Big Times (1945)

Brown, Ruth
Jazz Festival (1955), Rhythm and Blues Revue (1956), Rock 'n' Roll Revue (1955)

Brown, Tom
Uncle Remus' First Visit to New York (1914)

Brown, Troy
Moo Cow Boogie (1943), Rhythm Rodeo (1938)

Bryant, Marie
The Bronze Venus (1943), The Duke Is Tops (1938), Jammin' the Blues (1944)

Bryant, Melvin
Shoe Shine Boy (1945)

Bryant, Pauline
Jungle Jamboree (1943)

Bryant, Willie
Keep Punching (1939), Rock 'n' Roll Review (1955), Rhythm & Blues Revue (1956).

Buck and Bubbles
Black Cat Tales (1933), Black Narcissus (1929), Buck and Bubbles Laff Jamboree (1945), Cabin in the Sky (1943), Darktown Blues (1929), Dark Town Follies (1930), Fowl Play (1929), Harlem Bound (1935), High Toned (1930), Honest Crooks (1930), In and Out (1935), Mantan Messes Up (1946), Night in a Night Club (1937)

Buckner, Teddy
St. Louis Blues (1958)

Bufford, Daisy
Deep South (1937), Son of Ingagi (1940)

Bunn, John
Moon Over Harlem (1939)

Bunny and the Cotton Girls
Slow Poke (1932)

The Burch Mann Dancers
Back Beat Boogie (1944)

Burelle, Vera
The Notorious Elinor Lee (1940)

Burke, Georgia
Anna Lucasta (1958)

Burley, Dan
Jivin' in Be-Bop (1946), Oop Boop Sh'Bam (1947)

Burnes, Mary
Low Down: A Bird's Eye View of Harlem (1929)

Burns, A.
Realization of a Negro's Ambition (1916)

Burns, Fanetta
His Great Chance (1923)

Burns, Jim
Symbol of the Unconquered (1920)

Burns, Sandy
His Great Chance (1923), Lem Hawkins' Confession (1935), Murder in Harlem (1935)

Burrell, Mrs. Hamer
Injustice (1919), Loyal Hearts (1919)

Burrell, Rosa
Pitch a Boogie Woogie (1948)

Burris, Jim
Sport of the Gods (1921)

Burt and Grant
Grafter and the Maid (1913)

Burton, John
Flames of Wrath (1923)

Burton-Huyrain, Marie
Grafter and the Maid (1913)

Burwell, Myra
Ten Nights in a Bar-Room (1926)

Bush, Anita
The Bull Doggers (1923), Crimson Skull (1921)

Butler, Helen
Go Down, Death! (1944)

Butler, William
Flaming Crisis (1924)

Butterbeans and Susie
Nine Lives (1926)

The Bye Trio
Get with It (1943)

Byrd, Anthony D.
Lovie Joe's Romance (1914), One Large Evening (1914)

Byrd, Joe
The Daughter of the Congo (1930), Gig and Saddle (1933), Hello Bill (1927), Scandal (1933)

Byrd, Sarah Green
Mandy's Choice (1914), One Large Evening (1914)

Byrd, William
The Betrayal (1948)

Byron, Lillian
Dark and Cloudy (1919)

Byron and Bean
Sun Tan Ranch (1948)

The Cabaliers, (Palmer Brothers)
Blues in the Night (1942), Skunk Song (1942), Virginia, Georgia and Caroline (1942)

The Cabin Kids
All's Fair (1938), Easy Pickin' (1936), Gifts in Rhythm (1936), Life of the Party (1935), Pink Lemonade (1936), Radio Rascals (1935), Rhythm Saves the Day (1937), Spooks (1936), Swanee Smiles (1943), Trailer Paradise (1937), Way Down Yonder (1934), Way Out West (1935)

The Cabots
Mr. Black Magic (1956)

Calhoun, Red (Orchestra)
Juke Joint (1947), Woman's a Fool (1947)

Callender, George "Red"
Jammin' the Blues (1944), St. Louis Blues (1958)

Calloway, Cab
All-colored Vaudeville Show (1935), Beale St. Revue (1955), Blowtop Blues (1945), Blues in the Night (1942), Bosko and the

Pirate (1937), Cab Calloway's Hi-De-Ho (1934), Cab Calloway's Jitterbug Party (1935), Cab Calloway Melody (1945), Dixieland Jamboree (1935), Ebony Parade (1947), Foo, a Little Ballyhoo (1945), Green Pastures (1938), Hi-De-Ho (1934), Hi-De-Ho (1937), Hi-De-Ho (1947), Jazz Festival (1955), I Was Here When You Left Me (1945), Meet the Maestros (1938), Minnie the Moocher (1932), Minnie the Moocher (1942), Rhythm and Blues Revue (1955), St. Louis Blues (1958), Skunk Song (1942), Stormy Weather (1943), Virginia, Georgia and Caroline (1942), Walking with My Honey (1945), We the Cats Shall Hep Ya (1945)

Calloway, Ernest
Beware (1946)

Calloway, Howard
Dirty Gertie from Harlem, U.S.A. (1946)

Calloway, Star
Girl from Chicago (1932)

Calmers, Lee
Bronze Buckaroo (1938)

Cameron, Earl
Simba (1955)

Campbell, Dick
What Goes Up (1939)

Campbell, Irene
Go Down, Death! (1944)

Campbell, Tim
George Washington Carver (1940)

Campbell, William
Hi-De-Ho (1947), Killer Diller (1948)

Caps, Red
Mantan Messes Up (1946)

Carey, James
Deceit (1921)

Carlisle, Una Mae
Boarding House Blues (1948), Fuzzy Wuzzy (1945), Hep Cat Serenade (1947), I Like It Cause I Love It (1944), I'm a Good Good Woman (1944), The Joint Is Jumping (1948), Stars on Parade (1946), Taint Yours (1944)

Carns, W.
He Was Bad (1914)

Carpenter, Eliot
The Broken Earth (1939)

Carr, Jack
Way Down South (1939), Four Shall Die (1940)

Carroll, Connie
Rockin' the Blues (1955)

Carroll, Diahann
Carmen Jones (1954), Porgy and Bess (1959)

Carroll, Judy
Jim (1941)

Carrols, Vivian
Modern Cain (1921)

Carson, Charles
Cry, the Beloved Country (1958), Sanders of the River (1935)

Carter, Barrington
Thirty Years Later (1928)

Carter, Benny (Orchestra)
Case o' the Blues (1942), Harlem Harmony (1935), Harlem Wednesday (1959), King Cole and His Trio (1950), King Cole Trio and Benny Carter (1950), Stars on Parade (1946)

Carter, Bruxton
Lovie Joe's Romance (1914)

Carter, Frank
Foolish Lives (1921)

Carter, Freddie
Jivin' in Be-Bop (1946)

Carter, Jack
Devil's Daughter (1939), Miracle in Harlem (1948), Murder Rap (1945), St. Louis Gal (1938), Sepia Cinderella (1947), Straight to Heaven (1939), Take My Life (1941)

Carter, Laveda
Harlem Follies of 1949 (1950), Miracle in Harlem (1948)

Carter, Lorene
Lionel Hampton and Herb Jeffries (1955)

Carter, Monica
Negro Sailor (1945)

Carver, George Washington
George Washington Carver (1940), We've Come a Long, Long Way (1943)

Caterio, Lucy
Corn Pone (1945)

Catlett, Sid "Big"
Boy! What a Girl! (1946), Harlem Follies of 1949 (1950), Jammin' the Blues (1944)

Catlett, Walter
Shoe Shine Boy (1945)

Cato, Minto
Girl from Chicago (1932)

Cats and the Fiddle
The Bronze Venus (1943), The Duke Is Tops (1938), Two-Gun Man from Harlem (1938)

Cavanaugh, Joann
Old Dan Tucker (1946)

Caviness, Cathryn
The Blood of Jesus (1941)

Challis, Beth
Shake It Up (1929)

Chambers, Gertie
Low Down: A Bird's Eye View of Harlem (1929)

The Chanticleers
Ain't My Sugar Sweet (1943), Hep Cat Serenade (1947), If You Treat Me to a Hug (1943), Jumpin' Jack from Hackensack (1943), Lovin' Up a Solid Breeze (1943), Rocco Blues (1947)

Chappelle, Thomas
Black Network (1936)

The Charioteers
Dark Town Strutter's Ball (1941), Oh, Susannah (1941), Ride, Red, Ride (1941), Swing for Sale (1941)

Chase, Bill
Souls of Sin (1949)

Chatman, Frank
Foolish Lives (1921)

Chenault, Lawrence
Birthright (1924), Burden of Race (1921), Call of His People (1922), Children of Fate (1929), Crimson Fog (1932), Crimson Skull (1921), Devil's Disciple (1926), Ghost of Tolston's Manor (1934), Gunsaulus Mystery (1921), Harlem After Midnight (1934), House Behind the Cedars (1924), A Prince of His Race (1922), Scar of Shame (1927), Schemers (1922), Secret Sorrow (1922), Son of Satan (1924), Spitfire (1922), Sport of the Gods (1923), Symbol of the Unconquered (1920), Ten Minutes to Live (1932), Ten Nights in a Bar-Room (1926), Veiled Aristocrats (1932), Within Our Gates (1919)

Chester, Alfred "Slick"
Girl from Chicago (1932), Harlem After Midnight (1948), Harlem Is Heaven (1932), Lem Hawkins' Confession (1935), Miracle in Harlem (1948), Paradise in Harlem (1940)

Chester, Marie
The Flaming Crisis (1924)

Chestnutt, Charles
Idlewild (1927)

Childers, Helen
By Right of Birth (1921)

Childress, Alvin
Anna Lucasta (1958), Crimson Fog (1932), Dixie Love (1933), Hell's Alley (1938), Keep Punching (1939)

Chiyo, Princess
International Rhythms (1938)

The Chocolateers
Harlem Rhumba (1942), Peckin' (1942), Tweed Me (1942)

Christian, Hattie
Gunsaulus Mystery (1921)

Christmas, Gertrude
Realization of a Negro's Ambition (1916)

Christmas, Leonard
Harlem Rides the Range (1939), Lady Luck (1940), Lucky Ghost (1941), Mystery in Swing (1940)

Churchill, Savannah
Devil Sat Down and Cried (1942), Harlem Follies of 1949 (1950), Miracle in Harlem (1948), Souls of Sin (1949), What to Do (1942)

Cines, Henry "Gong"
Lying Lips (1939)

Clark, Anice
Look-Out Sister! (1948)

Clark, Bobby
Bad Boy (1939)

Clark, Wyatt
Junction 88 (1947)

The Clark Brothers
Killer Diller (1948)

Clarke, Angela
Harlem Globetrotters (1951)

Clayton, William A., Jr.
Children of Fate (1929), Easy Street (1930), A Prince of His Race (1922), Ten Minutes to Live (1932), Ten Nights in a Bar-Room (1926), Wages of Sin (1928), When Men Betray (1929)

Clements, Flo
Within Our Gates (1919)

Clinton, Larry
Chant of the Jungle (1943)

Clissby, Jack
Double Deal (1939)

Clough, Inez
Crimson Fog (1932), Easy Money (1921), Gunsaulus Mystery (1921), Secret Sorrow (1921), The Simp (1921), Ties of Blood (1921)

The Clovers
Basin Street Revue (1955), Jazz Festival (1955), Rock 'n' Roll Revue (1955)

Cobb, John
Lure of a Woman (1921)

Cobbs, Ruth
Mistaken Identity (1941), Murder with Music (1941)

Codero, Thelma
Tall, Tan and Terrific (1946)

Coffin, Ida
Am I Guilty? (1940), Lady Luck (1940), Lucky Ghost (1941), Racket Doctor (1945)

Cohee, Regina
Lure of a Woman (1921)

Coke, Harold
Midnight Menace (1946)

Colbert, Frank
Flames of Wrath (1923)

Colby, Anita
Sweet Shoe (1947)

Coldwell, J.
Deceit (1921)

Cole, Bill
Pullman Porter (1910)

Cole, Cozy
Blues in the Night (1942), Minnie the Moocher (1942), Skunk Song (1942), Virginia, Georgia and Caroline (1942)

Cole, Louis
Murder in Swingtime (1937)

Cole, Nat "King"
Basin St. Revue (1955), Come to Baby Do (1946), Downbeat Revue (1955), Errand Boy for Rhythm (1946), Frim Fram Sauce (1945), Got a Penny Benny (1946), Harlem Jazz Festival (1953), I'm a Shy Guy (1946), Is You or Is You Ain't My Baby (1944), Killer Diller (1947), King Cole and Benny Carter (1950), King Cole and His Trio (1950), Nat King Cole and Joe Adams Orchestra (1951), Nat King Cole and Russ Morgan Orchestra (1953), Nat King Cole Musical Story (1955), Oh-h-e-e My, My (1945), Revue in Rhythm (1955), Rock 'n' Roll Revue (1955), St. Louis Blues (1958), Stars on

Parade (1940), Stars Over Harlem (1956), Who's Been Eating My Porridge (1944)

Coleman, J.W.
Injustice (1919), Loyal Hearts (1919)

Coles, Erostine
Let My People Live (1938)

Coles, Honi
Rock 'n' Roll Revue (1955)

Coles and Atkins
Rock 'n' Roll Revue (1955)

Collier, Estelle
Loyalty of a Race (1918)

Collins, Claude
The Lady Fare (1929)

Collins, Leroy
The Betrayal (1948)

Collins, Shad
Blues in the Night (1942), Minnie the Moocher (1942), Skunk Song (1942), Virginia, Georgia and Caroline (1942)

Columbus, Christopher (Swing Crew)
It Happened in Harlem (1945), Look-Out Sister! (1948), Moon Over Harlem (1939)

Colvin, George
Flying Ace (1926)

Comathiere, A.B.
Black King (1932), The Brute (1920), Deceit (1921), Drums o' Voodoo (1933), The Exile (1931), Harlem After Midnight (1934), Harlem Big Shot (1936), Louisiana (1938), The Midnight Ace (1928), She Devil (1940), Thirty Years Later (1928)

Comfort, Joe
King Cole and His Trio (1950)

The Conga Night Club Band
Lady Luck (1940), Lucky Ghost (1941)

Conn, Irene
In the Depths of Our Hearts (1920)

Connor, Edgar
Rufus Jones for President (1933)

Connor, Ellen
Zoot (1946)

Cook, Charles
Chatter (1943)

Cook, Louise
Exile (1931), Yamekraw (1930)

Cook, Sam
Spitfire (1922)

Cook and Brown
Harlem Bound (1935), Jungle Jamboree (1943), Toot That Trumpet (1943)

Cooke, Earl Brown
Dungeon (1922)
Cooke, Marie
Boarding House Blues (1948), Junction 88 (1947)
Cooley, Isabelle
Anna Lucasta (1958)
Cooper, Kinky
Grafter and the Maid (1913)
Cooper, Ralph
Am I Guilty? (1940), Bargain with Bullets (1937), The Bronze Venus (1943), Dark Manhattan (1937), The Duke Is Tops (1938), Gang War (1939), Gangsters on the Loose (1944), Racket Doctor (1945), Stormy Weather (1943)
Cormick, Walter
Midnight Ace (1928)
Cornall, Anna
Harlem Follies of 1949 (1950)
Cornell, Ann
Boy! What a Girl! (1946)
Cornell, Billy (Chorus)
Pitch a Boogie Woogie (1948)
Costell, Frank
Lying Lips (1939)
The Cotton Club Chorus
Black and Tan (1929), The Lady Fare (1929)
Couch, Robert
Hallelujah (1929)
The Counts and the Countess
Five Salted Peanuts (1945), I've Got to Be a Rug Cutter (1945), Oh-h-e-e My, My (1945)
Covan, DeForrest
Mr. Washington Goes to Town (1940), Murder Rap (1948), No Time for Romance (1948), Prison Bait (1944), Reform School (1939), Take My Life (1939)
Covan, Willie
The Bronze Venus (1943), The Duke Is Tops (1938)
Cowan, Verlie
The Betrayal (1948)
Cox, Ida
Woman's a Fool (1947)
Cox, Jewel
Foolish Lives (1921)
Cox, Jimmie
Disappearance of Mary Jane (1921)
Crawford, Lou
We Pitched a Boogie Woogie (1946)

Crawford, Sam (Captain)
As the World Rolls On (1921)
The Creole Chorus
Spirit of Youth (1937)
Criner, Jeanette
Injustice (1919), Loyal Hearts (1919), Man's Duty (1919)
Criner, John
Gang Smashers (1938), Gun Moll (1944), Midnight Shadow (1939), Professor Creeps (1941)
Criner, Lawrence J.
Am I Guilty? (1940), Bargain with Bullets (1937), Black Gold (1928), The Bronze Venus (1943), The Brute (1920), The Duke Is Tops (1943), The Flying Ace (1926), Gang Smashers (1938), Gang War (1939), Gangsters on the Loose (1944), His Harlem Wife (1944), The Lady Fair (1929), Life Goes On (1938), The Millionaire (1927), Miracle in Harlem (1948), Mr. Smith Goes Ghost (1940), Night Club Girl (1944), One Dark Night (1939), Pigmeat's Laugh Hepcats (1944), Racket Doctor (1945), Up Jumped the Devil (1941), What a Guy (1947), While Thousands Cheer (1940)
Crockett, J.
Ten Thousand Dollar Trail ($10,000 Trail) (1921)
Cromer, Harold
Boarding House Blues (1948)
Cross, Archie
Moon Over Harlem (1939)
Cross, James
Boarding House Blues (1948)
Crothers, Scatman
King Cole and His Trio (1950), King Cole Trio and Benny Carter (1950)
Crowell, T.C.
Birthright (1924)
Crowell, William F. (Big Bill)
Dungeon (1922), Ghost of Tolston's Manor (1934), House Behind the Cedars (1924)
Crum, Robert
Adventure in Boogie Woogie (1946)
Cryer, Jessie
Lady Luck (1940), Lucky Ghost (1941), Professor Creeps (1941)
Cumby, William
Green Pastures (1936)
Curry, Nathan
Harlem on the Prairie (1938), Lady Luck

(1940), Lucky Ghost (1941), Music Hath Harms (1929)

Curtis, Al
What a Guy (1947)

Custard, Virgil
Custard Nine (1921)

Dabney, Ardella
Broken Violin (1926), Thirty Years Later (1928)

Dalthy, Regina
Siren of the Tropics (1927)

Dandridge, Dorothy
Blackbird Fantasy (1942), Bright Road (1953), Carmen Jones (1954), Condemned Men (1948), Congo Clambake (1942), Cow-Cow Boogie (1942), Easy Street (1941), Ebony Parade (1947), Flamingo (1947), Four Shall Die (1940), Frenzy (1946), Harlem Globetrotters (1951), Jungle Jig (1941), Moo Cow Boogie (1943), Porgy and Bess (1959), Swing for Your Supper (1941), A Zoot Suit (With a Reet Pleat) (1942)

Dandridge, Putney
Gig and Saddle (1933), Harlem Is Heaven (1932), Harlem Rhapsody (1932), Scandal (1933)

Dandridge, Ruby
Cabin in the Sky (1943), Midnight Shadow (1939)

Dandridge, Vivian
Bright Road (1953)

Daniels, Billy
Mr. Black Magic (1956), Sepia Cinderella (1947), There Are Eighty-Eight Reasons Why (1945)

Daniels, Dimples
Beware (1946)

Daniels, Iris
Dusky Virgin (1932)

Daniels, Lyons
Flying Ace (1926)

Darden, Tasmania
Man's Duty (1919)

Darnell, Larry
Jazz Festival (1955), Rock 'n' Roll Revue (1955)

Davies, Marshall
Colored American Winning His Suit (1916)

Davis, Dr. A. Porter
Lure of a Woman (1921)

Davis, Amon
Darktown Revue (1931)

Davis, Carl "Chicago"
Harlem Follies (1950)

Davis, James
Harlem on the Prairie (1938), Look-Out Sister! (1948), Rhythm Rodeo (1938)

Davis, Martha
Basin Street Revue (1955), Rhythm and Blues Revue (1956), Rock 'n' Roll Revue (1955)

Davis, Sammy, Jr.
Anna Lucasta (1958), Porgy and Bess (1959), Rufus Jones for President (1933)

Dawn, Marpessa
Black Orpheus (1959)

Dawson, Rudolph
The Daughter of the Congo (1930)

Day, Ward
Midnight Ace (1928)

Day, Dawn and Dusk
Cash Ain't Nothing but Trash (1945), Ebony Parade (1947), Fare Thee Well (1945), Faust (1945), Sleep Kentucky Babe (1945)

Deans, William
When Good Luck Comes Our Way (1917)

Deary, Clarissa
Marching On! (1943), Where's My Man To-Nite? (1944)

De Bulger, Louis
Deceit (1921), Gunsaulus Mystery (1921)

Debuse, Eddie
The Blood of Jesus (1941)

Dee, John, Jr.
Mantan Runs for Mayor (1946)

Dee, Ruby
The Fight Never Ends (1947), The Jackie Robinson Story (1950), Love in Syncopation (1946), St. Louis Blues (1958), That Man of Mine (1947), What a Guy (1947)

The Deep River Boys
Booglie Wooglie Piggy (1941), Hark! Hark! The Lark (1941), Shadrach (1941), Toot That Trumpet! (1941)

De Gaston, Gallie
Gig and Saddle (1933), Scandal (1933), Ten Minutes to Live (1932)

De Knight, Fanny Belle
Hallelujah (1929)

Delavalade, Herman
In the Depths of Our Hearts (1920)

De Legge, Boise
Flying Ace (1926)

The Delta Rhythm Boys
Choo Choo Swing (1943), Dry Bones (1945), Fan Tan Fanny (1945), Give Me Some Skin (1941), I Dreamt I Dwelt in Harlem (1941), Jack, You're Playing the Game (1941), Just a-Sittin' and a Rockin' (1945), Rhythm and Blues Revue (1956), Rigoletto Blues (1941), Rock 'n' Roll Revue (1955), Snoqualomie Jo Jo (1945), Stars Over Harlem (1956), Symphony in Swing (1949), Take the "A" Train (1941)

Demetrius, Claude
Get It Off Your Mind (1946), House-Rent Party (1946), Sho Had a Wonderful Time (1946)

Dennis, E.M.
Ten Thousand Dollar Trail ($10,000 Trail) (1921)

Desmond, Cleo
Am I Guilty? (1940), Deceit (1921), The Hypocrite (1922), The Millionaire (1927), Mr. Washington Goes to Town (1940), Racket Doctor (1945), Spirit of Youth (1938)

DeYoung, Francis
The Betrayal (1948)

Diaz, Hazel
Swing (1938)

Dickerson, Dudley
Boogie Woogie (1944), Cow-Cow Boogie (1942), Fuzzy Wuzzy (1945), The Green Pastures (1936), Hep Cat Serenade (1947), The Outskirts of Town (1942), Roll 'Em (1944)

Dickerson, Milton
Hallelujah (1929)

Dickerson, Tiny
Rockin' the Blues (1955)

Dillard, Bill
Mistaken Identity (1941), Murder with Music (1941)

Dillon, Linda
Cry of Jazz (1958)

Dirkson, Sherman
Straight to Heaven (1939)

The Dixiairs
Dear Old Southland (1941)

The Dixie Jubilee Singers
Hallelujah (1929)

Dixon, Allen D.
Deceit (1921)

Dixon, Alonzo
Lure of a Woman (1921)

Dixon, Gabrielle
The Revue des Revues (1927)

Dixon, Henry
Flaming Crisis (1924)

Dixon, Ivan
Porgy and Bess (1959), Carmen Jones (1954)

Dockstader, Lew
Everybody Works but Father (1905)

Domino, Fats
Jamboree (1957)

Dones, Sidney Preston
Injustice (1919), Loyal Hearts (1919), Reformation 1919), The Ten Thousand Dollar Trail ($10,000 Trail) (1921)

Dorsey, Princess
Burlesque in Harlem (1955)

Dots and Dash
Temptation (1936)

Douglas, Frederick
Frederick Douglas's the House on Cedar Hill (1953)

Douglas, Joan
Negro Sailor (1945)

Dove, Marie
Son of Satan (1924)

Downs, Johnny
Bad Boy (1939)

Droughan, Amos
Go Down, Death! (1944)

Dryfus, Miss
Injustice (1919), Loyal Hearts (1919)

Dudley, Sherman H.
Easy Money (1921), Reckless Money (1926), The Simp (1921)

Dudley, Susie
Lure of a Woman (1921)

Dugas, Oscar Roy
Midnight Ace (1928)

Dumas, Wade
Harlem Rides the Range (1939)

Dumont, Dorothy Yvonne
Injustice (1919), Loyal Hearts (1919), Reformation (1919), The Ten Thousand Dollar Trail ($10,000 Trail) (1921)

Duna, Steffi
Way Down South (1939)

Dunbar, Dorothy
The Flaming Crisis (1924)

Dunbar, Louise
The Green Eyed Monster (1921)
Duncan, Andrew
Cry of Jazz (1958)
Duncan, Leonard
Juke Joint (1947)
Duncan, Melody
Juke Joint (1947)
Duncan, Vernon
The Betrayal (1948), The Homesteader (1918)
Duncan's Beauty Show Girls
Juke Joint (1947)
Dunham, Katherine (Troupe)
Carnival of Rhythm (1944), Cuban Episode (1942), Flamingo (1942), Spirit of Boogie Woogie (1942), Stormy Weather (1943)
Dunmire, James
The Black King (1932), Harlem Big Shot (1932)
Dunsmore, James
Chicago After Dark (1946), Hi-De-Ho (1947), Midnight Menace (1946)
Duree, Robert
Are Working Girls Safe (1918), Black and Tan Mix Up (1918), Black Sherlock Holmes (1917), Bully (1918), Busted Romance (1917), Comeback of Barnacle Bill (1918), Dat Blackhand Waitah Man (1917), Devil for a Day (1917), Do the Dead Talk? (1918), Fixing the Faker (1918), Ghosts (1917), Good Luck in Old Clothes (1918), Hypocrites (1917), Janitor (1918), Luck in Old Clothes (1918), Mercy, the Mummy Mumbled (1917), Milk-Fed Hero (1918), Porters (1918), Reckless Rover (1918), Shine Johnson and the Rabbit Foot (1917), Some Baby (1918), Spooks (1917), Spying the Spy (1918), When Cupid Went Wild (1917), When You Are Scared, Run (1918), When You Hit, Hit Hard (1918), Wrong All Around (1917)
Duvall, Al
Bargain with Bullets (1937), Gangsters on the Loose (1944)
Dyer, E.C.
Georgia Rose (1930)
Earle, Walter
Beware (1946), Big Timers (1945), Dusky Virgin (1932)
Easton, Sidney
Black and Blue (1932), Boarding House

Blues (1948), Fight That Ghost (1946), Killer Diller (1948), Murder on Lenox Ave. (1941), Paradise in Harlem (1940), Sunday Sinner (1940), What Goes Up (1939)
The Ebony Players
Are Working Girls Safe (1918), Black and Tan Mix Up (1918), Black Sherlock Holmes (1917), Bully (1918), Busted Romance (1917), Comeback of Barnacle Bill (1918), Dat Blackhand Waitah Man (1917), Devil for a Day (1917), Do the Dead Talk? (1918), Fixing the Faker (1918), Ghosts (1917), Good Luck in Old Clothes (1918), Hypocrites (1917), Janitor (1918), Luck in Old Clothes (1918), Mercy, the Mummy Mumbled (1917), Milk-Fed Hero (1918), Porters (1918), Reckless Rover (1918), Shine Johnson and the Rabbit Foot (1917), Some Baby (1918), Spooks (1917), Spying the Spy (1918), When Cupid Went Wild (1917), When You Are Scared, Run (1918), When You Hit, Hit Hard (1918), Wrong All Around (1917)
The Ebony Trio
Bipp Bang Boogie (1944)
Eckstine, Billy
Flicker Up (1946), Harlem After Midnight (1947), Harlem Jubilee (1949), I Cried for You (1946), I Want to Talk About You (1946), Lonesome Lover Blues (1946), Play It Brother (1947), Rhythm in a Riff (1946), You Call It Madness (1946)
Eckstine, June
Love in Syncopation (1946)
Edison, Harry
Jammin' the Blues (1944)
Edmondson, William
Bubbling Over (1934), The Midnight Ace (1928), The Millionaire (1927), Thirty Years Later (1928).
Edwards, Aurora
Veiled Aristocrats (1932)
Edwards, Frog
The Joint Is Jumping (1945)
Edwards, Grant
Within Our Gates (1919)
Edwards, James
Anna Lucasta (1958), Joe Louis Story (1953)
Edwards, John (Junk)
Butting In (1914), Coon Town Suffragettes (1914), Father Said He'd Fix It (1915), Haunted House (1915), He Was Bad (1914),

In Zululand (1913), It Happened on Wash Day (1915), Just a Note (1914), New Way to Win (1915), Rakoon Hose Company (1915), Rastus Knew It Wasn't (1914), Sam and the Bully (1914), Swami Sam (1914), The Tail of a Chicken (1915), The Undertaker's Daughter (1915)

Edwards, Josephine
Mystery in Swing (1940), You Can't Fool About Love (1943)

Edwards, Mattie
Coon Town Suffragettes (1914), Father Said He'd Fix It (1915), Haunted House (1915), He Was Bad (1914), In Zululand (1913), It Happened on Wash Day (1915), Just a Note (1914), New Way to Win (1915), Rakoon Hose Company (1915), Sam and the Bully (1914), Swami Sam (1914), The Tail of a Chicken (1915), The Undertaker's Daughter (1915), Within Our Gates (1919)

Edwards, Ralph
George Washington Carver (1940)

The Eight Black Streaks
Minstrel Days (1930)

The Eight Covan Dancers
Bargain with Bullets (1937), Gangsters on the Loose (1944)

Eldridge, Roy
Smash Your Baggage (1932)

Elkas, Edward
Birthright (1924)

Ellen, Lou
Backstage Blues (1943)

Ellenwood, Grace
By Right of Birth (1921)

Ellington, Duke
Black and Tan (1929), A Bundle of the Blues (1933), Cabin in the Sky (1943), Check and Double Check (1930), Dancers in the Dark (1932), A Date with Duke (1946), Duke Ellington and His Orchestra (1943), Flamingo (1942), Hot Chocklate (1941), I Got It Bad and That Ain't Good (1942), Jam Session (1942), Jazz Festival (1955), The Negro in Entertainment (1950), Revue in Harlem (1955), Rock 'n' Roll Revue (1955), Salute to Duke Ellington (1950), Symphony in Black (1935), Symphony in Swing (1949), Upbeat in Music (1943)

Ellis, Byron
No Time for Romance (1948)

Ellis, Evelyn
Easy Money (1921)

Ellison, Curley
The Betrayal (1948)

Europe, James Reese
Clef Club Five Minutes for Train (1918)

Evans, Chick
Girl from Chicago (1932)

Evans, Emmory
Straight to Heaven (1939)

Evans, Estelle
Quiet One (1958)

Evans, Rudolph
Man of the Worlds (1946)

Evans, Warren
Baby Don't You Cry (1943), I Miss You So (1943), I'm Making Believe (1945)

Everett, Francine
Big Timers (1947), Dirty Gertie from Harlem, U.S.A. (1946), Ebony Parade (1947), Keep Punching (1939), Paradise in Harlem (1940), Stars on Parade (1947), Tall, Tan and Terrific (1941), Toot That Trumpet (1943), Toot That Trumpet (1946)

Everett, John
Girl from Chicago (1932)

Everett, Munzell
Modern Cain (1921)

Fairley, Freeman
The Black King (1932), Harlem Big Shot (1932)

Farmer, Jacque
Nobody's Children (1920)

Farmer, Oliver
His Harlem Wife (1944), Life Goes On (1940)

The Fast Steppers
Sing and Swing (1943)

Feltenburg, Henry (Master)
Ten Thousand Dollar Trail ($10,000 Trail) (1921)

Felway, Bruce
As the World Rolls On (1921)

Fenderson, Reginald
Am I Guilty? (1940), Bargain with Bullets (1937), Condemned Men (1948), Four Shall Die (1940), Gang Smashers (1938), Gang War (1939), Gangsters on the Loose (1944), Green Pastures (1936), His Harlem Wife (1944), Lady Luck (1940), Life Goes On (1938), Lucky Ghost (1941), Prison Bait (1944),

Racket Doctor (1945), Reform School (1939), While Thousands Cheer (1940)

Fetchit, Stepin
Baby Don't Go Away from Me (1946), Big Timers (1945), Broadway and Main (1946), Harlem Follies of 1949 (1950), Hearts of Dixie (1929), I Ain't Gonna Open That Door (1949), Miracle in Harlem (1948), Moo Cow Boogie (1943), Slow Poke (1932), Swingtime Jamboree (1949)

Fields, Florence
Lady Luck (1940), Lucky Ghost (1941)

Fisher, Mamie
Girl in Room 20 (1946)

Fitzgerald, Bobby
Square Joe (1922)

Fitzgerald, Ella
St. Louis Blues (1958)

Fitzgerald, Lillian
Temptation (1936)

The Five Blazers
Black and Tan (1929)

The Five Racketeers
All-colored Vaudeville Show (1935), Dixieland Jamboree (1935), Doin' the Town (1935)

Fleming, Walter
Veiled Aristocrats (1932)

Flemings, Margaret
Gang Smashers (1938), Gun Moll (1944)

The Flennoy Trio
Gee (1944), Steak and Potatoes (1944), Yankee Doodle Never Went to Town (1944)

Fletcher, Dusty
Boarding House Blues (1948), Hi-De-Ho (1947), Killer Diller (1947), King for a Day (1934), Open the Door Richard (1947), Rufus Jones for President (1933)

Fletcher, Ethel
Troubles of Sambo and Dinah (1914)

Fletcher, Orville
Shadowed by the Devil (1916)

Fletcher, Tom
Custard Nine (1921)

Florent, Napolean
Man of the Worlds (1946)

Flowers, Pat
Dixie Rhythm (1945), Ebony Parade (1947), Scotch Boogie (1945)

Flowers, "Tiger"
The Fighting Deacon (1927)

Fluellen, Joel
The Jackie Robinson Story (1950), The Negro Sailor (1945), No Time for Romance (1948), Porgy and Bess (1959), Sun Tan Ranch (1948), While Thousands Cheer (1940)

Fluker, Eddie L.
Going to Glory, Come to Jesus (1946)

Forbes, Herman
Pitch a Boogie Woogie (1948)

Forbes Randolph Kentucky Jubilee Singers
Cotton-Pickin' Days (1934), Kentucky Jubilee Singers #1 (1928), Kentucky Jubilee Singers #2 (1929), Old Black Joe (1931), On a Plantation (1930), The Road Home (1931), Slave Days (1930), The Water Boy (1929), Welcome (1931)

Foreman, Tom
Pitch a Boogie Woogie (1948)

Fortson, Robert
Injustice (1919), Loyal Hearts (1919)

Fortune, John
Moon Over Harlem (1939)

Foster, Chuck (Orchestra)
Harriet (1945), I Left My Heart in Texas (1945)

Foster, Daisy
Broken Violin (1926)

Foster, Rose Marie
Burlesque in Harlem (1955)

Foster, Rube
As the World Rolls On (1921)

Fountaine, William E.
The Dungeon (1922), Fool's Errand (1922), Hallelujah (1929), Uncle Jasper's Will (1922), The Virgin and the Seminole (1922)

The Four Blackbirds
Harlem on the Prairie (1938)

The Four Congaroos
Killer Diller (1948)

The Four Ginger Snaps
Keep Smiling (1943), Rocco Blues (1947), Wham (1943)

The Four Hamptons
Lionel Hampton and Herb Jeffries (1955)

The Four Horsemen (Male Quartet)
Sweet Shoe (1947)

The Four Knobs
Dispossessed Blues (1943)
The Four Step Brothers
Barbershop Blues (1937), Claude Hopkins and His Orchestra (1933)
The Four Tones
Baby, Are You Kiddin'? (1946), The Bronze Buckaroo (1938), Harlem on the Prairie (1938), Harlem Rides the Range (1939), Mantan Messes Up (1946), Night Club Girl (1944), One Dark Night (1939), Rhythm Rodeo (1938), Satchel Mouth Baby (1946), Shout, Brother, Shout (1946), Two-Gun Man from Harlem (1938)
The Four Toppers
Jump In (1942), Let's Go (1942), Life of Florence Mills (1940), Mystery in Swing (1940), Son of Ingagi (1940), Toppers Take a Bow (1941), You Can't Fool About Love (1943)
Fowler, Billy (Band)
Darktown Scandal's Revue (1930)
Fox, George
Fall of the Mighty (1913)
Fraction, Edward
The Betrayal (1948)
Francis, Anne H.
Going to Glory, Come to Jesus (1946)
Francis, Mae
Straight to Heaven (1939)
Frank, Piano
Dirty Gertie from Harlem, U.S.A. (1946)
Franklyn, Louise
Lady Luck (1940), Look-Out, Sister! (1948), Lucky Ghost (1941), Negro Sailor (1945), No Time for Romance (1948)
Freddy and Flo (Robinson)
Basin Street Revue (1955), Rhythm and Blues Revue (1956)
Fredericks, Gertrude
Dusky Virgin (1932)
Freeland, Jeni
Sun Tan Strut (1946)
Freeman, Bea
Harlem After Midnight (1934), Lem Hawkins' Confession (1935), Murder in Harlem (1935), The Phantom of Kenwood (1933), Underworld (1937)
Freeman, Charles
Going to Glory, Come to Jesus (1946)
Freeman, Dusty
Sepia Cinderella (1947)

Freeman, Kenneth
Miracle in Harlem (1948), What a Guy (1947)
Freeman, Ruth
Giant of His Race (1921), Shot in the Night (1922)
Frisbie, Maud
Love Bug (1920)
Fullen, Louise
Come Back (1922)
Fuller, Alva
The Blood of Jesus (1941)
Fuller, James
Green Pastures (1936), Romance on the Beat (1945), Straight to Heaven (1939)
Fuller, Walter (Orchestra)
Sepia Cinderella (1947)
Gabriel, Angel
Underworld (1937)
Gaby, Ray
Black Thunderbolt (1921)
Gafford, Luther "Soldier Boy"
Murder in Swingtime (1937)
Gaillard, Slim (Trio)
Dunkin' Bagels (1946), Go, Man, Go (1954), O'Voutie O'Rooney (1947)
Gains, Charles
Regeneration (1923)
Gains, Harris
The Betrayal (1948)
The Gainsborough Girls
Dusky Melodies (1930)
Gale, Rozelle
The Joint Is Jumping (1948)
Galloway, Howard
Girl in Room 20 (1946), Juke Joint (1947)
Galloway, Marion
Straight to Heaven (1939)
Gant, Cecil
No Mr. Ghost, Not Now (1947)
Gardner, Chappie
News Reel, #1 (1930)
Gardner, Sammy
God's Stepchildren (1938)
Garrett, Mabel
Ten Minutes to Live (1932), Veiled Aristocrats (1932)
Garrison, Harold
Gang War (1939), Lady Luck (1940), Lucky Ghost (1941), Mr. Washington Goes to

Town (1940), Prison Bait (1944), Reform School (1939)

Garvey, Marcus
Negro News Reel (1923)

Gary, Erwin
Girl from Chicago (1932)

Gates, Emily
Lure of a Woman (1921)

Gaytzera, Anthony
Midnight Ace (1928)

George, Beatrice
By Right of Birth (1921)

George, William
Homesteader (1918)

Gertrude, Josephine
Going to Glory, Come to Jesus (1946)

Gibbens, Bessie
Wages of Sin (1928), When Men Betray (1929)

Gibson, Harry "Hipster"
Harry the Hipster (1944), Opus 12 EEE (1944)

Gibson, Judith
Sinner Kissed an Angel (1942)

Gibson, Mae
Hearts of the Woods (1921)

Gilbert, Don
Dirty Gertie from Harlem, U.S.A. (1946), Juke Joint (1947)

Gilbert, Mercedes
Body and Soul (1924), The Call of His People (1922), Moon Over Harlem (1939)

Gilbert, Raye
George Washington Carver (1940)

Gillespie, Dizzy
Ee Baba Leba (1947), Harlem Dynamite (1947), Harlem Jubilee (1949), Harlem Rhythm (1947), Jivin' in Be-Bop (1946), Night in Harlem (1947), Oop Boop Sh'Bam (1947)

Gilliam, Allie
Uncle Remus' First Visit to New York (1914)

Gilpin, Charles
Mandy's Choice (1914), One Large Evening (1914), Ten Nights in a Bar-Room (1926)

Ginn, Sam
Music Hath Harm (1929)

Girard, Adele
Harp Boogie (1946)

Giuffre, Jimmy (Trio)
Sound of Jazz (1957)

Givens, Bessie
Midnight Ace (1928)

Givens, Ruth
Night Club Girl (1944), One Dark Night (1939)

Gladden, W.W.E. (Chaplain)
Injustice (1919), Loyal Hearts (1919)

Gladden, W.W.E. (Mrs.)
Injustice (1919), Loyal Hearts (1919)

Gleaves, Abraham
Green Pastures (1936)

Glenn, Roy
Carmen Jones (1954), Dark Manhattan (1937)

Glenn, Tyree
Blues in the Night (1942), Minnie the Moocher (1942), Salute to Duke Ellington (1950), Skunk Song (1942), Virginia, Georgia and Caroline (1942)

Glover, Henry
Souls of Sin (1949)

Glover, Rubeline
Dark Manhattan (1937)

Godfrey, Everett
For His Mother's Sake (1922)

The Golden Slipper All Girl Band
Tall, Tan and Terrific (1946)

Goldthwaite, Rogenia
The Blood of Jesus (1941)

Gomez, Phil
It Happened in Harlem (1945)

Gomez, Thomas
Harlem Globetrotters (1951)

Gooding, Sally
Notorious Elinor Lee (1940)

Goodman, J.K.
The Dungeon (1922)

Gordon, Charles
Double Deal (1939)

Gordon, Fred D.
Mantan Runs for Mayor (1946), Sepia Cinderella (1947)

Gordon, Gwendoline
Injustice (1919), Loyal Hearts (1919)

The Gorgeous Astor Debutantes
Tall, Tan and Terrific (1946)

Gorman, Grant
Within Our Gates (1919)

Grace-Boon, Margaret
Injustice (1919), Loyal Hearts (1919)

Grady, Lottie
Grafter and the Maid (1913), Pullman Porter (1910), Railroad Porter (1912)

Grainger, Porter
Jailhouse Blues (1934)

Granger, Reginald
Dusky Virgin (1932)

Grant, Alfred
Am I Guilty? (1940), Condemned Men (1948), Four Shall Die (1940), Mystery in Swing (1940), Night Club Girl (1944), One Dark Night (1939), Prison Bait (1944), Racket Doctor (1945), Reform School (1939), Son of Ingagi (1940), The Well (1951)

Grant, John
Beware (1946)

Granville, Max
Harlem Follies (1950)

Graves, Edith
Lucky Gamblers (1946)

Graves, Jesse
Son of Ingagi (1940)

Gray, Bernice
Temptation (1936)

Gray, Ethel
Man's Duty (1919)

Gray, Harry
The Black King (1923), Hallelujah (1929), Harlem Big Shot (1932)

Grayson, Jesse
Night Club Girl (1944), One Dark Night (1939)

Greaves, William
The Fight Never Ends (1947), Miracle in Harlem (1948), Souls of Sin (1949)

Greeley, Aurora
Close Shave (1942)

Green, Cora
Cora Green (1929), Moon Over Harlem (1939), Swing (1938)

Green, Eddie
Black Network (1936), Comes Midnight (1940), Crap Game (1930), Dress Rehearsal (1939), Eddie Green and Company, Sending a Wire (1929), Eddie Green's Rehearsal (1916), Eddie's Laugh Jamboree (1944), Mantan Messes Up (1946), Mr. Atom's Bomb (1949), One Round Jones (1946), What Goes Up (1939)

Green, Hazel
Hazel Green and Company (1928)

Green, Herman
Murder on Lenox Ave. (1941), Paradise in Harlem (1940), Sunday Sinners (1941)

Green, Jimmie (Orchestra)
Go Down, Death! (1944)

Green, Joe
Nobody's Children (1920)

Green, Virginia
Hi-De-Ho (1947)

Greene, Jackie
Alabamy Bound (1941)

Greene, Marion
Burlesque in Harlem (1955)

Gregg, Richard
Dixie Love (1934)

Griffin, Alex
Nobody's Children (1920)

Griffin, Douglas
House Behind the Cedars (1924)

Griffin, Frank C.
Cannibal King (1915)

Griffith, Bea
Reet-Petite and Gone (1947)

Griggers, Roscoe
Music Hath Harm (1929)

Grimes, Chinky
Emily Brown (1943), Harlem Follies (1950)

Grimes, Tiny (Orchestra)
Joseph 'n' His Brudders (1945), Never Too Old to Swing (1945), Romance Without Finance (1945), Swingin' in the Grove (1945), T.G. Boogie Woogie (1945)

Gross, Adella
Burlesque in Harlem (1955)

Gross, Leon (Orchestra)
God's Stepchildren (1938), Swing (1938)

Guilford, Willor Lee
The Daughter of the Congo (1930), Easy Street (1930), Ten Minutes to Live (1932), Veiled Aristocrats (1932)

Gulfport, Billy
Spider's Web (1926)

Guster, Al
Harlem After Midnight (1947)

Guy, Barrington
Veiled Aristocrats (1932)

Guyse, Sheila
Boy! What a Girl! (1946), Harlem Follies of 1949 (1950), Miracle in Harlem (1948), Sepia Cinderella (1947)

Gwynn, Bobbye
Life of Florence Mills (1940)
Hackett, Birdina
Woman's a Fool (1947)
Haily, Bert
Reformation (1919)
Hairston, Jessie (Choral)
Cherished Melodies (1950), Melodic Spirituals (1950), Melodies Reborn (1950), Southern a Cappella (1950), Symphonic Shades (1950), Tradition (1950), Tunes That Live (1950)
Hale, Teddy
Straight to Heaven (1939)
Hall, Adelaide
All-colored Vaudeville Show (1935), Dancers in the Dark (1932), Dixieland Jamboree (1935)
Hall, Beulah
Realization of a Negro's Ambition (1916)
Hall, Earl
Night Club Girl (1944), One Dark Night (1939)
Hall, Iris
Homesteader (1918), Symbol of the Unconquered (1920)
Hall, Juanita (Choir)
Harlem Follies of 1949 (1950), Miracle in Harlem (1948), Paradise in Harlem (1940)
Hall, Lindsay J.
Sport of the Gods (1921)
Hall, Milton
Prison Bait (1944), Reform School (1939)
Hall, Teddy
Lying Lips (1939)
The Hall Johnson Choir
Black and Tan (1929), Cabin in the Sky (1943), Camp Meeting (1936), Deep South (1937), Green Pastures (1936), Message from Dorothy Maynor (1949), Mississippi Moods (1937), St. Louis Blues (1929), Syncopated Sermon (1930), That Man Samson (1937), Way Down South (1939)
Hamilton, Benjamin (Bernie)
Jackie Robinson Story (1950), Well (1951)
Hamilton, Curtis
Look-Out Sister! (1948)
Hammed, Tosh (Company)
Dance Your Old Age Away (1944)
Hamner, Curley
Lionel Hampton and Herb Jeffries (1955)

Hampton, Lionel
Basin Street Revue (1955), Harlem Jazz Festival (1955), Harlem Variety Revue (1955), Jazz Festival (1955), Lionel Hampton and Herb Jeffries (1955), Lionel Hampton and His Orchestra (1949), Rhythm and Blues Revue (1955), Rock 'n' Roll Revue (1955)
Handy, W.C.
Negro in Entertainment (1950), Satchmo the Great (1954)
Hanna, David
Lem Hawkins' Confession (1935), Murder in Harlem (1935)
Harbin, Suzette
Look-Out, Sister! (1948)
Hardcastle, Lew (Band)
Dusky Melodies (1930)
Hardeman, Reather
The Blood of Jesus (1941)
Hardin, Rollie
The Bronze Buckaroo (1938)
Harding, Daisy
The Daughter of the Congo (1930)
Harding, Halley
Bargain with Bullets (1937), Gangsters on the Loose (1944), Mystery in Swing (1940)
Hardy, Babe
Cannibal King (1915)
Hargraves, Clarence
Mr. Washington Goes to Town (1940)
Hargreaces, Bobby (Orchestra)
Temptation (1936), Underworld (1937)
The Harlem Cuties
Backstage Blues (1943), Block Party Revels (1943)
The Harlem Dead End Kids
Murder Rap (1948), Take My Life (1941)
The Harlem Globetrotters
Go, Man Go (1954), Harlem Globetrotters (1951)
The Harlem Honeys
Foolin' Around (1943), Jackpot (1943), Melody Takes a Holiday (1943), Quick Watson, the Question (1943), Rhythm Mania (1943)
Harleman, Ann
Policy Man (1938)
The Harlemania Orchestra
The Bronze Venus (1943), The Duke Is Tops (1938), Sugar Hill Baby (1937)

The Harlemaniacs
Boy! What a Girl! (1946)

Harley, Eileen
Anna Lucasta (1958)

Harper, Billy
Mandy's Choice (1914)

Harper, Irene
Going to Glory, Come to Jesus (1946)

Harper, Leonard (Chorines)
Exile (1931)

The Harpstones
Rockin' the Blues (1955)

Harrington, Hamtree
Bubbling Over (1934), The Devil's Daughter (1939), Gayety (1929), Jittering Jitterbugs (1943), Keep Punching (1939), Mill's Blue Rhythm Band (1933), Rufus Jones for President (1933)

Harris, Aranelle
Lady Luck (1940), Lucky Ghost (1941)

Harris, Ariel
Up Jumped the Devil (1941)

Harris, Bud
Bud Harris and Frank Radcliffe (1929), Girl from Chicago (1932), Moon Over Harlem (1939)

Harris, Clifford
Hearts of the Woods (1921)

Harris, Connie
Harlem on the Prairie (1938), Murder in Swingtime (1937)

Harris, Consuelo
God's Stepchildren (1938)

Harris, Cora
Harlem Hot Shots (1945)

Harris, Edna Mae
Green Pastures (1936), Harlem on Parade (1948), Harlem Serenade (1942), I Gotta Go to Camp and See My Man (1943), Jive Comes to the Jungle (1942), Leg's Ain't No Good (1942), Lying Lips (1939), Murder on Lenox Ave. (1941), The Notorious Elinor Lee (1940), Paradise in Harlem (1940), Rhythm on the Run (1942), Solid Senders (1941), The Spirit of Youth (1938), Sunday Sinners (1949), Tall, Tan and Terrific (1946), That Man Samson (1937), Tuxedo Junction (1942)

Harris, Harriett
Modern Cain (1921)

Harris, Henry
Foolish Lives (1921)

Harris, Leorine
Scapegoat (1920), Uncle Remus' First Visit to New York (1914)

Harris, Mary Lou
Flicker Up (1946)

Harris, Rhina
That Man of Mine (1947)

Harris, Sarah
Rhythm in a Riff (1946)

Harris, Theresa
Bargain with Bullets (1937), Gangsters on the Loose (1944), Outskirts of Town (1942)

Harris, Vivian
Burlesque in Harlem (1955)

Harris, Wallace
Going to Glory, Come to Jesus (1946)

Harris and Hunt
Foolin' Around (1943), Rhythm Mania (1943)

Harris and Scott
Souls of Sin (1949)

Harrison, Richard B.
Easy Street (1930), Grafter and the Maid (1913), How High Is Up (1923)

Hart, Fred
His Great Chance (1923)

Hastings, Henry
Lady Luck (1940), Lucky Ghost (1941)

Haven, Shirley
No Time for Romance (1948)

Hawkins, Alfred
Dirty Gertie from Harlem, U.S.A. (1946)

Hawkins, Charles
The Bronze Venus (1943), Double Deal (1939), The Duke Is Tops (1943), Gang Smashers (1938), Gang War (1939), Gun Moll (1944), Midnight Shadow (1939), Mr. Washington Goes to Town (1940)

Hawkins, Erskine (Orchestra)
Deviled Hams (1937), Hot in the Groove (1942), Paper Doll (1942)

Hawkins, Flo
That Man of Mine (1947)

Hawkins, Tuffy
Straight to Heaven (1939)

Hawley, Monte
Am I Guilty? (1940), The Bronze Venus (1943), Double Deal (1939), The Duke Is Tops (1938), Gang Smashers (1938), Gang War (1939), The Ghost of Tolston's Manor

(1934), His Harlem Wife (1944), Lady Luck (1940), Life Goes On (1938), Look-Out Sister! (1948), Lucky Ghost (1941), Mantan Messes Up (1946), Merrie Howe Carfe (1939), Miracle in Harlem (1948), Mr. Smith Goes Ghost (1940), Mr. Washington Goes to Town (1940), Murder Rap (1948), Mystery in Swing (1940), Night Club Girl (1944), One Big Mistake (1940), One Dark Night (1939), Pigmeat's Laugh Hepcats (1944), Prison Bait (1944), Racket Doctor (1945), Reform School (1939), Son of Satan (1924), Take My Life (1941), Tall, Tan and Terrific (1946), Toot That Trumpet (1946), What a Guy (1947), While Thousands Cheer (1940)

Haynes, Betty
That Man of Mine (1947)

Haynes, Daniel L.
Hallelujah (1929)

Haywood, Billy
I Can't Dance (1944)

Heard, "Crip"
Boarding House Blues (1948)

Heathman, Josephine
Hello Bill (1927)

The Heavenly Choir
The Blood of Jesus (1941), Go Down, Death! (1944), Spiritual Sing-a-Long 1-A (1948), Spiritual Sing-a-Long 2-B (1948), Spiritual Sing-a-Long 3-C (1948), Spiritual Sing-a-Long 4-D (1948)

Hemmings, John
Girl in Room 20 (1946)

Hemmings, Myra
Girl in Room 20 (1946), Go Down, Death! (1944), Marching On! (1943), Where's My Man To-Nite? (1944)

Henderson, Frances
Ten Thousand Dollar Trail ($10,000 Trail) (1921)

Henderson, Harry
Children of Fate (1929), A Prince of His Race (1922), St. Louis Blues (1958), The Scar of Shame (1927), Smiling Hate (1924), Ten Nights in a Bar-Room (1926)

Hensley, E.
Return of Mandy's Husband (1948)

Hepburn, Phillip
Bright Road (1953)

Herbert, Holmes
Bad Boy (1939)

Hereford, Leon (Orchestra)
The Lady Fare (1929), Music Hath Harms (1929), My First Love (1921)

Hernandez, Juano
Girl from Chicago (1932), Lying Lips (1940)

Herndon, Cleo
Dark Manhattan (1937)

Heywood, Donald (Choir)
Darktown Revue (1931), Exile (1931), Ten Minutes to Live (1932)

The Hi-Hatters
Life of Florence Mills (1940)

Higginbotham, J.C.
Count Me Out (1946), Crawl Red Crawl (1946), Drink Hearty (1946), House on 52nd Street (1944), Mop (1946)

Higgins, Billy
Father Said He'd Fix It (1915), Gig and Saddle (1933), Hello Bill (1927), Scandal (1933)

Higgins, Johnny
Charleston (1927), Crap Game (1930)

Higgins, W.
He Was Bad (1914)

Hill, Florence
Gone Harlem (1939)

Hill, Lethia
Slow Poke (1932)

Hill, Nellie
Killer Diller (1948), Murder with Music (1941)

Hill, Ruby
Ebony Parade (1947), Put Your Arms Around Me, Honey (1943)

Hill and Robinson
Contrast in Rhythm (1945)

Hilliard, Joseph
Beware (1946)

Hilton, Milt
Blues in the Night (1942), Minnie the Moocher (1942), Skunk Song (1942), Virginia, Georgia and Caroline (1942)

Hines, Eleanor
Pitch a Boogie Woogie (1948)

Hite, Les (Orchestra)
Bargain with Bullets (1937), Devil Sat Down and Cried (1942), Gangsters on the Loose (1944), Murder in Swingtime (1937),

Pudgy Boy (1942), That Ol' Ghost Train (1942), What to Do (1942)

Hix, Tommy
Beware (1946)

Holden, Rusha
Harp Boogie (1946)

Holder, Geoffrey
Carib Gold (1956), Shango (1953)

Holder, Roland
Exile (1931)

Holeby, Walter
Giant of His Race (1921)

Holiday, Billie
Sound of Jazz (1957), Sugar Chile Robinson (1950), Symphony in Black (1935)

Holland, Clifford
Prison Bait (1944), Reform School (1939)

The Hollywood Jitterbugs
Woman's a Fool (1947)

Holmes, Rubber Neck
The Bronze Venus (1943), The Duke Is Tops (1938), Solid Senders (1941)

Holt, Anna
The Barber (1916)

Homes, Mabel
Giant of His Race (1921)

Hopkins, Claude
Barber Shop Blues (1937), By Request (1935), Claude Hopkins and His Orchestra (1933), Claude Hopkins and His Orchestra (1935)

Hopkins, Jack
For His Mother's Sake (1922)

Hopkins, Linda
Rockin' the Blues (1955)

Horance, John Shadrack
Along the Navajo Trail (1945), It's Me, Oh Lord (1945)

Horne, Boots
Broken Violin (1926)

Horne, Lena
Boogie Woogie Dream (1942), Boogie Woogie Dream (1944), The Bronze Venus (1943), Cabin in the Sky (1943), The Duke Is Tops (1938), G.I. Jubilee (1942), Harlem Hotshots (1945), Harlem on Parade (1948), Hi-De-Ho Holiday (1944), Jivin' the Blues (1946), Mantan Messes Up (1946), My New Gown (1944), Stormy Weather (1943), Unlucky Woman (1944), We've Come a Long, Long Way (1943)

Horton, Dorothea
Cry of Jazz (1958)

Hosay, Professor
Ghost of Tolston's Manor (1934)

Hough, Earl
Moon Over Harlem (1939)

Houston, Eddye L.
Go Down, Death! (1944)

Hoveler, Winnie (Dancers)
Riff 1943)

Howard, Bob
Bob Howard's House Party (1947), Dinah (1944), Gifts in Rhythm (1936), I'd Love to Be a Cowboy (1944), The Joint Is Jumping (1948), Junction 88 (1947), Murder with Music (1941), She's Too Hot to Handle (1944), Shine (1944), Stars on Parade (1946), Trailer Paradise (1937)

Howard, Gertrude
Hearts of Dixie (1929)

Howard, Gloria
Burlesque in Harlem (1955)

Howard, Peggy
Let My People Live (1938)

Howard, Shingzie
Children of Fate (1929), The Dungeon (1922), Fool's Errand (1922), Ghost of Tolston's Manor (1934), The House Behind the Cedars (1924), A Prince of His Race (1922), St. Louis Blues (1929), Son of Satan (1924), Uncle Jasper's Will (1922), The Virgin of the Seminole (1922)

Howard, Willie
How to Go to a French Restaurant (1941)

Howlett, Lloyd
Going to Glory, Come to Jesus (1946)

The Hubba Hubba Girls
Oop Boop Sh'Bam (1947)

Huey, Richard
Caldonia (1945)

Huff, Carrie
Drums o' Voodoo (1933), She Devil (1940)

Humes, Helen
Basin Street Revue (1955), Ee Baba Leba (1947), Jivin' in Be-Bop (1946)

Hunter, Ed
Big Timers (1945)

Hunter, Elveta
Big Timers (1945)

Hunter, Floyd
Hello Bill (1927)

Hunter, Mabel
Burlesque in Harlem (1955)
Hunter, Patsy
Murder in Swingtime (1937)
Hurley, Jess
Murder in Swingtime (1937)
The Hurricanes
Rockin' the Blues (1955)
Hyson, Roberta
Framing of the Shrew (1929), Georgia Rose (1930), The Lady Fare (1929), Melancholy Dame (1929), Music Hath Harms (1929)
Ingram, Clifford
Hearts of Dixie (1929)
Ingram, Rex
Anna Lucasta (1958), Cabin in the Sky (1943), Emperor Jones (1933), Green Pastures (1936), Harlem After Midnight (1934), Let My People Live (1938)
The Ink Spots
Ink Spots (1955)
Inma, Daniel
Go Down, Death! (1944)
International Sweethearts of Rhythm
Jump Children (1946), She's Crazy with Heat (1946), Sweethearts of Rhythm (1947), That Man of Mine (1946), That Man of Mine (1947)
Invador, Lord
House Rent Party (1946)
Irving, Roland
The Daughter of the Congo (1930)
Jacks, S.T.
The Millionaire (1927)
Jacks, Samuel "Sambo"
Are Working Girls Safe (1918), Black and Tan Mix Up (1918), Black Sherlock Holmes (1917), Bully (1918), Busted Romance (1917), Comeback of Barnacle Bill (1918), Dat Blackhand Waitah Man (1917), Devil for a Day (1917), Do the Dead Talk? (1918), Fixing the Faker (1918), Ghosts (1917), Good Luck in Old Clothes (1918), Hypocrites (1917), Janitor (1918), Luck in Old Clothes (1918), Reckless Rover (1918), Shine Johnson and the Rabbit Foot (1917), Some Baby (1918), Spooks (1917), Spying the Spy (1918), When Cupid Went Wild (1917), When You Are Scared, Run (1918), When You Hit, Hit Hard (1918), Wrong All Around (1917)

Jackson, Al
Boy! What a Girl (1946), Do I Worry? (1943), Git It (1943), Hair Raid (1948), Harlem Follies of 1949 (1950), Killer Diller (1948), Mama, I Wanna Make Rhythm (1943)
Jackson, Alonzo
Children of Fate (1926)
Jackson, Bull-Moose
Big Fat Mammas (1946), Boarding House Blues (1948)
Jackson, Carol
Little Carol Jackson (1942)
Jackson, Columbus
God's Stepchildren (1938), Swing (1938)
Jackson, Emmett
Marching On! (1943), Where's My Man To-Nite? (1944)
Jackson, Eugene
Hearts of Dixie (1929), Look-Out Sister! (1948), Moo Cow Boogie (1943), Murder Rap (1948), Prison Bait (1944), Reform School (1939), Take My Life (1941)
Jackson, Freddie
Double Deal (1939), Merrie Howe Carfe (1939), Prison Bait (1944), Reform School (1939)
Jackson, J.A.
Birthright (1939)
Jackson, Louise
Souls of Sin (1949)
Jackson, Mahalia
Imitation of Life (1959), St. Louis Blues (1958)
Jackson, Mike
The Black King (1932), Harlem Big Shot (1932)
Jackson, Quentin
Blues in the Night (1942), Minnie the Moocher (1942), Skunk Song (1942), Virginia, Georgia and Caroline (1942)
Jackson, Stringbeans
Harlem Hot Shots (1945)
The Jackson Brothers
Rhythm Rodeo (1938)
Jacquet, Illinois
Jammin' the Blues (1944)
James, Ida
Can't See for Looking (1944), Devil's Daughter (1939), Hi-De-Ho (1946), Hi-De-Ho (1947), His Rockin' Horse Ran Away (1944), Is You or Is You Ain't My

Baby (1944), Romance on the Beat (1945), Whose Been Eating My Porridge (1944)

James, Olga
Carmen Jones (1954)

Jeanette, Joe
Square Joe (1926)

Jefferson, Hilton
Blues in the Night (1942), Minnie the Moocher (1942), Skunk Song (1942), Virginia, Georgia and Caroline (1942)

Jeffries, Herbert (Herb)
The Bronze Buckaroo (1938), Flamingo (1947), Frenzy (1946), Harlem on the Prairie (1938), Harlem Rides the Range (1939), Harlem Variety Revue (1955), Jazz Festival (1955), Lionel Hampton and Herb Jeffries (1955), Rhythm and Blues Revue (1956), Sarah Vaughn and Herb Jeffries (1950), Two-Gun Man from Harlem (1939)

Jenkins, Bo
Gang Smashers (1938), Gun Moll (1944), Mantan Messes Up (1946)

Jenkins, Margaret
Harlem Is Heaven (1932), Harlem Rhapsody (1932)

Jenkins, Wesley
Custard Nine (1921)

The Jitterbug Johnnies
Juke Joint (1947)

Johnny and George
I Had a Dream (1945), Tall, Tan and Terrific (1946), There Are Eighty-Eight Reasons Why (1945), Write That Letter Tonight (1945)

Johnson, Alice
Lure of a Woman (1921)

Johnson, Ben
Simba (1955)

Johnson, Bobby
Look-Out Sister! (1948)

Johnson, Cee Pee (Orchestra)
Jump In (1942), Jungle Jig (1941), Let's Go (1942), Mystery in Swing (1940), Swing for Your Supper (1941), You Can't Fool About Love (1943)

Johnson, Charles
Beware (1946)

Johnson, Dora Dean
Georgia Rose (1930)

Johnson, Dots
Big Timers (1945), Joe Louis Story (1953),

Reet-Petite and Gone (1947), Tall, Tan and Terrific (1946)

Johnson, Eva
Man's Duty (1919), One Large Evening (1914)

Johnson, Frederick
Hi-De-Ho (1947), Lucky Gamblers (1946)

Johnson, Honey Boy
What Goes Up (1939)

Johnson, J. Lewis
Lying Lips (1939), Reet-Petite and Gone (1947)

Johnson, J. Rosamond
Keep Punching (1939)

Johnson, Jack
As the World Rolls On (1921), Black Thunderbolt (1921), For His Mother's Sake (1921), Man in Ebony (1918)

Johnson, Jesse
The Betrayal (1948)

Johnson, John Lester
Bargain with Bullets (1937), The Flames of Wrath (1923), Gangsters on the Loose (1944), Lady Luck (1940), Lucky Ghost (1941), Mr. Washington Goes to Town (1940), Mystery in Swing (1940), One Dark Night (1939), Professor Creeps (1941), Square Joe (1926), Story of Dr. Carver (1939)

Johnson, Keg
Blues in the Night (1942), Minnie the Moocher (1942), Skunk Song (1942), Virginia, Georgia and Caroline (1942)

Johnson, Mae
Keep Punching (1939)

Johnson, Marvin
Murder in Swingtime (1937)

Johnson, Maud
Love Bug (1920)

Johnson, Max
Nobody's Children (1920)

Johnson, Maxine
Love in Syncopation (1946)

Johnson, Myra
Ain't Misbehavin' (1945), Hark! Hark! The Lark (1941), Here 'Tis Honey, Take It (1943), Honeysuckle Rose (1941), Jimmie Lunceford and His Dance Orchestra (1936), The Joint Is Jumpin' (1941), Let's Get Down to Business (1943), Quick Watson, the Question (1943), Tall, Tan and Terrific (1946)

Johnson, Noble
Law of Nature (1918), Realization of a Negro's Ambition (1916), Trooper of Company K (1916)

Johnson, Norma
Girl in Room 20 (1946)

Johnson, Paul
Drums o' Voodoo (1933), She Devil (1940)

Johnson, Pete
Boogie Woogie Dream (1942), Boogie Woogie Dream (1944), My New Gown (1944), Unlucky Woman (1944)

Johnson, Ralph
Within Our Gates (1919)

Johnson, Robert
Gang War (1939)

Johnson, Sol
Underworld (1937)

Johnson, Susette
Up Jumped the Devil (1941)

Johnson, William
Ten Nights in a Bar-Room (1926)

Johnson and Johnson
Murder with Music (1941)

Johnston, Johnny
Sinner Kissed an Angel (1942)

Johnstone, Norman
Deceit (1921), Scar of Shame (1927)

Jones, Albert Reese
Boogiemania (1946)

Jones, Alma
Midnight Menace (1946)

Jones, Clayborn
Butting In (1914)

Jones, Clyde
Hair Raid (1948)

Jones, Darry
The Broken Earth (1939)

Jones, David
The Betrayal (1948)

Jones, Dolly
Go Down, Death! (1944)

Jones, Ernestine
Eddie Green's Laugh Jamboree (1944)

Jones, Gus
The Lady Fare (1929)

Jones, Harry
Injustice (1919), Loyal Hearts (1919)

Jones, Isaac
Anna Lucasta (1958)

Jones, Isham (Orchestra)
Meet the Maestros (1938)

Jones, James B.
The Blood of Jesus (1941)

Jones, Joe
Jammin' the Blues (1944)

Jones, Jonah
Blues in the Night (1942), Minnie the Moocher (1942), Skunk Song (1942), Virginia, Georgia and Caroline (1942)

Jones, July
Beale Street Mama (1946), Dirty Gertie from Harlem, U.S.A. (1946), Girl in Room 20 (1943), Juke Joint (1947)

Jones, Lenore
Lure of a Woman (1921)

Jones, Lila Walker
Regeneration of Souls (1921)

Jones, Lollypop
Chicago After Dark (1946), Lucky Gamblers (1946), Midnight Menace (1940)

Jones, Matthew
Am I Guilty? (1940), Racket Doctor (1945)

Jones, Maude
Scapegoat (1920), Uncle Remus' First Visit to New York (1914)

Jones, Quincy
Harlem Jazz Festival (1955)

Jones, Robert Earl
Lying Lips (1939), The Notorious Elinor Lee (1940)

Jones, Ruth
Mantan Runs for Mayor (1946)

Jones, Samuel H.
Go Down, Death! (1944)

Jones, Wesley
Uncle Remus' First Visit to New York (1914)

The Jones Boys
Super Sleuths (1947)

Jonny and Henny
Jivin' in Be-Bop (1946)

Jordan, Louis (Tympany Five)
Beware (1946), Buzz Me (1945), Caldonia (1945), Caldonia (short) (1945), Down, Down, Down (1942), Five Guys Named Moe (1942), Fuzzy Wuzzy (1942), Fuzzy Wuzzy (1945), G.I. Jive (1944), Hep-Cat Serenade (1945), Honey Chile (1945), If You Can't Smile and Say Yes (1944), Jordan Jive (1944), Jordan Melody #1 (1946), Jordan Melody #2 (1946), Jumpin' at the Jubilee (1944), Look-Out Sister! (1948), Old Man Mose (1942), Outskirts of Town

(1942), Ration Blues (1945), Reet-Petite and Gone (1947), Rocco Blues (1945), Swingtime Jamboree (1949), Tillie (1945), Toot That Trumpet (1946)

Jordan, Sam
Flying Ace (1926)

Jore, R.
Girl in Room 20 (1946)

Joyce, Adrian
For His Mother's Sake (1922)

Joyce, Billie
When You and I Were Young, Maggie (1944)

Joynes, Roxie
Caldonia (1945)

The Jubalaires
Brother Bill (1945), Noah (1946), Preacher and the Bear (1945), Ten Thousand Years Ago (1945)

The Jungle Jivestors
Jungle Jamboree (1943)

Junior, Herbert
Junction 88 (1947)

Kalana, Thais Nehli
Injustice (1919), Loyal Hearts (1919)

The Kandy Kids
Grafter and the Maid (1913)

Kauffin, Ida Belle
Crooked Money (1945), Gridiron Graft (1940), While Thousands Cheer (1940)

Keith, Charles
Vanities (1946)

Keith, Rosaline
Bad Boy (1939)

Kelly, Georgia
Marching On! (1943), Where's My Man To-Nite? (1944)

Kelly, Howard
The Barber (1916)

Kelly, Mabel
Midnight Ace (1928), Thirty Years Later (1928)

Kelly, Robert A.
Lovie Joe's Romance (1914)

Kelson, Anna
Flames of Wrath (1923)

Kemp, Mae
Call of His People (1921)

Kennedy, Ann
Scar of Shame (1927)

Kenney, Isadore
Loyalty of a Race (1918)

The Kentuckians
Children of Circumstance (1937)

The Kentucky Jubilee Singers
Cotton-Pickin' Days (1934), Kentucky Jubilee Singers #1 (1928), Kentucky Jubilee Singers #2 (1929), Old Black Joe (1931), On a Plantation (1930), The Road Home (1931), Slave Days (1930), The Water Boy (1929), Welcome (1931)

Keyes, Evelyn
Stepping Along (1943), Sweet Kisses (1943)

Kid Herman
Ten Thousand Dollar Trail ($10,000 Trail) (1921)

Kinbrough, Baby Ruth
By Right of Birth (1921)

King, F.
Colored American Winning His Suit (1916)

King, John
Dirty Gertie from Harlem, U.S.A. (1946)

King, Webb
By Right of Birth (1921), Georgia Rose (1930), A Man's Duty (1919), Realization of a Negro's Ambition (1916), Reformation (1919)

The Kings of Harmony (Quartette)
Those Pullman Porters (1930)

Kirby, John (Band)
Close Shave (1942), Harlem Follies of 1949 (1950), Sepia Cinderella (1947), Tweed Me (1942)

Kirk, Andy (Orchestra)
Killer Diller (1948)

Kirkpatrick, Sidney
Scapegoat (1920)

Kit and Kat
Juke Joint (1947)

Kitt, Eartha
Anna Lucasta (1958), St. Louis Blues (1958)

Knight, Terry
Mantan Runs for Mayor (1946), Return of Mandy's Husband (1948)

Knox, Walter
Mr. Washington Goes to Town (1940)

The Korn Kobblers
Listen to the Mocking Bird (1940)

LaBek, Una
Slow Poke (1932)

The Lafayette Players
Black Gold (1928), Eyes of Youth (1920)

Lane, Francey
Junior (1946)
Lane, Joy
Ink Spots (1955)
Lane, Lovey
Murder Rap (1948), Take My Life (1941)
Lane, Richard
Jackie Robinson Story (1950)
Lane, Sammie
Eleven PM (1928)
Lane, Willa Mae
Devil's Daughter (1939)
Langford, Sam
The Brute (1920), Haynes Newsreel No. 1
(1914), Haynes Newsreel No. 3 (1917)
La Redd, Cora
That's the Spirit (1932)
The Larks
Basin Street Revue (1955), Jazz Festival
(1955), Rhythm and Blues Revue (1956)
Larrimore, Rosalie
Beale Street Mama (1946)
Larry, Dene
Murder on Lenox Ave. (1941), Sunday Sin-
ners (1941)
La Rue, Jean
Woman's a Fool (1947)
La Rue, John
Reckless Money (1928)
La Rue, Reese
Rockin' the Blues (1955)
Latorre, Charles
Lying Lips (1939)
Lavassor, Vera
Injustice (1919), Loyal Hearts (1919), Ref-
ormation (1919)
Lavette, Harry
Crooked Money (1945), Gridiron Graft
(1940), While Thousands Cheer (1940)
Lawrence, Helen
Lem Hawkins' Confession (1935), Murder
in Harlem (1935)
Lawrence, Marilyn
Going to Glory, Come to Jesus (1946)
Lawrence, Richard
The Betrayal (1948)
Lawson, Belford (Attorney)
Lionel Hampton and Herb Jeffries (1955)
Lawson, Bob "Fighting"
Fighting Deacon (1925)
Ledbetter, Huddie
Three Songs by Leadbelly (1945)

Lee, Barbara
The Betrayal (1948)
Lee, Canada
Ask the OPA (1945), Cry, the Beloved
Country (1952), Henry Brown Farmer
(1944), Keep Punching (1939)
Lee, Dick
For His Mother's Sake (1922)
Lee, Don D.
Lying Lips (1939)
Lee, Dorothy
Pitch a Boogie Woogie (1948)
Lee, Eldridge
Injustice (1919), Loyal Hearts (1919)
Lee, Flo
Murder on Lenox Ave. (1941)
Lee, John (Johnny)
Boarding House Blues (1948), Come On,
Cowboy (1946), Mantan Runs for Mayor
(1946), Return of Mandy's Husband (1948),
St. Louis Blues (1929), She's Too Mean for
Me (1948)
Lee, Mabel
Baby Don't Go Away from Me (1946), Cats
Can't Dance (1945), Chicken Shack Shuffle
(1943), Dancemania (1943), Dreamer (1948),
Ebony Parade (1947), Everybody's Jumpin'
Now (1946), Foolin' Around (1943), Half
Past Jump Time (1945), O'Voutie O'Rooney
(1947), Pigmeat Throws the Bull (1945),
Reet-Petite and Gone (1947), Rhythm Mania
(1943), Sizzle with Sissle (1946)
Lee, Vicky
Lionel Hampton and Herb Jeffries
(1955)
Lee, Will
Smash Your Baggage (1932)
Lee, William
Steppin' High (1924)
Leedy, Glenn
Look-Out Sister! (1948)
Legon, Jeni
Double Deal (1939), Hi-De-Ho (1947),
Merrie Howe Carfe (1939), Murder Rap
(1948), Take My Life (1941), While Thou-
sands Cheer (1940)
Leighton, Fred
Colored American Winning His Suit
(1916)
Lemonier, Tom
Troubles of Sambo and Dinah (1914)

LeNoire, Rosetta
Anna Lucasta (1958)

The Lennox Trio
Rhythm Sam (1946)

Leonardo and Zolo
Harlem Follies of 1949 (1950), Sepia Cinderella (1947)

Le Shine, Count
Harlem After Midnight (1934)

Lester, Ezella
Burlesque in Harlem (1955)

Levette, Harry
Four Shall Die (1940), Murder Rap (1948), Take My Life (1941)

Lewis, Edward W.
Life in Harlem (1940)

Lewis, Ferdie
Harlem Is Heaven (1932), Harlem Rhapsody (1932)

Lewis, George (Stock Company)
Are Working Girls Safe (1918), Black and Tan Mix Up (1918), Black Sherlock Holmes (1917), Bully (1918), Busted Romance (1917), Comeback of Barnacle Bill (1918), Dat Blackhand Waitah Man (1917), Devil for a Day (1917), Do the Dead Talk? (1918), Fixing the Faker (1918), Ghosts (1917), Good Luck in Old Clothes (1918), Hypocrites (1917), Janitor (1918), Luck in Old Clothes (1918), Mercy, the Mummy Mumbled (1917), Milk-Fed Hero (1918), Porters (1918), Reckless Rover (1918), Shine Johnson and the Rabbit Foot (1917), Some Baby (1918), Spooks (1917), Spying the Spy (1918), When Cupid Went Wild (1917), When You Are Scared, Run (1918), When You Hit, Hit Hard (1918), Wrong All Around (1917)

Lewis, J. Henry (Professor)
Loyalty of a Race (1918)

Lewis, Jacqueline
God's Stepchildren (1938)

Lewis, Lee
Dirty Gertie from Harlem, U.S.A. (1946)

Lewis, Lucille
Veiled Aristocrats (1932)

Lewis, Mae Evelyn
Greatest Sin (1922)

Lewis, Meade Lux
Boogie Woogie (1944), Fuzzy Wuzzy (1945), Hep Cat Serenade (1947), Low Down Dog (1944), Roll 'Em (1944), Spirit of Boogie Woogie (1942)

Lewis, Sybil
Am I Guilty? (1940), Boy! What a Girl! (1946), Broken Strings (1940), Midnight Menace (1946), Miracle in Harlem (1948), Mystery in Swing (1940), Racket Doctor (1945)

Lewis and White
Boarding House Blues (1948)

Leyea, Claire
Anna Lucasta (1958)

Lillard, Joe
Reet, Petite and Gone (1947)

Lincoln, Rose Lee
Absent (1928), Murder in Swingtime (1937), Rhythm Rodeo (1938), Two-Gun Man from Harlem (1939)

Lindsey, Powell
Love in Syncopation (1946)

The Lindy Lenox Hoppers
Tuxedo Junction (1942)

Liney, Jack
Dark Manhattan (1937)

Litterson, Edgar
Railroad Porter (1912)

Little, Joe
Pitch a Boogie Woogie (1948)

Little Buck
Basin Street Revue (1955), Rhythm and Blues Revue (1956), Rock 'n' Roll Revue (1955)

The Little Four Quartet
Cha-Chi-Man (1944), Chilly 'n' Cold (1945), Love Grows on a White Oak Tree (1944)

Lloyd and Willis
Deed I Do (1944)

Lochart, Ida
Fall of the Mighty (1913)

Logan, Ruby
Night Club Girl (1944), One Dark Night (1939)

Long, Johnny (Orchestra)
Boogie Man (1943), Caterpillar Shuffle (1943), Chop Sticks (1943), Hanover Hangover (1946), It Must Be Jelly (1946), It's a Sin to Tell a Lie (1946), Johnny Peddler (1941), Junior (1946), Let's Get Away from It All (1943), The Long and Short of It (1943), Maria Elena (1943), My Girl Loves a Sailor (1943), Watch Out! (1946), Watcha Know, Joe? (1941)

Long, Walter
The Devil's March (1923), A Giant of His Race (1921), His Great Chance (1923), A Shot in the Night (1922)

Lorain, Harry
Cannibal King (1915), Swami Sam (1914)

Louis, Joe
The Brown Bomber (1939), Easy to Get (1943), The Fight Never Ends (1947), The Real Joe Louis (1946), The Roar of the Crowd (1953), Sergeant Joe Louis on Tour (1943), The Spirit of Youth (1938), We've Come a Long, Long Way (1943)

Love, Garfield
Rhythm in a Riff (1946)

Lovejoy, Alec
Birthright (1939), Black and Tan (1929), God's Stepchildren (1938), Lem Hawkins' Confession (1935), Moon Over Harlem (1939), Murder in Harlem (1935), Murder on Lenox Ave. (1941), Paradise in Harlem (1940), Sunday Sinners (1940), Swing (1938)

Loveless, Henrietta
Lem Hawkins' Confession (1935), Murder in Harlem (1935), Spider's Web (1926)

Lowe, James
Uncle Tom's Cabin (1927)

Lucas, Charles D.
The Homesteader (1918), Within Our Gates (1920)

Lucas, Lt. Eugene
Injustice (1919), Loyal Hearts (1919)

Lucas, George
Deceit (1921)

Lucas, Sam
Uncle Tom's Cabin (1914)

Lucasta, Anna
What a Guy (1947)

Lunceford, Jimmie (Orchestra)
Jimmie Lunceford and His Dance Orchestra (1936)

Lyles, Aubrey
Harlem Knights (1929), Harlem Mania (1929), Jim Town Cabaret (1929), Mayor of Jimtown (1929), Midnight Lodger (1930), Miller and Lyles (1929), Their Groceries (1929), They Know

Lynch, Thelma
Going to Glory, Come to Jesus (1946)

Lynn, Eddie
Murder Rap (1948), Prison Bait (1944), Reform School (1939), Take My Life (1941)

Lynn, Lee
Rockin' the Blues (1955)

Lynn, Mauri
Nat "King" Cole and Joe Adams' Orchestra (1951)

Lyons, Cleophus
Pitch a Boogie Woogie (1948)

Mabley, Jackie "Moms"
Big Timers (1947), Boarding House Blues (1948), Emperor Jones (a.k.a. J. Mayble) (1933), Killer Diller (1947)

Mac and Ace
Juke Joint (1947)

Macbeth's Calypso Band
House-Rent Party (1946)

McBride, Sue
The Betrayal (1948)

McCalla, Vernon
Am I Guilty? (1940), The Bronze Venus (1943), Double Deal (1939), The Duke Is Tops (1938), Four Shall Die (1940), Gang Smashers (1938), Lady Luck (1940), Lucky Ghost (1941), Mr. Smith Goes Ghost (1940), One Dark Night (1939), Pigmeat's Laugh Hepcats (1944), Prison Bait (1944), Racket Doctor (1945), Reform School (1939)

McCarty, Dorothy
Burlesque in Harlem (1955)

McClain, Billy
Bargain with Bullets (1937), Gangsters on the Loose (1944), Rhapsody in Black (1934)

McClain, Florence
Aladdin Jones (1916), Black and White in Darktown (1916), Money Talks in Darktown (1916), A Natural Born Shooter (1914), Two Knights in Vaudeville (1916)

McClane, Lorenzo
Lem Hawkins' Confession (1935), Murder in Harlem (1935)

McClennan, Frank H.
The Blood of Jesus (1941)

McCoo, Arthur
The Betrayal (1948)

McCord, Montgne
Girl in Room 20 (1946)

McCormack, Pearl
Phantom of Kenwood (1933)

McCoy, Austin (Band)
No Time for Romance (1948), Sun Tan Ranch (1948)

McDaniel, Hattie
Colored American Cavalcade (1939), Mississippi Moods (1937)

McDaniels, Sam
Am I Guilty? (1940), Bargain with Bullets (1937), Dark Manhattan (1937), Gangsters on the Loose (1944), Racket Doctor (1945)

McGarr, Jules
Fall of the Mighty (1913)

McGarrity, Everett
Hallelujah (1929)

McGinty, Antiebelle
Chicago After Dark (1946), Junction 88 (1947)

McGlynn, Frank, Jr.
Story of Dr. George Washington Carver (1935)

McGowan, Ira O.
Deceit (1921)

McGuire, Lawrence
Hearts of the Woods (1921)

Machen, Yvonne
Betrayal (1948)

McHugh, Frances
Juke Joint (1947)

Mack, Baby
New Way to Win (1915)

Mack, Cecil (Choir)
International Rhythms (1938)

Mackellar, Helen
Bad Boys (1939)

McKinley, Ray
Basin Street Boogie (1942)

McKinney, Chick
Drums o' Voodoo (1933), She Devil (1940)

McKinney, Nina Mae
Black Network (1936), Devil's Daughter (1939), Gang Smashers (1938), Gangsters on the Loose (1944), Hallelujah (1929), Life Is Real (1936), Mantan Messes Up (1946), Minstrel Days (1930), Pie Pie Blackbirds (1932), Pinky (1949), Racket Doctor (1945), St. Louis Gal (1938), Sanders of the River (1935), Straight to Heaven (1939), Swanee Showboat (1945)

McLane, Lorenzo
Spider's Web (1926)

McMillen, Allen
Chicago After Dark (1946)

McMillion, Walter
Go Down, Death! (1944)

McMowan, Edward
For His Mother's Sake (1922)

McNeely, Howard Louis
Jackie Robinson Story (1950)

McQueen, Thelma "Butterfly"
Cabin in the Sky (1943), Killer Diller (1947)

McRae, Teddy
Blues in the Night (1942), Minnie the Moocher (1942), Skunk Song (1942), Virginia, Georgia and Caroline (1942)

McZekkashing, Mickey
Marching On! (1943), Where's My Man To-Nite? (1944)

Mahon, Carl
Exile (1931), Girl from Chicago (1932), Ten Minutes to Live (1932), Veiled Aristocrats (1932)

Maize, Andrew
Mistaken Identity (1941), Murder with Music (1941)

Makeba, Miriam
Come Back, Africa (1959)

Makumbi, Eseza
Man of the Worlds (1946)

Mallon, Ozzy (Jitterbugs)
House-Rent Party (1946)

Malneck, Matty (Orchestra)
Ah, Yes, There's Good Blues Tonight (1946)

Mankins, Roxie
Flames of Wrath (1923)

Mann, Joan
Watch Out! (1946)

Manning, Ambrose
The Song of Freedom (1938)

Manning, Sam
Quarry Road (1943), Willie Willie (1943)

Mariann's Mediterreans
Yamekraw (1930)

Maris, Marian
Hello Bill (1927)

Markham, Dewey "Pigmeat"
Am I Guilty? (1940), Burlesque in Harlem (1955), Fight That Ghost (1946), Hellcats (1947), House-Rent Party (1946), Junction 88 (1947), Mr. Smith Goes Ghost (1940), One Big Mistake (1940),

Pigmeat Throws the Bull (1945), Pigmeat's Laugh Hepcats (1947), Racket Doctor (1945), Shut My Big Mouth (1947), Swanee Showboat (1945), The Wrong Mr. Wright (1947)

Marley, John
Joe Louis Story (1953)

Marshall, Jimmie
Aladdin Jones (1915)

Marshall, Matt
Troubles of Sambo and Dinah (1914)

Martin, Daisy
Spitfire (1922)

Martin, Edgar
Boarding House Blues (1948), Hi-De-Ho (1947), Killer Diller (1948)

Martin, Hugo
Marching On! (1943), Where's My Man To-Nite? (1944)

Martin, Ray
Bargain with Bullets (1937), The Bronze Venus (1943), The Duke Is Tops (1938), Gangsters on the Loose (1944), Green Pastures (1936), No Time for Romance (1948), One Dark Night (1939)

Martin, Sarah
Darktown Scandal's Revue (1930), Hello Bill (1927)

Martin and Williams
Straight to Heaven (1939)

Martins, Orlando
Man of the Worlds (1946), Simba (1955), The Song of Freedom (1938)

Mason, Bernardine
Veiled Aristocrats (1932)

Mason, John
Boarding House Blues (1948), Harlem Is Heaven (1932), The Joint Is Jumping (1948)

Mason, Julia
Are Working Girls Safe (1918), Black and Tan Mix Up (1918), Black Sherlock Holmes (1917), Bully (1918), Busted Romance (1917), Comeback of Barnacle Bill (1918), Dat Blackhand Waitah Man (1917), Devil for a Day (1917), Do the Dead Talk? (1918), Fixing the Faker (1918), Ghosts (1917), Good Luck in Old Clothes (1918), Hypocrites (1917), Janitor (1918), Luck in Old Clothes (1918), Mercy, the Mummy Mumbled (1917), Milk-Fed Hero (1918), Porters

(1918), Reckless Rover (1918), Shine Johnson and the Rabbit Foot (1917), Some Baby (1918), Spooks (1917), Spying the Spy (1918), When Cupid Went Wild (1917), When You Are Scared, Run (1918), When You Hit, Hit Hard (1918), Wrong All Around (1917)

Mason, Ruby
Sport of the Gods (1921)

Mason, Ruth
Harlem Follies (1950)

Mason, Youth
Modern Cain (1921)

Massey, P.
Wife Hunter (1922)

Matthews, Babe
King for a Day (1934)

Matthews, Bessie
Realization of a Negro's Ambition (1916)

Maurice, Richard
Eleven PM (1928), Nobody's Children (1920)

Maurice, Vivian
Nobody's Children (1920)

Maxwell, M.C.
Regeneration (1923)

May, Mabel
Sound of Sacrifice (1918)

Maynard, Geraldine
Of One Blood (1944)

Maynor, Dorothy
Message from Dorothy Maynor (1949)

Mayo, Stella
Regeneration (1923)

Mays, Betti
Boy! What a Girl! (1946)

Mays, Willie
Willie Mays Story (1955)

Meehan, Lew
By Right of Birth (1921)

Mello, Brenoo
Black Orpheus (1959)

Mercer, Mabel
Harlemesque Revue (1943)

Metcaff, Clarence
Nat "King" Cole and Joe Adams' Orchestra (1951)

Metcalfe, Ralph
Easy to Get (1944)

Michaels, Daniel
The Black King (1932), Harlem Big Shot (1932), Love and Undertakers (1918)

Michaux, Elder Solomon Lightfoot
Negro Marches On (1938), We've Got the Devil on the Run (1934)

Micheaux, Oscar
Lem Hawkins' Confession (1935), Murder in Harlem (1935)

Mickey, Arline
Children of Fate (1926), Prince of His Race (1926), Ten Nights in a Bar-Room (1926)

Middleton, Velma
I'll Be Glad When You're Dead, You Rascal You (1942), Swingin' on Nothin' (1942)

Milburn, Amos
Rhythm and Blues Revue (1956)

Miles, Viola
Deceit (1921)

Miller, Fay
Hell's Alley (1931)

Miller, Flournoy E.
The Bronze Buckaroo (1938), Come On, Cowboy (1949), Double Deal (1939), Harlem Knights (1929), Harlem Mania (1929), Harlem on the Prairie (1938), Harlem Rides the Range (1938), Jimtown Cabaret (1929), Lady Luck (1940), Lucky Ghost (1941), Mantan Runs for Mayor (1946), Mayor of Jimtown (1929), Midnight Lodger (1931), Miller and Lyles (1929), Mr. Creeps (1938), Mr. Washington Goes to Town (1940), Mystery in Swing (1940), Professor Creeps (1941), Return of Mandy's Husband (1948), Rockin' the Blues (1955), She's Too Mean for Me (1948), Stormy Weather (1943), That's the Spirit (1933), They Know Their Groceries (1929)

Miller, Fred
Square Joe (1922)

Miller, Irvin C. (Brownskin Revue)
Darktown Scandal's Revue (1930), Pitch a Boogie Woogie (1948), Where's My Man To-Nite? (1944)

Miller, Mrs. Irvin C.
Deceit (1921)

Miller, James
Cry of Jazz (1958)

Miller, Johnny
Come to Baby Do (1946), Errand Boy for Rhythm (1946), Frim Fram Sauce (1945), Got a Penny Benny (1946), I'm a Shy Guy (1946), Is You or Is You Ain't My Baby (1944), Oh-h-e-e My, My (1945), Who's Been Eating My Porridge? (1944)

Miller, Taps
Song and Dance Man (1932)

Miller, Veronica
Lure of a Woman (1921)

Miller and Lyles
Harlem Knights (1929), Harlem Mania (1929), Jim Town Cabaret (1929), Mayor of Jimtown (1929), Midnight Lodger (1930), Miller and Lyles (1929), They Know Their Groceries (1929)

Miller Brothers & Louis
Hi-De-Ho (1947), Hi-De-Ho (1947)

The Miller Sisters
Rockin' the Blues (1955)

Millie and Bubbles
Straight to Heaven (1939)

Millinder, Lucky (Orchestra)
Because I Love You (1942), Big Fat Mamas (1946), Boarding House Blues (1948), Four or Five Times (1941), Gig and Saddle (1933), Hair Raid (1948), Harlem on Parade (1940), Harlem Serenade (1942), Hello Bill (1946), I Want a Big Fat Mama (1941), I Want a Man (1946), Lonesome Road (1942), Lucky Millinder (1946), Paradise in Harlem (1940), Play It, Brother (1947), Readin', Writin' and Rhythm (1939), Rhythm on the Run (1942), Scandal (1934), Shout! Sister, Shout! (1941)

Mills, Billy
Jailhouse Blues (1934), Love Bug (1920)

Mills, Gertrude
Shadowed by the Devil (1916)

Mills, Jerry
Grafter and the Maid (1913), Pullman Porter (1910), Railroad Porter (1912)

Mills, Maude
Darktown Scandal's Revue (1930)

Mills Blue Rhythm Band
Mills' Blue Rhythm Band (1933)

The Mills Brothers
Bosko and the Pirate (1937), Caravan (1942), Cielito Lindo (1944), Ebony Parade (1947), The Fight Never Ends (1947), Hot Frogs (1942), I Ain't Got Nobody (1932), Lazy River (1944), Rockin' Chair (1942), Till Then (1944), You Always Hurt the One You Love (1944)

Milton, Roy (Orchestra)
Forty-Seventh Street Jive (1944), Hey, Lawdy Mama (1944), Ride On, Ride On (1944)

Milton, William
Smiling Hate (1924)

Mines, Callie
Birthright (1924)

Mitchell, Abbie
Eyes of Youth (1920), Night in Dixie (1926), Scape Goat (1917), Uncle Remus' First Visit to New York (1914)

Mitchell, Billy
Blackbird Fantasy (1942), Professor Creeps (1941)

Mitchell, Dora
By Right of Birth (1921)

Mitchell, Knolly
The Black King (1932), Harlem Big Shot (1932)

Mitchell, Tressie
Ten Minutes to Live (1932)

The Mitchell Brothers
Sweet Kisses (1943)

M'Kosi, Lewis
Come Back, Africa (1959)

Modisane, Blake
Come Back, Africa (1959)

Molyneux, Tom
When Giants Fight (1926)

Monagas, Lionel
Drums o' Voodoo (1940), Keep Punching (1939), Lem Hawkins' Confession (1935), Louisiana (1933), The Millionaire (1927), Murder in Harlem (1935), Paradise in Harlem (1940), Romance on the Beat (1946), She Devil (1940), Straight to Heaven (1939)

Monk, Thelonius
Sound of Jazz (1957)

Monroe, Clark
Harlem Follies (1950)

Monroe, Millie
Lady Luck (1940), Lucky Ghost (1941), Mr. Smith Goes Ghost (1940), One Big Mistake (1940), Pigmeat's Laugh Hepcats (1944)

Montgomery, Frank
Aladdin Jones (1916), Black and White (1914), Money Talks in Darktown (1916), A Natural Born Shooter (1914), Two Knights in Vaudeville (1916)

Moore, Charles
The Daughter of the Congo (1930), Exile (1931), God's Stepchildren (1938)

Moore, Dauphine
Juke Joint (1947)

Moore, Edward
Ten Nights in a Bar-Room (1926)

Moore, Mrs. Eugene L.
Square Joe (1922)

Moore, Mrs. Fred
Square Joe (1922)

Moore, Gertrude
His Great Chance (1923)

Moore, Johnnie (Three Blazers)
Along the Navajo Trail (1945), It's Me, Oh Lord (1945)

Moore, Juanita
Imitation of Life (1959)

Moore, Judy
Grafter and the Maid (1913)

Moore, Katherine
Dirty Gertie from Harlem, U.S.A. (1946), Girl in Room 20 (1946), Juke Joint (1947)

Moore, Margery
Girl in Room 20 (1946)

Moore, Marian
Square Joe (1922)

Moore, Matt
Bad Boy (1939)

Moore, Monette
Low Down: A Bird's Eye View of Harlem (1929)

Moore, Oscar
Come to Baby Do (1946), Errand Boy for Rhythm (1946), Frim Fram Sauce (1945), Got a Penny Benny (1946), I'm a Shy Guy (1946), Is You or Is You Ain't My Baby (1944), Oh-h-e-e My, My (1945), Who's Been Eating My Porridge? (1944)

Moore, Perita
Moon Over Harlem (1939)

Moore, Phil (Four)
Chair Song (1945), I Want a Little Doggie (1945), The Joint Is Jumping (1948), Lazy Lady (1945), Stars on Parade (1946), Who Threw the Whiskey in the Well? (1945)

Moore, Ray
Rhythm in a Riff (1946)

Moore, Tim
Boy! What a Girl! (1946), Darktown Revue (1931), His Great Chance (1923)

Moore, Tommie
Mystery in Swing (1940), That Man of Mine (1947)

Moore, Tommiwitta
The Broken Earth (1939)

Moore, Vernetties
The Betrayal (1948)

Moore, Vernol
Reformation (1919)

Mordecai, Jimmy
St. Louis Blues (1929), Yamekraw (1930)

Morehouse, Clarence
Mr. Washington Goes to Town (1940)

Moreland, Mantan
Basin St. Revue (1955), Cabin in the Sky (1943), Come On, Cowboy (1946), Condemned Men (1948), The Dreamer (1948), Ebony Parade (1947), Four Shall Die (1940), Gang Smashers (1938), Harlem on the Prairie (1938), Jazz Festival (1955), Lady Luck (1940), Lucky Ghost (1941), Mantan Messes Up (1946), Mantan Runs for Mayor (1946), Mr. Creeps (1938), Mr. Washington Goes to Town (1940), Night Club Girl (1944), One Dark Night (1939), Professor Creeps (1941), Racket Doctor (1945), Return of Mandy's Husband (1948), Rhythm and Blues Revue (1956), Rock 'n' Roll Revue (1955), Rockin' the Blues (1955), She's Too Mean for Me (1948), Spirit of Youth (1938), Super Sleuths (1947), Tall, Tan and Terrific (1946), That's the Spirit (1933), Two-Gun Man from Harlem (1938), Up Jumped the Devil (1941), What a Guy (1947), While Thousands Cheer (1940)

Moreland, Marcella
Am I Guilty? (1940), Racket Doctor (1945)

Morrell, Stanley
Exile (1931)

Morris, Earl J.
Broken Strings (1940), The Bronze Buckaroo (1938), Mystery in Swing (1940), Son of Ingagi (1940)

Morris, Lea
Lem Hawkins' Confession (1935), Murder in Harlem (1935)

Morris, Mae
Why Worry? (1923)

Morris, Marlowe
Jammin' the Blues (1944)

Morrison, Ernest "Sunshine Sammy"
Pickaninny (1921), Stepping Along (1929), Sunshine Sammy (1929)

Morrow, Guernsey
Am I Guilty? (1940), The Bronze Venus (1943), The Duke Is Tops (1938), Gang Smashers (1938), Murder Rap (1948), One Dark Night (1939), Racket Doctor (1945), Take My Life (1941)

Morton, Edgar Lewis
Chicago After Dark (1946)

Morton, Edna
The Burden of Race (1921), The Call of His People (1922), Easy Money (1921), The Ghost of Tolston's Manor (1934), The Jazz Hounds (1922), The Schemers (1922), Secret Sorrow (1922), The Simp (1921), Son of Satan (1924), Spitfire (1922), The Sport of Gods (1923), Uncle Remus' First Visit to New York (1914)

Morton, Tommy
Watch Out! (1946)

Mosby, Curtis (Orchestra)
The Broken Earth (1939)

Moses, Ethel
Birthright (1939), Cab Calloway's Jitterbug Party (1935), God's Stepchildren (1938), Gone Harlem (1939), Harlemania (1938), Policy Man (1938), Temptation (1936), Underworld (1937)

Moses, Lucia
Scar of Shame (1927)

Mosley, Thomas M.
Colored American Winning His Suit (1916), Crimson Fog (1932), Harlem Is Heaven (1932), Harlem Rhapsody (1932), Hell's Alley (1931), Straight to Heaven (1939)

Moss, Carlton
The Negro Soldier (1944), The Phantom of Kenwood (1933)

Moss and Fry
How High Is Up (1923)

Mozart, George
The Song of Freedom (1938)

Mukwanazi, David
Magic Garden (1952)

Murphy, Bert
Aladdin Jones (1915), Are Working Girls Safe (1918), Black and Tan Mix Up (1918), Black and White (1914), Black Sherlock Holmes (1917), Bully (1918), Busted

Romance (1917), Comeback of Barnacle Bill (1918), Dat Blackhand Waitah Man (1917), Devil for a Day (1917), Do the Dead Talk? (1918), Fixing the Faker (1918), Ghost (1917), Good Luck in Old Clothes (1918), Hypocrites (1917), Janitor (1918), Luck in Old Clothes (1918), Mercy, the Mummy Mumbled (1917), Milk-Fed Hero (1918), Money Talks in Darktown (1916), Natural Born Shooter (1913), Porters (1918), Reckless Rover (1918), Shine Johnson and the Rabbit Foot (1917), Some Baby (1918), Spooks (1917), Spying the Spy (1918), Two Knights of Vaudeville (1916), When Cupid Went Wild (1917), When You Are Scared, Run (1918), When You Hit, Hit Hard (1918), Wrong All Around (1917)

Murray, Art
Bargain with Bullets (1937), Gangsters on the Loose (1944)

Murray, John "Rastus"
Fight That Ghost (1946), House-Rent Party (1946)

Murray, Kitty
Lionel Hampton and Herb Jeffries (1955)

Muse, Clarence
The Broken Earth (1939), Broken Strings (1940), Camp Meeting (1936), Custard Nine (1921), Deep South (1937), Hearts of Dixie (1929), Jam Session (1944), The Peanut Man (1947), Porgy and Bess (1959), The Spirit of Youth (1938), Toussaint L'Ouverture (1921), Way Down South (1939)

The Musical Madcaps
Hit That Jive Jack (1943), Linda Brown (1943), Rhythm Mad (1943), Rhythm of the Rhythm Band (1943), Shoot the Rhythm to Me (1943)

Nagel, George
Harlem Is Heaven (1932), Harlem Rhapsody (1932)

Neely, Lawrence "Pepper"
Marching On! (1943), Where's My Man To-Nite? (1944)

Nelson, Howard
Nobody's Children (1920)

Newcome, Nora
Exile (1931)

Newell, Inez
Dirty Gertie from Harlem, U.S.A. (1946), Juke Joint (1947)

Newman, Laura
Life of Florence Mills (1940)

Newsome, Carman
Birthright (1939), God's Stepchildren (1938), Lying Lips (1939), The Notorious Elinor Lee (1940), Swing (1938)

Newton, Frankie
Readin', Writin' and Rhythm (1939)

Newton, Jack
For His Mother's Sake (1922)

The Nicholas Brothers
All-colored Vaudeville Show (1935), Barbershop Blues (1937), Black Network (1936), Dixieland Jamboree (1935), Pie Pie Blackbird (1932), Stormy Weather (1943)

Nicholson, Calvin
Flaming Crisis (1924)

Nit, Johnny
Dusky Melodies (1930)

Nix, Victor
Greatest Sin (1922)

Noel, Hattie
King for a Day (1934)

Noisette, Katherine
The Daughter of the Congo (1930), The Exile (1931), Wages of Sin (1928)

Nolan, Kid
Come Back (1922), Regeneration of Souls (1921), Shoot 'Em Up, Sam (1922)

Norcom, Alfred
Black Gold (1928), Regeneration (1923)

Norman, Lee (Orchestra)
Boarding House Blues (1948), Jittering Jitterbugs (1943), Keep Punching (1939)

Norman, Maidie
Bright Road (1953), The Peanut Man (1947), The Well (1951)

Norton, Thelma
Sunday Sinners (1941)

O'Brien, Florence
Double Deal (1939), Lady Luck (1940), Lucky Ghost (1941), Mr. Smith Goes Ghost (1940), Mr. Washington Goes to Town (1940), Professor Creeps (1941), Up Jumped the Devil (1941), While Thousands Cheer (1940)

O'Daniel, Nicky
Boogie Mania (1946), Caldonia (1945), Dancemania (1943), Harlem After Midnight (1947), Harlem Hotcha (1946), It

Happened in Harlem (1945), Pollard Jump (1946), Rhythm of the Rhythm Band (1943)

O-Dee, Sporty
Caldonia (1945)

Offley, Hilda
Keep Punching (1939), Miracle in Harlem (1948)

Olden, Charles
Melancholy Dame (1929)

Oliver, George
Mistaken Identity (1941), Murder with Music (1941)

Oliver, Marjorie
Murder with Music (1941)

O'Neal, Frederick
Anna Lucasta (1958)

Ony, Edward
Prison Bait (1944), Reform School (1939)

The Original Swing Band
Streamlined Swing (1938)

Ory, Kid (Band)
Sarah Vaughn and Herb Jeffries, Kid Ory (1950)

Oscar, John
The Joint Is Jumping (1948)

Ovey, George
Dark and Cloudy (1919)

Owens, Jesse
Negro in Sports (1950)

Owens, Luella
Burlesque in Harlem (1955)

Owens, Robert
Injustice (1919), Loyal Hearts (1919)

Owens, Virgil
Absent (1928)

Owens, Wilhelmina
Injustice (1919), Loyal Hearts (1919)

Paige, Barry (Orchestra)
Breakfast in Rhythm (1943), Pardon Me, But You Look Like Margie (1943)

Pancho and Delores
Broken Violin (1926), Jivin' in Be-Bop (1946)

Paquin, Robert
Lying Lips (1939)

The Paradise Chorus
It Happened in Harlem (1945)

Parker, Delores
King Cole and His Trio (1950), King Cole Trio and Benny Carter (1950)

Parker, Fred
Chocolate Cowboys (1925)

Parker, Gloria
Broadway and Main (1946), Four Letters (1946), Here Comes the Fattest Man in Town (1946)

Parker, Sonny
Lionel Hampton and Herb Jeffries (1955)

Parrish, Bob
Emily Brown (1943)

Patrick, Edward
Prison Bait (1944), Reform School (1939), Ten Thousand Dollar Trail ($10,000 Trail) (1921)

Patterson, J. Patrick
The Joint Is Jumping (1948)

Patterson, Marguerite
Foolish Lives (1921)

Patterson, Sam
God's Stepchildren (1938)

Patterson, Tilford
Juke Joint (1947)

Patterson, Warren
Boy! What a Girl! (1946), Do I Worry? (1943), Git It (1943), Hair Raid (1948), Harlem Follies of 1949 (1950), Killer Diller (1948), Mama, I Wanna Make Rhythm (1943)

Patterson and Jackson
Boy! What a Girl! (1946), Do I Worry? (1943), Git It (1943), Hair Raid (1948), Harlem Follies of 1949 (1950), Killer Diller (1948), Mama, I Wanna Make Rhythm (1943)

Patton, Jonella
Foolish Lives (1921)

Paul, Manhattan
Harlem Follies (1950)

Paul, Marilyn
Harriet (1945)

Payne, Benny
Blues in the Night (1942), Minnie the Moocher (1942), Mr. Black Magic (1956), Skunk Song (1942), There Are Eighty-Eight Reasons Why (1945), Virginia, Georgia and Caroline (1942)

The Peachy Pinups
Where's My Man To-Nite? (1944)

Pearson, Charles
Flames of Wrath (1923)

Pearson, Josephine
Night Club Girl (1944), One Dark Night (1939)

Penalver, Clarence
Midnight Ace (1928)
Pennall, H.
He Was Bad (1914)
Peoples, Neva
The Bronze Venus (1943), The Duke Is
Tops (1943), Gang Smashers (1938), Gun
Moll (1944), Mantan Messes Up (1946)
Percy, Esme
Sing of Freedom (1938)
Perkins, Alberta
Drums o' Voodoo (1933), Murder on Lenox
Ave. (1941), She Devil (1940), Sunday Sin-
ners (1941)
Peters, Brock
Porgy and Bess (1959), Carmen Jones (1954)
The Perkins Sisters
Hi-De-Ho (1947)
Petti, Emile (Orchestra)
Sun Tan Ranch (1948)
Pettus, William E.
Scar of Shame (1927)
Phil and Audrey
Jivin' in Be-Bop (1946)
Piano, John
Boarding House Blues (1948)
Pickens, Albertine
Law of Nature (1917)
Pickett, Bill
The Bull-Dogger (1923), Crimson Skull
(1921), Scarlet Claw (1921)
Pierson, Don
Hearts of the Woods (1921)
Pillot, Bernice
Hearts of Dixie (1929), Story of Dr. Carver
(1939)
Pitts, Juanita
It Happened in Harlem (1945)
Pitts, Pitter-Patter
It Happened in Harlem (1945)
The Plantation Boys' Choir
Spirit of Youth (1937)
The Plantation Club Chorus
Gone Harlem (1939), Policy Man (1938)
Platts, Harold
Flying Ace (1926)
Pleasants, Henry
Secret Sorrow (1921), Ties of Blood (1921)
Poitier, Sidney
Cry, the Beloved Country (1958), Porgy
and Bess (1959)

Poke, Leon
Midnight Menace (1946)
Polk, Oscar
Cabin in the Sky (1943), Green Pastures
(1936), Underworld (1937)
Pollard, Frank
Are Working Girls Safe (1918), Black and
Tan Mix Up (1918), Black Sherlock Holmes
(1917), Bully (1918), Busted Romance
(1917), Comeback of Barnacle Bill (1918),
Dat Blackhand Waitah Man (1917), Devil
for a Day (1917), Do the Dead Talk? (1918),
Fixing the Faker (1918), Ghosts (1917),
Good Luck in Old Clothes (1918), Hyp-
ocrites (1917), Janitor (1918), Luck in Old
Clothes (1918), Mercy, the Mummy Mum-
bled (1917), Milk-Fed Hero (1918), Porters
(1918), Reckless Rover (1918), Shine John-
son and the Rabbit Foot (1917), Some Baby
(1918), Spooks (1917), Spying the Spy (1918)
When Cupid Went Wild (1917), When You
Are Scared, Run (1918), When You Hit, Hit
Hard (1918), Wrong All Around (1917)
Pope, Emma
Hair Raid (1948)
Pope, Leo
Eleven PM (1928)
Pope, Lucille
Dixie Love (1934)
The Pope Sisters
Temptation (1936), Underworld (1937)
Portee, Joesfred
Vanities (1946)
Porter, Charles
Just a Note (1914)
Porter, Harry
Music Hath Harms (1929), My First Love
(1921)
Porter, Jean
How to See a French Doctor (1941)
Porter, Uriel
Man of the Worlds (1946)
Porteur, Esther Mae
Pitch a Boogie Woogie (1948)
Powell, Bud
Cootie Williams and His Orchestra (1944)
Preer, Evelyn
Birthright (1924), Brown Gravy (1929), The
Brute (1920), The Conjure Woman (1926),
Deceit (1921), The Devil's Disciple (1926),
The Dungeon (1922), Framing of the Shrew

(1929), Georgia Rose (1930), The Gunsaulus Mystery (1921), The Homesteader (1918), The Hypocrite (1922), The Lady Fare (1929), Melancholy Dame (1928), Music Hath Harms (1929), My First Love (1921), Oft in the Silly Night (1929), The Spider's Web (1926), The Widow's Bite (1929), Within Our Gates (1920)

Press, Gloria
God's Stepchildren (1938)

Preston, Billy
St. Louis Blues (1958)

Price, Mildred
Are Working Girls Safe (1918), Black and Tan Mix Up (1918), Black Sherlock Holmes (1917), Bully (1918), Busted Romance (1917), Comeback of Barnacle Bill (1918), Dat Blackhand Waitah Man (1917), Devil for a Day (1917), Do the Dead Talk? (1918), Fixing the Faker (1918), Ghosts (1917), Good Luck in Old Clothes (1918), Hypocrites (1917), Janitor (1918), Luck in Old Clothes (1918), Mercy, the Mummy Mumbled (1917), Milk-Fed Hero (1918), Porters (1918), Reckless Rover (1918), Shine Johnson and the Rabbit Foot (1917), Some Baby (1918), Spooks (1917), Spying the Spy (1918), When Cupid Went Wild (1917), When You Are Scared, Run (1918), When You Hit, Hit Hard (1918), Wrong All Around (1917)

Price, Naomi
Harlem Is Heaven (1932), Harlem Rhapsody (1932)

Price, Victor
Come Back (1922)

Prince, Henry
Murder in Swingtime (1937)

Proctor, John
Anna Lucasta (1958)

Proctor, June
Sepia Cinderella (1947)

Proctor, Lyn (Trio)
Miracle in Harlem (1948)

Pryne, Alberta
House-Rent Party (1946)

Pryor, H.L.
Easy Money (1921)

Pumis, W.C.
The Bronze Buckaroo (1938)

Purlow, Carol
What Goes Up (1939)

Purty, Jessie
Wife Hunter (1922)

Purvis, Evelyn
Swing Cats Ball (1943)

Qubeka, Harriet
Magic Garden (1952)

Quick, Thomas
Going to Glory, Come to Jesus (1946)

Quinn, Fred
Colored American Winning His Suit (1916)

Raber, Vivianne
The Black King (1932), Harlem Big Shot (1932)

The Radio Aces
Meetin' Time (1943)

Rae, Charlie Mae
Souls of Sin (1949)

Rahn, Muriel
King for a Day (1934)

Rainey, Pat
Dreamer (1948), Reet-Petite and Gone (1947)

Ramires, Ram
Boy! What a Girl! (1946)

Ramokgopa, Tommy
Magic Garden (1952)

Randall, Lloyd
Romance on the Beat (1945)

Randol, George
The Exile (1931), Green Pastures (1936), That Man Samson (1937)

Randolph, Amanda
Black Network (1936), Comes Midnight (1940), Lying Lips (1939), Swing (1938)

Randolph, Forbes (Singers)
Cotton-Pickin' Days (1934), Kentucky Jubilee Singers #1 (1928), Kentucky Jubilee Singers #2 (1929), Old Black Joe (1931), On a Plantation (1930), The Road Home (1931), Slave Days (1930), The Water Boy (1929), Welcome (1931)

Randolph, Lillian
Am I Guilty? (1940), His Harlem Wife (1944), Life Goes On (1938), Mr. Smith Goes Ghost (1940), One Big Mistake (1940), Pigmeat's Laugh Hepcats (1944), Racket Doctor (1945)

Ransom, Ernie
Murder on Lenox Ave. (1941), Sunday Sinners (1941)

Rathbe, Dorothy
Jim Comes to Jo'Burg (1950)
Rathebe, Dolly
Magic Garden (1952)
Ray, Arthur
Am I Guilty? (1940), The Bronze Venus (1943), The Burden of Race (1921), Double Deal (1939), The Duke Is Tops (1938), Gang Smashers (1938), Lady Luck (1940), Lucky Ghost (1941), Mr. Washington Goes to Town (1940), Murder Rap (1948), Night Club Girl (1944), One Dark Night (1939), Professor Creeps (1941), Racket Doctor (1945), Son of Ingagi (1940), Take My Life (1941), Thirty Years Later (1938), Ties of Blood (1921), Up Jumped the Devil (1941)
Ray, Ellen
Come Back (1922)
Reavis, Teddy
Chocklate Cowboys (1925)
The Red Lily Chorus
Harlem Hot Shots (1945)
Redd, Clarence
The Daughter of the Congo (1930)
Redd, Frances
Midnight Shadow (1939)
Redman, Don (Orchestra)
Don Redman and His Orchestra (1935), I Heard (1932)
Reed, Cora
Injustice (1919), Loyal Hearts (1919)
Reed, Mrs. Crystal
Injustice (1919), Loyal Hearts (1919)
Reed, George
Absent (1928), Green Pastures (1936), Realization of a Negro's Ambition (1916)
Reed, Leonard
Rock 'n' Roll Revue (1955)
Reed, Nat
Swing (1938)
Reese, Charles M.
Girl in Room 20 (1946)
Reeves, McKinley
Mantan Runs for Mayor (1946), Return of Mandy's Husband (1948)
Renard, Ken
Killer Diller (1948), Mistaken Identity (1941), Murder with Music (1941), Sugar Hill Baby (1932)
Reynolds, George
Lying Lips (1939)

Reynolds, Steve "Peg"
Black Gold (1928), The Bull-Dogger (1923), The Crimson Skull (1921), The Flying Ace (1926), Regeneration (1923)
Rhodes, Dotty
It Happened in Harlem (1945), Romance on the Beat (1945)
Rhuebottom, Doris
Smash Your Baggage (1932)
The Rhythm Pals
Murder in Swingtime (1937)
Rhythm Rascals Orchestra
Girl from Chicago (1932)
Rice, Versia
As the World Rolls On (1921)
Richards, Ruby
Fuzzy Wuzzy (1942)
Richardson, Daisy
Jivin' in Be-Bop (1946)
Richardson, Emory
Beware! (1946), Boarding House Blues (1948), Sepia Cinderella (1947), Souls of Sin (1949)
Richardson, Jack
Free and Equal (1925)
Richardson, Walter
Moon Over Harlem (1939)
Richmond, June
Baby Don't You Love Me Any More? (1945), The Dreamer (1948), Ebony Parade (1947), Forty-Seventh Street Jive (1944), Hey Lawdy Mama (1944), Joseph 'n' His Brudders (1945), Mr. Jackson from Jacksonville (1945), Murder in Swingtime (1937), My Bottle Is Dry (1946), Reet-Petite and Gone (1947), Ride On, Ride On (1944), Time Takes Care of Everything (1946), Who Dunit to Who (1946)
Ridley, Ethel
Troubles of Sambo and Dinah (1914)
Riley, Juanita
The Blood of Jesus (1941)
Rio, Rita (All-Girl Band)
Sticks and Stones (1943), Sweet Shoe (1947)
Ritchie, Louise
Look-Out Sister (1948)
Rivers, Moke Fletcher
Cabin in the Sky (1943)
Robbins, James
Bad Boy (1939)
Roberts, Beverly
Do I Worry? (1941)

Roberts, Elyce
Rockin' the Blues (1955)
Roberts, Henry
Gang War (1939)
Roberts, Shepard
Hi-De-Ho (1947)
The Roberts Brothers
Swing and Swing (1943)
Robertson, Edward
His Harlem Wife (1944), Life Goes On (1940)
Robertson, R.L.
The Blood of Jesus (1941)
Robeson, Eslanda
Big Fella (1938), Borderline (1929)
Robeson, Paul
Africa Speaks (1930), Big Fella (1938), Body and Soul (1924), Borderline (1929), Easy to Get (1943), Emperor Jones (1933), Jericho (1937), My Song Goes Forth (1947), Sanders of the River (1935), The Song of Freedom (1938), We've Come a Long, Long Way (1944)
Robinson, Bill "Bojangles"
By an Old Southern River (1942), Harlem Is Heaven (1932), Harlem Rhapsody (1932), Hello Bill (1929), Hot Frogs (1942), King for a Day (1934), Let's Shuffle (1942), The Negro in Entertainment (1950), Stormy Weather (1943), We've Come a Long, Long Way (1943)
Robinson, Frankie "Sugar Chile"
All American News Reel (1945), Sugar Chile Robinson (1947), Sugar Chile Robinson (1950)
Robinson, Freddie
Boarding House Blues (1948), Killer Diller (1948), Moon Over Harlem (1939)
Robinson, Jackie
Jackie Robinson Story (1950)
Robinson, James
Tenderfeet (1928)
Robinson, Louise
Murder in Swingtime (1937)
Robinson, Madame
The Daughter of the Congo (1930), Thirty Years Later (1928)
Robinson, Ollie Ann
Midnight Shadow (1939)
Robinson, Orlando
Barbershop Blues (1937), Claude Hopkins and His Orchestra (1933)

Robinson, Sam
Are Working Girls Safe (1918), Black and Tan Mix Up (1918), Black Sherlock Holmes (1917), Bully (1918), Busted Romance (1917), Comeback of Barnacle Bill (1918), Dat Blackhand Waitah Man (1917), Devil for a Day (1917), Do the Dead Talk? (1918), Fixing the Faker (1918), Ghosts (1917), Good Luck in Old Clothes (1918), Hypocrites (1917), Janitor (1918), Luck in Old Clothes (1918), Mercy, the Mummy Mumbled (1917), Milk-Fed Hero (1918), Porters (1918), Reckless Rover (1918), Shine Johnson and the Rabbit Foot (1917), Some Baby (1918), Spooks (1917), Spying the Spy (1918), When Cupid Went Wild (1917), When You Are Scared, Run (1918), When You Hit, Hit Hard (1918), Wrong All Around (1917)
Robinson, Walter
Son of Satan (1924)
Robinson, Willard
Syncopated Sermon (1930)
Robinson and Hill
Contrast in Rhythm (1945)
Rocco, Maurice
Beat Me Daddy (1943), Rhumboogie (1943), Rocco Blues (1943), Rocco Blues (1947), Rock It for Me (1943)
Rodgers, Gene
Big Fat Butterfly (1944), Juke Box Boogie (1944), My Ain't That Somethin' (1944)
Rodriquez, Asenio
Black Thunderbolt (1921)
Rogers, Hilda
Everyday Is Saturday in Harlem (1944), I Can't Give You Anything But Love (1944), Rhapsody of Love (1944), Temptation (1936).
Rogers, Leonard
Hi-De-Ho (1947)
Rogers, Marshall
Spider's Web (1926)
Rogers, Timmy
G.I. Jubilee, George Dewey Washington (1942)
Ronnell and Edna
Love in Syncopation (1946)
Roseborough, David
Haunted House (1915), It Happened on Wash Day (1915), New Way to Win (1915), Rakoon Hose Company (1913)

Rosemond, Clinton
Dark Manhattan (1937), Green Pastures (1936), Midnight Shadow (1939), The Story of Dr. George Washington Carver (1935), The Story of Dr. Carver (1939), That Man Samson (1937)

Rosette, Belle
Quarry Road (1943), Willie Willie (1943)

Ross, Clinton
Ten Thousand Dollar Trail ($10,000 Trail) (1921)

Ross, Shelly
Dirty Gertie from Harlem, U.S.A.(1946)

Roth, Murray
Yamekraw (1930)

Rout, Maria
Burlesque in Harlem (1955)

Rowland, Nine
Ten Thousand Dollar Trail ($10,000 Trail) (1921)

Roy, Harry (Orchestra)
Harlemesque Revue (1943)

Rucker, Clarence
Regeneration (1923)

Ruffin, James D.
Within Our Gates (1919)

Rushing, Jimmy
Sound of Jazz (1957), Take Me Back, Baby (1941)

Russell, Alice B
The Betrayal (1948), Broken Violin (1926), The Daughter of the Congo (1930), Easy Street (1930), Girl from Chicago (1932), God's Stepchildren (1938), Lem Hawkins' Confession (1935), Murder in Harlem (1935), Ten Minutes to Live (1932), Wages of Sin (1928), When Men Betray (1929)

Russell, Julia Theresa
Boarding House Blues (1948)

Russell, Nipsey
Basin Street Revue (1955), Jazz Festival (1955), Rhythm and Blues Revue (1956), Rock 'n' Roll Revue (1955)

Russell, Sam
His Great Chance (1923)

Rutledge and Taylor
The Lady Fare (1929)

R'Wanda, Princess
Harlem Follies (1950)

Sahji
Jivin' in Be-Bop (1946)

San, Wahneta
Murder on Lenox Ave. (1941)

Sanders, Barbara Ann
Bright Road (1953)

Sandfier, F.
Deceit (1921)

Sanford, Rusti
Swing Cats Ball (1943)

Santos, Emily
Murder on Lenox Ave.

Sarr, Mamamou
Afrique sur Seine (1955)

Saulter, Dotty
I Was Here When You Left Me (1945), Underworld (1937), Walking with My Honey (1945)

Saunders, Gertrude
Big Timers (1945), The Joint Is Jumping (1948)

Saunders, W.H.
Man's Duty (1919)

Savage, Archie
Carnival of Rhythm (1944), Jammin' the Blues (1944)

Savannah Club Chorus
Harlem Follies (1950)

The Savoy Lindy-Hoppers
Policy Man (1938)

Sawyer, Ruth
Carib Gold (1956)

Sayles, Olive
Burlesque in Harlem (1955)

Schooler, Lewis
Deceit (1921)

Scott, Bob
Look-Out Sister (1948)

Scott, Cecil (Orchestra)
Contrast in Rhythm (1945), Don't Be Late (1945), I'm Making Believe (1945), Mr. X Blues (1945)

Scott, Dorothy
Girl in Room 20 (1946)

Scott, Fred
Reformation (1919)

Scott, Henry
Anna Lucasta (1958)

Scott, Luke
Father Said He'd Fix It (1915), Rakoon Hose Company (1913), Tale of a Chicken (1914), Undertaker's Daughter (1915)

Scott, Mabel
Gee (1944), Steak and Potatoes (1944), Yankee Doodle Never Went to Town (1944)

Scott and Whaley
Life Is Real (1935), Minstrel Days (1930), Swanee Showboat (1945)

Scotty and Harris
Two of a Kind (1955)

Seager, Mrs. James
Injustice (1919), Loyal Hearts (1919)

Seagures, Elinor
Comes Midnight (1940)

Seamans, Dorothy
Look-Out Sister! (1948)

Selby, J.G.
Wife Hunter (1922)

The Sepia Steppers
Chatter (1943), Poppin' the Cork (1943), Stepping Along (1943), Sweet Kisses (1943), Toot That Trumpet (1943)

Sewall, Alma
Birthright (1924)

The Sewanee Sweethearts
Jivin' the Blues (1946)

Seymour, Larry
Swing (1938), Underworld (1937)

Shackeford, Floyd
Absent (1928)

The Shadrach Boys
Jonah and the Whale (1944), Lazy River (1944)

Shaklett, Gwendolyn
Burlesque in Harlem (1955)

Shannon, Alex K.
Easy Money (1921), The Simp (1921)

Shaw, Freida (Choir)
The Broken Earth (1939)

Sheffield, Maceo B.
Double Deal (1939), Gang War (1939), Harlem on the Prairie (1938), Lady Luck (1940), Look-Out Sister (1948), Lucky Ghost (1941), Mr. Washington Goes to Town (1940), Prison Bait (1944), Professor Creeps (1941), Reform School (1939), Up Jumped the Devil (1941)

Shepard, Billy
Crimson Fog (1932)

Shepard, Norma
Harlem Follies of 1949 (1950)

Sherman, Kathryn
Flaming Crisis (1924)

Shockley, Milton
Bargain with Bullets (1937), Gangsters on the Loose (1944)

Shore, Byron
Lem Hawkins' Confession (1935), Murder in Harlem (1935)

Simmon, Bobby
Night Club Girl (1944), One Dark Night (1939), Prison Bait (1944), Reform School (1939)

Simmons, John
Jammin' the Blues (1944)

Simmons, Maude
Junction 88 (1947)

Simms, Hilda
Joe Louis Story (1953)

Simms, Margaret
Yamekraw (1930)

Simpson, Napolean
Am I Guilty? (1940), Racket Doctor (1945)

Simpson, Ronald
The Song of Freedom (1938)

Simpson, Walter
As the World Rolls On (1921)

Singleton, Zutie
Stormy Weather (1943)

Sissle, Noble
Bob Howard's House Party (1947), Chocolate Dandies (1924), Everybody's Jumpin' Now (1942), Joe, Joe (1946), Junction 88 (1947), Murder with Music (1941), Noble Sissle and Eubie Blake (1927), Sissle and Blake (1923), Sissle and Blake (1930), Sizzle with Sissle (1946), Snappy Tunes (1923), That's the Spirit (1933)

Six Cheerful Steppers
Shake It Up (1929)

The Six Knobs
Block Party Revels (1943), Dispossessed Blues (1943)

Skeets, Bonnie
Comes Midnight (1940)

Skekeeter, Evon
Are Working Girls Safe (1918), Black and Tan Mix Up (1918), Black Sherlock Holmes (1917), Bully (1918), Busted Romance (1917), Comeback of Barnacle Bill (1918), Dat Blackhand Waitah Man (1917), Devil

for a Day (1917), Do the Dead Talk? (1918), Fixing the Faker (1918), Ghosts (1917), Good Luck in Old Clothes (1918), Hypocrites (1917), Janitor (1918), Luck in Old Clothes (1918), Mercy, the Mummy Mumbled (1917), Milk-Fed Hero (1918), Porters (1918), Reckless Rover (1918), Shine Johnson and the Rabbit Foot (1917), Some Baby (1918), Spooks (1917), Spying the Spy (1918), When Cupid Went Wild (1917), When You Are Scared, Run (1918), When You Hit, Hit Hard (1918), Wrong All Around (1917)

Skinner, Herbert
The Lady Fare (1929), Murder Rap (1948), Night Club Girl (1944), One Dark Night (1939), Take My Life (1941)

Skipper, Bill
Watch Out! (1946)

Skylight
Big Timers (1945)

The Slam Stewart Trio
Boy! What a Girl! (1946), Harlem Follies of 1949 (1950)

Slap and Happy
Rug Cutters Holiday (1943)

Slappey, Florian
Music Hath Harms (1929)

Slater, Bob
Square Joe (1922)

Slater, Mark
His Great Chance (1923)

Slatten, Edna
Straight to Heaven (1939)

Slick and Slack
It Happened in Harlem (1945), The Joint Is Jumping (1948)

Slim, A.K.
Night Club Girl (1944), One Dark Night (1939)

Slim and Sweets
Tap Happy (1943)

Slim Sham
Dancemania (1943)

Slip and Slide
Burlesque in Harlem (1955)

Small's Paradise Entertainers
Smash Your Baggage (1932)

Smallwood, Mildred
Ghost of Tolston's Manor (1934), Son of Satan (1924)

Smart, Bobby
The Devil's Mark (1923), His Great Chance (1923), A Shot in the Night (1922)

Smith, Albert
Juke Joint (1947)

Smith, Alma
Harlem Is Heaven (1932), Harlem Rhapsody (1932)

Smith, Bessie
St. Louis Blues (1929)

Smith, Byron
Why Worry? (1923)

Smith, Corrine
How High Is Up (1923)

Smith, Effie
Night Club Girl (1944), One Dark Night (1939)

Smith, Elwood
Boy! What a Girl! (1946), The Fight Never Ends (1947)

Smith, Ethel
Broken Violin (1926), A Prince of His Race (1926), Smiling Hate (1924), Ten Minutes to Live (1932), Ten Nights in a Bar-Room (1926), Wages of Sin (1928), When Men Betray (1929)

Smith, Grace
Girl from Chicago (1932), Millionaire (1927)

Smith, Henry
Ten Thousand Dollar Trail ($10,000 Trail) (1921)

Smith, Inez
Homesteader (1918)

Smith, J. Agustus
Boarding House Blues (1948), Drums o' Voodoo (1933), Hi-De-Ho (1947), Junction 88 (1947), Killer Diller (1947), Louisiana (1934), Lucky Gamblers (1946), Murder on Lenox Ave. (1941), Sunday Sinners (1941)

Smith, Jeli
Harlem Is Heaven (1932), Harlem Rhapsody (1932)

Smith, Jewel
Spirit of Youth (1937)

Smith, Jimmie
Trooper of Troop K (1916)

Smith, Jules
Straight to Heaven (1939)

Smith, Katherine
Slow Poke (1932)

Smith, L.K.
Marching On! (1943), Where's My Man To-nite? (1944)

Smith, Mamie
Because I Love You (1942), Jailhouse Blues (1934), Murder on Lenox Ave. (1941), Paradise in Harlem (1940), Sunday Sinners (1940)

Smith, Merritt
Paradise in Harlem (1940)

Smith, Minnie
Colored American Winning His Suit (1916)

Smith, Ollie E.
Children of Circumstance (1937)

Smith, Pete
Midnight Ace (1928)

Smith, Ray
Oop Boop Sh'Bam (1947)

Smith, Russell
Blues in the Night (1942), Minnie the Moocher (1942), Skunk Song (1942), Virginia, Georgia and Caroline (1942)

Smith, Speedy
Sam and the Bully (1914)

Smith, Trixie
The Black King (1932), God's Stepchildren (1938), Harlem Big Shot (1932), Swing (1938)

Smith, Veronica
Injustice (1919), Loyal Hearts (1919)

Smith, Vivian
Hearts of Dixie (1929)

Smith, Wilbert
Let My People Live (1938)

Smith, William
Prince of His Race (1926), Within Our Gates (1919)

Smythe, Grace
Spider's Web (1926)

Smythe, Vanita
Back Door Man (1946), Does You Do, or Does You Don't (1946), Ebony Parade (1947), Get It Off Your Mind (1946), I Need a Playmate (1946), Low, Short and Squatty (1946), Reet-Petite and Gone (1947), Sho Had a Wonderful Time (1946), They Raided the Joint (1946)

Snap and Snappy
Rug Cutters Holiday (1943)

Snead, Mrs. E.
Colored American Winning His Suit (1916)

Snead, Edgar
Colored American Winning His Suit (1916)

Snead, Florence
Colored American Winning His Suit (1916)

Sneed, Ray
Jivin' in Be-Bop (1946)

Snelson, Gertrude
Broken Violin (1926), The Daughter of the Congo (1930), Thirty Years Later (1928), The Wages of Sin (1928), When Men Betray (1929)

Snow, Valaida
If You Only Knew (1946), Patience and Fortitude (1946)

Snyder, Gladys
Crooked Money (1945), Gang War (1939), Gridiron Graft (1940), While Thousands Cheer (1940)

South, Eddie
The Joint Is Jumping (1948), Stars on Parade (1946)

Southern, Tommy
Double Deal (1939), Harlem Rides the Range (1939), Look-Out Sister (1948), Mystery in Swing (1940), Spirit of Youth (1937), Two-Gun Man from Harlem (1938)

The Southernaires
Bubbling Over (1934)

Spears, Basil
Boy! What a Girl! (1946), Harlem Follies of 1949 (1950)

Spencer, Kenneth
Cabin in the Sky (1943), Rhythm of Africa (1947)

The Spirits of Rhythm
Yes! Indeed (1941)

Spivey, Victoria
Hallelujah (1929)

Sprage, Milton
George Washington Carver (1940)

Sprawl, Zenia
Music Hath Harms (1929)

Stanton, Myra
The Betrayal (1948)

Stapler, Maurice
Injustice (1919), Loyal Heart (1919)

Starks, Will
Are Working Girls Safe (1918), Black and

Tan Mix Up (1918), Black Sherlock Holmes (1917), Bully (1918), Busted Romance (1917), Comeback of Barnacle Bill (1918), Dat Blackhand Waitah Man (1917), Devil for a Day (1917), Do the Dead Talk? (1918), Fixing the Faker (1918), Ghosts (1917), Good Luck in Old Clothes (1918), Hypocrites (1917), Janitor (1918), Luck in Old Clothes (1918), Mercy, the Mummy Mumbled (1917), Milk-Fed Hero (1918), Porters (1918), Reckless Rover (1918), Shine Johnson and the Rabbit Foot (1917), Some Baby (1918), Spooks (1917), Spying the Spy (1918), When Cupid Went Wild (1917), When You Are Scared, Run (1918), When You Hit, Hit Hard (1918), Wrong All Around (1917)

Steele, Geraldine
Reformation (1919)

Steptoe, Zoreta
Mr. Washington Goes to Town (1940)

Stevens, James
Call of His People (1921)

Stevens, V.
Wife Hunter (1922)

The Stevens Sisters
The Broken Earth (1939)

Stewart, Dink
Ghost of Tolston's Manor (1934)

Stewart, Lawrence
That Man Samson (1937)

Stewart, Nicodemus
Cabin in the Sky (1943), Dark Manhattan (1937), Stormy Weather (1943)

Stewart, Robert
Love Bug (1920)

Stockton, Sadie
Quiet One (1958)

Stoderling, Walter
Story of Dr. George Washington Carver (1935)

Stokes, Al
Green Pastures (1936)

Strange, Mary
Injustice (1919), Loyal Hearts (1919)

Stuart, Julia
Injustice (1919), Loyal Hearts (1919)

Stump and Stumpy
Boarding House Blues (1948)

Sublette, John (Bubbles)
Black Cat Tales (1933), Black Narcissus (1929), Buck and Bubbles Laff Jamboree (1945), Cabin in the Sky (1943), Dark-Town Follies (1929), Darktown Blues (1929), Fowl Play (1929), Harlem Bound (1935), High Toned (1930), Honest Crooks (1930), In and Out (1935), Mantan Messes Up (1946), Night in a Night Club (1937)

Sullivan, Maxine
Case o' the Blues (1942), Some of These Days (1942)

Sul-Te-Wan, Madam
Life of Florence Mills (1940), Uncle Tom's Cabin (1927)

Summer, Minnie
Square Joe (1922)

Sun Ra Orchestra
Cry of Jazz (1958)

The Sun Tan Four
Boogiemania (1946), Cootie Williams and His Orchestra (1944), Harlem Hotcha (1946), The Pollard Jump (1946), Swanee Showboat (1945)

The Sunkissed Brownskin Chorus
Sunday Sinners (1941)

Sutton, George T.
Girl in Room 20 (1946), Marching On! (1943), Where's My Man To-Nite? (1944)

Sutton, Susie
The Brute (1920), Comes Midnight (1940), Midnight Ace (1928)

Swain, Charles
Anna Lucasta (1958)

The Swanee Swingsters
Swanee Showboat (1945)

Swarz, Lou Sealia
Big Timers (1945), House-Rent Party (1946), Tall, Tan and Terrific (1946)

The Swing Maniacs
Jumpin' at the Jubilee (1944)

The Swing Stars
Old Dan Tucker (1946)

Sydnor, Earl
Murder on Lenox Ave. (1941), Sunday Sinners (1941)

Szony, Giselle
Mr. Black Magic (1956)

Tait, Walter
Hallelujah (1929)

Talley, Josephine
Smiling Hate (1924)
Tamariya, Hechla
Abyssinia (1931)
Tanner, Frank
Girl in Room 20 (1946)
Taps and Wilda
Chicago After Dark (1946), Love in Syncopation (1946)
Tarleton, Dr. W.A.
Injustice (1919), Loyal Hearts (1919)
Tarzana
Big Timers (1945)
Tatum, Art
Upbeat in Music (1943)
Tatum, E.G.
Birthright (1924), Body and Soul (1924), Custard Nine (1921), The Gunsaulus Mystery (1921), The Millionaire (1927), Son of Satan (1924), Symbol of the Unconquered (1920), Within Our Gates (1920)
Tatums, L.B.
Black Gold (1928)
Taylor, Al (Orchestra)
Policy Man (1938)
Taylor, Betty (Taylorettes)
Burlesque in Harlem (1955)
Taylor, Don
Hair Raid (1948)
Taylor, George R.
Swing (1938)
Taylor, Johnny
The Bronze Venus (1943), The Duke Is Tops (1943), Good-Nite All (1943), Jivin' Be Bop (1946), Mr. Smith Goes Ghost (1940), Mr. Washington Goes to Town (1940), One Big Mistake (1940), Pigmeat's Laugh Hepcats (1944)
Taylor, Roberto
Lure of a Woman (1921)
Taylor, Ruby
Fall of the Mighty (1913)
Taylor, Vivian Thompson
Loyalty of a Race (1918)
Taylor and Burley
Jivin' in Be-Bop (1946), Oop Boop Sh'Bam (1947)
Taylor and Harris
Caldonia (1945)
Teal, Joel
Ten Thousand Dollar Trail ($10,000 Trail) (1921)

Telbird, Audrey
Moon Over Harlem (1939)
Temple, Vera
Crimson Fog (1932)
Terry, Griffen Trixie
Burlesque in Harlem (1955)
Tharpe, Sister Rosetta
Four or Five Times (1941), Lonesome Road (1941), Shout! Sister, Shout! (1941)
Thomas, Dorothy
Going to Glory, Come to Jesus (1946)
Thomas, Joe Joe
Paradise in Harlem (1940)
Thomas, John
Condemned Men (1948), Four Shall Die (1940), Harlem Rides the Range (1939), Night Club Girl (1944), One Dark Night (1939)
Thomas, Norman
Harlem Mania (1929), Norman Thomas Quintette, Harlem Mania (1929)
Thomas, Peggy
Look-Out Sister (1948)
Thomas, Reed
As the World Rolls On (1921)
Thomas, Regina
Siren of the Tropics (1927)
Thomas, Slim
Green Pastures (1936), Jive Comes to the Jungle (1942), Legs Ain't No Good (1942), Lying Lips (1939), Moon Over Harlem (1939)
Thomas, Walter
Blues in the Night (1942), Minnie the Moocher (1942), Skunk Song (1942), Sport of the Gods (1921), Virginia, Georgia and Caroline (1942)
Thompson, Anita
By Right of Birth (1921), A Man's Duty (1919), Zircon (1923)
Thompson, Blanche
As the World Rolls On (1921), The Dungeon (1922), The Ghost of Tolston's Manor (1934)
Thompson, Charles
God's Stepchildren (1938)
Thompson, Chuck
Gone Harlem (1939)
Thompson, Creighton
Miracle in Harlem (1948)
Thompson, Donald
Quiet One (1958)

Thompson, Edward
Am I Guilty? (1940), Bargain with Bullets (1937), Broken Strings (1940), The Bronze Venus (1943), Brown Gravy (1929), Condemned Men (1948), Devil's Disciple (1926), Double Deal (1939), The Duke Is Tops (1938), Four Shall Die (1940), Framing of the Shrew (1939), Gang Smashers (1938), Gangsters on the Loose (1944), Georgia Rose (1930), His Harlem Wife (1944), The Lady Fare (1929), Lady Luck (1940), Life Goes On (1938), Lucky Ghost (1941), Melancholy Dame (1929), Music Hath Harms (1929), Mystery in Swing (1940), Oft in the Silly Night (1929), Prison Bait (1944), Reform School (1939), The Spider's Web (1926), While Thousands Cheer (1940), Widow's Bite (1929)

Thompson, Tommy
Jumpin' Jack from Hackensack (1943)

Thompson, Viola
Man of the Worlds (1946)

Thompson, Walker
Scapegoat (1920), Symbol of the Unconquered (1920)

Thornton, Cherokee
Girl from Chicago (1932), Lying Lips (1939)

Thornton, Fannie
Burlesque in Harlem (1955)

Thornton, Jack
Scapegoat (1920)

Thornton, Josephine
Scapegoat (1920)

The Three Brown Jacks
Jimmie Lunceford and His Dance Orchestra (1936)

The Three Businessmen of Rhythm
Basin Street Revue (1955)

The Three Chefs
Breakfast in Rhythm (1943), Pardon Me, But You Look Like Margie (1943)

The Three Peppers
Ain't She Pretty (1944), Mama Had a Little Lamb (1944), Rhythm Sam (1946), Straight to Heaven (1939), Take Everything (1945)

The Three Slate Brothers
Little Jive Is Good for You (1941)

The Three Sun Tan Girls
Caldonia (1945)

Tillman, Harrel
Fight Never Ends (1947), Love in Syncopation (1946), That Man of Mine (1947)

Tilton, Liz
Ah, Yes There's Good Blues Tonight (1946)

Tilton, Martha
Little Jive Is Good for You (1941)

Timblin, Slim
Revival Day (1929)

Tip, Tap and Toe
Claude Hopkins and His Orchestra (1935), By Request (1935)

Tisdale, Clarence
Clarence Tisdale (1929), Old Time Songs (1928)

Tolbert, Skeets (Orchestra)
Blitzkrieg Bombardier (1944), Corn Pone (1945), No, No, Baby (1945), Tis You, Babe (1945)

The Tolliver Brothers
Shot in the Night (1922)

Tomelty, Joseph
Simba (1955)

Tondelayo-Brillianis
Sepia Cinderella (1947)

Toombs, Rudolph
House-Rent Party (1946), Reet-Petite and Gone (1947), Tall, Tan and Terrific (1946)

Torrance, Lena
While Thousands Cheer (1940)

Toto, Ecce Homo
The Song of Freedom (1938)

Townsend, Babe
Phantom of Kenwood (1933)

Townsend, Edward
Wife Hunters (1922)

Tracy, Harry
Music Hath Harms (1929)

Treadville, Betty
Night Club Girl (1944), One Dark Night (1939)

The Tree Whippits
Dixieland Jamboree (1935)

The Treniers
Sarah Vaughn and Herb Jeffries, Kid Ory (1950)

Trible, Andrew
Darktown Revue (1931)

Truate, A.B.
Day in the Nation's Capital (1918)

Tucker, Earl "Snakehips"
Symphony in Black (1935)
Tucker, Lorenzo
The Black King (1932), The Daughter of the Congo (1930), Easy Street (1930), Harlem After Midnight (1934), Harlem Big Shot (1936), One Round Jones (1946), Reet-Petite and Gone (1947), Sepia Cinderella (1946), Straight to Heaven (1939), Temptation (1936), Ten Minutes to Live (1932), Underworld (1937), Veiled Aristocrats (1927), Wages of Sin (1928), When Men Betray (1929), Witching Eyes (1930)
Tullos, Lavilla
Swanee Swing (1944)
Turham, Frances
Bargain with Bullets (1937), Gangsters on the Loose (1944)
Turner, Harry
Harlem Hotcha (1946)
Turner, Joe
Boogie Woogie (1944), Low Down Dog (1944), Rhythm and Blues Revue (1955), Rock and Roll Revue (1955), Roll 'Em (1944), Stars Over Harlem (1956)
Turner, Mae
Am I Guilty? (1940), One Dark Night (1939), Racket Doctor (1945), Spirit of Youth (1937), Tow-Gun Man from Harlem (1938)
Turner, Walter Scott, Jr.
Loyalty of a Race (1918)
Tutt, J. Homer
Birthright (1924), Broken Violin (1926)
The Tyler Twins
God's Stepchildren (1938), Swing (1938)
Tynes, Gwendolyn
Fight Never Ends (1947)
Tyson, Cecily
Carib Gold (1956)
The Utica Jubilee Singers
Utica Jubilee Singers (1930)
The V's
Big Fat Butterfly (1944), Juke Box Boogie (1944)
Van, Gus
Macnamara's Band (1941)
Van Cleve, Virgil
Put Your Arms Around Me, Honey (1943)
Van Derzee, Stella
Going to Glory, Come to Jesus (1946)

Van Engle, Dorothy
Harlem After Midnight (1934), Lem Hawkins' Confession (1935), Murder in Harlem (1935), Swing (1938)
The Varietiettes Dancing Girls
Killer Diller (1948)
Vaughn, Sarah
Basin Street Revue (1955), Beale Street Revue (1955), Harlem Jazz Festival (1955), Rhythm and Blues Revue (1955), Sarah Vaughn and Herb Jeffries, Kid Ory (1950)
Vernon, Lou
The Betrayal (1948), The Exile (1931)
Verwayen, Percy
Body and Soul (1924), The Burden of Race (1921), The Call of His People (1922), Conjure Woman (1926), The Daughter of the Congo (1930), Easy Money (1921), Fight That Ghost (1946), Hello Bill (1929), Paradise in Harlem (1940), Romance on the Beat (1945), Secret Sorrow (1922), Sepia Cinderella (1947), Straight to Heaven (1939), Sunday Sinners (1941)
Verwayen, Ruby
Sepia Cinderella (1947)
Vic, Ace and Danny
Smash Your Baggage (1932)
Vieyra, Paulin Soumanou
Afrique sur Seine (1955)
Vincent, Bernice
Straight to Heaven (1939)
Vodery, Will (Girls)
Rufus Jones for President (1933)
The Wagenia Tribe Chief
Sanders of the River (1935)
Walcott, Joe
Haynes Newsreel No. 1 (1914), Haynes Newsreel No. 3 (1917)
Walker, Bill
Harlem Globetrotters (1951), No Time for Romance (1948), Sun Tan Ranch (1948)
Walker, Hughie
Rockin' the Blues (1955)
Walker, Jimmy
Midnight Menace (1946)
Walker, Ruth
For His Mother's Sake (1922)
Wallace, Coley
Carib Gold (1956), Joe Louis Story (1953)
Wallace, Emett "Babe"

Black Network (1936), Devil's Daughter (1939), Fight Never Ends (1947), G.I. Jubilee (1942), Rhythm in a Riff (1946), Smash Your Baggage (1933), Stormy Weather (1943)

Waller, Fred (Fats)
Ain't Misbehavin' (1945), Green Pastures (1938), Honeysuckle Rose (1941), Hot Frogs (1942), Joint Is Jumpin' (1941), Negro in Entertainment (1950), Stormy Weather (1943), Waller Medley (1946), Your Feet's Too Big (1941)

Waller, George
Cry of Jazz (1958)

Walpole, Stanley
Sport of the Gods (1921)

Walter, Ella Mae
Swing It Harlem (1941)

Walter, Jessie
Souls of Sin (1949)

Walton, J.T.
Wife Hunter (1922)

The Wanderers
Rockin' the Blues (1955)

Waples, Patrina
Moon Over Harlem (1939)

Ward, Norman
Modern Cain (1921)

Ware, Gene
Mr. Atom's Bomb (1949)

Ware, Toto
Sanders of the River (1935)

Wash and Wimpy
Marching On! (1943), Where's My Man To-Nite? (1944)

The Washboard Serenaders
A Bird's Eye View of Harlem (1929), Black Network (1936), That's the Spirit (1932)

Washington, Booker T.
George Washington Carver (1940), Leader of His Race (1922)

Washington, Charles
Go Down, Death! (1944)

Washington, Dinah
Basin Street Revue (1955), Downbeat Revue (1955), Harlem Jazz Festival (1955), Jazz Festival (1955), Revue in Rhythm (1955), Rock 'n' Roll Revue (1955)

Washington, Flora
Tenderfeet (1928)

Washington, Ford Lee (Buck)
Black Cat Tales (1933), Black Narcissus (1929), Buck and Bubbles Laff Jamboree (1945), Cabin in the Sky (1943), Darktown Blues (1929), Dark Town Follies (1930), Fowl Play (1929), Harlem Bound (1935), High Toned (1930), Honest Crooks (1930), In and Out (1935), Mantan Messes Up (1946), Night in a Night Club (1937)

Washington, Fred C. (Orchestra)
Georgia Rose (1930)

Washington, Fredi
Black and Tan (1929), Emperor Jones (1933), Hi-De-Ho (1947), Imitation of Life (1934), Mills' Blue Rhythm Band (1933)

Washington, Fredrica
Square Joe (1922)

Washington, George
St. Louis Blues (1958), Swingin' on Nothin' (1942)

Washington, George Dewey
George Dewey Washington #1 (1928), George Dewey Washington #2 (1929), George Dewey Washington #3 (1929), George Dewey Washington #4 (1929), George Dewey Washington #5 (1930), Ol' King Cotton (1931), Old Man Rhythm (1932), Rhythm on the River (1932)

Washington, Hazel
Imitation of Life (1934)

Washington, Isabel
St. Louis Blues (1929)

Washington, Kenny
Crooked Money (1945), Gridiron Graft (1940), Jackie Robinson Story (1950), While Thousands Cheer (1940)

Washington, Mildred
Dusky Virgin (1932), Hearts of Dixie (1929), Tenderfeet (1928)

Washington, William
The Broken Strings (1940)

Waters, Ella Mae
Notorious Elinor Lee (1940)

Waters, Ethel
Bubbling Over (1934), Cabin in the Sky (1943), Carib Gold (1956), Hot Frogs (1942), The Negro in Entertainment (1950), Pinky (1949), Rufus Jones for President (1933)

Watkins, Cornelious
Deceit (1921)

Watkins, Mary Jane
Black King (1932), Deceit (1921), Harlem Big Shot (1936)

Watson, Deek (Brown Dots)
Boy! What a Girl! (1946), Harlem Follies of 1949 (1950), Sepia Cinderella (1947)

Watson, Earl
Troubles of Sambo and Dinah (1914)

Watson, Ethel
Come Back (1922)

Watson, Hugh
Dirty Gertie from Harlem, U.S.A. (1946)

Watts, Ethel
Gunsaulus Mystery (1921)

Watts, James
Going to Glory, Come to Jesus (1946)

Watts, John
Going to Glory, Come to Jesus (1946)

Wayne, Billy
Jackie Robinson Story (1950)

Weave, Mattie
The Joint Is Jumping (1948)

Weaver, John
Crawl Red Crawl (1946), We Pitched a Boogie Woogie (1946)

Webb, Jean
Hell's Alley (1931)

Webb, Robert
Mystery in Swing (1940), Murder Rap (1948), Take My Life (1941)

Webb, Mrs. Seith
Injustice (1919), Loyal Hearty (1919)

Webster, Pete (Neil)
Broken Strings (1940), Condemned Men (1948), Four Shall Die (1940), Midnight Shadow (1939)

Welch, Elizabeth
Big Fella (1938), The Song of Freedom (1938)

Wells, Dickie
Smash Your Baggage (1932)

Wescort, Marcelle
Straight to Heaven (1939)

Wessels, Henri
Harlem Is Heaven (1932), Harlem Rhapsody (1932), Policy Man (1938)

West, Hank
For His Mother's Sake (1922)

Wharton, Evelyn
Pitch a Boogie Woogie (1948)

Wheeler, Thomas
Colored American Winning His Suit (1916)

Whipper, Leigh
The Negro Sailor (1945), Symbol of the Unconquered (1920)

White, Arthur (Lindy Hoppers)
Hot Chocklate (1941), Jittering Jitterbugs (1943), Sugar Hill Masquerade (1942), Swanee Showboat (1945)

White, Beverly
Killer Diller (1948)

White, Bob
Wife Hunter (1922)

White, Frank
Man's Duty (1919)

White, Lt. Journee
Injustice (1919), Loyal Hearts (1919)

White, Lenore
Straight to Heaven (1939)

White, Loray
Lionel Hampton and Herb Jeffries (1955)

White, Paul
Murder Rap (1948), Take My Life (1941), Walls Keep Talking (1942), Zoot Suit (1942)

White, Talford
Flaming Crisis (1924)

White, Thelma (Girl Orchestra)
Hollywood Boogie (1946), Zoot (1946)

Whitfield, Geraldine
Mr. Washington Goes to Town (1940)

Whiting, Napoleon
Look-Out Sister (1948)

Whiting, Nappie
Lady Luck (1940), Lucky Ghost (1941), Professor Creeps (1941)

Whitman, Ernest
Cabin in the Sky (1943), G.I. Jubilee, George Dewey Washington (1942), Green Pastures (1936), King for a Day (1934), Stormy Weather (1943)

Whitney, Salem Tutt
Birthright (1924), The Daughter of the Congo (1930), Marcus Garland (1928)

Whitten, Margarette
Mr. Washington Goes to Town (1940), Mystery in Swing (1940), Professor Creeps (1941), The Spirit of Youth (1938), Two-Gun Man from Harlem (1939), Way Down South (1939)

Wilburn, Amos
Basin Street Revue (1955)

Wilcox, Izinetta
Moon Over Harlem (1939)

Wilenehech, Clem
Bad Boy (1939)

Wiley, Arnold
Veiled Aristocrats (1932)

Wiley, Stella
Lovie Joe's Romance (1914)

Wilkens, Matty
For His Mother's Sake (1922)

Wilkes, Mattie
Gunsaulus Mystery (1921), Symbol of the Unconquered (1920)

Wilkins, Lester
Gang Smashers (1938), Gun Moll (1944)

Williams, Arthur
The Song of Freedom (1938)

Williams, Augusta
In the Depths of Our Hearts (1920)

Williams, Bert
Darktown Jubilee (1914), Fish (1916), Natural Born Gambler (1916)

Williams, Cootie (Orchestra)
Cootie Williams and His Orchestra (1944)

Williams, Cristola
Murder on Lenox Ave. (1941)

Williams, Duke
Big Timers (1945), Boy! What a Girl! (1946)

Williams, Edward
Spitfire (1922)

Williams, Egbert Austin (Bert)
Darktown Jubilee (1914), Fish (1916), Natural Born Gambler (1916)

Williams, Elizabeth
Burden of Race (1921)

Williams, Frances
Lying Lips (1939)

Williams, Fred
Modern Cain (1921)

Williams, George
Gig and Saddle (1933), Murder on Lenox Ave. (1941), Paradise in Harlem (1940), Scandal (1933), Sepia Cinderella (1947), Sunday Sinners (1941), Ten Minutes to Live (1932)

Williams, Gladys
The Betrayal (1948), Lying Lips (1939), The Notorious Elinor Lee (1940)

Williams, H. Marion
Eleven PM (1928)

Williams, "Hucklebuck" and His Orchestra
Rhythm and Blues Revue (1956)

Williams, Jack
Look-Out Sister (1948)

Williams, Joe
Jamboree (1957)

Williams, John
Melancholy Dame (1929), My New Gown (1944), Unlucky Woman (1944)

Williams, Lawrence & Lillian
Lionel Hampton and Herb Jeffries (1955)

Williams, Leon
One Large Evening (1914), Scapegoat (1920), Sport of the Gods (1921), Uncle Remus' First Visit to New York (1914)

Williams, Milton
Miracle in Harlem (1948), Murder with Music (1941)

Williams, Paul
Basin Street Revue (1955)

Williams, Pinky
Mistaken Identity (1941), Murder with Music (1941)

Williams, Rosetta
Moon Over Harlem (1939)

Williams, Rubber Legs
Smash Your Baggage (1932)

Williams, Ruth
Thirty Years Later (1928)

Williams, Skippy (Band)
Mistaken Identity (1941), Murder with Music (1941)

Williams, Spencer
Bad Boy (1939), Beale Street Mama (1946), Blood of Jesus (1941), The Bronze Buckaroo (1938), Brother Martin Servant of Jesus (1943), Brown Gravy (1929), Dirty Gertie from Harlem, U.S.A. (1946), Framing of the Shrew (1929), Georgia Rose (1930), Girl in Room 20 (1943), Glory Road (1945), Go Down, Death! (1944), Harlem on the Prairie (1938), Harlem Rides the Range (1939), Juke Joint (1947), The Lady Fare (1928), Melancholy Dame (1928), Music Hath Harms (1929), Of One Blood (1944), Oft in the Silly Night (1929), Son of Ingagi (1940), Tenderfeet (1928), Toppers Take a Bow (1941), Two-Gun Man from Harlem (1939), Widow's Bite (1929)

Williams, Theodore
Modern Cain (1921)
Williams, Tim
Harlem on Parade (1940)
Williams, Tunji
Man of the Worlds (1946)
Williams, Virgil
In the Depths of Our Hearts (1920)
Williams, Wilhelmina
The Daughter of the Congo (1930)
Williams, Zack
Hearts of Dixie (1929), The Lady Fare (1929), Murder in Swingtime (1937), Professor Creeps (1941), Son of Ingagi (1940)
Wills, Harry
Harry Wills in Training (1924)
Wilson, Arthur (Dooley)
Keep Punching (1939), Stormy Weather (1943)
Wilson, Don
Dirty Gertie from Harlem, U.S.A. (1946)
Wilson, Edgar
The Barber (1916)
Wilson, Eunice
All-colored Vaudeville Show (1935), Dixieland Jamboree (1935), Lem Hawkins' Confession (1935), Murder in Harlem (1935), No Time for Romance (1948), Sun Tan Ranch (1948)
Wilson, Frank
Beware! (1946), Bubbling Over (1934), Emperor Jones (1933), Girl from Chicago (1932), Green Pastures (1936), Melody Makers Series (1932), Paradise in Harlem (1941), Phantom of Kenwood (1927), Way Down Yonder (1934)
Wilson, Irene
Georgia Rose (1930)
Wilson, Marcellus
Boarding House Blues (1948)
Wilson, Speedy
The Daughter of the Congo (1930)
Wilson, Teddy (Orchestra)
Boogie Woogie Dream (1942), Harlem Hot Shots (1945), Harlem on Parade (1940), My New Gown (1944), Unlucky Woman (1944)
Wiltshire, George
Burlesque in Harlem (1955), Caldonia (1945), Hi-De-Ho (1947), It Happened in

Harlem (1945), Junction 88 (1947), Keep Punching (1939), Killer Diller (1947), Midnight Menace (1946), Straight to Heaven (1939)
Winburn, Anna Mae
Jump Children (1946), She's Crazy with Heat (1946), That Man of Mine (1946)
Witherspoon, Eloise
His Harlem Wife (1944), Life Goes On (1940)
Wolford, Bertha
Negro Soldier (1944)
Woode, Henry (Orchestra)
Adventure (1946), Broadway (1946), Love in Syncopation (1946), That Man of Mine (1947)
Wooding, Russell (Jubilee Singers)
Rufus Jones for President (1933)
Woods, Buck
The Broken Earth (1939), Double Deal (1939), Lady Luck (1940), Lucky Ghost (1941), Midnight Shadow (1939), Mystery in Swing (1940)
Woods, Johnny
Dinty McGinty (1946)
Woods, Milton
Beware! (1946), Big Timers (1945), Boy! What a Girl! (1946), Caldonia (1945), It Happened in Harlem (1945), Reet-Petite and Gone (1947), Tall, Tan and Terrific (1946)
Woods, Pearl
Rockin' the Blues (1955)
Woods, Trevy
Homesteader (1918)
Woodson, J.H.
Secret Sorrow (1921)
Woodward, William
Moon Over Harlem (1939)
Wright, Jimmy
Souls of Sin (1949)
Wright, Lamar
Blues in the Night (1942), Minnie the Moocher (1942), Skunk Song (1942), Virginia, Georgia and Caroline (1942)
Wright, Richard
Native Son (1951)
Yarbo, Lillian
Way Down South (1939)
Yeargan, Arthur
Flaming Crisis (1924)

York, Doris
It Must Be Jelly ... (1946)
Young, Al
Harlem Follies of 1949 (1950), Junction 88 (1947), Sepia Cinderella (1947), Sunday Sinners (1941)
Young, Artie
The Bronze Buckaroo (1938), Harlem Rides the Range (1939)
Young, Fay
Sports Cavalcade (1944)
Young, Jackie
Harlem Is Heaven (1932), Harlem Rhapsody (1932)
Young, Lee
St. Louis Blues (1958)
Young, Lester
Jammin' the Blues (1944)

Young, Mabel
Burden of Race (1921), Deceit (1921), Gunsaulus Mystery (1921), Scapegoat (1920), Spitfire (1922)
Young, Marie
Moon Over Harlem (1939), One Large Evening (1914)
Young, Marty
The Brone Buckaroo (1938), Harlem Rides the Range (1939)
Young, Tarza
Burlesque in Harlem (1955)
Young, Z.V.
Modern Cain (1921)
Ze Zullesttes
Jive Comes to the Jungle (1942)

APPENDIX B:
FILM COMPANIES

Acme Film Distribution Corporation
The Disappearance of Mary Jane (1921),
Harry Wills in Training (1924)

Les Actualités Françaises
Regard sur l'Afrique Noire (1947)

Aetna Films Corporation
Mystery in Swing (1940)

African Films
The Symbol of Sacrifice (1918), A Zulu's
Devotion (1916), Zulutown (1916), Zulu-
town Races (1916),

Afro-American Exhibitors Company
The Human Devil (1921)

Afro-American Film Company
Dandy Jim's Dream (1914), How Skinny
Made Good (1915), Love Me, Love My Dog
(1914), Lovie Joe's Romance (1914), Mandy's
Choice (1914), National Negro Business
League (1913), National Negro Business
League (1914), One Large Evening (1914),
The Tango Queen (1916), With the Help
of Uncle Eben (1915)

Ajax Pictures
Swanee Showboat (1945

Al Bartlett Film Manufacturing Company
The Fall of the Mighty (1913), Slim-the-
Cow-Puncher (1914)

Alexander Korda London Films
Sanders of the River (1935)

Alexander Production
Adventure (1946), Big Fat Mammas (1946),
Broadway (1946), By Line Newsreel (1950),
The Call to Duty (1946), The Fight Never
Ends (1947), Hair Raid (1948), Hello Bill
(1946), The Highest Tradition (1946), I
Cried for You (1946), I Want a Man (1946),
I Want to Talk About You (1946), Jivin' in

Be-Bop (1946), Jump Children (1946),
Lonesome Lover Blues (1946), Mistletoe
(1946), Rhythm in a Riff (1946), She's
Crazy with Heat (1946), Souls of Sin
(1949), That Man of Mine (1946), Two of
a Kind (1955), Vanities (1946), You Call It
Madness (1946)

All American News
All American News Reel (1945), All Amer-
ican News Reel, No. 4 (1945), Ask the OPA
(1945), Big Timers (1945), Boarding House
Blues (1948), Boogie Woogie Blues (1948),
Chicago After Dark (1946), Colored Amer-
ica on Parade (1940), Hi-De-Ho (1947), It
Happened in Harlem (1945), The Joint Is
Jumping (1948), Killer Diller (1948), Lucky
Gamblers (1946), Midnight Menace (1946),
Open the Door, Richard! (1947), Queen of
the Boogie (1947), Romance on the Beat
(1945), Second News Reel (1942), Sports
Calvacade (1944), Stars on Parade (1946),
Sugar Chile Robinson (1947), Toot That
Trumpet (1946)

Ambassador Films
My Song Goes Forth (1947)

Amegro Films
The Blood of Jesus (1941)

American Film Center
As Our Boyhood Is (1947), One Tenth of
Our Nation (1940)

American Missionary Association
Color of a Man (1946)

American Mutoscope / Biograph
Bally-Hoo Cake Walk (1901), A Bucket of
Cream Ale (1904), Cotton Spinning on the
Old Plantation (1904), Dancing Darkies
(1904), Darky Cake Walk (1904), Miss Jew-

ett and the Baker Family of Negroes, a Muffin Lesson (1905), Pickaninny's Dance (1903), Pie Eating Contest (1903), The Porters (1903), Porters' Parade (1903), They're Not Warm (1905), Watermelon Feast (1903), Way Down South (1903)

Anderson-Watkins Film Company
A Day at Tuskegee (1913)

Andlauer Production Company
As the World Rolls On (1921)

Argentina Sono / Classic Pictures / Walter Gould
Native Son (1951)

Argus Pictures
Double Deal (1939), Merrie Howe Carfe (1939)

Aristo Films / Rosebud Productions
Georgia Rose (1930)

Arthur Rank Productions
Simba (1955)

Artisan Productions / Nationl Association of Colored Women
Lifting as We Climb (1953)

Associated Features
Harlem on the Prairie (1938)

Associated Producers of Negro Motion Pictures
Flicker Up (1946), Rhythm in a Riff (1946), Sweethearts of Rhythm (1947), That Man of Mine (1947)

Astor Pictures Corporation
The Betrayal (1948), Beware! (1946), Buzz Me (1945), Caldonia (1945), Caldonia (1945), The Dreamer (1948), Ebony Parade (1947), Honey Chile (1945), Look-Out Sister (1948), Love in Syncopation (1946), Lucky Millinder (1946), Marching On! (1943), O'Voutie O'Rooney (1947), Reet-Petite and Gone (1947), Swingtime Jamboree (1949), Tall, Tan and Terrific (1946), Tillie (1945), Woman's a Fool (1947)

Baby Marie Productions
Sambo Comedies (1919)

Baccus *see* **M. W. Baccus Films Company**

Baker, Mary E.
The House of Mystery (1923)

Ben Roy Productions
The Man from Texas (1921)

Berne, Josef
Band Parade (1943)

Bilmore Film Company
News Reel #1 (1930)

Biograph (*see also American Mutoscope*)
Darktown Jubilee (1914), Everybody Works But Father (Blackface) (1905), Fish (1916), Natural Born Gambler (1916), The Nigger in the Woodpile (1904), The Thirteen Club (1905), The Wooing and Wedding of a Coon (1905), The Zulu's Heart (1910)

Birth of a Race Film Company
Birth of a Race (Lincoln's Dream) (1918)

Black Western Film Company
Shoot 'Em Up, Sam (1922)

Blackburn Velde Productions
For His Mother's Sake (1922)

Blackhawk Films
The St. Louis Blues (1929)

Blue Ribbon Pictures
Toussaint L'Ouverture (1921)

Board of Missions of Presbyterian Church
Rise of a Race (1922)

Bookertee Investment Company
My First Love (1921), The Ten Thousand Dollar Trail ($10,000 Trail) (1921)

Bourgeois-Jenkins Pictures
Brother Martin, Servant of Jesus (1942), Where's My Man To-Night? (1944)

British & French Pictorial Film Service
France's Dusky Warriors (1918)

British Film Company
Callalco (1937)

British Information Service
Mamprusi Village (1944)

British Lion–Hammer Production / Trio Exchange
The Song of Freedom (1938)

Brown-America Studios
Lincoln-Howard Football Game (1934)

Brown Lion-Hammer
Big Fella (1938)

Bryant Productions
George Washington Carver (1940)

Buckingham Films / Max Schach
Jericho (1937)

CAC News
Colored American Cavalcade (1939)

C.B. Campbell Studio
The Negro Today (1921)

Calverton Motion Picture Service
The Spirit of the Hellfighters (1932)

Carlton Moss
Frederick Douglass's the House on Cedar Hill (1953)

Castle Films
Let's Do the Black Bottom (1926)

Celebrity Pictures Cartoon
Little Black Sambo (1933)

Centrals Cinematographique
Siren of the Tropics (1927)

Century Productions
Mistaken Identity (1941), Murder with Music (1941), Bob Howard's House Party (1947)

Charles H. Turpin
Turpin's Real Reels (1916)

Chesterfield Company
The Negro in Entertainment (1950), The Negro in Sports (1950)

Christie Film Company
The Framing of the Shrew (1929), The Lady Fare (1929), Melancholy Dame (1929), Music Hath Harms (1929), Roll Along (1929)

Classic Pictures *see* **Argentina Sono**

Cocteau, Jean, and François Villiers
Rhythm of Africa (1947)

Cohen, Octavus
The Florian Slappey Series (1925)

Colonade Pictures Corporation
Murder on Lenox Ave. (1941), Sunday Sinners (1941)

Colored and Indian Film Company
Clef Club Five Minutes for Train (1918), Love and Undertakers (1918), Prize Drill Team (1919)

Colored Motion Picture Producers
Nine Lives (1926)

Colored Players Film Corporation of Phila.
Children of Fate (1926), A Prince of his Race (1926), The Scar of Shame (1927), Ten Nights in a Bar-Room (1926)

Columbia Pictures
The Harlem Globetrotters (1951), Jailhouse Blues (1934), Jam Session (1944), Jules Bledsoe (1929), On the Levee (1930), Porgy and Bess (1959)

Columbia Victor Gems
Old Man Trouble (1929)

Consolidated Pictures
The Peanut Man (1947)

Continental Pictures, Inc.
The Broken Earth (1939)

Cooper-Randol *see* **Renaldo Films**

Cornblum, Sherman
Frenzy (1946)

Cotton Blossom Film Company
Undisputed Evidence (1922)

Cramerly Picture Corporation
The Vicious Circle (1936)

Creative Cinema Corporation
Gone Harlem (1939), Harlem Mania (1938), Policy Man (1938), St. Louis Gal (1938), Sugar Hill Baby (1937)

Crusader Film Company
Tuskegee Finds a Way Out (1923)

Cyclone Pictures
A Chocolate Cowboy (1925)

D.W.D. Film Corporation
A Child in Pawn (1921)

Deforest Phonofilm
A Night in Dixie (1926)

Democracy Photoplay Corporation
Democracy, or a Fight for Right (1919), Injustice *see* Loyal Hearts, Loyal Hearts (Injustice) (1919), A Minister's Temptation (1919), Reformation (1919), Upward Path (1919)

Dixie National Pictures, Inc.
Lady Luck *see* Lucky Ghost, Lucky Ghost (Lady Luck) (1940), Mr. Washington Goes to Town (1940), Professor Creeps (1941), Up Jumped the Devil (1941)

Domino Film Corporation
The Devil's Daughter (1939)

Downing Film Company
Our Colored Fighters (1918)

Dudley Film Company
Reckless Money (1926)

Dunbar Film Corporation
The Fighting Fifteenth Colored Regiment (1921), The Midnight Ace (1928), The Negro Logging in Louisiana (1921), The Negro Rice Farmer (1922), The Southern Negro Baptism (1921), Tony's Shirt (1923)

Duo Art Pictures, Inc.
Life of Booker T. Washington (1940), Life of Florence Mills (1940), Life of George Washington Carver (1940)

E & H Distributing Company
The Devils (1923)

E.S.&L. Colored Feature Photoplay Company
Square Joe (1922)

Eagle Film Company
News Reel #1 (1922), News Reel #2 (1922)

Eagle Lion Films
The Jackie Robinson Story (1950)

Ebony Film Company
Are Working Girls Safe (1918), Black and Tan Mix Up (1918), A Black Sherlock Holmes (1917), The Bully (1918), A Busted Romance (1917), The Comeback of Barnacle Bill (1918), Dat Blackhand Waitah Man (1917), Devil for a Day (1917), Do the Dead Talk? (1918), Fixing the Faker (1918), Ghosts (1917), Good Luck in Old Clothes (1918), The Hypocrites (1917), The Janitor (1918), Luck in Old Clothes (1918), Mercy, the Mummy Mumbled (1917), A Milk-Fed Hero (1918), The Porters (1918), A Reckless Rover (1918), Shine Johnson and the Rabbit Foot (1917), Some Baby (1917), Spooks (1917), Spying the Spy (1918), When Cupid Went Wild (1917), When You Are Scared, Run (1918), When You Hit, Hit Hard (1918), Wrong All Around (1917)

Edison (*see also* Thomas A. Edison, Inc.)
Colored Troops Disembarking (1898), The Gator and the Pickaninny (1903), Jamaica Negroes Doing a Two Step (1907), The Possum Hunt (1910), Steamer Mascotte Arriving at Tampa (1898)

Editorial Film Productions
Introducing East Africa (1950)

Educational Film Corporation
All's Fair (1938), Easy Pickens (1937), Gifts in Rhythm (1936), Harlem Harmony (1935), Kinky (1923), The Life of the Party (1935), Pink Lemonade (1936), Radio Rascals (1935), Rhythm Saves Day (1937), Slow Poke (1932), Spooks (1936), Trailer Paradise (1937), Two Black Crows in Africa (1929), Way Down Yonder (1934), Way Out West (1935)

Elder Solomon Lightfoot Michaux
We've Got the Devil on the Run (1934)

Encyclopaedia Britannica Films
Pygmies of Africa (1938)

England
When Giants Fought (1926)

Enterprise Film Company
Come Back (1922)

Epinay Studios
Charleston (Sur un Air de Charleston) (1927)

Essanay
The Dancing Nig (1907)

Ethnographic Film Committee of the Museum
Afrique sur Seine (1955)

Exquisite Productions
Golden Pearls of Progress (1919)

Famous Artists Company
Hello Bill (1927)

Film Art Studios, Inc.
Keep Punching (1939)

Filmcraft Production
Adventure in Boogie Woogie (1946), Baby Don't Go Away from Me (1943), Back Door Man (1946), Boogiemania (1946), Broadway and Main (1946), Cats Can't Dance (1945), The Chair Song (1945), Come to Baby Do (1946), Count Me Out (1946), Crawl Red Crawl (1946), Dinty McGinty (1946), Does You Do, or Does You Don't (1946), Drink Hearty (1946), Errand Boy for Rhythm (1946), Everybody's Jumpin' Now (1946), Four Letters (1946), Frim Fram Sauce (1945), Get It Off Your Mind (1946), Got a Penny Benny (1946), Half Past Jump Time (1945), Hanover Hangover (1946), Harlem Hotcha (1946), Harp Boogie (1946), Harriet (1945), Here Comes the Fattest Man in Town (1946), I Left My Heart in Texas (1945), I Need a Playmate (1946), I'm a Shy Guy (1946), It Must be Jelly ('Cause Jam Don't Shake Like That) (1946), It's a Sin to Tell a Lie (1946), Joe, Joe (1946), Junior (1946), Lazy Lady (1945), Low, Short and Squatty (1946), My Bottle Is Dry (1946), Noah (1946), Old Dan Tucker (1946), Pigmeat Throws the Bull (1945), The Pollard Jump (1946), Rhythm Sam (1946), Romance Without Finance (1945), Sho Had a Wonderful Time (1946), Sizzle with Sissle (1946), Sun Tan Strut (1946), They Raided the Joint (1946), Time Takes Care of Everything (1946), Watch Out! (1946), We Pitched a Boogie Woogie (1946), Who Dunit to Who (1946), Who Threw the Whiskey in the Well? (1945)

Finely Film Company
Colored Troops at Chillicothe (1918)

Flowers, Tiger / Walt Miller
The Fighting Deacon (1925)

Folklore Research Films
Three Songs by Leadbelly (1945)

Foster Photoplay Company
The Barber (1916), Birth Mark (1911), Brother (1918) The Butler (1911), Colored Championship Baseball Game (1914), The Fall Guy (1913), Fool and Fire (1918), The Grafter and the Maid (1913), Mother (1917), The Pullman Porter (1910), The Railroad Porter (1912), A Woman's Worst Enemy (1918)

Fox — Movietone
Kentucky Jubilee Singers (1928), Kentucky Jubilee Singers (1929)

France
The Revue des Revues (1927)

Frank Hall Production
The Bar Sinister (1917)

Frederick Douglas Film Company
The Colored American Winning His Suit (1916), Heroic Negro Soldiers (1919), The Scapegoat (1920)

French Film Company
L'Afrique Vous Paris (1931)

Futurity Film Productions
Harlem Follies (1950)

Gaiety Comedies
Dark and Cloudy (1919)

Garrison Film Distribution Company
If a Boy Needs a Friend (1943)

Gate City Feature Films
Fought and Won (1921)

Gateway Productions
Bad Boy (1939)

Gaumont British Studios *see* **Lincoln**

George Randol Productions
Darktown Strutters' Ball (1940), Midnight Shadow (1939), Rhythm Rodeo (1938)

Ghana Information Service
Freedom for Ghana (1957)

Gjon Mili Films / Warner Bros.
Jammin' the Blues (1944)

Globe Pictures / Vintage Films
The Spirit of Youth (1937)

Goldberg Productions
Gig and Saddle (1933), The Negro Marches On (1938), Scandal (1933)

Goldberg, B. *see* **Pathé Nathan-Joinville / B. Goldberg**

Goldman Productions
Come On, Cowboy (1948), She's Too Mean for Me (1948)

Goldseal Productions *see* **Million Dollar Productions / Goldseal**

Gould, Walter *see* **Argentina Sons**

Gramercy Pictures
Children of Circumstance (1937)

Green, Eddie
Eddie Green's Rehearsal (1916)

Harlem Productions
Cavalcade of Harlem (1937)

Harlemwood Studios
Bipp Bang Boogie (1944), Go Down, Death! (1944), Juke Joint (1947)

Harman-Ising
Hot Frogs (1942)

Harmon Foundation Educational Films
Art in Negro Schools (1946), Calhoun — The Way to a Better Future (1945), Hampton Institute Programs for Education (1946), The Negro and Art (1947), Painting in Oil (1946), A Study of Negro Artist (1945), Xavier University — Negro Catholic College (1946), Y.W.C.A., Harlem, N.Y. (1945)

Harris Dickson Film Corporation
The Beauty Contest (1921)

Harris Dixon Film Company
The Custard Nine (1921)

Harvard University Dept. of Anthropology
Forest People of Central Africa (1920)

Harvard University Film Study Center
The Hunters (1958)

Haynes Photoplay Company
A Review of the B.M.C. and the Colored Business World ((1914), Uncle Remus' First Visit to New York (1914), Haynes Newsreel No. 1 (1914), Haynes Newsreel No. 2 (1916), Haynes Newsreel No. 3 (1917)

Herald Pictures, Inc.
Boy! What a Girl! (1946), Harlem Follies of 1949 (1950), Miracle in Harlem (1948), Sepia Cinderella (1947)

Herman, Will
Negro News Reel (1923)

Historical Feature Films
Aladdin Jones (1915), Black and White (1914), Money Talks in Darktown (1916),

Natural Born Shooter (1913), Two Knights of Vaudeville (1916)

Hollywood Pictures Corporation
Beale Street Mama (1946), Black Preview Trailers (1939), Boogie Woogie Dream (1942), Boogie Woogie Dream (1944), The Bronze Buckaroo (1938), Harlem Rides the Range (1939), My New Gown (1944), Son of Ingagi (1940), Toppers Take a Bow (1941), Two-Gun Man from Harlem (1938), Unlucky Woman (1944)

Hunter C. Haynes *see* **Haynes Photoplay Company**

Ideal-Gainsborough
Dusky Melodies (1930)

Idlewild
Idlewild (1927)

Imp
Pickaninnies and Watermelon (1912)

Ince, Thomas *see* **Thomas Luce**

Independent
The Quiet One (1958)

International Photoplay
Crap Game (1930)

International Road Show
Broken Strings (1940)

International Stage Play Pictures
Drums o' Voodoo (alt. titles: Louisiana; Voodoo Drums) (1933), Louisiana *see* Drums o' Voodoo, She Devil (1940), Voodoo Drums *see* Drums o' Voodoo

J.W. Fife Productions
A Modern Cain (1921)

Jan M. Perold
Lobola (1954)

Jenkins and Bourgeois *see* **Bourgeois-Jenkins Pictures**

Jubilee Pictures Corporation
Othello in Harlem *see* Paradise in Harlem, Paradise in Harlem (1940)

Kalem Studio
Florida Crackers (1921)

Keystone
Barber of Darktown (1915), A Dark Lover's Play (1915)

KHTB Productions
The Cry of Jazz (1958)

Lee DeForrest Phonofilms
Eubie Blake Plays (1929), Sissle and Blake (1923), Snappy Tunes (1923)

Len Films
Young Pushkin (1935)

Lenwall Productions (*see also* Million Dollar Productions / Lenwall)
Daughters of the Isle of Jamaica (1937)

Lewis, Edward W.
Battling Amateurs (1941), Colored Champions of Sport (1940)

Lichtman Theatre Enterprises
Mammy's Boy (1932)

Lincoln Motion Picture Company
By Right of Birth (1921), A Day with the Tenth Cavalry at Fort Huachuca (1922), The Law of Nature (1917), Lincoln Pictorial (1918), A Man's Duty (1919), The Realization of a Negro's Ambition (1916), Trooper of Troop K, (Trooper of Company K) (1916)

Lincoln Productions
Harlem Is Heaven (1932), Harlem Rhapsody *see* Harlem is Heaven (1932), The Unknown Soldier Speaks (1934)

Lincoln Productions / Gaumont British Studios
Life Is Real (1935)

Lionel Rogosin Productions
Come Back, Africa (1959)

LOL Production
Rug Cutters Holiday (1943)

Long Star Motion Picture Company
The Girl from the Pepper Patch (1922), The Stranger from Way Out Yonder (1922), Why Worry? (1923), The Wife Hunters (1922), Wrong All Around (1922), The Wrong Mr. Johnson (1922), You Can't Keep a Good Man Down (1922)

Longridge Enterprise, Inc.
Anna Lucasta (1958)

Lopert Films
Black Orpheus (1959)

Lord-Warner Pictures
Pitch a Boogie Woogie (1948)

Lubin Manufacturing Company
A Barnyard Mix-Up (1915), Butting In (1914), The Cannibal King (1915), Coffee Industry in Jamaica (1913), Coon Town Suffragettes (1914), The Cotton Industry of the South (1908) Father Said He'd Fix It (1915) The Haunted House (1915), He Was Bad (1914), How Rastus Got His Pork Chop (1908), In Zululand (1915), It Hap-

pened on Wash Day (1915), Just a Note (1914), A New Way to Win (1915), Rakoon Hose Company (1913), Rastus Among the Zulus (1913), Rastus Knew It Wasn't (1914), Sam and the Bully (1914), Swami Sam (1914), The Tale of a Chicken (1914), The Undertaker's Daughter (1915), Who's Who (1914), Zeb, Sack and the Zulus (1913)

Lucky Star Productions
Mantan Messes Up (1946), Mantan Runs for Mayor (1946), Return of Mandy's Husband (1948), What a Guy (1947)

M-G-M Movietone
George Dewey Washington, #1 (1928), George Dewey Washington, #2 (1929), George Dewey Washington, #3 (1929), George Dewey Washington, #4 (1929), George Dewey Washington, #5 (1930)

M.W. Baccus Films Company
From Cotton Patch to Congress (1910)

Madam C.J. Walker Manufacturing Company
Pythian Conclave and League Parley (1930)

Manor Films
The French Way (1952)

March of Time
Upbeat in Music (1943)

Markham and Heckle
Mr. Smith Goes Ghost (1940), One Big Mistake (1940)

Mascot Pictures Company
Africa Speaks (1930)

Maurice Film Company
Eleven PM (1928), Nobody's Children (1920), Return of Black Hawk (1921)

Mentone Production
Doin' the Town (1935)

Mesco Productions (*see also* Monarch)
In the Shadows (1923)

Meteor Film Production Company
Moon Over Harlem (1939)

Metro-Goldwyn-Mayer
Bosko and the Pirate (1937), Bright Road (1953), Cabin in the Sky (1943), Hallelujah (1929), Little Daddy (1931), Mayor of Jimtown (1929), Memories and Melodies (1935), Shoe Shine Boy (1945), Steppin' Along (1929), Story of Dr. Carver (1939), Streamline Swing (1938), Sunshine Sammy (1929), Uncle Tom's Cabana (1947)

Metropolitan Films
The Black King (1932), Harlem Hot Shots (1945)

Micheaux Book and Film Company
The Homesteader (1918), Within Our Gates (1919)

Micheaux Film Corporation
Birthright (1924), Birthright (1939), Black Magic (1932), Body and Soul (1924), The Brand of Cain *see* Murder in Harlem (1935), Broken Violin (1926), The Brute (1920), The Conjure Woman (1926), The Darktown Revue (1931) Darktown Scandal's Revue (1930), The Daughter of the Congo (1930), Deceit (1921), The Devil's Disciple (1926), The Dungeon (1922), Easy Street (1930), The Exile (1931), A Fool's Errand (1922), Ghost of Tolston's Manor (1934), The Girl from Chicago (1932), God's Stepchildren (1938), The Gunsaulus Mystery (1921), Harlem After Midnight (1934), The House Behind the Cedars (1924) The Hypocrite (1922), Jasper Landry's Will *see* Uncle Jasper's Will, Lem Hawkins' Confession, (Murder in Harlem) (1935), Lying Lips (1939), Marcus Garland (1928), The Millionaire (1927), Murder in Harlem *see also* Lem Hawkins' Confession (1935), The Notorious Elinor Lee (1940), Phantom of Kenwood (1933), Son of Satan (1924), The Spider's Web (1926), Swing (1938), The Symbol of the Unconquered (1920), Temptation (1936), Ten Minutes to Kill (1933), Ten Minutes to Live (1932), Thirty Years Later (1928), Uncle Jasper's Will (Jasper Landry's Will) (1922), Underworld (1937), Veiled Aristocrats (1932), The Virgin of the Seminole (1922), The Wages of Sin (1928), When Men Betray (1929)

Midnight Productions
Tenderfeet (1928)

Miller, Walt *see* Flowers, Tiger

Million Dollar Productions
Bargain with Bullets (1937), The Bronze Venus *see* The Duke Is Tops, Brown Bomber (1939), Condemned Men (1948) *see also* Four Shall Die, Crooked Money (1945) *see* While Thousands Cheer, The Duke Is Tops (The Bronze Venus) (1938), Four Shall Die (1940), Gang Smashers (1938), Gang War (1939), Gangsters on the

Loose (Bargain with Bullets) (1944), Gridiron Graft *see* While Thousands Cheer (1940), Gun Moll (Gang Smashers) (1944), His Harlem Wife (Life Goes On) (1944), Life Goes On (His Harlem Wife) (1938), Night Club Girl (One Dark Night) (1944), One Dark Night (1939), Prison Bait (1944) *see also* Reform School, Reform School (1939), While Thousands Cheer (1940)

Million Dollar Productions / Goldseal Productions
Take My Life (1941)

Million Dollar Productions / Lenwal Productions
Straight to Heaven (1939)

Millman, A.A.
Black Thunderbolt (1921)

Minoco Production
Basin Street Boogie (1942), Blues in the Night (1942), Honeysuckle Rose (1941), How to Go to a French Restaurant (1941), How to See a French Doctor (1941), The Joint Is Jumpin' (1941), Legs Ain't No Good (1942), Listen to the Mocking Bird (1941), Macnamara's Band (1941), Minnie the Moocher (1942), Oh, Susannah (1941), The Skunk Song (1942), Virginia, Georgia and Caroline (1942), Your Feet's Too Big (1941)

Monarch Productions / Mesco Productions
The Flaming Crisis (1924)

Monogram Pictures
Roar of the Crown (1938)

Monumental Pictures Corporation
A Day in the Nation's Capital (1918), Howard-Lincoln Football Game (1921), Monumental Monthly Negro Newsreel (1921), Monumental News Reel No. 2 (1921)

Motion Picture Service Corporation
Let My People Live (1938)

Mt. Olympus Distributing Co.
Darktown Affair (1921)

Movietone Studios / RKO Radio Pictures
Murder in Swingtime (1937)

Münchener Lichtspielkunst Emelka / Coloniale du Film
Samba (1928)

Mutual Film Corporation
Colored Americans (1918), Escapades of Estelle (1916)

National Archives Gift Collection
A Day in an African Village (1929), How Africa Lives (1929), How an Africa Tribe Is Ruled Under Colonial Government (1929), The Negro and Art (1931), Negro Education and Art in the United States (1931), Negro Life (1929), Song After Sorrow (1929), Tuskegee Trains New Pilots (1931)

National Association of Colored Women *see* **Artisan**

National Colored Soldier's Comfort Committee
The Loyalty of a Race (1918)

National Film Board of Canada
Family of Ghana (1958)

National Tuberculosis Association
Message from Dorothy Maynor (1949)

Negro Marches on Corporation
We've Come a Long, Long Way (1943)

NET
Slavery (1953)

Norman Film Manufacturing Company
Black Gold (1928), The Bull-Dogger (1923), The Crimson Skull (alt. title, The Scarlet Claw) (1921), A Debtor to the Law (1924), The Fighting Fool (1925), The Flying Ace (1926), The Green Eyed Monster (1921), The Love Bug (1920), Regeneration (1923), Scarlet Claw *see* The Crimson Skull (1921), Zircon (1923)

North State Film Corporation
The Devil's Match (1923), A Giant of His Race (1921), His Great Chance (1923), His Last Chance (1923), A Shot in the Night (1922)

Norwanda Pictures
No Time for Romance (1948), Sun Tan Ranch (1948)

Official Films
A Jungle Jinx (1932)

Organologue
Rhapsody in Black (1934)

P.D.C.
The Dixie Chase (1931)

Paragon Pictures
The Crimson Fog (1932), Dixie Love (1934), The Dusky Virgin (1932), Hell's Alley (1931)

Paramount
Brown Gravy (1929), A Bundle of Blues (1933), Cab Calloway's Hi-De-Ho (1934),

Cab Calloway's Jitterbug Party (1935), A Date with Duke (1946), Hi-De-Ho (1934), I Ain't Got Nobody (1932), Jasper Series (1946), Meet the Maestros (1938), Oft in the Silly Night (1929), Ol' King Cotton (1931), Old Man Rhythm (1932), Rhythm on the River (1932), St. Louis Blues (1958), Uncle Tom's Cabin (1918), The Widow's Bite (1929)

Pathé
Bessie Coleman (1922), Bessie Coleman (1923), Black Narcissus (1929), Chocolate Dandies (1924), Croix du Sud (1932), Dark Town Follies (1929), Darktown Blues (1929), Fowl Play (1929), The Funeral of Booker T. Washington (1916), Gluttonous Negro (1905), High Toned (1929), Honest Crooks (1929), In and Out (1929), The Pickaninny (1921)

Pathé / RCA Phonophone
The Water Boy (1929)

Pathé / RKO Radio Pictures
Duke Ellington and His Orchestra (1943)

Pathé Nathan-Joinville
Prinsesse Tam-Tam (1935)

Pathé Nathan-Joinville / B. Goldberg
Zouzou (1934)

Peacock Photoplay Company
Memorial Services at the Tomb of "Prince Hall" (1922), Peacock News Reel #1 (1921), Peacock News Reel #2 (1922)

Penn School Trustees
To Live as Free Men (1943)

Peter P. Jones Photoplay Company
Colored Soldiers Fighting in Mexico (1916), The Dawn of Truth (1916), For the Honor of the 8th Illinois Regiment (1914), Illinois National Half Century Exposition (1915), Negro Soldiers Fighting for Uncle Sam (1916), Progress of the Negro (1916), Re-Birth of a Nation (1916), The Slacker (1917), The Slaver (1917), Troubles of Sambo and Dinah (1914)

Pizor, William M.
Chocklate Cowboys (1925)

Pool Films
Borderline (1929)

Progress Picture Association
The Lure of a Woman (1921)

Pyramid Picture Producing Corporation
A Day in the Magic City of Birmingham (1920)

Quality Amusement Company
Eyes of Youth (1920), Home Brew (1920)

RCA Phonophone / RKO Radio Pictures (see also Pathé / RCA)
Black and Tan (1929)

RCM Production
Ah, Yes, There's Good Blues Tonight (1946), Ain't Misbehavin' (1945), Ain't My Sugar Sweet (1943), Ain't She Pretty (1944), Air Mail Special (1941), Alabamy Bound (1941), All Ruzzitt Buzzitt (1945), Along the Navajo Trail (1945), Am I Lucky? (1946), Babbling Bess (1943), Baby, Are You Kiddin'? (1946), Baby Don't You Cry (1943), Baby Don't You Love Me Anymore (1945), Back Beat Boogie (1944), Backstage Blues (1943), Beat Me Daddy (1943), Because I Love You (1942), Big Fat Butterfly (1944), Blackbird Fantasy (1942), Blitzkreig Bombardier (1944), Block Party Revels (1943), Blowtop Blues (1945), Boogie Man (1943), Boogie Woogie (1944), Boogie Woogie Piggy (1944), Booglie Wooglie Piggy (1941), Breakfast in Rhythm (1943), Brother Bill (1945), By an Old Southern River (1942), Cab Calloway Medley (1945), Can't See for Lookin' (1944), Caravan (1942), Case o' the Blues (1942), Cash Ain't Nothing But Trash (1945), Caterpillar Shuffle (1943), Cha-Chi-Man (1944), Chant of the Jungle (1943), Chatter (1943), Chicken Shack Shuffle (1943), Chilly 'n' Cold (1945), Chop Sticks (1943), Cielito Lindo (1944), Close Shave (1942), Congo Clambake (1942), Contrast in Rhythm (1945), Cootie Williams and His Orchestra (1944), Corn Pone (1945), Cow-Cow Boogie (1942), Cryin' and Singin' the Blues (1945), Cuban Episode (1942), Dance Your Old Age Away (1944), Dancemania (1943), Darktown Strutters' Ball (1941), Dear Old Southland (1941), Deed I Do (1944), The Devil Sat Down and Cried (1942), Dinah (1944), Dispossessed Blues (1943), Dixie Rhythm (1945), Do I Worry? (1941), Do I Worry? (1943), Don't Be Late (1945), Down, Down, Down (1942), Down on the Swanee River (1941), Dry Bones (1945), Dunkin' Bagels (1946), Easy Street (1941), Emily Brown (1943), Everyday Is Saturday in Harlem (1944), Fan Tan Fanny (1945),

Fare Thee Well (1945), Faust (1945), Five Guys Named Moe (1942), Five Salted Peanuts (1945), Flamingo (1942), Foo, a Little Ballyhoo (1945) Foolin' Around (1943), Forty-Seventh Street Jive (1944), Four or Five Times (1941), Fuzzy Wuzzy (1942), G.I. Jive (1944), Gee (1944), Get with It (1943), Git It (1943), Give Me Some Skin (1941), God's Heaven (1943), Good-Nite All (1943), Hark! Hark! The Lark (1941), Harlem Rhumba (1942), Harlem Serenade (1942), A Harlemesque Revue (1943), Harry the Hipster (1944), Here 'Tis Honey, Take It (1943), Hey, Lawdy Mama (1944), His Rockin' Horse Ran Away (1944), Hit That Jive Jack (1943), Hollywood Boogie (1946), Hot Chocklate (Cottontail) (1941), Hot in the Groove (1942), House on 52nd Street (1944), I Can't Dance (1944), I Can't Give You Anything But Love (1944), I Dreamt I Dwelt in Harlem (1941), I Got It Bad, and That Ain't Good (1942), I Gotta Go to Camp and See My Man (1943), I Had a Dream (1945), I Like It Cause I Love It (1944), I Miss You So (1943), I Want a Big Fat Mama (1941), I Want a Little Doggie (1945), I Was Here When You Left Me (1945), I Won't Miss You (1942), I'd Love to Be a Cowboy (1944), If You Can't Smile and Say Yes (1944), If You Only Knew (1946), If You Treat Me to a Hug (1943), I'll Be Glad When You're Dead, You Rascal You (1942), I'm a Good Good Woman (1944), I'm Making Believe (1945), I'm Tired (1944), Is You or Is You Ain't My Baby (1944), It's Me, Oh Lord (1945), I've Got to be a Rug Cutter (1945), Jack, You're Playing the Game (1941), Jackpot (1943), Jam Session (1942), Jim (1941), Jive Comes to the Jungle (1942), Johnny Peddler (1941), Jonah and the Whale (1944), Jordan Jive (1944), Jordan Melody #1 (1946), Jordan Melody #2 (1946), Joseph 'n' His Brudders (1945), Juke Box Boogie (1944), Jump in (1942), Jumpin' at the Jubilee (1944), Jumpin' Jack from Hackensack (1943), Jungle Jamboree (1943), Jungle Jig (1941), Just a-Sittin' and a Rockin' (1945), Keep Smiling (1943), Keep Waitin' (1943), Knock Me Out (1945), Lazy River (1944), Lazy River

(1944), Let's Get Away from It All (1943), Let's Get Down to Business (1943), Let's Go (1942), Let's Shuffle (1942), Linda Brown (1943), A Little Jive Is Good for You (1941), The Lonesome Road (1941), The Long and Short of It (1943), Love Grows on a White Oak Tree (1944), Lovin' Up a Solid Breeze (1943), Low Down Dog (1944), Mama Had a Little Lamb (1944), Mama, I Wanna Make Rhythm (1943), Maria Elena (1943), Meetin' Time (1943), Melody Takes a Holiday (1943), Mr. Jackson from Jacksonville (1945), Mr. X Blues (1945), Mop (1946), My, Ain't That Somethin' (1944), My Girl Loves a Sailor (1943), Never Too Old to Swing (1945), No, No, Baby (1945), Oh-e-e My, My (1945), Old Man Mose (1942), Opus 12 EEE (1944), The Outskirts of Town (1942), Paper Doll (1942), Pardon Me, But You Look Like Margie (1943), Patience and Fortitude (1946), Peckin' (1942), Poppin' the Cork (1943), Prancing in the Park (1943), The Preacher and the Bear (1945), Pudgy Boy (1942), Put Your Arms Around Me, Honey (1943), Quarry Road (1943), Quick Watson, the Question (1943), Ration Blues (1944), Rhapsody of Love (1944), Rhumboogie (1943), Rhythm Mad (1943), Rhythm Mania (1943), Rhythm of the Rhythm Band (1943), Rhythm on the Run (1942), Ride on, Ride On (1944), Ride, Red, Ride (1941), Riff (1943), Rigoletto Blues (1941), Rinka Tinka Man (1944), Rocco Blues (1943), Rock It for Me (1943), Rockin' Chair (1942), Roll 'Em (1944), Satchel Mouth Baby (1946), Scotch Boogie (1945), Shadrach (1941), She's Too Hot to Handle (1944), Shine (1942), Shine (1944), Shoot the Rhythm to Me (1943), Shout, Brother, Shout (1946), Shout! Sister, Shout! (1941), Sing and Swing (1943), A Sinner Kissed an Angel (1942), Sleep Kentucky Babe (1945), Sleepy Time Down South (1942), Snoqualomie Jo Jo (1945), Some of These Days (1942), A Song and Dance Man (1943), Spirit of Boogie Woogie (1942), Standin' Joe (1945), Steak and Potatoes (1944), Stepping Along (1943), Sticks and Stones (1943), Sugar Hill Masquerade (1942), Swanee Smiles (1943), Swanee Swing (1944), Sweet Kisses

(1943), Swing Cats Ball (1943), Swing for Sale (1941), Swing for Your Supper (1941), Swingin' in the Grove (1945), Swingin' on Nothin' (1942), T.G. Boogie Woogie (1945), Taint Yours (1944), Take Everything (1945), Take Me Back, Baby (1941), Take the "A" Train (1941), Tap Happy (1943), Ten Thousand Years Ago (1945), That Ol' Ghost Train (1942), There Are Eighty-Eight Reasons Why (1945), Till Then (1944), Tis You, Babe (1945), Toot That Trumpet! (1941), Toot That Trumpet (1943), Tuxedo Junction (1942), Tweed Me (1942), Walking with My Honey (1945), Waller Medley (1946), The Walls Keep Talking (1942), We the Cats Shall Hep Ya (1945), Wham (1943), What to Do (1942), Whatcha Know, Joe (1941), When You and I Were Young Maggie (1944), Where The Sweet Mammas Grow (1941), Who's Been Eating My Porridge? (1944), Willie Willie (1943), Write That Letter Tonight (1945), Ya Fine and Healthy Thing (1945), Yankee Doodle Never Went to Town (1944), Yes! Indeed (1941), You Always Hurt the One You Love (1944), You Can't Fool About Love (1943), Your Feet's Too Big (1946), Zoot (1946), A Zoot Suit (With a Reet Pleat) (1942)

Renaldo Films / Cooper-Randol
Dark Manhattan (1937)

Reol Productions
The Burden of Race (1921), The Call of His People (1921), Easy Money (1921), The Jazz Hounds (1922), The Leader of His Race (1922), The Schemers (1922), Secret Sorrow (1921), The Simp (1921), Spitfire (1922), The Sport of the Gods (1921), Ties of Blood (1921), A Tuskegee Pilgrimage (1922)

RKO Radio Pictures (*see also* Movietone; Pathé / RKO; Van Beuren–Meyer Davis; Variety)
Camp Meeting (1936), Check and Double Check (1930), Deep South (1937), Hi-De-Ho (1937), International Rhythms (1938), Mississippi Moods (1937), Readin', Writin' and Rhythm (1939), That Man Samson (1937), The Willie Mays Story (1955)

Rosebud Film Corporation
Absent (1928)

Royal Garden Film Company
In the Depths of Our Hearts (1920)

Royal Gospel Productions
Going to Glory, Come to Jesus (1946)

Sack Amusement Enterprises
Black and Tan (1929), Dark Manhattan (1937), Dirty Gertie from Harlem, U.S.A. (1946), Fuzzy Wuzzy (1945), Harlem Big Shot (The Black King) (1936), Harlem on Parade (1940), Harlem Rides the Range (1939), Hep Cat Serenade (1947), Jittering Jitterbugs (1943), Junction 88 (1947), Life in Harlem (1940), Moo Cow Boogie (1943), Of One Blood (1944), Rocco Blues (1947), Spiritual Sing-a-Long 1-A (1948), Spiritual Sing-a-Long 2-B (1948), Spiritual Sing-a-Long 3-C (1948), Spiritual Sing-a-Long 4-D (1948)

St. Paul Presbyterian Church
Seeking Kansas City in Action (1921)

Schach, Max *see* Buckingham

Selig Company
Interrupted Crap Game (1905)

Seminole Film Company
How High Is Up (1923)

Sepia-Art Pictures Company
Comes Midnight (1940), Dress Rehearsal (1939), Mr. Atom's Bomb (1949), One Round Jones (1948), What Goes Up (1939)

Southern Education Foundation
Jeans Teacher and Her Work (1940)

Southern Educational Film Production Service
Feeling Alright (1949)

Southern Motion Picture Company
When True Love Wins (1915)

Splendora Film Company
Carib Gold (1956)

Stillman Pond Production
Flamingo (1947)

Studio Films, Inc.
Basin Street Revue (1955), Beale Street Revue (1955), Downbeat Revue (1955), Harlem Jazz Festival (1955), Harlem Merry-Go-Round (1955), Harlem Variety Revue (1955), Jazz Festival (1955), Revue in Rhythm (1955), Rhythm and Blues Revue (1956), Rhythm in Harlem (1955), Rock 'n' Roll Revue (1955), Rockin' the Blues (1955), The Sound of Jazz (1957), Stars Over Harlem (1956)

Superior Arts Motion Picture Company
Hearts of the Woods (1921), Smiling Hate (1924), Steppin' High (1924)

Supreme Pictures Corporation
Am I Guilty (1940), Racket Doctor (Am I Guilty?) (1945)

Swan Films
The Magic Garden (1952)

Swanson, Donald
Jim Comes to Jo'Burg (1950)

T.H.B. Walker's Colored Pictures
The Man in Ebony (1918), Walker Newsreel No. 1 (1921)

T.N.T. Pictures Corporation
Burlesque in Harlem (1955)

Teaching Film Custodians
The Story of Dr. George Washington Carver (1935)

Thanhauser
The Judge's Story (1911), Uncle Tom's Cabin (1909)

Thomas A. Edison, Inc. (*see also* Edison)
Dancing Darkey Boy (1896), Native Woman Coaling a Ship at St. Thomas, D.W.I. (1895), Native Woman Washing Clothes at St. Vincent, D.W.I. (1895), Native Women Coaling a Ship and Scrambling for Money (1895), Ninth U.S. Cavalry Watering Horses (1898), A Scrap in Black and White (1903), Uncle Tom's Cabin (1903), A Watermelon Contest (1895), West Indian Boys Diving for Money (1897), West Indian Girls in Native Dance (1897), Wharf Scenes and Natives Swimming at St. Thomas, D.W.I. (1897)

Thomas Ince
Free and Equal (1925)

Tiffany Film Company
Cotton-Pickin' Days (1934), Jungle Drums (1929), Old Black Joe (1933), On a Plantation (1930), Pickin' Cotton (1930), The Road Home (1931), Slave Days (1930), Welcome Home (1931)

Toddy Pictures Company
The Bronze Venus (The Duke Is Tops) (1943), Buck and Bubbles Laff Jamboree (1945), Colored Americans in the Nation's Capitol (1946), Colored Men in White (1943), The Corpse Accuses (1946), Crime Street (1946), Eddie's Laugh Jamboree (1944), Fight That Ghost (1946), Fighting Americans (1943), Hell Cats (1947), House-Rent Party (1946), Ill Wind (1946), Mr. Creeps (1938), A Night with the Devil (1946), Pigmeat's Laugh Hepcats (1944),

Prairie Comes to Harlem (1946), Rufus Green in Harlem (1946), Sergeant Joe Louis on Tour (1943), Shut My Big Mouth (1947), Super Sleuths (1947), Voodoo Devil Drums (1946), Who's Who in Colored America (1945), The Wrong Mr. Wright (1947)

Toussaint Motion Pictures Company
Doing Their Bit (1918)

Tressie Saunders
Woman's Error (1922)

Triangle Film Company
Mr. Miller's Economics (1916)

Trinity Film Corporation
A Daughter of Pharaoh (1920)

Trio Productions
The Greatest Sin (1922)

Tropical Photoplay Company
Shuffling Jane (1921)

Trowship Film Company
What's the Use? (1918)

Turpin, Charles H. (*see also* Turpin Film Co.)
Phthian Parade and 19th Biannual Encampment (1920)

Turpin Film Company (*see also* Turpin, Charles H.)
In Honor of the 92nd Division (1917), Ninety-Second Division on Parade (1919)

Twentieth Century–Fox Film Corporation
Carmen Jones (1954), Hearts of Dixie (1929), A Modern Dixie (1938), Pinky (1949), Stormy Weather (1943), Zululand (1947)

Two Cities Film Company
Man of the Worlds (Kisenga, Man of Africa) (1946)

U. M. & M. TV Corporation
Symphony in Black: A Rhapsody of Negro Life (1935)

Unique Film Company
Shadowed by the Devil (1916)

United Artists
Cherished Melodies (1950), Cry, the Beloved Country (1952), Emperor Jones (1933), Folklore (1950), Glory Filled Spirituals (1950), Go, Man Go (1954), The Joe Louis Story (1953), Long Remembered (1950), Melodic Spirituals (1950), Melodies Reborn (1950), Satchmo, the Great (1954), Southern a Cappella (1950), Symphonic Shades (1950), The Tradition (1950), Tunes That Live (1950), The Well (Deep Is the Well) (1951)

United Films
Girl in Room 20 (1946)
United Stated Army
Easy to Get (1944)
United States Army, Air Force Production
Wings for This Man (1944)
United States Department of Agriculture
Henry Brown, Farmer (1944), The Negro Farmer (1938)
United States Navy Department
The Negro Sailor (1945),
United States War Department
From Harlem to the Rhine (1920), The Negro College in Wartime (1943), The Negro Soldier (1944), Our Colored Boys Over There (1921), Teamwork (1946)
Universal-International
The Ink Spots (1955), King Cole and His Trio (1950), Lionel Hampton and Herb Jeffries (1955), Lionel Hampton and His Orchestra (1949), Mr. Black Magic (1956), Nat "King" Cole and Joe Adams' Orchestra (1951), The Nat "King" Cole Musical Story (1955), Salute to Duke Ellington (1950), Sarah Vaughan and Herb Jeffries, Kid Ory, etc. (1950), Sugar Chile Robinson (1950), Symphony in Swing (1949)
Universal Studios
Baby Jewels (1937), Choo Choo Swing (1943), Harlem Bound (1935), Imitation of Life (1934), Imitation of Life (1959), King Cole Trio & Benny Carter (1950), Minstrel Days (1930), Nat "King" Cole and Russ Morgan's Orchestra (1953), A Night in a Night Club (1937), Uncle Tom's Cabin (1927), Voodoo in Harlem (1938)
Van Beuren–Meyer Davis / RKO Radio Pictures
Bubbling Over (1934)
Variety Film Company / RKO Radio Pictures
Way Down South (1939)
Villiers, François *see* **Cocteau, Jean**
Vintage Films *see* **Globe Pictures**
Vitagraph
Midnight Lodger (1930)
Vitaphone
Barbershop Blues (1937), Black Network (A Broadway Brevity) (1936), Bud Harris and Frank Radcliffe (1929), By Request (1935), Clarence Tisdale (1929), Claude Hopkins and His Orchestra (1933), Claude Hopkins and His Orchestra (1935), Cora Green (1929), Dixie Days (1928)
Walker, Madam C.J. *see* **Madam C.J. Walker Manufacturing Company**
Walker, T.H.B. *see* **T.H.B. Walker's**
Warner Bros. *see* **Gjon Mili Films**

APPENDIX C:
DIRECTOR CREDITS

Alexander, William D.
The Fight Never Ends (1947), Flicker Up (1946), Hair Raid (1948), The Highest Tradition (1946), Love in Syncopation (1946), Lucky Millinder (1946), Sweethearts of Rhythm (1947), That Man of Mine (1947), Two of a Kind (1955), Vanities (1946)

Anderson, Leonard (*see also* Birch, Maceo / Leonard Anderson)
Adventure (1946), Big Fat Mammas (1946), Broadway (1946), Hello Bill (1946), I Cried for You (1946), I Want a Man (1946), I Want to Talk About You (1946), Jivin' in Be-Bop (1946), Jump Children (1946), Lonesome Lover Blues (1946), Mistletoe (1946), She's Crazy with Heat (1946), That Man of Mine (1946), You Call It Madness (1946)

Barlow, Roger
Henry Brown, Farmer (1944)

Barton, Charles
Jam Session (1944)

Berne, Josef (*see also* Murphy, Dudley / Josef Berne)
Band Parade (1943), Dry Bones (1945), Hot Chocklate (Cottontail) (1941), Jam Session (1942), Paper Doll (1942), Shine (1942), Sleep Kentucky Babe (1945)

Binney, Josh
Boarding House Blues (1948), Chicago After Dark (1946), Hi-De-Ho (1947), The Joint Is Jumping (1948), Killer Diller (1948), Lucky Gamblers (1946), Midnight Menace (1946)

Birch, Maceo
Rhythm in a Riff (1946)

Birch, Maceo / Leonard Anderson
Rhythm in a Riff (1946)

Bitzer, G.W.
Natural Born Gambler (1916)

Blake, Ben K.
Harry the Hipster (1944), Opus 12 EEE (1944)

Bland, Edward
The Cry of Jazz (1958)

Bonafield, Jay
Duke Ellington and His Orchestra (1943)

Brodie, Don
Life of Florence Mills (1940)

Brown, Melville
Check and Double Check (1930)

Brown, Phil
The Harlem Globetrotters (1951)

Bruckner, August
Samba (1928)

Buell, Jed (*see also* Newfield, Sam / Jed Buell)
Mr. Washington Goes to Town (1940)

Burger, Hans
Boogie Woogie Dream (1942), Boogie Woogie Dream (1944), My New Gown (1944), Unlucky Woman (1944)

Calnek, Roy E.
Hearts of the Woods (1921), Ten Nights in a Bar-Room (1926)

Calnek, Roy / Bob Martin
A Prince of His Race (1926)

Camus, Marcel
Black Orpheus (1959)

Chenal, Pierre
Native Son (1951)

Chelin, John
Keep Punching (1939)

Cogine, Ray
Ol' King Cotton (1931)

Cohen, Octavus Roy
The Framing of the Shrew (1929)
Connelly, Marc *see* **Keighley, William**
Cooper, Ralph *see* **Fraser, Harry / Ralph Cooper**
Cornblum, Sherman
Frenzy (1946)
Cowan, Will
The Ink Spots (1955), King Cole and His Trio (1950), Lionel Hampton and Herb Jeffries (1955), Lionel Hampton and His Orchestra (1949), The Nat "King" Cole Musical Story (1955), Salute to Duke Ellington (1950), Sarah Vaughn and Herb Jeffries, Kid Ory, etc. (1950), Sugar Chile Robinson (1950)
Crouch, William Forest
Adventure in Boogie Woogie (1946), Baby Don't Go Away from Me (1943), Block Party Revels (1943), Boogiemania (1946), Buzz Me (1945), Caldonia (1945), Cats Can't Dance (1945), The Chair Song (1945), Come to Baby Do (1946), Count Me Out (1946), Crawl, Red, Crawl (1946), Dinah (1944), Dinty McGinty (1946), Does You Do, or Does You Don't (1946), Drink Hearty (1946), Errand Boy for Rhythm (1946), Everybody's Jumpin' Now (1946), Four Letters (1946), Frim Fram Sauce (1945), Get It Off Your Mind (1946), Got a Penny Benny (1946), Half Past Jump Time (1945), Hanover Hangover (1946), Harlem Hotcha (1946), Harp Boogie (1946), Harriet (1945), Hep Cat Serenade (1947), Here Comes the Fattest Man in Town (1946), Honey Chile (1945), I Left My Heart in Texas (1945), I Need a Playmate (1946), I'm a Shy Guy (1946), It Must Be Jelly ('Cause Jam Don't Shake Like That (1946), It's a Sin to Tell a Lie (1946), Joe, Joe (1946), Junior (1946), Lazy Lady (1945), Low, Short and Squatty (1946), Mop (1946), My Bottle Is Dry (1946), Noah (1946), Old Dan Tucker (1946), Pigmeat Throws the Bull (1945), The Pollard Jump (1946), Ration Blues (1944), Reet-Petite and Gone (1947), Rhythm Sam (1946), Romance Without Finance (1945), Sho Had a Wonderful Time (1946), Sizzle with Sissle (1946), Sun Tan Strut (1946), T.G. Boogie Woogie (1945), They Raided the Joint (1946), Tillie (1945), Time Takes Care of Everything (1946), Watch Out! (1946), We Pitched a Boogie Woogie (1946),

Who Dunit to Who (1946), Who Threw Whiskey in the Well? (1945)
Crowley, William Xavier
Lady Luck, *see* Lucky Ghost (1940), Lucky Ghost (Lady Luck) (1941), Up Jumped the Devil (1941)
Daly, William R.
Uncle Tom's Cabin (1914)
David, N.C.
A Reckless Rover (1918)
Dawley, J. Searle
Uncle Tom's Cabin (1918)
DeBaroncelli, J.
The French Way (1952)
De Forrest, Lee
Sissle and Blake (1923)
Dickinson, Thorrold
Man of the Worlds (Kisenga, Man of Africa) (1946)
Dones, Sidney P. *see* **Peacocke, Leslie / Sidney P. Dones**
Dreifuss, Arthur
Double Deal (1939), Murder in Swingtime (1937), Murder on Lenox Ave. (1941), Mystery in Swing (1940), Sunday Sinners (1941)
Dudley, S.H. / Robert Levy
Easy Money (1921)
Dudley, Sherman H., Jr.
Reckless Money (1926)
Edwards, J. Harrison
Square Joe (1922)
Elljat, Sam
Bipp Bang Boogie (1944)
Etierant, Henri *see* **Nalpas, Mario**
Fleischer, Dave
I Heard (1932), I'll Be Glad When You're Dead You Rascal You (1932)
Foster, William
Birth Mark (1911), Black Narcissus (1929), Brother (1918), The Butler (1911), Colored Championship Baseball Game (1914), Dark Town Follies (1929), Darktown Blues (1929), The Fall Guy (1913), Florida Crackers (1921), Fool and Fire (1918), Fowl Play (1929), The Grafter and the Maid (1913), High Toned (1929), Honest Crooks (1929), In and Out (1929), Mother (1917), The Railroad Porter (1912), A Woman's Worst Enemy (1918)
Foy, Bryan
Hazel Green and Company (1928)

Franklyn, Irwin R.
Harlem Is Heaven (1932), Harlem Rhapsody *see* Harlem Is Heaven

Franklyn, Irwin R. & Hazele
Gone Harlem (1939)

Fraser, Harry
Bargain with Bullets (1937), The Spirit of Youth (1937)

Fraser, Harry / Ralph Cooper
Dark Manhattan (1937)

Freeland, Thorton
Jericho (1937)

Freland, Fritz
Goldilocks and the Jivin' Bears (1944)

Freulich, Roman
The Broken Earth (1939)

Gant, Harry
Absent (1930), Georgia Rose (1930)

Gillstrom, Arvis
Melancholy Dame (1929)

Ginn, Haywood
The Custard Nine (1921)

Goldberg, Jack
The Unknown Soldier Speaks (1934), We've Come a Long, Long Way (1943)

Goodwins, Leslie
Deep South (1937), Mississippi Moods (1937)

Gordon, Robert
The Joe Louis Story (1953)

Gould, Dave
Ah, Yes, There's Good Blues Tonight (1946), Am I Lucky? (1946), Baby, Are You Kiddin'? (1946), Hollywood Boogie (1946), If You Only Knew (1946), Patience and Fortitude (1946), Satchel Mouth Baby (1946), Shout, Brother, Shout (1946), Your Feet's Too Big (1946), Zoot (1946)

Graham, Walter
Jittering Jitterbugs (1943), Music Hath Harms (1929)

Grahm, Chatty
How High Is Up (1923)

Green, Alfred E.
The Jackie Robinson Story (1950)

Green, Eddie
Dress Rehearsal (1939), Eddie Green's Rehearsal (1916), Mr. Atom's Bomb (1949), One Round Jones (1948), What Goes Up (1939)

Hall, Robert
All's Fair (1938)

Hammons, E.W.
Pink Lemonade (1936)

Hargrave, Myrtle
Dixie Love (1934)

Haynes, Hunter C.
Haynes Newsreel No. 1 (1914), Haynes Newsreel No. 2 (1916), Haynes Newsreel No. 3 (1917), The Tango Queen (1916), Uncle Remus' First Visit to New York (1914)

Henabery, Joseph
Barbershop Blues (1937), Jimmie Lunceford and His Dance Orchestra (1936)

Henle, Fritz
Shango (1953)

Herzig, Sid
Slow Poke (1932)

Heywood, Donald
The Black King (1932)

Hoerle, Arthur
Drums o' Voodoo (alt. title: Louisiana; Voodoo Drums) (1933), Louisiana *see* Drums o' Voodoo, Voodoo Drums *see* Drums o' Voodoo

Howe, James Wong
Go, Man, Go (1954)

Hurst, Brian D.
Simba (1955)

Ince, Thomas
Free and Equal (1925)

Iwerks, Ub
Little Black Sambo (1933)

Jason, Leigh
Bubbling Over (1934)

Jones, Peter P.
Colored Soldiers Fighting in Mexico (1916), The Dawn of Truth (1916), For the Honor of the 8th Illinois Regiment (1914), Illinois National Half Century Exposition (1915), Negro Soldiers Fighting for Uncle Sam (1916), Progress of the Negro (1916), Re-Birth of a Nation (1916), The Slacker (1917), The Slaver (1917), Troubles of Sambo and Dinah (1914)

Kahn, Richard C.
The Bronze Buckaroo (1938), Harlem Rides the Range (1939), Son of Ingagi (1940), Toppers Take a Bow (1941), Two-Gun Man from Harlem (1938)

Kane, Raymond
Rhythm Saves Day (1937)

Kazan, Elia
Pinky (1949)

Keighley, William / Marc Connelly
The Green Pastures (1936)

Kemp, Jack
Miracle in Harlem (1948)

Kohn, Joseph
Basin Street Revue (1955), Downbeat Revue (1955), Harlem Jazz Festival (1955), Harlem Merry-Go-Round (1955), Harlem Variety Revue (1955), Jazz Festival (1955), Rhythm and Blues Revue (1956), Rhythm in Harlem (1955), Rock 'n' Roll Revue (1955), Stars Over Harlem (1956)

Korda, Zolton
Cry, the Beloved Country (1952), Sanders of the River (1935)

Laven, Arnold
Anna Lucasta (1958)

Leonard, Arthur (*see also* Quigley, George P. & Arthur Leonard)
Boy! What a Girl! (1946), The Devil's Daughter (1939), Sepia Cinderella (1947), Straight to Heaven (1939)

Levy, Robert (*see also* Dudley, S.H. / Robert Levy)
Eyes of Youth (1920)

Lewis, Edward
Brown Bomber (1939), Colored America on Parade (1940), Colored Champions of Sport (1940), Life Harlem (1940)

Lieven, Henry
The Negro Sailor (1945)

Lindsay, Powell
Souls of Sin (1949)

Lockwood, Roy
Jamboree (Disc Jockey Jamboree) (1957)

Lord, William
Pitch a Boogie Woogie (1948)

Lubin, Fredric
How to Rastus Got His Pork Chop (1908)

Lubin, Sigmund
Butting In (1914), The Cannibal King (1915), Coffee Industry in Jamaica (1913), Coon Town Suffragettes (1914), The Cotton Industry of the South (1908), Father Said He'd Fix It (1915), The Haunted House (1915), He Was Bad (1914), In Zululand (1915), It Happened on Wash Day (1915), Just a Note (1914), A New Way to Win (1915), Rakoon Hose Company (1913), Rastus Among the Zulus (1913), Rastus Knew It Wasn't (1914), Sam and the Bully (1914), Swami Sam (1914), The Tale of a Chicken (1914), The Under-taker's Daughter (1915), Who's Who (1914), Zeb, Zack and the Zulus (1913)

MacCullough, Jack
Do the Dead Talk? (1918)

McGill, Lawrence B.
The Scapegoat (1920)

McGuire, Neil
Rhapsody in Black (1934)

Mack, Roy
All-Colored Vaudeville Show (1935), Black Network (A Broadway Brevity), By Request (1935), Hi-De-Ho (1937), The Mississippi (1934), Pie Pie Blackbirds (1932), Rufus Jones for President (1933), Syncopated Sermon (1930)

Mack, Roy & Joseph Henabery
Smash Your Baggage (1932)

Markham, Dewey and Heckle
Mr. Smith Goes Ghost (1940)

Martin, Bob *see* Calnek, Roy / Bob Martin

Maurice, Richard D.
Eleven PM (1928), Home Brew (1920), Nobody's Children (1920), Return of Black Hawk (1921)

Mayer, Gerald
Bright Road (1953)

Meyer, Herbert
Bad Boy (1939)

Meyer, T.
Going to Glory, Come to Jesus (1946)

Meyers, Sidney
The Quiet One (1958)

Micheaux, Oscar
The Betrayal (1948), Birthright (1924), Birthright (1939), Black Magic (1932), Body and Soul (1924), The Brand of Cain *see* Murder in Harlem (1935), Broken Violin (1926), The Brute (1920), The Conjure Woman (1926), The Darktown Revue (1931), Darktown Scandal's Revue (1930), The Daughter of the Congo (1930), Deceit (1921), The Devil's Disciple (1926), The Dungeon (1922), Easy Street (1930), The Exile (1931), A Fool's Errand (1922), Ghost of Tolston's Manor (1934), The Girl from Chicago (1932), God's Stepchildren (1938), The Gunsaulus Mystery (1921), Harlem After Midnight (1934), The Homesteader (1918), The House Behind the Cedars (1924), The Hypocrite (1922), Jasper Landry's Will *see*

Uncle Jasper's Will, Lem Hawkins' Confession (Murder in Harlem) (1935), Lying Lips (1939), Marcus Garland (1928), The Millionaire (1927), Murder in Harlem *see also* Lem Hawkins' Confession, The Notorious Elinor Lee (1940), Phantom of Kenwood (1933), Son of Satan (1924), The Spider's Web (1926), Swing (1938), The Symbol of the Unconquered (1920), Temptation (1936), Ten Minutes to Kill (1933), Ten Minutes to Live (1932), Thirty Years Later (1928), Uncle Jasper's Will (Jasper Landry's Will) (1922), Underworld (1937), Veiled Aristocrats (1932), The Virgin of the Seminole (1922), The Wages of Sin (1928), Within Our Gates (1919)

Mili, Gjon
Jammin' the Blues (1944)

Minnelli, Vincente
Cabin in the Sky (1943)

Montague, Brian *see* **Nicholson, Irene**

Moss, Carlton
Frederick Douglas's the House on Cedar Hill (1953)

Murphy, Dudley
Emperor Jones (1933), The St. Louis Blues (1929)

Murphy, Dudley / Josef Berne
Yes! Indeed (1941)

Murray, Warren
Honeysuckle Rose (1941), How to Go to a French Restaurant (1941), How to See a French Doctor (1941), Macnamara's Band (1941)

Muse, Clarence
Toussaint L'Ouverture (1921)

Nalpas, Mario / Henri Etierant
Siren of the Tropics (1927)

Narodistky, Arady
Young Pushkin (1935)

Newfeld, Sam
Am I Guilty (1940), Racket Doctor (Am I Guilty?) (1945), Fight That Ghost (1946), House-Rent Party (1946)

Newfeld, Sam / Jed Buell
Harlem on the Prairie (1938)

Nicholson, Irene & Brian Montague
Callalco (1937)

Nissotti, Arys
Zouzou (1934)

Nolte, William
The Duke Is Tops (The Bronze Venus) (1938),

His Harlem Wife (Life Goes On) (1944), Life Goes On (His Harlem Wife (1938)

Pal, George
Jasper Series (1946)

Pal, John
Mamprusi Village (1944)

Palmer, Harry
Escapades of Estelle (1916)

Parker, Ben
George Washington Carver (1940)

Peacocke, Captain Leslie T.
Reformation (1919)

Peacocke, Leslie / Sidney P. Dones
Injustice *see* Loyal Hearts, Loyal Hearts (Injustice) (1919)

Perugini, Frank
The Scar of Shame (1927)

Phillips, R.G.
A Black Sherlock Holmes (1917), Mercy, the Mummy Mumbled (1917)

Pollard, Bud
Beware! (1946), Big Timers (1945), Harlem Big Shot (The Black King) (1936), It Happened in Harlem (1945), Kilroy Lives Here (1940), Look-Out Sister (1948), Romance on the Beat (1945), Tall, Tan and Terrific (1946)

Pollard, Harry
Uncle Tom's Cabin (1927)

Popkin, Leo C. (*see also* Rouse, Russell)
Bronze Venus (1943), Four Shall Die (1940), Gang Smashers (1938), Gang War (1939), Gun Moll (Gang Smashers) (1944), Night Club Girl (One Dark Night) (1944), One Dark Night (1939), Prison Bait (1944) *see also* Reform School (1944), Reform School (1939)

Preminger, Otto
Porgy and Bess (1959)

Primi, John
Listen to the Mocking Bird (1941)

Quigley, George P.
Junction 88 (1947), Murder with Music (1941)

Quigley, George P. & Arthur Leonard
Mistaken Identity (1941)

Randol, George
Darktown Strutters' Ball (1940), Midnight Shadow (1939), Rhythm Rodeo (1938)

Randolph, Forbes
Slave Days (1930)

Reisner, Allen
St. Louis Blues (1958)

Renoir, Jean
Charleston (Sur un Air de Charleston) (1927)
Rieger, Jack
O'Voutie O'Rooney (1947)
Rodakiewiecz, Henwar
One Tenth of Our Nation (1940)
Rogosin, Lionel
Come Back, Africa (1959)
Roth, Murray
Yamekraw (1930)
Rouse, Russell & Leo C. Popkin
The Well (Deep Is the Well) (1951)
Ruth, Roy Del
Ham and Eggs (1927)
Sarr, Mamamou *see* **Vieyra, Paulin Souman**
Schwarzwald, Milton
Deviled Hams (1937)
Seiden, Joseph
Othello in Harlem *see* Paradise in Harlem, Paradise in Harlem (1940), Stars on Parade (1946)
Sennett, Mack
A Dark Lover's Play (1915)
Serk, Douglas
Imitation of Life (1959)
Sheehan, Winfield / Paul Sloan
Hearts of Dixie (1929)
Sherman, Vincent
S.S. Booker T. Washington (1942)
Simms, John M.
The Lure of a Woman (1921)
Sloan, Paul *see* **Sheehan, Winfield**
Smight, Jack
The Sound of Jazz (1957)
Smith, Basil
Jailhouse Blues (1934), Old Man Trouble (1929)
Smith, Pete
Story of Dr. Carver (1939)
Smith, Dr. William S.
Heroic Negro Soldiers (1919)
Snody, Robert R.
I Dreamt I Dwelt in Harlem (1941)
Stahl, John M.
Imitation of Life (1934)
Stone, Andrew L.
Stormy Weather (1943)
Swanson, Donald
Jim Comes to Jo'Burg (1950), The Magic Garden (1952)
Trent, William, Jr.
The Negro in Entertainment (1950), The Negro in Sports (1950)

Tyler, Ralph W.
The Loyalty of a Race (1918)
Ulmer, Edgar G.
Let My People Live (1938), Moon Over Harlem (1939)
Vidor, King
Hallelujah (1929)
Vieyra, Paulin Souman & Mamamou Sarr
Afrique sur Seine (1955)
Vorhaus, Bernard / Clarence Muse
Way Down South (1939)
Wade, John H.
The Midnight Ace (1928)
Waller, Fred "Fats"
Cab Calloway's Hi-De-Ho (1934), Cab Calloway's Jitterbug Party (1935), Hi-De-Ho (1934), Symphony in Black: A Rhapsody of Negro Life (1935)
Waston, William
The Lady Fare (1929), The Life of the Party (1935), Spooks (1936), Way Down Yonder (1934), Way Out West (1935)
Whipper, Leigh
A Regeneration of Souls (1921), Renaissance Newsreel (1921)
White, Bob
The Wife Hunters (1922)
Williams, Spencer
Beale Street Mama (1946), The Blood of Jesus (1941), Brother Martin, Servant of Jesus (1942), Dirty Gertie from Harlem, U.S.A. (1946), Girl in Room 20 (1946), Go Down, Death! (1944), Harlem Hot Shots (1945), Juke Joint (1947), Marching On! (1943), Of One Blood (1944), Rhapsody of Negro Life (1949), Tender-feet (1928), Where's My Man To-Nite? (1944)
Wills, J. Elder
Big Fella (1938), The Song of Freedom (1938)
Wilson, Ben D.
The Man from Texas (1921)
Wright, William Forest
Back Door Man (1946)
Wright, William Lord
Baby Jewels (1937)
Zamora, Ruby
Voodoo in Harlem (1938)
Zebba, Sam
Fincho (1958)

APPENDIX D:
PRODUCER CREDITS

Adams, Berle (*see also* Crouch, William Forest / R.M. Savini / Berle Adams)
Buzz Me (1945), Caldonia (1945), Honey Chile (1945), Look-Out Sister (1948), Tillie (1945)

Adler, Buddy
The Harlem Globetrotters (1951)

Alexander, William D.
Adventure (1946), Big Fat Mammas (1946), The Fight Never Ends (1947), Flicker Up (1946), Hair Raid (1948), Hello Bill (1946), The Highest Tradition (1946), I Cried for You (1946), I Want a Man (1946), I Want to Talk About You (1946), Jivin' in Be-Bop (1946), Jump Children (1946), Lonesome Lover Blues (1946), Love in Syncopation (1946), Lucky Millinder (1946), Mistletoe (1946), Rhythm in a Riff (1946), She's Crazy with Heat (1946), Souls of Sin (1949), Sweethearts of Rhythm (1947), That Man of Mine (1946), That Man of Mine (1947), Two of a Kind (1955), Vanities (1946), You Call It Madness (1946)

All American News
Ask the OPA (1945), The Negro Sailor (1945)

Allgret, Marc
Zouzou (1934)

Anderson, Byron O.
No Time for Romance (1948)

Baker, Mary E.
The House of Mystery (1923)

Bernard, L. Barry *see* **DeBaroncelli, J.**

Binney, Josh
Mammy's Boy (1932)

Blake, Ben K.
Harry the Hipster (1944), Opus 12 EEE (1944)

Blake, Sid
Life of Booker T. Washington (1940), Life of Florence Mills (1940), Life of George Washington Carver (1940)

Bland, Edward / Nelam Hill / M. Kennedy / E. Titus
The Cry of Jazz (1958)

Bordon, L. C. *see* **L. C. Bordon**

Bourgeois *see* **Jenkins-Bourgeois**

Briskin, Mort
The Jackie Robinson Story (1950)

Buell, Jed
The Bronze Buckaroo (1938), Harlem on the Prairie (1938), Lady Luck *see* Lucky Ghost, Lucky Ghost (Lady Luck) (1941), Professor Creeps (1941), Up Jumped the Devil (1941)

Buell, Jed & James K. Friedrich
Mr. Washington Goes to Town (1940)

Calnek, Roy
Smiling Hate (1924)

Celebrity Pictures
Little Black Sambo (1933)

Christie, Al
All's Fair (1938), Brown Gravy (1929), The Framing of the Shrew (1929), Gifts in Rhythm (1936), The Lady Fare (1929), The Life of the Party (1935), Melancholy Dame (1929), Music Hath Harms (1929), Oft in the Silly Night (1929), Pink Lemonade (1936), Rhythm Saves Day (1937), Roll Along (1929), Spooks (1936), Way Down Yonder (1934), Way Out West (1935), The Widow's Bite (1929)

Church, Gilbert
My Song Goes Forth (1947)

Clein, John
Keep Punching (1939)

Clifford, Lt. J. Williams
A Day in the Nation's Capital (1918)
Cochran, Gifford *see* **Krimsky, John**
Cocteau, Jean & François Villiers
Rhythm of Africa (1947)
Cohen, Octavus
The Florian Slappey Series (1925)
Connelly, Marc *see* **Keighley, William**
Cornblum, Sherman
Frenzy (1946)
Coslow, Sam
Hot Chocklate (Cottontail) (1941), Jam Session (1942), Paper Doll (1942), Shine (1942), Yes! Indeed (1941)
Cowan, Will
The Nat "King" Cole Musical Story (1955)
Crouch, William Forest
Adventure in Boogie Woogie (1946), Baby Don't Go Away from Me (1943), Block Party Revels (1943), Boogiemania (1946), Cats Can't Dance (1945), The Chair Song (1945), Come to Baby Do (1946), Count Me Out (1946), Crawl Red Crawl (1946), Dinah (1944), Dinty McGinty (1946), Does You Do, or Does You Don't (1946), Drink Hearty (1946), Errand Boy for Rhythm (1946), Everybody's Jumpin' Now (1946), Four Letters (1946), Frim Fram Sauce (1945), Get It Off Your Mind (1946), Got a Penny Benny (1946), Half Past Jump Time (1945), Hanover Hangover (1946), Harlem Hotcha (1946), Harp Boogie (1946), Harriet (1945), Here Comes the Fattest Man in Town (1946), I Left My Heart in Texas (1945), I Need a Playmate (1946), I'm a Shy Guy (1946), It Must Be Jelly ('Cause Jam Don't Shake Like That) (1946), It's a Sin to Tell a Lie (1946), Joe, Joe (1946), Junior (1946), Lazy Lady (1945), Low, Short and Squatty (1946), Mop (1946), My Bottle Is Dry (1946), Noah (1946), Old Dan Tucker (1946), Pigmeat Throws the Bull (1945), The Pollard Jump (1946), Rhythm Sam (1946), Ration Blues (1944), Romance Without Finance (1945), Sho Had a Wonderful Time (1946), Sizzle with Sissle (1946), Sleep Kentucky Babe (1945), Sun Tan Strut (1946), T.G. Boogie Woogie (1945), They Raided the Joint (1946), Time Takes Care of Everything (1946), Watch Out! (1946), We Pitched a Boogie Woogie (1946), Who Dunit to Who (1946), Who Threw the Whiskey in the Well? (1945)
Crouch, William Forest / R.M. Savini / Berle Adams
Reet-Petite and Gone (1947)
Currier, Dick
Black and Tan (1929)
Deans, William
When Good Luck Comes Our Way (1917)
DeBaroncelli, J. / L. Barry Bernard
The French Way (1952)
De Forrest, Lee
Sissle and Blake (1923)
Dones, Sidney P.
My First Love (1921), Reformation (1919), The Ten Thousand Dollar Trail ($10,000 Trail) (1921)
Dreifuss, Arthur / Jack Goldberg
Murder on Lenox Ave. (1941), Mystery in Swing (1940), Sunday Sinners (1941)
Dudley, Sherman H., Jr.
Reckless Money (1926), The Scar of Shame (1927)
Editorial Film Productions
Introducing East Africa (1950)
Fielding, Sol P.
Bright Road (1953)
Fife, J.W.
A Modern Cain (1921)
Fleischer, Max
I Heard (1932), I'll Be Glad When You're Dead You Rascal You (1932), Minnie the Moocher (1932)
Flowers, Tiger & Walt Miller
The Fighting Deacon (1925)
Folklore Research Films
Three Songs by Leadbelly (1945)
Foster, William
Birth Mark (1911), Black Narcissus (1929), Brother (1918), The Butler (1918), Colored Championship Baseball Game (1914), Darktown Blues (1929), The Fall Guy (1913), Florida Crackers (1921), Fool and Fire (1918), Fowl Play (1929), The Grafter and the Maid (1913), High Toned (1929), Honest Crooks (1929), In and Out (1929), Mother (1917), The Pullman Porter (1910), The Railroad Porter (1912), A Woman's Worst Enemy (1918)

Fox, William
Hearts of Dixie (1929)
Franklyn, Irwin & Hazele
Policy Man (1938)
Freed, Arthur
Cabin in the Sky (1943)
Friedrich, James K. *see* **Buell, Jed & James K. Friedrich**
Friendly, Fred *see* **Murrow, Edward R.**
Frye, Ben
Jazz Festival (1955), Rhythm and Blues Revue (1955), Rock 'n' Roll Revue (1955)
Futter, Walter
Jericho (1937)
Gant, Harry
Absent (1928)
Ghana Information Service
Freedom for Ghana (1957)
Gilroy, Bert
Deep South (1937), Mississippi Moods (1937)
Glucksman, E.M.
Big Timers (1945), Boarding House Blues (1948), Cab Calloway's Hi-De-Ho (1934), Hi-De-Ho (1947), Killer Diller (1948)
Goldberg, Bert
Beale Street Mama (1946), Dirty Gertie from Harlem, U.S.A. (1946), Harlem Is Heaven (1932), Harlem Rhapsody *see* Harlem Is Heaven, Juke Joint (1947)
Goldberg, Jack (*see also* **Dreifuss, Arthur; Harwin, Dixon R.;** *following three entries*)
Harlem Follies of 1949 (1950), Miracle in Harlem (1948), The Negro Marches On (1938)
Goldberg, Jack & Dave
Boogie Woogie Dream (1942), Boogie Woogie Dream (1944), Harlem on Parade (1940), My New Gown (1944), Othelloin Harlem *see* Paradise in Harlem, Paradise in Harlem (1940), Unlucky Woman (1944)
Goldberg, Jack / Arthur Leonard
Boy! What a Girl! (1946), Sepia Cinderella (1947)
Goldberg, Jack / Elder Micheaux
We've Come a Long, Long Way (1943)
Golder, Lew
The Spirit of Youth (1937)
Goldman, Lawrence
The Flaming Crisis (1924)

Goldwyn, Samuel
Porgy and Bess (1959)
Gordine, Sacha
Black Orpheus (1959)
Granz, Norman
Jammin' the Blues (1944)
Green, Clarence *see* **Popkin, Leo C.**
Green, Eddie
Dress Rehearsal (1939), Eddie Green's Rehearsal (1916), Eddie's Laugh Jamboree (1944), One Round Jones (1948), What Goes Up (1939)
Green, Ira
George Washington Carver (1940)
Groner, Louis *see* **Starkman, David / Louis Groner**
Groupe Africain
Afrique sur Seine (1955)
Hackel, A.W.
Am I Guilty (1940), Racket Doctor (Am I Guilty?) (1945)
Hammons, E.W.
Slow Poke (1932)
Harding, Halley
Colored American Cavalcade (1939)
Harmon, Sidney
Anna Lucasta (1958)
Harvard University Dept. of Anthropology
Forest People of Central Africa (1920)
Harwin, Dixon R. / Jack Goldberg
Double Deal (1939)
Haven, H.C.
Pygmies of Africa (1938)
Haynes, Hunter C.
Haynes Newsreel No. 1 (1914), Haynes Newsreel No. 2 (1916), Haynes Newsreel No. 3 (1917), Love Me, Love My Dog (1914), Mandy's Choice (1914), The Tango Queen (1916), Uncle Remus' First Visit to New York (1914)
Hentoff, Nat / Whitney
The Sound of Jazz (1957)
Herman, Will
Negro News Reel (1923)
Hersh, Ben
Ah, Yes, There's Good Blues Tonight (1946), Am I Lucky? (1946), Baby, Are You Kiddin'? (1946), Hollywood Boogie (1946), If You Only Knew (1946), Patience and Fortitude (1946), Satchel Mouth Baby (1946), Shout, Brother, Shout

(1946), Your Feet's Too Big (1946), Zoot (1946)

Hill, Nelam *see* **Bland, Edward**

Hubley, John
Harlem Wednesday (1959)

Hunter, Ross
Imitation of Life (1959)

I.B.P.O.E.
Hello Bill (1927)

Ince, Thomas
Free and Equal (1925)

Jarwood, Arthur
Harlem Follies (1950)

Jenkins-Bourgeois
Girl in Room 20 (1946)

Johnson, George P.
A Man's Duty (1919)

Jones, Peter P.
Colored Soldiers Fighting in Mexico (1916), The Dawn of Truth (1916), For the Honor of the 8th Illinois Regiment (1914), Illinois National Half Century Exposition (1915), Negro Soldiers Fighting for Uncle Sam (1916), Progress of the Negro (1916), Re-Birth of a Nation (1916), The Slacker (1917), The Slaver (1917), Troubles of Sambo and Dinah (1914)

Jordan, Louis
Caldonia (1945)

Julian, Hubert *see* **Micheaux, Oscar & Hubert Julian**

Kahn, Richard C.
Harlem Rides the Range (1939), Son of Ingagi (1940), Two-Gun Man from Harlem (1938)

Keighley, William / Marc Connelly
The Green Pastures (1936)

Kennedy, M. *see* **Bland, Edward**

Kier, H.W.
Of One Blood (1944)

Korda, Alexander
Sanders of the River (1935)

Korda, Zoltan
Cry, the Beloved Country (1952)

Krimsky, John & Gifford Cochran
Emperor Jones (1933)

L.C. Bordon Productions
Broken Strings (1940)

Laemmle, Carl, Jr.
Imitation of Life (1934), Minstrel Days (1930), Uncle Tom's Cabin (1914)

Lantz, Walter
Voodoo in Harlem (1938)

Leader, Anton M.
Go, Man, Go (1954)

LeBaron, William
Check and Double Check (1930), Stormy Weather (1943)

Lee, A.W.
Long Remembered (1950)

Leonard, Arthur H. (*see also* **Goldberg, Jack / Arthur Leonard; Quigley, George P. & Arthur Leonard)**
The Devil's Daughter (1939)

Lessor, Sol
Way Down South (1939)

Levy, Robert
Secret Sorrow (1921), The Sport of the Gods (1921)

Lewis, Edgar
The Bar Sinister (1917)

Lewis, Edward W.
Brown Bomber (1939), Colored America on Parade (1940), Colored Champions of Sport (1940), Life in Harlem (1940)

Louis, Will
Rakoon Hose Company (1913)

Lubin, Fredric
How Rastus Got His Pork Chop (1908)

Lubin, Sigmund
A Barney Mix-Up (1915), Butting In (1914), The Cannibal King (1915), Coffee Industry in Jamaica (1913), Coon Town Suffragettes (1914), The Cotton Industry of the South (1908), Father Said He'd Fix It (1915), The Haunted House (1915), He Was Bad (1914), In Zuzuland (1915), It Happened on Wash Day (1915), Just a Note (1914), A New Way to Win (1915), Rastus Among the Zulus (1913), Rastus Knew It Wasn't (1914), Sam and the Bully (1914), Swami Sam (1914), The Tale of a Chicken (1914), The Undertaker's Daughter (1915), Who's Who (1914), Zeb, Zack and the Zulus (1913)

Mahuzier, A.
Regard sur l'Afrique Noire (1947)

March of Time
Upbeat in Music (1943)

Markham, Dewey and Heckle
Mr. Smith Goes Ghost (1940), One Big Mistake (1940)

Maurice, Richard D.
Eleven PM (1928), Home Brew (1920), Nobody's Children (1920), Return of Black Hawk (1921)

Meyers, Sidney, Janet Loeb
The Quiet One (1958)

Michaux, Elder Solomon Lightfoot (see also Goldberg, Jack / Edler Micheaux)
We've Got the Devil on the Run (1934)

Micheaux, Oscar
The Betrayal (1948), Birthright (1924), Black Magic (1932), Body and Soul (1924), Broken Violin (1926), The Brute (1920), The Conjure Woman (1926), Deceit (1921), The Devil's Disciple (1926), The Dungeon (1922), A Fool's Errand (1922), God's Stepchildren (1938), The Gunsaulus Mystery (1921), The Homesteader (1918), The House Behind the Cedars (1924), The Hypocrite (1922), Jasper Landry's Will see Uncle Jasper's Will, Lying Lips (1939), Marcus Garland (1928), The Millionaire (1927), Murder in Harlem (1935) see also Lem Hawkins' Confession, Son of Satan (1924), The Spider's Web (1926), The Symbol of the Unconquered (1920), Temptation (1936), Ten Minutes to Kill (1933), Thirty Years Later (1928), Uncle Jasper's Will (Jasper Landry's Will) (1922), Underworld (1937), Veiled Aristocrats (1932), The Virgin of the Seminole (1922), The Wages of Sin (1928), When Men Betray (1929), Within Our Gates (1919)

Micheaux, Oscar & Hubert Julian
The Notorious Elinor Lee (1940)

Micheaux, Swan
The Midnight Ace (1928)

Miller, Walt see Flowers, Tiger

Million Dollar Production
Murder Rap (1948)

Minz, Robert see Weiss, Louis

Monumental Pictures Corporation
Monumental Monthly Negro Newsreel (1921)

Morris Wax Management Company
The Vicious Circle (1936)

Moss, Carlton
Frederick Douglas's the House on Cedar Hill (1953)

Murrow, Edward R. / Fred Friendly
Satchmo, the Great (1954)

Muse, Clarence
Toussaint L'Ouverture (1921)

Nalpas, Alex
The Revue des Revues (1927)

National Anti-Tuberculosis Association
Let My People Live (1938)

NET
Slavery (1953)

Nissotti, Arys
Prinsesse Tam-Tam (1935)

Norman Film Manufacturing Company
Black Gold (1928), The Bull-Dogger (1923), The Crimson Skull (1921) (alt. title The Scarlet Claw), A Debtor to the Law (1924), The Fighting Fool (1925), The Flying Ace (1926), The Green Eyed Monster (1921), The Love Bug (1920), Regeneration (1923), Scarlet Claw see The Crimson Skull, Zircon (1923)

Pal, George
A Date with Duke (1946), Jasper Series (1946)

Pathé
The Beauty Contest (1921), Dark Town Follies (1929)

Patric, Fitz
Memories and Melodies (1935)

Paton, Tony
The Peanut Man (1947)

Peacocke, Leslie
Injustice see Loyal Hearts, Loyal Hearts (Injustice) (1919)

Perold, Jan M.
Lobola (1954)

Pizor, William M.
Chocklate Cowboys (1925)

Pollard, Bud
Beware! (1946), Harlem Big Shot (The Black King) (1936), Tall, Tan and Terrific (1946)

Pollard, Fritz
Rockin' the Blues (1955)

Pond, Stillman
Flamingo (1947)

Popkin, Harry M.
Bargain with Bullets (1937), Crooked Money see While Thousands Cheer, The Duke Is Tops (The Bronze Venus) (1938), Gang Smashers (1938), Gridiron Graft see While Thousands Cheer, Gun Moll (Gang Smashers) (1944), Life Goes On (1938), Straight to Heaven (1939), While Thousands Cheer (1940)

Popkin, Leo C. & Clarence Green
The Well (Deep Is the Well) (1951)
Porter, Edwin S.
Uncle Tom's Cabin (1903)
Prades, James
Native Son (1951)
Progress Picture Association
The Lure of a Woman (1921)
Quigley, George P.
Murder with Music (1941)
Quigley, George P. & Arthur Leonard
Mistaken Identity (1941)
Quimby, Fred
Uncle Tom's Cabana (1947)
Randol, George
Midnight Shadow (1939), Rhythm Rodeo
(1938)
Randol, George / Ben Rinaldo
Dark Manhattan (1937)
Randol, George / Bert Goldberg
Darktown Strutters' Ball (1940)
Rieger, Jack
O'Voutie O'Rooney (1947)
Rinaldo, Ben see Randol, George / Ben Ri-
naldo
Roach, Hal
Little Daddy (1931)
Rogosin, Lionel
Come Back, Africa (1959)
Rosebud Productions
Georgia Rose (1930)
Rossen, Robert & Jack
The Unknown Soldier Speaks (1934)
Russell, A. Burton
Birthright (1939), The Darktown Revue
(1931), The Daughter of the Congo (1930),
Easy Street (1930), Ghost of Tolston's
Manor (1934), The Girl from Chicago
(1932), Harlem After Midnight (1934),
Lem Hawkins' Confession (Murder in
Harlem) (1935), Phantom of Kenwood
(1933), Swing (1938), Ten Minutes to Live
(1932)
Sack, Alfred
Bipp Bang Boogie (1944), The Blood of
Jesus (1941), Children of Circumstance
(1937), Fuzzy Wuzzy (1945), Hep Cat Ser-
enade (1947), Junction 88 (1947), March-
ing On! (1943), Rocco Blues (1947), The St.
Louis Blues (1929), Where's My Man To-
Nite? (1944)

Sack, Alfred N. / Spencer Williams
Go Down, Death! (1944)
Sanforth, Clifford
Four Shall Die (1940), Gang War (1939)
Sarigny, Peter de
Simba (1955)
Saunders, Tressie
Woman's Error (1922)
Savini, R.M. see Crouch, William Forest /
R.M. Savini / Berle Adams
Schiffman, Frank
The Exile (1931)
Schlesinger, Leon
Coal Black and de Sebben Dwarfs (1942),
Jungle Jitters (1942)
Scott, Emmett J.
Birth of a Race (Lincoln's Dream) (1918)
Silliphant, Stirling
The Joe Louis Story (1953)
Smith, Pete
Story of Dr. Carver (1939)
Smith, Robert
St. Louis Blues (1958)
Smith, Dr. W.
Howard-Lincoln Football Game (1921)
Southland Pictures
The Black King (1932)
Starkman, David
Children of Fate (1926)
Starkman, David / Louis Groner
A Prince of His Race (1926), Ten Nights in
a Bar-Room (1926)
Strasser, Ben
A Giant of His Race (1921), His Great
Chance (1923), A Shot in the Night (1922)
Swanson, Donald
Jim Comes to Jo'Burg (1950), The Magic
Garden (1952)
Titus, E. see Bland, Edward
Toddy, Ted
Colored Americans in the Nation's Capitol
(1946), Colored Men in White (1943),
Fight That Ghost (1946), House-Rent
Party (1946), Mantan Messes Up
(1946), Mantan Runs for Mayor (1946),
A Night with the Devil (1946), Prairie
Comes to Harlem (1941), Rufus Green in
Harlem (1946), Sergeant Joe Louis on Tour
(1943), She's Too Mean for Me (1948), Shut
My Big Mouth (1947), Super Sleuths
(1947), Voodoo Devil Drums (1946), What

a Guy (1947), Who's Who in Colored America (1945), The Wrong Mr. Wright (1947)

Tuller, Joseph
Burlesque in Harlem (1955)

Turpin, Charles H.
In Honor of the 92nd Division (1917), Ninety-Second Division on Parade (1919), Pythian Parade and 19th Biannual Encampment (1920), Turpin's Real Reels (1916)

Ulmer, Edgar G.
Moon Over Harlem (1939)

United States Office of War Information
The Negro College in Wartime (1943)

United States War Department
Heroic Negro Soldiers (1919), The Negro Soldier (1944), Our Colored Fighters (1918)

Vidor, King
Hallelujah (1929)

Villiers, François *see* **Cocteau, Jean**

Vitaphone
Black Network (A Broadway Brevity) (1936)

Walker, C.J.
Pythian Conclave and League Parley (1930)

Waller, Fred "Fats"
Honeysuckle Rose (1941), How to Go to a French Restaurant (1941), How to See a French Doctor (1941), Listen to the Mocking Bird (1941), Macnamara's Band (1941)

Warner, John
Pitch a Boogie Woogie (1948)

Warner Bros.
Pie Pie Blackbirds (1932)

Waters, Ethel
Carib Gold (1956)

Weiss, George

Junior Jeeps (1947)

Weiss, Louis / Robert Minz
Drums o' Voodoo (alt. title: Louisiana; Voodoo Drums) (1933), Louisiana *see* Drums o' Voodoo, Voodoo Drums *see* Drums o' Voodoo

Whipper, Leigh
Come Back (1922), A Regeneration of Souls (1921), Renaissance Newsreel (1921)

White, Charles Allman
The Crimson Fog (1932), The Dusky Virgin (1932)

Whitney *see* **Hentoff, Nat**

Wilder, A.W. Lee
Cherished Melodies (1950), Folklore (1950), Glory Filled Spirituals (1950), Southern A Cappella (1950), The Tradition (1950), Tunes That Live (1950)

Williams, Spencer (*see also* Sack, Alfred N. / Spencer Williams)
Hot Biscuits (1929), Rhapsody of Negro Life (1949), Tenderfeet (1928)

Wills, J. Elder
The Song of Freedom (1938)

Wilson, Ben D.
The Man from Texas (1921)

World Artist, Inc.
Marian Anderson (1953)

Yorke, Emmerson
Message from Dorothy Maynor (1949)

Zanuck, Darryl F.
Pinky (1949)

Zebba, Sam
Fincho (1958)

Zukor, Adolph
Hi-De-Ho (1958), Symphony in Black: A Rhapsody of Negro Life (1935)

APPENDIX E:
FILMS BY YEAR

1895

Native Woman Coaling a Ship and Scrambling for Money
Native Woman Coaling a Ship at St. Thomas, D.W.I.
Native Woman Washing a Negro Baby in Nassau, B.I.
Native Woman Washing Clothes at St. Vincent, D.W.I.
A Watermelon Contest

1896

Dancing Darkey Boy

1897

West Indian Boys Diving for Money
West Indian Girls in Native Dance
Wharf Scenes and Natives Swimming at St. Thomas, D.W.I.

1898

Colored Troops Disembarking
Ninth U.S. Cavalry Watering Horses
Steamer Mascotte Arriving at Tampa

1900

Sambo and Jemima

1901

Bally-Hoo Cake Walk

1903

The Gator and the Pickaninny
Pickaninny's Dance
Pie Eating Contest
The Porters
Porters' Parade
A Scrap in Black and White
Uncle Tom's Cabin
Watermelon Feast
Way Down South

1904

A Bucket of Cream Ale
Cotton Spinning on the Old Plantation
Dancing Darkies
Darky Cake Walk
The Nigger in the Woodpile

1905

Everybody Works But Father (Blackface)
Gluttonous Negro
Interrupted Crap Game
Miss Jewett and the Baker Family of Negroes
A Muffin Lesson
They're Not Warm
The Thirteen Club
The Wooing and Wedding of a Coon

1907

The Dancing Nig
Jamaica Negroes Doing a Two Step

1908

The Cotton Industry of the South
How Rastus Got His Pork Chop

1909

Uncle Tom's Cabin

Pre–1910

American Soldier in Love & War, No. 3
Barnstormers
Cake Walk
A Close Call
Comedy Cake Walk
Dixon-Chester Leon Contest
The Feud and the Turkey
The Guerrilla
A Hard Wash
His Trust
His Trust Fulfilled
How Charlie Lost the Heiress
A Kiss in the Dark
Laughing Ben
The Mis-Directed Kiss
Nellie, Beautiful Housemaid
Paul J. Rainey's African Hunt
Pompey's Honey Girl
The Seeress
The Snowman
The Subpoena Server
Under the Old Apple Tree
What Happened in the Tunnel
While Strolling in the Park
Who Said Chicken?

1910

The Confederate Spy
From Cotton Patch to Congress
The Possum Hunt
The Pullman Porter
Sam Langford–Jim Flynn Prize Fight
The Zulu's Heart

1911

Birth Mark
The Butler
The Judge's Story

1912

The Debt
Jack Johnson vs. Jim Flynn
Pickaninnies and Watermelon
The Railroad Porter

1913

Coffee Industry in Jamaica
A Day at Tuskegee
The Fall Guy
The Fall of the Mighty
The Grafter and the Maid
National Negro Business League
Natural Born Shooter
Rakoon Hose Company
Rastus Among the Zulus
Zeb, Zack and the Zulus

1914

Black and White
Butting In
Colored Championship Baseball Game
Coon Town Suffragettes
Dandy Jim's Dream
Darktown Jubilee
For the Honor of the 8th Illinois Regiment
Haynes Newsreel No. 1
He Was Bad
Just a Note
Love Me, Love My Dog
Lovie Joe's Romance
Mandy's Choice
National Negro Business League
One Large Evening
Rastus Knew It Wasn't
A Review of the B.M.C. and the Colored
    Business World
Sam and the Bully
Slim-the-Cow-Puncher
Swami Sam
The Tale of a Chicken
Troubles of Sambo and Dinah
Uncle Remus' First Visit to New York
Uncle Tom's Cabin
Who's Who

1915

Alladin Jones
Barber of Darktown
A Barnyard Mix-Up
The Cannibal King
A Dark Lover's Play
Father Said He'd Fix it
The Haunted House
How Skinny Made Good
Illinois National Half Century Exposition
In Zululand
It Happened on Wash Day
A New Way to Win
The Undertaker's Daughter
When True Love Wins
With the Help of Uncle Eben

1916

The Barber
The Colored American Winning His Suit
Colored Elks Parade
Colored Soldiers Fighting in Mexico
The Dawn of Truth
Eddie Green's Rehearsal
Escapades of Estelle
Fish
The Funeral of Booker T. Washington
Haynes Newsreel, No. 2
Mr. Miller's Economics
Money Talks in Darktown
Natural Born Gambler
Negro Soldiers Fighting for Uncle Sam
Progress of the Negro
The Realization of a Negro's Ambition
Re-Birth of a Nation
Shadowed by the Devil
The Tango Queen
Trooper of Troop K (Trooper of Company K)
Turpin's Real Reels
Two Knights of Vaudeville
A Zulu's Devotion
Zulutown
Zulutown Races

1917

The Bar Sinister
A Black Sherlock Holmes
Booker T. Washington Industrial School

A Busted Romance
Dat Blackhand Waitah Man
Devil for a Day
Ghosts
Haynes Newsreel, No. 3
The Hypocrites
In Honor of the 92nd Division
The Law of Nature
Mercy, the Mummy Mumbled
Mother
Shine Johnson and the Rabbit Foot
The Slacker
The Slaver
Some Baby
Spooks
When Cupid Went Wild
When Good Luck Comes Our Way
Wrong All Around

1918

Are Working Girls Safe
Birth of a Race (Lincoln's Dream)
Black and Tan Mix Up
Brother
The Bully
Clef Club Five Minutes for Train
Colored Americans
Colored Troops at Chillicothe
The Comeback of Barnacle Bill
A Day in the Nation's Capital
Do the Dead Talk?
Doing Their Bit
Fixing the Faker
Fool and Fire
France's Dusky Warriors
Good Luck in Old Clothes
The Homesteader
The Janitor
Lincoln Pictorial
Love and Undertakers
The Loyalty of a Race
Luck in Old Clothes
The Man in Ebony
A Milk-Fed Hero
Our Boys at Camp Upton
Our Colored Fighters
Our Hell Fighters
The Porters
A Reckless Rover
Spying the Spy

The Symbol of Sacrifice
Uncle Tom's Cabin
What's the Use?
When You Are Scared, Run
When You Hit, Hit Hard
A Woman's Worst Enemy

1919

Dark and Cloudy
Democracy, or a Fight for Right
Golden Pearls of Progress
Heroic Negro Soldiers
Loyal Hearts (Injustice)
A Man's Duty
A Minister's Temptation
Ninety-Second Division on Parade
Prize Drill Team
Reformation
Sambo Comedies
Upward Path
Within Our Gates

1920

The Brute
A Daughter of Pharaoh
A Day in the Magic City of Birmingham
Eyes of Youth
Forest People of Central Africa
From Harlem to the Rhine
Home Brew
In the Depths of Our Hearts
The Love Bug
Nobody's Children
Pythian Parade and 19th Biannual Encampment
The Scapegoat
The Symbol of the Unconquered

1921

As the World Rolls On
The Beauty Contest
Black Thunderbolt
The Burden of Race
By Right of Birth
The Call of His People
The Charge of the Black Brigade
A Child in Pawn
The Crimson Skull (The Scarlet Claw)

The Custard Nine
Darktown Affair
Deceit
The Disappearance of Mary Jane
Easy Money
The Fighting Fifteenth Colored Regiment
Florida Crackers
Foolish Lives
A Fool's Promise
Fought and Won
A Ghost Hunt
A Giant of His Race
The Green Eyed Monster
The Gunsaulus Mystery
Hearts of the Woods
Hot Dogs
Howard-Lincoln Football Game
The Human Devil
The Lure of a Woman
The Man from Texas
The Matchless Key
A Modern Cain
Monumental Monthly Negro Newsreel
Monumental News Reel, No. 2
My First Love
The Negro Logging in Louisiana
The Negro Today
Our Colored Boys Over There
Peacock News Reel, #1
The Pickaninny
A Regeneration of Souls
Renaissance Newsreel
Return of Black Hawk
Secret Sorrow
Seeing Kansas City in Action
Shuffling Jane
The Simp
The Southern Negro Baptism
The Sport of the Gods
The Ten Thousand Dollar Trail
Ties of Blood
Toussaint L'Ouverture
Walker Newsreel No. 1

1922

Bessie Coleman
Come Back
A Day with the Tenth Cavalry at Fort
  Huachuca
The Dungeon
A Fool's Errand

For His Mother's Sake
The Girl from the Pepper Patch
The Greatest Sin
The Hypocrite
Jasper Landry's Will *see* Uncle Jasper's
   Will
The Jazz Hounds
The Leader of His Race
Lure of the Woods
Memorial Services at the Tomb of "Prince
   Hall"
The Negro Rice Farmer
News Reel, #1
News Reel, #2
Peacock News Reel, #2
The Perfect Dreamer
The Schemers
Shoot 'Em Up, Sam
A Shot in the Night
Spitfire
Square Joe
The Stranger from Way Out Yonder
A Tuskegee Pilgrimage
Uncle Jasper's Will (Jasper Landry's Will)
Undisputed Evidence
The Virgin of the Seminole
The Wife Hunters
Woman's Error
Wrong All Around
The Wrong Mr. Johnson
You Can't Keep a Good Man Down

1923

Bessie Coleman
The Bull-Dogger
The Devils
Devil's Match
Flames of Wrath
His Great Chance
His Last Chance
The House of Mystery
How High Is Up
In the Shadows
Kinky
Negro News Reel
Regeneration
Sissle and Black
Snappy Tunes
Tony's Shirt
Tuskegee Finds a Way Out

Why Worry?
Zircon

1924

Birthright
Body and Soul
Chocolate Dandies
The Dayton Guide
A Debtor to the Law
The Flaming Crisis
Harry Wills in Training
The House Behind the Cedars
Smiling Hate
Son of Satan
Steppin' High

1925

Bathing Beauty Parade, Pacific Beach
The Black Boomerang
Chocolate Cowboy
The Fighting Deacon
The Fighting Fool
The Florian Slappey Series
Free and Equal

1926

Broken Violin
Children of Fate
The Conjure Woman
The Devil's Disciple
The Flying Ace
Let's Do the Black Bottom
A Night in Dixie
Nine Lives
A Prince of His Race
Reckless Money
Saddle Daze
The Spider's Web
Ten Nights in a Bar-Room
When Giants Fought

1927

Charleston (Sur un Air de Charleston)
Ham and Eggs
Hello Bill
Idlewild
The Millionaire

Noble Sissle and Eubie Blake
The Revue des Revues
The Scar of Shame
Siren of the Tropics
Uncle Tom's Cabin
Willie and Eugene Howard in a Theater
    Manager's Office

1928

Absent
Black Gold
Dixie Days
Eleven PM
George Dewey Washington, #1
Hazel Green and Company
Kentucky Jubilee Singers
Marcus Garland
The Midnight Ace
Old Time Songs
Samba
Southern Revellers
Tenderfeet
Thirty Year Later
The Wages of Sin
Willie and Eugene Howard, Music Makers

1929

Black and Tan
Black Narcissus
Borderline
Brown Gravy
Bud Harris and Frank Radcliffe
Clarence Tisdale
Cora Green
Dark Town Follies
Darktown Blues
A Day in an African Village
Eddie Green and Company, Sending a Wire
Eubie Blake Plays
Fowl Play
The Framing of the Shrew
Gayety
George Dewey Washington, #2
George Dewey Washington, #3
George Dewey Washington, #4
Hallelujah
Harlem Knights
Harlem Mania
Hearts of Dixie

High Toned
Honest Crooks
Hot Biscuits
How Africa Lives
How an African Tribe Is Ruled Under Colo-
    nial Government
In and Out
Jim Town Cabaret
Jules Bledsoe
Jungle Drums
Kentucky Jubilee Singers
The Lady Fare
Low Down: A Bird's Eye View of Harlem
Mayor of Jimtown
Melancholy Dame
Miller and Lyles
Minstrel Days
Music Hath Harms
Negro Life
Norman Thomas Quintette, Harlem Mania
Oft in the Silly Night
Old Man Trouble
Revival Day
Roll Along
The St. Louis Blues
Shake It Up
Song After Sorrow
Steppin' Along
Sunshine Sammy
They Know Their Groceries
Two Black Crows in Africa
The Water Boy
When Men Betray
The Widow's Bite
Willie and Eugene Howard, My People

1930

Africa Speaks
Check and Double Check
Crap Game
Darktown Scandal's Revue
The Daughter of the Congo
Dusky Melodies
Easy Street
George Dewey Washington, #5
Georgia Rose
Kid Chocolate and Jack Kid Berg
Midnight Lodger
Minstrel Days
News Reel, #1

On a Plantation
On the Levee
Pickin' Cotton
Pythian Conclave and League Parley
Sissle and Blake
Slave Days
Syncopated Sermon
Those Pullman Porters
Utica Jubilee Singers
The Witching Eyes
Yamekraw

1931

Abyssinia
L'Afrique Vous Paris
The Darktown Revue
The Dixie Chase
The Exile
Hell's Alley
Little Daddy
The Negro and Art
Negro Education and Art in the United States
Ol' King Cotton
The Road Home
Tuskegee Trains New Pilots
Welcome Home

1932

The Black King
Black Magic
The Crimson Fog
Croix du Sud
Dancers in the Dark
The Dusky Virgin
The Girl from Chicago
Harlem Is Heaven
Harlem Rhapsody *see* Harlem Is Heaven
I Ain't Got Nobody
I Heard
I'll Be Glad When You're Dead You Rascal You
A Jungle Jinx
Mammy's Boy
Melody Makers Series
Minnie the Moocher
Old Man Rhythm
Pie Pie Blackbirds
Rhythm on the River
Slow Poke
Smash Your Baggage

The Spirit of the Hellfighters
Ten Minutes to Live
That's the Spirit
Veiled Aristocrats

1933

Black Cat Tales
A Bundle of Blues
Claude Hopkins and His Orchestra
Drums o' Voodoo (Louisiana; Voodoo Drums)
Emperor Jones
Gig and Saddle
Little Black Sambo
Mills' Blue Rhythm Band
Old Black Joe
Phantom of Kenwood
Rufus Jones for President
Scandal
Ten Minutes to Kill

1934

Bubbling Over
Cab Calloway's Hi-De-Ho
Cotton-Pickin' Days
Dixie Love
Ghost of Tolston's Manor
Harlem After Midnight
Hi-De-Ho
Imitation of Life
Jailhouse Blues
King for a Day
Lincoln-Howard Football Game
The Mississippi
Rhapsody in Black
The Unknown Soldier Speaks
Way Down Yonder
We've Got the Devil on the Run
Zouzou

1935

All-colored Vaudeville Show
By Request
Cab Calloway's Jitterbug Party
Claude Hopkins and His Orchestra
Dixieland Jamboree
Doin' the Town
Don Redman and His Orchestra
Hall Johnson Choir in a Syncopated Sermon

Harlem Bound
Harlem Harmony
Life Is Real
The Life of the Party
Memories and Melodies
Murder in Harlem (The Brand of Cain; *see also* Lem Hawkins' Confession)
Prinsesse Tam-Tam
Radio Rascals
Sanders of the River
The Story of Dr. George Washington Carver
Symphony in Black: A Rhapsody of Negro Life
Way Out West
Young Pushkin

1936

Black Network (A Broadway Brevity)
Camp Meeting
Gifts in Rhythm
The Green Pastures
Harlem Big Shot (The Black King)
Jimmie Lunceford and His Dance Orchestra
Pink Lemonade
Spooks
Temptation
The Vicious Circle
We Work Again

1937

Baby Jewels
Barbershop Blues
Bargain with Bullets
Bosko and the Pirate
Callalco
Cavalcade of Harlem
Children of Circumstance
Clean Pastures
Dark Manhattan
Daughters of the Isle of Jamaica
Deep South
Deviled Hams
Easy Pickens
Hearts in Bondage
Hi-De-Ho
Jericho
Life of Today
Mississippi Moods
Murder in Swingtime

A Night in a Night Club
Rhythm Saves Day
The Spirit of Youth
Sugar Hill Baby
That Man Samson
Trailer Paradise
Underworld

1938

All's Fair
Big Fella
The Bronze Buckaroo
The Duke Is Tops (The Bronze Venus)
Gang Smashers
God's Stepchildren
The Green Pastures
Harlem Mania
Harlem on the Prairie
International Rhythms
Let My People Live
Life Goes On (His Harlem Wife)
Meet the Maestros
Mr. Creeps
A Modern Dixie
The Negro Farmer
The Negro Marches On
Policy Man
Pygmies of Africa
Rhythm Rodeo
Roar of the Crowd
St. Louis Gal
The Song of Freedom
Streamlined Swing
Swing
Two-Gun Man from Harlem
Voodoo in Harlem

1939

Bad Boy
Birthright
Black Preview Trailers
The Broken Earth
Brown Bomber
Colored American Cavalcade
The Devil's Daughter
Double Deal
Dress Rehearsal
Gang War
Gone Harlem

Harlem Rides the Range
Keep Punching
Lying Lips
Merrie Howe Carfe
Midnight Shadow
Moon Over Harlem
One Dark Night
Readin', Writin' and Rhythm
Reform School
Story of Dr. Carver
Straight to Heaven
Way Down South
What Goes Up

1940

Am I Guilty
Broken Strings
Colored America on Parade
Colored Champions of Sport
Comes Midnight
Darktown Strutters' Ball
Four Shall Die
George Washington Carver
Harlem on Parade
Kilroy Lives Here
Lady Luck *see* Lucky Ghost
Life in Harlem
Life of Booker T. Washington
Life of Florence Mills
Life of George Washington Carver
Mr. Smith Goes Ghost
Mr. Washington Goes to Town
Mystery in Swing
The Notorious Elinor Lee
One Big Mistake
One Tenth of Our Nation
Paradise in Harlem (Othello in Harlem)
She Devil
Son of Ingagi
While Thousands Cheer (Gridiron Graft)

1941

Air Mail Special
Alabamy Bound
Battling Amateurs
The Blood of Jesus
Booglie Wooglie Piggy
Dark-Town Strutters' Ball
Dear Old Southland
Do I Worry?

Down on the Swanee River
Easy Street
Four or Five Times
Give Me Some Skin
Hark! Hark! The Lark
Honeysuckle Rose
Hot Chocklate (Cottontail)
How to Go to a French Restaurant
How to See a French Doctor
I Dreamt I Dwelt in Harlem
I Want a Big Fat Mama
Jack, You're Playing the Game
Jeans Teacher and Her Work
Jim
Johnny Peddler
The Joint Is Jumpin'
Jungle Jig
Listen to the Mocking Bird
A Little Jive Is Good for You
The Lonesome Road
Lucky Ghost (Lady Luck)
Macnamara's Band
Mistaken Identity
Murder on Lenox Avenue
Murder with Music
Oh, Susannah
Prairie Comes to Harlem
Professor Creeps
Ride, Red, Ride
Rigoletto Blues
Shadrach
Shout! Sister, Shout!
Solid Senders
Sunday Sinners
Swing For Sale
Swing for Your Supper
Swing It Harlem
Take Me Back, Baby
Take My Life
Take the "A" Train
Toot That Trumpet!
Toppers Take a Bow
Up Jumped the Devil
Whatcha Know Joe?
Where the Sweet Mammas Grow
Yes! Indeed
Your Feet's Too Big

1942

Basin Street Boogie
Because I Love You
Blackbird Fantasy
Blues in the Night
Boogie Woogie Dream
Brother Martin, Servant of Jesus
By an Old Southern River
Caravan
Case o' the Blues
Close Shave
Coal Black and de Sebben Dwarfs
Congo Clambake
Cow-Cow Boogie
Cuban Episode
The Devil Sat Down and Cried
Down, Down, Down
Five Guys Named Moe
Flamingo
Fuzzy Wuzzy
G.I. Jubilee, George Dewey Washington
Harlem Rhumba
Harlem Serenade
Hot Frogs
Hot in the Groove
I Got It Bad, and That Ain't Good
I Won't Miss You
I'll Be Glad When You're Dead, You Rascal
    You
Jam Session
Jive Comes to the Jungle
Jump In
Jungle Jitters
Legs Ain't No Good
Let's Go
Let's Shuffle
Little Carol Jackson
Minnie the Moocher
Old Man Mose
The Outskirts of Town
Paper Doll
Peckin'
Pudgy Boy
Rhythm on the Run
Rockin' Chair
S.S. Booker T. Washington
Second News Reel
Shine
A Sinner Kills an Angel
The Skunk Song

Sleepy Time Down South
Some of These Days
Spirit of Boogie Woogie
Sugar Hill Masquerade
Swingin' on Nothin'
That Ol' Ghost Train
Tuxedo Junction
Tweed Me
Virginia, Georgia and Caroline
The Walls Keep Talking
What to Do
A Zoot Suit (With a Reet Pleat)

1943

Ain't My Sugar Sweet
Babbling Bess
Baby Don't Go Away from Me
Baby Don't You Cry
Backstage Blues
Band Parade
Beat Me Daddy
Block Party Revels
Boogie Man
Breakfast in Rhythm
Bronze Venus (The Duke Is Tops)
Cabin in the Sky
Caterpillar Shuffle
Chant of the Jungle
Chatter
Chicken Shack Shuffle
Choo Choo Swing
Chop Sticks
Colored Men in White
Dancemania
Dispossessed Blues
Do I Worry?
Duke Ellington and His Orchestra
Emily Brown
Fighting Americans
Foolin' Around
Get with It
Git It
God's Heaven
Good-Nite All
A Harlemesque Revue
Here 'Tis Honey, Take It
Hit That Jive Jack
I Gotta Go to Camp and See My Man
I Miss You So
If a Boy Needs a Friend

If You Treat Me to a Hug
Jackpot
Jittering Jitterbugs
Jumpin' Jack from Hackensack
Jungle Jamboree
Keep Smiling
Keep Waitin'
Let's Get Away from It All
Let's Get Down to Business
Linda Brown
The Long and Short of It
Lovin' Up a Breeze
Mama, I Wanna Make Rhythm
Marching On
Maria Elena
Meetin' Time
Melody Takes a Holiday
Moo Cow Boogie
My Girl Loves a Sailor
The Negro College in Wartime
Pardon Me, But You Look Like Margie
Poppin' the Cork
Prancing in the Park
Put Your Arms Around Me, Honey
Quarry Road
Quick Watson, the Question
Rhumboogie
Rhythm Mad
Rhythm Mania
Rhythm of the Rhythm Band
Riff
Rocco Blues
Rock It for Me
Rug Cutter's Holiday
Sergeant Joe Louis on Tour
Shoot the Rhythm to Me
Sing and Swing
A Song and Dance Man
Stepping Along
Sticks and Stones
Stormy Weather
Swanee Smiles
Sweet Kisses
Swing Cats Ball
Tap Happy
To Live as Free Men
Toot That Trumpet
Upbeat in Music
The Way to Happiness
We've Come a Long, Long Way
Wham

Willie Willie
You Can't Fool About Love

1944

Ain't She Pretty
Back Beat Boogie
Big Fat Butterfly
Bipp Bang Boogie
Blitzkrieg Bombardier
Boogie Woogie
Boogie Woogie Dream
Boogie Woogie Piggy
Can't See for Lookin'
Carnival of Rhythm
Cha-Chi-Man
Cielito Lindo
Cootie Williams and His Orchestra
Dance Your Old Age Away
Deed I Do
Dinah
Easy to Get
Eddie's Laugh Jamboree
Everyday Is Saturday in Harlem
Forty-Seventh Street Jive
Gangsters on the Loose (Bargain with Bullets)
Gee
G.I. Jive
Go Down, Death!
Goldilocks and the Jivin' Bears
Gun Moll (Gang Smashers)
Harry the Hipster
Henry Brown, Farmer
Hey, Lawdy Mama
Hi-De-Ho Holiday
His Harlem Wife (Life Goes On)
His Rockin' Horse Ran Away
House on 52nd Street
I Can't Dance
I Can't Give You Anything but Love
I Like It Cause I Love It
I'd Love to be a Cowboy
If You Can't Smile and Say Yes
I'm a Good Good Woman
I'm Tired
Is You or Is You Ain't My Baby
Jam Session
Jammin' the Blues
Jonah and the Whale
Jordan Jive

Juke Box Boogie
Jumpin' at the Jubilee
Lazy River
Love Grows on a White Oak Tree
Low Down Dog
Mama Had a Little Lamb
Mamprusi Village
My, Ain't That Somethin'
My New Gown
The Negro Soldier
Night Club Girl (One Dark Night)
Of One Blood
Opus 12 EEE
Pigmeat's Laugh HepCats
Prison Bait (Reform School *re-release*)
Ration Blues
Rhapsody of Love
Ride on, Ride On
Rinka Tinka Man
Roll 'Em
She's Too Hot to Handle
Shine
Sports Cavalcade
Steak and Potatoes
Story of the American Negro Theatre
Swanee Swing
Taint Yours
Till Then
Unlucky Woman
When You and I Were Young, Maggie
Where's My Man To-Nite?
Who's Been Eating My Porridge?
Wings for This Man
Yankee Doodle Never Went to Town
You Always Hurt the One You Love

1945

Ain't Misbehavin'
All American News Reel
All American News Reel, No. 4
All Ruzzitt Buzzitt
Along the Navajo Trail
Ask the OPA
Baby Don't You Love Me Anymore
Basie's Boogie
Big Timers
Blowtop Blues
Brother Bill
Buck and Bubbles Laff Jubilee

Buzz Me
Cab Calloway Medley
Caldonia
Calhon — The Way to a Better Future
Cash Ain't Nothing But Trash
Cat's Can't Dance
The Chair Song
Chilly 'n' Cold
Contrast in Rhythm
Corn Pone
Cryin' and Singin' the Blues
Dixie Rhythm
Don't Be Late
Dry Bones
Fan Tan Fanny
Fare Thee Well
Faust
Five Salted Peanuts
Foo, a Little Ballyhoo
Frim Fram Sauce
Fuzzy Wuzzy
Glory Road
Half Past Jump Time
Harlem Hot Shots
Harriet
Honey Chile
I Had a Dream
I Left My Heart in Texas
I Want a Little Doggie
I Was Here When You Left Me
I'm Making Believe
It Happened in Harlem
It's Me, Oh Lord
I've Got to Be a Rug Cutter
Joseph 'n' His Brudders
Just a-Sittin' and a Rockin'
Knock Me Out
Lazy Lady
Mr. Jackson from Jacksonville
Mr. X Blues
The Negro Sailor
Never Too Old to Swing
No, No, Baby
Oh-h-e-e My, My
Pigmeat Throws the Bull
The Preacher and the Bear
Racket Doctor (Am I Guilty?)
Rise of a Race
Romance on the Beat
Romance Without Finance
Scotch Boogie

Shoe Shine Boy
Sleep Kentucky Babe
Snoqualomie Jo Jo
Standin' Joe
A Study of Negro Artists
Swanee Showboat
Swingin' in the Groove
T.G. Boogie Woogie
Take Everything
Ten Thousand Years Ago
There Are Eighty-Eight Reasons Why
Three Songs by Leadbelly
Tillie
Tis You, Babe
Walking with My Honey
We the Cats Shall Hep Ya
Who Threw the Whiskey in the Well?
Who's Who in Colored America
Write That Letter Tonight
Ya Fine and Healthy Thing
Y.M.C.A., Harlem, N.Y.

1946

Adventure
Adventure in Boogie Woogie
Ah, Yes, There's Good Blues Tonight
Am I Lucky?
Art in Negro Schools
Baby, Are You Kiddin'?
Back Door Man
Beale Street Mama
Beware!
Big Fat Mammas
Boogiemania
Boy! What a Girl!
Broadway
Broadway and Main
The Call to Duty
Chicago After Dark
Color of a Man
Colored Americans in the Nation's Capitol
Come to Baby Do
The Corpse Accuses
Count Me Out
Crawl, Red, Crawl
Crime Street
A Date with Duke
Dinty McGinty
Dirty Gertie from Harlem, U.S.A.
Does You Do, or Does You Don't

Drink Hearty
Dunkin' Bagels
Errand Boy for Rhythm
Everybody's Jumpin' Now
Fight That Ghost
Flicker Up
Four Letters
Frenzy
Get It Off Your Mind
Girl in Room 20
Going to Glory, Come to Jesus
Got a Penny Benny
Hampton Institute Programs for Education
Hanover Hangover
Harlem Hotcha
Harp Boogie
Hello Bill
Here Come the Fattest Man in Town
The Highest Tradition
Hollywood Boogie
House-Rent Party
I Cried for You
I Need a Playmate
I Want a Man
I Want to Talk About You
If You Only Knew
Ill Wind
I'm a Shy Guy
It Must Be Jelly ('Cause Jam Don't Shake
  Like That)
It's a Sin to Tell a Lie
Jasper Series
Jivin' in Be-Bop
Jivin' the Blues
Joe, Joe
Jordan Melody #1
Jordan Melody #2
Jump Children
Junior
Lonesome Lover Blues
Love in Syncopation
Low, Short and Squatty
Lucky Gamblers
Lucky Millinder
Man of the Worlds (Kisenga, Man of Africa)
Mantan Messes Up
Mantan Runs for Mayor
Midnight Menace
Mistletoe
Mop
My Bottle Is Dry

A Night with the Devil
Noah
Old Dan Tucker
Painting in Oil
Patience and Fortitude
The Pollard Jump
The Real Joe Louis
Rhythm in a Riff
Rhythm Sam
Rufus Green in Harlem
Satchel Mouth Baby
She's Crazy with Heat
Sho Had a Wonderful Time
Shout, Brother, Shout
Sizzle with Sissle
Stars on Parade
Sun Tan Strut
Tall, Tan and Terrific
Teamwork
Temple Belles
That Man of Mine
They Raided the Joint
Time Takes Care of Everything
Toot That Trumpet
Vanities
Voodoo Devil Drums
Waller Medley
Watch Out!
We Pitched a Boogie Woogie
Who Dunit to Who
Xavier University — Negro Catholic College
You Call It Madness
Your Feet's Too Big
Zoot

1947

As Our Boyhood Is
Bob Howard's House Party
Ebony Parade
Ee Baba Leba
The Fight Never Ends
Flamingo
Harlem After Midnight
Harlem Dynamite
Harlem Rhythm
Hell Cats
Hep Cat Serenade
Hi-De-Ho
Juke Joint
Junction 88

Junior Jeeps
My Song Goes Forth
The Negro in Art
Night in Harlem
No Mr. Ghost, Not Now
Oop Boop Sh'Bam
Open the Door, Richard!
O'Voutie O'Rooney
The Peanut Man
Play It, Brother
Queen of the Boogie
Reet-Petite and Gone
Regard sur l'Afrique Noire
Rhythm of Africa
Rocco Blues
Sepia Cinderella
Shut My Big Mouth
Sugar Chile Robinson
Super Sleuths
Sweet Shoe
Sweethearts of Rhythm
That Man of Mine
Uncle Tom's Cabana
What a Guy
Woman's a Fool
The Wrong Mr. Wright
Zululand

1948

The Betrayal
Boarding House Blues
Boogie Woogie Blues
Come On, Cowboy
The Dreamer
Hair Raid
The Joint Is Jumping
Killer Diller
Look-Out Sister
Miracle in Harlem
Murder Rap
No Time for Romance
One Round Jones
Pitch a Boogie Woogie
Return of Mandy's Husband
Set My People Free
She's Too Mean for Me
Singin' the Blues
Spiritual Sing-a-Long 1-A
Spiritual Sing-a-Long 2-B
Spiritual Sing-a-Long 3-C

Spiritual Sing-a-Long 4-D
Sun Tan Ranch

1949

Bobbling Over
Feeling Alright
Harlem Jubilee
I Ain't Gonna Open That Door
Lionel Hampton and His Orchestra
Message from Dorothy Maynor
Mr. Atom's Bomb
Pinky
Rhapsody of Negro Life
Souls of Sin
Swingtime Jamboree
Symphony in Swing

1950

Baltimore News Revue
By Line Newsreel
Cherished Melodies
Folklore
Glory Filled Spirituals
Harlem Follies
Harlem Follies of 1949
Introducing East Africa
The Jackie Robinson Story
Jim Comes to Jo'Burg
King Cole and His Trio
King Cole Trio & Benny Carter
Long Remembered
Melodic Spirituals
Melodies Reborn
The Negro in Entertainment
The Negro in Sports
Salute to Duke Ellington
Sarah Vaughn and Herb Jeffies, Kid Ory, etc.
Southern a Cappella
Sugar Chile Robinson
Symphonic Shades
Those Who Dance
The Tradition

1951

The Harlem Globetrotters
Nat "King" Cole and Joe Adams' Orchestra
Native Son
The Well (Deep Is the Well)

1952

Cry, the Beloved Country
The French Way
The Magic Garden
The Negro In Industry
Selected Negro Work Songs

1953

Bright Road
Frederick Douglas's the House on Cedar Hill
The Joe Louis Story
Lifting as We Climb
Marian Anderson
Nat "King" Cole and Russ Morgan's Orchestra
Shango
Slavery

1954

Carmen Jones
Go, Man, Go
Lobola
Satchmo, the Great

1955

Afrique sur Seine
Basin Street Revue
Beale Street Revue
Big Bill Broonzy
Burlesque in Harlem
Downbeat Revue
Harlem Jazz Festival
Harlem Merry-Go-Round
Harlem Variety Revue
The Ink Spots
Jazz Festival
Lionel Hampton and Herb Jeffries
The Nat "King" Cole Musical Story
Revue in Rhythm
Rhythm in Harlem
Rock 'n' Roll Revue
Rockin' the Blues
Simba
Two of a Kind
The Willie Mays Story

1956

Big Bill Blues
Carib Gold
Mr. Black Magic
Rhythm and Blues Revue
Stars Over Harlem

1957

Freedom for Ghana
Jamboree (Disc Jockey Jamboree)
The Sound of Jazz

1958

Anna Lucasta
The Cry of Jazz

Family of Ghana
Fincho
The Hunters
The Quiet One
St. Louis Blues

1959

Africa's Future
Black Orpheus
Come Back, Africa
Harlem Wednesday
Imitation of Life
Porgy and Bess

INDEX

References are to entry numbers.